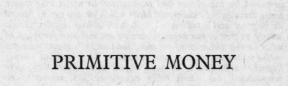

PRIMITIVE MONEY

"... For, when all is said and done, our resemblances to the savage are still far more numerous than our differences from him; what we have in common with him and deliberately retain as true and useful, we owe to our savage forefathers who slowly acquired by experience and transmitted to us by inheritance those seemingly fundamental ideas which we are apt to regard as original and intuitive. ... Reflection and enquiry should satisfy us that to our predecessors we are indebted for much of what we thought most of our own, and that their errors were not wilful extravagances or the ravings of insanity, but simply hypotheses justifiable as such at the time when they were propounded, but which fuller experience has proved to be inadequate. ... Therefore in reviewing the opinions and practices of ruder ages and races we will do well to look with leniency upon their errors and inevitable slips made in the search for truth, and give them the benefit of that indulgence which we ourselves may one day stand in need of."

SIR JAMES G. FRAZER, *The Golden Bough*

PRIMITIVE MONEY

IN ITS ETHNOLOGICAL, HISTORICAL
AND ECONOMIC ASPECTS

by

PAUL EINZIG

EYRE & SPOTTISWOODE
LONDON

First published 1948
Reprinted 1951

*This book is printed for Eyre & Spottiswoode
(Publishers) Ltd., 15, Bedford Street, London,
W.C. 2, by The Thanet Press, Margate.*

PREFACE

Books written on money could fill libraries. The number of volumes devoted to the description of primitive communities is probably even larger. The present volume is, however, the first of any substantial size that is devoted entirely to the subject of primitive money. The publication of this volume on primitive money requires, therefore, no apology. That the task is undertaken by one who has hitherto specialized exclusively in modern monetary problems calls, however, for an explanation.

For some time past I had felt that the early phases of the evolution of money have not been dealt with adequately either by economic history or by anthropology, and least of all by economic theory. It was not until the second World War, however, that I conceived the idea of attempting to repair this deficiency. My decision was perhaps due to some extent to the desire to escape from the horrors of the present into the remote past and from the complications of our civilization into the simpler conditions of backward communities. At the same time I felt a strong desire to probe into the question, raised by Keynes in his *Treatise on Money*, whether in the distant past the inadequacy of the monetary system had ever hindered the progress of mankind in the same way as it did in recent times.

Thus it came about that, after having written forty books on modern monetary and economic problems, I decided to devote some years of research on primitive money. It was only when I was well on my way with this work that I began to realize how formidable my self-imposed task was. I found that there was no short cut to securing the factual material by relying on some scores of authoritative standard works. I had to search for evidence in thousands of books and periodicals, published in several languages, none of which contained more than a fraction of the material required. I was handicapped in my research by the absence of a large number of library books removed to safety, and by the deplorable loss of many books through enemy action. Also it was impossible for me to complete my research by paying visits to the principal libraries abroad. Notwithstanding these difficulties, I have collected many times more factual evidence than any author dealing with the subject. This does not in any way affect my debt of gratitude to them for having provided me with part of my material, and for having indicated sources from which I was able to secure more.

It would undoubtedly have served a useful purpose to investigate unpublished records of Government Departments and elsewhere. All this would have taken, however, considerable time, and rightly or wrongly I felt that the additional material I might be able to secure would not justify the additional delay involved. The number of primitive currencies still in existence—apart from those temporarily adopted by civilized communities in times of difficulties—is diminishing rapidly. I was anxious, therefore, that this book should be available before they had disappeared altogether. For I hope that the material it contains will assist ethnologists, before it is too late, in investigating the remaining primitive currencies from a broader theoretical point of view, and that it might inspire them to approach their subject from new angles. To that end I felt justified in omitting some evidence which might have been of value. After all, that evidence will always remain available, but the sands are running out fast so far as the investigation of the surviving primitive monetary systems is concerned.

As my previous writings on money had dealt mainly with the practical side of the subject I had assumed my present task without being committed in advance to any preconceived monetary theory in any way. I endeavoured to act as an impartial arbiter between the conflicting theories, and tried to reconcile them with each other. Most of them contain part of the truth, and a combination of them is bound to contain a very substantial part. I found it impossible, however, to remain entirely neutral, for I could not help arriving at very definite conclusions of my own on many subjects. And I strongly felt the need for supplementing and correcting some existing theories, and even for replacing some of them. In particular I realized the need for laying stress on the non-commerical origin of money and on the possibility of the existence of credit before money, of money before barter and of barter before private property or division of labour in the generally accepted sense of these terms. Furthermore, I felt the need for putting forward a social theory of money, in which money is regarded not as a technical instrument but a social institution providing the driving force in primitive and modern communities alike, even though in a different way. Finally, I had to fill some blanks by elaborating some new theories peculiar to the working of primitive money.

Since this book breaks new ground in many respects, it would be little short of a miracle if it succeeded in fully achieving its manifold aims. As far as the factual material is concerned, it had to cover a wide field in space and in time. I have no doubt that specialists who made one period or one country or one particular type of currency the study of a lifetime will find many imperfections in the chapters presenting in a nutshell the subjects of their speciality. Before condemning me too severely for any such faults, perhaps they will consider in all fairness that if I had specialized in their particular subject I could never have produced a general picture calculated to enable them in turn to see their special subject in its true perspective, as part of the whole vast subject of primitive money. They should also allow for the fact that, for considerations of space, I had to jettison much of the evidence, and especially much background material.

As far as the theoretical use of the factual material is concerned, I am undoubtedly open to criticism on the ground that I have failed to explore adequately every conceivable line of approach opened up by the factual material I provided. To this charge, too, I plead guilty. I have no doubt that there are others better qualified to analyse my material once it had become easily accessible to them. It is largely for their benefit that I have provided the factual evidence. I admit that I have hardly gone beyond suggesting tentatively some hitherto unexplored lines of theoretical approach. In the original draft of this book, the Theoretical Section was much more extensive. It included a number of chapters on the various systems and functions of primitive money, on the transition from primitive to modern money, and the relapse into the use of primitive money. Considerations of space compelled me, however, to sacrifice that material.

The general reader may find much of the Theoretical Section too abstruse and intricate; but most of the factual material, occupying the greater part of the volume, requires no specialized preliminary study. The reader might also gain a glimpse at historical progress from a new angle. If he is interested in interpretations as well as facts he may find many of the theoretical chapters intelligible. As far as possible I sought to avoid obscurities, even at the risk of failing to impress some academic economists who are inclined to regard as shallow and superficial any argument which is not obscure or over-involved.

I obtained most of my material from the British Museum, the London Library, and the Libraries of the University of London, the London School of Economics, the Anthropological Institute, the Royal Geographical Society, the Royal Empire Society, the Royal Institute of International Affairs, the Institute of Bankers, the Colonial Office and the India Office. I owe a debt of gratitude to the librarians and staffs of all these institutions. Notwithstanding war-time difficulties, they have succeeded in maintaining a remarkably high standard of efficiency; and, with unfailing devotion to duty, they carried on their jobs in highly vulnerable reading rooms during the endless alerts of 1944.

Suffolks,

Ashurst Wood, East Grinstead, Sussex,

September, 1947.　　　　　　　　　　　　　　　　　　　　　P.E.

CONTENTS

Chapter		Page
	INTRODUCTORY	
1	THE STUDY OF PRIMITIVE MONEY	15
2	PRIMITIVE MONEY—TERRA INCOGNITA	19
3	THE BACKGROUND TO PRIMITIVE MONEY	25
4	TREATMENT OF THE SUBJECT	33

BOOK I—ETHNOLOGICAL

Part I. *Oceania*

1	MAT AND BARK CLOTH MONEY IN SAMOA	41
2	WHALES' TEETH CURRENCY OF FIJI	44
3	OTHER CURRENCIES OF THE EASTERN PACIFIC	45
4	THE STONE MONEY OF YAP	48
5	THE BEAD CURRENCY OF PELEW	53
6	OTHER MICRONESIAN CURRENCIES	56
7	PIG EXCHANGES ON THE NEW HEBRIDES	58
8	THE FEATHER MONEY OF SANTA CRUZ	63
9	SHELL LOANS ON THE BANKS ISLANDS	64
10	SHELL AND TEETH CURRENCIES ON THE SOLOMON ISLANDS	67
11	THE INTRICATE CURRENCY OF ROSSEL ISLAND	72
12	DEBTS IN DOGS' TEETH ON THE ADMIRALTY ISLANDS	75
13	SHELL AND YAM CURRENCIES OF THE TROBRIAND ISLANDS	79
14	THE "SACRED" MONEY OF NEW BRITAIN	83
15	NEW GUINEA'S BOAR TUSK AND SHELL CURRENCIES	88

Part II. *Asia*

16	RICE STANDARD IN THE PHILIPPINES	93
17	THE DRUM CURRENCY OF ALOR	95
18	BRONZE GUNS, BEES' WAX AND BUFFALOES AS MONEY IN BORNEO	98
19	OTHER MONEYS OF THE INDONESIAN ARCHIPELAGO	100
20	"HOMERIC" CURRENCIES IN FRENCH INDO-CHINA	102
21	GAMBLING COUNTERS AS MONEY IN SIAM	103
22	TIN INGOTS AND GOLD DUST IN MALAYA	104
23	WEIGHED SILVER AND LEAD CURRENCY IN BURMA	105
24	TEA BRICK CURRENCY IN BACKWARD PARTS OF CHINA	107
25	COCONUT STANDARD ON THE NICOBARS	110
26	GRAIN MEDIUM OF EXCHANGE IN INDIA	113
27	REINDEER AND CATTLE STANDARD IN ASIATIC RUSSIA	115
28	CURRENCIES AT THE PERSIAN GULF	118

Part III. Africa

Chapter		Page
29	IRON CURRENCY IN ANGLO-EGYPTIAN SUDAN	120
30	SALT MONEY OF ETHIOPIA	123
31	LIVESTOCK STANDARD IN KENYA	126
32	BEAD MONEY OF TANGANYIKA	129
33	COWRIES AS CURRENCY IN UGANDA	132
34	OTHER EAST AFRICAN CURRENCIES	135
35	CALICO CURRENCY IN RHODESIA	137
36	CLOTH, METALS AND SLAVES AS CURRENCY IN FRENCH EQUATORIAL AFRICA	138
37	COWRIE CRISES IN THE FRENCH SUDAN	141
38	COWRIES, SLAVES, CLOTH AND GIN MONEY OF NIGERIA	146
39	GOLD DUST CURRENCY OF THE GOLD COAST AND ASHANTI	153
40	OTHER MONEYS OF THE GUINEA BAY	155
41	DEBASED BRASS ROD CURRENCY OF THE BELGIAN CONGO	160
42	SHELL MONEY OF ANGOLA	166
43	CATTLE AND BEAD MONEY OF SOUTH-WEST AFRICA	168
44	CATTLE CURRENCY IN SOUTH AFRICA	170

Part IV. America

45	FUR CURRENCY IN ALASKA	172
46	SHELL, FUR AND BLANKET CURRENCY OF CANADA	173
47	WAMPUM AND OTHER SHELL CURRENCIES IN THE UNITED STATES	177
48	COCOA BEAN CURRENCY OF MEXICO	182
49	MAIZE MONEY OF GUATEMALA	185
50	CATTLE STANDARD IN COLOMBIA	186
51	ARROWS AND GUNS AS CURRENCY IN BRAZIL	188
52	SNAIL SHELL CURRENCY IN PARAGUAY	189
53	OTHER LATIN AMERICAN CURRENCIES	190

BOOK II—HISTORICAL

Part I. Ancient Period

1	PREHISTORIC CURRENCIES	195
2	COPPER UNIT OF ACCOUNT IN ANCIENT EGYPT	201
3	BARLEY AND SILVER MONEY OF BABYLONIA AND ASSYRIA	210
4	SEALED INGOTS IN CAPPADOCIA	217
5	SHEEP AND SILVER CURRENCY IN THE HITTITE EMPIRE	218
6	LIVESTOCK AND WEIGHED SILVER MONEY OF THE JEWS	219
7	SLOW DEVELOPMENT OF COINAGE IN PHŒNICIA AND CARTHAGE	223
8	INVENTION OF COINAGE IN LYDIA	225
9	LIVESTOCK STANDARD IN ANCIENT PERSIA	227
10	OX AND BASE METAL CURRENCIES IN GREECE	228
11	CRUDE BRONZE CURRENCY OF ANCIENT ITALY AND ROME	234
12	BRONZE AXES AND WHEELS AS CURRENCIES IN GAUL	239
13	CATTLE CURRENCY OF THE ANCIENT GERMANS	241

Chapter		Page
14	IRON SWORD CURRENCY OF BRITAIN	242
15	SLAVE GIRL MONEY OF IRELAND	247
16	CATTLE CURRENCY OF INDIA	249
17	SHELL, SILK AND METAL CURRENCIES OF CHINA	253

Part II. Medieval Period

18	RINGS AND WEIGHED METAL CURRENCIES OF THE BRITISH ISLES	259
19	CATTLE MONEY IN IRELAND	262
20	CATTLE, CLOTH AND WEIGHED METAL IN GERMANY	265
21	LEATHER CURRENCY IN ITALY AND FRANCE	268
22	CATTLE, CLOTH AND FISH CURRENCY OF ICELAND	269
23	RING MONEY OF DENMARK	272
24	CATTLE AND CLOTH CURRENCY OF SWEDEN	273
25	BUTTER AS CURRENCY IN NORWAY	274
26	CALVES AS MONETARY UNIT IN HUNGARY	276
27	FUR MONEY OF RUSSIA	277
28	OTHER EUROPEAN CURRENCIES	280
29	COWRIES AS CURRENCY IN INDIA	281
30	LIVESTOCK STANDARD OF THE MONGOLS	282
31	SALT MONEY OF CHINA	285
32	GOLD DUST MONEY OF JAPAN	286

Part III. Modern Period

33	COMMODITY-CURRENCIES OF THE UNITED STATES	287
34	LEATHER MONEY OF THE BRITISH ISLES	295
35	CATTLE CURRENCY OF IRELAND	297
36	RUM CURRENCY IN AUSTRALIA	297
37	FUR AND WHEAT CURRENCY IN CANADA	299
38	SUGAR MONEY OF BARBADOS	300
39	TOBACCO MONEY OF THE BERMUDAS	301
40	TOBACCO AND SUGAR MONEY OF THE LEEWARD ISLANDS	302
41	MAHOGANY LOGS AS CURRENCY IN BRITISH HONDURAS	304
42	UNCOINED SILVER MONEY IN RUSSIA	305
43	GRAIN MONEY IN FRANCE	306
44	COMMODITY UNITS OF ACCOUNT IN GERMANY AND AUSTRIA	307
45	OTHER EUROPEAN CURRENCIES	309
46	ALMONDS AS CURRENCY IN INDIA	310
47	FICTITIOUS MONETARY UNIT IN CHINA	311
48	RICE MONEY IN JAPAN	313

BOOK III—THEORETICAL

Part I. What is Primitive Money?

1	DEFINITION OF PRIMITIVE MONEY	319
2	WHAT IS NOT PRIMITIVE MONEY?	327
3	REQUIREMENTS OF PRIMITIVE MONEY	330
4	CLASSIFICATION OF PRIMITIVE MONEY	335

Part II. The Origin of Money

5 MONEYLESS COMMUNITIES 340
6 EVOLUTION OF BARTER 346
7 ORIGIN OF MONEY—THE MEDIUM OF EXCHANGE THEORY 353
8 ORIGIN THROUGH EXTERNAL TRADE 356
9 ORIGIN THROUGH INTERNAL TRADE 361
10 THE STANDARD OF VALUE THEORY 364
11 THE STORE OF VALUE THEORY 368
12 ORIGIN FROM STANDARD OF DEFERRED PAYMENTS 372
13 ORIGIN THROUGH ORNAMENTAL AND CEREMONIAL FUNCTIONS 376
14 RELIGIOUS ORIGIN 379
15 POLITICAL ORIGIN 386
16 MATRIMONIAL ORIGIN 392

Part III. The Value of Primitive Money

17 PRIMITIVE V. MODERN MONETARY THEORY 395
18 THE SUPPLY AND DEMAND THEORY 397
19 THE QUANTITY THEORY 401
20 THE QUALITY THEORY 407
21 THE COST OF PRODUCTION THEORY 411
22 THE STATE THEORY 416
23 GRESHAM'S LAW 419
24 PRICE LEVELS IN SEMI-NATURAL ECONOMIES 421
25 DUAL CHARACTER OF PRIMITIVE MONEY 425
26 MULTIPLE CURRENCIES 428
27 LIMITED CURRENCIES 431

Part IV. Primitive Monetary Policy

28 ACTIVE AND PASSIVE ATTITUDE OF THE STATE AUTHORITY 434
29 RESTRICTIONIST MONETARY POLICY 439
30 STABILIZATIONIST POLICY 444
31 EXPANSIONIST MONETARY POLICY 446
32 FOREIGN EXCHANGE POLICY 449

Part V. The Philosophy of Primitive Money

33 THE ECONOMIC ROLE OF PRIMITIVE MONEY 452
34 A SOCIAL THEORY OF MONEY 456
35 THE HISTORICAL ROLE OF PRIMITIVE MONEY 460
36 MONEY AND CIVILIZATION 465
37 THE FUTURE OF PRIMITIVE MONEY 470

BIBLIOGRAPHY 476
INDEX 507

INTRODUCTORY

INTRODUCTORY

CHAPTER 1

THE STUDY OF PRIMITIVE MONEY

THE study of primitive money is justified on three grounds. It adds to human knowledge on a special subject. It provides material for the use of other branches of learning. And it provides some material for practical use.

The aim of adding, however slightly, to the ever-increasing volume of human knowledge is worth pursuing even for its own sake. It will be a sad day for mankind when those in search of new knowledge become entirely utilitarian and confine their investigations to subjects offering immediate practical benefit. Primitive money is well worth studying for its own sake, especially since our knowledge of the subject is far from adequate and there is ample scope for adding to it. Being one of the many comparatively neglected sections of economics and of anthropology, primitive money is a subject on which further research has long been overdue.

An enquiry into primitive money is worth undertaking also for the sake of furthering the progress of economic science as a whole. It provides new material for the economic and monetary historian, and it enables the theoretical economist to place his conclusions on a broader basis. It should also help in the establishment of closer links between economics and other branches of learning. It furthers co-operation between economics and numismatics. It should assist in the anthropological approach to economics and in the economic approach to anthropology, to the benefit of both sciences. Archæologists and ethnologists can give a great deal to economists, and can in turn receive a great deal from them. Historians, too, stand to gain from a study of primitive money. In many instances it may assist them in understanding historical events and developments which have never been adequately explained.

Finally, the study of primitive money is worth undertaking even for the immediate practical benefit it can offer. Merchants and colonial authorities stand to benefit by being able to compare their problems arising from the use of primitive money with the problems of others in similar situations. Admittedly, the potential benefit derived in this respect from a study of primitive money is dwindling rapidly, owing to the decline in the use of primitive currencies. Nevertheless, there are still many primitive communities which are using primitive money, or which are using modern money in a primitive spirit. What is perhaps even

more important, there is from time to time a tendency to revert to the
use of primitive money not only in primitive communities but even in
highly developed modern communities. Hitherto, the authorities confronted with such situations were inclined to adopt an ostrich-like policy
by pretending to ignore such retrograde tendencies instead of trying to
regulate them. Perhaps, as a result of closer study of past experience in
this sphere, some of the Governments concerned may be inclined to
revise their attitude.

The study of primitive money is not a mere matter of economics. It
embraces the study of mankind from its remote past right to the present
day. It is the study of the evolution of civilization from its earliest beginnings. For this purpose it is not sufficient to ascertain the economic
factors which determined the progress of mankind or which were determined by its progress. The scope of the study of primitive money must
extend over the field of general history and of social evolution. We have
to study man's reaction to non-economic as well as economic influences.
Subjects such as marriage, religion, social ambitions of primitive peoples
lie within our scope.

The period which our enquiry must cover extends over more than
five thousand years for which there is written evidence. We have also to
try to probe into dark ages which lie beyond this period, and into
blanks that exist, unfortunately, even in the historical period. The communities we have to deal with range from savage cannibal tribes to
highly civilized nations. In the course of our study we have to follow the
rise and fall of empires, the development and decline of civilizations.
This is a comparatively easy part of the task, because of the advanced
intellectual standard of the historical races even in the early phases of
their history. We are in a position to follow the working of the mind of
an Ancient Greek or even of an Ancient Egyptian because they were
more or less of our standard of intelligence. Allowing for the difference
due to the accumulation of additional knowledge over a period of many
centuries, the outstanding personalities of the Ancient Period are in no
way inferior to the best brains of our period; nor is the average mental
capacity of ancient civilized races in any way inferior to ours. Consequently, we are in a reasonably good position to understand their attitude towards the use of money which is in substance identical with our
own attitude. The real difficulty comes when we have to deal with races
at a primitive stage of evolution. Their intellectual standard is inferior
and their mentality is totally different from ours. We are, so to say, not
on the same wavelength. Their attitude towards money differs fundamentally from ours in many respects. Unless we duly appreciate this
difference, we have no means of understanding primitive money.

The study of primitive money is the study of contrasts. There is an
infinite variety of systems with the aid of which communities at early
phases of development sought, consciously or otherwise, to solve their

monetary problems within the limit of their intellectual capacity and in accordance with the stage of their technical and economic progress. In studying primitive money we encounter some systems of touching simplicity. Peoples without any developed sense of value or capacity for measuring value sell jars and bowls for the quantity of grain or liquid they contain. Weight is exchanged for weight in some communities at the most primitive stage. Thus a slave is worth his weight in salt. We also encounter, however, extremely involved systems requiring a highly developed if one-sided intellectual capacity far above the standard achieved even in the majority of modern communities. We discover among the primitive monetary systems materials that impress primitive minds by their bulk or weight, but also small ornaments selected for monetary use because they are suitable for being carried in large numbers on the person of their possessors. We come across objects of practical use in everyday life, but also absurd and useless objects. There are among the primitive moneys staple products which the communities concerned choose because they handle them day after day and understand the meaning of values expressed in them. On the other hand, we also encounter fictitious monetary units which are used for measuring values, even though they have no concrete existence at all. Some communities use for money popular utensils, or tools, or weapons. Other communities use objects surrounded with mystery. Some currencies can be picked up in large quantities, at the cost of the effort to bend down for them. Others are extremely scarce, and their collection or production requires immense effort. Among the objects used for monetary purposes are raw materials or very crudely finished products, but also highly finished goods the production of which requires elaborate care and no mean skill. Primitive moneys include some repulsive objects, but also some creations of art and beauty. The choice and use of certain primitive currencies implies unconscious humour; that of others suggests tragedy and brutality.

There are some moneys which only measure value very approximately in accordance with the undeveloped sense of value of their users. There are other currencies which constitute a highly accurate standard. Many currencies were chosen because their material is valuable; others were entirely worthless, and derived their value solely from the monetary use to which they were put. There are some moneys which constitute obvious units of a high degree of uniformity and which have only to be counted when passing from hand to hand. In other words, they pass by tale. There are others which have to be weighed, or measured, and the quality of which has to be assayed or tested on every occasion when used in payment. The extent to which primitive money possesses the monetary qualities which the modern economist considers indispensable varies within extreme limits.

Contrasts between primitive moneys are not confined to their outward form and other physical qualities. There are also extreme differences in respect of their employment. Some primitive moneys perform all the main functions which, according to textbooks, money is supposed to fulfil. Others, on the other hand, are only used for one or two of the main functions while the remaining functions are fulfilled by different objects. There are also wide differences in the degree to which primitive moneys fulfil their functions. Some are used as media of exchange universally within their communities, subject only to limitations due to the survival of pure barter. Other media of exchange have only a limited use. They are accepted for only certain goods or services, or they may be employed by certain classes of the community. Again, transactions in some primitive currencies are on the borderline of barter. Others, though primitive in form, are in substance very highly advanced and fulfil their monetary functions in a reasonably satisfactory manner. The use of some of the primitive currencies arises naturally from the conditions in the communities in which they are used. Others are just freaks and their adoption adds to the innumerable puzzles encountered by students of primitive peoples. Or they are adopted as a result of external influences. Some serve only internally, others only in relations with outside communities. Some are adopted and function spontaneously. Others are imposed on the community by the tribal or state authority.

Even if the task of studying primitive money were confined to fact-finding it would be formidable. But much more is required. From the mass of accumulated evidence there must emerge some principles, a set of theoretical rules to indicate the evolution and functioning of primitive money. Many of our facts lend themselves to classification into conventional categories. They fit into the rules of well-established monetary theories. Others defy all the known rules. Instead of supporting each other's evidence, they often tend to cancel each other out. If we are honest in presenting our material of evidence without any attempt at selecting our facts to fit certain preconceived theories, the result is apt to be a mass of apparently contradictory conclusions. But then, human nature, which is the foundation of all monetary systems, is full of contradictions and the study of it cannot be oversimplified with impunity.

It would be indeed strange if such an immense variety of races existing in different stages of cultural development and amidst widely different conditions had worked out substantially identical solutions for the task money is called upon to perform, or if all the various systems they adopted in their widely divergent circumstances obeyed absolutely identical laws. Indeed, what is remarkable is not the extent to which the variety of monetary systems differ but the extent to which they obey certain identical laws.

The rules that can be applied to individual systems but are inapplicable as general principles are bound to be manifold. It would be comfortable to adopt the line of least resistance by resorting to empiricism, and to abandon any attempt at arriving at a general system. Our task is, however, to find some broad general principles. If there are exceptions from those principles, it is necessary to attempt to find the rules that govern the exceptions. It must be the ultimate goal of the study of primitive money to try to find the common denominator—in so far as it exists— in terms of which both the well-established rules of modern money and the apparently conflicting conclusions on primitive money can be expressed.

Above all, it must be the object of the study of primitive money to ascertain how the early evolution of money links up with general economic progress, with social evolution, with trends of general history and with the progress of civilization as a whole. How far was the evolution of money a cause and how far an effect? How far did it help and how far did it hinder the advancement of mankind? Was money, at its early stages, a "root of all evil," or was it a means for achieving a higher degree of human welfare? These are the questions that really matter. For money, like every other institution, must be judged not as an end in itself but as a means to the supreme end of human happiness.

CHAPTER 2

PRIMITIVE MONEY — TERRA INCOGNITA

On the face of it the choice of the title of this chapter may appear absurd, seeing that primitive money has in reality a wealth of literature. Numismatists have dealt with it to some extent in the introductory sections of works on early coinage, and also in innumerable monographs. Students of archæology published much highly valuable material on prehistoric currencies. Evidence on the currencies of primitive communities published by ethnologists, explorers and travellers adds up to a very considerable total. Nevertheless, the remark made by Jevons in 1875 that "the natural history of money is an almost virgin subject" still holds good. In particular as far as economic science is concerned, the circumstances of the origin and early development of money, and the laws which it obeyed at its early phase, are indeed a practically uncharted territory.

Theoretical economists are, generally speaking, not interested in economic history. But even most economic historians prefer to confine themselves to the general aspects of their subject and fight shy of detailed monetary history. And even monetary historians prefer to confine themselves largely, if not entirely, to the study of the evolution of money in comparatively recent periods. Finally, even the minority of monetary historians who have taken up the investigation of ancient monetary history usually devote a very small proportion of their time and space to primitive money. Research into early monetary history receives very scant encouragement, judging by the reception given to some books dealing with that subject. A reviewer of high standing dealing with a book on monetary history complained that the author "wasted" one-third of his space before he got through the ancient period, and that he only devoted half a page to Alfred Marshall; as if enough had not been written about Marshall to justify the allocation of a little space to the sadly neglected subject of early monetary history!

The worst of it is that even though most economists have spent very little time on investigating primitive money, textbooks on monetary history and on monetary or economic theory dutifully register in a few brief paragraphs their author's views on the origin and early evolution of money. No economist worthy of that name would think of writing, however briefly, on contemporary Chinese currency without first making a carefully study of the subject and its background. Yet economists whose names are household words committed themselves unhesitatingly to views on primitive money without taking the trouble to study even such material on the subject as is easily accessible. They have devoted no original research and very little original thought to primitive money before venturing to tell their readers just how money has come into being. Most of them still live on the few casual remarks on the subject in Adam Smith's *Wealth of Nations*. They take in each others highly inadequate washing and do not even trouble to find original instances, or to invent new fictitious examples, to illustrate the well-worn conventional theory which they put forward with an amazing degree of self-assurance.

Admittedly there are a few economists who provide an exception from this rule. Those who have taken the trouble to study primitive money outside the meagre material provided by economic literature include Jevons, Knies, Roscher, Helfferich and Menger. A number of American monetary theorists published chapters on the primitive money used in the old American colonies. Considering the wealth of factual material available and the opportunities for original research, the extent to which this source of evidence has been drawn upon must be regarded, however, as far from adequate. What is even more remarkable is that British economists have ignored almost completely the material published on American primitive money by their American colleagues, and also the material published by Chalmers and others on primitive money in the early British colonies in the West Indies and elsewhere.

Bearing in mind the inadequacy of the effort on the part of theoretical economists to study primitive money, it is as astonishing as it is gratifying that some of them at any rate should have managed to arrive at conclusions which withstand the test of investigation in the light of historical and anthropological research. Since Jevons is one of the few economists who has taken some trouble over studying primitive currency it is not surprising that he has been able to arrive at the conclusion that in many instances the use of primitive money as a store of value preceded its other monetary uses. But Rist, even though he did not particularly investigate primitive currency, was also able to appreciate the overwhelming importance of that role of money. Theoretical economists such as Menger and Cassel realized the absurdity of the conventional theory according to which money was necessarily invented when the commercial turnover reached such an advanced stage that barter conditions became intolerable. Although Keynes confessed to have had no time to study early monetary history in detail, he duly realized that when a medium of exchange is not used also as a standard of value the community concerned can hardly be considered to have emerged from the stage of barter. Credit is due to these and other economists who, on purely or largely hypothetical grounds, were able to use their reasoning power to such advantage. A few swallows do not, however, make a summer. In the majority of instances the conclusions reached by economists without studying primitive money are only too obviously affected by the deficiency of their factual foundations.

On the other hand, even the most thorough research, resulting in the accumulation of much valuable evidence, is in itself not sufficient for the elaboration of theories on the evolution of money in the absence of an adequate theoretical background. Many historians and ethnologists have not been saved by their wealth of knowledge of the relevant facts from arriving at entirely wrong conclusions. Indeed, many of them outdistance even theoretical economists in the dogmatic character of their treatment of the subject. Our Theoretical Section contains much criticism of authors who cannot plead ignorance of the facts in mitigation of the grossly one-sided character of their arguments.

The collection of factual evidence is only half the battle. And even that half is still far from having been won. The factual evidence available for the elaboration of theory is indeed very patchy. We know a great deal about the primitive currencies of certain periods in history and next to nothing about other periods. The primitive money of certain savage communities in recent times has been subject to careful and detailed study by members of a rising generation of economic anthropologists. The predominant majority of primitive currencies that is, or was until quite recently, still in existence has never been sufficiently investigated, however, even for the purpose of ascertaining the facts, let alone from the point of view of ascertaining their theoretical implications. And even such factual evidence as has been ascertained is often not easily accessible to anyone capable of appreciating its significance. Few economists have the time and energy to peruse thousands of books and periodicals in order to piece together sufficient factual material to enable them to study the primitive monetary systems.

The task of securing historical material is not facilitated by the misguided patriotism of many historians and archæologists studying the

early history of their own countries. Many of them consider any facts
pointing towards the use of primitive currencies by their ancestors as a
proof of the low state of cultural development of their country in its
early history. Consequently, they consider it their patriotic duty to go
out of their way to suppress or discredit any such facts, and seek to prove
that their country adopted coinage at a very early stage. It was probably
for this reason that very few economic historians have provided any
material indicating the survival of primitive currencies in their countries
side by side with the use of coined money, especially during the Middle
Ages. A similar attitude is noticeable also on the part of many authors
writing about the colonies of their respective countries, and on the part
of many educated natives of primitive though progressing communities.

Early explorers and travellers rendered great service to the study of
primitive money by their casual references to monetary systems operating in the countries they had visited. They can hardly be blamed for not
going into details, seeing that their visits were not undertaken with the
object of studying primitive monetary systems. The inadequacy of most
of the material provided by ethnologists is more open to criticism.
Until comparatively recently, most of them were more concerned with
the religion, folklore, sexual life, etc., of the savages, and it was only
incidentally that they picked up some crumbs of knowledge on primitive
money when they discovered some connecting link between it and the
subjects in which they were primarily interested.

It was not until after the first World War that the monetary systems
of savages came to be studied systematically, and by then many interesting primitive currency systems had ceased to exist. Writing in 1922,
Malinowski, one of the leading economic anthropologists, observed:
"Ethnology is in the sadly ludicrous, not to say tragic, position that at
the very moment when it begins to put its workshop in order, to forge
its proper tools, to start ready for work on its appointed task, the
material of its study melts away with hopeless rapidity. Just now when
the methods and aims of scientific field ethnology have taken shape,
when men fully trained for the work have begun to travel into savage
countries and study their inhabitants, these die away under our very
eyes." Although he wrote this in a general sense it applied remarkably
well to the state of research into primitive monetary systems. And what
was true a quarter of a century ago holds good to a considerably increased degree now. In the meantime many, indeed most, of the primitive communities have adopted modern money, so that they are no
longer suitable fields for the study of primitive money.

Unfortunately, even during the inter-war period ethnological research
failed to make full use of its dwindling opportunities. It is true, some
primitive communities were thoroughly investigated from the point of
view of their monetary systems. We know a great deal about the currencies of a few of the Pacific islands and of a few African communities,

but no ethnologist adequately equipped with the necessary economic knowledge ever studied on the spot the predominant majority of the remaining primitive currencies. Credit is due to the few exceptions. Malinowski, Firth, Armstrong, Thurnwald and a few others performed splendid work in respect of the communities which they investigated. They could not be everywhere, however. We have also obtained much valuable incidental information from ethnologists who had been able to observe the working of monetary systems in primitive communities even though their main interest was in a different sphere. Generally speaking, however, most ethnologists and travellers are exasperatingly vague when referring to the primitive currency systems of the tribes they visited. Many of them make some casual remarks on the subject and give just enough information to be tantalizing without being really instructive.

Lord Hailey's *African Survey* complains that there is no reference book which provides full information about the primitive currencies used in various parts of Africa. The same may be said about the other continents. The only systematic attempts at providing a comprehensive list of primitive currencies in use were made by two Germans, Noback and Klimpert. Their reference books published during the 19th century are, however, hopelessly out of date, and not easily accessible outside Germany. German ethnologists spent much time and effort on the investigation of the primitive currencies of the former German colonies. There is also a certain amount of detailed though not very up-to-date information available about the primitive monetary systems of some French and Dutch colonies. The information concerning primitive moneys in most British colonies is, however, on the whole, remarkably scant.

If we disregard incidental references to primitive money, literature on the subject may be classified into three categories. There are works by numismatists or monetary historians such as Lenormant, Babelon, Mommsen, Burns, Ridgeway, Nolan, etc. The second group includes ethnologists covering the subject from an ethnological rather than an economic point of view. Outstanding amongst them are: Schurtz, Ilwof, Lenz, Thilenius, Regling and Andrée. They have treated their subject with German thoroughness but, generally speaking, with little theoretical background. Finally, there is a group of economic anthropologists, Malinowski, Firth, Thurnwald, Herskovits, Viljoen, etc. Even the members of this latter group treated their subject from an anthropological rather than an economic point of view and were, as a rule, more concerned with classifying their facts than analysing the broader theoretical implications of their findings.

The investigation of primitive currencies was handicapped largely by the lack of co-operation between economists and ethnologists. The former practically ignored the very existence of the latter. They never heard of those few ethnologists who have done very good work in the sphere of research on primitive money, even though their names were well known among students of ethnology. Ethnologists, on their part, undertook their task without adequate preparation in economic theory. They collected valuable facts without being able to appreciate the significance of their discoveries from the point of view of monetary theory. In fact-finding they were handicapped by lack of adequate knowledge of the kind of facts that are necessary from a theoretical point of view. For instance, some ethnologists took much trouble in ascertaining the objects which were generally or widely acceptable in payment among the primitives. Very few of them took the trouble of ascertaining, however, whether and to what extent those objects were required for the purpose of direct consumption or for the purpose of using them for future purchases. Yet the answer to that question is in many instances conclusive in determining whether objects given and accepted in exchange can be regarded as money.

One of the results of the inadequate theoretical background of ethnologists was the development of unilateral theories by them. In particular, those engaged in field work were inclined to generalize from the small number of communities they investigated. Most of them failed to realize the almost infinite variety of systems that were in existence outside the sphere of their special interest.

Another cause of the erroneous views economists take about primitive money is that they are inclined to regard problems of primitive communities from a modern point of view without allowing for the fundamental differences existing between primitive man and modern man, and between primitive community and modern community. Because barter would be extremely difficult and inconvenient in our highly developed community, economists imagine that it is almost as inconvenient and difficult in primitive communities having reached a certain stage in their economic progress. They fail to realize that barter may suit conditions in a community which has not reached a very advanced stage. It is largely because of their preconceived notion about the extreme difficulty of barter that economists gave an entirely false picture of the evolution of money. They assumed that money necessarily arose from the realization of these inconveniences, and were unaware that long before barter had reduced itself to absurdity, indeed in many instances before barter even existed, non-commercial factors may have led to the evolution of money.

Yet another instance of the tendency to regard primitive conditions from a modern point of view was provided by Keynes, who tentatively suggested that the fall of the Egyptian and Sumerian Empires may have been due to a decline in their supply of monetary metals. Because in modern communities shortage of currency handicapped production in the 19th and 20th centuries, he was inclined to assume that ancient empires were inconvenienced by the same factor in a similar way. What he failed to realize was that money played an incomparably less important part in the life of Egypt than in our life, and that in Babylonia any shortage of silver was largely corrected by the monetary use of barley.

Evidently, the study of primitive money is uncharted territory both from the point of view of its factual material and from that of its theoretical implications. Many economic anthropologists made admittedly valuable contributions towards the building up of a theory of primitive money. None of them has made so far a systematic effort to ascertain the extent to which modern monetary theory can be applied to primitive money and to examine the need and justification for an independent theory of primitive money. They did not seek to ascertain the place primitive money occupies in the evolution of the economic and social system and in the progress of civilization. Both the philosophical aspects of primitive money and its technico-theoretical aspects were left largely unexplored.

When we come to the study of primitive monetary policy we are on almost entirely unexplored ground. Apart from the notable exception of Burns, authors dealing with the broader aspects of primitive money ignored the very existence of monetary policy in primitive communities. The general assumption was that in primitive communities money is a spontaneous development and the State authority abstains from interfering with it until a more advanced stage is reached. The many known instances of monetary policy in primitive communities have hardly been studied. Nor have the instances of monetary policy pursued by advanced communities using primitive money been adequately investigated. Indeed, relapses into the use of primitive money in recent times have been almost completely ignored by theoretical economists who regard them as freak phenomena, the treatment of which should be left to daily journalism. It was only quite recently that economists began to take notice of the "cigarette standard" that was adopted in many parts of Europe and in Eastern Asia during or after the second World War.

In the light of the above facts—and the selection of similar instances could be prolonged considerably—it seems justified to describe the study of primitive money as being largely a *Terra Incognita*. Although the quantity of the material available is considerable, much more is needed before its manifold deficiencies can be said to have been corrected to a reasonable degree.

CHAPTER 3

THE BACKGROUND TO PRIMITIVE MONEY

Money does not exist in a vacuum. It is not a mere lifeless object, but a social institution. Without its background it has as little meaning as a verb divorced from its context. An axe or a table has obvious uses which are inherent in its nature and qualities. On the other hand, the use of an object chosen for monetary purposes depends not only on its inherent qualities but on the character of its users and the conditions in the community in which it is used. For this reason it is important to study the background of primitive currencies if we want to understand their use. That background is provided by the intellectual standard, character and customs of the peoples concerned, and their economic, political, social and cultural systems and institutions.

A detailed study of the background of the large number of primitive currencies dealt with in this book would be an immense task requiring many volumes. The author had necessarily to confine himself here to a few general observations. What matters is that the reader should realize the high degree to which the nature of a primitive currency depends not only on its inherent qualities but on the background against which it is used.

The study of primitive money should be conceived not as a mere study of the function of economic factors. It is because many economists have so conceived it that they still believe that the adoption of money was decided upon when barter became too inconvenient; that the nature of the money chosen was always determined by the economic requirements of the community; and that the process of improvement of the monetary system culminating in the adoption of coinage was necessarily determined by economic considerations. In reality the convenience of trade was only one of the many factors responsible for the origin and evolution of primitive monetary systems. To find most of the other factors, we must study primitive character and primitive social institutions.

The result of our enquiry into the background to primitive money is a picture of the human species trying to work out his salvation by trial and error, very often without any precise idea, or indeed without any idea whatsoever, of what he is after. Primitive man is not a rationally calculating being. He is apt to grope his way forward in the dark. He does not know what is best for him and his fellow human beings. And even if he did, he might still prefer some other solution on some apparently irrational ground, or at any rate on some purely non-economic ground. His progress towards the adoption and improvement of money is very often unconscious. He is apt to do the right thing for the wrong reason, and to discover improved systems without knowing what he is doing or why he is doing it.

The story of primitive money is part of the general story of mankind drifting towards its destiny through a series of reverses, often stumbling on the correct solution by sheer accident. We ought to bear in mind that primitive man had not as a rule the benefit of the experience of other primitive communities. While in many instances he may have been able to imitate the systems of neighbouring tribes, much more often each community had to work out its own solution. Moreover, in the absence of written records, knowledge acquired by one generation was apt to be lost by the next if meanwhile the system fell into disuse. It is only at a comparatively advanced stage that primitive communities established sufficiently close contact with each other, both through space and through time, to be able to imitate each other's currencies systematically and to learn by the mistakes of their ancestors or neighbours.

Unfortunately, we know very little about the human background of prehistoric primitive money. By the time the "historic" races had emerged from their prehistoric phase they had reached a fairly advanced intellectual standard. Even though the use of primitive money may have survived for some time their advance in other spheres, it was used by comparatively civilized races in a comparatively civilized way. Almost all "historic" races, even in their earliest *recorded* stages of development, far exceeded the present-day or recent cultural and intellectual standard of most "unhistoric" races. The survival of primitive money was in their case largely anachronism, or it was forced on them by economic conditions. Our information about those phases of their development when the use of primitive currencies really corresponded to their contemporary primitive intellectual standards and economic systems is in most instances very vague.

We have, of course, much more evidence concerning the use of primitive currencies forced on advanced races by the unsatisfactory working of the modern monetary system. While that information may be helpful in enabling us to observe the functioning of primitive money, it is not very helpful for the elaboration of a theory of its early evolution. For that purpose we have to rely largely on evidence obtained through the investigation of present-day or recent primitive communities. In order to make such use of that evidence as a basis for a theory of the evolution of money, however, it would be necessary for us to assume that at an early stage the historic races were at the same stage of intellectual development as the unhistoric races were until recently or still are even in our days. To some extent such an assumption is, in fact, supported by the comparison of evidence contained in the historical and ethnological sections of this book. If we compare the earliest known monetary systems with those used by recent primitive communities, there is at times a striking degree of similarity. The Code of Hammurabi contains provisions which are largely identical with those of present-day tribal law and custom in some primitive communities. The same objects which were used as currencies during the early stages of development of the historic races are still used or were used until quite recently by many unhistoric races.

Nevertheless, it would be dangerous to take it for granted that the behaviour of present-day savage tribes in the Pacific or Africa is necessarily identical with, or even similar to, that of the ancestors of the present European races thousands of years ago. It is open to argument whether present-day primitive races have merely failed to develop for lack of opportunity or whether they are fundamentally incapable of ever reaching an advanced stage of civilization. Until the controversy is settled we have to exercise the utmost caution in applying our ethnological evidence for the purpose of elaborating our theory of the evolution of the money of the historic races. At the same time, since the study of ethnological evidence is largely our only possible way of approach, we can hardly afford to discard it.

The first fact that emerges forcefully from the study of primitive character is that there is no such thing as a primitive character, except in such a vague sense as to be almost meaningless for practical purposes. There is an immense range of differences between the character of different primitive peoples at any given moment, and between the character of the same race at various stages of its development. It is essential to resist the temptation to infer sweeping conclusions from observations concerning a limited number of primitive communities which happened to have a largely similar outlook on some particular point.

For instance, it is widely assumed that all primitive communities are highly conservative and that they tend to resist to the utmost any influencies making for changes in their monetary systems. While this may be true so long as the evolution of their monetary systems is not subject to external influence, it is largely incorrect as far as the attitude of many primitive communities towards the penetration of external monetary systems is concerned. The speed with which certain African tribes adopted various imported objects as their money for internal purposes was in sharp contrast with the dogged determination of certain Pacific tribes to hang on to their ancient primitive monetary system.

It is a frequently employed method of modern writers to represent primitive communities precisely in the way that suits their thesis. Adherents of the classical economic doctrine of *laisser-faire* present the unspoilt savage as the true personifier of the type of the Economic Man. This enables them to argue that any departure from the unrestricted exercise of the pursuit of self-interest as the main economic motive power constitutes a departure from the natural state of affairs. Yet the study of our ethnological evidence, and even to some extent of our historical evidence, clearly indicates that this picture is entirely false. *Laisser-faire* does not truly represent the primitive character. The fact is that the predominant majority of primitive communities had controlled economies and savages were found to be guided by self-interest to a much less degree than modern men. Indeed, if we were to describe the primitive type as the Non-Economic Man we would be much nearer the truth than by trying to present him as the Economic Man—though in this respect, too, we must guard ourselves against sweeping generalizations.

Another extreme misinterpretation of the primitive character and the primitive system is represented by the theory put forward by Socialist writers, according to whom the original system of mankind was Communism and that by returning to it we would simply return to the natural state of affairs from which we had departed. Without going into the extremely involved question of ownership in primitive communities, let it be sufficient to point out that in many instances a high degree of private ownership existed at a very early stage and that the tendency was towards an increase in the relative importance of private property when the size of the primitive community progressed from the stage of the family through the stages of the clan and tribe towards the stages of race, nation and empire. In any case, what is often loosely described as original Communism very often amounted in reality to ownership by the chief of the tribe and not common ownership by members of the tribe. Indeed, while in many instances the prevailing system in primitive communities is distinctly Communistic, in other instances private ownership is carried to extremes unknown in the most highly individualistic modern communities. In many tribes the belongings of primitive man are individual to such a degree that on his death they are buried with the owner or destroyed rather than allowed to pass into other hands.

Another one-sided popular picture is that of the easy-going savage, the primitive man who does not work unless he is actually hungry and stops working as soon as he has satisfied his immediate hunger. This savage type is described as improvident in the extreme, in that he wastes the surplus products he is unable to consume immediately and makes no provision whatsoever for the future. Beyond doubt, the description fits a large number of known instances. On the other hand, it is entirely incorrect in at least an equally large number of known instances. Many primitive communities are indeed the scene of feverish activity. Their members are engaged in production to the utmost limit of their capacity and the turnover of their products is very considerable. This activity is not prompted by profit motive. They do not produce in order to sell at a profit, nor do they exchange goods for the sake of material gain. The reason why they exert themselves is to gain prestige by outdoing other members of their communities in competitive exchanges or in religious sacrifices, or in their subscriptions to secret societies, or in giving away presents, or in arranging lavish feasts, or even in destroying the largest possible quantity of wealth. In conjunction with these activities they contract huge debts and make the utmost effort to meet them. This is certainly not in accordance with the picture of the easy-going savage of the popular imagination. Curiously enough, the South Sea savage is generally regarded as the typical representative of the idle and improvident primitive man, the carefree playboy of nature. Yet in no other part of the globe can we encounter so many instances of feverish economic activity stimulated by the desire to secure large supplies of primitive money in order to gain prestige.

Yet another one-sided picture arising through generalization is the type of the greedy savage. It originates from the experience of travellers in backward countries. In a large number of accounts of such travels prominence is given to the insatiable greed with which savage tribes sought to exploit and rob white travellers. It would be interesting to ascertain to what extent this attitude was due to special circumstances arising from the contact between two fundamentally different civilizations. In many instances those who had an opportunity of studying the attitude of savages towards each other give an account of almost unlimited selfless generosity, of a kind entirely unknown in modern commmunities which could afford it much more easily than primitive peoples living on a bare subsistence level. Nobody is allowed to go hungry in many a savage village so long as there is some food to go round. In some primitive communities—especially in Polynesia—no tribesman can refuse a request for any of his belongings. It is easily understandable, however, that when the savage encounters travellers of a foreign race who possess goods which he is entirely unable to produce, his greed is aroused and he seeks to gain possession of those goods by fair means or foul. Possibly as a result of the introduction of a limited quantity of modern goods the savages became greedy also in their dealings with each other. Until then they were in a position to produce in excess of their immediate needs most kinds of goods they consumed and they could often well afford to give them away to each other on a basis of reciprocity. The introduction of a limited quantity of much-coveted modern manufactures tends, however, to create a spirit of selfishness and greed and, since most of those who described the savage only know him after his contact with modern civilization, they imagine that unbounded greed is inherent in the primitive character.

Admittedly even before they become "contaminated" through contact with advanced civilization savages are apt to be very anxious to secure for themselves the largest possible proportion of certain of the goods their community produces. We saw above that their desire for prestige induces them to engage in competitive exchanges and other kinds of economic activity prompted largely by non-economic motives. According to Galbraith Welch, there is a term in many African languages that means "to give a small present in order to catch a bigger present." In a large proportion of instances, however, the desire to secure more is prompted by the desire to be able to give away more. Greed for prestige and not greed for wealth characterizes these communities. In many instances the savages resent being given valuable presents which they are not in a position to reciprocate. It is true, in other instances they are only induced to reciprocate for fear of the consequences of not doing so.

Many writers are inclined to indulge in sweeping generalizations about the mental capacity of savage races. Yet that capacity varies immensely. Many primitive races are utterly incapable of counting beyond two or three, or at any rate beyond the number of their fingers and possibly their toes. They check their livestock not by counting them but by remembering the appearance of their animals or by marking them. Other savages, equally primitive in many other respects, are, on the other hand, able to count in very high figures and somehow manage to carry out advanced arithmetical operations. Most transactions are concluded verbally, and to remember them is a no mean feat of memory. In Africa, where after the depreciation of cowries payments ran into very big figures, the rapidity with which tens of thousands of cowries were counted would have put to shame any modern bank cashier.

There is also a tendency to generalize from known instances in which savages showed themselves reluctant to engage in exchanges. Beyond doubt, this is the characteristic attitude in many primitive communities. It is probably partly in order to overcome this reluctance, making as it does for stagnation, that the various tribal customs leading to competitive exchanges and other forms of artificially stimulated turnover in goods have developed. It is often stated that primitive man does not exchange his product unless and until he particularly wants to acquire some definite object. Beyond doubt there are many instances to confirm this theory. On the other hand, there are innumerable instances to show that in many primitive communities the exchange of goods is a favourite pastime. Primitive markets constitute the principal means of entertainment, and those who participate in it, especially womenfolk, thoroughly enjoy bartering even for its own sake. In many instances they are described as very hard bargainers, but in other instances they are extremely easy-going, so that in this respect, too, it is impossible to generalize regarding the character of savages. Instances have been recorded in which native sellers of products were rigidly obstinate and preferred to leave their products unsold rather than reduce the price. In other instances, however, prices quoted by native producers and traders are extremely elastic and adapt themselves to supply and demand.

From the foregoing it is evident that the character of primitive peoples is at least as varied as that of modern peoples. If there is one respect in which it is justifiable to some extent to generalize, it is in respect of the relative importance of non-economic factors in the life of the large majority of primitive communities. Social considerations play relatively a much more important part as the motives for their economic activities than in modern communities.

All these and many other considerations influence directly or indirectly the development of money in primitive communities. The study of primitive money is, therefore, for obvious reasons not an exact science. It would be futile to attempt to ascertain any definite relationship between certain phases of civilization and the use of certain types of money.

To understand a primitive monetary system, we must know something not only about the inherent qualities of the objects used and their actual and potential quantity, but also about the people who used it and their economic conditions, social institutions and cultural background. We have to know a great deal about these matters in order to form a correct idea of their monetary systems. Superficial descriptions by travellers lacking local knowledge have been the source of many misleading conclusions. After all, even if we arrive in some foreign city which is at the same stage of development as our own community, and the language of which we can speak, it takes some time before we can adapt ourselves to the differences of habits and mentality and before we even begin to understand their actions and the motives behind their actions. It is easy to imagine, therefore, how much more difficult it must have been for the European traveller to become acquainted with the system of a community at a totally different stage of cultural development, speaking a strange language and ruled by traditions with which he had no means of being acquainted. It necessarily takes years of patient field work before any intruder in a primitive community could possibly form a really reliable idea about the working of a primitive monetary system.

The study of the background to primitive moneys used in historic instances is incomparably simpler. Apart from any other reasons, in most historic instances the use of primitive money is attributable to material circumstances rather than to the character of its users. Nevertheless, early monetary history, too, has its puzzles to which human character provides the key. But in the overwhelming majority of instances the knowledge of the material background should suffice to enable us to answer the question why many communities preferred to use, say, scrap metals by weight rather than coins, or why peoples acquainted with modern money were prepared to put up with commodity currencies.

The reason why it is particularly important for us to become acquainted with the background to primitive money adopted in primitive communities is that the realization of the existence of extreme contrasts in the circumstances and character of various communities will help us to discount various one-sided theories. Economists, with an enviable degree of confidence in their infallibility, sought to explain the origin and early development of money on the ground of one over-simplified theory with the exclusion—tacit or expressed—of all other possible explanations. Perhaps if they had duly realized the immense discrepancies in the mental make-up and material circumstances of the communities over the five continents they might have allowed for the possibility of alternative explanations. They might not have taken it for granted that all communities in all ages and throughout the world necessarily resorted to precisely the same solution for precisely the same reasons. The study of the background to primitive money is perhaps the best way of making the student realize the need for humility in his approach to the subject. Surrounded as it is on all sides with unknown factors, it calls for an open-minded attitude.

A fact that is liable to impress one more than anything else as a result of a study of the background to primitive money is the possibility of a wide variety of causes leading to the same solution, and of the same cause leading to a wide variety of solutions. Also the student cannot fail to be impressed by the remarkably slow pace of evolution. After having studied the background to primitive money, he is bound to realize that the predominant majority of writers on early monetary evolution is guilty of gross over-simplification. The neat "streamlined" theories they produced are utterly divorced from reality. In real life the evolution of money was a highly involved process—a process, moreover, that was apt to differ widely from place to place.

CHAPTER 4

TREATMENT OF THE SUBJECT

Chapter 2 gave some idea of the immense gaps that exist in our knowledge of primitive money. The object of this book is to fill many of these gaps. It would be impossible, however, for any single human being to fill all of them, even if he were to devote his whole life to the task. It is far beyond the capacity of any one student to ascertain by direct personal investigation on the spot more than a negligible fraction of the relevant factual material. Nor is it possible for anybody who has not an extensive research organization at his disposal to accumulate and study within the brief space of a lifetime all the published evidence secured by others.

At the very outset of his enquiry the author had to face a particularly difficult dilemma. He had to decide whether to arrive at a preconceived definition before embarking on his ethnological and historical research, or whether to allow the definition to emerge subsequently from the material collected. This dilemma which confronts the monetary historian or anthropologist engaged in research on primitive money is clearly stated by Laum in his *Heiliges Geld*. He points out that unless the meaning of the term "money" is defined in advance, students may extend their research over objects which could not properly be described as primitive money, or they would omit others which should have been

C

included. On the other hand, if they accept one of the innumerable definitions put forward by economists, their research becomes both restricted and prejudiced by that preconceived definition. Most anthropologists considered the first alternative the lesser evil and proceeded with their investigations without a preliminary definition. The result was often a loose and indiscriminate application of the term "money," leading to much confusion of thought, arguments at cross-purposes, and the production of much misleading or irrelevant information. Some anthropologists, on the other hand, adopt in advance a strict and comparatively narrow definition which subordinates their ethnological research to economic dogmatism. As for economists, they usually simply proceed on the basis of their favourite definition of modern money.

In this book an attempt is made to reconcile the two methods. In the Ethnological and Historical Sections practically all objects which have been claimed by responsible writers to have been used for monetary purposes are dealt with. The author usually indicates the extent to which he is inclined to endorse these claims, without binding himself in advance to a cut and dried definition. It is not until after the presentation of the factual evidence that he attempts to solve the problem of finding a definition on the basis of that evidence. The material is at the disposal of others who may prefer some totally different definition.

Another difficulty of procedure with which the author was faced was the determination of the dividing line between the historical and the ethnological material. History deals with the so-called historic races and ethnology with the so-called unhistoric races. This sounds simple enough. Unfortunately, it is often a matter of opinion whether a given race is historic or unhistoric. What is worse, in many communities historic and unhistoric races live together and to a large extent use the same primitive currencies. It also occurred in a number of instances that races which had had great historical past had subsequently declined into primitive communities. This is the case, for instance, with the Mongols, who were in many respects a relatively advanced nation in the Middle Ages but have subsequently become a comparatively primitive community. In the absence of a clear dividing line, it was necessary to divide much of the material in an arbitary manner.

Although chronologically the Historical Section should precede the Ethnological Section, the author reversed this order, because logically the description of the least advanced communities should come first. And the overwhelming majority of communities dealt with in the Ethnological Section is at a lower stage of evolution than even the least advanced community covered in the Historical Section.

The chapter headings in the Ethnological and Historical Sections could not possibly cover all primitive currencies dealt with in the chapters concerned. They indicate the currency or currencies that, in the author's opinion, are the most characteristics of the primitive monetary systems of the communities during the periods covered by the chapters.

Most authors dealing with primitive money classify their material according to the objects used for monetary purposes, and not according to the nationality of the users. They follow, for instances, ring money from its early beginnings in Ancient Egypt right to its present-day use in West Africa. They describe the use of the cattle standard from Homeric days to present-day pastoral communities. Since our object in the Ethnological and Historical Sections is to provide raw material for the Theoretical Section, and for others who may want to write on the subject, the author thought it more convenient to arrange his ethnological material for the purpose of reference according to countries, and to divide the history of primitive money in various advanced or comparatively advanced countries into the conventional three main historical periods.

The book does not claim to be a practical guide for merchants desirous of engaging in trade with primitive communities. Nevertheless, it contains much information which merchants wanting to trade with primitive communities still using primitive currencies may find useful. They will be able to compare their experience with that of many other communities trading in a similar way. From this point of view the book may contain some helpful material also for Colonial administrations and for Governments of countries with backward territories. When they are confronted with some problem arising from the use of a primitive currency they may be able to compare their experience with that of other administrative authorities faced with somewhat similar problems in various parts of the world during various periods. In this respect colonial authorities having to deal with problems arising from the use of primitive money are at present working under a considerable disadvantage. If they are faced with a problem arising from modern money, they can draw upon the immense wealth of experience accumulated in modern times all over the world—experience which was published in an accessible form and commented upon by the world's leading experts whose writings were translated into each other's languages. As far as primitive money is concerned, however, the Governments anxious to ascertain how others before them acted in a given situation, have often no opportunity to search for obscure references contained in long-forgotten volumes kept in inaccesible libraries. Even Colonial Offices adequately equipped for such enquiries are not always in a position to undertake such research at short notice. And even if the facts are obtained, there is no way of benefiting by accumulated expert knowledge relating to them, for the simple reason that they have never been subject to searching enquiries similar to those undertaken in connection with modern monetary problems. To help to overcome this difficulty to some extent is one of the objects of this book.

The foregoing observation brings us to the theoretical aspects of this enquiry. The facts relating to primitive money are in themselves interesting, but their accumulation within the covers of this book is largely a means to an end. The main purpose of the study of these facts is to provide raw material for the elaboration of a monetary theory based on the broadest possible factual foundations.

The Theoretical Section is concerned with primitive money in general, not with each type of primitive money separately. It would be justifiable to examine in detail the full theoretical implications of every system of primitive money, in the same way as the various types of gold standard, bimetallism, paper currency, etc., are often investigated separately. There is an almost infinite variety of primitive monetary systems, each obeying a peculiar set of rules. While there are laws which affect equally the ox standard, the wheat standard and the cowrie standard, there are essential differences in their actual application. To describe and analyse thousands of systems based on the various monetary objects would in itself be an immense task. But owing to the multiplicity of currencies in primitive communities we would have to deal with the infinite variety of combinations of these monetary objects—a task that is too formidable to be feasible. We have to content ourselves by trying to ascertain the general rules applicable to a sufficiently large number of primitive monetary systems to be accepted as general.

The author endeavoured to follow up most lines of theoretical approach initiated by those writing on the subject before him, and also to originate a number of new lines of approach. While primarily concerned with primitive money, the Theoretical Section necessarily has to deal with money in general, viewed in the light of the evidence produced by the enquiry on primitive money.

In the concluding chapters, the broadest aspects of primitive money are examined. These include the part it plays in the economic system, its historical role and its role in the evolution of civilization. The author puts forward a Social Theory of Money, endeavouring to present money as a social institution which in primitive as well as modern communities provides the incentive to produce goods beyond immediate requirements. He seeks to prove that, even though this role is played in a totally different way in primitive and modern communities, in final results primitive money as modern money is the driving force making for the better utilization of economic resources and productive capacity.

The book concludes with a series of suggestions concerning further research and with a forecast of the prospect of primitive money. The author feels that he is far from having exhausted the subject of his choice and that there is ample scope both for general works carrying his investigation further and for a large number of monographs dealing with particular countries, particular periods or particular primitive currencies. He also feels that, in spite of the decline of the use of primitive money, it should be studied by the monetary authorities and those qualified for advising them, owing to the ever-present possibility of a relapse into their use during an emergency or a difficult period. Over and above all, he feels that monetary theory and other branches of learning could greatly benefit by a thorough investigation of the nature and working of the primitive monetary systems still in existence, and by the full utilization of the factual material thus obtained by the theoretical economists and students of sister-sciences.

During recent years the trend of progress of monetary science has been mainly in the direction of "mechanization"—that is, monetary functions were sought to be expressed in mathematical formulæ, and their results were sought to be ascertained with the aid of statistical tables. The present book does not attempt to contribute towards progress in that direction; indeed its special subject does not lend itself to such treatment. Instead of swimming with the fashionable tide of mathematical and statistical approach, the author has chosen the somewhat neglected biological approach. In other branches of learning the importance of studying existing systems, institutions, objects, by probing into their origins and earliest evolution has long been recognized. The author feels it is high time monetary science developed in that direction.

BOOK I
ETHNOLOGICAL

PART I: OCEANIA

CHAPTER 1

MAT AND BARK CLOTH MONEY IN SAMOA

THE question whether or not the Samoan group of islands had a primitive currency before the second World War is highly controversial. Raymond Firth and George Brown hold strongly the view that the mats and native bark cloth which were, and probably still are, used frequently in exchanges do not constitute a currency. According to Brown,[1] the value of fine mats depends not only on the fineness of the thread and the size, but is also affected by historical associations. Many old mats had distinct names and acquired great sentimental value as a result of having been used as the "top mat" on some great occasion, such as a famous wedding or the conclusion of a peace treaty. Many of the most valuable mats are old and torn. It stands to reason that any such heirlooms cannot possibly be considered as currency. Helfferich quotes a document in the archives of the German Colonial Government of Samoa, a petition from High Chief Mataafa to the Governor of Samoa, asking him to decree mats as unpawnable as they were sacred and had the same significance for the inhabitants of Samoa as orders of chivalry and titles had for Germans.[2]

Mats with historical or sentimental associations constitute, however, only a small fraction of the number of mats in existence in Samoa. The overwhelming majority of mats have no such significance and change hands quite freely. Indeed, the entire economic and social system of Samoa is built on the frequency of exchanges in which mats, and to a less extent native bark cloth, play a prominent part.

The mats are made by women, and their size is between two and three yards square. Many months and even years are sometimes spent over the making of a single mat. These fine mats are considered the most valuable property of the Samoans and, according to Turner, "form a sort of currency which they give and receive in exchange."[3]

Their values varied before the second World War between two shillings and forty shillings. Fine mats constitute the principal store of value. Indeed, they may be considered to be practically the only possible form of store of value in that primitive community which is essentially

[1]George Brown, *Melanesians and Polynesians* (London, 1910), pp. 303-4.
[2]Karl Helfferich, *Money* (London, 1927), Vol. I, p. 14.
[3]George Turner, *Samoa a Hundred Years Ago* (London, 1884), p. 120.

Communistic, like most communities in Polynesia. Ownership of land is rather indistinct. Anybody having any movable objects, including modern money, must be prepared to give them up at the request of a kinsman of a friend, or be prepared to find them missing.[4] Fine mats, precisely because there is sentimental value attached to some of them, cannot be claimed, however, by others, though their owners have to part with them through obligatory exchanges.

Ordinary fine mats serve to a large extent as a medium of exchange in Samoa. A number of authors who have studied the system on the spot for more or less prolonged periods hold this opinion. Thus Schulz-Ewerth: "Fine mats are highly valuable. They serve as a medium of exchange."[5] According to Pritchard: "Fine mats in Samoa are a medium of exchange and a standard of wealth."[6] In the opinion of Reinecke: "Mats play the part of money for the purposes of paying for certain services and objects."[7] Kraemer says: "Fine mats are a fixed medium of exchange, similar to the *Diwara* shell money of the Melanesians and the *Fei* stone money of Yap."[8]

Wages are paid in fine mats, among others to artisans engaged for the building of houses and boats.[9] The services of the tattooer and magician are rewarded in payments of mats.[10] They are given as presents in consideration for the use of land,[11] which is the peculiar form assumed by rent in Samoa. On the other hand, George Brown[12] claimed that fine mats had no fixed negotiable value, by which he probably meant that their exchange value was a matter of negotiation.

Above all, mats play a vital part in exchanges connected with marriage. In this respect, native bark cloth fulfils a similar role. The relatives of the bride have to give to the bridegroom and his friends, on the celebration of the wedding, a large quantity of fine mats and native bark cloth prepared by women. The bridegroom in turn has to give the family of his bride canoes, pigs, tools, garments, ornaments, etc.[13] "No lover of money was ever fonder of gold than a Samoan was of his fine mats," observes Turner.[14] In order to secure the largest possible number of mats, chiefs usually married a large number of women—indeed, marriage constituted the main economic incentive and barter arising from it represented a very large percentage of the turnover of goods.

To some extent fine mats constitute the unit of account in Samoa.[15]

---

[4]Felix M. Keesing, *Modern Samoa* (London, 1934), p. 325.
[5]Erich Schulz-Ewerth, *Samoa* (Das Eingeborenenrecht. Edited by Erich Schulz-Ewerth and Leonhardt Adam, Stuttgart, 1930), p. 676.
[6]W. T. Pritchard, *Polynesian Reminiscences* (London, 1886), p. 13.
[7]F. Reinecke, *Samoa* (Berlin, 1902), p. 150.
[8]A. Kraemer, *Die Samoa-Inseln* (Stuttgart, 1902), Vol. I, p. 28.
[9]Reinecke, p. 150.   [10]Turner, p. 40.
[11]Robert W. Williamson, *The Social and Political Systems of Central Polynesia* (Cambridge, 1924), Vol. III, p. 247.
[12]Brown, p. 434.   [13]Turner, p. 93.   [14]Turner, p. 176.
[15]Margaret Mead, *Coming of Age in Samoa* (Penguin Books, London, 1943), p. 26.

To a much larger extent they serve as a standard for deferred payments. The Royal Commission investigating native affairs in the mandated islands of Samoa during the 'twenties questioned a former native district judge who was dismissed because he disobeyed the order forbidding transactions in fine mats by repaying debt in that form. This appeared to have been a customary transaction.[16]

Fine mats are used extensively for unilateral payments. They are used for the payment of compensation to outraged husbands.[17] Fines, blood money, etc., are fixed in mats. On the occasion of the election of chiefs and kings, the candidates distribute mats among the electors. Whoever has most mats to distribute stands the best chance of being elected. The successful candidate, in return, receives mats from the people, so that on balance he may even have gained.[18] In inter-tribal wars allies could be bought with mats.[19]

The value of mats in modern money has increased considerably since the concluding years of the nineteenth century, in spite of their partial demonetization through the penetration of modern money because their output has declined. The use of modern money has resulted in a decline in the production of mat and bark cloth money.[20] Whilst in 1897-8, the value of ordinary mats was, according to Kraemer, between fifty and two hundred marks; in 1899 it was, according to Reinecke, between eighty and three hundred marks. Shortly before the first World War it reached one hundred to four hundred marks, according to Finsch who added that white traders were willing to lend eighty to one hundred marks on the security of a mat.[21] The value of mats declined, however, between the two wars.

Whether the ethnologist or the economist is satisfied or not that mats constitute a currency in Samoa, there can be no doubt about the views held on the subject by the Samoans themselves. In the course of his evidence before the Royal Commission referred to above, the dismissed native district judge demanded that the law forbidding financial dealings in fine mats should be repealed. Samoans did not consider that it was a good law, because "there is no difference between the fine mats and gold and silver. The European works and saves money in the bank for his children; Samoan children have fine mats. They are the coin of the Samoans or Samoan wealth."[22]

---

[16]N. A. Rowe, *Samoa Under the Sailing Gods* (London, 1930), pp. 207-8.
[17]Mead, p. 67.   [18]Reinecke, p. 149.   [19]Kraemer, p. 28.
[20]Mead, p. 163.
[21]O. Finsch, *Südsee-Arbeiten*. Abhandlungen der Hamburgischen Kolonial Institute, Vol. XIV (Hamburg, 1914), p. 408.
[22]Rowe, p. 208.

CHAPTER 2

WHALES' TEETH CURRENCY IN FIJI

The natives of Fiji are as Communistic in their attitude towards property as those of any Pacific islands. For this reason no primitive currency system has had a real chance of developing to any considerable extent. Nevertheless, it seems that the teeth of the sperm whale enjoyed until recently such a degree of preference among the articles of exchange that we are justified in classing them amongst the limited primitive currencies.

According to Laura Thompson[1] the beautiful polished "ivory" teeth of the sperm whale serve as a means by which wealth can be accumulated, condensed and stored. The same author also claims that they serve as a medium of exchange. She does not regard whales' teeth as a standard of value because "its ceremonial significance imparts to it an immeasurably sacred value which cannot be compared with the exchange value of other objects."[2] Since most of the turnover in goods assumes the form of gift exchange with no strict equivalence between the goods given and received, the question of the use of a standard of value may not arise. On the other hand, whales' teeth figure prominently enough in such exchanges to be regarded as a favourite medium of barter, and possibly a medium of exchange.

Whales' teeth were only used for big transactions in the 'forties of the last century. One single whale's tooth was said to have been sufficient to buy a big canoe. It was also accepted as blood money for a murdered man.[3] It was extensively used as bride money. According to Basil Thompson, such was the power of a whale's tooth that he who accepted it could not refuse the request it carried with it, whether it be for a mere gift, or for an alliance, or for a human life.[4] At the beginning of the 19th century, whales' teeth were held in such great esteem that it would have been dangerous for anybody but a great chief to be known to have a whale's tooth in his possession.[5] On the other hand, according to the report of the Fijian Commission on Depopulation in 1893, modern money does not particularly attract the native of Fiji. When he takes produce to the market it is not from any desire for possession of money. He has in his mind a definite object on which the proceeds are to be spent. If he has no such object in mind, he will let the surplus product of his garden or fishing net decay rather than undergo the trouble of taking it to the market for the sake of receiving merely money.[6]

[1]Laura Thompson, *Fijian Frontier* (San Francisco, 1940), pp. 85-6.
[2]Thompson, p. 86.   [3]Finsch, p. 206.
[4]Nancy Walker, *Fiji* (London, 1936), p. 71.
[5]John Martin, *William Mariner's Account of the Natives of the Tongo Islands* (London, 1817), Vol. I, p. 315.
[6]Roberts, *Problems of the Pacific*, p. 224. Quoted by I. C. Greaves, *Modern Production among Backward Peoples* (London, 1935), p. 160.

CHAPTER 3

OTHER CURRENCIES OF THE EASTERN PACIFIC

One of the few Polynesian communities which is claimed to have possessed a native currency is Easter Island. The "currency"—if it can be regarded as such—consisted of rats. This at any rate is alleged by Macmillan Brown.[1] The "edible" rats of the Pacific area are considered a favourite delicacy and are eaten raw. They were "so highly valued as a luxury that they became favourite medium of barter, and perhaps a medium of exchange. No one would refuse a bunch of rats when anyone made an offer for any of his goods."[2] If a man wanted anything another man had, he went out to hunt rats and was able to amass as much of the "coin" of the realm as would purchase the coveted object.[3]

There is no independent evidence to corroborate Macmillan Brown's statement. But then, he is one of the leading authorities on Easter Island and on the ethnology of the Pacific in general. Nor is he, generally speaking, inclined to assume too lightly that objects which are used in barter play the part of currency. Indeed he refuses to consider the fine mats of Samoa or the whales' teeth of Fiji as currencies. "The only Polynesian island that ever developed the concept of a medium of trade" he observes, "was Easter Island and its currency was rats."[4]

He fails to enlighten us, however, whether the rats taken in payment were always consumed by the recipients or whether on many occasions the latter used them in turn for payment. Nor does he inform us whether prices were regularly quoted in terms of rats. There can be no doubt, however, that rats were more freely acceptable than anything else, so that they may possibly have played a monetary role. Since, however, dead rats are essentially perishable, especially under a hot climate such as that of Easter Island, it is open to doubt whether their recipient could possibly envisage its use in subsequent exchanges.

The idea of a unit of account in Hawaii does not appear to have arisen until after the arrival of the Europeans on the scene. Imported silver coins gave rise to the notion of a standard of value.[5] Even after the import of such coins, most exchanges were done by barter, but the goods came to be exchanged on the basis of their value in silver money.[6]

Sandalwood, which for a long time was the staple export of Hawaii, also became a unit of account. Obligations in traders' accounts were stated in terms of piculs of sandalwood, not in currency, during the early part of the 19th century.[7] The Hawaiian chiefs were keen purchasers of foreign goods and offered promissory notes for large amounts

---

[1]J. Macmillan Brown, *The Riddle of the Pacific* (London, 1924), p. 177.
[2]Brown, p. 177.   [3]Brown, p. 23.   [4]Brown, p. 23.
[5]Freycinet, *Voyage autour du Monde*, Vol. II, p. 617. Quoted by R. S. Kuykendall, *The Hawaiian Kingdom*, 1778-1819 (Honolulu, 1938), p. 84.
[6]Kuykendall, p. 84.   [7]Kuykendall, p. 85.

payable in sandalwood.[8] One of the Hawaiian kings bought eight sailing vessels worth more than 300,000 dollars payable in sandalwood.[9] Huge debts in sandalwood accumulated during the first quarter of the 19th century. In 1826 a United States sloop of war was despatched to enforce the acknowledgment of these debts. A head tax was levied under which every man had to contribute half a picul, or four Spanish dollars. As a result the full amount of the debt was cleared,[10] but the sandalwood supply became exhausted.

No evidence is available as to what extent sandalwood became a currency for internal transactions. It stands to reason, however, that since there was a persistent demand for debt payment and export well in excess of the supply available, everybody readily accepted sandalwood logs in payment for his goods and services.

Natives on Tikopia are in the habit of acquiring bark cloth, not only for their immediate personal use but also to keep it as a "prime stand-by in the resources of a person wishing to demonstrate his liberality or to implement any sudden payment."[11] This appears to imply that bark cloth is used extensively as a store of value. According to Firth both bark cloth and sinnet can serve as "embryonic media of exchange" because of their durability. To some extent the two are alternative or even convertible in terms of each other, there being a number of transactions in which either a coil of sinnet or a piece of bark cloth can be offered.[12] To a large extent bark cloth is a fiduciary currency. The reckoning is made in terms of the *maro* as a whole, that is, of the bundle irrespective of whether it contains half a dozen or two pieces of bark cloth.[13]

Firth emphasizes, however, that as measures of exchange value both sinnet and bark cloth operate only to a very limited degree "because of the limitations of sphere which social convention puts upon them." By this he means that only certain classes of goods are exchangeable for bark cloth and sinnet. It would be contrary to convention to exchange bark cloth or sinnet either for goods belonging to a lower category, such as food, or for goods belonging to a higher category, such as canoes. This fact would not, however, disqualify bark cloth and sinnet from being regarded as a medium of exchange within the limited sphere in which they are used for that purpose.[14] For, in spite of the limitation of their use, Firth lays stress on the frequency with which they are liable

[8]Andrew W. Lind, *An Island Community* (Chicago, 1938), p. 10.
[9]Jean Hobbs, *Hawaii—A Pageant of the Soil* (Stanford, California, 1935), p. 23.
[10]Hobbs, p. 24.
[11]Raymond Firth, *Primitive Polynesian Economy* (London, 1939), p. 253.
[12]Firth, p. 343.   [13]Firth, p. 253.
[14]In his article on Primitive Currency in the *Encyclopædia Britannica* (14th Edn.), Firth readily recognizes the monetary status of some of the objects used for monetary purposes in Africa, even though they, too, are used as media of exchange in limited spheres only and their scope is, therefore, comparable to that of bark cloth and sinnet in Tikopia.

to change hands as a result of commercial or ceremonial transactions. Even so, he feels we cannot regard these objects as currency. In this respect Rivers shares his views, in spite of his much more elastic conception of primitive money.[15] According to him, "Mats, bowls, hooks, bark cloth and other objects are exchanged freely, but there is no commodity used as a medium of exchange which can be regarded as money." It appears, nevertheless, that on the basis of a broader interpretation of primitive currency, bark-cloth and sinnet in Tikopia can be classed as such.

The French Colony of New Caledonia had two kinds of objects serving as currency—the fur of the flying fox and various types of shells. Belts made of fibre with hair of the flying fox attached to it were described by Finsch as being a very current medium of barter, to such an extent that it might be considered as a kind of money.[16] No adequate information is, however, available to ascertain to what extent this object fulfilled the requirements of a currency. According to Archey, it originally served decorative purposes before it became "a kind of currency."[17]

On the other hand, there is evidence showing that shells played a monetary role in New Caledonia. According to Père Lambert,[18] shell strings were a medium of exchange. They were measured by the arm's length. They appeared to be highly valuable, considering that half an arm's length bought a small boat. Père Lambert came across an instance of forged shell money. The forger was caught and his counterfeit currency was withdrawn from circulation.

In addition, there were strings of shell discs alternating with knots in monetary use; their value in 1911 was six cents a foot and it was used extensively by traders in dealing with natives. There were also strings of shell beads alternating with pieces of fur.[19] This was highly valuable and, according to the natives, it corresponded to the gold coins of the white man. It was only used by chiefs.

The red fur under the ears of the flying fox constituted the material chosen as the medium of exchange of the Loyalty Islands.[20] Trade is done, however, mostly by means of barter and the natives are reputed to be very easygoing in their dealings with each other. According to Hadfield,[21] at the market where people from fishing and gardening villages meet when a member of the fishing village enquires the price of yam, the answer is: "Oh, just give me as much fish as you would think it is worth"—and the bargain is closed. At the end of the day,

[15]W. H. R. Rivers, *The History of Melanesian Society* (Cambridge, 1914), p. 330.
[16]Finsch, p. 173.
[17]G. Archey, *South Sea Folk* (Auckland, 1937), p. 54.
[18]Père Lambert, *Moeurs et Superstitions des Néo-Calédoniens* (Nouméa, 1900), pp. 168-9.
[19]A. B. Lewis, *Melanesian Shell Money in the Field Museum Collection* (Chicago, 1929), (Field Museum of Natural History Publication No. 268), p. 34.
[20]R. H. Codrington, *The Melanesians* (Oxford, 1891), pp. 324-5.
[21]E. Hadfield, *Among the Natives of the Loyalty Group* (London, 1920), pp. 220-1.

each party hands over the unsold products to the other party. Under such a system, there can only be limited scope for the development of a currency.

CHAPTER 4

THE STONE MONEY OF YAP

The monetary use of large stone discs on Yap is surely one of the strangest systems human brain has ever devised. Its Spartan austerity is nothing if not impressive. Nor is the system a matter of distant past history. It was still in function on the eve of the outbreak of the war with Japan.[1] Those who are opposed to the liberal use of the term "primitive currency" naturally object to the inclusion of the "stone money of Yap" among them. Even Melville Herskovits, although in favour of a broad and elastic interpretation of the term, emphasizes that the stone money of Yap could not properly be included among their ranks.[2] Nevertheless, it seems that under a liberal and broad definition this borderline case may reasonably be classed as a currency.

Photographs of the stone money of Yap (known under the name of _fé_ or _fei_) show irregular shaped "millstones" of varying size. Their material is aragonite, which is a type of calcite. It was shipped mainly from the quarries of Pelew and Guam. Its size varies from that of a plate[3] to a gigantic disc with a diameter of more than twice the size of a full-grown man. There is a hole in the middle of each stone to facilitate its transportation with the aid of a pole thrust through it. Some of the stones are believed to be more than 200 years old.[4] According to Hernsheim[5] the older stones are full of inscriptions, for it is customary to engrave on them the name of those who quarried it and shipped it across to Yap, and also the name of each new owner.

The value of the stone money depends largely on its size measured in spans, which in Yap means the stretch of the index finger and thumb.[6] In addition to its size, its shape and quality also affect its value. The stones imported from Guam are worth more than those shipped from Pelew, possibly because of a difference in quality, but more probably because Guam is more distant and the journey is more dangerous.

[1]The most recent published information is provided by Tadao Yanaihara, _Pacific Islands under Japanese Mandate_ (Shanghai, 1939), Ch. VI.

[2]M. J. Herskovits, _The Economic Life of Primitive Peoples_ (New York 1940), pp. 215-6.

[3]Franz Hernsheim, _Südsee-Erinnerungen_, 1875-1880 (Berlin, 1883), p. 20. According to J. Kubary (Journal of the Museum Godefroy, Vol. IV, p. 20) the small change consists of stones of the size of a dollar.

[4]W. Müller, _Yap—[Ergebnisse der Südsee-Expedition._ II Ethnographie, B. Mikronesien (Hamburg, 1917)], p. 132.

[5]Hernsheim, p. 20.

[6]W. H. Furness, _The Island of Stone Money_ (Philadelphia, 1910), p. 96.

There is absolutely no practical non-monetary use for the stone money of Yap. It does not constitute an implement, nor can its material be used for any non-monetary purpose. Nor is it considered to be ornamental, excepting the very large specimens. It owes its value to the following circumstances:—

1. *Scarcity*—Its material cannot be found in Yap and its quantity could not be increased indefinitely by import, owing to the difficulty of transport in small native boats.

2. *Cost of production*—Its quarrying and transport involved a considerable amount of labour. Teams of men engaged in its production and transport had to be paid for their efforts in the form of food. In addition, suitable presents had to be given to the King of Pelew for his permission to quarry the stone on his island.[7]

3. *Risk*—Heavy loads had to be carried by frail native craft. It is said that from an expedition to Guam, only one out of twenty boats returned.

The stones are not valued because they are old, nor is there any idea of sanctity attached to them.[8] It is true, according to legend, the stone money is of divine origin. But the people of Yap possess sufficient unconscious humour to believe that it was one of their wicked gods who inspired the creation of their strange currency with the object of sowing the seeds of dissension among them.[9]

Photographs of the Island show an impressive display of some of the largest stones in front of the houses of their owners and of the communal buildings. Evidently the inhabitants are proud of their possessions and consider their stone money ornamental. Indeed, according to F. W. Christian,[10] stone money "is more for show and ornament than use." It is not, of course, the white man's idea of ornament, and it is doubtful whether even the Yap Islanders adopted it because they thought the clumsy stones beautiful. It seems reasonable to assume that the stones came to be considered ornamental because they were valuable, and did not acquire their value because they were first used as ornament. In any case small stones are valuable even though they are not considered ornamental. They are not displayed by their owners, partly because it would be easy to steal them and partly because they do not consider they have any reason to be proud of the possession of small "coins" measuring a mere foot or two in diameter.

Stones, big and small, perform the functions of a store of value. They are practically the only form of mobile investment of the inhabitants in addition to their boats. Everybody is anxious to accumulate his capital in the form of stone money.

Stone money also serves the purpose of a medium of exchange,

[7]Hernsheim, p. 20.   [8]Furness, p. 100.
[9]Willard Price, *Japan's Islands of Mystery* (London, 1944), p. 76.
[10]F. W. Christian, *Caroline Islands* (London, 1899), p. 236.

D

though to a considerably less degree. In this respect it is necessary to discriminate between large stones and small ones. The latter circulate freely within the community.[11] Price describes a scene in which a queen proceeded to a shopping expedition with two muscular slaves carrying two smallish stones.[12] These small "coins" change hands frequently. On the other hand, the large stones hardly ever change hands. Everybody prefers to have a few large stones rather than a large number of small ones. The very large specimens cannot possibly be used in everyday transactions. It is for this reason that many ethnologists hold the view that the stone money of Yap is in reality no money. They are undoubtedly right as far as the large specimens are concerned, but the fact that these do not act as a medium of exchange does not disqualify small stones from being regarded as money.

Admittedly, the use of stone money as medium of exchange has its limitations:—

1. It is purely an internal money. Trade with other islands is transacted largely on a barter basis.

2. Even within Yap the bulk of trade assumes the form of barter without the intermediary of any kind of money.[13]

3. There are other currencies in use in Yap besides the stone money.
   (a) The large pearl shell (*jar*) which is second in popularity to stone money.[14]
   (b) Shell strings made of discs of the *Chama Pacifica* (*gau*).
   (c) Dyestuff made out of the roots of the Curcuma (*reng*).[15]
   (d) Coconuts which form very frequently a means of payment, especially in buying from white traders.[16]
   (e) Tobacco, used especially in payment for goods sold to traders.
   (f) Baskets of taro, or cups of syrup, which serve as units of account.
   (g) Mats are an international currency in that part of the Pacific.

4. Modern money is also making some progress, but until the eve of the war in the Pacific it did not succeed in displacing the stone money and other subsidiary currencies to any noteworthy extent. The German Colonial Administration made an effort to stop the use of native money,

[11]Richard Andrée, *Ethnographische Parallellen und Vergleiche* (Berlin, 1876), p. 232.

[12]Price, p. 75. Large stones are not moved when they change ownership. Their physical possession is not considered essential. A large stone which fell into the ocean is still considered to form part of the possessions of the heirs of those who had owned it.

[13]Christian, p. 270, Price, p. 79.

[14]A. Senfft, *Die Rechtsitten der Yap-Eingeborenen* (Globus, Vol.XLI, 14th March, 1907), p. 151.

[15]Senfft, p. 15.

[16]Price (p. 106) quotes the figure of two coconuts for one match, ten coconuts for one roll of bread or for one packet of cigarettes, twenty-five coconuts for ten leaves of tobacco and forty coconuts for a beer-bottle of petroleum. Furness (p. 106) mentions the purchase of a cooking stove for 20,000 coconuts.

because it hampered the development of commerce and of German enterprises. After the change of régime, the Japanese Government made the use of yen compulsory in shops. Notwithstanding this, yen were only accepted by the natives in the immediate vicinity of the harbour, while farther inland it was entirely impossible to buy anything with modern coins, let alone notes. The inhabitants of Yap do not like any foreign money and do not trust it. As Price pointed out, they had no means of knowing how long the latest variety of foreign money would be good. First Spanish money came when Yap was a Spanish colony; then it was displaced by German money after the transfer of the island to the Second Reich, and Spanish money was no longer of any use. Then Japanese money came after the first World War, and German money was no longer acceptable. (Since Price's visit Japanese money has also ceased to be valid.) On the other hand, they firmly believed that the Yap's stone money is always good.[17] In any case, the natives did not appear to understand the value of foreign money.[18]

Even traders settled on the island are perfectly willing to accept stone money in payment for their goods. Its possession enables them to buy within the island anything they wish.

No information is available about the extent to which stone money serves as a unit of account. Presumably owing to the fact that its value varies not only according to its size but also according to its quality, it is not used frequently for expressing prices. On the other hand, it is used extensively as a standard of deferred payments. Debts are frequently contracted in terms of stone money. Indeed, traders actually encourage the accumulation of debts in the hope that they will be paid with large stones instead of small ones.[19] Loans are granted in stone money. No interest is charged for three to four months, thereafter interest is paid in the form of pearl shells.[20]

Stone money is also used for political payments. A large specimen is sufficient to buy the active support of a neutral tribe in an inter-tribal war.[21] During the German régime fines were fixed, however, in terms of coconuts.[22] Native chiefs collect occasional levies in stone money or pearl shells or food.[23]

The prices quoted by various authors in terms of stone money vary widely. Kubary, writing in the 'eighties, emphasized the very low purchasing power of stone money, allowing for its weight and quantity. On the other hand, subsequent writers lay stress on the large volume of goods these millstones can buy. Furness[24] states that a three-span stone of good whiteness and shape purchases fifty baskets of food (a basket

[17]Price, p. 80.   [18]Christian, p. 270.   [19]Price, p. 80.
[20]Senfft, p. 152.   [21]Hernsheim, p. 20.
[22]A. Senfft, *Ethnographische Beiträge über Karolinen-Insel Yap* (Dr. A. Petermann's Mitteilungen, 1903, Vol. XLIX), p. 50.
[23]Senfft, *Die Rechtsitten der Yap-Eingeborenen*, p. 172.   [24]Furness, p. 101.

being about eighteen inches long and ten inches deep and containing
taro roots, husked coconuts, yams and bananas), or a pig weighing
between eighty and one hundred pounds, or one thousand coconuts.
According to Hernsheim,[25] against the smallest piece of stone money a
family can obtain a month's supply of yam, taro, fish and other foodstuffs. The high value of stone money is even more striking if expressed
in terms of modern currency. Museums trying to buy specimens found
that the prices quoted by the natives for large specimens were prohibitive. According to Price[26] a Guam wheel a foot in diameter costs
about seventy-five U.S. dollars. A stone man high is worth many villages
and plantations, and a stone two men high is entirely beyond price.

The appreciation of the stone money in recent decades is all the more
remarkable as during the 'eighties an enterprising Irish ship-owner,
Captain O'Keefe, transported to Yap many large-size stones from
Pelew and Guam in return for copra. He became an almost legendary
figure because in possession of his vast wealth in stone money he was
able to buy up anything and anybody he wanted in Yap. Others followed
his example, so that towards the close of the 19th century, Yap secured
all the stones it could possibly absorb.

Notwithstanding this, the value of stone money in Yap before the
second World War was as high as ever, and the owners of large specimens were as reluctant as ever to part with their precious possession.
Perhaps the explanation is that the cost of labour also increased materially, so that it cost much more to produce and transport the stone
wheels to Yap than it did fifty years earlier. In any case, the import of
new stones practically ceased some time ago.

On the basis of all relevant evidence available, it is perhaps permissible to answer the question whether the "stone money of Yap" could
really be considered money in a somewhat hesitant affirmative.

It seems that the upheaval caused by the war in the Pacific reduced
the monetary use of the stone money. Modern money in the form of
military dollar notes has come to be adopted to a large extent, as a
result of the American occupation of the island in 1945. The United
States Navy spent large amounts in dollars in return for goods and
services, and the islanders accepted the dollars because they were able
to spend them on the purchase of American stores.[27] No information is
available about the extent to which dollar notes are used as money by
natives when dealing with each other. Possibly stone money still reigns
supreme in their internal trade.

[25]Hernsheim, p. 20.   [26]Price, p. 80.
[27]The author is indebted for this up-to-date information to Mr. James Callaghan,
M.P., who obtained it first-hand during his visit to Yap in 1945 while serving in the
Royal Navy.

CHAPTER 5

THE BEAD CURRENCY OF PELEW

Pelew Islands have a highly involved monetary system which is the basis of one of the strangest economic and social systems ever devised. Most of the great variety of beads used at Pelew form part of a highly developed system of primitive currency, even though the multiplicity of the units necessarily limits the scope of any one of them.

There are seven main types of bead money.[1] The most valuable of them is called *brak*. According to Semper,[2] only three or four specimens were in existence at the time of his investigation. It is a yellow stone of some kind but complete mystery surrounds the exact nature of its material.[3] German and Japanese experts tried in vain to ascertain the material of this type of money and also of some inferior types of money. Second in rank is the *mungugau* which is a red jaspis stone worn by women of royal rank on State occasions. Third in rank is the *kalebukub* which is an agate in cylindrical form. These three are the moneys of princes and hardly ever reach the ordinary people. Next in rank is the *kaldoir* which is followed by the *kluk*, a polished enamel bead. The latter is used as a medium of exchange in ordinary large and medium-sized transactions.[4] Finally, the lowest types are called *adelobok* (half a *kluk*) and *Kaymon a kvae* which are pieces of white or green glass polished into odd shaped beads. These are the small change and are barely sufficient for buying bananas.[5] Within these categories there is a large and somewhat indefinite number of sub-categories. According to Kubary[6] there are at least twenty-five kinds of *kalebukubs* and at least twenty-six kinds of *kluks*, and nearly twenty kinds of *adeloboks*. Beyond doubt Pelew holds the record regarding the number of currency units of different denomination in use at the same time.

The money of Pelew is believed to be of foreign origin. From time to time various types of Pelew money are unearthed in Yap. Considering that one of the Pelew Islands is partly inhabited by exiles from Yap, it seems highly probable that the Pelew money originated in part at least from the "Island of stone money."[7] When Pelew was discovered by Captain Henry Wilson in 1783 its strange money appears to have been already in use. Wilson's *Journals* contain references to beads made of baked earth worn by the king and to glass beads used by his subjects.

[1]For detailed description see J. Kubary, *Ethnographische Beiträge zur Kenntnis des Karolinen-Archipel* (Leyden, 1889), pp. 7-8; Friedrich Ratzel, *The History of Mankind* (London, 1896), Vol. I, pp. 246-7; and Emil Rogner, *Gesellschaft und Wirtschaft auf den Palau-Inseln* (Nürnberg, 1939), p. 64.
[2]Karl Semper, *Die Palau Inseln* (Leipzig, 1873), p. 61.
[3]According to Andrée (p. 232) a single piece is valued at £750.
[4]Price, p. 123.   [5]Semper, p. 61.
[6]Kubary, p. 10.   [7]Kubary, pp. 23-5.

He thought that the latter were made of simple pieces of broken bottles which had been got out of his wrecked ship, the "Antelope."[8]

There can be little doubt that the origin of the monetary use of the various types of beads and stones in Pelew was their ornamental use. Each one has a hole through it so that it can be worn. Only the most valuable specimens fulfil the functions of the store of value. The less valuable types are not hoarded. Indeed they are actually required to remain in circulation, as we shall see later.

All articles of daily use can be bought with bead money.[9] The smaller denominations are used regularly as a medium of exchange, to a much larger extent than is the stone money of Yap. Payment for taro, tobacco and similar goods is made with the lower-grade types, while boats are purchased with the more valuable types. There has been at times an acute shortage in moneys of small denominations. Arm-rings have been broken up, *kluk* beads have been divided, in order to meet the need for small change.[10]

The inferior types of stones and beads are not the sole media of exchange on Pelew. There are the following subsidiary currencies:—

1. Betel nuts and betel leaves, which are said to serve as small change.[11]
2. *Chama Pacifica* shells (for trade with other islands).[12]
3. Mats (for trade with other islands).[13]
4. Tortoise-shell discs (for transactions between women only).[14]
5. Tobacco (for trade with whites only).[15]

The entire society of Pelew is sharply graded into classes, and money evidently conforms to this system. There are separate types of money for the use of various social classes.

The monetary character of the beads and stones of Pelew is indicated particularly distinctly by their use as units of account. The entire system is based on the unit of ten baskets of taro. Each one of the various types of money bears fixed relation to this unit.

When in 1882, two British warships undertook a punitive expedition against the Island of Molegojok of the Pelew group for the plunder of Captain O'Keefe's wrecked ship, an indemnity of $4,600 was imposed on the community. Security was demanded in the form of Pelew money and the basis of calculation was one basket of taro being equal to one shilling.[16]

While nominal parities between the various types of money are fixed,

---

[8]George Keate, *An Account of the Pelew Islands, Composed from the travels and communications of Captain Henry Wilson.* 4th Edn. (London, 1789), p. 188.

[9]T. Yanaihara, p. 103.

[10]Augustin Kraemer, *Palau [Ergebnisse der Südsee-Expedition.* II Ethnographie, B. Mikronesien, Vol. III, Part III (Hamburg, 1926)], p. 160.

[11]Kraemer, p. 160.

[12]A. Senfft, *Ethnographische Beiträge über die Karolinen-Insel Palau* (Dr. Petermann's Mitteilungen, Vol. XLIX, 1903), p. 83.

[13]Senfft, p. 83.   [14]Price, p. 124.   [15]Senfft, p. 83.

[16]Kubary, p. 11.

their exchange rates in relation to each other vary very widely. Anyone wanting particularly to change one type of money into another has to pay heavily for his preference. Exchange transactions are nevertheless frequent, and form an important political, social and economic function. They are extremely involved. It is not a matter of simple arithmetic to calculate the equivalent of one currency in another, which depends on the rank of the parties concerned. Different rates are allowed in transactions between equals and in transactions with inferiors.[17] Both in Pelew and in Yap men of higher rank must pay more for everything than men of lower rank.[18]

Bead money is used very extensively as a standard of deferred payments. The Islands have a very highly developed credit system. Very often if somebody does not possess the type of money required for the occasion, he borrows it rather than exchange a superior type. Loans are granted on security and interest is deducted in advance. Although interest rates are very high, they compare favourably with the loss sustained through an exchange transaction.[19]

Pelew money is extensively used for unilateral payments. Fines are fixed in terms of the various types. In Pelew any punishment for political, social or religious offence can be commuted into money payment.[20] Fines are the main revenue of the chiefs. On occasions of weddings, moneys are exchanged.[21] Relations between individuals and also between tribes are largely based on swapping money. This aspect of the subject, as many of its other aspects, has not been adequately explored.

According to Kubary, in social life in Pelew everybody is compelled by custom to undertake definite expenditure in accordance with his standing in the community. "It is amazing that in spite of the limited amount of money available, the inhabitants are able to effect all the numerous kinds of payments and it is therefore understandable that demand for money and the zeal to acquire it is very high. To satisfy the demand, custom in Pelew seeks also to regulate the turnover of money."[22] Chiefs are not allowed to hoard money. Custom determines their liabilities in relation to the people and to other chiefs. As a result, money which finds its way to the chief through fines is returned into circulation. There is a rule that nobody is allowed to live on his own products. Everybody must sell the objects which he produces and must buy the identical goods and pay for them.[23] Prices and payments are fixed and are unalterable. They are known by everybody.

The quantity of Pelew money remains unchanged. No new supplies are imported to any extent apart from the occasional pieces discovered

---

[17]Kubary, p. 11.
[18]K. Regling, *Geld—Reallexikon der Vorgeschichte* (Berlin, 1926), Vol. IV, p. 204.
[19]Kubary, p. 11.   [20]Kubary, p. 21.
[21]Kraemer, p. 159.   [22]Kubary, p. 23.
[23]Kubary, p. 23. It is to be deplored that these interesting observations, though quoted by many ethnologists, have not been corroborated.

in the soil of Yap. It is perhaps for this reason that the system of price fixing is thoroughly effective.

Owing to the high relative value of Pelew money, it would be surprising if no European had tried to take advantage of it by supplying the natives with manufactured imitations. In fact, Captain O'Keefe had an opposite number on Pelew, who hoped to grow rich by importing a large number of pieces similar in appearance to those highly valued on Pelew. He tried to sell them for copra and bêche-de-mer, but the natives refused to accept them. They could easily recognize that the imported beads were not genuine. According to Semper, imitations are rejected because "they are made by man, while the original money is of celestial origin."[24] According to Andrée[25] the imitation of glass money, which can be counterfeited comparatively easily, is a punishable offence.

Trade with other Caroline Isles is conducted with the aid of mats which are largely an international currency in Micronesia. Modern money did not seem to make more headway before the second World War in Pelew than in Yap. According to the account of Price in the middle 'thirties, the beads and stones were as popular in Pelew as ever. Tobacco was used widely as the unit in trading with whites.[26]

The high stage of development reached by the Pelew monetary system is indicated by the fact that the Pelew Islanders have words for "exchange," "lending," "repayment," "interest," "security" and "pawn."[27]

[24]Semper, pp. 62-3.   [25]Andrée, p. 232.
[26]Senfft, p. 83.   [27]Kraemer, p. 169.

CHAPTER 6

OTHER MICRONESIAN CURRENCIES

Fish-hooks made of shells are said to have been a currency in the Gilbert Islands. It was claimed that they were a highly valuable currency at one time.[1] In addition, the teeth of the sperm whale constituted an important medium of exchange.[2] Finally, discs of coconut shells and sea shells strung on long cords of coconut fibre, black and white alternatively, are claimed to have played the part of money.[3]

On Nauru Island very little modern money is in circulation. Eggs appear to be a favourite form of limited currency. Even stamps in the post-office are paid for in eggs.[4]

A shell ornament made of *Spondylus* shells is claimed to have played a monetary role on the Marshall Islands. This view is not shared by all authors. According to Senfft[5] before the advent of the Europeans all

[1]Finsch, p. 132.   [2]Finsch, p. 206.   [3]Ratzel, p. 248.
[4]A. Brandeis, *Ethnographische Beobachtungen über die Nauru-Insulaner* (Globus, 31st January, 1907), Vol. XLI, p. 74.
[5]A. Senfft, *Marshall Insulaner*, p. 454.

trade was transacted through barter. Even barter is said to have been practised to a very limited extent only.[6] Subsequently bars of tobacco became the general means of payment used by whites. Taxes were collected by the Japanese authorities in copra.[7]

Sarfert describes seven kinds of shell currencies in Kusaie.[8] Most of these currencies were made of pearl shells. They were cut in various shapes. Some of them were made into the shape of fish-hooks, and constituted a very valuable currency. It actually had the name of "fish-hook money."[9] Some large pieces of shell money bore the inscription of the finder's name. Among shell rings in use, those of large size were also ornaments. The smaller ones were used for monetary purposes only; they served for paying wages and for contributions to festivities.[10] Modern money has now largely replaced primitive currency in trading with whites, but not in dealings of natives amongst themselves. Moreover, modern money is not considered by natives as a store of wealth. It is spent on European goods as soon as it is earned.[11]

According to Yanaihara, no money of any sort existed on Ponapé.[12] On the other hand, Hambruch and Eilers[13] maintain that sleeping mats represented the island's currency. A big war canoe for two men was bought for ten sleeping mats; a small dinghy for two men for one big mat.

The nearest thing to a medium of exchange on Truk was a yellow or brown powder made from the root of curcuma which was used for painting the body, and is believed by the natives to possess protective and healing qualities. It was employed for monetary purposes right to the eve of the second World War.[14] For some time this powder, called by the natives *taik*, served as a unit of account. The value of commodities was expressed in terms of so-and-so-many *taik* cakes. Kraemer quotes the price of various shells or shell ornaments in *taik*.[15] Matsuoka quotes in *taik* the prices of mat sails, loin cloth, and hatchets.[16] Gradually some prices became standardized. *Taik* was also used in trade with other islands. It fulfils the functions of money in external trade, since it was found to be a convenient means of measuring the values of commodities.[17]

[6]Yanaihara, p. 84.

[7]P. H. Clyde, *Japan's Pacific Mandate* (New York, 1935), p. 93.

[8]E. Sarfert, *Kusaie [Ergebnisse der Südsee-Expedition.* II Ethnographie, B. Mikronesien, Vol. xiv (Hamburg, 1919)], p. 213.

[9]Sarfert, pp. 215-6. [10]Sarfert, p. 219.

[11]Sarfert, p. 218. [12]Yanaihara, p. 88.

[13]P. Hambruch and A. Eilers, *Ponapé. [Ergebnisse der Südsee-Expedition.* II Ethnographie, B. Mikronesien, Vol. vii, Part ii (Hamburg, 1936)], p. 183.

[14]Yanaihara, p. 84.

[15]A. Kraemer, *Truk. [Ergebnisse der Südsee-Expedition.* II Ethnographie, B. Mikronesien, Vol. ii (Hamburg, 1938)], p. 161.

[16]S. Matsuoka, *Ethnography of Micronesia* (1927), (in Japanese). Quoted by Yanaihara, p. 85.

[17]Yanaihara, p. 85.

Trade on Faraulip was mainly barter, but coconuts were said to have been used as "small" money, and mats constituted the larger unit. A small boat was worth three mats and a mat was worth a hundred coconuts.[18] According to Hambruch, Pelew bead money was also in use to some extent.

According to Yanaihara,[19] the Marianas had no properly developed money. On the other hand, according to Featherman, there was a rather advanced type of money in circulation. It consisted of polished tortoise-shells pierced with one or several holes. The unit was called *lailai*. Their value was as many times three *lailai* as there were holes in them.[20] This is claimed to be one of the instances of primitive currency in which the value is determined by the tribal authority. It is impossible, however, to obtain confirmation of Featherman's uncorroborated evidence, and he does not quote his source of information.

Ratzel claims that polished beads of coconut shell, bracelets of tortoise-shell and *Spondylus* armlets were used on the Mortlock Islands as currency.[21] Kubary considered shell necklaces as the nearest thing to a currency, at the same time as being favourite objects in interinsular trade.[22] According to Matsuoka, however, these objects were only used in barter with other islands.[23]

[18]Hans Damm, *Zentral-Karolinen* [*Ergebnisse der Südsee-Expedition.* II Ethnographie, B. Mikronesien, Vol. x, Part ıı (Hamburg, 1938)], p. 173.
[19]Yanaihara, p. 84.
[20]A. Featherman, *Social History of the Races of Mankind.* 2nd Division (London, 1887), p. 386.
[21]Ratzel, p. 248.
[22]J. Kubary, *Die Bewohnreder Mortlock Inseln* (Mitteilungen der Geographischen Gesellschaft, Hamburg, 1878-9), p. 270.
[23]Matsuoka. Quoted by Yanaihara, p. 85.

CHAPTER 7

PIG EXCHANGES ON THE NEW HEBRIDES

The pig standard in the New Hebrides is in some ways the strangest and probably one of the most highly developed among the known livestock standards. Pigs of a definite type constitute the foundation of an involved currency and credit system and the entire economic, political and social life centres around their monetary use. Only boars with curved tusks are reckoned as currency. On some islands, however, inter-sex pigs, which also grow tusks, are the only type eligible.[1] It is not the size nor condition of the pigs that matters, but solely the elongation of their tusks.[2] The natives knock out two teeth from the pig's upper jaw to

[1]A. J. Marshall, *The Black Musketeers* (London, 1937), pp. 129-32.
[2]J. Layard, *Stone Men of Malekula—The Small Island of Vao* (London, 1942), p. 249.

encourage the growth of the tusk. Pigs corresponding to the prescribed requirements are valued in the New Hebrides primarily because they are prospective victims at sacrificial feasts.[3]

Boars are a store of value in the New Hebrides. The wealth of a man is judged by the number of pigs that he posseses.[4] It is the oldest form of capital on the islands. This was noted as early as 1774 on Eromanga.[5]

Pigs are used extensively as a medium of exchange throughout the group with the exception of a few islands. They are primarily used for large payments in connection with the purchase of land.[6] At markets which are held periodically on every island they are used for the acquisition of various objects.[7] Workers are paid in pigs,[8] and so are magicians, dancers, mortuary officials, etc.[9] It is true, pigs are not the universal medium of exchange. They are far too valuable for most everyday transactions. Various other currencies serve as smaller units; most important among them are mats.

Pigs constitute a standard of value in various kinds of transactions.[10] There is, however, little actual evidence that prices are regularly quoted in terms of pigs, or that barter is conducted on the basis of pig values.

Pig currency is the principal form of bride money.[11] Blood money, ransom, fines for infringing taboos, are paid in pigs. Above all, payment for admission into "men's clubs" or "secret societies" and for promotion of members takes place in the form of pigs. These societies dominate the life of the community. Social and political advancement is only possible within these societies, and it is therefore the ambition of most men to become members and be able to buy promotion. Use of pigs for this purpose alone should be sufficient to secure an almost unlimited demand.[12]

Pigs serve extensively as a standard and means of deferred payments. A most elaborate and extensive credit system in terms of pigs has developed in the New Hebrides.[13] For the purpose of buying a bride, or of gaining admission into a secret society, a young man must borrow pigs from his relatives, or from fellow-members of secret societies if he is already a member. These debts must be repaid with interest. The rate of interest is equal to the growth of the tusk—that is, the extent to which

---

[3]Layard, p. 249. Tom Harrison, *Savage Civilization* (London, 1937), pp. 25-6.
[4]A. Bernard Deacon, *Malekula* (London, 1934), p. 193.
[5]C. R. Humphries, *The Southern New Hebrides* (Cambridge, 1926), p. 70.
[6]Layard, p. 437. Evelyn Cheeseman, *Backwaters of the Savage South Seas* (London, 1933), p. 51.
[7]Dr. Felix Speiser, *Ethnographische Materialen aus den Neuen Hebriden und den Banks Inseln* (Berlin, 1923), p. 278.
[8]Layard, p. 364.   [9]Layard, pp. 355, 371, 556.
[10]Layard, p. 276.   [11]Layard, pp. 193, 196, 198.
[12]Deacon, p. 193. According to A. J. Marshall (p. 129) the rank and title of chiefs depend on the number of pigs they have ceremonially slaughtered. Evelyn Cheeseman (p. 197) mentions an instance of eight hundred pigs having been sacrificed when a wealthy and powerful man became a king.
[13]Speiser, pp. 278-280. Layard, pp. 252-3. Harrison, pp. 26-8.

the tusk would have grown during the period of the loan. Repayment must be made, therefore, by returning pigs with bigger tusks; and since it usually takes a long time to repay the loans, the tusks must be considerably more developed. This means that the pigs to be returned have to be much more valuable and more expensive than those received.

The increase in the value of pigs through the growth of their tusks on Atchin in the 'thirties is illustrated by Layard.[14] The value of a crescent (quarter of a circle) tusker was then about £4; that of a curved (half circle) tusker £6. For a re-entrant (three-quarters of a circle) tusker between £10 and £15 was demanded, while circle tuskers fetched anything from £30 upwards. He quotes Godefroy a few years later, describing a circle tusker as fetching £40, and a circle plus re-entrant tusker (i.e., a boar with tusks describing a complete circle and a half) as commanding as much as between £50 and £60. Owing to the appreciation of pigs with the growth of their tusks, interest on pig debts is exceptionally heavy, even for primitive communities where 100 per cent per annum is usually the standard rate.

The burden represented by pig debts is very considerable. No man would dare to default, since in doing so he would ruin his chance of economic, political and social advancement. Young men have to concentrate therefore on breeding pigs and lending them to other people who need them and who will be his debtors. They will also have to work for chiefs or other rich men to receive payment in pigs. During more recent times, the opportunity has arisen for them to earn modern money and to invest their earnings in pigs. The rising trend in pig prices may be due to the growing purchasing power of young men who undertake working for others.

Another reason for the expansion in the amount of pig debts is that it is safer for owners of pigs to lend them, because in doing so they avoid the risk of loss through the death of the animals. A situation has developed in which practically everybody on the islands is both a creditor and a debtor in pigs. When a man feels he is approaching death, he calls together his debtors and his creditors and at his deathbed they try to disentangle the situation.[15] Various methods of inducing and shaming defaulting debtors into paying, or of bringing pressure to bear on them, have been devised. Even the services of the pig-magician are enlisted; by his spells and incantations he puts it into the heads of debtors to repay their debts.[16] A high proportion of the disputes and murders are over the payment or non-payment of pig debts.[17]

Possession of pigs is not aimed at for its own sake, nor even for the sake of being able to exchange them for other objects, but first and foremost for the sake of being in a position to make huge sacrifices and to

[14]Layard, pp. 254-5.   [15]Layard, p. 253.
[16]H. W. Krieger, *Island Peoples of the Western Pacific* (Washington, 1943), p. 86.
[17]Marshall, p. 130.

contribute lavishly towards festivities, in addition to being able to buy membership and promotion in secret societies.

The entire economic system of the New Hebrides is based on the reciprocity of gifts. Rich men are in a position to entertain on a generous scale and to make such generous presents that the recipients are not in a position to reciprocate adequately, so therefore they lose face and have to acknowledge their inferiority.

This involved system of reciprocal indebtedness is in its way fully as complicated as our own financial system. At any given moment the total number of pigs owed is in excess of the number of pigs in existence. Rich men acquire political power with the aid of this system partly by buying promotion in the all-powerful secret societies and partly by placing a large number of young men under obligation through lending or giving them pigs. It is through the possession of pigs that men can achieve the rank of chiefdom. There is a great deal of inter-tribal competition for supremacy following the same lines as competition within a tribe. The rich chief who is able to become a creditor of other tribes or who outshines other chiefs by his generous sacrifices and contributions to festivities is liable to become the ruler of a group of tribes.

Pig currency has a very high velocity of circulation. All transactions take place in public, in what Speiser describes as "pig Bourses." There are periodic meetings connected with sacrifical feasts, providing occasion for creditors to call in their pigs from their debtors. Pigs are borrowed, exchanged, repaid on such occasions. Within a few hours, the same pig may change hands a number of times.[18]

The quantity of pig currency is apt to fluctuate widely through natural causes, according to the frequency and extent of sacrifices and feasts, and as a result of foreign trade. There is a great deal of traffic between the islands and communities which do not attach so much importance to highly developed tusks and exchange their boars for tuskless pigs or for other goods. When the Europeans arrived on the scene they, too, took a hand. During the middle of the 19th century there was a strong demand by Europeans for sandalwood and payment was made mostly in pigs. In the year 1860 alone some 8,000 were shipped to the New Hebrides. This, according to Harrison, upset the very foundation of native culture and currency.[19] It seems, however, that the New Hebrides succeeded in absorbing the abnormal influx, and, judging by the prices quoted above, there was a rising trend in the value of pigs at the time of Layard's visit.

According to the most recent information available, in spite of the penetration of modern civilization in the Pacific, pig currency continued to reign supreme right to the eve of the second World War. There were, however, also other currencies in use. Trade with whites was largely

[18]Speiser, pp. 278-80.   [19]Harrison, p. 141.

conducted in terms of tobacco. According to Harrison[20] tobacco has become universal currency in import trade with Europeans and its value was at one time fixed at threepence a stick. In Malekula natives who are reluctant to work unless they are in need of money willingly render minor services against payment in sticks of tobacco or boxes of matches.[21]

The New Hebrides have several kinds of subsidiary currencies also for internal trading. The importance of these currencies compared with that of pigs varies from island to island and even between different parts of the larger islands, according to the extent to which the cult of sacrificial pigs prevails in the communities concerned. The best known subsidiary currencies are mats, shells, stones and feathers.

On some islands such as Mævo and Aoba mats are more important than pigs. On Malekula they play the part of small change. On islands where they play a subsidiary role, mats depreciate as and when their fringes are worn away.[22] On the other hand, on islands where they play a leading part they appreciate as they grow older. Indeed, according to Speiser,[23] on Mævo they are kept in separate houses and a fire is continually burning there in order that they should become covered with soot. A man has to watch the process constantly and his wages gradually increase the value of the mats in proportion to the time during which they are subject to the smoking process. These smoked specimens are only used for purchasing club advancement, not for current everyday transactions. They are never moved even when they change ownership.[24] They are lent, and interest is obtained through the repayment of older and smokier mats.

On North Pentecôte coloured mats in good condition are used for current trading. One mat is worth five shillings. On Vao mats are used as currency sometimes even in trade with Europeans at the rate of one shilling per mat.[25] According to Rivers[26] in Pentecote two kinds of mats are used; red being the "sacred" colour, red mats are more valuable than the others.

Mats are the principal store of value in some islands, and are displayed as evidence of riches.[27] Many authors do not consider them as currency, but it is advisable to differentiate between the old specimens which seldom, if ever, change hands and the new ones which circulate freely.

Shells are used as valuable ornaments throughout the group of isles, but their monetary use is confined to a few islands only. They are considered money on Espirito Santo, on Marlo and on Ambrim.[28] According to Harrison, in some parts of the group, especially in the far north,

[20]Harrison, p. 228.   [21]Cheeseman, p. 81.   [22]Layard, p. 249.
[23]Speiser, p. 274.
[24]W. Coote, *The Western Pacific* (London, 1883), p. 65.
[25]Speiser, p. 274.   [26]Rivers, p. 386.   [27]Speiser, p. 271.
[28]Speiser, p. 273. Harrison, p. 50.

shell beads of a certain type are almost as important as pigs. Marlo trades them against pigs with islands where the cult of pigs predominates.

Stone money, made of quartzite, is particularly popular on Eromanga, where it is considered very valuable.[29] According to Speiser,[30] the largest specimen is rather less than two feet in diameter, a mere trifle compared with the stone giants of Yap. It is used mainly for the purchase of wives, and plays no part in everyday transactions. It has no standard unit.

Cowries, which are used as ornaments in many parts of Oceania, are said to serve as means of payment on Eromanga.[31]

Feathers are used as currency on Marlo and some of the islands. They are fastened on strings, and a string of about 30 cms. constitutes the unit.[32] They do not compare in importance with the other subsidiary currencies.

[29]Finsch, p. 267.
[30]Speiser, p. 273. Andrée, p. 233.
[31]J. E. Hertz, *Über Verwändung und Verbreitung der Kaurimuschel.* Mitteilungen der Geographischen Gesellschaft in Hamburg (1880-81), p. 25.
[32]Speiser, p. 273.

CHAPTER 8

THE FEATHER MONEY OF SANTA CRUZ

The feather money of Santa Cruz Islands, which was still in use in the late 'thirties, is regarded by ethnologists as one of the outstanding characteristics of that group. According to Codrington among others, the red feathers used are those of the parrot *Trichoglossus Massena*.[1] According to Archey,[2] they are the feathers of a scarlet honey-eater named by Krieger[3] *Myzomela Cardinalis*. Whichever version may be correct, this feather money consists of strip-like coils of fibre about fifteen feet long and up to two to three feet wide, completely covered on the outer side with overlapping rows of red feathers.

The area within which this currency circulated originally included also the Duff and Wilson groups and the Reef Islands.[4] On the eve of the second World War the monetary use of red feathers was confined to the Santa Cruz group, and the other islands where it had circulated exported them to that group. Both the capture of the birds and especially the preparation of the coils involves a considerable amount of labour, which accounts partly for the high value of this type of primitive money. Each bird yields only a few feathers suitable for the purpose, and a great many are needed for a whole roll.[5] According to Archey the

[1]Codrington, p. 324.
[2]Archey, p. 51.
[3]Krieger, p. 81.
[4]Krieger, p. 81.
[5]Felix Speiser, *Two Years with the Natives in the Western Pacific* (London, 1913), p. 283.

value of the feather coils is partly due to the wooden emblems and charms attached to them.

Feather money is used to a very large extent as a store of value.[6] It is carefully guarded and stored in a dry, warm place to preserve the colour and elasticity of the coils. Rich men sometimes build special huts for their feather money. As the feathers wear off, the coils depreciate in value.[7]

Archey[8] claims that the feather coils are actually used as medium of exchange. Four coils of good quality would purchase an ocean-going canoe, and a bride would cost ten coils or more according to her looks and reputed industry. Owing to its high value the feather money is not used in everyday transactions. No information is available how far it is used as a unit of account. It is known to serve as a means for special payments such as ransoms, fines and blood money. In one known instance, the life of an Englishman, threatened by an infuriated crowd, was ransomed through the payment of a number of coils of feather money.[9] On Nukapu, Reef Islands, the native who murdered Bishop Patterson in 1871 was fined four coils of feather money.[10]

Formerly strings of shell discs were used in Santa Cruz as a secondary currency, but now they only serve as ornaments.[11] In the 'eighties, blue beads were the rage on the islands, and with them practically everything the native had could be bought. Also small pieces of iron, eight inches long and one and a half inches wide, were in great request, and their value was about a penny each.[12]

[6]Florence Coombe, *Islands of Enchantment—Many-Sided Melanesia* (London, 1911).   [7]Coombe, p. 189.   [8]Archey, p. 51.
[9]Coombe, p. 179.   [10]Coombe, p. 210.   [11]Archey, p. 51.
[12]Coombe, p. 99.

CHAPTER 9

SHELL LOANS ON THE BANKS ISLANDS

The Banks Islands have a very highly developed currency and credit system which is closely connected with its system of men's clubs or secret societies. While pigs play an important part in exchanges, their principal currency consists, or consisted until recently, of strings of shell discs. These shells are rough and unfinished. They do not serve as ornaments. It is not their quality but their quantity that matters.[1] Originally the shell strings may possibly have been ornaments, but if so they have long ceased to serve that purpose; they have come to serve no other purpose than that of currency.[2] The shell discs are not even

[1]Codrington, p. 325.   [2]Rivers, p. 385.

polished. They are manufactured chiefly on a small coral islet off Rowa and are acquired from their producers against taro and yam.[3]

The shell strings are valued by the length measured from one shoulder to the tip of the fingers of the other hand, which is about four feet. For this length, according to Rivers,[4] it is possible to obtain ten yams which provides vegetable food for five persons for a week. A woman working for one day from sunrise to sunset is able to make a fathom of this money.

The shell money of Banks Islands is used as a store of value, and also as a medium of exchange, but its main functions are to buy admission and promotion in secret societies and to be loaned out against high interest. Even if it played no part in commercial transactions, this alone would be sufficient to justify describing shell strings on Banks Islands as a form of primitive currency.

Firth is opposed to applying the definition of money to objects which "only" serve as means of payment in connection with the activities of secret societies. Yet he has contributed more than most ethnologists towards making us realize the immense importance of such societies in the economic, political and social systems of primitive communities. The direct or indirect economic importance of such transactions is far greater than that of the total of commercial transactions proper. In any case, if an object serves as the means of payment of subscriptions to secret societies it is bound to become a medium of exchange to some extent. Most men want to acquire it and accept it therefore in payment for their goods or their labour. Others, too, are likely to be willing to accept it because they can depend on a steady demand which should enable them to use those objects in payment.

In his *History of Melanesian Society*, Rivers gives a detailed account of the functioning of "men's clubs" or "secret societies" on the Banks Islands and explains the way in which such activities link up with the currency and credit system of the communities concerned. In the most important type of these societies, known under the name of *Suqe*, candidates were expected to produce sixty fathoms of shell money.[5] Further sums were required to be paid in order to buy promotion in that society. This process is, however, by no means a one-way traffic. The *Suqe* does not accumulate the money but redistributes it among its members. Participation in the "dividends" is according to rank. A man who has spent a large amount of shell money in order to gain high promotion in the *Suqe* is entitled to receive a large share from the contributions of those initiated later or of those who subsequently paid for promotion. Since it is only the rich who can advance far in the organization, the whole system results in the perpetuation, and even accentuation, of differences in social rank; for this rank is dependent on the

[3]Rivers, p. 168.   [4]Rivers, p. 168.
[5]Rivers, p. 64.

E

possession of wealth to a larger degree than in most modern communities.[6] An increase of wealth is, in turn, simply the means to the end of securing still further advancement in the organization.

The problem for poor people is to find ways to provide the shell money required to pay for their initiation and promotion. One of the most widespread practices to that end is to lend money against interest. The standard rate is 100 per cent for any period. If the prospective candidate already possessed ten fathoms of shell money, he would lend it to ten of his friends, a fathom to each. After some months they would repay this loan with 100 per cent interest, so that the candidate would then possess twenty fathoms. The process can be repeated until the candidate has a sufficient amount of money to pay for his initiation.[7]

It may well be asked why anybody should borrow money at such an exorbitant rate, without any apparent benefit to himself, for the sole purpose of enabling another man to double his capital. The answer is given by Codrington[8] who states that in the Banks Islands a man is entitled to *impose* a loan on an unwilling borrower and the latter is under inescapable moral obligation to accept the loan and repay subsequently at a 100 per cent interest. This may sound like a passage from *Erewhon* or from *Alice in Wonderland*. But Codrington is a reliable observer, and can be depended upon.

Indeed, Banks Island appears to be a creditor's paradise. There is a very highly developed credit system that favours the creditor at the expense of the debtor. The treatment of defaulting debtors is very drastic. All the members of the creditor's household proceed to the defaulter's house and stay there, eating up all his food. They remain there until his friends help him to settle his debt.[9] It is worth while for a debtor in difficulty to postpone the day of reckoning by borrowing the amount he has to repay, even though in doing so he redoubles his liability. Florence Coombe summed up the position with the following words: "In these islands everybody is always in debt. Our own fiscal policy appears to many lay minds a trifle intricate. It is clear as daylight when compared with the financial laws that run through this part of Melanesia."[10]

As a rule no written documents change hands, but all credit business is transacted in public. A great deal of the time and energy of the population is expended in an eternal effort to obtain payment from one's debtors to be able to pay one's creditors. Owing to the fact that every debtor is due to repay twice the amount he borrows, the amount payable is liable to exceed the total amount of money available, in spite of the fact that new money is constantly produced. The whole system is of a snowball-like character. On Mota, "creditors are for ever roaming

[6]Rivers, p. 141.
[7]Rivers, p. 65.   [8]Codrington, p. 326.
[9]Codrington, p. 326. Florence Coombe, pp. 61-2.
[10]Coombe, p. 61.

about, trying to raise at least some of the money and pigs due to them, that they in turn may satisfy their own creditors."[11]

In addition to the shell money, there are other primitive currencies on the Banks Islands. Pigs are the most important amongst them. There is a strong and steady demand for pigs in connection with the activities of the secret societies. Beads are also used for small purchases.[12] On Vanikolo turtle shells play an important part as a currency.[13] On Santa Maria and Meraclava they have a curious feather currency made up from the small feathers around the eyes of fowls, tied on strings and dyed fine crimson. They are mainly ornamental but also pass in the way of money.[14]

Torres Island has a most involved monetary system which has not yet been adequately studied. Its chief currency is claimed to be arrows which are very neatly made and are ornamental.[15] In addition, mats circulate as small change.[16] Strangest of all, pigs' jawbones are said to be used as currency.[17] Formerly boars' tusks were a medium of exchange. Beads serve as small change.[18] No information is available whether and to what extent there are fixed ratios between these various kinds of currencies, nor has their relative importance been ascertained.

[11]Codrington, p. 326.
[12]Coombe, p. 77.   [13]Rivers, p. 386.   [14]Codrington, p. 324.
[15]Rivers, p. 386. British Museum, *Handbook to the Ethnographical Collections* (London, 1910), p. 125.
[16]Rivers, p. 386.   [17]Layard, p. 249.   [18]Codrington, p. 327.

CHAPTER 10

SHELL AND TEETH CURRENCIES ON THE SOLOMON ISLANDS

Most islands of the Solomons group used both shells and teeth as currency. The types of shells and teeth that are used on particular islands or groups of islands vary, and so does the relative importance of these currencies. Even within the same islands different kinds of money are sometimes in use. For instance, each part of Mala fancies its own kind of shell money and affects to despise the money used in other parts.[1]

Both shell disc strings and shell rings are widely used as currency on all islands. There is an immense number of combinations in which the various coloured discs are strung, sometimes by themselves and sometimes together with teeth. The unit seldom consists of a single disc or even a single string, but a combination of a number of strings. Single shells are only used by the islanders for the reconciliation of their offended deities who are apparently satisfied with small change.

The value of the strings varies generally according to their colour. As

[1]Walter G. Ivens, *The Island Builders of the Pacific* (London, 1930), p. 276.

in other parts of Melanesia, red is considered the sacred colour and red shells are valued very highly. Indeed, it is almost impossible to induce natives to part with red shell strings. Most chiefs in Malaita, San Christobal, Guadalcanal and Gela hide their supply of red shell strings in secret places.[2]

The name of one of the popular varieties of shell money is *rongo* which in many Melanesian languages means "sacred."[3] It is produced on reef islets near Malaita, and has a wide sphere of circulation.[4] On Rubiana a different kind of shell currency is manufactured out of the shells of a giant clam. They are made into arm-shells which are used as a currency all over the Solomons. An ordinary string is worth a hundred coconuts, but particularly reddish strings are worth anything between a thousand and two thousand coconuts.[5]

On Bougainville and Buka Islands two kinds of shell strings are used which are somewhat similar to the *diwara* of the Bismarck Archipelago. The cheaper kind has a fixed value of five shillings, while the more expensive kind is not used in everyday transactions but is only used for ceremonial purposes, as bride money. It is also taken for pigs and as compensation for theft in return for the release of the culprit.[6]

In the South-Eastern Solomons shell money is put to the following uses: bride price, blood money, buying of canoes, payment of fees and fines, redemptive offerings to spirits, buying of pigs and food.[7]

Fines, blood money, the penalty for adultery, the fee of the rainmaker, etc., are fixed in Buin in amounts such as ten, twenty, forty fathoms according to circumstances. Various kinds of shell money differ, however, in value. There is a special kind for the use of women only which is worth twice as much as the standard money. While the ordinary shell strings are worth a shilling per fathom, the strings of red discs imported from Alu or Rubiana are worth a pound. Packets of a hundred fathoms of the ordinary shell money are deposited in the sleeping houses. Thurnwald records a popular belief that on such packets the spirits of ancestors take up their abode. Having regard to the ancestor-worship of primitive peoples, this belief gives some idea of the high regard in which shell money is held.[8]

On Buin the use of shell money appears to be linked up with the cult of the pig. Thurnwald suggests that originally the shell strings were used as tokens acknowledging the receipt of a pig, and that their value was

[2]O. Schneider, *Muschelgeld-Studien* (Dresden, 1905), p. 75.
[3]W. H. R. Rivers, *Psychology and Ethnology* (London, 1926), p. 295.
[4]Schneider, p. 75.
[5]C. Ribbe, *Zwei Jahre unter den Kannibalen der Salomo Inseln* (Dresden, 1903), p. 240.
[6]Beatrice Blackwood, *Both Sides of the Buka Passage* (Oxford, 1931), p. 447.
[7]Ivens, *Melanesians of the South-East Solomon Islands* (London, 1927), p. 391.
[8]R. Thurnwald, *Pigs and Currency on Buin. Observations about Primitive Standard of Value and Economy* (Oceania, December, 1934), Vol. v, No. ii, p. 123.

derived from their convertibility with pigs. "We may then fairly speak of a pig standard of currency."[9]

The advent of modern money has not displaced shell money; indeed, traders buy native shell money for the purpose of taking advantage of the wide differences between its value in various islands of the Solomons group and other parts of Melanesia. They buy, for instance, the shell moneys of North Malaita and use it to buy coconuts or copra on Florida.[10]

Shell money is certainly used as a unit of account and there are elaborate schedules of prices expressed in it. Coote gives the following table of values:—

> 10 coconuts=1 string of white money=1 stick of tobacco.
> 10 strings of white money=1 string of red money=1 dog's tooth.
> 10 strings of red money=50 porpoise teeth.
> 500 porpoise teeth=1 wife of good qualities.
> 1 "marble" (strong shell) ring=1 human head=1 very good pig= 1 young male slave of medium qualities.[11]

To form an idea about the important part shell money plays in the life of inhabitants of the Solomons, it is sufficient to study their poetry. A love song quoted by Thurnwald[12] is characteristic in this respect. "I broke off a long string of small shell beads and gave it to you, but you refused," chants a bemused lover, "therefore I am dissolved in tears. Surely your heart is longing for shell money." In another song quoted by Thurnwald a story is told about a chief who is blamed by his subjects for having spent the tribal shell money without distributing the proceeds among the tribesmen. His defence was that he had only used up a small amount for himself and that in the past he had always distributed generously on occasions of death feasts.[13]

Shell money is used on some islands of the Solomons for the purchase of food and of domestic animals.[14] Canoes are purchased with shell money.[15] Single strings of varying lengths are in common use for making current purchases.[16]

Several authors refer to the use made by white traders of shell money. According to Schneider, in 1896 there was strong demand for *rongo* for export to British New Guinea where it was used for the purchase of gold dust. Strings obtainable on the Solomons for one shilling fetched in British New Guinea twenty shillings.[17] The Government prohibited,

---

[9]Thurnwald (1934), pp. 138-9. He claims that boar tusks in New Guinea, dogs' teeth on Manus and *Tridacna* rings on Choiseul also became currencies through their use as a token acknowledging the receipt of pigs.

[10]Ivens (1930), p. 276.   [11]Coote, pp. 146-7.

[12]R. Thurnwald, *Forschungen auf den Salomo Inseln und den Bismarck Archipelago. Lieder und Sagen aus Buin* (Berlin, 1912), Vol. i, p. 229.

[13]Thurnwald (1912), pp. 51-4.

[14]H. A. Bernatzik, *Owa Raha* (Vienna, 1936), p. 48.

[15]Ivens (1930), p. 278.   [16]Ivens (1927), p. 391.

[17]Schneider, p. 75.

however, the use of shell money or tooth money in any transactions involving white people owing to the trouble arising over its valuation.[18]

The value of shell strings between the two wars ranged between 5s. and £1 per fathom, according to the degree of its redness.[19] Thin shell rings were a medium of exchange at one shilling in Rubiana, Isabel, Choiseul, Shortland and South-East Bougainville.[20] Old shell money depreciates and has to be exchanged for new, at the rate of one new for two old. The old shells are then restrung and put into circulation again.[21] Shells are also restrung for storage, for which purpose the strings are made several fathoms long.[22]

Shell money is widely used for payment of bride price. According to Ivens, its purchasing power in this sphere has depreciated considerably. Formerly a chief's daughter cost ten strings of shell money and a thousand porpoise teeth; now they ask up to thirty and even fifty strings in some instances.[23] In connection with marriages on Buin, pigs and shell money are constantly exchanged between the families of the bride and the bridegroom.[24]

Shell money plays an important part in political payments. It was the custom of the eastern Solomon Islands to put a price on the head of any man who had rendered himself obnoxious. The price consisted of a considerable amount of shell money which was offered by the friends of a murdered man for the head of the murderer.[25]

According to Ribbe, hooks made of mother-of-pearl shells were used as money in Rubiana, Wella-la-Wella, Renongo, Simbo, Choiseul and Isabel Islands. One hook was equal to a tobacco bar or to ten Pfennige German money.[26]

Teeth are nearly as important in the currency system of the Solomons as shells. The teeth of the dog, porpoise and the flying fox are used for monetary purposes. Amongst them, dogs' teeth are by far the most valuable, because only the two upper eye teeth are used for monetary purposes. It is no wonder they are more valuable than the porpoises' teeth, considering that a porpoise has 150 teeth. The hunting of porpoises by the coastal peoples of Mala is a religious function and can only be undertaken on certain special days.[27] Presumably this religious restriction was devised in order to avoid inflation of porpoises' teeth currency. The chief hunting ground for porpoises for monetary purposes has been at the coast of North Mala. Porpoises' teeth have been

[18]Blackwood, p. 448.
[19]S. G. C. Knibbs, *Savage Solomons as They Were and Are* (London, 1929). According to Blackwood (p. 448) some ceremonial shell string currencies are valued as high as £5.
[20]Schneider, p. 81.   [21]Ivens (1930), p. 277.
[22]Ivens (1930), p. 276.   [23]Ivens (1930), p. 101.
[24]Thurnwald (1934), p. 123.
[25]H. B. Guppy, *The Solomon Islands and Their Natives* (London, 1887), p. 17.
[26]Schneider, p. 81.
[27]Ivens (1930), p. 170.

imported in recent years from some of the Micronesian Islands in order
to make good the deficiency in the Solomons caused by the cessation of
porpoise hunting on Mala.[28]

The shell money unit consisting of ten strings is exchanged for fifty
large porpoise teeth or two hundred medium-sized ones. Traders paid
£1 for a hundred medium-sized teeth.[29] Porpoise teeth are extensively
used for payment of fines. Florence Coombe quotes an instance in which
on Gela a white trader was placed under taboo by the native chief by
putting a fine of a hundred porpoise teeth on selling coconuts to him.[30]
Porpoise teeth are used also for ceremonial payments and for the purchase of wives and pigs.[31] Teeth of the flying fox are used for similar
purposes.

Dogs' teeth were produced mainly on San Christobal, where a large
number of dogs were kept for the sake of their two money teeth. They
were not worth more than a penny apiece in San Christobal, but at
Gela they sold for sixpence each.[32] As the extraction of teeth involved
great cruelty, the Government decreed that only two dogs per hunter
were allowed to be kept. The breeding of large numbers of dogs for
currency purposes is no longer permissible.[33] The dogs' teeth strings
which were in circulation were freely accepted at a fixed value by white
traders.[34] According to Finsch, one dog's tooth was equal to one hundred coconuts or fifty porpoise teeth or ten sticks of tobacco. One
hundred dogs' teeth was the purchase price of a woman or a young boy.
During the 'eighties of the last century, this currency was no longer so
valuable.[35]

The Handbook of the Ethnographical Collections of the British
Museum states that shields constituted also currency on the Solomon
Islands.[36]

In their dealings with white people, natives used copra, coconuts and
tobacco as media of exchange. According to Blackwood, all purchases
from white men or Chinese store-keepers are usually paid for in copra,
the rates varying with the current market price of that commodity.
"Sticks of tobacco, and to a smaller extent shillings, are now coming
into favour as the means of trading among the natives themselves, three
sticks of tobacco being recognized as the equivalent of a shilling or
goods to that value."[37] Most dealing between natives is still done by
barter. Prices are fixed by tradition, but they are fixed independently of
each other. Thus, if, for instance, ten coconuts are equal to twenty taros
and twenty taros are equal to one large fish, it does not at all follow that
ten coconuts can be exchanged for one fish. Quite possibly the tradi-

[28]Ivens (1930), p. 170. [29]Ivens (1930), p. 278.
[30]Coombe, p. 311. [31]Blackwood, p. 448. [32]Coombe, p. 233.
[33]Caroline Mytinger, *Headhunting in the Solomon Islands* (London, 1943), p. 42.
[34]Mytinger, pp. 83-4. [35]Finsch, p. 184.
[36]*Ethnographical Collections*, p. 125.
[37]Blackwood, p. 446.

tional rate of exchange between fish and coconuts is something quite different.[38]

Until the eve of the second World War the use of modern money apparently failed to dislodge the various types of native money. Young men working for white people earn wages in modern money, and two-thirds of their wages are required by law to be deferred until their contract is completed in order that they should take the cash back to their villages.[39] Once back in their villages, they share out their money amongst their relatives in accordance with ancient custom. In any case modern money would be useless for young men for paying bride price which must be paid in shell money and teeth money. By distributing his modern money, he establishes a claim for contributions of his relatives towards the bride price.[40] This statement is contradicted, however, by Hogbin,[41] according to whom most natives in Malaita are much more firmly attached to their modern money than to their other possessions. They give away liberally their shell money, their food supplies, and their labour, but will think twice before presenting a neighbour with a shilling. This is said to be partly because, in order to earn modern money it is necessary to work for whites on plantations, partly because modern money is needed for taxes, and partly because it can buy a variety of European goods.

One of the features of the social system on the Solomons is the lack of desire to make profit on either labour or goods. Sellers in many instances try to outdo buyers in generosity, giving more than the value received. "For the only profit a man can make in a deal in this absurd society is a reputation for generosity."[42] Nevertheless, the strong desire of natives for holding primitive currency as store of value has generated selfishness and greed manifesting itself in a desire to hold the shell money or porpoise tooth money by burying it.

[38]Ivens (1930), p. 262.
[39]Mytinger, p. 79.   [40]Ivens (1930), p. 279.
[41]H. Ian Hogbin, *Experiments in Civilization* (London, 1939), p. 170.
[42]Mytinger, p. 148.

CHAPTER 11

THE INTRICATE CURRENCY OF ROSSEL ISLAND

One of the most complicated systems of means of payment ever devised by tortuous human mind is the system used on Rossel Island. Its savage cannibal inhabitants have a monetary system—if it can be regarded as such—that is more intricate than any monetary system operating in modern communities. We owe our knowledge of this extraordinary system to W. E. Armstrong, who studied it on the spot with great care and produced one of the most interesting accounts of any primitive means of payment.[1] There is no reason to suppose that even the upheavals of the World War have made any difference to the deeply rooted system.

Rossel Island has two kinds of "money." The one called *ndap* consists of individual pieces of *Spondylus* shell. The second type of "money" is called *nko* and consists of sets of ten shell discs made probably from a giant clam.[2] There are twenty-two different values of *ndap* and sixteen different values of *nko*. The difference between the two is that *ndap* represents higher values and its highest units are treated with religious reverence and only its lower units circulate freely, while all units of *nko* circulate freely. Another difference is that *ndap* is regarded as men's money, while *nko* is regarded as women's money.

As in many other instances of primitive currencies, the natives believe the currencies of Rossel Island to be of supernatural origin. They are claimed to have been made by the Island's chief deity Wonajo, the snake-god. Fresh supplies of shells out of which *ndap* is made reach the island through expeditions undertaken by special canoes owned by the chiefs who thereby possess the control of the monetary supply.[3] No additional *nko* money is created and all existing supplies appear to be very ancient. The thirteen highest denominations of *ndap* have individual names each. They can be recognized owing to their irregular shape and to difference in their colour.

Armstrong gives the names of the twenty-two denominations of *ndap*, but for the sake of simplicity he subsequently refers to them by their number, "one" being the least value and "twenty-two" the highest. He says that the difference in the value of the various units is not due to their relative degree of scarcity. For example, number four, although by far the commonest kind on the island, has a greater value than numbers one, two or three. The value of each unit is determined by custom, and the law of supply and demand does not appear to affect it.

The parities between the various values follow a very peculiar system. The higher values are not simple multiples of the lower values, but represent a lower value plus the equivalent of the accumulated interest on that lower value for a certain period. Thus, if somebody borrows number four for a brief period, he has to repay a number five. If the loan is for a longer period, he has to repay a number six, or an even higher number, according to the length of the period. There is, however, no arithmetical proportion between the length of the period and the interest due for the loan. This system operates for all units up to number seventeen; numbers eighteen to twenty-two follow different rules. Debtors

[1]W. E. Armstrong, *Rossel Island* (Cambridge, 1928), Chapters v and vi.
[2]Armstrong, p. 59.
[3]According to Armstrong (p. 60) it may be that the importance of chieftainship on Rossel rests primarily on the privilege of making *ndap* money.

borrowing units up to number seventeen need not ever repay a higher
unit than number seventeen. Anyone borrowing a higher unit has to
repay the same unit and interest is paid in the form of a smaller unit.
Number eighteen is regarded as sacred and can only be passed from one
holder to another in a crouching position. Numbers nineteen to twenty-
two are considered even more sacred.

The relation between the sixteen different values of *nko* money are
governed by rules similar to those concerning *ndap* money. All of them,
including the highest denomination, circulate freely. The five highest
denominations are considered to be highly valuable, though less so than
the five highest denominations of *ndap* money.

There are special uses for each denomination and they are not freely
interchangeable. It is not possible, for instance, to use in payment several
pieces of lower denomination instead of a higher unit, or several *nko*
moneys instead of a *ndap* money. Tradition has fixed the amount and
the denomination of the units which are payable on every ceremonial
occasion.[4] Such cermonial occasions are connected with marriage or
various kinds of festivities such as the slaughter of a pig, or the eating
up of a man sentenced to the cooking-pot for some minor offence. The
chances are that the person who has to make the payment does not
possess the particular unit required. It would be indeed contrary to the
law of averages if such a coincidence occurred too frequently, considering that the total proportion of *ndap* money is, according to Armstrong, only about two per head of the population. In the predominant
majority of instances it is necessary to borrow the particular unit
required, even if the man who is to make the payment is a wealthy man.
Occasionally it is possible to swap a higher unit and a lower unit between relatives. Much more frequently it is necessary to borrow the unit
required giving in security a higher unit whenever possible.

The frequency of such loan operations has given rise to a profession
which corresponds to our bankers or bill-brokers. "The members of this
profession on Rossel," writes Armstrong,[5] "render an important service
by transferring the possession of coins, i.e., by borrowing from one who
does not want a particular coin and lending to another who does. Their
profit is made by borrowing at a lower rate of interest and discounting
at a higher. In practice a form of magic is employed by means of which
these brokers, and others who are not members of this profession, claim
to act on the minds of their debtors, making them repay within the
customary time, while the minds of their creditors are affected in the
reverse way."[6] In the highly developed "monetary" system of Rossel,
both interest and discount operations are known. It goes without saying
that the arithmetical faculties of the Rossel Islander are very highly
developed. They can easily reckon in high figures and they are very pro-
ficient in counting.

[4]Armstrong, pp. 64-5.   [5]Armstrong, p. 66.   [6]Armstrong, p. 66.

We are greatly indebted to Armstrong for having collected all this valuable information about this remarkable system. It is a pity that there is not enough evidence to show to what extent, if at all, *ndap* and *nko* are used as a medium of exchange in everyday transactions, apart from the purchase of pigs. Nor is there any evidence to show to what extent, if at all, prices are quoted in everyday life in *ndap* or in *nko*. It is argued sometimes that because the higher denominations of *ndap* are not mere units but have names of their own and are individually recognizable, they cannot be regarded as money, the essential characteristic of which is that it is entirely objective. In fact, it is only the higher units which are individual, while lower units circulate freely and are paid and received by tale. Even if they are not used extensively in everyday transactions, *ndap* and *nko* may be considered to play a limited monetary role, owing to the important part of ceremonial payments and transactions in pigs, and owing to the highly developed credit system and advanced banking operations based on the currencies.

The main reason why the monetary status of *ndap* and *nko* is open to doubt is that they do not confer on their owner indiscriminate purchasing power. Each unit can only be used for a certain well-defined purpose. Even though similar limitation of the use of primitive currencies is fairly frequent, in the case of Rossel Island it is carried to extreme. Nor are the various units freely interchangeable. Finally, there is no evidence to show, how far the shell "currency" on Rossel provides incentive for increased economic activity. It seems reasonable, however, to assume that the desire to possess *ndap* and *nko* stimulates the savages to breed pigs and possibly to produce other goods in excess of their own immediate requirements.

CHAPTER 12

DEBTS IN DOGS' TEETH ON THE ADMIRALTY ISLANDS

The Admiralty Islands had until the eve of the second World War, and possibly still have, two currencies of approximately equal importance— shell strings and dogs' teeth. Although in ordinary exchanges barter is usually preferred to sale against either of these currencies, both play, nevertheless, a very important part in the economic life of the communities.

The shell money consists of strings of white shell discs, measured mostly in strings or half strings. There are also special shells of rarer quality for the purchase of pigs and for the purposes of bride money.[1]

[1]Hans Nevermann, *Admiralitäts-Inseln*. [*Ergebnisse der Südsee-Expedition*, 1908-10. II Ethnographic Section, B. Melanesien, Vol. III (Hamburg, 1934)], p. 299.

Dogs' teeth serve as a money either singly or stringed. Both shells and dogs' teeth are used as store of value. They also act to a considerable extent as medium of exchange. Parkinson quotes the following prices in terms of shell strings:—

    10 obsidian spearheads=3 fathoms.

    A large container of coconut oil=33½ fathoms.

    2 blocks of obsidian (for 30 spearheads each)=10 fathoms.

    Small packet of manganese earth for blackening bodies=3 fathoms.

    Bead strings=length for length.

    String of 100 dogs' teeth=belt of 30 shell strings.[2]

Both dogs' teeth and shell strings are used for payments in connection with religious rites. The value of both shell money and dogs' teeth fluctuates according to supply and demand. Dogs' teeth lost a great deal of their value when, before 1914, white traders imported large quantities from China and Turkey.[3] A pot which formerly cost one tooth cost ten teeth in 1929.[4] Shell money was affected in a similar way through the import of glass beads, owing to the fact that many natives came to prefer these to shells for ornamental purposes.

In 1900 a shell money string about a foot long was worth two marks.[5] Bride money consisted of one hundred strings of shell money. In 1910, 2·39 metres of special shell string was worth one hundred dogs' teeth. In 1929, a dog's tooth was worth ten taro roots or ten coconuts or forty betel nuts. Three eggs cost two teeth.[6] In 1932 four to five dogs' teeth were worth a shilling.[7]

Both currencies are used extensively as units of account. Their principal role consists, however, in serving as standards of deferred payment and means for exchanges arranged in connection with marriages. As the origin of debts lies largely in these exchanges, it is necessary to deal with the system in some detail. Much information on the subject has been derived from Margaret Mead's essay on *The Manus of the Admiralty Islands*.[8]

Under the social system on the island of Manus and other islands of the Admiralty group, on the occasion of each marriage, the bridegroom's side has to contribute bride money in the form of currency or imperishable capital goods such as canoes, while the bride's side has to contribute perishable goods, such as food, of an equal value. The system provides strong inducement for a very considerable turnover in goods and in money. The prestige of a man within his community depends on the amount of wealth which has passed through his hands. What matters is not that large profit should be made on the transactions.

[2]R. Parkinson, *Dreissig Jahre in der Südsee* (Stuttgart, 1907), pp. 390-1.
[3]Margaret Mead, *Growing Up in New Guinea* (London, 1931), p. 236.
[4]Margaret Mead, *Melanesian Middle Men* (Natural History, Vol. xxx), p. 122.
[5]Schneider, p. 59.   [6]Mead (xxx), p. 121.   [7]Nevermann, p. 300.
[8]*Co-operation and Competition among Primitive Peoples* (New York, 1937), p. 210.

It is the ambition of the Manus that the volume of his exchange should be as large as possible. The amount of one single exchange is sometimes as high as 10,000 dogs' teeth. In the case of poor couples, wealthy men "adopt" the bride or the bridegroom and put up the necessary money for goods, in order to have an opportunity for participating in exchanges which, under the prevailing social system, are only effected in conjunction with marriages. The system has developed into exchanges between groups rather than between individuals. A wealthy man assumes leadership of the group and he provides and receives the largest payments and the major part of the prestige derived from it. Members of the groups have to contribute their share and have to endeavour to repay the debts contracted in connection with their marriage.

The entire system serves unconsciously the purpose of stimulating to the utmost the turnover of goods and of money. As in many other primitive communities, there seems to be among the Manus no natural desire for trading for economic motives. But for the social motive introduced in conjunction with the use of the primitive currency of the community, there would be utter economic stagnation. In the absence of trade the family would have to remain a self-sufficient economic unit and would not produce beyond its immediate needs. It is thanks to the non-economic motive introduced by the peculiar system that artificially stimulated trade can develop.

Although marriage simply serves as an excuse for exchanges, in the course of time the two institutions have become inseparable. For inscrutable reasons, the natives consider themselves inhibited from trading unless they can link up their transactions with marriage. Rather than try to overcome this inhibition, they very often arrange marriages solely for the sake of having a pretext to trade. At an early age a young boy and a girl are betrothed, and on the occasion of their betrothal the relatives of the boy give a large amount of dogs' teeth and shell money to the relatives of the girl. They receive this money from the group to which they belong, thereby contracting a debt. The relatives of the girl have to repay the money received by instalments of pigs, coconut oil, sago, taro, etc. They, too, have to be helped by their group. This exchange is repeated several years later on the occasion of the marriage and again later when the married couple celebrate their silver wedding.

"Everyone in the community is engaged in a network of economic obligations involving everybody else. . . . These obligations are often made suddenly and become unexpectedly due, by death or divorce. Nearly everyone is always engaged in a violent effort to keep up with events."[9]

The whole religious system of the community aims at inducing the native to work harder and to consume less for the sake of being able to

[9] R. F. Fortune, *Manus Religion and Ethnographical Study of the Manus Natives of the Admiralty Islands* (Philadelphia, 1936), p. 49.

contribute to the exchanges to the utmost limit of his capacity. If he does not do so, the spirits are offended and retribution follows. "The oracles are relentless in finding people behindhand and in spurring them on by a diagnosis that illness in the house is due to debts or obligations not fulfilled in time. . . . If a man is one day late in contributing his sago for instance, and his baby is ill on the night of the day when it should have been contributed, this slight delay is diagnosed as the cause."[10]

The credit system that has thus been created is even more delicately balanced than that of over-trading and over-speculating modern communities. Default by one debtor is liable to lead to quite a series of defaults on the part of his creditors who in turn are themselves debtors. For this reason the utmost moral and religious pressure is brought to bear on every debtor not to default. Likewise it is everybody's duty to his group not to commit any act which would compromise the delicately balanced exchange position between the groups. Fighting with groups with which they are in exchange relations must be avoided if possible.

There can be no doubt that the volume of production has greatly benefited by this system of exchanges. A great deal is produced for its sake which would not be produced otherwise. "The constant circulation of the imperishable valuables creates debts which must be met by fishing, trading and manufacturing; the community relies upon using, eating and wearing goods which have been distributed in this indirect manner."[11]

The Manus are very honest people, and "are ridden by an anxiety neurosis on the question of debt." Margaret Mead found it a far more effective way of ensuring a steady supply of fish to advance tobacco against future catches than simply to announce her willingness to buy.[12]

Anxiety in Manus about the possibility of debt repayment is always very marked. Every man is worried, irritable, apprehensive, restless, counting and recounting his debts. Every man is running an endless race with his own obligations, playing one creditor off against another, apportioning his goods among half a dozen different demands.[13]

On consideration of the above facts, it would not be easy to deny that both dogs' teeth and shell strings play the part of money on the Admiralty Islands. It may be objected that everyday trade, as distinct from the special exchanges dealt with above, is conducted mainly on the basis of barter. It is said to be unusual for a native to go to the market to buy taro in the ordinary way and pay with dogs' teeth. In accordance with the custom, taro is exchanged in the market against fish, and anyone who has no fish to offer has to wait till all the fish has been exchanged for taro and there is still some taro left for sale against money.[14]

Allowing for these and other limitations, there can be no doubt

[10]Fortune, p. 50.   [11]Mead (1931), p. 218.
[12]Mead (1931), p. 232.   [13]Mead (1931), p. 233.
[14]Herskovits, pp. 228-9.

that the importance of affinal exchanges is sufficiently large to justify the view that the objects that serve the purpose of such exchange constitute a currency. Moreover, dogs' teeth and shell money are extensively used as units of account and the value of most things is expressed in them, even if they change hands by means of barter. Herskovits is right in concluding, therefore, that to refuse to recognize these tokens of value as money would be simply to attach a greater importance to a definition than to the realities of the economic system in which the objects defined function.[15]

Contact with whites has resulted in the adoption of British money and tobacco as subsidiary currencies. Modern money is used even for the payment of small ceremonial debts, of magicians' fees, and also in ordinary trade relations between peoples of different tribes. Tobacco has even assumed a definite part as a currency in the mortuary ritual. Natives often borrow tobacco for that purpose. Workmen helping in house building are also often paid in tobacco. On the other hand, neither tobacco nor modern money play any part in the all-important affinal exchanges between the relations of bride and bridegroom.

[15]Herskovits, p. 229.

CHAPTER 13

SHELL AND YAM CURRENCIES OF THE TROBRIAND ISLANDS

Have the Trobriand Islands a primitive currency system or are they on a basis of pure natural economy? Malinowski, the leading authority on the Trobriand Islands—indeed practically the only scientific authority who has made their economic system the subject of special study—emphatically denies that there is anything in the nature of currency in use on the islands. His immense and well-deserved authority as an economic anthropologist makes it tempting to accept his conclusion without further investigation. He is contradicted, however, by another anthropologist of considerable authority, Marcel Mauss, who in his *Essai sur le don*[1] asserts that the shell ornaments of Trobriand are a kind of currency. This conflict between the views of two such eminent experts makes it particularly important to examine with care the available factual evidence. Most of this evidence was provided by Malinowski himself in his two books of outstanding importance, *Argonauts of the Western Pacific* and *Coral Gardens and their Magic*. It appears from this factual material that there is room for two different opinions on the question whether or not the Trobriands have a currency.

On general grounds there is no reason to rule out in advance the

[1]*L'Année Sociologique* (Paris, 1923-4), Nouvelle Série, Vol. i, p. 69.

possibility of the Trobriand community possessing a monetary system. After all, it forms part of Melanesia where a great many communities have, some more or less, developed primitive currency. While Polynesia is highly Communistic, in Melanesia private property is highly developed and the natives are strongly inclined towards exchanging goods in a businesslike way. Preliminary conditions for the operation of a currency system appear to exist, therefore, on the Trobriand Islands.

There are two objects which may be claimed to serve—or have served at any rate until recently—as currency. These are shells and yam. Malinowski examines with great care and in great detail the part both play in Trobriand economy.

Two types of shell ornaments come into consideration. There are single armshells and long *Spondylus* shell strings. Although they are used as ornaments on special occasions, this is not the primary object of their possession. Indeed, as Malinowski emphasizes,[2] at least 90 per cent of the armshells are of too small a size to be worn even by young boys and girls. The main object of both types of shells is to serve for ceremonial exchanges between Trobrianders and other island dwellers, and also for special payments within the Trobriand community itself.

Malinowski gives an interesting account of the way in which these valuables are systematically exchanged in the course of visits to islands belonging to the circuit within which the system operates. In exchange for armshells, *Spondylus* shell strings are given, and *vice versa*. The exchange, known under the name of *Kula*, is effected without any bargaining and with the utmost grace and dignity. It serves no economic purpose, for on an early occasion the exchange is reversed. On the other hand, the opportunity of these ceremonial visits is taken for exchanging also goods of practical use by means of ordinary barter on a strictly give-and-take basis.

Obviously, this strange function of the Trobriand shell valuables is not a monetary function, and if the shell ornaments served no other purpose it would be easy to conclude that they do not by any means constitute money. It seems, however, from the evidence provided by Malinowski himself, that they do perform other functions besides being the objects of ceremonial non-economic exchanges.

Malinowski states that shell valuables represent "condensed wealth," which means that they are used for the purpose of store of value.[3] There is reason to believe that they are also used as a limited medium of exchange, notwithstanding Malinowski's emphatic statement to the contrary. He admits that white pearl traders regularly pay native pearl fishers in armshells and ornaments made of *Spondylus* shell discs for really good pearls for which the natives would not be prepared to accept tobacco. Shell valuables are, according to Malinowski, exchanged for

[2] B. Malinowski, *Argonauts of the Western Pacific* (London, 1922), p. 88.
[3] Malinowski (1922), p. 511.

yam. He also states that chiefs use them for payments for services rendered to them. Admittedly these scraps of evidence in themselves are not sufficient to enable us to arrive at the conclusion that shell valuables are used as a medium of exchange on any noteworthy scale. Since, however, they are highly desired for considerations of prestige, and since there is a permanent demand for them also for certain special payments, it should be possible to acquire almost anything in Trobriand against payment in them. There is no evidence, however, to show that shell valuables are used as a unit of account, and in all probability prices are not expressed in them systematically.

According to Malinowski shell valuables are not used as a standard of deferred payment, apart from other reasons, because there are no deferred payments in Trobriand. This statement, however, appears to be contradicted by his own evidence. He says that sometimes as much as a year or more may elapse between payments in shell valuables.[4] There are also deferred payments of bride money in the form of shell ornaments. In this respect the system prevailing in Trobriand appears to be very similar to that prevailing on the Admiralty Islands, according to the description given in the previous chapter by Margaret Mead.[5] On Trobriand annual payments are received at harvest time by a man from his wife's brothers in the form of food. In return for this, he gives shell valuables or pigs to his wife's brothers from time to time. While Margaret Mead represents this exchange between the relatives of bride and bridegroom as the very foundation of the economic and social life of the primitive community she had investigated, Malinowski fails to appreciate adequately its economic importance. Nevertheless, it seems reasonable to assume that this exchange of shells for food in connection with marriage is a most important institution and the role played in it by shell valuables is similar to that played by shells and dogs' teeth on the Admiralty Islands—which is a decidedly monetary role. Indirectly shell valuables provide a stimulus to production and trade, since their exchange is accompanied by barter between islands, which would not take place otherwise.

Allowing for all these facts, it seems to be permissible to disagree with Malinowski, notwithstanding the high authority his views command, and to consider shell valuables as a limited currency in Trobriand. Admittedly it is not the only currency, perhaps not even the most important currency. Its part in everyday transactions is probably very limited. For the requirements of everyday life yam appears to be the principal form of currency in exchanges between natives. Malinowski denies that yam plays the part of currency, any more than shell ornaments do. Nevertheless in this respect his own evidence points even

[4] Malinowski (1922), p. 95.
[5] *Co-operation and Competition among Primitive Peoples* (New York, 1937), pp. 214 *et seq.*

F

more emphatically towards the opposite conclusion than in respect of shell ornaments.

For limited periods yam is undoubtedly used as a store of value. It is produced well in excess of requirements for the purpose of consumption. In any average year twice as much yam is produced than is consumed.[6] It is true, the unused excess supply is destroyed when the new harvest becomes available. Between the two harvests it certainly serves, however, as a store of value. Natives always accept yam in payment for most goods and services, even if they possess enough for their present and future requirements. They simply add the new supply to their reserve. Beyond doubt there is a great deal of pure barter between agricultural and fishing communities. Nevertheless basketfuls of yam are used for a variety of payments, especially for industrial labour. What is even more important from the point of view of enabling us to ascertain the monetary status of yam is the fact, admitted by Malinowski, that prices are expressed regularly in standard yam baskets.[7] "In ordinary barter," Malinowski observes,[8] "a basketful of yams is the only commercial unit which functions as a measure of value." Although the bundle of taro is also used in a similar way, it is not used to anything like the same extent.

There is also a third object which can claim to be regarded as a limited currency, namely, sticks of tobacco. As in other parts of Melanesia, it is used extensively for the purposes of payment by white traders for objects of comparatively small value and for minor services.[9] Malinowski says that "in everything which an ethnographer might need from a native either as specimens or services, tobacco has become their universal currency." The trader can best obtain most objects with tobacco. What is important is Malinowski's statement that on rare occasions even shell valuables can be purchased against tobacco when the person in possession of the shell valuables needs a large quantity of tobacco for distribution.[10] This indicates that tobacco is acquired by the islanders not solely for the purpose of direct consumption, but also for the purpose of using it in turn in payment for goods or services.

According to M. K. Gilmour, ceremonial axe blades serve as a currency in the Trobriands. They are used for buying pigs, food, canoes and even land; for procuring sorcery; for blood money and tribute to enemies, etc. Loan transactions are made in axe blades.[11]

Malinowski quotes in support of his contention that there is no currency in Trobriand the fact that there are abnormal discrepancies between prices quoted in tobacco or in yams. "If you wanted to purchase a valuable with tobacco, you would have to pay perhaps a thousand or two thousand sticks, that is about ten or twenty times its price in yams."

[6]Malinowski (1922), p. 58. B. Malinowski, *Coral Gardens and Their Magic* (London, 1935), p. 8.

[7]Malinowski (1935), p. 20.   [8]Malinowski (1935), p. 45.

[9]Malinowski (1935), p. 44.   [10]Malinowski (1935), p. 45.

[11]C. G. Seligmann, *The Melanesians of British New Guinea* (Cambridge, 1910), p.518.

He explains this discrepancy by the fact that the exchange of shell valuables for yams conforms to the traditionally obligatory type of exchange, while when trying to acquire shell valuables for tobacco the white traders have to make it well worth the natives' while to effect the unusual exchange.[12] The existence of such wide discrepancies does not, however, in itself disprove the existence of a monetary system. After all, in several primitive communities which have adopted modern money there are noteworthy discrepancies between the value of coins of various denomination. For sentimental or other reasons, natives prefer one denomination to another. This fact does not in any way alter the monetary character of the coins in question.

Had it not been for Malinowski's strong bias in favour of his conception of what money is,[13] he might possibly have arrived at the conclusion that in Trobriand no less than in many other Melanesian communities there is a monetary system consisting of several types of currencies, each one with a limited use. Had Malinowski investigated the New Hebrides or the Banks Islands or Rossel Island, in all probability he would have concluded that those communities too are moneyless. On the other hand, had Trobriand been investigated by Margaret Mead or W. E. Armstrong, with a less rigid definition of primitive money, they would undoubtedly have discovered a fairly advanced monetary system there. This is a somewhat perturbing thought.

[12]Malinowski (1935), p. 45.
[13]Malinowski's definition of money is implied in the following remark:—"There is no regular market (in Trobriand), hence no prices, hence no established mechanism of exchange, hence no room for currency" (1935, pp. 45-6). In his view, shared by many economists, the existence of money pre-supposes the existence of "a system of markets where haggling determines the price."

CHAPTER 14

THE "SACRED" MONEY OF NEW BRITAIN

The sacred character of money is very pronounced in New Britain, as is indicated by the name given to the principal shell money that was until recently, and probably still is to some extent, in use there. It is called *tambu*, a variant of the word *taboo* which means "sacred" or, to be accurate, "forbidden for religious reasons." On the Gazelle Peninsula, the origin of *tambu* is surrounded with an atmosphere of mystery that accounts largely for its prestige. On the Duke of York Island where the same money is called *diwara*, it is believed that the spirits have created it, and it is handled with reverential awe.[1]

Most ethnologists agree that the *diwara* or *tambu* is the most highly developed form of currency in the Pacific area. Even authors who are

[1]R. Parkinson, *Im Bismarck-Archipel* (Leipzig, 1887), p. 83.

otherwise reluctant to admit the monetary character of various objects used for payment in primitive communities, readily admit that the shell strings used in certain parts of the Bismarck Archipelago qualify to be considered a currency.[2]

The origin of the shells out of which these strings are made is shrouded in mystery—but for a very worldly reason. Most communities receive it through a chain of intermediary tribes, each one of which tries to conceal the source from which it acquired the shells in order not to lose its profitable intermediate trade. There can be no doubt, however, that some of the shells which reach the Duke of York group of islands come from Nakanai. In return the shells called *pele* which serve as currency at Nakanai are found in the Duke of York group. Here is an instance of two primitive communities swapping currencies. It provides a safeguard against inflation. The chiefs have the means of controlling the influx of shell money, as their permission is necessary for its import.[3] This monetary management is sometimes circumvented through unauthorized import of shells—judging by the frequent stories about people possessing "super-natural" powers to create shell money.[4]

Some of the *diwara* shells are found in Blanche Bay. Their collection requires diving operations which explains partly their comparative scarcity and their high value. In New Ireland the same shells are used as currency in some districts but their adoption is believed to be comparatively recent.[5] There, and also in New Britain and in the Duke of York group, *diwara* is the inter-tribal currency. While each tribe has also subsidiary internal currencies of its own, *diwara* is of overwhelming importance also in internal trade throughout the territory where it is in use.

One of the great advantages of *diwara* is that it can be divided very easily. The unit is the fathom and prices are quoted in fractions of a fathom. Moreover, individual shells can be removed from the strings for the purpose of making small payments. It would be idle to pretend that the sub-division of the unit is ideal or that the standard is absolutely accurate. After all, as the fathom is measured as being the distance between the two hands when they are stretched out straight in opposite directions, there is ample scope for discrepancies and disagreement. "A man is praised according to the good full measure he gives and execrated according to the short measure he may give."[6] Nevertheless, if we allow for the fact that the system operates in primitive conditions, its accuracy may be said to be adequate for the requirements.

Diwara is a very important store of value. It is kept in coils containing

²For the sake of simplicity the shell money will be referred to by its more popular name of *Diwara* for the rest of the chapter.
³Heinrich Schnee (Editor), *Deutsche Kolonial-Lexikon* (Leipzig, 1920), p. 692.
⁴Parkinson, pp. 83-4.   ⁵Finsch, p. 20.
⁶Benjamin Danks, *On the Shell Money of New Britain* (Journal of the Anthropological Institute of Great Britain and Ireland, Vol. xvii, London, 1888), p. 307.

between fifty and two hundred fathoms. Such coils are stored away in carefully guarded money houses and they are exhibited from time to time as a sign of great wealth.[7] Apart from an amount varying between a half fathom and four fathoms, which a man carries on him for current requirements, and a number of strings kept at home, his possession of *diwara* is deposited in the *diwara* house. When the enemy approaches, men, women and children seize *diwara* packets to take them to safety. It is said that in an emergency a woman would rather abandon her child than her *diwara*.[8] *Diwara* deposited in the house is only withdrawn for important purposes, such as the purchase of a wife. The native is proud when depositing a roll of fifty or more strings. The drums are beaten to summon the neighbours who watch the event with covetous eyes.[9]

Diwara decidedly fulfils the functions of the principal medium of exchange. It can be used in payment for goods and services of every description. Although barter continues to prevail to a large degree, the natives are aware that when they buy something with *diwara* they are not engaged in barter but in purchase. They have separate words for "purchase" and "barter."[10] *Diwara* is used for every kind of purchase, from the smallest to the largest. "A man wanting betel nuts would twist off a few shells and tender them as recognized payment."[11] On the other hand, *diwara* is also used when a man buys up the whole of his neighbour's crop. Danks himself purchased crops for between ten fathoms and twenty-five fathoms of shell strings.[12]

Right to the eve of the war in the Pacific *diwara* remained a medium of exchange.[13] During German colonial rule over the Bismarck Archipelago an attempt was made to eliminate it in order to be able to introduce German colonial currency. The adoption of modern currency had made no headway, however, and even white traders among themselves had taken to transacting business in *diwara*. A decree in 1902 prohibited the use of *diwara* in trade with whites. This measure produced some effect in the coastal areas. By 1904 German money was freely circulating along the North coast of the Gazelle Peninsular. *Diwara* remained, however, the dominant currency in internal regions, and even on the coast natives continued to use it in trade amongst themselves.[14]

Diwara plays an important part also as a standard of value. Most prices are quoted regularly in *diwara*. According to Finsch[15] a string bought between fifty and eighty taro roots; chickens cost between a

[7]George Brown, p. 296.   [8]Parkinson (1887), p. 105.
[9]Parkinson (1887), p. 105.   [10]Danks, p. 307.
[11]Brown, p. 296.   [12]Danks, p. 307.
[13]S. W. Reed, *The Making of Modern New Guinea* (Philadelphia, 1943), p. 47.
[14]Finsch, p. 19.
[15]Finsch, p. 15. Parkinson (1887, p. 104) quotes the following prices: A pig of 60 kilos = 10 strings; a bag of fresh copra = 1½ strings; 80 taros or 60 yams = 1 string; an older woman = 20 strings; a young girl = 50-100 strings.

quarter and half a string; pigs between six and forty strings; young girls between fifty and two hundred strings; elder women between twenty and fifty strings. Fish, yam, taro, lime, bananas, puddings, birds, pigs, canoes, slaves, turtle-shell and wives all had their recognized value in *diwara*. This value was, however, subject to fluctuations according to supply and demand.[16]

Payment of bride money and also fines, ransom, blood money, etc., is made in *diwara*. According to Parkinson a native can appease his bitterest enemy through the payment of *diwara*, even though he may have killed his nearest relative. The blood money to the next-of-kin of slayed victims is between twenty and fifty strings.[17] According to Danks, every wound inflicted in the fight had to be paid for in *diwara*.[18] The German Colonial Government collected fines in *diwara* during the 'nineties. Its revenue in 1896 included an item of 923 strings of *diwara*.[19]

Shell money in New Britain and in the other territories where it is in use fulfils in some respects even more extensive functions than modern money does in civilized communities. It is possible to make good, through payments in *diwara*, offences or crimes, including murder.[20] In the *diwara* area there is certainly one law for the rich and another law for the poor. Inter-tribal wars and feuds between individuals can be avoided through making payments in *diwara*. When peace is concluded, the number of those killed on both sides is counted and amends are made through paying the difference to the party which lost more men. Under this peculiar principle the victor pays "reparations" to the vanquished.

Above all, *diwara* plays a most important part as a standard of deferred payments. There is a very elaborate credit system in the Duke of York group. The standard rate of interest is ten per cent. The natives have a word for "usury" on the Duke of York Islands. In New Britain, the idea of interest is not so clear. There the extra fathom which is repaid for each ten fathoms of loan is regarded as a way of expressing gratitude for the loan. One of the reasons why credit is used extensively is the New Britain natives' aversion to break a coil of *tambu*. If he requires change, he prefers to mortgage his coil and spend the proceeds.[21]

There is a banker in each community with whom wealthy men lodge their shell money and who lends shell money on interest. He has great influence and power. Most young men are unable to pay for their wives unless they borrow money for that purpose. If a man defaults, he is a marked man; his character is gone; he is called an embezzler—nobody will lend him money in the future.[22]

Another way in which credit is granted is by the distribution of food, weapons and ornaments among a community by a rich man. On a fixed day, known to all who have accepted his goods, the debtors have to

[16]Brown, p. 296.   [17]Parkinson (1887), pp. 104-5.   [18]Danks, p. 314.
[19]Finsch, p. 15.   [20]Finsch, p. 15.   [21]Danks, pp. 307-8.
[22]Danks pp. 309-10.

come to make payment on the occasion of festivities arranged by the creditor. During the course of the festivities the shell strings are laid at the banker's feet.[23] Money for the purchase of a wife or for ceremonial fees is lent usually without security, especially if the lender is sufficiently powerful to enforce payment. While loans are outstanding debtors have to assist their creditors in any work or fight.[24]

Shell money enters into every phase of native life. Already children are taught how to use it. They make a sort of imitation money out of shells of inferior value and use it in their play, which consists generally in imitating their elders' activities. They drive as hard a bargain amongst themselves as their fathers would do with the genuine shell money.[25]

There is in various parts of the Bismarck Archipelago a different kind of money used mainly for the purchase of pigs. A pigtail is attached to the shell string with each purchase. For sentimental reasons the value of the string increases with the number of pigtails.[26] In New Ireland there is a local shell currency called *kokonon*, the finer specimens of which are used mainly for bride money.[27] There is also a reddish shell called *ledara* which is scarce and its value is three times that of *diwara* in certain places. Other types of subsidiary currencies are far cheaper than *diwara*.[28]

The local currency in Lesu is *tsera*, consisting of an arm's length of tiny flat shell discs strung together. It is made on a nearby island Lawongai, north of New Ireland, where there are only a few men who can make it. While engaged in making the currency, the men must be continent.[29] This currency had for some time a fixed ratio with the Australian currency. One *tsera* was equal to five Australian shillings. The *tsera* is used extensively as a medium of exchange and prices of most goods are expressed in it. The value of various objects in *tsera* is rigidly fixed. The price of pigs, on the other hand, varies according to the resources of the purchaser. A rich person might pay five *tsera* for a pig for which another man would pay four. To pay a higher price for the same object confers prestige on the buyer.[30] The services of magicians are paid in *tsera*. There is magic for every occasion, for winning the girl of a man's choice, for securing a coveted pig, for causing the death of an enemy, etc., and all this can be secured for payment in *tsera*.[31]

Tobacco was easily adopted in New Britain as a suitable currency in addition to shell strings.[32]

[23]Reed, p. 47.   [24]Brown, p. 298
[25]H. H. Romilly, *The Western Pacific and New Guinea* (London, 1886), p. 25.
[26]Joachim Graf Pfeil, *Studien und Beobachtungen aus der Südsee* (Braunschweig, 1899), pp. 106-7.
[27]O. Finsch, *Ethnologische Erfahrungen und Belegstücke aus der Südsee* (Descriptive catalogue of a collection in the Naturhistorische Hofmuseum, Vienna, 1888), Vol. III, pp. 127-8.
[28]Pfeil, pp. 110-1.   [29]Hortense Powdermaker, *Life in Lesu* (London, 1933), p. 200
[30]Powdermaker, p. 201.   [31]Powdermaker, p. 205.   [32]Brown, p. 297.

CHAPTER 15

NEW GUINEA'S BOAR TUSK AND SHELL CURRENCIES

There is an immense variety of objects that may be claimed to have played the part of primitive currencies in New Guinea and the surrounding smaller islands, which is only natural, considering the size of the island, and its many tribes belonging to various races and at various cultural stages. "It is easier to account for the lack of a territory with standard money," observed Reed, "than it is to explain how communities which are ordinarily at feud come to share a single system of currency."[1] Even when they are not at war with each other, the tribes display a high degree of economic nationalism. While some currencies are inter-tribal, most tribes like to retain their own local currency. For instance, for the Seleo people shell bracelets are the local standard, and for the Pultalul people arrows. When somebody wants to pay a Pultalul with shell bracelets they are scornfully rejected with the following words: "You are not in Seleo, you have to pay in arrows."[2] Gradually, however, several tribes have adopted the same currency.

Those New Guinea tribes which are at the lowest stages of culture have hardly even reached the stage of systematic barter, let alone money. More advanced tribes have adopted certain objects as their store of value, though the degree to which these objects also serve as a medium of exchange and standard of value varies very widely. Over most parts of New Guinea, some kind of shell money is in use, whether in the form of single shells, or shell rings, or strings of small shell discs.[3] There are three grades of armshells in the Massim area; they are made in the Trobriands. The most valuable specimens have individual names.

In most communities in and around New Guinea, shell money is used extensively, though by no means exclusively, for the payment of bride price, for the purchase of pigs, and various ceremonial payments and other unilateral payments. In the majority of instances, however, various other kinds of valuables and currencies are included in the same transactions. The scope of shell money in New Guinea is distinctly narrower than in New Britain or New Ireland.

There is, however, one kind of shell which plays an important part in the economic system of some tribes of the interior; it is the cowrie shell. In the course of an expedition, Wirz found a tribe on the Dika river, Dutch New Guinea, where the life of the whole community was remarkably dominated by their worship of this form of primitive currency.

[1]Reed, p. 48.

[2]Richard Thurnwald, *Papuanisches und Melanesisches Gebiet südlich des Equators, einschliesslich Neu-Guinea*, p. 624.

[3]For such detailed information as is available the reader is referred to C. G. Seligmann, *The Melanesians of British New Guinea* (Cambridge, 1910), pp. 514-29; Finsch, *Südsee-Arbeiten*, and above all, O. Schneider, *op. cit.*

Cowries were literally worth their weight in gold there. When his expedition wanted to trade with the natives and displayed the goods brought for barter purposes such as tobacco, iron goods, mirrors, red cotton cloth, the response was very lukewarm. On the other hand, when the natives discovered that the expedition had cowries, they grew very excited and refused to accept anything else. A single cowrie shell was worth to them more than many knives and axes. While in other countries in which cowries are the currency their value is usually very low and prices are fixed in terms of thousands and tens of thousands of cowries, among this New Guinea tribe ten cowries were considered a fortune.[4]

Cowries were not accepted, however, on the Dika River indiscriminately. Only one special kind was accepted. Not knowing this, Wirz had brought from the coast, at heavy expense, three cases of cowries, but much to his dismay the predominant majority of them proved to be quite useless. Even a blind savage rejected them. The wrong kind of cowries were taken only for ornaments for children. In the three cases there were only two dozens of the right kind of shells.

Within that tribe, cowries were certainly not only a store of wealth but also the chief medium of exchange. Anything could be acquired with them. A pig cost between three and six cowries, and an unlimited supply was forthcoming at that absurd price.[5] Native porters were willing to carry the heaviest loads on a day's journey for a single cowrie. Ten cowries spaced out on a string constituted the standard bride price. All prices were expressed in terms of cowries.[6] That the quantity theory of money is apt to operate even in such a primitive community was shown by the fact that within a few weeks from the arrival of the expedition prices began to rise rapidly. Porters had to be paid three or four cowries for a day's journey. The purchasing power of cowries was falling almost from hour to hour.[7]

J. V. de Bruijn, a district officer in the Central Dutch New Guinea before and during the war, registered similar experience in the Wissel Lakes district. As a result of an influx of cowries through missionaries in 1939, their value began to depreciate. Bruijn had to intervene to check uncontrolled import of cowries, and to fix new prices based on their depreciated value.[8] The Japanese invading forces distributed cowries freely, "thus endangering the economic and financial stability of the district." Bruijn, who remained in New Guinea during the occupation, received several parachuted consignments of cowries to finance his activities.[9]

[4] P. Wirz, *Im Lande des Schneckengeldes* (Stuttgart, 1931), p. 70.
[5] Wirz, p. 76.   [6] Wirz, p. 122.   [7] Wirz, p. 132.
[8] Lloyd Rhys, *Jungle Pimpernel. The Story of a District Officer in Central Netherlands New Guinea* (London, 1947), pp. 56-9. According to Bruijn the Elkari have thirty-two sorts of cowries, divided into four categories. The lowest grade is hardly used for monetary purposes. The monetary cowries are divided into three grades according to their colour. Prices are quoted in terms of specified grades.
[9] Rhys, p. 116.

The difference between the value of cowries on the coast and inland is accounted for partly by the cost of transport. Meek makes the same observation concerning coarse salt which is a favourite currency in many parts of the interior of New Guinea. "In the mountain district a hundredweight of coarse salt would feed a dozen boys for three or four months."[10]

More important currencies than salt are dogs' teeth and boars' tusks. Dogs' teeth change hands either singly or on strings. For the purpose of large payment for pigs or canoes, strings are measured by the fathom.[11] Boars' tusks are the "money" in many parts of New Guinea for big transactions. The most valuable pieces are those of spiral shape. They are worth some two hundred dogs' teeth. However, even boars' tusks have depreciated. According to Zahn, in the good old days it was possible to get a pig for a single tusk, while in the time of his stay the purchase price of pigs was two tusks and in addition also other valuables.[12] Boars' tusks do not, however, conform to any standard; their monetary character requires careful investigation.

Several authors mention tomahawks and stone axes as being among the objects used as currency in New Guinea and on the surrounding islands. According to Armstrong[13] tomahawk stones were used as a medium of exchange on the south-east of the island. Meek also mentions tomahawks as playing the part of money in big transactions, especially on Woodlark Island where they are made of jade quarried locally.[14] Landtman found in the western division of British New Guinea abnormally large sized axe blades which could not possibly be used for practical purposes. These large axe blades were used as a medium of exchange.[15] In the south-eastern districts, too, finely polished ceremonial axe blades called *benam*, too large and thin to be used as tools, are a currency.[16] It is difficult to ascertain from the material available how far these tomahawk stones and axe blades were used mainly for ceremonial purposes and as store of value and how far they actually served as a medium of exchange. Seligmann considered the ceremonial axe blades as being merely articles of trade.[17]

It goes without saying that pigs play a certain monetary part in New Guinea as the purchase price of women and in other large transactions. They freely exchange for boars' tusks at a steady rate.[18] It has been

[10]A. S. Meek, *A Naturalist in Cannibal Land* (London, 1913), p. 153.
[11]Heinrich Zahn, *Die Jabim—Deutsch Neu Guinea*. Edited by R. Neuhauss (Berlin, 1911), Vol. III, p. 314. According to R. W. Williamson, *The Mafulu—Mountains People of British New Guinea*, the Mafulu pay for pigs with dogs' teeth strings of the length of the pig's body (p. 232).
[12]Zahn, *Die Jabim*, p. 314; Seligmann, p. 517; Reed, p. 47.
[13]Armstrong, p. 113.
[14]A. S. Meek, pp. 73 and 154.
[15]G. Landtman, *The Kiwai Papuans of British New Guinea* (London, 1927), pp. 34-5.
[16]Seligmann, pp. 33 and 517.   [17]Seligmann, pp. 33 and 517.
[18]R. Thurnwald, *Die Menschliche Gesellschaft* (Berlin, 1932), Vol. V, p. 37.

alleged that human heads were also used as currency, but there is no acceptable evidence to that effect. Headhunters were, on various occasions, prepared to barter their cherished trophies when the goods offered by white traders were too tempting to resist.

Slaves were used as a standard of value throughout the western parts of New Guinea. Prices of calico or other trade goods were expressed in terms of slaves.[19]

In addition to the above-mentioned objects which were originally limited currencies in New Guinea, various objects have become adopted for monetary use as a result of contact with whites. Beads have to some extent replaced shell money and are in use as small change.[20] As in other parts of Melanesia, tobacco is, of course, extensively used as a currency with which whites can pay for smaller purchases and services. This imported tobacco currency assumes the usual form of pressed sticks. Home-grown tobacco is also used at the Empress Augusta River where it is packed in bundles and is offered in payment for everything. There are three standard sizes of bundles.[21] Some Negrito tribes of New Guinea are said to be using as a currency "a certain type of large, flat, polished seed."[22] No particulars are vailable. According to Thurnwald, pots are a kind of standard of value among tribes specializing in their production. Wives are bought for ten pots, representing the value of their lost labour for three years.[23]

The extent to which it is justified to describe these various objects as moneys differs widely. Beyond doubt most of them play the part of a store of value and many of them serve for ceremonial occasions and for special payments. On the other hand, their very multiplicity, not only as between various tribes, but even within the same tribes, seems to show that their use as a medium of exchange is limited. In the majority of instances these various objects described as currencies were on the borderline between popular media of barter and limited currencies.

It is quite certain that hardly any of the various monetary objects actually serve as a unit of account to a noteworthy extent. As for deferred payments, they appear to play a relatively subordinate part in the life of the natives of New Guinea, though in some parts competitive exchanges have led to the development of the credit system. Pigs and other objects of value are exchanged between persons representing their clans. The object of these competitions is to break the individual in whose honour the feast is given, as under the prevailing custom he is

[19]G. W. Earl, *The Native Races of the Indian Archipelago* (London, 1853), p. 84.
[20]Meek, p. 154; A. F. K. Woollaston, *Pygmies and Papuans, The Stone Age To-day in Dutch New Guinea* (London, 1912), p. 62.
[21]Otto Reche, *Der Kaiserin Augusta Fluss.* [*Südsee-Ergebnisse*, A. Melanesien (Hamburg, 1913)], Vol. I, p. 285.
[22]M. W. Stirling, *The Native Peoples of New Guinea* (Smithsonian Institute, War Background Studies No. 9. Washington, 1943), p. 17.
[23]R. Thurnwald, *Die Gemeinde der Banaro* (Stuttgart, 1921), pp. 42-3.

placed under obligation to return presents of even higher value. Members of their clans contribute to support their representatives. The victor in this contest acquires great social prestige, while the vanquished is doomed to disgrace and poverty. The clans share in the glory or disgrace as the case may be.[24] Among the Arapech a present—mostly meat— given cannot be refused and must be repaid sometime. Giving meat is therefore "a way of banking."[25]

It appears that much thorough-going study of local conditions in various parts of New Guinea is needed in order to be able to ascertain the extent to which the various objects can be considered as currencies.

At the beginning of this century it was almost impossible to spend modern money in New Guinea. Even the tribes near trading stations and missionary posts preferred to be paid in sticks of tobacco.[26] Meanwhile modern money has, of course, become more acceptable.

[24]Stirling, p. 21.
[25]Margaret Mead, *The Arapech of New Guinea* (*Co-operation and Competition among Primitive Peoles*) (New York, 1937), p. 33.
[26]Ernst v. Hesse-Wartegg, *Samoa. Bismarckarchipel und Neu-Guinea* (Leipzig, 1902), p. 83.

PART II: ASIA

CHAPTER 16

RICE STANDARD IN THE PHILIPPINES

WHILST in some parts of the Philippines modern money has been current for centuries, it is impossible to ascertain the existence of any money in other parts. As elsewhere, many Negrito tribes are at such a primitive stage of civilization that they only transact a limited volume of barter of a very rudimentary type. In more advanced parts of the Philippines rice has long been used as the principal primitive currency. Captain Forrest wrote in 1775 that the vassals of the Sultans of Magindan (Mindanao) paid taxes mostly in unhusked rice.[1]

Unthreshed rice is, or was until recently, the currency of some of the remote tribes. The Bontoc Igorot (or Ifugao) and the Tinguian use it, and although otherwise they are very primitive races, they have developed its monetary use to a very advanced stage. The unit is the *manojo* (handful) of *palay* (unthreshed rice) tied up immediately below the fruit heads. An elaborate system has been evolved, with fixed denominations rising from one handful to a thousand handfuls.[2] The Tinguian use also cleaned rice, the unit being one coconut shell-full.[3]

Rice is extensively used as a store of value. If money is paid for the products of the natives, it is invariably converted into *palay*.[4] It is suitable to act as a store of value because it can be kept for eight to ten years without deterioration.

Palay is employed as a medium of exchange. Most kinds of goods are bought and sold with it.[5] Cloths, clay and metal pipes are mentioned by Jenks as being traded for *palay*. Wages are paid in *palay*. Five handfuls of *palay* are the daily wages of the wood-gatherer in the mountains, of the builder of granaries and of agricultural labourers in general.[6] Its value is very stable in terms of labour and products. There is a constant demand for it by manufacturing Igorot villages.[7]

Rice is widely used also as a standard of value, not only when it is used in payment for goods and services, but also for the purposes of

[1] E. B. Christie, *The Subanua of Sindangan Bay* (Division of Ethnology Publications, Vol. VI, Part I, Manila, 1909), p. 27.

[2] A. E. Jenks, *The Bontoc Igorot* (Department of Interior Ethnological Survey Publications, Vol. I., Manila, 1905), p. 156.

[3] Fay Cooper Cole, *The Tinguian—Social, Religious and Economic Life of a Philippine Tribe*. Field Museum of Natural History. Publication No. 209 (Chicago, 1922), p. 395.

[4] Jenks, p. 153.   [5] Jenks, p. 155.   [6] Jenks, p. 137.
[7] Jenks, p. 153.

barter. "The value of all things, from a five cent block of Mayinit salt to a seventy peso *carabao* (water buffalo) is measured in *palay*. To-day as formerly, every bargain between Igorot is made on the basis of the *palay* value of the articles bought or sold. This is so even though the payment is in money."[8]

Loans are granted in rice, repayable with interest out of the next crop. The Ifugao even have a form of discount, deducted in advance from the amount of loans for one year.[9]

From the foregoing it is evident that *palay* among the Igorot is a very advanced type of primitive currency. It has most of the qualities a good primitive money is required to have. *Palay* is sufficiently uniform for the requirements of the Igorot. Being the staple food, it is always in demand. "Except when used for the purchase of clothing it is seldom heavier or more difficult to transport than is the object for which it is exchanged."[10] And it cannot be counterfeited. Rice fulfils among the Igorot all the essential functions of modern money. The main difference is that it is not applied in trade universally. In addition to transactions of direct barter, there are transactions in which a larger unit is used, the *carabao*, which is a domestic animal that was valued at forty to seventy pesos at the beginning of this century. Land values are expressed in terms of *carabaos*. The *carabao* is also a store of value. It is seldom traded outside the community and is consumed chiefly on ceremonial occasions. Gold ear-rings are traded against *carabaos*.[11]

Moreover, each community has its local medium of exchange in addition to *palay*. The use of modern money has also made progress. To Americans the Igorot prefer to sell against modern money. Most of the clothing made of cotton is bought for modern money.[12] Nevertheless, in everyday transactions, *palay* plays the part of money, whether as a medium of exchange or as a unit of account.

In other parts of the Philippines too, rice is used as primitive currency, though we do not possess the same detailed information about the extent of its use. The monetary use of rice is linked up with religion. Entry into the rice storehouse is subject to religious rituals. Only men are allowed to enter.

Some Philippine tribes use native or European cloth as a standard of value. The unit is a piece of cloth as long as the spread of a man's arms —it is called the *kumpau*, and is used in measuring the value of gongs, jars, glassware, as well as perishable goods. Fines are fixed in cloth. Christie quotes an instance of a fine of about 215 metres of cotton cloth having been imposed on an adulterer.[13]

According to Bücher, old Chinese porcelain vessels served as money

[8]Jenks, p. 156.
[9]R. F. Barton, *Ifugao Law*. Quoted by Herskovits, p. 203.
[10]Jenks, p. 155.   [11]Jenks, p. 107.   [12]Jenks, p. 154.
[13]Christie, p. 65. There are separate units for measuring the value of durable and perishable objects.

among the Bagobo in Mindanao.[14] Beyond doubt, various other objects were also used as currency in other backward parts of the Philippines, but no adequate information is available.

Early in the 16th century, according to De Morga, the famous Governor of the Philippines, metal bells (gongs?) imported from China were used for payment.[15] Gold dust was another early form of currency.[16]

Modern money was introduced in one known instance by Government action. Governor Frederick Johnson of the Province of Aguan, Mindanao, in 1910 found the natives exploited by traders who charged to the natives 1,500 per cent interest on goods advanced against payment in products. He made the use of modern currency compulsory, and the Government competed with traders by selling trade goods on the basis of 25 per cent net profit.[17]

[14]Karl Bücher, *Industrial Evolution* (New York, 1901), p. 69. See also Schadenberg, *Zeitschrift für Ethnographie*, 1885, pp. 10, 19 and 29. Quoted by Schurtz, *Grundriss einer Enstehungsgeschichte des Geldes* (Weimar, 1898), p. 69.
[15]Sir R. C. Temple, *Beginnings of Currency* [(Journal of the Royal Anthropological Institute (London, 1899)], Vol. xxix, p. 110.
[16]Montero y Vidal, *Historia de Filipinas*, Vol. i, p. 63. Quoted by F. W. Atkinson, *The Philippine Islands* (Boston, 1905), p. 62.
[17]W. Cameron Forbes, *The Philippine Islands* (Boston, 1928), p. 618.

CHAPTER 17

THE DRUM CURRENCY OF ALOR

Alor, a small island to the north of Timor, possesses—or possessed up to 1941—a highly developed primitive monetary system. We have a great deal of detailed information about it, thanks to Cora du Bois, who visited the island shortly before the second World War, primarily for the purpose of studying the psychology of the natives. It occupies such a predominant position in the thoughts of the natives that it would have been hardly possible to study their psychology without coming across a wealth of material on the subject. Indeed, Cora du Bois observed on one occasion with some apparent irritation that the native whom she questioned about his dreams kept talking about drums and gongs, the principal currencies of the island.

On Alor all the hard work is done by the women. Men have no time for gardening or other similar physical labour, for they have a full-time job on hand by looking after the highly involved financial system.[1] Indeed, this division of labour is in force to such extent that a woman who shows an interest in finance is referred to as a "man-woman," while

[1]Cora du Bois, *The People of Alor* (Minneapolis, 1944), p. 22.

a man who finds time for gardening or gathering wood is referred to as a "woman-man."[2]

The principal currencies of Alor are metal kettle-drums called *mokos*, and brass gongs. Pigs may also be regarded as a limited currency, while arrows are used as small change.

As in other communities where pigs serve as a kind of currency, their value is relatively high. They are only eaten at feasts and their value is included in "the interminable and complex monetary accounting that is basic to ceremonial procedure." Should a pig be killed accidentally, a ceremonial feast of one sort or another is improvised to justify its consumption[3] and since festivities provide occasion for creditors to collect their claims, it often happens that creditors shoot their debtor's pig in order to find such an opportunity for forcing him to pay up.[4]

Among the gongs, only those which are damaged are used for currency, for the perfect specimens are retained by their owners for ceremonial purposes. Far more important than either gongs or pigs in the monetary system of Alor are the *mokos*. Some specimens of these bronze drums are supposed to have been found buried in the earth.[5] Most of the drums have, however, been imported in modern times from East Java. Although the Alor people know the difference between the genuine article and the imitation, they readily accept the latter.

The value of the *mokos* ranges from one rupiah to 3,000 rupiahs.[6] Each denomination has a separate name. In recent years, their value has been rising owing to the fact that in 1914—until when *mokos* were "the general money of Alor"—the Dutch Colonial Government, in an effort to encourage the use of modern money, banned the import of *mokos*. It went even further—it bought up hundreds of *mokos* and scrapped them or threw them into the sea.[7]

Mokos together with gongs are the most highly valued possession of the natives and serve as their principal store of value. They are also used in current transactions as a medium of exchange. To quote actual instances:—A native informant of Cora du Bois told her that he intended to sell rice for *mokos*.[8] Another native told her that he sold a pig for a *moko*.[9] There are, however, many other objects which are accepted in exchange for rice or pigs. Most trade is done in the form of barter. Nor is there any evidence that *mokos* served as units of account in these deals. There appears to be a fixed ratio between pigs and *mokos*. A pig is worth a certain type of *moko*, valued at about five rupiahs.[10] The

[2]du Bois, p. 95.
[3]du Bois, p. 22.   [4]du Bois, p. 148.
[5]Ernst Vatter, *Ata Kiwan—Unbekannte Bergvölker im Tropischen Holland* (Leipzig, 1932), p. 239.
[6]du Bois, p. 23; Vatter, p. 239.
[7]Vatter, p. 239. According to Vatter, in 1916 there were still over 2,000 *mokos* in Alor. The number is given by du Bois as 20,000. Even if we were to consider the smaller figure to be correct, it represents a fair number for a small island.
[8]du Bois, p. 195.   [9]du Bois, p. 198.   [10]du Bois, p. 23.

mokos differ in value considerably, but conform to a complicated standard with a fixed ratio between the various denominations.

Drums and gongs form an indispensable part of bride price which largely accounts for the persistent demand for them. The purchase of a wife is not a single transaction, but a series of highly complicated exchanges between the two families concerned. Burial feasts, too, lead to a series of transactions in pigs, gongs and *mokos*. Finally, the building of "lineage houses" entails complicated financial operations, in which gongs and *mokos* play a prominent part.[11]

By far the most important part played by *mokos* and gongs is in the sphere of credit. The total circulation of *mokos* in Alor serves as a basis for an inverted pyramid of credit structure not unlike that of our modern communities. On Alor, wealth consists essentially of a series of outstanding credits, not of accumulated property.[12] Natives are busily engaged in looking after their drum and gong investments, or are trying to find drums and gongs to repay their debts. Those owning a number of these valuables are not happy unless and until they have succeeded in lending them—if only in order to protect them from being seized by their creditors. It always requires an immense effort to force debtors to pay, and festivities which provide occasion for it are the scenes of furious haggling between creditors and debtors.

When the creditors assemble in the debtor's house in order to collect the drums and gongs the latter owes them, their own creditors in turn are also present in order to lay claim to the drums and gongs the moment they change hands. The result is that in addition to the quarrels centring on the liquidation of the principal debt, there is also a series of subsidiary quarrels being waged on the side.[13]

To form an idea of how fully this credit system dominates the minds of the natives, Cora du Bois quotes a number of specimens of their poetry in which there is very frequent reference to the none too poetic subject of relations between debtors and creditors.

"The lack of standardized currencies, the contest devices and the chicanery associated with wealth, the difficulties attendant upon feasts, the competitive system in which only a fraction of the male population can be successful, all contribute to the frustrations and irritations of gaining prestige," Cora du Bois remarks. "In addition, no one can relax his efforts once the goal has been reached. There are too many socially recognized pressures to permit him to withdraw and still maintain his status rating."

Pantar is another island of the same group where *mokos* and gongs are the currency.[14]

[11]du Bois, p. 23. [12]du Bois, p. 143. [13]du Bois, p. 145.
[14]Vatter, p. 269.

9

CHAPTER 18

BRONZE GUNS, BEES' WAX AND BUFFALOES AS MONEY IN BORNEO

The best known amongst the primitive currencies of Borneo are bronze cannons, gongs, buffaloes, bees' wax, gold dust and bundles of cloth. The origin of the monetary use of bronze cannons dates from the bad old days when petty kings and chiefs were engaged in warfare against each other. Later the cannons were retained as one of the principal forms of store of value and as ornaments. They played, until recently, also the part of a standard of value. Prices were expressed in terms of so many *piculs* of bronze cannon, and barter was largely based on this unit of account. Evans believes the Sarawak Government still fined, in the early 'twenties, recalcitrant tribes so many *piculs* of bronze cannon.[1] It was also a medium of exchange which was readily taken and received in payment. Indeed, according to Evans, bronze cannons, together with gongs, buffaloes and standard rolls of cloth, became a sort of legal tender.[2] Fixed ratios were established between the various types of currencies.

The large brass gongs which are used in various ceremonies for dancing and for signalling, and of which there is a number in every house, constituted right up to the 'twenties "one of the best recognized standards of value and the most important form of currency."[3]

During the 'twenties buffaloes also served as an abstract unit of account. Although a large part of the population had grown used to coins and even to paper currency, a high proportion of their trade was still carried on by barter, and though a native may tell you that such and such an article is worth so many *piculs*, he is probably himself calculating its value in buffaloes and converting the result into dollars for your benefit. The price of buffaloes does not vary extensively from year to year.[4] Credit transactions take place in terms of buffaloes. Many disputes arise over such transactions and in many instances creditors take out summonses to secure a buffalo calf as interest on the buffalo they lent.[5]

Another type of loan is granted in rice, usually on the security of bronze objects which are worth a good deal more than the rice lent. The creditors reckon with the improvident nature of their debtors and hope to keep the bronze object through the non-payment of their claims.

---

[1]Ivor H. N. Evans, *Among the Primitive Peoples in Borneo* (London, 1922), p. 136.
[2]Evans, p. 136.
[3]Charles Hose, *Natural Man—A Record from Borneo* (London, 1926), p. 88.
[4]Evans, pp. 135-6.
[5]Evans, p. 136.

More often than not, the calculation proves to be correct.[6] According to Ling Roth, the annual interest of loans granted in paddy depends on the relative scarcity of paddy in the district.[7]

Around the rivers where gold dust is washed, gold dust played the part of money.[8] In the Sambao country, bees' wax was the principal currency. "It is melted but not refined, and cast into moulds of an oblong square, and a rattan withy to lift them by is cast in the wax. A piece weighs a quarter of a *picul* and the *picul* is valued in payments at forty shillings. They have also for smaller payments pieces of one-eighth and one-sixteenth *picul* and for small money they have cowries."[9] Bars of iron were used for small change in some parts of Borneo.[10]

According to Temple, plaited fibre armlets passed as currency in Borneo, at the rate of three cents of the trade dollar per bundle of fifteen armlets.[11] Among the Battak a much more primitive form of currency—if it can be regarded as such—consisted of human skulls during the 19th century.[12] It is even alleged that traders had captured natives and slaughtered them, in order to use their skulls in payment for sandal-wood.[13] Even if this information is authentic, it seems probable that the skulls only played the part of a favourite medium of barter.

Other monetary materials in the interior included salt, pieces of copper imported by the Rajah of Sarawak,[14] and rice. We have already referred to its use as a means of deferred payments; it was also used as a medium of exchange. In British North Borneo, a certain charm against disease could be bought only by rice. If the would-be purchaser had only coins, he had first to buy rice.[15] The Dayaks are said to have used Chinese procelain vessels as currency.[16]

Much of the trade is still done by barter. The Dayaks in the more backward regions are unable to grasp the possibility of buying something for a third object instead of direct barter.[17]

[6]Evans, pp. 137-9.
[7]Henry Ling Roth, *The Natives of Sarawak and British North Borneo* (London, 1896), p. 186.
[8]Ling Roth, p. 176.
[9]Captain Alexander Hamilton, *A New Account of the East Indies*. Pinkerton's Travel Series, Vol. VIII (1811), p. 460.
[10]Captain R. Mundy, *The Journals of James Brooke* (London, 1848), Vol. II, p. 350.
[11]Sir R. C. Temple, *The Evolution of Currency and Coinage*, Lectures on the Method of Science (Oxford, 1906), p. 188.
[12]*Ausland*, Vol. MDCCCLXXXII, p. 327.
[13]V. Schleinitz in *Zeitschrift der Gesellschaft für Erdkunde* (Berlin, 1877), p. 258. Quoted by Schurtz, p. 45.
[14]H. C. Millies, *Recherches sur les monnaies des indigènes de l'Archipel Indien et de la Péninsule Malaie* (The Hague, 1871), p. 157.
[15]I. H. N. Evans, *Orang Dusun*, p. 156. Quoted by Elizabeth Ellis Hoyt, *Primitive Trade* (London, 1926), p. 84.
[16]Bücher, p. 69. British Museum Handbook to the Ethnological Collection (London, 1910), p. 91.
[17]Friedrich Noback, *Münz-, Mass-, und Gewichtsbuch*. 2nd Edn. (Leipzig, 1879), p. 343.

CHAPTER 19

OTHER MONEYS OF THE INDONESIAN ARCHIPELAGO

A large part of the Sumatran population trade with each other and with other communities largely by barter, without apparently using any standard of value. On the other hand, there are races on the island which adopted primitive currencies centuries ago. According to a Chinese author, Tung Hli Yung K'An, writing in the early 17th century, "when the men of Jambi bargain for goods, the price is agreed upon in gold, but they pay only with pepper, e.g., if something costs two *taels* of gold, they pay a hundred *piculs* of pepper or thereabouts. They like to buy foreign women, and girls from other countries are often brought here and sold for pepper."[1] Gold dust by weight was extensively used as a currency in many parts of Sumatra during the 18th and 19th centuries.[2]

In Tappanuli, the natives reckoned the value of goods in benzoe cakes or in buffalo hides.[3] Coffee is said to have served as a currency on Sumatra.

On the Alu islands near Sumatra, small pieces of cotton cloth were used as a currency, according to Cheng-lo, in 1415.[4] Other objects mentioned as having served as a currency include tampans, brass wire, or brass beads, and buffaloes. All these are claimed to have served as standards of value to assist transactions of barter. For small payments salt was extensively used.[5]

On the island of Nias, west of Sumatra, commercial transactions were effected by barter but were based on gold as the abstract standard of value.[6] By the beginning of this century, the Nias and Dayak tribes came to use coins in their contact with Europeans. Among themselves they still practised barter with gold as the standard of value.[7]

According to Ibn Batuta who visited Sumatra in 1345-6, trade was then done with the aid of lumps of tin and native gold.[8]

On Nassau Island, off Sumatra, "a sort of iron hatchet or handbill served as the standard for the value of various commodities such as coconuts, poultry, etc."[9] The natives are said to have been still strangers

---

[1]Sir R. C. Temple, *Notes on Currency and Coinage among the Burmese* (Reprinted from the Indian Antiquary, Vol. XLVIII, 1919), p. 19.

[2]W. Marsden, *History of Sumatra* (London, 1811), p. 171. Quoted by Ridgeway, p. 172.

[3]Noback, p. 856.

[4]W. W. Rockhill, *Notes on the Relations and Trade of China with the Eastern Archipelago and the Races of the Indian Ocean during the fourteen century* (T'Oung Pao, Vol. XV, 1914), p. 141.

[5]A. Featherman, p. 298.　　　　　　　　[6]Featherman, p. 351.

[7]H. Breitenstein, *Sumatra* (Leipzig, 1902), p. 176.

[8]H. C. Millies, p. 58.

[9]John Crisp, *An Account of the Inhabitants of the Poggy or Nassau Islands.* (Asiatic Researches, Vol. VI. Reprinted for the Straits branch of the Royal Asiatic Society, 1886), pp. 71-2.

to the use of coin of any kind towards the close of the 19th century, and a metal coat button would be of equal value in their estimation to a piece of gold or silver coin, either of which would be immediately hung about the neck as ornament.

Some of the most primitive communities in Sumatra, long before they were acquainted with the use of money, became acquainted with the blessings of credit. The primitive Sakai tribes are granted by Chinese traders very large amounts of credits. Their I.O.U. consists of a string with as many knots as are owed in dollars. Their creditor collects his claims on maturity in products.[10]

In the distant past, rice which was the staple product of Majapahit served as a medium of exchange in Java, not because the population was unacquainted with coins but owing to the scarcity of coins, as a result of which prices tended to be unduly low.[11] The dynastic history of the Sung Dynasty (A.D. 960-1279) records that the Javanese during that period cut leaves of silver and used them as money.[12]

According to Grubauer, the Foradja people in Celebes fixed fines in terms of buffaloes.[13] Credit is granted in terms of rice on security.

In the mountain villages of the island of Ili Mandiri ivory is the chief store of value. The number of ivory tusks and their size determines the social standing of the natives. To-day it is no longer used as currency, but there is reason to believe that in a not too distant past it served as a medium of exchange. It is still the principal form of bride money.[14]

Pieces of cloth measuring 15 × 15 cms. and 17 × 17 cms. served as a currency on Buton Island during the 19th century. Its name was *kampuna*, which means "head cloth of a king." It was originally introduced as the chief means of payment of the Sultan and the leading noblemen who had the monopoly of its issue. It was produced by special looms. Only the officially produced pieces of cloth were valid as currency, other kinds of cloth were valueless except as goods. From time to time this cloth money was withdrawn from circulation and was replaced by metallic money. During a later period subordinate officials and priests were also allowed to issue it. The cloth issued by the various Sultans differed in design. It is only comparatively recently that his money was entirely replaced by silver coins.[15] In the Sulu Archipelago, too, during the first half of the 19th century pieces of cotton cloth circulated as currency. They were imported by the Sultans who fixed their value which

[10]M. Moszkowski, *Auf Neuen Wege durch Sumatra* (Berlin, 1909), p. 101.

[11]J. S. Furnivall, *Netherlands India—A Study in Plural Economy* (Cambridge, 1939), p. 9.

[12]W. B. Groeneweldt, *Notes on the Malay Archipelago and Malacca* (Batavia, 1817), p. 16.

[13]A. Grubauer, *Celebes* (The Hague, 1923), p. 69.

[14]Vatter, p. 77.

[15]Johann Elbert, *Die Sunda-Expedition des Vereins für Geographie und Statistik zu Frankfurt am Main* (Frankfurt, 1911), Vol. I, pp. 185-6.

was unaffected by the fluctuation of its supply.[16] More recently, paddy or rice was used for small payments, though Chinese copper coins were the principal currency.[17]

According to Duarte Barbosa, trade on the Moluccas and Banda Islands during the early period of colonization was conducted on the basis of Javanese gongs in terms of which prices were quoted. "The kings and great men set great value on these and kept them, both great and small, as a treasure and estate."[18] On the other hand, according to Furnivall, at the end of the 16th century, the Spice Islands did not use any money and sold their products for cloth from Coromandel. "The market of cloth was limited, and when the people had all the cloth they wanted they had no wish to sell or even cultivate their supplies."[19]

Gongs, small brass cannons and elephant tusks constituted the store of value of the Aru people. They used these objects as bride money and hoarded them.[20]

[16] *Ausland*, 1848, p. 955. Quoted by G. Thilenius, p. 5, *Primitives Geld* (*Archiv für Anthropologie*, 1920, Vol. XVIII, New Series).
[17] Featherman, Part II, p. 416.
[18] Mansel Longworth Dames, *The Book of Duarte Barbosa* (London, 1921), Hakluyt Society, Vol. II, pp. 302-3.
[19] Furnivall, p. 22.
[20] A. R. Wallace, *The Malay Archipelago* (London, 1890), p. 360.

CHAPTER 20

"HOMERIC" CURRENCIES IN FRENCH INDO-CHINA

In Cambodia buffaloes and oxen were used to a large extent as units a thousand years ago. An inscription dating from A.D. 960 found near Angkor, gives an account of land acquired against payments in buffaloes and oxen.[1] Among the Bahnars the same means of payment were employed until recently as in Homeric Greece: cattle, tripods and small axes.[2] A slave—which was a large monetary unit—was worth a number of buffaloes, according to his age, strength, skill, etc. A buffalo was worth seven earthenware jars.[3]

Until recently, buffaloes were used in part of French Indo-China as a limited unit of account. The prices of red earthenware jars which are the chief store of value of the Moi were quoted in buffaloes.[4] Cowries were used until recently as currency in Luang Prabong.[5] In the Laos province, cowries had fixed ratio to the Indo-Chinese piastre. Each shell

[1] Etienne Aymonier, *Le Cambodge* (Paris, 1904), Vol. III, p. 10.
[2] E. Babelon, *Les Origines de la Monnaie* (Paris, 1897), p. 14.
[3] E. Aymonier, *La Cochinchine Française* (Paris, 1887), Vol. XIII, pp. 296-7.
[4] H. Baudesson, *Indo-China and its Primitive People* (London, 1919), p. 24.
[5] J. G. Andersson, *Children of the Yellow Earth* (London, 1934), p. 301.

was worth piastre 0.0002.[6] Laos had also an iron currency consisting of small bars of about 120 grams each. It was particularly used in southern Laos.[7] At Sting Treng in Cambodia, too, small iron bars were in use as currency. Garnier remarked on it that its nominal value was eight or nine times its metallic value.[8] The smallest monetary unit of the Bahnars was the iron hoe. In the 'seventies it was equated to ten centimes of European goods, and was a popular unit of account.

As in other parts of Further India, metals by weights were used as means of payment. Already in the 10th century fines were fixed in weights of gold or silver. The objects which were used in Cambodia for the payment of fines included slaves, cattle, buffaloes, horses, pigs and elephants.[9]

Rice has always played a part in various parts of Indo-China as a means of payment. According to a description of Cambodia by the Chinese Ambassador Theou-la-Kuan, in the 13th century in small transactions payment was made in rice, grain, or cloth, in large transactions in gold and silver.[10] At the beginning of this century, the main tax was the *dîme du riz*, the most ancient of all taxes in Indo-China, payable in rice.[11] Loans were granted in rice and also in other commodities at an interest rate of 50 per cent if repayable at the end of the next season.[12]

There was also a fictitious unit of account called *muk*; a jar was worth four *muks*.[13]

Before the French occupation of the left bank of the Mekong valley the following currencies were in circulation there: cowries, legally fixed by the Siamese Government at 6,400 per *tical*; small copper ingots called *lat*, worth twenty-four per *tical*; small iron bars, ten per *tical*; and silver bars in the shape of a loaf.[14]

[6]Lucien de Rheinach, *Le Laos* (Paris, 1911), p. 330. Cowries were seen in circulation in Luan Prabong in the latter part of the nineteenth century (Andersson, p. 301).
[7]Rheinach, p. 330.
[8]Etienne Aymonier, *Voyage dans le Laos* (Paris, 1895), Vol. I, p. 22; *La Cochinchim Française*, XIII, pp. 296-8.
[9]Aymonier (1904), p. 557. [10]Aymonier (1904), p. 629. [11]Aymonier (1904), p. 75.
[12]Aymonier (1904), p. 86. See also J. B. Alberti, *L'Indochine d'autrefois et d'aujourdhui* (Paris, 1934), pp. 110-12.   [13]Aymonier (1887), XIII, pp. 296-7.
[14]A. Schroeder, *Annam—Etudes Numismatiques* (Paris, 1905), pp. 586-7.

CHAPTER 21

GAMBLING COUNTERS AS MONEY IN SIAM

In the 14th century cowrie shells were used in Siam as a currency and bore a fixed ratio of 10,000 cowries to twenty taels in paper money.[1] In the 17th century there was a fixed ratio between cowries and in

[1]Rockhill, p. 105.

prevailing monetary unit, the *cattu*.[2] For a long time, cowries remained the favourite medium of exchange in Siam for small transactions. It was not until 1865 that they were replaced through the issue of lead token money.[3] Eight varieties of cowries were in use at the same time as currencies for hundreds of years.[4]

The most curious form of primitive currency that was until recently in use in Siam consisted of Chinese gaming counters. When Hallett arrived at Zimmé in the 'eighties, he was astonished to find that traders gave back small octagonal porcelain gaming counters as change. These counters bore Chinese inscriptions and were reckoned to be worth two annas and four annas. It was explained to him that the monopolists of gaming houses had a right to issue such counters and that they were in general use among the people as small change. They remained current as long as the Chinese monopolist was solvent or had the monopoly. If his monopoly was discontinued, he called in the tokens by sending a crier round beating a gong and informing the people that he was ready to exchange the tokens for money.[5] After three days following the announcement the counters ceased to be acceptable and holders frequently suffered losses.[6] Such gambling counters formed the sole small change at Zimmé before the Bangkok copper currency supplanted them.

Up to 1874, salt was used as currency for purchases in the Zimmé market.[7] Lumps of silver, the shape and weight of which vary in different localities, are still in use as money in remote districts.[8] In the gold producing districts gold dust was until recently the sole currency. Taxes were paid in it. According to Aymonier, in the olden days gold dust was so plentiful that it was not even weighed. A tube of gold dust, ten centimetres in length and the thickness of the thumb, was the price of a buffalo.[9]

After the second World War cigarettes became the favourite medium of exchange and unit of account for a short time. Advertisements appearing in Siamese newspapers quoted prices in cigarettes.

[2]John Fryer, *A New Account of East India and Persia* (Hakluyt Society, 2nd Series, XX, 1912), Vol. II.
[3]H. S. Hallett, *A Thousand Miles on an Elephant in the Shan State* (London, 1890), p. 164.
[4]Virginia Thompson, *Thailand the New Siam* (New York, 1941), pp. 566-7.
[5]Hallett, p. 234. See also Adolf Bastian, *Reisen in Siam im Jahre 1863* (Jena, 1867), pp. 22 and 213, and Aymonier (1895), pp. 314-5.
[6]Aymonier (1895), pp. 314-5.   [7]Hallett, p. 164.
[8]W. A. Graham, *Siam* (London, 1924), Vol. I, p. 343.
[9]Aymonier (1895), pp. 134-6.

CHAPTER 22

TIN INGOTS AND GOLD DUST IN MALAYA

Primitive money on the Malayan Peninsula was less evident than on many islands of the Malayan Archipelago or in other parts of the mainland of South Eastern Asia. The reason for this is that while the backward tribes on the Peninsula are, or were until recently, at a too low stage of economic development to use any kind of money, the more advanced tribes are fully familiar with the use of modern money. The Sakai and Semang tribes of Negritos do very little trade, even in the form of barter, although in recent years contact with European and Asiatic traders, and with more advanced tribes, has resulted in some progress.

Some of the Sakai tribes have actually become familiar with modern money but it serves almost exclusively as a unit of account. The bridegroom generally pays ten dollars to his father-in-law, but if he is a chief, he is required to pay thirty dollars. Presumably these sums are paid in kind, as no ordinary Sakai bridegroom would have such a large amount in cash.[1]

A rudimentary unit of account among the Sakai is the supply of food for a family for a specified period. According to de Morgan, a blowpipe and quiver with darts are valued at a fortnight's food supply for a family, and a loin cloth is priced at a month's supply of food.[2]

The Benua-Jakun tribe used coarse china plates and saucers as a rudimentary currency for the purpose of imposing fines.[3] Gold dust packed in pieces of cloth changed hands by weight as a form of limited medium of exchange. The packages usually weighed one *tael* each.[4] Tin ingots were also used as means of payment and were weighed on a scale. Models of animals made of tin were used as currency according to weight.[5] White cloth figures so frequently in bride money and in every kind of other payment in various tribes that it may be regarded as a limited currency.[6] According to a manuscript attributed to either Magellan or Duarte Barbosa, the City of Malacca had such a quantity of gold in the 16th century, that the big merchants always reckoned in *bahars* (400 lbs.) of gold.[7]

[1]W. W. Skeat and C. O. Blagden, *Pagan Races of the Malay Peninsula* (London, 1906), Vol. II, pp. 60-1.
[2]Skeat and Blagden, p. 502.　　　　[3]Skeat and Blagden, p. 515.
[4]Sir R. C. Temple, *Notes on Currency and Coinage among the Burmese* (Reprinted from the Indian Antiquary, Vol. XLVIII, Bombay, 1919), p. 19.
[5]Temple, p. 3.
[6]Skeat and Blagden, pp. 78, 82 and 85.
[7]Sir Frank Swettenham, *British Malaya* (London, 1908), p. 17.

CHAPTER 23

WEIGHED SILVER AND LEAD CURRENCY IN BURMA

In 1879, Noback's reference book of currencies gave weighed silver and lead as the currencies of Burma.[1] As long ago as 1795, Symes reported

[1]Noback, pp. 753-4.

from Ava the existence of the same currencies:—"The Birmans, like the Chinese, have no coins; silver bullion and lead are the current monies of the country; weight and purity are, of course, the standard of value, and in the ascertainment of both, the natives are extremely scrupulous and expert."[2]

According to Bastian, who paid a visit to Burma in 1861-2, anybody wanting to transact business on the market must be provided with a lump of silver, a hammer, a chisel, weighing scales and weights. When the potential buyer asks the seller to state his price, the latter responds by asking his customer to show his money. Having formed an opinion about the fineness of the lump of silver produced, he then quotes a price in weight. Thereupon they proceed to cut off from the lump of silver a corresponding piece which is then weighed. Often the operation has to be repeated several times until the correct weight is achieved. Needless to say, much silver becomes lost in the process. To avoid this, the buyer often asks the seller how much of his goods he is prepared to give for his lump of silver such as it is. Alternatively, change is given in the form of rice.[3]

Flouet, writing of Pegu and Rangoon in 1786, stated that the current money in the bazaars and markets was lead, cut into lumps of various sizes. The sellers put into one scale the goods they were selling and in the other scale the lumps of lead. Meat and fish were sold sometimes weight for weight. For 25 lbs. of meat the buyer paid 25 lbs. of lead. Vegetables and other goods of lower value were sold in proportion. Flouet remarks that this currency was seldom used for large payments.[4]

Lumps of spelter or pewter were used as currency already in the 16th century. According to Cæsar Frederick in about 1567 the current money in the city of Pegu and throughout the entire kingdom was called *ganza* or *gamca*, an alloy of copper and lead. It was not issued by the king; anyone was entitled to stamp it.[5]

General Macmahon, an authority on the Karens quoted by Temple,[6] stated that "among the most valued possessions of the Hill Karens is the *kyee-zee*, consisting of a copper spelter cylinder of about a quarter of an inch in thickness, averaging about two feet in length, and of somewhat greater diameter at one end, which is closed with the same kind of

[2]Michael Symes, *Embassy to Ava*. Pinkerton's Voyages (London, 1811), Vol. IX, p. 503.
[3]Adolf Bastian, *Reisen in Birma in den Jahren* 1861-2 (Leipzig, 1866), pp. 57-8. Bastian found that while in the towns token money was freely accepted, in the backward regions it was rejected (p. 284).
[4]*T'Oung Pao*, Vol. II, 1941, quoted by Temple (1919), pp. 19-20.
[5]*Purchas Pilgrims*, Vol. III (1717-18), quoted by Temple (1919), p. 22. See also Gabriel Ferrand, *Les Poids, Mesures et Monnaies des Mers du Sud aux XVIe et XVIIe Siècle*, *Journal Asiatique*, July-Dec., 1920, p. 85.
[6]Sir R. C. Temple, *Beginnings of Currency*, *Journal of the Anthropological Institute*, Vol. XXIX (London, 1899), p. 110.

metal, the smaller end being left open. The possession of *kyee-zee* is what constitutes a rich Karen. No one is considered rich without them, whatever may be his other possessions. Everyone who has money endeavours to turn it into *kyee-zee*." There is no evidence whether *kyee-zee* are used as a medium of exchange or a standard of value.

Macmahon also stated in 1845 that "the value of all property is estimated by the Maliah Khonds in "lives," a measure which requires some adjustment every time it is applied. A buffalo, a bullock, a goat, a pig or a fowl, a bag of grain or a set of brass pots being each, with anything that may be agreed upon, a "life." A hundred lives on an average may be taken to consist of ten bullocks, ten buffaloes, ten sacks of corn, ten sets of brass pots, twenty sheep, ten pigs and thirty fowls."[7]

A brick of tea was, according to Temple, not only worth a rupee, but in a certain sense *was* a rupee.[8] In the market of Bamo, the currency consisted of flat discs of China tea and balls of Shan tea.[9] Glass jars and bottles are claimed to have served as currency in Burma a thousand years ago, according to Chinese observers. During expeditions in Upper Burma in the 'seventies, it was found that empty bottles were very popular among the Shans.[10] There is no evidence, however, that they played any other part than that of a favourite medium of barter.

Rice was used until recently as a currency. Only useless broken rice, unsuitable for food or seed, was used for that purpose. Apparently it was possible to find buyers for unlimited amounts of good rice; only what was spoiled in handling was used as money.[11] This observation was first made by the British Resident at the Court of Ava in 1797, according to Temple. According to Temple the quantity of such broken rice in monetary circulation has its natural limits, owing to the demand for food and for seed. Under native governments revenue was estimated in baskets of rice.[12]

[7]Temple (1899), p. 105   [8]Temple (1899), p. 109.
[9]Clement Williams, quoted by Temple (1899), p. 190.
[10]Temple (1899), pp. 109-10.   [11]Temple (1899), pp. 111-2.
[12]Temple (1899), p. 109.

CHAPTER 24

TEA BRICK CURRENCY IN BACKWARD PARTS OF CHINA

The primitive currencies of China, as those of India, have a very ancient history. Various primitive currencies have survived to some extent to our days in the backward provinces, but even in the most advanced parts of China such as the former Treaty Ports, the adoption of coins and of paper currency has not replaced altogether the use of the ancient fictitious silver unit, the *tael*. This system is described in some detail in the Historical Section of this book, and we propose to refer to it here only briefly. Although until recently most large transactions were concluded in terms of *taels*, there were no actual coins called *tael*. The metal that actually changed hands consisted of shoe-shaped silver ingots called *sycee*. The *tael* represents a certain weight of such ingots of a certain fineness.[1]

On the China-Tibet border, silver by weight constituted until recently both the standard of value and the medium of exchange. In Attensé, towards the close of the last century, musk was sold for seven times its weight in silver, and gold at eighteen times its weight in silver.[2]

In some of the backward parts of China it was found difficult to popularize modern money. Silver coins are still taken as a piece of ornament rather than a currency in the towns of the Gobi desert. Their value depends largely on whether the people approve or disapprove of their design. The dollar bearing the head of Yuan Shik-Kai was favourably received, but when a new coin stamped with the effigy of Sun Yat-Sen was issued the inhabitants of Gobi towns refused to accept it because the new President's head was small and unimpressive. In Tunkwang, each coin is valued individually a little higher or a little lower than its face value, according to the degree of preference of the people, independently of intrinsic values.[3] In some towns in the Gobi desert and Sinkiang gamblers' counters made of bamboo or base metals served until recently as a currency.[4]

In Tibet sheep were used as a measure of value.[5] As in other parts of Inner Asia, tea was, and probably still is, extensively used as a medium of exchange.[6] Lumps of gold and gold dust by weight, and silver *yambu* were also media of exchange.[7] Turquoise beads were also said to have been used as a kind of money.[8] In Sinkiang, too, tea bricks and sheep served as currency.[9]

In Mongolia and in other parts of Central and Western Asia, livestock played an important part as a currency for many centuries. Until recently sheep continued to serve as a unit of account. They represent a fairly flexible standard according to Karamisheff.[10] The grown-up ram, the grown-up sheep, the one-year-old ram and sheep, the lamb, each had its fixed value. For instance, a grown-up bull was worth ten grown-up rams or twenty grown-up sheep, or thirty one-year-old sheep, or sixty lambs.

[1]The best description of this system is to be found in Eduard Kann, *The Currencies of China* (Shanghai, 1921), 2nd Edition, p. 65 *et seq.*
[2]Prince Henri d'Orleans, *From Tonkin to India* (London, 1898), p. 242.
[3]Mildred Cable and Francisca French, *The Gobi Desert* (London, 1942), p. 70.
[4]Cable and French, p. 88. According to G. N. Roelich, *Trails in Inmost Asia* (New Haven, 1931), p. 97, small bamboo sticks are issued by gambling houses on the road to Urumchi, with the names of the house on them. They are universally accepted.
[5]Regling (1926), p. 208.
[6]W. Ridgeway, *The Origin of Metallic Currency and Weight Standards* (Cambridge, 1892), p. 23.   [7]Noback, p. 871.   [8]Ridgeway, p. 23.
[9]W. Karamisheff, *Mongolia and Western China* (Tientsin, 1925), pp. 38-9.
[10]Karamisheff, pp. 38-9.

During the early part of the century, sheep were largely displaced as currency by brick tea. Owing to the strong demand for it throughout Inner Asia, it is generally acceptable.[11] It is divisible for small payments. The value of goods sold in the markets and shops was reckoned by numbers of tea bricks. During the 19th century tea bricks were given by the Chinese to the Mongols to pay for troops.[12] During the 'seventies in Urga a sheep was worth from twelve to fifteen bricks, a camel from 120-150 bricks, a Chinese pipe from two to five bricks. Anyone desirous of making purchases in the market took with him a sackful or a cartload of tea bricks.[13] Haslund quotes an instance of the purchase of a house for tea bricks in Kiakt.[14] Extensive credit transactions were concluded in tea bricks.[15] Tea currency has its disadvantages. It is very bulky and heavy. One brick weighs four and a half lbs. and the transport of a quantity of it worth a hundred dollars would require the services of a camel. Moreover, its value is unstable; it largely depends on the quantity available.[16] Owing to this inconvenience, in more recent years tea bricks were replaced by the silver *sycee*, current in other parts of China. Scrap silver is also used, while in remote corners barter continues to prevail on a basis of tea or sheep as units of account.[17]

In addition to sheep and tea, various local products served as limited currencies in particular districts. In Northern Mongolia, the unit of account was the squirrel skin, and Mongols near the Salenga river used furs as a medium of exchange.[18] Haslund quotes the instance of a rich lama in the 'thirties, to whom most people in the district owed money, collecting his debts in the form of furs.[19] In certain parts of the steppes, horses or cattle were valued in terms of puds of butter.[20]

A very large part of the home trade of Mongolia was until recently on a barter basis. Barter was often transacted according to the value of goods expressed in Chinese dollars.[21] Silver, whether in the form of *sycee* or coins, is largely used as a store of wealth.

Rice was for a long time used in Korea as currency. In addition, during the 14th century pieces of flax tissue served as money. In 1357 it was decided to seal pieces of linen in order to make them legal tender.[22]

More recently the currency consisted entirely of brass coins of very small value, between 2,000 and 2,800 being equal to one Mexican dollar. To pay a sum of £10 or £20 the hire of oxen and of six to eight coolies

[11]M. P. Price, *Siberia* (London, 1912), p. 279.

[12]Ritter, *Asien*, Vol. III, p. 252. Quoted by W. Roscher, *Principles of Politica Economy* (Chicago, 1878), p. 357.

[13]N. Prejevalsky, *Mongolia, the Tangut Country and the Solitudes of Northern Tibet* (London, 1876), Vol. I, p. 10.

[14]Henning Haslund, *Tents in Mongolia* (London, 1934), pp. 208.

[15]Price, p. 281.   [16]Karamisheff, p. 38.   [17]Karamisheff, p. 39.

[18]Haslund, pp. 185-6.   [19]Haslund, p. 31.   [20]Haslund, p. 153.

[21]Haslund, p. 31.

[22]Maurice Courant, *Journal Asiatique*, Vol. II, 1893, pp. 270 *et seq*. Quoted by E. Babelon, *Les Origines de la Monnaie* (Paris, 1897), p. 13.

became necessary. In spite of the inconvenience of this Spartan system, no gold or silver coins were introduced in the country.[23] The mining of both gold and silver was, until the Japanese conquest, strictly prohibited and even punished with death. The idea was to avoid penetration of foreign interests attracted by the mineral wealth of the country.[24]

[23]A. Henry Savage-Landor, *Korea* (London, 1895), pp. 38-9.
[24]Ernest Oppert, *A Forbidden Land—Voyages to Korea* (London, 1880), pp. 170-3.

CHAPTER 25

COCONUT STANDARD ON THE NICOBARS

The currency of Car Nicobar consists of coconuts. There is ample evidence of its monetary role during the late 19th century and during the present century right to the eve of the second World War, and it is probable that at present it is still in monetary use. Car Nicobar produces a large exportable surplus of coconuts. They constitute the staple food of the inhabitants as well as their staple exports. Anybody in possession of coconuts finds no difficulty in exchanging them freely for goods or services.

Coconuts play the part of a store of value mainly for brief periods. Traders accumulate them pending their sale to shippers. Natives, too, hold supplies until they use their coconuts for purchases. Coconuts are considered part of the riches of the inhabitants of Nicobar.[1] They cannot be kept, however, indefinitely without deterioration.

The custom of Indian traders of keeping their coconut supplies in primitive "safes" consisting of courtyards screened by palm leaf fences led to much litigation with the natives whose pigs were quite capable of cracking these safes and, what is much more difficult, also the shells of the coconuts. Mahommedan traders, when catching the pigs in the act, usually rushed out with spears to drive the unclean beasts away. They even slayed them on occasions, and retained the carcass in compensation for the damage suffered. When the conflict arising from such extreme action was brought before the British Government Agent, George Whitehead, he delivered a judgment worthy of the wisdom of King Solomon at his best, by ruling that, since the Nicobarese had been there with their pigs long before the Indian traders came, it was the business of the traders to make sufficiently strong fences around their premises to prevent the pigs getting at their nuts; and that while the traders were entitled to inflict bodily harm on the intruders in defence

[1]"A man is rich on the Nicobars when he possesses above 400 rupees, plenty of pigs, nuts and sons"—F. A. de Roepstorff, *Vocabulary of Dialects spoken in the Nicobar and Andaman Isles* (Calcutta, 1875), p. 14.

of their property, if as a result of their action the animal was killed the carcass must be surrendered to its rightful owner.[2]

The main store of value of the natives consists of silver-plated spoons and forks. They spend most of their coconut surplus on buying these from the traders, thinking presumably that they are silver.[3]

While coconuts play a secondary part as a store of value, they play a most important part both as a medium of exchange, standard of value and standard of deferred payments. They are practically the only medium of exchange on Car Nicobar, and to a less extent on other islands of the group. They are accepted by traders in payment for anything.[4] For instance, imported rice, which is a most important food, is paid in coconuts in the local shops.[5] Indeed, traders prefer nuts to coins. The Government made an effort to introduce the Indian coinage, and to that end it was made illegal to refuse to give or to accept coins for goods on sale. In practice, however, coconuts remained the means of payment. For one thing, the traders are more inclined to trust their employees with coconut "petty cash" than with silver coins; in this instance, at any rate, difficult transportability is considered an advantage. Moreover, in selling their goods for coconuts they are able to make a profit both ways, since they re-sell the coconuts to shippers at a profit.[6] Sometimes a transaction runs into thousands of coconuts. Natives trading amongst themselves also freely accept coconuts in payment, even for valuable objects such as boats. Car Nicobar bought some twenty-five ships from Chowra Island every year for 100,000 coconuts.[7] Wages are also paid largely in coconuts. Those engaged in husking the coconuts are paid one nut for each ten nuts husked.[8]

The use of coconuts as a medium of exchange is not without disadvantages. If coconuts were an ordinary commodity they would be sold when they are ripe. As it is, the nuts are kept until their owners wish to use them in payment for goods and services.

Although to some extent coins are used, they disappear quickly as they are either hoarded or are converted into ornaments. "The rupee is a foreign coin with which they are familiar and they will buy it with their own currency, the coconut."[9] There exists a discrepancy between

[2]George Whitehead, *In the Nicobar Isles* (London, 1924), pp. 83-4.
[3]G. Boden Kloss, *In the Andamans and Nicobars* (London, 1903), p. 81. According to W. Swoboda, *Die Bewohner des Nicobaren Archipels*, (Leipzig, 1903) Part II, p. 5., silver is hoarded in the form of spoons, coins and ornaments.
[4]Mrs. Talbot Clifton, *Pilgrims to the Isle of Penance* (London, 1911), p. 177.
[5]E. H. Mann, *The Nicobar Islands and their People* (London, 1933), p. 113.
[6]Whitehead, pp. 78-9.
[7]*Papers relating to the Nicobar Islands* (Selections from the records of the Government of India, No. 77. Calcutta, 1870), p. 182.
[8]Kloss, p. 319.
[9]H. S. Montgomerie, *The Nicobar Islands* (Geographical Journal, January, 1922, Vol. LIX, No. I), p. 42, Whitehead (p. 79), who spent some years on the island, only remembers one occasion to have seen rupees used on a large scale, and then they were buried in the coffin of the wife of a rich Nicobarese.

the coconut value of coins of various denominations. According to official information, in 1901 the silver piece of two annas was valued at sixteen coconuts, while the silver piece of one rupee was valued at a hundred coconuts.[10] Since there are sixteen annas in a rupee, the corresponding value for one rupee should be 128 coconuts, not 100. The explanation of the discrepancy, put forward by Temple, is that the little piece of silver is used for one sort of ornament and the big piece for another sort, and their value in coconuts to these people depends on their relative value as ornaments and not on their relative nominal monetary value.[11]

Most important of all is the role of coconuts as a standard of value. Trade between the natives is conducted largely on a basis of barter, but the value of each article is assessed in coconuts. This is done even on the occasion of large transactions such as the purchase of a canoe. A concrete instance is quoted in an official document showing that in 1896, the people of Car Nicobar bought from Chowra a large racing canoe valued at 35,000; payment was made in various articles, the list of which included cloth, spoons, baskets, two-anna pieces, silver wire, silver rings, knives, forks, pigs, fowls, beads, fish-hooks, rupees, axes, etc. Each article was reckoned according to its coconut value and the total thus arrived at was exactly 35,000.[12]

Another officially quoted instance is that of the purchase of land valued at 10,000 nuts paid for by about fifty manufactured articles valued in the aggregate at 10,000 nuts.[13] The Census of India for 1901 contains lists of trade articles valued in coconuts in 1896 and in 1857. Unfortunately, the items in the two lists are not strictly comparable. It would be interesting to see the change in the price level in terms of coconuts.

The value of the coconuts in terms of rupees has undergone a spectacular appreciation during recent decades. Up to 1885, 500 coconuts were equal to one rupee. Later, the "parity" was 300.[14] In 1901 the rate quoted in the Census of India was 100 per rupee. When it was decided after the first world war to impose an export duty on all goods exported from the islands, the exchange rate was officially fixed at 200 nuts per rupee.[15] Subsequently the value of the rupee was reduced once more to 100 nuts, and later to 64.[16] At that latter rate it was worth exactly one pie, the smallest Indian monetary unit. According to Montgomerie,

[10]*Census of India*, 1901, Vol. III. The Andaman and Nicobar Islands (Calcutta, 1903), p. 242.
[11]Temple (1899), p. 104.
[12]*Local Gazetteer, The Andaman and Nicobar Islands* (Calcutta, 1908), p. 108.
[13]*Imperial Gazetteer*, All India Provincial Series, Andaman and Nicobar Islands (Calcutta, 1909), p. 50.
[14]Swoboda, p. 5.
[15]Mann, pp. 30-31. Coconut was thus given "a definite value as well as official recognition as a form of currency."
[16]Whitehead, p. 78.

however, while in theory the rupee may have been equal to 64 nuts, in practice "it seems that 48 nuts are now more nearly equivalent to it."[17]

Practically all debts on Car Nicobar are expressed in coconuts. When Whitehead first arrived to take charge as British Government Agent, he learned to his consternation that the natives were in debt to the traders to the tune of millions of nuts. Since that time there has been a Commission investigating the amount of indebtedness and cutting down very considerably the claims of the traders. It was also declared to be illegal to contract any new debt in coconuts, and that, since the rupee was legal tender, any debts contracted in coconuts could be repaid in rupees. Notwithstanding this, natives continued to contract and repay debts in coconuts.[18]

It seems that the coconut standard suits admirably the primitive requirements of the Nicobarese. "Because it acts as a sufficient currency, they have no use for money as Europeans understand it."[19] The coconut currency is never liable to be inflated, for if there is no adequate demand for coconuts when they are ripe, then the natives just do not trouble to collect them. Nor is there any evidence that the increase in the value of coconuts from 500 to the rupee in 1885 to 48 to the rupee forty years later—an appreciation of 900 per cent—has in any way upset the primitive economy of Nicobar. They just think in terms of coconuts, and if the rupee costs less coconuts then so much the worse for the rupee.

[17]Montgomerie, p. 42.
[18]Mann, p. 101.   [19]Whitehead, p. 9.

CHAPTER 26

GRAIN MEDIUM OF EXCHANGE IN INDIA

India had primitive currencies which were in use for many centuries B.C. even in those parts of the sub-continent which had reached an advanced civilization. These are dealt with in the Historical Section. In this section we are only concerned with the primitive currencies which are still in existence, or were in existence until recently, in backward parts of India. Most important amongst them is grain, which was the principal medium of exchange in a large number of Indian agricultural districts. Almost all economic transactions in many villages were carried out without the use of money.[1] In many villages coins are even to-day only a store of value, not a medium of exchange. When they happen to be rich in money they hoard it in coins which serve as ornaments. Until recently the use of modern money in remote villages was rare, whether for effecting exchanges or remunerating services. Grain was the standard

[1]Radhakamal Mukerjee, *The Foundation of India Economics* (London, 1916), p. 34.

H

of value, and it was used by the villagers in their exchanges with each other.[2] Even now, grain is to some extent used as a medium of exchange in remote districts.[3]

Grain is also used even now as a standard of deferred payments. A large proportion of loans in backward rural areas is contracted in terms of grain. In particular sowing seed is often borrowed, as well as food to last till the next crop. The usual arrangement is that double the quantity borrowed shall be repaid at harvest time.[4] Considering that interest charged on loans in rupees in backward districts is between twenty-four and thirty-six per cent per annum, this rate is exorbitant, though it is necessary to allow for the fact that grain is cheaper at harvest than at seed time. In the Punjab and also in Bengal and other parts of India there are a number of so-called grain banks, a special type of small credit societies in which thrift dealings are transacted in grain. In the Punjab there were nineteen such banks in July, 1927, with a working capital of 27,900 rupees. These grain banks are meant as a co-operative experiment for backward communities where most people hardly even see coins, much less use them.[5]

In districts where rice is the staple product it plays a part somewhat similar to that of grain in other districts. In Malabar agricultural wages are paid mainly in paddy.[6] Paddy seed is borrowed at an interest of sixty per cent.[7]

In Assam a wide variety of primitive currencies is claimed to be still in use. Each tribe has a different kind of currency. The Ao Nagas use brass discs of twelve inch diameter with a highly convex surface. These discs have been in use for some time, but the natives accept also modern imported discs. Formerly there were in use bars of iron between six and seven inches long.[8]

The Sema Nagas in the Vachumi country use small flat cakes of salt and also blades of worn out knife-like weapons, one of which was reckoned to be worth one cock or eight annas. Strings of broken shell beads alternating with pieces of bamboo are said to have also been currency in the Sema country. Strings of brass beads were also used. Most trade is done, however, by barter.[9] Animals are loaned, and their value is determined by the length of their horns and by the girth behind their shoulder. The debtor is required to pay interest by returning to his creditors animals with slightly longer horns and greater in girth.[10]

[2]G. B. Jathar and S. G. Beri, *Indian Economics* (Bombay, 1928), p. 154.
[3]S. C. Roy, *The Oraons of Chota Nagpur* (Ranchi, 1915), p. 189.
[4]J. Fawcett, *The Highlands of Central India* (London, 1871), p. 153.
[5]L. C. Jain, *Indigenous Banking in India* (London, 1929), p. 200.
[6]Gilbert Slater, *Economic Studies*, Vol. I. *Some South Indian Villages* (London, 1918), p. 155.
[7]Slater, p. 175.
[8]J. P. Mills, *The Ao Nagas* (London, 1926), p. 102.
[9]J. H. Hutton, *The Sema Nagas* (London, 1921), pp. 58-9.
[10]Hutton, p. 162.

The currency of the Angami Nagas is conch shell and iron. Small iron hoes brought from Manipur are also currency. The iron currency is roughly key-shaped and it is possible that it was used originally as a spear. Its length is about eight inches and it has now no other use except as currency. It is called the *chabili* and one of these strange pieces of iron pays for one day's labour. Large numbers can be seen in rich men's houses. The Chang use flat metal gongs which were worth eight annas in the early 'twenties, but were formerly worth a great deal more.[11]

In Manipur among the Naga tribes fines were fixed in cows. Bride money was paid in buffaloes. Debts are frequently incurred; after one year the amount repayable is doubled.[12] The Meitheis of Manipur have a bell-metal coinage made of melted down gongs. Originally coins bore no punch-marks, but recently they have been punch-marked.[13] Cowries were the original currency of the Meitheis in the late 19th century; they were worth four hundred to the anna.[14]

The currency of the Rengma Nagas was specially made large spear-heads which were never sharpened. Nowadays they are only used in marriage price. Some of the tribes have a fixed ratio between cattle and rice—fifty baskets of rice being equal to one cow. According to an old Angami table of barter, one male slave was worth one cow and three conch shells; one female slave three cows and three or five conch shells; one cow ten conch shells; one pig two conch shells; one goat two conch shells. Among the Eastern Rengmas, double-edged daggers of a special type and small iron digging hoes were also said to have been a currency.[15]

Various authors have alleged that in Assam animal skulls are used as currency in inter-tribal trade.[16] The claim is too fantastic, however, to be accepted without adequate corroborative evidence.

[11]J. H. Hutton, *The Angami Nagas* (London, 1921), pp. 71-2.
[12]T. C. Hodson, *The Naga Tribes of Manipur* (London, 1911), pp. 106-8.
[13]T. C. Hodson, *The Meitheis* (London, 1908), p. 37.
[14]Sir R. C. Temple, *Indian Antiquary*, Vol. XXVII, p. 169. Quoted by Hodson (1908), p. 38.
[15]J. P. Mills, *The Rengma Nagas* (London, 1937), p. 72.
[16]Andrée, p. 240.

CHAPTER 27

REINDEER AND CATTLE STANDARD IN ASIATIC RUSSIA

The entire economy of many tribes of Northern Siberia is based on the domesticated reindeer. It is no wonder, therefore, that reindeer should have served as their primitive currency. It is held in high esteem; the Tungus are most reluctant to part with their reindeer and they do not kill it except when it breaks its leg or is otherwise incapacitated.[1] The Arctic reindeer-breeding tribes of Siberia reckon their fortunes in terms of reindeer; it is still their chief store of value, even if furs and subsequently roubles have become the medium of exchange.[2] Until recently in some communities it acted as the main medium of exchange for large transactions. It was also the standard of value among the Samoyedes.[3] Loans were granted in reindeer among the Northern Tungus.[4] Bride money consisted largely of reindeer among the Ostyak.[5] Taxes, too, were paid largely in the same form.[6] Ridgeway quotes a traveller writing that among the Samoyedes a certain contract was undertaken for five hundred reindeer, and that in the 'eighties the reindeer was for monetary purposes generally considered to be equal to five roubles.[7]

Skins and small furs also became a medium of exchange among the hunting tribes. They also formed part of the bride money and were used for payment of taxes.[8] The Tungus adopted them as a store of value after the penetration of Chinese and Russian traders.[9] The fee of Tungus courtesans was so many ermine skins.[10] Among the Ostyaks the squirrel skin was the recognized unit of value.[11] According to Regling,[12] in some parts of Arctic Siberia, skins and furs had a fixed value in coins.

From time to time certain trade goods assume such a degree of popularity among the natives that they become practically universal media of exchange in their community. In the olden days, it was alcohol that played such a part. More recently Russian tobacco leaf, pressed in one lb. packets, served as money among the Tchuktchee. Tea bricks, sugar, iron goods, tools and arms are also mentioned among the money-substitutes.[13] In the early 'thirties jam was introduced by the Soviet Trading Stations. The natives liked it and the trading agents were overwhelmed with urgent demands. "Jam is now almost a recognized currency among the tribes."[14]

In certain backward parts of Southern Siberia, tea bricks played the part of currency among races such as Bashkirs and Kalmuks,[15] and near the Mongolian border.

[1]M. A. Czapliczka, *My Siberian Years* (London, 1916), p. 96.
[2]Czapliczka, p. 136. [3]Ridgeway, p. 4.
[4]S. M. Shirokogoroff, *Social Organization of the Northern Tungus* (Shanghai, 1929), p. 296.
[5]M. A. Czapliczka, *Aboriginal Siberia—A Study in Social Anthropology* (Oxford, 1914), p. 127.
[6]Czapliczka (1916), p. 66.
[7]V. A. L. Morier in *Murray's Magazine*, August, 1889, p. 18. Quoted by Ridgeway, p. 4.
[8]Czapliczka (1916), p. 286. [9]Shirokogoroff, p. 301.
[10]Czapliczka (1916), p. 136. [11]Ridgeway, p. 4.
[12]Regling, p. 209.
[13]Oskar Iden-Zeller, *Ethnographische Beobachtungen bei den Tchucktschen.* (*Zeitschrift für Ethnographie*, 1911), Vol. XLIII, p. 843.
[14]L. Metters, *Through the Kara Sea* (London, 1932), p. 235.
[15]Franz Ilwof, *Tauschhandel und Geldsurrogate in alter und neuer Zeit* (Graz, 1882), p. 55.

In pre-historic graves in Caucasia and Armenia, in certain regions of the Urals, and along the Volga, bronze rings were found which are believed to have served as money. The weight of the various sizes is claimed to conform to certain weight standards.[16]

Until recently, horses and sheep were the money of the Kirghiz. Wolf and lamb skins were used as small change.[17] Fines were fixed in horses,[18] which were also the principal form of store of value.[19] According to Ratzel[20] a wealthy Kirghiz on the upper Irtysh lends his beasts at the usual interest of 100 per cent. For a long time, the Kirghiz distrusted modern money. They were afraid that they might be cheated. To be on the safe side they either flatly refused to sell for modern money or demanded exaggerated prices.[21]

Cattle was, until comparatively recently, the chief currency of the Chefsurs in Caucasia. Fines for injuries and blood money were fixed in cows. After the adoption of Russian money, fixed ratios were established between the rouble and the cow, one cow being equal to five silver roubles. The Ossetes had a highly developed cattle currency.[22] They reckoned everything in cows or fractions of cows. Values were expressed as being ten times or a hundred times the value of a cow. An ox was worth two cows and a cow ten sheep.[23] A cow was reckoned to be equal to five roubles. The Tcherkess used oxen as their standard of value.[24] An observation by Jenkinson may indicate that cattle was used in Bukhara as a medium of exchange.[25]

The inhabitants of the Darwaz district are said to have used cakes made of dried mulberries as their unit of account and also to some extent as their medium of exchange. Mulberries constituted their staple food and it was almost their sole means of subsistence. They bought with this currency rough matting and sheeps' skins, and even their taxes were paid with it.[26] Trade was, however, mainly by barter. There was little coined money in the country.[27]

[16]J. de Morgan, *Revue Archéologique*, Vol. II, 1889, pp. 177-87 and 291. Quoted by Babelon, p. 82.
[17]v. Haxthausen, *Studien*, Vol. II, p. 371. Quoted by Roscher, p. 353.
[18]Regling, p. 208.
[19]H. J. Nieboer, *Slavery as an Industrial System* (The Hague, 1900), p. 269.
[20]Ratzel, p. 328.
[21]A. de Levchine, *Descriptions des hordes et des steppes des Khirgies-Kazaks* (Paris, 1840).
[22]Ridgeway, p. 4.
[23]Haxthausen, *Transkaukasia*, Vol. II, p. 30. Quoted by Babelon, p. 30.
[24]Roscher, p. 353.
[25]*Account of Independent Tartary*. Pinkerton's Voyages, Vol. IX (London, 1811), p. 33.
[26]*A short account of the Khanates of Bokhara and Khiva*. Translated from the Russian by E. Beard. (*Journal of the United Service Institution of India*, 1893), Vol. XXII, p. 258. Quoted by Temple (1919), p. 35.
[27]H. Lansdell, *Russian Central Asia* (London, 1885), p. 54.

CHAPTER 28

CURRENCIES AT THE PERSIAN GULF

One of the objects which is said to have served as currency in Ceylon during the Middle Ages was the tamarind seed.[1] Until comparatively recently, taxes in Ceylon were levied in grain or paddy and all rural wages were paid in these or other products.[2]

The Maldives Islands have been, since time immemorial, the principal finding place of cowries which until comparatively recently served as a most important currency in Southern Asia and in a large part of Africa. Vast quantities have been exported throughout the centuries. As cowries were the staple export of the Maldives, this alone qualified them to act as currency, since they had always been assured of an unlimited demand. To some extent, cowries were used as money also in their country of origin. According to Abu'l Hasan Ali, in A.D. 916 the Queen of the Maldives had no other money but cowries.[3] Edrisi, writing in the 12th century, stated that the King preserved the shells in his Treasury and possessed the greater portion of them.[4]

In more recent centuries the principal currency of the Maldives was not, however, the cowrie shell, but a corrupted silver fish-hook called *larin*. It was issued by the King, and later it was duly stamped as the result of which it became a coin proper. For the requirements of trade for small change *larins* were cut into pieces, even though in doing so they lost one-twelfth of their value.[5]

The early forms of primitive currency in Persia are dealt with in the Historical Section. The nomadic races in Persia are said to have used in recent times sheep, grain, straw or wool as their currency. In some parts of Persia dates were the medium of exchange. The smallest token coin was made in the shape of date stones.[6] Shawls were said to have circulated in business transactions almost like money. "In every good house part of the liquid wealth is kept in the form of shawls."[7] Sometimes these shawls were cut into pieces as small money. It was possible to sew them together again invisibly. *Larins* (corrupted silver fish-hooks) were used as a currency in Southern Persia. They derived their name from the city of Larr.

In Arabia the camel was the unit of payment among the nomadic tribes. In a feud between two Meccan tribes the manslayer had the

---

[1] H. W. Codrington, *Ceylon—Coins and Currency* (Colombo, 1924), p. 12.
[2] Sir John B. Phear, *The Aryan Village in India—Ceylon* (London, 1880), pp. 214 et seq.
[3] Albert Gray, *The Voyage of François Pyrard de Laval* (Hakluyt Society, London, 1890), Vol. II, p. 429.
[4] Gray, p. 432.　　　　　　　　　　　[5] Gray, pp. 232-5.
[6] Ritter, *Erdkunde. Asien*, Vol. VIII, p. 386. Quoted by Roscher, p. 353.
[7] Polack, *Persien*, Vol. I, p. 153. Quoted by Schurtz, p. 29.

alternative of paying a hundred camels or bringing fifty of his kin to take "oath of purgation."[8] Camels were, and probably still are, the chief standard of value among the nomadic tribes. Doughty repeatedly expressed the value of horses and other objects in terms of camels.[9] The actual medium of exchange is the silver *rial*, and gold coins are also in use. Nevertheless, among pastoral tribes payment is often made in goats[10] or other animals. Bride money is always expressed in camels.[11] There are in Nejd small bars of silvered brass, which bear bad Arabic inscriptions. Ridgeway regards them as the last surviving descendants of the old fish-hook money.[12] Coffee beans were used as small change until comparatively recently even in towns.[13]

[8]Robertson Smith, *Kinship in Arabia*, p. 53. Quoted by F. Seebohm, *Tribal Custom in Anglo-Saxon Law* (London, 1911), p. 3.   See also Ilwolf, p. 59.

[9]C. M. Doughty, *Wanderings in Arabia* (An Abridgment of *Travels in Arabia Deserta*, London, 1926), pp. 64, 126, 151.

[10]Doughty, p. 145.   [11]Doughty, p. 150.   [12]Ridgeway, pp. 29-30.

[13]Burckhardt, *Reisen in Arabien*, p. 587. Quoted by Schurtz, p. 180.

PART III: AFRICA

CHAPTER 29

IRON CURRENCY IN THE ANGLO-EGYPTIAN SUDAN

IN the backward parts of the Anglo-Egyptian Sudan cattle is still the main store of value. The Dinka, Shilluk, Nuer and other tribes still consider possession of cattle the main object of their life. The Nuer judge wealth entirely by the number of cattle and sheep a man possesses.[1] They often grant loans in cattle and the creditor is entitled to receive back bigger or better beasts than those he lent.[2] Such is the reluctance of debtors to repay what they owe that creditors often have to steal the cows owed to them as the only possible way of collecting their claims. Sometimes they employ the services of the magician whose job is to cast a spell on the defaulting debtor, so that he may not guard his herds on the day for which the theft is planned.[3] They have, or had until recently, no other currency, indeed they have hardly any barter with other tribes, for the simple reason that all they are in a position to give in exchange is cattle, and they are not prepared to part with that easily. "A rich Dinka may own 500 to 1,000 heads of cattle, but seldom trades any of them, except a few odd cows, for the small necessities of an utterly savage life."[4]

Nevertheless, to some extent cattle did, and still does, serve as a medium of exchange.[5] It was also used as a unit of account. A horse was valued at the time of El-Tounsy's visit a hundred years ago at twenty heads of cattle.[6] Above all, cattle is the means with which to purchase wives.[7]

The principal medium of exchange in backward parts of the Anglo-Egyptian Sudan was, however, iron mainly in the shape of hoes. In the countries of the Upper Nile, iron is scarce and its value is equal to that of copper.[8] Rüppel, a traveller writing about conditions in the years 1824-5, remarks that in Obeid for small outlays they used small pieces

[1] Melville J. Herskovits, *The Cattle Complex in East Africa* (American Anthropologist. New Series, Vol. xxviii, 1926), p. 230.
[2] E. E. Evans-Pritchard, *The Nuer—A description of the Mode of Livelihood and political institutions of a Nilotic People* (Oxford, 1940), p. 91.
[3] Evans-Pritchard, p. 165.
[4] C. W. Domville-Fife, *Savage Life in the Black Sudan* (London, 1927), p. 132.
[5] H. A. MacMichael, *The Tribes of Northern and Central Kordofan* (Cambridge, 1912), p. 67.
[6] Mohammed Ebn-Omar El-Tounsy, *Voyages au Darfour* (Paris, 1845), p. 321.
[7] Domville-Fife, p. 791.
[8] A. Woermann, *Über Tauschhandel in Afrika* (Mitteilungen der Geographischen Gessellschaft, Hamburg, 1880-81), p. 32.

of iron about three inches in size and of the shape of an anchor. He states that these pieces were issued by the Government of Kordofan.[9] Presumably he was referring to the hoe-shaped pieces of iron to which reference is made also by El-Tounsy who says that they were used at Ras-el-Fyl for the purchase of goods of small value.[10] Another traveller in the first half of the 19th century, Hoskins, found in 1833 at Dongola rudely shaped pieces of iron which he was told were Darfur money.[11] J. Pallme wrote in 1844 that there was a small coin of iron struck by the Sultan of Darfur in the form of an obtuse anchor; 150 of these pieces were formerly considered equal to one dollar; they subsequently depreciated to 250, and their value at the time Pallme was writing was 800 to the dollar.[12] The Mombattu on the Nile used shapeless lumps of iron, the size of a fist, or semi-circular rings.[13] Reference is made by Schweinfurth to the use of spades as currency along the course of the Upper Nile.[14]

It seems possible that ostrich egg beads (known as Bushman beads) which played an important part as currency in South Africa, were at one time used as a medium of exchange in the Sudan. In mounds in the central Kordofan district very large numbers of such beads have been found.[15] Conceivably, however, these beads were merely ornaments.

In more recent times rings of gold and silver, such as had been used as money in Ancient Egypt, were employed in a similar capacity in Sennar and neighbouring countries.[16] Tin rings were one of the currencies at Fader, the place of residence of the Sultan, for the purchase of everyday requirements.[17] Tin plates were a standard of value at Darfur towards the close of the 19th century.[18] El-Tounsy gives us a detailed list of the various objects that he claims have served as currency in the various districts. At Fader, in addition to tin rings, cotton cloth also played the part of currency, four pieces being equal to a Spanish dollar.

Slaves were used as a unit of account. The standard unit was a black slave of certain measurements. Houses were quoted as being worth three slaves. The value of a slave was thirty pieces of cotton or six oxen, or ten dollars.[19]

[9]Quoted by MacMichael, *A History of the Arabs in the Sudan* (Cambridge, 1922).
[10]El-Tounsy, p. 320.
[11]E. A. Wallis Budge, *The Egyptian Sudan* (London, 1907), p. 105.
[12]J. Pallme, *Travels in Kordofan* (London, 1844), p. 303. Quoted by MacMichael, *The Tribes of Northern and Central Kordofan*, p. 67. MacMichael observes that the hoes were originally genuine articles for practical use, but after they had been adopted as currency, small sized specimens were specially issued for that purpose alone.
[13]Woermann, p. 32.
[14]George Schweinfurth, *The Heart of Africa* (London, 1873), Vol. I, pp. 278-9.
[15]MacMichael (1922), p. 30   [16]MacMichael (1922), p. 30.
[17]El-Tounsey, p. 315.
[18]O. Lenz, *Wanderungen in Afrika* (Vienna, 1895), p. 206.
[19]El-Tounsy, pp. 315-6.

In Guely bars of salt were used for the purchase of cheap goods. They changed hands not by weight but by the number of bars and their length.[20] At Kouca very strong tobacco was the chief medium of exchange.[21] At Ryl and elsewhere bundles of twenty cotton threads were the monetary unit for moderately-priced objects; for very cheap objects payment was made in raw cotton by approximate weight.[22] In the Noumleh district, onions are said to have been the principal medium of exchange.[23] At Temourkeh, cylindrical-shaped copper was the currency.[24]

Each district had a different local currency, and the object which was money in one place was considered an object of inferior value elsewhere. The Sultan did not seek to establish any degree of uniformity in the monetary system.[25] General Gordon stated in a letter to a relative, dated the 20th November, 1875, that the money in use in Moogie was the *dhoora* (millet).[26] He also states in a letter dated the 17th July, 1877, that the money of Darfur was cloth, certain pieces having certain values.[27] According to Woermann, both Maria Theresa dollars and cowries were used in the Sudan mainly by Mohammedans.[28]

During recent decades the adoption of modern money made much progress in all but the most remote and backward areas. General Gordon himself made an effort to popularize the use of coins. In one of his letters he gave an account of his attempt to initiate the black man into the mysteries of civilization by teaching him the use of money: "I have had great work with the native Chiefs in teaching them the use of money. Up to the present time the habit has been to give the Chief of tribe some beads or calico and he makes his men bring wood or do any work. Now I want to break through the feudal system of Chiefs; the only way to do this is to let their subjects see that they can stand on their own feet. Before I began the system which I hope to establish, the Chief would keep the mass of the things given to him and give only a few to his subjects. I began by paying each man who worked some beads; next day I gave each man who worked half a piaste (one penny) in copper and offered to sell him beads to that amount. They soon saw it and would not buy. They said: 'We will keep the money till we get more and can buy more expensive things.' I have fixed certain prices for certain things and made out little lots of beads and wire to sell for certain prices. . . .

---

[20]El-Tounsy, p. 318.
[21]El-Tounsy, p. 318.   [22]El-Tounsy, pp. 318-9.
[23]El-Tounsy, pp. 319-20.   [24]El-Tounsy, p. 320.   [25]El-Tounsy, p. 321.
[26]*Colonel Gordon in Central Africa*, 1874-79, from original letters and documents edited by G. B. Hill, 2nd Edn. (London, 1884), pp. 145-6. The use of dhoora as medium of exchange is referred to also by Burckhard, quoted by MacMichael (1912), p. 67.
[27]Colonel Gordon, p. 249. According to G. Nachtigal, strips of loosely-woven cotton cloth were used as small change at Darfur (*Sahara-Sudan*, Berlin, 1879, Vol. III). pp. 306-7.
[28]Woermann, p. 33.

A Chief brought a tusk and wanted two bells for cows to wear around their necks in exchange, I said: 'No, I will give you two dollars for the tusk.' He said: 'Yes'—and so I gave him two dollars. 'Now,' I said, 'I will give you two bells for a dollar each'—which he agreed and bought them. This was a great step to make. He has brought some more tusks since for which I gave him money and he has bought from me copper wire."[29]

[29]Colonel Gordon, pp. 39-50.

CHAPTER 30

SALT MONEY OF ETHIOPIA

At the time of the Italian invasion, the currency of Ethiopia consisted almost exclusively of Maria Theresa dollars and salt. The former cannot properly be classed among the primitive currencies since it is a silver coin changing hands by tale. It has always been a mystery why many millions of natives in East Africa have adopted and used that coin for a century and a half in preference to any other coin. According to one explanation, the Empress with her ample bust corresponds to African ideas of the perfect feminine beauty. However this may be, these coins have been readily taken in exchange for goods and services over wide areas of East Africa. Nevertheless, it is possible to argue that they are an advanced form of primitive money, and not money in the modern sense of the term.[1]

The use of salt as currency in Ethiopia has an even longer history than that of the Maria Theresa dollars. Reference was made to it by Alvarez, one of the early European explorers of Ethiopia covering the beginning of the 16th century, and Captain Alexander Hamilton who paid a visit to the country at the beginning of the 18th century. The latter observed that "the current small money of Ethiopia is salt."[2] It was first intro-duced into Ethiopia by the Amole tribe and a bar of salt serving as currency is known as *amole* to this day.[3] It is used mainly in the Amharic provinces,[4] but as small change it is popular throughout the Empire. In particularly backward regions it constitutes the only currency. Cheese-man found that in remote villages people refused Maria Theresa dollars

[1]C. F. Rey, *In the Country of the Blue Nile* (London, 1927), "Maria Theresa Thaler is more a commodity of facile use than a medium of exchange," p. 185.
[2]Captain Alexander Hamilton, *A New Account of the East Indies* (Pinkerton's Travel Series, Vol. VIII, London, 1811), p. 272.
[3]Sir E. A. Wallis Budge, *A History of Ethiopia* (London, 1928), Vol. I, p. 136.
[4]Ratzel, p. 233.

and accepted salt only, observing: "We cannot eat dollars."[5] The bars used as currency are pieces of rock salt of the shape of a whetstone, ten to twelve inches long and one and a half inches thick. Their weight is just over a pound.[6] According to Rey, the bars in circulation are black with handling, but according to W. Cornwallis Harris[7] the colour of the rock salt is naturally black.

It is not surprising that salt should be a favourite currency in Ethiopia, seeing that natives have an exceptionally strong liking for its taste. It is considered a great luxury. The Ethiopians say of a millionaire, "he eateth salt."[8] Nevertheless, the monetary value of salt in Ethiopia is not based entirely on its non-monetary use as a favourite article of consumption. Only the black bars are accepted as a medium of exchange. White salt of much finer quality is only taken at its commodity value which is much lower. Moreover, in many districts only faultless bars are accepted as money.

To some extent at any rate salt serves as a store of value. Slave traders invest their profit in *amoles*.[9] To a much larger extent the salt bars constitute the medium of exchange in most districts. A woman goes to the market with a bar, and when small purchases are made she breaks off a bit of salt and pays with it.[10] This habit of dividing salt bars existed already in Hamilton's days. Ethiopians are so expert in dividing the pieces that "they err not above five per cent more or less in their calculation of weight."[11] Although primarily used as small change, even valuable properties such as slaves are purchased with it. According to Burton, at Harar at the time of his visit the price of a slave was a donkeyload of salt bars.

Salt bars are also used extensively as a standard of value. The ratio between salt and Maria Theresa dollars is subject to fluctuations according to changes in the market price of silver.[12] At the time of Hamilton's visit, 20 lbs. of salt currency was worth about a shilling. More recent authors quote widely different parities. Thus according to Cheeseman, the number of salt bars equal to one dollar was between three and five; according to Rey it was between five and six; according to Maydon[13] it was eight; according to Budge it varied between ten and forty, while Sievers and Hahn state definitely that in Adowa forty-eight bars were equal to one dollar.[14] There may have been discrepancies in the size of the bars as there is no standard size for the whole country even at any given moment, and the size in use is liable to change over a period of

[5]R. E. Cheeseman, *Lake Tana and the Blue Nile* (London, 1936), p. 184.
[6]Budge, p. 136.
[7]W. Cornwallis Harris, *The Highlands of Ethiopia* (London, 1844), Vol. I, p. 377.
[8]R. F. Burton, *First Footsteps in East Africa or an Exploration of Harar* (London, 1856), p. 136.
[9]Harris, p. 377.   [10]Cheeseman, pp. 184-5.
[11]Hamilton, p. 272.   [12]Cheeseman, p. 184.
[13]H. C. Maydon, *Simen and its Heights and Abysses* (London, 1925), pp. 236-7.
[14]W. Sievers and F. Hahn, *Africa*, 2nd Edn. (Leipzig, 1901), p. 133.

time. Above all, the value of salt differs widely even at a given moment, according to the distance from the salt-producing district.[15]

Cartridges having a certain bore of rifle were, and possibly still are, extensively used as a kind of currency in various districts of Ethiopia. Travellers often came across Ethiopian warriors armed with spears only, but carrying nevertheless bagfuls of cartridges—a fact which indicates that their monetary use was not entirely based on their non-monetary use. They were so used not only in remote parts but even in the vicinity of Addis Ababa, and there the value was between three and four to the dollar.[16] Landor found that in some parts of Ethiopia he had great difficulty in buying anything as they would not accept money and only Gras cartridges were accepted in payment for their goods. His servant bought a chicken and six eggs as well as some barley bread for one cartridge the value of which was about twopence.[17]

In the 16th century spade-shaped iron was used as currency.[18] Formerly in Abyssinia each district had its own imported bead money, circulating within the district only.[19]

Among the Borana, in Southern Ethiopia, cloth, white metal bracelets and cubes, beads, cowries and chewing tobacco are said to have served as a means of payment. These metal cubes served no non-monetary purposes. On the occasion of his journey, Dracopoli bought a sheep for 250 cubes.[20]

Taxes and fines were fixed at one time in oxen and in cows.[21] Alvarez stated that tributes fixed in horses were dischargeable in cows.[22]

Gold by weight was the means of payment towards the beginning of the 16th century. The use of coined money was actually forbidden.[23]

The tribes inhabiting British and Italian Somaliland are largely pastoral races, and their favourite beast is the camel. It is only natural, therefore, that camels should be the principal store of value. Among the Somali a man's wealth was entirely reckoned by the number of camels he possessed. Before the advent of the rupee, all debts, presents and compensations were paid in camels.[24] The blood money for a man killed was a hundred she-camels, but half this number was considered

---

[15]According to Kürchhoff, *Die Geldverhältnisse im Heutigen Afrika in ihrer Entwickelung* (Mitteilungen der Geographischen Gesellschaft in Hamburg, 1907, Vol. XXII, p. 17), the following parities prevailed in various parts of Abyssinia between salt and the dollar:—Adowa, 40; Tatsher Diver, 15; Amas, 12-13; Egibie, 10-12; Galla, 4-5 bars to the dollar.

[16]Maydon, p. 25.

[17]A. H. Savage-Landor, *Across Wildest Africa* (London, 1907), pp. 59 and 148-9.

[18]Francisco Alvarez, *Narrative of the Portuguese Embassy in Abyssinia* (Hakluyt Society, London, 1881), p. 117.

[19]Burckhardt, *Reisen in Nubien*, p. 409. Quoted by Schurtz, p. 63.

[20]I. N. Dracopoli, *Through Jubaland to the Lorian Swamps* (London, 1914), pp. 234 and 309.

[21]Babelon, p. 21.   [22]Alvarez, pp. 37, 54, 331.

[23]Alvarez, 60.

[24]R. E. Drake-Brockman, *British Somaliland* (London, 1912), p. 125.

enough for a woman. For the loss of an eye or permanent disablement of a limb, fifty camels had to be paid. If blood was drawn from the head, thirty camels were demanded, and even for a bruise the demand was for three or four camels.[25]

Camels, and to a lesser extent other livestock, were used for large purchases; beads were used for trifling purchases; together with tobacco they served for small change.[26]

The standard of value at Berberah was formerly two cubits of blue cotton cloth called *sauda*.[27] This was made equal to four pice after the adoption of coins.

Dates are also said to have been used as small change.[28] Millet was until recently a medium of exchange on the Somali coast. It was reckoned by the hollow of the hand.[29]

[25]H. G. C. Swain, *Seventeen Trips Through Somaliland* (London, 1895), pp. 13-14.
[26]Burton, p. 86.
[27]Burton, p. 419. See also Dracopoli, p. 308.
[28]Haggenmacher (Petermann's Mitteilungen, Ergänzungsheft x), p. 40. Quoted by Schurtz, p. 136.
[29]Justus Strandes, *Die Portugiesenzeit von Deutsch-und Englisch-Ostafrika* (Berlin, 1899), p. 332.

CHAPTER 31

LIVESTOCK STANDARD IN KENYA

Goats and cattle were until comparatively recently the principal currency of a large part of Kenya. The relative degree of their use varied according to district and tribe, but in general both were used, goats representing the "small change" and having a fixed ratio to cattle.

It is amongst the Masai that the cattle cult has achieved the most advanced stage. This warlike pastoral race has practically no other store of value, and its primitive economy is based entirely on values expressed in cattle. Owing to the fact that cattle is, or was until recently, the sole currency of the Masai, they are grossly overstocked, far beyond economic requirements. Quality is neglected, for old and diseased cattle are kept for the sake of possessing the largest possible number of this token of wealth. Before British control over the territories inhabited by them in Kenya and Tanganyika became effective, the difficulties of overstocking were overcome through raids on agricultural communities whose population was destroyed or enslaved, and whose cultivated land was turned into pasturage. Now that this can no longer be done, overstocking tends to cause soil erosion. Once the cattle has eaten off the land every blade of grass, the soil turns into dust under the scorching, tropical sun, and the wind blows it away, leaving nothing but bare rocks. This is a problem of first-rate gravity that preoccupies the Colonial

Administrations in Kenya and other countries of East and South Africa. Deficiency of water supplies is also aggravated by overstocking.

The remedy lies in inducing the natives to abandon the monetary use of cattle and other livestock, or, to quote Lord Hailey's *African Survey*, "so to change the attitude of the native towards his domestic animals that they become not tokens of wealth or a form of currency but a source of income."[1] In the report of the Kenya Agricultural Commission Sir Daniel Hall suggested the issue of coins bearing the image of cows or goats, or to provide special tokens shaped like livestock and convertible into modern money, to bridge the psychological gap between the use of animal and mineral tokens of exchange.[2]

Nothing could be more characteristic of the attitude of natives towards cattle-currency than the following story related by Negley Farson: "The agricultural expert of Nakuru . . . had been down arguing with some of the Wakambas about not keeping their old and diseased cattle. Then one of the old Wakamba said to him: 'Listen, Master—here are two pound notes. One is old and wrinkled and ready to tear—this one is a new one. But they are both worth a pound, aren't they? Well, it's the same with cows. They are both a cow'."[3]

To anyone realizing the profound religious and social foundations of the cattle currency in Africa, and the low standard of education of the natives concerned, Julian Huxley's suggestion that the tribes might be sufficiently impressed by a report of a committee consisting of, say, Mr. McKenna, Lord Keynes and Professor Pigou, to give ear to their recommendations,[4] must sound touchingly naïve. As if these names, distinguished as they are, could possibly have conveyed anything to the illiterate Masai or other tribesmen. A more realistic suggestion which has been considered is a progressive stock tax rising with the animals' age.[5]

The part played by goats in the Gikuyu country is ably described in a book by Jomo Kenyatta, a native of that country. Kenyatta was trained at the London School of Economics under Malinowski who contributed an introduction to his book. We have it on his evidence that before the introduction of the European monetary system, sheep and goats were regarded by the Gikuyu as the standard currency. The price of almost everything was determined in terms of sheep and goats. This system still operated on the eve of the war of 1939 among the majority of the Gikuyu people who have not yet grasped the idea of a modern monetary system.[6]

[1]Lord Hailey, *African Survey* (London, 1938), pp. 1068-9. Its chapters dealing with this matter were contributed by Mr. A. E. G. Robinson.
[2]*Report of the Kenya Agricultural Commission*, 1929, p. 31. Quoted by Hailey, p. 1069.
[3]Negley Farson, *Behind God's Back* (London, 1940), p. 264.
[4]Julian Huxley, *Africa View* (London, 1931), p. 83.
[5]Hailey, p. 1111.
[6]Jomo Kenyatta, *Facing Mount Kenya—The Tribal Life of the Gikuyu* (London, 1938), p. 66.

Goats and sheep play there the part of a store of value. Natives fee]
that modern money is not a good investment for one shilling does not
bear another shilling, whereas a sheep or goat does bear another sheep
or goat.[7] These are still required for bride money, and are used for
religious sacrifices, which itself secures for them a steady demand. The
parents of the bride do not accept modern money, for to them the
coins have very little meaning and have no religious or sentimental
associations. The value of goat currency depreciated between the two
wars, and while formerly bride money in the case of a chief's daughter
was about seventy goats, by 1935 it had risen to ninety.[8]

The reason why modern money was slow to make headway among the
Gikuyu is said to lie in its small size. Since times immemorial the Gikuyu
have been accustomed to barter goods of approximately equal size or
weight against each other. They cannot easily accommodate themselves
to giving bulky goods and receiving in exchange tiny coins.[9]

The Kipsings transact most of their trade with the aid of cattle. They
are a pastoral people who employ the same word for going to work as
for going to war, for the object in both cases is to obtain cattle. Cattle
is the only medium through which large transactions can be carried
out.[10] It is the sole form of investment. It is the only acceptable form of
bride-wealth, and of blood money.[11]

The Turkana use the cow as their standard of value.[12] The Elgeyo are
in the habit of converting into cattle at the earliest opportunity all their
money earnings beyond the amount required for imported food or for
taxes. They lend their cows to poorer members of their community.[13]

Various beads, cotton cloth and brass and copper wire played in the
past a more or less important part as the white man's currency for the
purchase of native products.[14] Iron currency was used in Northern districts.[15] There was supposed to be, however, one currency in respect of
which Kenya was original—a kind of red brick dust which is said to
have been readily accepted in exchange in the vicinity of the Tana River.[16]

Where at the beginning of this century it would have been impossible

[7]Kenyatta, p. 66.
[8]Richard C. Thurnwald, *Black and White in East Africa* (London, 1935), p. 109.
[9]C. Cagnolo, *The Akikuyu* (Nyeri, Kenya, 1933), pp. 42-3.
[10]Diedrich Westermann, *Africa To-day and To-morrow* (London, 1939), p. 67.
[11]J. G. Peristany, *The Social Institutions of the Kipsings* (London, 1939), p. 149.
[12]Melville J. Herskovits, *The Cattle Complex in East Africa* (American Anthropologist, New Series, 1926), Vol. xxviii, p. 352.
[13]J. A. Massam, *The Cliff Dwellers of Kenya* (London, 1927), pp. 126-7. See also
J. G. Peristany, pp. 149-50.
[14]W. S. and K. Routledge, *With a Prehistoric People—The Akikuyu of East Africa*
(London, 1910), p. 106. In 1903 beads were the sole medium in which payment was
accepted.
[15]H. Stigand, *To Abyssinia through an Unknown Land* (London, 1910), p. 297.
[16]W. W. A. Fitzgerald, *Travels in the Coastlands of British East Africa and the
Islands of Zanzibar and Pemba* (London, 1898), p. 337. Unfortunately the author
does not give any particulars about this strange currency, nor has it been possible to
corroborate his statement from any independent source.

to buy provisions with modern currency, to-day refusal of coins is considered exceptional.[17] This in spite of the fact that early experience with coins was not very fortunate. The Government considered it necessary to change the coinage after the population had grown used to the rupee system, as the distrust of the natives towards the new nickel cents was considerably increased when many of the buried coins had disintegrated into a grey metallic powder.[18]

[17]W. S. and K. Routledge, p. 116.
[18]W. MacGregor Ross, *Kenya from Within* (London, 1927), p. 200.

CHAPTER 32

BEAD MONEY OF TANGANYIKA

The principal standard of value in Tanganyika was cattle or other livestock. Saving assumed the form of accumulating cattle in olden times; in fact cows were considered the capital which should be preserved and it was only their milk and blood that was used up.[1] Nevertheless Thurnwald notes a certain degree of weakening of the "cattle complex." He quotes a native boy representing the attitude of the new generation as having said: "What is the use of being rich in cows, sheep and goats if the man goes in cow skins?" Evidently there is a growing desire for European luxuries and refinements of life which cannot be satisfied if saving assumes the form of accumulating livestock for its own sake.

Livestock was extensively used as a medium of exchange. In the Irangi district, goats, sheep and donkeys were until recently the principal form of currency.[2] Livestock played also the part of a standard of value. When the missionaries arrived in Usambra in the 'nineties of the last century, the "symbols of value" were cattle, sheep and goats and smaller values were represented by fowls.[3] In Majita the old currency consisted of cows and goats. Twenty-five goats were estimated to equal one cow or ox; one goat was equal to one hoe.[4] The ratio between oxen and goats varied according to district, but was stable over long periods of years within the same region.[5] Amongst themselves the Masai were until recently still trading only in livestock. They pay five goats for an ass. An iron spear costs two goats, a big cattle bell or a small axe is bought for one goat.[6] "The Hehe value their cattle chiefly as currency. . . . Cattle are used to make large transfers of property."[7]

[1]Thurnwald (1935), p. 136.
[2]Franz Stuhlmann, *Mit Emin Pasha ins Herz von Afrika* (Berlin, 1894), p. 804.
[3]Thurnwald, p. 108.   [4]Thurnwald, p. 109.   [5]Thurnwald, p. 110.
[6]Max Weiss, *Die Völkerstämme in Norden Deutsch-Ostafrikas* (Nürnberg, 1910), pp. 381-2.
[7]G. Gordon Brown and A. McD. Bruce Hutt, *Anthropology in Action—An Experiment in the Iringa District* (London, 1935), pp. 144-5.

I

With the advent of European and Arab traders, various other kinds of primitive currencies came to be adopted. Beads served as small change. They became the principal currency in the market of Ujiji at the time of Cameron's voyage. According to him, everything was priced in beads called *sofi*, something in appearance like small pieces of broken pipe stem. "At the commencement of the market, men with wallets full of these beads deal them out in exchange for others with people desirous of making purchases; and when the mart is closed, they receive them again from the market people, making a profit on both transactions after the manner usual amongst money changers."[8] Another description of the beads current in the Ujiji market states: "Here for the first time, we find a regular currency or money in use by the natives; it consists of strings of blue and white cylindrical beads, each string containing twenty beads. Bunches of ten strings are called *fundo*. From nine to eleven *fundos* are given in exchange for four yards of thin Manchester calico and from twelve to fifteen *fundos* for four yards of good heavy American calico, the value varying daily according to the quantity of cloth in the market."[9]

Beads were not nearly as stable a standard as livestock. Whenever Europeans imported too many of a kind they depreciated, and the value of a type which was still scarce rose.[10] Of beads there were towards the middle of the 19th century about four hundred varieties, some of which had even three or four different names.[11] When several types of beads were in circulation, the cheaper varieties were accepted in payment for grain and vegetables, but would not purchase fowls, milk and eggs.[12] The attitude of natives towards various types of beads (as indeed towards many other kinds of primitive currencies) was entirely incalculable. According to Burton, "in 1858 the Wajiji rejected with contempt the black porcelains. At first they would not receive the white porcelains; and afterwards, when the Expedition had exchanged, at a considerable loss, their large stock for small blues, they demanded the former."[13]

Cowries, too, became popular as a medium of exchange and a standard of value. The following prices are quoted by Stuhlmann as having prevailed in Bukoba in May, 1892: a chicken, fifty cowries; a large bunch of bananas, thirty to fifty cowries; a large basket of flour, fifty cowries; an egg, three to five cowries; a pot of banana wine, fifty cowries; two balls of soap, a hundred cowries.[14]

---

[8]Verney Lovett Cameron, *Across Africa* (London, 1885), p. 183.
[9]Edward C. Hore, *On the Twelve Tribes of Tanganyika*. (*Journal of the Anthropological Institute*, Vol. xii, London, 1883), p. 9.
[10]H. Graf von Schweinitz, *Deutschostafrika im Krieg und Frieden* (Berlin, 1894), p. 91.
[11]Richard F. Burton, *The Lake Regions of Central Africa* (London, 1860), Vol. i, p. 146.
[12]Burton, p. 398.   [13]Burton, pp. 73-5.   [14]Stuhlmann, p. 706.

Cloth was used extensively as a currency in most parts of Tanganyika. At the time of Stanley's visit to Ujiji, it was used simultaneously with beads. In 1876 a goat was worth two pieces of sheeting cloth four yards long, a sheep one and a half pieces, a bullock ten pieces, a slave-boy sixteen pieces, a slave-girl fifty to eighty pieces if under thirteen, eighty to two hundred pieces between thirteen and eighteen.[15] Speke quotes prices prevailing in Usagaru in yards of American sheeting.[16]

The use of brass wire as a currency caused considerable inconvenience to the Post and Telegraph Department of Tanganyika. The removal of hundreds of yards of wire by the Watusi led to frequent interruptions of the telegraph service.[17] But, then, if coins or notes were left unattended in remote parts of any modern country, many civilized people would find it difficult to resist the temptation.

Barter continued to prevail to a large degree. There were credit transactions in goods. Dempwolf quotes an instance of millet having been delivered to the blacksmith after harvest.[18] This appears to indicate that between harvests blacksmiths work on a credit basis and are paid out of the proceeds of the new crop. Millet was extensively used throughout East Africa as a money for small payments.[19]

During recent years modern money has gradually replaced primitive currencies in Tanganyika. Nevertheless, the attitude of the natives towards modern money has remained largely primitive. A Majita woman thinks it shameful to buy food with modern money. She would prefer to starve. Modern money in her mind is for buying beads, cloths, ornaments and luxury.[20] Natives frequently quote exorbitant prices in modern money; being at a loss what prices to quote, they prefer to err on the safe side.[21] They are perturbed by the fluctuation of prices under the new standard.

To a large degree modern money, as also some kinds of primitive money, is used in Tanganyika only as common denominator to facilitate barter transactions. This is partly because there is not enough coined money in circulation within the tribe to finance all the necessary transactions.[22]

Notwithstanding all difficulties modern money has been gaining ground slowly but surely. Even bride money is often paid or reckoned nowadays in modern money.

Among the former German East African colonial territories Urundi

[15]Henry M. Stanley, *Through the Dark Continent* (London, 1878), Vol. I, pp. 4-5.
[16]J. H. Speke, *The Discovery of the Source of the Nile* (Everyman Edn., London, 1906), p. 52.
[17]G. Alexander, *Tanganyika Memories* (London, 1936), p. 70.
[18]Otto Dempwolf, *The Sandawe* (Hamburg. 1916), p. 105.
[19]Strandes, p. 322.   [20]Thurnwald, (1935), p. 110.
[21]A native asked 10 cents for one onion in Usambra. Hans Meyer, *Der Kilimandjaro* (Berlin, 1900), p. 262. Objects formerly obtainable for bead strings worth 10 Pfennige (1d.) came to be quoted at a rupiah.
[22]Gordon Brown and Hutt, p. 157.

is probably among the least advanced economically. While in the neighbouring district of Ruanda money traffic has developed, in inner Urundi trade is, or was until recently, confined mainly to the exchange of land products by the natives amongst themselves.[23] During German colonial rule coins did not penetrate into the interior and were only reluctantly accepted near the few trading stations and main lines of communications. The main store of value was cattle. Such was the attachment of the natives to their cattle, that during the famine of the early 'thirties, Ruanda-Urundi people died in large numbers rather than slaughter their animals.

Beads were a favourite medium of exchange, and the German Government's efforts to introduce German colonial currency or even rupees failed to produce any results. The most widely used bead money consisted of strings of pink beads. There were also more valuable violet beads but the natives rejected yellow, green and black beads. The value of beads was subject to fluctuation according to their supply and demand. Under German rule a string of pink beads paid for a bunch of twenty bananas or a double handful of flour or a handful of salt. An iron hoe was worth six strings; a goat, ten strings.[24]

Among the Wahima, cotton cloth was the most current means of payment. Smaller purchases of vegetables were paid in beads.[25]

[23]Hans Meyer, *Die Barundi—Eine völkerkundliche Studie aus Deutschostafrika* (Leipzig, 1916), p. 74.
[24]Meyer, p. 77.   [25]Weiss, p. 56.

CHAPTER 33

COWRIES AS CURRENCY IN UGANDA

Cattle and to a smaller degree goats constituted until recently, and to some extent still constitute, an important form of currency in Uganda. Cattle is the main store of value of the natives. They will frequently face starvation rather than kill their cattle because they wish to leave untouched what they regard as the family cattle.[1]

The question as to what extent livestock serves as a medium of exchange is not easy to answer. It is the tribal custom of the Ankole that, while cows may change masters within the tribe from one cowman to another, they cannot pass to a man of another tribe.[2] Among the Lango tribe livestock is freely convertible into grain.[3] While it is a widespread rule not to sell livestock outside the tribe if it can possibly be avoided, it

[1]H. P. Thomas and Robert Scott, *Uganda* (London, 1935), p. 196.
[2]John Roscoe, *The Soul of Central Afrika* (London, 1922), p. 61.
[3]J. H. Driberg, *The Lango—a Nilotic Tribe of Uganda* (London, 1923), p. 93. He observes (p. 94) that a transaction involving a cow or a bull is not complete until the party acquiring it has paid a spear for its tail, which had to be bought separately.

seems to be used as a medium of exchange within the tribe. Slaves are bought for cows or bulls.[4] The Baganda people buy with cattle and goats.[5] There is usually a fixed exchange rate between cattle and goats. The latter circulate more freely than the former and are used for buying weapons or salt.[6]

While the extent to which livestock served as a medium of exchange may be open to argument, there can be no doubt that it served to a large extent as a standard of value. Ivory and slaves were often valued in cattle.[7] Prices were based on the value of the cow.[8] Livestock served also as a standard of deferred payments, and especially as a means of deferred payments.[9] The chief frequently sent goats to his subjects to be kept for him, and he received every third kid that is born in lieu of interest.[10] Livestock is extensively used for special payments. Bride money usually includes cattle or goats.[11] Fines are often fixed in terms of goats.[12]

During the period that preceded the penetration of Arab traders, ivory discs were a favourite medium of exchange. They were produced by the king's men and, while other people were not prohibited from producing them, it was not easy for them to procure ivory since they were forbidden to kill elephants or to have ivory in their possession without special permission from the king. Moreover, only a limited number of men had the expert knowledge required for producing the discs.[13]

Before the introduction of cowrie shells a blue bead was used as a means of payment. It was very badly finished, but was considered none the less to be highly valuable. It was equated to one ivory disc or a hundred cowrie shells.[14] When cowries first made their appearance, they, too, were very valuable. It was possible to buy not only cloth and food but even boats and slaves with cowries.[15] Two cowrie shells would purchase a woman.[16] Subsequently large quantities found their way into

[4]John Roscoe, *The Banyankole* (Cambridge, 1923), p. 78.
[5]Weiss, p. 142.
[6]Roscoe (1922), pp. 61-2. Keynes quotes a District Commissioner in Uganda as having remarked that it was part of his official duties to decide, in cases of disputes, whether a given goat is or is not too old or too scraggy to constitute a standard goat for the purpose of discharging debt. (*A Treatise on Money*, I, p. 13.)
[7]Roscoe, *The Baganda* (London, 1911), p. 456.
[8]Roscoe (1922), p. 61.
[9]John Roscoe, *The Bagesu and other Tribes of the Uganda Protectorate* (Cambridge, 1924), p. 18.
[10]Roscoe (1911), p. 422.
[11]Driberg, p. 157. Roscoe (1924), pp. 18, 88, 134. Rats are also claimed to have been a means of payment, five of them buying a bunch of plantain and three a basket of about 20 lbs. of grain (Roscoe, 1911, p. 422).
[12]Roscoe (1911), p. 422.
[13]Roscoe (1911), pp. 269, 412-3, 457. Speke (p. 422) also refers to the use of ivory as money.
[14]Roscoe (1911), p. 457.   [15]Stuhlmann, p. 182.
[16]Roscoe (1911), p. 457.

the country. They became the principal medium of exchange and were also extensively used as a standard of value.[17] In 1911 the value of a cow was 2,500 cowries, that of a goat was equal to 500 cowries; a fowl was sold for 25 cowrie shells and a cock for 50; an ivory tusk weighing 62 lbs. sold for 1,000 cowrie shells.[18] In some parts of Uganda cowries had an artificially high value. The Sultans ensured that they should not depreciate through an excessive increase of their quantity. They withdrew into their Treasuries any surplus supplies.[19]

With the penetration of European civilization through the construction of the Uganda railway, coins gradually took the place of cowries. As a result, cowries depreciated. In 1896, cowries were exchanged for about 200 to the rupee, but by 1901 the exchange rate rose to 800. After 31st March, 1901, cowries ceased to be acceptable in payment of taxes. At the same time the Government placed an embargo on the import of cowries, having received information that large amounts were being imported from German East Africa. The Government's own stock was eventually burned for lime. It was estimated that in 1902 after the destruction of the Government's stock there were still some three hundred million shells in circulation in Uganda. For a long time thereafter cowries remained a medium of exchange in trade between natives for petty transactions.[20]

Among some tribes native beer is claimed to have been a form of limited currency. The Lango paid wages largely in the form of beer. One pot of beer was the fee for the consecration of a goat or for the manufacture of a shield. The usual fee payable to the barber was one pot of beer and one chicken.[21] Since, however, the recipients usually consumed their wages the arrangement only amounted to payment in kind.

Cotton cloth was for a long time a favoured means of payment. Gunpowder, too, played the part of a medium of exchange.[22] In the last years of the 19th century iron and brass as well as cloth and beads still continued to serve as media of exchange.[23]

The Makaraka, in the Lado Enclave, make special spearheads which are used as a medium of exchange and which are always included in the bride money.[24] The Kuku use arrows as a limited currency. Among the Madi a man is allowed to pass a night with an unmarried girl if he makes her a present of five arrows.[25] As women have no use for arrows, the fact that payment is made in that form seems to indicate that arrows can be used fairly freely for purchases. Speke's expedition carried six

---

[17]According to L. P. Mair, *An African People in the Twentieth Century* (London, 1934), p. 145, the Baganda even now express values in terms of cowries.
[18]Roscoe (1911), p. 456.
[19]*Deutsche Geographische Blätter* (Bremen, 1897), p. 22. Quoted by Kürchhoff, p. 9.
[20]Thomas and Scott, p. 231.   [21]Driberg, pp. 58, 60, 82.
[22]Stuhlmann, p. 182.   [23]Thomas and Scott, p. 231.
[24]C. H. Stigland, *Equatoria—The Lado Enclave* (London, 1923), pp. 62-3.
[25]Stigland, p. 154.

hundred *majembe* (iron spades), "two of which were expended daily for their board and lodging on the way."[26]

[26]Speke, p. 401.

CHAPTER 34

OTHER EAST AFRICAN CURRENCIES

Until comparatively recently the currency of Madagascar consisted of pieces of cut silver coins changing hands by weight. The standard coin was the Spanish dollar which was also a medium of exchange in an uncut form, especially in the ports. A very large proportion of the dollars that found their way to Madagascar were, however, cut into pieces by "money brokers." W. Ellis, describing a market scene at Tamatave remarked: "The money changers were busy cutting up dollars, half and quarter dollars and smaller pieces, cut silver valued by weight being the universal currency."[1] Other foreign silver coins, especially French five franc pieces, were also chopped up likewise to serve for the payment of small sums. The use of weights and scales is strictly regulated by law.[2] Originally, the money changers charged a small fee for cutting up the coins; subsequently, however, cut coins went to a discount compared with whole dollars. Occasionally this discount amounted to something like one-sixth or more of the weight of dollars. An official limit of one-sixteenth was fixed, however, for the premium on whole dollars.[3]

The units of account consisted of certain fractions of the dollar, each one of which had a special name. The smallest fraction was equal to 1/72nd of the Spanish dollar; it was also equal to ten grains of rice which was used for even smaller payments.[4]

Cattle are the store of value in Madagascar. All modern money is invested in cattle and the greatest ambition of a poor man is to acquire at least two or three beasts. Bride money is paid in oxen.[5] The fine for theft was fixed at fifteen oxen.[6]

The islands Nossi-bé and Mayotte near Madagascar adopted the same currency system. Coins accepted in payment were cut into pieces

[1]W. Ellis, *Three Visits to Madagascar* (London, 1859), p. 125.
[2]G. W. Parker, *On the New Code of Law for the Hova Kingdom of Madagascar* (*Journal of the Anthropological Institute*, Vol. XII, London, 1883), p. 314. According to Frank Vincent, *Actual Africa* (London, 1895), the money current in Tamatave is French coin, but for the journey to Antananarivo "cut money" is employed "and, in fact, only this sort is current in the capital and generally in the interior of the island," p. 223.
[3]S. P. Oliver, *Madagascar* (London, 1886), Vol. II, p. 207.
[4]Oliver, pp. 205-6.   [5]Friedrich Ratzel, p. 461.   [6]Ilwof, p. 68.

and weighed. Everybody carried scales for the purpose.[7] On Anjouan the French five franc coins and the Portuguese piastres were cut into ten pieces and were passed on by weight.[8]

In Mozambique unbleached calico was the favourite medium of exchange. In interior districts beads, bracelets of lead and copper, cowries, copper and brass wire and blue cloth was used as currency.[9] In Sofala millet was used for the purchase of objects of small value.[10] In the hinterland of Delagoa Bay cattle, rifles, bullets and powder were media of exchange.[11] Between the Limpopo and the Zambesi brass discs served as currency.[12]

The Wabena have always differentiated between articles regarded as currency and those regarded as commodities pure and simple. Right up to the second World War cattle, goats, cloth and hoes were currencies, accepted for the settlement of debt, and so were formerly, rifles which have subsequently become too rare and precious to be exchanged at all. On the other hand, food, chickens, ducks or dogs were not necessarily accepted by creditors in payment of their claim. Ceremonial payments, too, could only be made in objects which were, so to say, legal tender.[13]

The cattle standard in Portuguese East Africa gave way to the hoe standard, but the latter has also gone out of fashion since the introduction of modern money and of cheap imported hoes. At one time the value of hoes was very high; some of the old hoes were seldom, if ever, used for agricultural work but served almost entirely as currency.[14]

Zanzibar deserves attention not so much on account of its own primitive currencies as in its capacity as a purveyor of primitive currencies for the African mainland. A very large proportion of the cowries in circulation in Africa originates in Zanzibar. Originally most shipments came from the Maldives, but subsequently it was found more convenient to import cowries from closer quarters. The blue Zanzibar cowries are larger than the white Maldive cowries and the latter are considerably more valuable, partly because of the higher cost of transport to Africa, and partly because, once in Africa, they can be transported more easily and cheaply owing to their smaller weight.

The markets of Zanzibar supplied explorers, travellers and traders also with wire, cloth and bead currencies required on the African mainland. Credit transactions were frequent in terms of such primitive currencies—especially in cloth—which were taken by traders to the East

---

[7]S. R. Steinmetz, *Rechtsverhältnisse von Eingeborenen Völkern in Afrika und Oceanien* (Berlin, 1903), p. 395.

[8]Alfred Voeltzkow, *Reise in Ostafrika* (Stuttgart, 1914), Vol. ı., p. 226. See also Baron Carl Claas von der Decken, *Reisen in Ostafrika* (Leipzig, 1869), Vol. ı, p. 330.

[9]Noback, p. 623.　　　　　　[10]Ferrand, p. 67.　　　　　　[11]Kürchhoff, p. 28.

[12]Ilwof, p. 68.

[13]A. T. and G. M. Culwick, *Ubena of the Rivers* (London, 1935), p. 290.

[14]Culwick, pp. 294-5.

African coast or the interior to exchange for local products. Interest charged on such credits was exorbitant even for conditions prevailing in Africa.[15]

Until the middle of the 19th century, millet played the part of small change owing to the shortage of token money. Broken sums were paid in it, a certain measure constituting the equivalent of a dollar.[16] In 1845, the British authorities introduced large quantities of pice from India to relieve the shortage of small change. Nevertheless, even to this day change for small amounts is often given in millet in country shops.[17] Another currency which in the past is said to have played some part in Zanzibar was cotton cloth called *doti*, the unit being a piece twelve feet (eight cubits) long.[18] Before that beads were a medium of exchange.

[15]R. F. Burton, *Zanzibar* (London, 1872), p. 407.
[16]Burton, p. 405. See also W. H. Ingrams—*Zanzibar, Its History and Its People* (London, 1931), p. 329.
[17]Ingrams, p. 329.   [18]Burton, p. 405.

CHAPTER 35

CALICO CURRENCY IN RHODESIA

Cattle, in addition to being a store of value, are also used at times as a medium of exchange for large transactions. The purchase price of land is occasionally paid in this form.[1]

On the Great Plateau, calico is the main medium of exchange. For most purposes, it takes the place of "hard cash." Men draw their rations in calico, marriage dowries are often paid in calico. "In brief, calico is to the Plateau what cowrie shells are to the South Sea Islanders, and were it not that Lotusland expresses more or less aptly the mental attitude of both white and black, one would be tempted to christen the Plateau calico country."[2]

In other parts salt served and possibly still serves as currency. In the Basanga district, salt is produced by filling baskets with saline earth and pouring water through it. The salt water gained is evaporated and the salt is gathered into baskets one foot long and three inches wide. Such baskets were a form of currency; five of them were equal to a male calf, three were equal to a sucking calf and twenty to a heifer.[3] Near Kasama the natives prefer to use salt for their everyday purchases rather than modern money. It can be broken into fractions of smaller value

[1]E. W. Smith and A. N. Dale, *The Ila Speaking Peoples of Northern Rhodesia* (London, 1920), Vol. I, p. 388.
[2]C. Gouldsbury and H. Sheane, *The Great Plateau of Northern Rhodesia* (London, 1911), p. 10.
[3]Smith and Dale, p. 148.

than the smallest coin; besides women often want salt in a hurry and they agree to sell for it anything required.[4]

The Africans are still far from being accustomed to the use of coins. At the beginning of this century an amateur financier found that the new penny served as well as a shilling in one of the western districts. But those days are past.[5] Nevertheless, even to-day, the Africans fail to grasp the fact that the possession of money confers on them indiscriminate purchasing power. They are utterly reluctant to spend coins on food. A few years before the second World War, an old woman was discovered dying of starvation with a two shilling piece tied in the fold of her cloth. It had apparently never occurred to her to use the money to buy supplies.[6]

[4]Audrey I. Richards, *Land, Labour and Diet in Northern Rhodesia* (London, 1939), p. 225.
[5]Gouldsbury and Sheane, p. 10.
[6]Richards, p. 220.

CHAPTER 36

CLOTH, METALS AND SLAVES AS CURRENCY IN FRENCH EQUATORIAL AFRICA

In Gabon the monetary unit was ivory and blocks of sandalwood and ebony. Prices were quoted in weights of ivory and in numbers of blocks of timber.[1] Another type of currency which was in use was bell-shaped pieces of iron, four of them tied together, or snail-shaped pieces of iron likewise linked. There were also iron bars and arrow point shaped pieces of iron.[2] Flag-shaped pieces of iron constituted the small change of the Fan on the Ogowe River. They changed hands in bundles of a hundred. The quality of the iron was so good that it was found impossible in Germany to imitate this currency for trading purposes.[3]

On the Loango coast, as on other parts of the coast of West Africa, the monetary unit was called *long*, which originally referred to cotton cloth of a certain length, but which became subsequently a fictitious unit of account. Prices were widely quoted in *longs*.[4] Another fictitious unit in Gabon Bay and at the Lower Ogowe was the "dollar," which did not represent a coin or a note, but goods to the value of between 1.25 francs and 1.75 francs. Natives trusted Europeans, and accepted in payment for food and services vouchers called "book" payable in goods at

[1]Noback, p. 346.
[2]*Bulletin de la Société de Géographie* (Paris, 1886), p. 339. Quoted by Schurtz, p. 144.
[3]Woermann, p. 32. See also Mary Kingsley, *Travel in West Africa* (London, 1897), p. 51.
[4]Woermann, p. 33.

sight at any trading station. Some of these vouchers were only presented after years.[5]

In the Cameroons the store of value consisted of wives, goats and bead necklaces, while the medium of exchange and standard of value was the cowrie. A wife cost anything from 15,000 to 50,000 cowries and a sheep or goat averaged about 1,000.[6] Although in 1911 the import of cowries was prohibited, they were still in current use at the time of the first World War. Hoards of them still existed at the outbreak of the second World War. Towards the end of the German régime 1,000 cowries were equivalent to one silver mark.[7]

Goats and sheep played the part of bride money and standard of deferred payments. In order to be able to marry, young men had to borrow goats and sheep. No rate of interest was fixed in advance, but the creditor expected to receive young sheep and young goats as interest.[8] Other objects that are said to have served as currency in the Cameroons included soap, fish-hooks and gunpowder.[9]

In the early days of German colonization, fines were fixed in ivory. As a result the colonial administration accumulated large stocks of ivory.[10]

A monetary unit in the Cameroons was the "brass," a brass ring of one yard in circumference. It was equal to a handful of small beads, or twenty beads or ten eggs. There was, above all, the *kroo*, a purely fictitious standard of value. Usually the unit was a given quantity of the staple trade goods. Originally it was a hollow measure of palm oil. Eventually it became equal to twenty marks.[11] The exact value of the *kroo* varied, however, from place to place at any given moment, and changed from time to time.[12]

The Bakwiri used cattle and women as monetary units for large transactions.[13] The Banaka and Bapuku used among other objects, rifles, powder, salt, tobacco, rum and printed cotton goods; they did not use cowrie shells.[14] The Bulu used cloth, the Basa employed tobacco, while

[5]G. Bruel, *La France Equatoriale Africaine* (Paris, 1935), pp. 422-3. The working of this system, and the role played in its working by missionaries, is described in detail by Mary Kingsley (p. 148). The "books" were for three amounts: five "fura" = one dollar, one "fura" = one franc, and half a "fura" = fifty centimes. The value given for these "books" (which were either handwritten or printed) was the same in Government trading stations, private trading stations and missions. The latter do not trade for profit, but keep stores which are practically banks, since they are engaged in the conversion of "books" into goods. All the native personnel of the stations are paid in such "books." When missionaries are away on a journey they pay for their food and the wages of their canoe crews in the same form. For several hours every week-day the missionaries have to devote themselves to store work. Each class of article used in this traffic—and there are hundreds of them—has a definite and acknowledged value.
[6]F. C. C. Egerton, *African Majesty* (London, 1938), p. 139.
[7]Egerton, p. 140.   [8]Egerton, p. 141.
[9]H. R. Rudin, *Germans in the Cameroons* (London, 1938), pp. 223-4.
[10]Rudin, p. 200.   [11]*Ausland*, 1889, p. 116.   [12]Rudin, p. 224.
[13]Steinmetz, p. 26.   [14]Steinmetz, p. 55.

the Banankan and Batanga transacted business mainly in terms of sheep.[15]

In Logone the money consisted of curved iron bars. The Sultan collected his tribute in such bars and their value fluctuated according to whether tribute was being collected or purchases were being made by the Sultan. Merchants speculated on these fluctuations which could be anticipated.[16] The official value of the currency was settled by proclamation every Wednesday.[17]

Types of money used in the French Congo included cloth, brass wire, spiral spring coiled in the form of cylinders, salt, shovels and hoes, iron blades, bars and iron double bells.[18] The most important currency consisted, however, of copper rods. They were accepted in payment for goods by natives, not for their own use but on the assumption that they could be used in payment for other objects.[19] The currencies of exclusively local origin were all metallic and were all of base metals. Beads and shells used as currency were of foreign importation. Most of the metals employed for monetary purposes were made in shapes which could easily be transformed into useful tools or utensils.[20]

In the Gribingui district iron arrows about twenty cms. long were the principal currency. They were extensively though not exclusively used as a medium of exchange. Chickens were worth three arrows before the first World War; eggs, one arrow; goats, sixty arrows; a big fish, six arrows; a dog, twelve arrows; a litre of sesame oil, twenty arrows. Often other goods were also included in the purchase price; for instance, an elephant tusk of twenty kgs. was bought for 360 arrows, two knives and five copper bracelets.[21]

In the Bagirmi country strips of cotton cloth were the most used currency for small payments. Larger articles were bought with shirts, the value of which according to their size and quality varied from seventy to a hundred and fifty strips. Barth sold a few cheap looking-glasses for one shirt each, while a better type of looking-glass, bought in London for eighteen pence, fetched four shirts.[22] In Kanem, north of Lake Chad, many things were bought with the common white Bornu shirts which form the general dress of the people.[23] Raphia fibre mats were

[15]Julius Lips, *Kamerun* (*Das Eingeborenerecht*. Edited by E. Schulz-Ewerth and Leonhardt Adam—Stuttgart, 1930), p. 198.

[16]H. Schnee, *Deutsche Kolonial-Lexikon* (Leipzig, 1920, Vol. II), p. 692.

[17]Major Denham, Captain Clapperton and Dr. Oudney, *Narrative of Travels and Discoveries in Northern and Central Africa*. 2nd Edn. (London, 1826), Vol. II, pp. 17-8.

[18]A. L. Cureau, *Savage Man in Central Africa—A Study of Primitive Races in French Congo* (London, 1915), p. 238.

[19]Cureau, p. 252.   [20]Cureau, p. 253.

[21]Fernand Gaud and C. van Overbergh, *Les Mandja* (*Congo Français*). (Brussels, 1911), pp. 413-5.

[22]Henry Barth, *Travels and Discoveries in North and Central Africa* (London, 1857), Vol. III, p. 381.

[23]Barth, Vol. III, p. 75.

among the objects serving as a medium of exchange.[24] Another unusual type of currency in Bagirmi was iron throwing discs.[25] They were the only currency accepted for grain. Tobacco, too, was an important medium of exchange.

Slaves played the part of the standard of value for big transactions. The unit was a slave of medium qualities and the value of better slaves was expressed in terms of this standard slave. Wealth was reckoned in terms of "heads." When after a successful slave raid the number of slaves for sale was large, the effect was the same as of a sudden increase of the monetary circulation in civilized communities. The price of all goods, horses, arms, chains increased in terms of the slave currency.[26]

Cattle is the chief wealth of the Wadai people and also their monetary unit for large transactions. There was also a cotton cloth unit of standard size and quality.[27] It was seventeen metres long and sixty-five cms. wide. During Nachtigal's stay in the country the import of such cloth had for a long time been inadequate and the market was short of money. This produced the same deflationary effect as scarcity of money does in modern communities. Prices were low and goods were difficult to sell. Nachtigal himself had to put up with the disadvantages of this deflation. He wanted to dispose of some of his trading goods and found it very difficult to find buyers even at low prices. For the purposes of daily food requirements, native cloth made in Kano was accepted.[28]

East of the Shari River in Mofu the means of payment were cowries and beads, but rolls of tobacco were very popular and widely acceptable means of barter.[29]

[24]G. Bruel, p. 421.
[25]Richard Andrée, *Die Metalle bei den Naturvölkern* (Leipzig, 1884), p. 27.
[26]Ilwof, p. 66.   [27]Barth, p. 558.
[28]G. Nachtigal, *Sahara-Sudan* (Berlin, 1879), Vol. III, pp. 67-8.
[29]Nachtigal, Vol. II, pp. 578.

CHAPTER 37

COWRIE CRISES IN THE FRENCH SUDAN

Cowries were until recently the principal currency in French Sudan. Their use was referred to already in the 16th century by Leo Africanus, who stated that in Timbuctoo "in matters of small value they use certaine shels brought hither out of the Kingdome of Persia, four hundred of which shels are worth a ducate."[1] The area in which cowries were in use extended over the southern half of French Sudan. In the northern half Timbuctoo was the only place where they were used; in the country surrounding Timbuctoo it was not accepted by the Tuareg.[2]

[1]Leo Africanus, *A Geographical Historie of Africa* (London, 1600, Published by the Hakluyt Society, London, 1896), Vol. III, p. 825.
[2]E. Baillaud, *Sur les Routes du Soudan* (Toulouse, 1902), p. 70.

Hoards of cowries were often buried or kept in reserve. They played, however, a much more important part as a medium of exchange. The daily purchases of necessities were paid for mainly in cowries. In Sokolo, west of the Niger, an egg cost five cowries and chickens between thirty and forty cowries during the 'eighties.[3] On the market of Yamina at the beginning of this century salt was sold retail in portions varying from five to a hundred cowries. An entire bar of salt was worth 20,000 cowries, the same as the price of a "captive."[4] At the end of the last century, five cowries were enough at Segou to pay for a meal at a time when the value of cowries was fifty for five centimes.[5] Valuable objects were also regularly purchased with cowries. Frequently forty to fifty thousand cowries changed hands in a single transaction.[6]

Since the quantity of cowries was often not adequate to meet requirements, other types of local currencies had to be used in order to be able to transact trade. The value of everything was usually reckoned, however, in terms of cowries even if payment was made in other currencies.[7]

The arithmetic of accounting in cowries must appear very strange to the logical European mind. Nominally the decimal system was in operation. Nevertheless 8 × 10 was reckoned as 100; 10 × 80 (nominally 100) was reckoned as 1,000; 10 × 800 (nominally 1,000) was reckoned as 10,000 and 8 × 8,000 (nominally 10,000) was reckoned as 100,000, so that what they called 100,000 was really only 64,000.[8] This system may appear to us crazy, but there was method in the madness of those who devised it and applied it. It was simply one way of securing advantage to retail trading. If five bars of salt were sold in a single transaction for 100,000 cowries, the seller only received 64,000 cowries. If, on the other hand, they were sold retail in very small items, the sellers received a full total of 100,000 cowries.[9]

The value of cowries was subject to wide fluctuations. Their quantity in each community depended on imports from other towns and countries, which was often not easy. Fluctuations were caused by seasonal influences, the political situation, and even weather conditions affecting the movements of caravans.[10] There were also very marked discrepancies between their value at any given moment in various parts of French Sudan. In rich communities with an exportable surplus of goods the purchasing power of cowries was usually low because cowries were always in good supply. In regions where salt or some other object served as a subsidiary currency cowries tended to be cheaper than in regions where they were the exclusive currency for small purchases, because monetary demand in districts with subsidiary currencies was not so strong. As a general rule the value of cowries tended to be higher the

[3]Oskar Lenz, *Timbuktu* (Leipzig, 1884), Vol. II, p. 214.
[4]M. E. Mage, *Voyages dans le Soudan Occidental* (Paris, 1908), p. 188.
[5]Baillaud, p. 70.   [6]Lenz, p. 156.   [7]Lenz, p. 156.
[8]Mage, p. 191.   [9]Baillaud, p. 71.   [10]Lenz, pp. 155-6.

further East the community was situated,[11] because they were imported through West African ports, and the cost of their Eastward transport tended to add to their value.

During the second half of the 19th century, the value of cowries depreciated materially. At the time of Barth's visit in the 'fifties a *mit-khal* of gold was worth between 3,000 and 4,000 cowries. Some thirty years later, the value of gold and of salt more than doubled.[12] While such major changes in its value over long periods were inevitable, the French Colonial authorities endeavoured to prevent local fluctuations. In Timbuctoo the rate was fixed for some time at 5,000 cowries for five francs.[13]

An even more important problem than the prevention of fluctuations in the value of cowries was the prevention of the development of local shortages. From time to time such shortages created conditions not dissimilar to deflationary crises in modern communities. They were entirely due to maldistribution of the supply of cowries. At Segou the French authorities accumulated at one time over twenty million cowries. It would have been impossible to unload there such a quantity in the ordinary way without causing a sharp rise in prices. At Djenne (a distance of some 150 miles), on the other hand, the Administrator accepted cowries in taxes, but used them up in his current expenditure and did not accumulate any. Local shortages in various districts created very awkward conditions, for although it was possible to make larger payments with the aid of livestock, salt, cotton cloth, or slaves, there was nothing to take the place of cowries for current small transactions. To relieve a shortage in Dori, Zinder and Say, the French authorities sent on one occasion four million cowries to be spent in those communities.[14]

For the purpose of medium-size payments "guinea pieces" were used extensively in various parts of the French Sudan as in the greater part of north-west Africa in general. They were cotton cloth of about fifteen metres long and seventy cms. wide. Originally they were imported from India and were first used on the Guinea coast, hence their name. They were extensively used both as a medium of exchange and as a standard of value. In Sahel it was the regular practice of merchants to grant credits in guinea pieces to natives and to receive repayment in gum.[15] Within the triangle of the Senegal, the Niger and the Sahara, guineas were undoubtedly a very important currency. They were liable to change their value in the course of time and also there were discrepancies in their value at the same time in various districts. At a particular spot and at a given moment, however, the value indicated by "guineas" was

[11]Baillaud, p. 71.   [12]Lenz, pp. 150-1.   [13]Baillaud, p. 117.
[14]Baillaud, p. 73.
[15]Baillaud, p. 32. The value of guinea pieces was reckoned above its market value, while that of gum was accepted below its market value. This was the method of circumventing the Mahommedan ban on charging interest.

something very definite; it did not represent simply fifteen metres of cloth—it had come to be regarded as an amount of money. At Niore, for instance, a guinea piece meant six francs even though the actual value of fifteen metres of guinea cloth may have been worth seven and a half francs. The authorities at Niore tried to fix the price of guineas at six francs and from time to time sold large quantities to prevent a rise. The experiment was not a success, however, owing to the fluctuation of the quantity of imports.[16]

Native cloth also served as currency in the form of narrow strips of considerable length.[17] At the time of the visit of Denham, Clapperton and Oudney to Bera, forty fathoms of this cloth were valued at a dollar.[18]

Slaves constituted the most important form of currency for large transactions. A horse was valued at two to five "captives"; if it was of exceptional quality, its price was as high as seven to ten captives. A fine ox was worth one captive, an ordinary ox half a captive. In Segou the price of everything of substantial value was quoted in terms of slaves or fractions of slaves. Fractions were paid in cowries at the fixed rate of 20,000 per slave.[19] Alternatively, the price of half a slave could be paid through the transfer of an inferior slave or a slave child.[20] Definite parities were established between slaves and other currencies of smaller value. Thus among the Kasonké an adult male slave was worth five guinea pieces, or fifty lengths of native cloth, or five hundred measures of millet.[21] While originally slaves were a medium of exchange, subsequently their monetary role became confined to that of a unit of account. In 1907, a slave in the French Sudan simply meant a hundred francs.[22]

Salt was yet another currency, at the same time as being the principal commodity in Sudanese trade. To the north and west of the Niger, where cowries were valueless, salt bars and guinea pieces were the chief medium of exchange.[23] At Samatiguila, at the time of Cailié's visit, a slave sold roughly for his weight in salt in time of peace. When, however, the negroes went to war, salt became extra dear and slaves extra cheap owing to the capture of prisoners of war. In such circumstances the value of a man declined to a fraction of his weight in salt. In small transactions, too, salt was used as currency, often at the rate of a few grains at a time.[24]

The real medium of exchange in Asben at the time of Barth's visit was

[16]Baillaud, pp. 37-8.
[17]Charles Monteil, Les Khassonké—Monagraphie d'une Peuplade du Soudan Française (Paris, 1915), p. 121.
[18]Denham, Clapperton and Oudney, p. 191.   [19]Mage, p. 192.
[20]Andrée (1876), p. 250.
[21]Monteil, p. 122.
[22]A. de Foville, La Monnaie, 2nd Edn. (Paris, 1907), p. 17.
[23]J. E. Hertz, Über Verwendung und Verbreitung der Kaurimuschel. (Mitteilungen der Geographischen Gesellschaft in Hamburg, 1880-81), p. 24.
[24]Galbraith Welch, The Unveiling of Timbuctoo (London, 1938), p. 185.

millet. "With this article a man may buy everything at a much cheaper rate than with merchandise."[25] In more recent times, too, millet was used as a currency in parts of the Sudan.[26] Monteil considers millet as the most ancient medium of exchange of the Kasonké.[27]

For large transactions cattle was also used as a currency.[28] Cattle consituted an important form of store of value. It also was a standard of deferred payments. Loans were granted in terms of cattle free of interest, but if a cow which is lent has a calf during the period of loan, the calf is claimed by the creditor.[29]

Gold and silver were not used for current payments by the Kasonké, but were extensively used as a store of value.[30] In Timbuctoo and other towns gold by weight was a medium of exchange. The unit was the ancient Arabic unit of weight, the *mitkhal*, equivalent to the weight of ninety-six grains of wheat.[31]

Schurtz claims that camphor, to which magic qualities are attributed, was a currency in parts of the Sudan.[32] Another unusual kind of currency was bitter almonds which served as small change, as it did in parts of India in past centuries.[33]

All the currencies mentioned above—apart from cowries—had a practical as well as a monetary use. The only currency that served no non-monetary purpose and is in no way useful or ornamental is the little pieces of red cloth one and a half inches square, used by Caillié for payment on his way to Timbuctoo. He also claims to have made payments with sheets of writing paper.[34] Kola nuts are also sometimes referred to as a currency.

French coins have gained ground since the beginning of the century, though for a long time they were hoarded as soon as they were received. Both gold and silver coins were often converted into jewellery, and in that form they were known under the name of "dead money."[35]

Let us now deal briefly with the currencies of the Sahara. While the Mediterranean countries of North Africa have long been acquainted with the use of coins, their districts adjacent to the Great Desert continued to use until comparatively recently various kinds of primitive currencies. Thus in Fezzan, Southern Libya, smaller payments were made in corn at the beginning of the 19th century. Spanish dollars were the current money and one dollar was generally worth three gallons of corn.[36] In the Murzuq area silk strings are said to have served as cur-

---

[25]Barth, Vol. I, pp. 477-78.   [26]Steinmetz, p. 137.   [27]Monteil, p. 120.
[28]Monteil, p. 122. Steinmetz, p. 137.   [29]Steinmetz, p. 180.
[30]Monteil, p. 123.   [31]Barth, p. 23.   [32]Schurtz, p. 151.
[33]Stewart, *Sahara and Sudan*, Vol. III, p. 43. Quoted by Schurtz, p. 139.
[34]Welch, p. 155. The use of writing paper as currency is also mentioned by Schurtz, p. 151.
[35]Monteil, p. 123.
[36]G. F. Lyon, *A Narrative of Travels in Northern Africa in the Years* 1818-1820 (London, 1921), p. 278.

K

rency.[37] In the Algerian Sahara the Maria Theresa dollar was in use; salt and cotton cloth were also media of exchange. Five kilos of salt were equal to one dollar.[38]

In Tibesti, eastern Sahara, unbleached European cotton cloth was the principal standard of value and medium of exchange.[39] At the beginning of the 19th century the Maria Theres a dollar found its way into the Tuareg Oasis which, however, continued to use also cotton cloth. The coins were cut into half and quarter pieces to serve as small change.[40]

In Arguin, Spanish Sahara, on the west coast, the old Arabic unit of weight, the *mitkhal*, became a fictitious monetary unit worth, according to Cadamosto, about one ducat. This unit was very widely used throughout Northern Africa for many centuries.[41] It was a unit of weight determining a quantity of gold dust that served as the monetary unit of the Tuareg. The metal probably did not pass from hand to hand owing to the inconvenience of handling gold dust.[42]

[37]Ilwof, p. 65.   [38]Kürchhoff, p. 19.   [39]Nachtigal, p. 201.
[40]Kürchhoff, p. 5.   [41]Kürchhoff, p. 10.
[42]Francis Rennell Rodd, *People of the Veil* (London, 1926), p. 22.

CHAPTER 38

COWRIES, SLAVES, CLOTH AND GIN MONEY OF NIGERIA

Already in the 16th century cowries played an important part as a currency in Nigeria. In 1589 Bird and Newton, two London merchants visited the Benin River and in their account they remarked: "Their money is pretie white shels, for golde and silver we saw none."[1] Throughout the 17th and 18th centuries and the greater part of the 19th century, cowries were imported into Nigeria mainly through the port of Lagos both from the Maldives and from Zanzibar.[2] They displaced to a large extent cloth money but had never been universally accepted throughout Nigeria. There were many districts in which anyone who had no other currency than cowries would have starved.

Cowries had official status in some parts of Nigeria. In the Sultanate of Bornu, both Maria Theresa dollars and cowries were officially adopted as currency.[3] In the markets of the Ibo tribes the Women's Councils which were in charge fixed the rate of the cowrie exchange.[4] In the market of Kano the Sheikh fixed the prices of all goods and charged a small

[1]Hakluyt's *Voyages* (Everyman Edn.), Vol. IV, p. 297. The merchants observed that the natives sold them two gallons of honey and honeycombs for 100 shells.
[2]The import of cowries through Lagos amounted to 65,496 cwt. in 1868; 56,040 cwt. in 1869; and 50,340 cwt. in 1870. (R. E. C. Stearns, *A Study in Primitive Money*, Smithsonian Institute Annual Report, Washington, 1887, p. 303).
[3]Kürchhoff, p. 9.
[4]G. T. Basden, *Among the Ibos of Nigeria* (London, 1921), p. 195.

commission. For the purpose of calculating this commission, the exchange rate was fixed at 2,000 cowries per dollar.[5]

Cowries served until recently as a store of value. The tendency to hoard cowries was still very strong even after the first World War. Basden had been in some treasure houses where the store of cowries reminded him of heaps of newly threshed corn.[6]

Cowries were used to a very large extent as a medium of exchange. During the 'twenties in the markets of the Ibo tribes there was no barter; everything was sold against cowries. "*A* buys *B's* yam for cowries and *B* buys *A's* oil for cowries also; they make no attempt at direct exchange."[7] Even after the penetration of British coins, cowries were preferred for a long time by the natives. The purchasing power of cowries was for some time actually higher than that of the metal coinage on the basis of the market exchange rate between the two, because shells were much more readily accepted.[8] On the other hand, in Barth's time cowries were only useful for buying small articles for which purpose they were infinitely more convenient than cotton strips.[9] So long as the coined currency was not adapted to native needs by the provision of suitable small coins, such as one-tenth of a penny, the Africans preferred to use cowries for small purchases.[10]

Cowries served extensively also as a standard of value. In some parts of Nigeria forty cowries were called a "string," fifty strings a "head," and ten heads a "bag."[11] Among the Yoruba the unit was thirty-two cowries and was called one *rotl*; prices were quoted in *rotls*.[12] At Bornu, the parity between the *rotl* and the Maria Theresa dollar was fixed from time to time. At the time of Nachtigal's visit the dollar was worth between 120 and 130 *rotls*.[13] In the olden days the Royal Niger Company simplified its trading operations by using a head of cowries as unit of account and fixing its value at one shilling and threepence. If a native brought five shillings worth of palm oil, the agent allowed him to select cotton goods, salt, etc., to the value of four heads of cowries. "The local market rate of cowries requires as careful daily attention as the rate of silver in Bombay."[14]

In some districts even in 1942 payments were expressed more often in cowries than in modern money. The original exchange rate was 8d. per 2,000 cowries; later it rose to 1s. per 2,000 cowries. This exchange

[5]Major Denham, Captain Clapperton and Dr. Oudney, *Narrative of Travels and Discoveries in Northern and Central Africa in the Years* 1822-24. (2nd Edn. 1826), Vol. II, p. 253.

[6]Basden, p. 199.   [7]Basden, p. 197.

[8]Basden, p. 199.   [9]Barth, Vol. II, p. 311.

[10]Allan McPhee, *The Economic Revolution in British West Africa* (London, 1926), p. 236.

[11]P. Amaury Talbot, *The Peoples of Southern Nigeria* (London, 1926), Vol. III, p. 875.

[12]Barth, p. 311.   [13]Lenz, *Timbuktu*, p. 158.

[14]A. F. Mockler and F. Ferryman, *Imperial Africa* (London, 1898), Vol. I, p. 726

rate was applied at the time of Nadel's investigation whenever figures were quoted in cowries.[15] Cowries are also used in Nigeria, at any rate in the Kingdom of Nupe, for the payment of bride price and for certain traditional gifts and payments,[16] even though bride money is now paid to a large and increasing extent in modern money.[17] Fees for membership and promotion in secret societies among the Ibo tribes were often fixed in cowries.

Beyond doubt cowries compared favourably with various other types of primitive currencies which were at one time in use in Nigeria. They, too, had their grave disadvantages, however. For one thing, owing to the large amounts payable in cowries, it was necessary for primitive and illiterate savages to be able to count in big figures. Apparently, however, they developed the advanced arithmetical faculty required for the purpose.

A much graver disadvantage was the difficulty of transporting large quantities of cowries. C. H. Robinson, in the course of his expedition in Hausaland, came to be confronted with this problem in a particularly acute form. One of the horses of the expedition became ill and was incapable of continuing its journey for many days. "The trouble is that we cannot sell it," Robinson remarked, "as its value in cowries would require fifteen extra porters to carry, to whom we should have to pay all the money they carried and a great deal more besides; there is in fact nothing which we could get in exchange for it which it would pay to carry with us."[18] Evidently by that time cowries were only suitable for local or short-distance trading.

After 1900 cowries appreciated considerably following on their persistent depreciation during the second half of the 19th century. This was due to the prohibition of their import. While within living memory the exchange rate was about 1,500 cowries to the shilling, during the early years of this century it recovered to between 620 and 780. More recently, however, it depreciated again, reaching new low records.

Second only in importance to cowries as a primitive currency were slaves. While cowries were essential for everyday requirements, slaves were equally essential for large transactions. Their use was particularly developed in communities lacking a valuable staple commodity which could be used as currency for big payments. A report of the early 'nineties said of the slave in Nigeria: "He has been the cheque book of the country and has been necessary for all large payments. Unfortunately he has a trick of dying while passing from hand to hand."[19]

[15]S. F. Nadel, *A Black Byzantium—The Kingdom of Nupe in Nigeria* (London, 1942), pp. 314-5.
[16]Nadel, p. 314.
[17]Daryl Forde and Richenda Scott, *The Native Economies of Nigeria* (London, 1946), p. 75.
[18]C. H. Robinson, *Hausaland* (London, 1896), p. 46.
[19]McPhee, p. 234.

Several authors blamed for the existence of slavery the absence of an easily portable currency of high value. Slaves were needed both as a currency which provides its own transport and as carriers of other bulky and heavy currencies. Native potentates and merchants, when travelling some distance, spent on their way not only the currencies which their slaves carried in payment for their current requirements, but also the slaves themselves.[20] The view was often expressed in those days that the introduction of coins would go a long way towards doing away with slavery. There can be no doubt that the penetration of modern money was in fact helpful in that direction. Conversely, the disappearance of slavery went a long way towards reducing primitive currency in Africa to absurdity, for in the absence of slaves the cost of transport of most kinds of primitive currencies in long-distance traffic became prohibitive.[21] Before that stage was reached, however, the expansion of trade, brought about by closer contact with Western civilization, actually increased for some time the use of slave currency owing to the increased requirements.[22]

Slaves were used as a store of value to a large extent. Rich men amassed slaves as their European counterparts amassed money.[23] Slaves also served extensively both as a medium of exchange and as a standard of value. As the value of slaves varied widely it was necessary for each transaction to assess each one individually in terms of the unit, which was the standard slave of a certain age. This practice did not by any means simplify transactions in slaves; but as McPhee reminds us, the hand-minted coins of early times, too, had to be assessed separately owing to the inequality of their metal content.[24]

Slaves became at one time the principal medium of exchange,[25] especially large transactions. They were also used for making unilateral payments such as tribute. The Emir of Adamawa is said to have paid for many years 10,000 slaves annually to the Sultan of Sokoto.[26]

In Nigeria gin fulfilled for a long time most of the essential functions of money. Very frequently bottles or cases passed from hand to hand for years without being consumed.[27] In evidence given before the Liqueur Traffic Commission, mention was made of the practice of purchasing gin to hold it as a treasure.[28] Its popularity as an investment was due in part at least to the fact that the Government steadily increased the rate of duty on imported spirits, and consequently the value

---

[20]Mockler and Ferryman, p. 371.
[21]McPhee, pp. 235-6. About 30s. worth of either brass rods or *manillas* was calculated as the load for one man. To carry such commodities to any distance, slave labour was essential, because the remuneration of free labour would have swallowed up the whole value of the goods. (Annual Report of the Niger Coast Protectorate for 1896-7, p. 8).
[22]McPhee, p. 251.
[23]A. C. Burns, *History of Nigeria* (London, 1929), p. 208.
[24]McPhee, p. 234.   [25]A. C. Burns, p. 208.   [26]McPhee, p. 251.
[27]McPhee, p. 233.   [28]Basden, p. 200.

of the stocks always appreciated. Many chiefs possessed large stocks of gin until the first World War when imports were cut down.[29] Indeed, in some cases, gin represented the entire wealth of chiefs.[30] Members of the Native Races Commission reported that they visited the house of a chief in the Central Province and saw a large quantity of gin in old cases purchased thirty years before.[31]

The same report also contains evidence indicating the extent to which gin was used as a medium of exchange. A Bishop giving evidence said that, when travelling in some parts of the Niger Delta, it was not possible to purchase food unless one was prepared to pay for it in gin. Other witnesses confirmed that unless they paid with gin they were liable to starve. The Commission arrived at the conclusion that in many parts of the country trade spirits, especially gin, were "a substitute for currency."[32] According to Talbot, gin became a currency especially in the central and eastern parts of Nigeria.[33] When the Government prohibited the import of trade spirits this brought the use of trade gin as a currency to an end, and added greatly to the shortage of silver currency that developed after the first World War.[34]

What matters particularly from the point of view of ascertaining the monetary character of gin is that it was used as a medium of exchange not only in trade between natives and Europeans, but also between natives among themselves.[35] There is no evidence that prices were quoted regularly in terms of gin, but owing to its extensive use as a medium of exchange it seems possible that this was done.

Palm oil was another liquid form of currency. On the so-called oil rivers trade with Europeans was based largely on the palm oil standard. The unit was the *kroo*, a hollow measure, the size of which varied from place to place. Its original definition was a quantity of palm oil, but subsequently it came to be used as an abstract unit of account for measuring the value of any commodity.[36] Already at the beginning of the 19th century, the *kroo*, equal to twelve gallons of palm oil, was a unit at Calabar.[37]

Manillas are among the oldest currencies of Nigeria. Some sources attribute its introduction to the ancient Phœnicians who had traded along the west coast of Africa. Early Portuguese traders found the willingness of the Africans to accept unlimited numbers of these bracelets very convenient.[38] Reference is made to their use as a medium of exchange in 1505 at Calabar. One copper *manilla* was worth a big ele-

[29]A. C. Burns, p. 180.   [30]A. C. Burns, p. 243.
[31]Native Races Commission, the Liqueur Traffic in Southern Nigeria 1909, quoted by A. G. MacDonald, *Trade Politics and Christianity in Africa and the East* (London, 1916), p. 92.
[32]MacDonald, p. 92.   [33]Talbot, Vol. III, p. 876.
[34]Address to the Nigerian Legislative Council, 1924, quoted by McPhee, p. 234.
[35]C. Partridge, *Cross Rover Natives* (London, 1905), p. 253.
[36]Woermann, p. 36.   [37]Talbot, Vol. I, p. 191
[38]P. Amaury Talbot, *Tribes of the Niger Delta* (London, 1932), pp. 282-4.

phant tooth, and a slave cost between eight and ten *manillas*.[39] Bird and Newton reported their presence in 1589 on the Benin River.[40] Dapper, too, came across *manillas* in 1688 in Calabar. He stated that Dutch traders bought slaves against payment in rough grey copper armlets which had to be very well made, otherwise the natives rejected them by the hundred.[41]

A report by T. J. Hutchinson, British Consul of Fernando Po, dated 20th June, 1856, states that there were five different patterns of *manillas* in use in Nigeria. "Although the casual observer could scarcely discriminate between them," he wrote, "yet the practised eye of the natives does it at once and cannot be deceived. The '*Antony Manilla*' is good in all interior markets; the '*Congo Simgolo*' or 'bottle necked' is good only at Opungo market; the '*Onadoo*' is best for the Ibo country between Bony and New Calabar; the '*Finniman Fawfinna*' is passable in Juju Town and Qua market; but it is only half the worth of the '*Antony*'; and the '*Cutta Antony*' is valued by the people at Umballa."[42]

In more recent times, *manillas* were still in use, especially among the Ibo tribe.[43] *Manillas* were, until comparatively recently, a medium of exchange at Wukai. A deep bowl filled with corn was considered equal to one large *manilla*. A cup-shaped receptacle filled with salt was worth one small *manilla*.[44]

The value of *manillas* is by no means stable. Its fluctuations are relatively narrow over short periods, but its value is apt to undergo considerable changes over long periods.[45] The Native Currency Proclamation of 1902 prohibited the import of *manillas* except with the High Commissioner's permit.[46] This was done in order to encourage the use of coined money. Nevertheless, the use of *manillas* in Nigeria survived right to our days. It is, in fact, one of the few primitive currencies which still constitute an administrative problem.

Brass rods formed an important element in the involved primitive currency system of Nigeria. According to some authors, they originated through the straightening out of *manillas*. At the beginning of the century, brass rods were the most popular currency in many parts of Nigeria. They had a fixed value of threepence.[47] After the first World

---

[39]Talbot (1926), p. 184. At Benin, too, captives were bought against *manillas*; their price was from 12-15 brass or copper *manillas*, p. 156.

[40]Talbot (1926), p. 159.

[41]C. K. Meek, *Law and Authority in a Nigerian Tribe* (London, 1937), p. 5.

[42]Sir W. N. M. Geary, *Nigeria under British Rule* (London, 1927), p. 82.

[43]Talbot (1926), Vol. III, p. 877. Talbot produced a unique table showing the currencies used by various sub-tribes in Southern Nigeria. Even though he does not indicate the extent of the monetary use of the various currencies, his material is extremely valuable.

[44]C. K. Meek, *A Sudanese Kingdom—An Ethnological Study of the Jukim Speaking Peoples of Nigeria* (London, 1931), pp. 452-4.

[45]G. T. Basden, *Niger Ibos* (London, undated), p. 338.

[46]Partridge, p. 252.

[47]Partridge, p. 251.

War, the cash value of brass rods among the Awka was sixpence.[48] At Calabar in 1830 copper rods were mostly a fictitious currency, though occasionally they actually changed hands.[49]

Iron hoes were used in the early 'fifties of the last century as a form of currency; forty of them bought a slave.[50] The currency of Kororofa is claimed to have been for a time a small hoe with a long spike at one end.[51] Hoe-shaped currency must have been widely used at one time throughout the northern provinces as such objects have been dug up on the sites of ancient towns in the north. Even at present, hoes are an integral part of the bride price among most of the semi-Bantu speaking tribes of the Plateau Province.[52] At Benue small hoes changed hands in bundles of thirty-six, one bundle being equal to a slave.[53]

Other iron currencies included iron bars. At Bonny, towards the middle of the 19th century, pilot's fees and port dues were fixed in bars. Actual payment was made in such goods as were brought by the ships for barter, but the valuation of the goods was in bars.[54] Fish-hooks, too, are said to have served as currency in parts of the Awgu Division,[55] while in the district of Moko, the currency is claimed to have been a flat piece of iron in the form of a fish.[56]

Arrow points and tin-tack shaped pieces of iron were among the metallic currencies. Secret societies issued their own currency resembling small squashed tin-tacks with arrow-shaped heads and with stems the thickness of a large pin.[57] Between Awka and Enugu, similar arrow heads were in use and were worth about forty-five to a penny.[58]

The non-metallic currencies included salt which was already used at Benin in 1789 in pieces valued at 2s. 6d.[59] This was equal to one "bar" at Bonny. Cones of salt still served as currency in the 'twenties of this century.[60]

Barth gives a description of shirts of all kinds and sizes used as currency for buying larger objects. The coarsest and smallest of these shirts were quite unfit for non-monetary use, and were equal to six *rotls* of cowries, while the large ones were worth between fifty and sixty *rotls*.[61] At the middle of the last century anyone wanting to buy corn in the Kukawa market could not do so with the aid of cowries or dollars. If he had only dollars, he had to exchange them first for shells, then with the

[48]Basden (1921), p. 201.
[49]Talbot, *Southern Nigeria*, Vol. I, p. 191.
[50]C. K. Meek (1931), p. 452.
[51]Dr. Baikie, *Exploring Voyage*, p. 114. Quoted by Meek (1931), p. 452.
[52]Meek (1931), p. 452.   [53]Mockler and Ferryman, p. 374.
[54]Talbot (1926), Vol. I, pp. 265-6.
[55]Meek (1937), p. 104.   [56]Meek (1937), p. 5.
[57]F. W. Butt-Thompson, *West African Secret Societies* (London, 1929), p. 33.
[58]G. T. Basden, *Niger Ibos*, p. 339.
[59]Talbot (1926), Vol. I, pp. 169-70.
[60]Talbot (1926), Vol. III, p. 876.
[61]Barth, Vol. II, p. 311.

shells he had to buy shirts and with the aid of the shirts he was able to buy corn.[62]

A piece of cloth called "pawn" worth about two shillings was used as a standard of value at Benin. Subsequently the "pawn" became one of the numerous fictitious units of the West African coastal regions.[63] Narrow strips of native cotton cloth were the principal currency in the interior before they were replaced by cowries. At the time of Rohlfe's visit, the cotton strip standard was still in force in the southern part of Bornu. The unit was the length from the tip of the middle finger to the point of the elbow; the difference between tall men and short men caused frequent disputes.[64]

Tobacco was used so much in barter, especially in the central and eastern parts, that it probably assumed the part of a currency.[65] In the central and eastern parts of the country, dried fish was a popular medium of exchange.[66]

Yams, either singly or five at a time, and bowls of oil palm kernels still function in Umor, Southern Nigeria, as a local currency for the purchase of goods in small quantities.[67]

[62]Barth, Vol. I, p. 312. He remarks that near the village Pirtwa he tried in vain to buy provisions with shells. A member of his expedition succeeded, however, in purchasing a goat with his servant's shirt. "This article, even if much worn, is always regarded as ready money in the whole of Negroland, and as long as a man has a shirt he is sure not to starve" (Vol. II, p. 354).

[63]Talbot (1926), Vol. III, p. 875.

[64]G. Rohlfs, *Geld in Afrika* (Dr. A. Petermann's Mitteilungen, 1889), Vol. XXXV, p. 190.

[65]Talbot (1926), Vol. III, p. 876.   [66]Talbot (1926), Vol. III, p. 876.

[67]Forde and Scott, p. 49.

CHAPTER 39

GOLD DUST CURRENCY OF THE GOLD COAST AND ASHANTI

In the Gold Coast for a long time gold dust was the only "coin" of the realm. "It is handier than one would suppose; even a farthing can be paid in it by putting one or two grains upon a knife tip."[1] In an official report it was stated that all payments were made in gold dust. At the time of its publication in 1848 gold dust was valued on the Gold Coast at £4 per ounce.[2] In another official publication, however, the general rate at which rock gold and gold dust passed currently was given at £3 12s. per ounce. The ounce, which served as the monetary unit, was sub-divided for monetary purposes into sixteen *ackies* of 4s. 6d. each,

[1]R. F. Burton and V. L. Cameron, *To the Gold Coast for Gold* (London, 1883), Vol. II, p. 154. But for the high authority of the authors one might be inclined to regard this statement as a mild exaggeration.

[2]*The Currency of the British Colonies*. H.M. Stationery Office (London, 1848), p. 25.

and the *ackie* into six *takus* of 9d. each. Larger units were the *benda*, equal to two ounces (£7 4s. 0d.), and the *periquin*, equal to two and a half ounces (£9).[3] The kings were able to obtain revenue by using a special set of weights rather heavier than those employed in ordinary trade; therefore they secured an advantage when gold dust was weighed out to them.[4]

Cowries were still used in the market place at Accra in 1883, and also in other towns of the eastern district for small purchases.[5] On the other hand, in Ashanti the import of cowries was prohibited so that they should not compete with gold dust as a currency.[6]

For large transactions slaves were a most important currency. They served largely as a standard of value.[7] In Ashanti a garment made of cotton, linen or silk was used fairly extensively as a medium of exchange. It was called *pawn*.[8]

Aggri beads were a store of value to a considerable degree. They fetched an equal weight in gold, and at times even more.[9] There is no reason to believe the aggri bead had ever served as a medium of exchange or a standard of value. On the other hand, it was known to have been used for the purposes of bride price. Its high value is indicated by the fact that if an aggri bead was stolen the thief was fined seven slaves.[10]

Various forms of iron currency were in use in the Gold Coast at various times. At the beginning of the 17th century big iron needles with a semi-circle at one end were employed as small money.[11] In more recent times small iron rods served as currency.[12]

In 1935 a number of iron discs of about two and five-eigths to two and seven-eighths inches were found near the village Odumase during gold prospecting operations. In 1929 the District Commissioner of Juaso (in which district Odumase is situated) noticed pieces of iron stored away within the precincts of the "palace" of the Omanhene of Juaben (the native capital of the district). He was informed that they were iron currency, formerly made at Juaben, and issued under the authority of the Omanhene.[13]

[3]Robert Chalmers, *A History of Currency in the British Colonies* (London, 1893), p. 212.
[4]W. D. Hambly, *Source Book for African Anthropology* (Chicago, 1937), p. 612.
[5]F. O. Adrian, *Currency of the Colonies* (Colonial Office, London, 1883), p. 44.
[6]Richard Andrée, *Geographie des Welthandels* (Stuttgart, 1872), Vol. ii, p. 62. Quoted by Kürchhoff, p. 8.
[7]Kürchhoff, p. 10.
[8]Noback, p. 344.
[9]J. Edward Price, *On Aggri Beads* (*Journal of the Anthropological Institute*, 1883, Vol. xii), p. 64.
[10]R. A. Freeman, *Travels and Life in Ashanti and Jaman* (London, 1898), p. 403.
[11]*Bibliothek der Geschichte der Menschheit*, Vol. ii, p. 144. Quoted by Schurtz, p. 144.
[12]Noback, p. 344.
[13]R. P. Wild, *Iron disc currency from Ashanti* (*Man.*, May, 1936).

CHAPTER 40

OTHER MONEYS OF THE GUINEA BAY

In the 17th century debased gold was extensively used as a medium of exchange on the coast of Guinea. Much of the pure gold was mixed with silver and copper and cast into fetishes. The latter were cut into small bits which were used for the purchase of daily necessities such as bread or fruit. The negresses knew the exact value of these bits so well at sight that they were never mistaken, and the bits changed hands without being weighed, just as if they had been coins. The Dutch garrisons then stationed on the Guinea coast were paid their subsistence money in these pieces and they were able to buy food from the negroes. Apparently one of the reasons why these debased bits of gold were so freely acceptable was that the natives mixed it with good gold and thus tried to pass it on to the Europeans. This was done systematically. The debased metal changed hands frequently and even though much of it was exported to Europe at about forty shillings an ounce, the natives were making them faster than the Europeans were exporting them.[1]

An even more ancient currency which, however, continued to circulate in Guinea until recent times was the *manilla*. In the early 16th century, Portuguese traders imported large quantities of this currency. The accounts of the trading station of San Jorge da Mina state that during the period between 1504 and 1507, the station received from Portugal 287,813 *manillas*.[2]

A unit of account was a *kroo* of rice. The same unit was also used on part of the Pepper coast, where one *kroo* of pepper was equal to two *kroos* of rice.[3]

Above all, guinea cloth, as its name implies, was extensively employed as currency in Guinea. It is through the ports of Guinea that this currency penetrated into the interior to become one of the most important currencies for a long period over a vast territory of Africa. It remained a standard of value long after it ceased to be a medium of exchange.

Slaves were a favourite unit of account for large transactions. Before the colonization, European ships had to pay to the native kings port dues to the value of seven or twelve slaves according to the number of their masts.[4]

Cowries were also used as a currency, and in time of wars large quantities were walled in.[5]

[1]William Bosman, *A New and Accurate Description of the Coast of Guinea* (1700) Pinkerton's Travels and Voyages, Vol. XVI, 1814, p. 373.
[2]J. W. Blake, *Europeans in West Africa*, 1450-1560. Hakluyt Society (London, 1842), Vol. I, p. 107.
[3]Noback, p. 343.
[4]P. E. Isert, *Reise nach Guinea* (Copenhagen, 1788), p. 151. The same author makes a reference to a string of coral beads being worth two slaves, p. 186.
[5]Isert, p. 64.

Natives of Gambia have long been acquainted with the notion of a standard of value. Jobson, writing in 1623, describes a bartering scene on the Gambia River. The European merchants asked the Mandingo which should be the staple commodity to pitch the price upon, to value other things by. The natives showed the Europeans a piece of cloth.[6] They apparently fully understood the idea of selecting an article which was to serve as a standard of value to facilitate barter.

In their internal trade the Mandingo had by then developed a primitive currency. "Now through the whole Countrey there is no use of any coyne or money, neither have they any, but every man to choppe and barter one thing for another and the only nominated thing is matts, as in asking the price of this or that they desire, the word is 'How many matts shall I give you?' so they are still in use."[7] They used kola nuts as bride money, the price of a wife being fifty of these nuts.[8] In more recent times gold dust was used as a medium of exchange.[9] Wealth in Gambia is invested in cattle; until recently natives knew no other form of investment.[10]

East and North-East of the Senegal River, in inner Senegambia, black cotton cloth was the medium of exchange in Walata. Gold dust was also extensively used as a medium of exchange, while millet and guinea cloth acted both as a medium of exchange and a standard of value. Ostrich feathers in trade with Europeans were used regularly, at a fixed value in relation to guinea cloth.

Senegambia had its fictitious unit, the "bar"—which at the time of Dapper's visit was still a real bar and only became fictitious later—and the "packet," also called *fazenda*, representing the value of a selection of European goods.[11]

Along the River Gambia modern money is treated by the Africans as a medium of barter. When an African gives coins in exchange for goods he thinks he is selling the coin against payment in grain, or cotton cloth. He does not ask the merchant how many francs (or shillings) the goods cost. He asks him how much rice or calico or sugar he is prepared to give for his coin. And the price of the units of measure remains always the same; it is the size of the measure that fluctuates. After a good harvest the standard hollow measure of grain that is equivalent to a certain coin is increased. Between harvests it becomes gradually reduced.[12]

Until recently the currency of Dahomey consisted of cowries; 2,000 cowries were called one head. Nominally a head was equal to one dollar, but owing to the scarcity of metallic currency, the silver dollar was eagerly taken at 2,400 to 2,600 cowries.

[6]Richard Jobson, *The Golden Trade or a Discovery of the River Gambia and the Golden Trade of the Ethiopians.* (1623—Reprinted in the Mary Kingsley Travel Books), p. 113.

[7]Jobson, p. 156.   [8]Jobson, p. 171.   [9]Noback, p. 346.

[10]F. B. Archer, *The Gambia Colony and Protectorate* (London, 1906), p. 10.

[11]Noback, pp. 347-8.   [12]de Foville, p. 18.

The kings of Dahomey paid in strings of cowries prepared by their wives. A string of 1,500 shells counted for 2,000—an instance to show that despots in primitive communities had the power even to alter the laws of arithmetic.[13] More recently thirty to thirty-five shells, wrapped in leaves, counted for forty.

Herskovits gives an interesting account of the fluctuation of the value of cowries in Dahomey. In 1883 it was worth 500 to the franc. After the occupation of the country by the French, cowries depreciated to about 800 to the franc, and at that level they remained stable in the region of Gaoua until 1918. After the first World War, during the period corresponding to the fall of the franc, cowries appreciated; in the view of the natives they were better money than the depreciating paper franc. There were also violent fluctuations due to speculative operations. After the disappearance of silver franc coins from circulation, a five-franc note was exchanged for 600 cowries. There were, however, interesting seasonal fluctuations in the cowrie-franc rate. From November to February the franc appreciated year after year, owing to the necessity of acquiring francs for the payment of taxes. The francs were bought from Sudanese pedlars who took advantage of the seasonal demand. In 1931 the rate rose from 600 cowries for a five franc note in October to 800 in November, 1,500 in December and 2,000 in January, dropping abruptly to the normal figure after the payment of taxes when the need for French money ceased to be pressing. These fluctuations reacted on commodity prices. Ever since taxes came to be payable in francs instead of in kind, active markets developed where money-changers converted notes into cowries and *vice versa*.[14]

In Togo cowries were currency to some extent right up to the 'twenties. In earlier times they were the general means of payment. They remained until recently a popular means of payment in the distant regions of the North, but coined money gradually displaced them. Certain goods such as palm wine are, or were until recently, still paid for in cowries.[15] In Akposso, in the olden days, even slaves were paid for in cowries.[16]

Under German rule there was a fixed ratio between cowries and the mark, which had to be adjusted as and when the cowries depreciated. Among the Moba, the price of a horse was fixed in cowries but actual payment was made in cows.[17] When supply and demand fluctuated, changes of prices were not expressed by quoting a larger or smaller number of cowries for the unit of measure of the various goods; it was the number of the units of measure for a fixed amount of cowries that was adjusted—thus instead of reducing the price of a litre of corn from

[13]Dalzel, *Geschichte von Dahomey*, p. 35. Quoted by Schurtz, p. 90.
[14]Herskovits, pp. 218-20.
[15]A. Schlettwein, *Togo* (*Das Eingeborenerecht*, Stuttgart, 1930), p. 72.
[16]Schlettwein, p. 74.   [17]Schlettwein, p. 72.

a hundred cowries to fifty cowries, the measure worth a hundred cowries was increased from one litre to two litres.[18]

Hoes were used as currency in Akpafu, one hoe being worth fifty pfennige.[19] In Anecho, objects of small value such as small quantities of pepper, onions, salt, or oil, to a value of less than a pfennig, were paid for in small bundles of tobacco which was worth half a pfennig. In Namba, payment was made in chickens.[20] Rubber balls are also said to have served as a medium of exchange. There were two standard sizes.[21]

Slaves were for a long time the chief currency of the Ivory Coast for large payments. Later gold dust was the principal currency, and it changed hands by weight. Cowries, too, were used.[22]

Among the Agni, salt, leaf tobacco, native cloth, hoes and beads served as money. Several of these goods were subject also to loan transactions.[23] Pieces of iron were used in the Seguela district. In various parts of the country *manillas* were used in packets of twenty for four francs. Some tribes used *manillas* for bride price.[24] Native traders sold their goods to Europeans against *manillas* which they kept until they wanted to buy fresh supplies of products in the interior. The *manilla* was, therefore, "a kind of bank for the black trader, something he can put his wealth into when he wants to store it for a time."[25]

Although many of the inhabitants of Liberia were used to coins, there was for a long time not enough modern money in circulation, so that payment was made in produce money. One dollar meant simply an abstract unit of account representing a given quantity of palm oil or palm kernels. Debts contracted in dollars were paid in either of the two commodities, and since the debtor had the choice whether to pay in palm oil or palm kernels he was likely to choose the one which at the moment was the cheaper. The situation was in this respect somewhat similar to that liable to develop under bimetallism in modern countries.[26]

In addition to this dual standard, various local currencies were in use in various districts. The Kpelle used salt, iron rods, kola nuts, slaves and cattle. Objects of high value were generally calculated in slaves. A slave was equal to 300 salt packets or 100 iron bars or 400 kola nuts.[27] In Eastern Buziland kola nuts were a means of payment.[28]

In Loma the money was the iron rod. 100 rods were equal to a slave

[18]F. Hupfeld, *Land und Leute im Basari* (1899-1900), p. 176.
[19]Dr. Asmis, *Die Stammesrechte der Bezirke Misakohe, Anecho und Loma-Land* (Zeitschrift für Vergleichende Rechtswissenschaft, Vol. xxvi, 1911.)
[20]Schlettwein, p. 72.   [21]Schurtz, p. 180.
[22]Noback, p. 344.
[23]F. J. Clozel and Roger Villamur, *Des Coutumes Indigènes de la Côte d'Ivoire* (Paris, 1902), pp. 88, 125, 127 and 159.
[24]Clozel and Villamur, pp. 267, 445, 469 and 501.
[25]Mary Kingsley, *West African Studies* (London, 1899), p. 82.
[26]Woermann, pp. 40-1.
[27]Diedrich Westermann, *Die Kpelle—Ein Negerstamm in Liberia* (Göttingen, 1921), p. 38.
[28]P. Germann, *Die Völkerstämme im Norden von Liberia* (Leipzig, 1933).

or to an ox. In Djaiaimai iron and salt were the favourite currencies.[29]
The Kissi and the Toma formerly used glass lozenges as medium of
exchange. Before the first World War it was entirely replaced by elon-
gated T-shaped pieces of iron which were of no practical use whatever.
The natives were very particular about these pieces of iron and refused
them in the case of the least imperfection.[30]

A monetary unit for trading on a large scale was 100 lbs. of ivory. It
was a fictitious unit and represented an assortment of European goods.[31]

The fictitious unit in Sierra Leone in the 17th century was the "bar."
A bar of gunpowder was two pounds of gunpowder; a bar of silver an
ounce of silver; a bar of gun flints two hundred gun flints, and so on.
In the 18th century Mungo Park put the value of a bar in cash at two
shillings.[32]

The Sherbro used iron strips as their chief currency, one strip being
equivalent to a penny. Alldridge met once in the bush several native
women who were going to the market with their purses under their arms
in the shape of a mat containing perhaps a couple of dozen of these
pieces of iron.[33] When Alldridge first visited the country, coins were
practically unknown. On the occasion of his more recent visit, however,
they were universally known and willingly accepted by the natives.[34]

The Bubi of Fernando Po used for their currency small discs cut from
the *Achatectonia* shell.[35] There were two kinds of shell strings in use as
currency.[36] Shell discs were made from the *Conus Papilionoceus* in the
shape of coins.[37] The shell strings looked very old and polished through
wear, though they were still being produced in the 'eighties. They were
the only valuables of the Bubi.[38]

The shell currency of the Bubi shared the fate of many other currencies, primitive or modern, in that it depreciated in terms of goods. Some
time ago one shell string bought ten eating yams or one chicken, but by
the early 'twenties its purchasing power declined by about half.[39]

[29]Walter Volz, *Reise Durch das Hinterland von Liberia* (Berne, 1911), p. 38.
[30]H. Neel, *Notes sur deux Peuplades de la Frontière Libérienne* (L'Anthropologie,
Vol. xxv, 1913), pp. 435-6.
[31]Noback, p. 343.
[32]F. W. Butt-Thompson, *Sierre Leone in History and Tradition* (London, 1926),
p. 41.
[33]T. J. Alldridge, *The Sherbro and its Hinterland* (London, 1901), p. 216.
[34]T. J. Alldridge, *A Transformed Colony—Sierre Leone* (London, 1910), pp. 186-7.
[35]Kingsley (1897), p. 59.   [36]Noback, p. 345.
[37]*Mitteilungen der Geographischen Gesellschaft* (Vienna, 1893), p. 27. Quoted by
Schurtz, p. 102.
[38]O. Baumann, *Fernando Po und die Bubie* (Vienna, 1888), pp. 83-4.
[39]G. Tessmann, *Die Bubi auf Fernando Po* (The Hague, 1923), p. 176.

CHAPTER 41

DEBASED BRASS ROD CURRENCY OF THE BELGIAN CONGO

Few countries have provided so much material for the study of primitive money as the Belgian Congo. Within her vast territory a variety of primitive currencies have been in use, some of them over a very long period. Wauters states that the money of the natives varied from one district to another, according to the riches of the people, their requirements, their tastes of the day. Although native trade was transacted as a rule by barter, there was nearly always a monetary unit, some object of common use or of a value well known to all.[1]

There were certain objects which served as money over a vast area. Amongst them brass rods played a very prominent part. Originally they were said to have been produced through melting down brass ornaments, but subsequently they came to be imported on a large scale from Europe. European traders, travellers and missionaries carried with them coils of thick brass wire which were cut into small pieces according to requirements.[2] These rods were not quite so thick as a slate pencil; their length varied from district to district and was liable to changes. Representing a favourite raw material for ornaments, weapons, tools and utensils, they served as a store of value. They were used extensively as a medium of exchange, and were accepted in payment for goods of every kind from the smallest to the biggest. Everything had its price in brass rods; eggs, fowls, cloth, male and female slaves, etc. Weeks quotes an instance of a purchase of land for which the headman of the village originally demanded 5,000 brass rods, but eventually 1,500 were accepted.[3] Apparently ivory was the only object the price of which was not quoted in brass rods but always in slaves.[4] Wages were paid in brass rods. When the Missionary Society to which Weeks belonged built its house, it engaged the help of a few natives at twenty rods per month as pay, five rods per week for food rations, and one fathom of cloth per month for wear.

Brass rods were used extensively as a standard of deferred payments. Credit was frequently given by native traders and others, and since debtors were on the whole reluctant to pay, the tribal laws gave to creditors extensive powers to collect their debts. To penalize defaulting debtors, a creditor is entitled to break pots and saucepans and anything he finds outside the debtor's house. Should this be of no avail, the creditor and his friends are entitled to seize the debtor's wife and keep

[1] A. J. Wauters, *L'état indépendant du Congo*. Quoted by Albert Thonnar, *Essai sur le système économique des primitifs* (Brussels, 1901), pp. 331-2.
[2] Sir Harry Johnston, *George Grenfell in the Congo* (London, 1908), Vol. ii, p. 795.
[3] John H. Weeks, *Among the Congo Cannibals* (London, 1913), p. 39.
[4] Grenfell, quoted by Johnston, Vol. ii, p. 796.

her a prisoner as a security for the outstanding debt. Since a woman was considered to be worth about 3,000 rods, debtors had every financial inducement, apart altogether from any sentimental considerations, to pay debts of smaller amounts. If they failed to do so within a reasonable time, the creditor was entitled to keep the woman as his wife, or, if she was a slave, to sell her.[5]

The history of the monetary use of brass rods in the Congo provides an outstanding example for currency debasement and inflation in a primitive community. Towards the middle of the last century when the quantity of rods in circulation was very small, and when their length was twenty-seven inches, their purchasing power was very high. Grenfell notes in his diary in 1889 that forty years earlier ten cakes of manioc paste could be bought for one brass rod, while in 1889 one cake cost fifteen brass rods.[6] The reason for this depreciation was partly the heavy influx of brass rods manufactured in Europe, but largely the debasement of these rods by the natives themselves. It was a widespread practice for anyone who came into possession of many brass rods, to cut a bit off each, so as to procure free of charge brass for ornaments, and to pass on the brass rods thus shortened. When it was realized that the rods were becoming shorter, prices went up. Weeks, writing in 1914, states that thirty years earlier a good fowl could be bought for two or three rods, but at the time of writing 150 rods had to be given for a fowl of the same size.[7] A missionary recorded the following experience: "In 1894 we noticed that a large number of rods in the Church Treasury Box were more than twice the length of those then current; we therefore cut them down to the current length of ten inches and sold the little pieces to local blacksmiths. By keeping the rods, their value had more than doubled."[8] What the missionaries did not realize was that the profit was purely a book-keeping profit, for the purchasing power of the shortened rods was probably considerably less than half that of the original rods at the time when they were deposited in the Church Treasury Box.

The combined effect of debasement and inflation was that brass rods eventually became a drug in the market, even though they continued to be accepted for small payments.

Iron bars were also among the metallic currencies in the Congo. They were regarded by all Europeans who had the misfortune of having to deal with them as a most inconvenient currency which was apt to reduce itself to absurdity because of the disproportionately high cost of its transport. The square or round bars of iron, cut into lengths of about one foot each, were extremely heavy. At the low rate at which they were accepted in payment it practically meant that one had to employ one

[5]Weeks, p. 115. [6]Johnston, Vol. II, p. 796.
[7]John H. Weeks, *Among the Primitive Bakongo* (London, 1914), p. 202.
[8]W. H. Bentley, *Pioneering on the Congo* (London, 1900), Vol. II, p. 398.

L

man to carry every eight shillings' worth of this money. Moreover, the Bakongo coveted the iron bars to such an extent that they could hardly be trusted with them.[9] The value of a load of iron bars represented only a few days' wages for their carrier.[10] What is puzzling is that in spite of the strong desire of the Africans for iron bars, their value was not higher.

Yet another type of metallic currency was copper ingot of Katanga in the shape of a St. Andrew's Cross. Copper crosses of all sizes, from very small to twelve inches across are said to have been in use since long before 1600. The small ones were found buried in small clay pots. They formed part of payments of bride money.[11]

Knives of various descriptions, especially throwing knives, were and possibly still are used as currency by certain tribes, especially by the Bushongo;[12] in fact that tribe received its name from the use of this peculiar currency, the translation of "Bushongo" being "people of the throwing knife."[13] As a result of the adoption of the throwing knife for monetary use, the Africans became increasingly reluctant to use it as a weapon, for if they missed their target and were unable to recover the weapon, they would literally be throwing money away.[14]

Spearheads served as currency at Yakusa, where the unit was a normal-sized spearhead, but there were also units of larger denomination; the biggest of them was six feet long. One of these would buy a canoe thirty-five to forty-five feet long.[15] Bolongole possessed large numbers of fancy-shaped spears which were displayed at the dancing feasts. The ambition of the natives was to surpass each other in producing new forms.[16] It seems doubtful whether this type of spear was sufficiently standardized to change hands by number or size. If it was used for monetary purposes at all, it was probably within a very restricted scope.

Both spears and knives were used extensively as bride money. Among the Ababua, spears and knives were necessary to pay the bride price in exogamic marriages.[17] There were two types of knives which were originally made exclusively for the payment of bride money. Through their use for that purpose they eventually became true medium of exchange. Prices were quoted in them and there were fixed rates between them; thus a spear or a sword was worth three of these knives, a hatchet two, an ordinary knife half a special knife.[18]

[9]M. W. Hilton-Simpson, *Land and People of the Kasai* (London, 1911), p. 287.
[10]E. Torday, *On the Trail of the Bushongo* (London, 1925), p. 234.
[11]Information supplied by the Chase National Bank's Collection of Moneys.
[12]Torday, p. 145.
[13]*British Museum Handbook to the Ethnographical Collections* (London, 1910), p. 223.
[14]H. Schurtz, *Das Wurfmesser der Neger* (Leyden, 1889), p. 10.
[15]Bentley, Vol. II, p. 295.
[16]Leo Frobenius, *The Childhood of Man* (London, 1909), p. 450.
[17]J. Halkin and E. Viaene, *Les Ababuas (Congo Belge)*. (Brussels, 1911), p. 510.
[18]Halkin and Viaene, pp. 513-4.

As in other parts of Africa, copper and iron wire was used as means of payment in Nyangwe.[19] Hoe blades of small size were a currency in the east and south of Congoland.[20] In the Lokele country such hoe blades were in 1903 worth about sixpence each circulated as cash. According to Grenfell, they were made in the Kasongo country.[21]

Iron beads were yet another type of metallic primitive currency, produced between the Rubi and Aruwimi rivers. One chain of these beads was worth a goat, twenty chains a woman.[22]

A much more important currency was blue beads produced by the natives themselves through some primitive process over a long period in the Katanga district.[23] These beads constituted the standard of value, especially around San Salvador.[24] They changed hands in bunches of a thousand and could be exchanged for any goods.[25] Beads of other kinds were also popular as a means of payment at various times and places, but were not nearly as widely used.

Shells, too, were among the wide variety of primitive currencies in the Belgian Congo. In the west small shells called *Olivella Nana* imported from the coast of Angola were widely used, especially on the Kwango and thence eastward to the Kasai. Further east, cowries imported from the Zanzibar coast through East Africa were used.[26] In some parts of the Congo they were accepted in payment even for goods of high value, including slaves. In 1910 the value of a hen was 500 cowries, that of a goat 15,000 cowries; male slaves changed hands at between 30,000 and 60,000 cowries and female slaves between 40,000 and 80,00 cowries. Fines and blood money were paid in cowries.[27]

There were also shell disc currencies made of shells of the fresh water oyster and snail shells. According to unsupported evidence of Johnston strings of the teeth of leopards, wild pigs and human beings were amongst the oldest currencies in the Congo.[28]

Rubber was said to have been used for monetary purposes among the Babunda and the Bapindji. Weekly markets were held in the open plains to the west of Alela where the natives exchanged among themselves rubber for food-stuffs and other goods. As a rule, rubber was not brought to the Europeans by those who collected it but by those who accepted it in payment. The greatest care was taken that the Europeans should not be allowed to attend the markets and thus ascertain at what price rubber changed hands.[29] It is not clear, however, from the evidence we possess, how far rubber really performed monetary functions.

[19]A. Woermann, p. 33.
[20]Johnston, Vol. II, p. 791.   [21]Johnston, Vol. II, p. 797.
[22]Frobenius, p. 62.   [23]Johnston, Vol. II, p. 790.
[24]Weeks (1914), pp. 201-2.   [25]Bentley, Vol. I, p. 73.
[26]Johnston, Vol. II, p. 792.
     [27]E. Torday and T. A. Joyce, *Notes ethnographiques sur les peuples communément appelés Bakuba ainsi que les peuplades apparentées les Bushongo* (Brussels, 1910), pp. 93-4.
[28]Johnston, Vol. II, pp. 790-1.   [29]Hilton-Simpson, p. 266.

The Congo Basin is poor in salt, and for this reason salt was a very acceptable form of currency, especially for small payments. On the upper Kwango salt in crystalline form was a most popular currency.[30] On the Kwilu River, salt neatly wrapped up in banana leaves was used to a large extent as currency in the district.[31] Wages to carriers were often paid in salt.[32] Ivory also became a kind of currency for large payments as a result of the steady demand for it by whites.

According to Johnston, following on the invasion of the country by the black rat from the Nile Valley, rat traps became so necessary that after some unknown genius had invented the construction of them out of palm rind, cane or some other elastic fibre, they were easily disposed of in all directions and became a kind of currency.[33] There is no reason to suppose, however, that their role exceeded that of a favourite medium of barter.

Other objects which are claimed to have played a monetary role include strips of zebra hide, arrow poison, and the highly valued feathers of a stork-like bird called *minda*.[34] Fantastic as some of these and similar uncorroborated claims may sound, it would be a mistake to reject them without further investigation; for nothing seems to be impossible in the sphere of the currency system of the Congo.

A much more important form of currency was cloth. The earliest type in use was native cloth made of grass or fibre, especially in the cataract region and the country between the Congo and the Kwango.[35] In Kabinda cloth of raphia fibre was until recently still used extensively as currency.[36] Various kinds of European and American cotton cloth (the latter was known under the popular name of *Merikani*) also came to be adopted as a means of payment, even though some local chiefs tried to stop their import by threatening with instantaneous execution any of their subjects found wearing such material.[37] To a large extent cloth assumed the role of a standard of value. Barter transactions were concluded on the basis of prices expressed in pieces of cloth. A "piece" was twelve yards of standard quality cloth.

Weeks gives a detailed description of the characteristic method of bargaining through the intermediary of a native broker talking Portuguese to the white trader and in a Congo language to the native trader. The white trader offered for the elephant tusks for sale 400 pieces of cloth, whereupon the broker informed the native in the latter's language that the white man was prepared to give him 180 pieces. The native replied that he wanted 450 pieces but by the time the broker translated

[30]E. Torday, *Camp and Tramp in African Wilds* (London, 1913), p. 224.
[31]Hilton-Simpson, p. 263.   [32]Simpson, p. 297.
[33]Johnston, Vol. II, pp. 790, 791, 795.
[34]Information supplied by the Chase National Bank Collection of Moneys.
[35]Johnston, Vol. II, p. 795.
[36]Information supplied by the Chase National Bank Collection of Moneys.
[37]Hilton-Simpson, p. 310.

it into Portuguese it became 500 pieces. Eventually, after much haggling, the white man increased his offer to 450 pieces while the broker brought down the native trader's quotation to 360 pieces. The difference was the honest broker's profit. The real difficulty was yet to be overcome, however. The next step was to agree on the trade goods chosen by the native as equivalent to the "pieces"; for payment was not made in cloth but in a large variety of other goods. Thus a case of beads may have equalled eight pieces, a piece of fine cloth four pieces, a demijohn of rum four pieces, etc.[38] It all had to be argued out and settled, so that agreement on the number of pieces payable really meant very little in itself.

Guns constituted a somewhat similar monetary unit. Although they were actually used as a medium of exchange, to a much larger extent they provided a standard of value to facilitate barter. When white men first came to the Congo in 1879-85 as a ruler, goods in the region of the lower Congo were principally reckoned in guns—that is, the trade price of guns.[39] Ivory was bought for so many guns; each gun represented a certain quantity of cotton cloth, some salt, brass wire, hoop iron, crockery, powder, spirit and in some places a big brass pan.[40] Johnston described an argument between Grenfell and three carriers at the Mission Station of Palabale who demanded that before they started they must be given the value of two guns each and in addition a commission of half a gun to the chief. When Grenfell refused this, they promptly increased their demand to four guns' worth of cloth. A gun in those days meant about four shillings' worth of cloth or trade goods.[41]

Gin and rum, too, served as means of payment with the usual destructive effect on the physique and morals of the natives.

Livestock was used as a currency to a much smaller extent than in East Africa. Cameron, on arriving at Nyangwe, found that goats were among the currencies of the place.[42]

Slaves were a most important medium of exchange and standard of value. Their value was kept steady by the fact that a slave was always equal to so many pounds of meat. "If he fell sick and could not work for you, you could eat him."[43] The monetary value of a slave could never decline below the "consumption point," that is the level at which his owner considered it more profitable to eat his money rather than spend it. Later, the realization of the economic value of slave labour conferred on slaves an intrinsic value of a different kind.

Most of the currencies in use in the Congo possessed an intrinsic value. Even if some of the fancy-shaped iron spears, knives and hoes were useless for practical purposes in the form in which they circulated,

[38]Weeks, pp. 211-2.   [39]Johnston, p. 795.
[40]Bentley, Vol. I, p. 73.   [41]Johnston, Vol. I, p. 397.
[42]Cameron, p. 397.
[43]Johnston, Vol. II, p. 790.

they could easily be converted by the blacksmiths into ornaments, tools, impliments or weapons. All the blacksmiths in the Stanley Falls district depended on the iron currencies for their raw material supplies needed in making axes, knives, spears, arrow-heads, etc. Demand for such purposes exceeded at times the supply available, so that there was ample scope for traders to use iron currency imported from Europe. The imitation spears or hoes were, however, not always acceptable, owing to differences in their shape or, in some instances, the inferiority of their quality.[44]

Brass bars, too, had an intrinsic value because of the demand for the material for ornaments. Likewise beads and shells had an alternative use to their monetary use. Cloth had its full intrinsic value, and so had staple exports such as rubber or ivory. The only currency without any intrinsic value mentioned in the very exhaustive account of Johnston was old grass mats which became in time a useless bundle of tangled hay but continued nevertheless to circulate.[45]

In the Belgian Congo modern money was not forced on the natives in the same way as it was in some other European Colonies in Africa or the Pacific area. There was no legislation forbidding the use of primitive currency. The Government paid its employees in francs, and so did the railway company. The traders, on the other hand, accepted produce in payment for their goods and paid for the goods of the natives either in francs or in trade goods. Even in the absence of any coercion, however, modern money succeeded gradually in displacing primitive currencies. This may have been due to some extent to the unfavourable experience with the brass rod currency referred to above. When brass rods reached an advanced stage in their depreciation, they practically ceased to be acceptable except at such a low rate that the white man who had no other form of money found the cost of living higher in a native village than in a first-class European hotel. As for the natives themselves, they reverted to barter pure and simple, after which retrograde step the adoption of coins, which do not lend themselves to debasement quite so simply as the discredited brass rod currency did, was a comparatively easy matter.

[44]Johnston, Vol. II, p. 797.   [45]Johnston, Vol. II, p. 790.

CHAPTER 42

SHELL MONEY OF ANGOLA

There is a fair amount of material about the currencies of Angola during the 16th and 17th centuries. Already Leo Africanus referred to the shells found at Loanda which in the Congo and the countrysides adjoining are used instead of money.[1] In the 17th century, Angelo and Carli provided much more detailed information. They observed that very little minted money passed in Loanda; instead, mats, cotton cloth and slaves were used as currencies. The mats were made of straw and they were a yard long. Ten of them were worth 100 reis. The cotton cloth used as currency was made in India and cost 200 reis a piece.

The unit of slave currency was a young black about twenty years of age worth twenty milreis. There were also shells coming from the Congo "for which all things are to be bought as if they were money." 2,000 of these shells were worth a mat.[2] The authors remarked that the people of the Congo valued the shells though they were of no use to them but only to trade with other Africans "who adore the sea and call these shells, which their country does not afford, 'God's children,' for which reason they look upon them as a treasure and take them in exchange for any sort of goods they have. Among them he is the richest and happiest who has most of them."[3]

A few years later Father J. Merolla da Sorrento described the currency system of Benguela: "The current coin of this country is little beads of glass coral brought hither by the Portuguese."[4] He confirms the information of Angelo and Carli about straw mats and cotton cloth being used as currency in Angola. According to him there was also a third type of currency, more valuable than the other two, consisting of finer cotton cloth.[5]

Dapper stated in the 17th century that in Angola pieces of cloth were money; in Lovando (Loanda) in addition there were also mats woven from the fibre of the matombe tree, and snail shells.[6] Blocks of red timber one foot long were used in payment for fruit, chickens, etc.[7]

In more recent times on the coast of Angola the use of the fictitious unit "piece" or "long" was adopted as a standard of value. A "long" was a piece of cotton cloth six yards long. Payment was not made, however, in cotton cloth as a rule, but in an assortment of various goods worth six yards of cloth. Usually there was a definite assortment which

[1]Africanus. The book described conditions at the beginning of the 16th century. Its reference to Congo concerned mainly Portuguese Congo because the territories which are to-day Belgian Congo were hardly known to European observers at that time.

[2]Michael Angelo and Denis de Carli, *A Curious and Exact Account of a Voyage to Congo in the Years* 1666-67 (Pinkerton's Voyages and Travels, Vol. XVI, 1814, p. 157). The Portuguese Government had the mats stamped, and they had them become an official currency (R. Andrée, *Ethnographische Parallellen und Vergleiche*, Stuttgart, 1878, p. 246).

[3]Angelo and Carli, p. 158.

[4]Father J. Merolla da Sorrento, *A Voyage to the Congo and Several other Countries chiefly in Southern Africk* (Pinkerton's Voyages and Travels, Vol. XVI, 1814, p. 213).

[5]Merolla da Sorrento, p. 298.

[6]The use of shells of land snails (*Achatina monetaria*), is referred to by E. V. Martin, *Zeitschrift für Ethnologie*, 1872, p. 67. Quoted by Schurtz, p. 102.

[7]O. Dapper, *Naukeurige Beschrijwinge der Afrikaansche Gewesten van Egypten, Barbaryen, etc.* (Amsterdam, 1676), Vol. II, pp. 217 and 233-4.

natives in certain districts were accustomed to regard as representing a "long." If one article was missing, the natives were liable to refuse to conclude the deal or to charge too much. Likewise, prices were at times fixed in terms of rifles but payment was made in a variety of goods. In one instance, for the purpose of big elephant tusks, the assortment included between fifty and sixty kinds of goods corresponding to the value of a rifle.[8] Slaves were also used as a unit of account in the 'eighties in the ports of Portuguese West Africa. A slave represented an assortment of goods.[9] Kürchhoff refers to the use of the fictitious monetary unit *fazenda*.[10]

The natives were reluctant to part with their ivory. The way in which European traders induced them to do so was to sell them goods on a credit basis against the security of ivory. Formerly women were left with the traders as a security, but often they were not redeemed; as a result of losses thus suffered the traders decided to insist on ivory.[11]

Cotton cloth was used extensively as a medium of exchange in Benguela. First the natives sold their ivory or wax for the cotton cloth, then the latter was given in payment for arms, powder, rum, beads, etc., "because cotton stuffs are, so to speak, the current money of this traffic."[12] In the distant inland districts of Angola cloth serves not only as a medium of exchange and a standard of value but also a store of value. This is due to its use at funerals as shroud for which purpose very large quantities are used. In order to have the cloth in readiness in case of need, large quantities are acquired and hoarded.[13]

Whetstone-like salt bars were used as a currency by the Kissama in Angola.

[8]Woermann, p. 38.   [9]Woermann, p. 35.
[10]Kürchhoff, p. 28.   [11]Woermann, p. 39.
[12]Serpa Pinto, *How I Crossed Africa* (London, 1883), p. 36.
[13]Büttner, *Reisen im Congolande*, p 91. Quoted by Schurtz, p. 43.

CHAPTER 43

CATTLE AND BEAD MONEY OF SOUTH-WEST AFRICA

Cattle and beads were the original currencies of South-West Africa during the early days of colonization. Among the Herero, before the rindpest of 1897, wealthy individuals are said to have possessed as many as 10,000 heads of cattle.[1] It was the only form of store of value and is still used extensively for special payments such as bride money. Among the Nama, Bergdama and Namib tribes, cattle was until recently the

[1]S. Viljoen, *The Economics of Primitive Peoples* (London, 1936), p. 133.

general medium of exchange.[2] The Ovambo, too, used cattle as a medium of exchange, in addition to beads.[3]

Debts were also incurred in cattle. In Namaland many of the chiefs owed traders more than a hundred oxen. These debts were often the cause of raids into Hereroland, so that the chiefs could repay their debts without reducing their own livestock.[4]

A favourite currency among the Ovambo, Herero, Nama and Bergdama was the so-called "bushmen's beads." They consisted of discs cut out of ostrich egg shells pierced with an arrow and strung. They were used primarily as ornaments, but also served as a medium of exchange, especially in inter-tribal trade.[5] The Ovambo also used iron beads as a means of payment.[6]

According to Vedder, ivory and ostrich feathers were a medium of exchange among the Nama.[7] As they were staple exports, the steady demand for them made them suitable for that role. Strangest of all, a strong intoxicating herb called *dagga* is said to have been at one time the Bergdama's money. They grew this herb which was smoked, worked into cakes and used in this form as a means of exchange. The Bergdama had to pay their annual tribute to their overlords, the Saan, in the form of *dagga* cakes.[8]

Rifles and ammunition served as a medium of exchange in the 19th century. They also served as a store of value. Rich chiefs accumulated large supplies, not for the purpose of waging wars but as an investment.[9]

Tobacco and skins are also among objects formerly used as a medium of exchange in various parts of South-West Africa.

European money has displaced to a large degree these various forms of primitive currencies. On the other hand, the advance of civilization produced at times also the opposite effect, in that some tribes reverted to barter instead of using primitive currency. The explanation is that the number of types of goods imported by the primitive peoples increased to such an extent that none of them was any longer in sufficiently general demand to serve as a medium of exchange.

The Herero adopted modern money as a unit of account to facilitate barter. Often exaggerated values were demanded in pounds, but whites were able to overcome the difficulty by charging equally exaggerated prices for their manufactures.[10]

[2]Max Schmidt, *Die Nama, Bergdama and Namib Buschleute* (*Das Eingeborenerecht* Stuttgart, 1930), p. 364.
[3]Noback, pp. 312, 325 and 344.
[4]Heinrich Vedder, *South-West Africa in Early Times* (London, 1938), p. 186.
[5]Heinrich Vedder, *Die Buschmänner* (*Das Eingeborenerecht* Stuttgart, 1930), pp. 429-30.
[6]Berengar v. Zastrov, *Die Herero* (Das Eingeborenerecht), p. 259.
[7]Vedder (1938), p. 176.   [8]Vedder (1938), p. 175.
[9]K. Schwabe, *Mit Schwert and Pflug in Deutsch-Südwestafrika* (Berlin, 1899), p. 354.
[10]Schwabe, pp. 362-3.

CHAPTER 44

CATTLE CURRENCY IN SOUTH AFRICA

This chapter covers the Union of South Africa and also the adjoining British Protectorates. In the 17th century trade was transacted with the Hottentots with the aid of brass rods and wire, tobacco, glass beads and clay-pipes.[1] Subsequently the natives' demand for brass appears to have been satisfied and its place has been taken by copper in the form of beads or plates.[2] Some of these objects continued to serve as a medium of exchange until more recent times. The Hottentots had demanded in the 19th century in payment for oxen tobacco sticks to a length reaching from the horns of the animal to the end of its tail.[3] Tobacco was a limited medium of exchange in Bechuanaland. Smaller objects could be bought with it, but cattle could only be exchanged for iron and tools.[4]

The Basuto used special beads or corals for the purpose of blood money and tribute.[5] Early colonists also paid with spirits and later with rifles.[6] Ivory, spear-heads and rings of iron, copper or brass, were also used as a medium of exchange by Kaffirs.[7] Rings sometimes changed hands strung on belts containing three to four hundred. Among the Malepa in Transvaal, clay pottery was also a form of money in inter-tribal trade.[8]

Above all, cattle was, and to some extent still is, extensively used as a currency in various parts of South Africa. In East Griqualand, taxes were generally paid in kind, even in the late 19th century. Livestock was the currency chiefly handled by Government officials. In November, 1865, a certain Apolis Bloem was appointed "one of the Treasurers of the Government Treasury and of the Government revenues like cattle, horses, goats and sheep."[9] Cattle are the principal medium of exchange of the Pondo. Fines for illicit sexual relations are levied in cattle; they are used also as bride money.[10] According to Letourneau, "the Kaffirs have no money, their cattle serve the purpose; and this four-footed currency has all the advantages and inconveniences of our own. . . . With money, that is cattle, a Kaffir can buy children, whom

[1] D. Moodie, *The Record—A Series of Official Papers of the Condition and Treat ment of the Native Tribes of South Africa* (Capetown, 1838), Part II, pp. 108, 113, 114 119, 126, 273 and 301.

[2] Moodie, Part II, p. 301; Part III, p. 73.

[3] Merensky, *Beiträge Zur Kenntniss Süd-Afrikas* (1878), p. 87. Quoted by Kürch hoff, p. 33.

[4] Viljoen, p. 221.

[5] Merensky, *Abhandlungen der Berliner Gesellschaft für Anthropologie* (1882), p. 543. Quoted by Schurtz, p. 104.

[6] Kürchhoff, p. 33. [7] Ilwof, p. 67. Steinmetz, p. 359.

[8] *Abhandlungen der Berliner Gesellschaft für Anthropologie* (1894), p. 69. Quoted by Schurtz, p. 151.

[9] J. S. Marais, *The Cape Coloured People 1652-1937* (London, 1939), p. 68. See also Steinmetz, p. 359.

[10] Monica Hunter, *Reaction to Conquest* (Oxford, 1936), p. 69.

poor parents are always ready to sell; with cattle he can procure as many wives as he pleases. . . . Finally, with cattle political influence may be acquired. . . . Cattle is money, that is to say, food, clothing, influence, everything."[11] Writing of the Kaffirs in 1927, Pitt-Rivers stated: "We may perhaps say that the cattle form the money of the people."[12]

In Bechuanaland, Basutoland and Swaziland cattle constitutes the principal form of store of wealth. It no longer acts as a medium of exchange to anything like the extent it did in the past; nevertheless owing to its role as bride money and as a means of other special payments, it may still be regarded as a limited currency. For this reason the natives keep much larger stocks than is economically necessary and justified. As a result, in Bechuanaland water supplies are not nearly sufficient and there are now many places where cattle do not obtain enough water for their requirements even in normal years. Conditions in Basutoland are even worse. Large areas which were rich pasture a few decades ago have become reduced to bare rocky slopes from which every trace of soil has disappeared. In Swaziland, too, over-stocking due to the monetary use of cattle leads to soil erosion.[13]

During recent decades the use of coins has, of course, developed considerably even in the most backward regions of the Union of South Africa and the native Protectorates. Nevertheless, in some regions modern money is still not fully used as a store of value but is merely regarded as a convenient means of discharging debts and satisfying new wants. The man who receives his pay invests it in cattle or spends it at once.[14]

As in many other primitive communities, in many villages the supply of money is not sufficient to meet all the requirements of trade, partly because most of the money is spent outside the communities and partly because it is required for the payment of Government taxation. Consequently grain is still a very common form of internal currency. It is used for the purchase of sugar, tea, coffee or soap.[15]

Barter continues to play an important part in backward districts. A pot is exchanged for its contents of mealies, or twice its contents of unhusked peanuts, or half its contents of Kaffir corn.[16]

[11]Ch. Letourneau, *Property: Its Origin and Development* (London, 1892), p. 86.
[12]G. H. Lane-Fox Pitt-Rivers *The Clash of Cultures and the Contact of Races* (London, 1924), p. 208.
[13]I. Schapera, *The Bantu-Speaking Tribes of South Africa* (London, 1937), p. 366.
[14]B. A. Marwick, *The Swazi* (Cambridge, 1940), p. 75.
[15]W. M. MacMillan, *Complex South Africa—An Economic Footnote to History* (London, 1930), pp. 167 and 176.
[16]H. A. Junod, *The Life of a South African Tribe*, 2nd. Edn. (London, 1927), Vol. II, p. 140. See also H. A. Stayt, *The Bavenda* (London, 1931), p. 76.

PART IV: AMERICA

CHAPTER 45

FUR CURRENCY IN ALASKA

THE social system of the Eskimos in Greenland was, and still is, essentially Communistic. There was, therefore, no scope for the development of any distinct currency for internal use, though to some extent blue fox furs and other furs are used for the purpose of valuation.[1]

In their dealings with Eskimos, white traders used as a kind of currency tobacco which the natives wanted mainly for snuff, and accepted at one time in payment for all services and purchases. Glass beads, too, served similar purposes. Modern money was for a long time unable to penetrate into the country. During the 19th century a gold coin and the smallest copper coin had for the Eskimo the same value.[2] To some extent dried fish became a kind of medium of exchange and standard of value, as in Iceland and Newfoundland.[3]

The Alaskan Eskimos and Indians appear to have had several units of account long before the advent of the Europeans. Their units were articles of wearing apparel, beads, or furs.[4] In the very early days the skin of the full-grown land otter was considered the unit of value in the Yukon district. Subsequently the beaver skin replaced the otter skin. All other skins, furs and articles of trade were sold in prices expressed in multiples or fractions of a "skin," by which they meant a beaver skin. The pelt of a wolf was worth several "skins" in trade, while a number of pelts of musk rats or marmots were required to equal the value of one "skin."[5]

The usual practice was to bundle together enough skins of a certain kind to make a *parka*, and these parcels constituted a standard of value for wholesale trading purposes. The number of skins included in the parcel varied according to the skin.[6]

[1]The author is indebted for this information to Wing-Commander E. A. A. Shackleton, M.P., who spent some years among the Eskimos.
[2]Ilwof, p. 81.   [3]Ilwof, p. 82.
[4]H. D. Anderson and W. C. Ellis, *Alaska Natives* (Stamford University, 1935), p. 82.
[5]E. W. Nelson, *The Eskimo About Bering Straits* (18th Annual Report of the Bureau of American Ethnology, Part I, Washington, 1899), p. 232. Pieces of stamped walrus skin, employed by Russians in Alaska in paying native trappers before the territory was acquired by the United States, represented a definite number of roubles or blankets (Eliot, *Alaska*, p. 8. Quoted by Ridgeway, p. 47).
[6]Anderson and Ellis, p. 82.

The Chase National Bank's Collection of Moneys contains what is described as "Alaskan fur buyers' trading beads."

After the advent of Europeans during the period of the gold rush, gold dust became the currency of Alaska. A traveller during the early part of this century wrote that there was no silver, and no currency of any kind in the country to meet the requirements of small change. To provide the means with which his expedition could purchase fish, his agent weighed out a number of little packets of gold dust, carefully sealed up in stout writing paper like medicine powders, some worth a dollar, some worth two dollars, the value written on the face. He found them readily accepted by the natives and very convenient. Two years later he heard of some of these packets, unbroken, still in circulation on the Kobuk.[7]

Some native tribes used *dentalium* shells as their currency right to the second half of the 19th century. Furs were paid for in such shells. Larger European species of *dentalia* were imported for the requirements of this trade.[8]

[7]Hudson Stuck, *Ten Thousand Miles with a Dog Sledge* (London, 1914), p. 64.
[8]R. E. C. Stearns, *Shell-Money* (The American Naturalist, Vol. III, March, 1869), p. 3.

CHAPTER 46

SHELL, FUR AND BLANKET CURRENCY OF CANADA

The present chapter deals only with primitive currencies of aboriginal Canadian races, Indians and Eskimos. Primitive currencies used during early colonial days by advanced peoples who immigrated from Europe are dealt with in the Historical Section.

The original currency of the Indian tribes of Canada was the *wampum* which consists of a string of shell beads made out of shells of clams. Longfellow's *Hiawatha* contains a number of references to *wampum* as a store of value. In addition to its monetary use, *wampum* was also used as an ornament, as a means of conveying messages of importance, as a token of friendship, as a record of historical events and as a pledge at the conclusion of Treaties. Any *wampum* belts which served such purposes had usually a sentimental value that disqualified them from serving as a medium of exchange.[1]

It is only loose beads or strings, not belts, that were used for monetary purposes. The strings were measured by the fathom and were used extensively as a medium of exchange not only in trade amongst the Indians themselves, but also in trade with whites.[2] It is recorded that a

[1]J. McLean, *The Indians of Canada* (London, 1892), p. 17.
[2]D. Jenness, *The Indians of Canada* (National Museum of Canada, Ottawa, 1932).

trader in the 18th century, when returning from a six months' journey, had his gross receipts entirely in the form of *wampum* beads, of which he had 14,000.[3] *Wampum* strings were also used for payment for special services, for instance to performers at Indian feasts.[4] To some extent they served as a standard of value. White and purple shells had different values. The Iroquois estimated their wealth by the number of beads they possessed.[5]

The quantity and value of *wampum* was necessarily affected by the contact with whites. As a result of the introduction of iron tools, the output increased a hundredfold. The natives of the East coast who were primarily affected by this inflation flooded the tribes residing further inland with *wampum* beads. Early in the 19th century, fur traders introduced faked porcelain beads, and, as a result, the monetary use of *wampum* became reduced to absurdity.[6]

Shells of other kinds were also used as currency in Canada. The Nootka, before adopting blankets as their currency, used small shells from the coast bays. In the 'seventies, they were still used by some of the more remote tribes.[7] Shell money was used to a large extent by the maritime tribes of British Columbia for payment of fines and blood money. Among the Haida murder was settled with the relatives of the victim by the payment of large sums of shell money. Among the Karok, outraged husbands were placated with shell money at about the rate that would be paid for murder.[8] Bride money, too, was paid in the form of shells. No marriage was legal and binding unless preceded by the payment of shell money.[9]

The use of furs as currency played a particularly important part in trade relations between natives and whites. Already before the advent of European immigrants, skins of various animals, especially beavers, were used as money by natives. Beaver skins owed this use to some extent to religious associations. The beaver was regarded as a sacred animal by many Indian tribes, and there prevailed a curious and, to the civilized mind, somewhat perplexing fiction according to which the hunter was supposed to kill the beavers with the animals' tacit consent, or at any rate its forgiveness could be earned by the observation of solemn rites in burying those of its remains for which he had no use either as food or as a currency.[10]

Skins of animals were extensively used as a store of value. There is also ample evidence in the accounts of the Hudson Bay Company and

[3] *Jesuit Relations*, Vol. xxxiii, p. 185. Quoted by Jenness, p. 113.
[4] McLean, p. 18.   [5] Jenness, p. 113.   [6] Jenness, p. 114.
[7] Grant, *Journal of the Royal Geographical Society*, Vol. xxvii, p. 307. Quoted by H. H. Bancroft, *The Native Races of the Pacific States of North America* (London, 1875), p. 192.
[8] Stearns, p. 332.   [9] Stearns, p. 333.
[10] Frank G. Speek Naskap, *The Savage Hunters of the Labrador Peninsula* (Norman, 1935), pp. 112-3.

elsewhere to show the extent to which they were used as a medium of exchange. Everything was sold for "made beaver" which was the currency of the country towards the middle of the 19th century.[11] "In olden times when an Indian wanted a rifle, the rifle was stood on end and the Indian laid furs flat on the ground till they were heaped to the top of the gun barrel; then the Indian took the rifle worth possibly fifty dollars, and the Hudson's Bay Company took the furs worth from a hundred dollars to a thousand dollars."[12] Furs were not always used as a standard of value in such a primitive fashion. As a general rule they were exchanged on the basis of an established scale. In 1748 a beaver skin was worth half a pound of beads, one and a half pounds of powder at Albany and Moose, or a brass kettle or two pounds of sugar. Prices in beaver skins were somewhat higher at York and Churchill. One blanket was worth six beavers at Moose, twenty fish-hooks, one beaver, a gun, twelve beavers, etc.[13] At Fort Edmonton, Saskatchewan in 1854, a horse was worth about twenty made beavers, a good robe two, a wolf skin half, a red fox one, a silver or black fox five, a scalping knife one, ten balls or a quarter of a pound of powder one made beaver.[14] To be qualified as a chief among the Kutchin, a man had to possess beads to the value of two hundred beavers.[15] The trade turnover of the various trading stations of the Hudson's Bay Company was valued in terms of beaver skins. Thus for the season 1722-23, furs collected at Churchill amounted to 6,488½ made beaver skins, that is, when the skins of other animals had been valued according to the established ratio, their total equivalent in beaver was that figure.[16]

Rare furs of the sea otter were said to have been the standard of value and medium of exchange of the Haida of British Columbia, until they were superseded by the trade blanket.[17]

During the 19th century a fictitious currency developed, the unit being a "skin," but no particular skin. It was equal to half a dollar. A beaver was worth ten such imaginary skins and a fine silver fox hide three hundred, a musk rat hide was worth one-tenth of a skin, etc.[18]

Spirits came to be widely accepted as a means of payment. At Fort

[11]H. J. Moberly and W. B. Cameron, *When Fur was King* (London, 1929), p. 35.

[12]Lee Merrithew, *Cosmopolitan* (November, 1899). Quoted by J. Davidson, *The Natural History of Money* (Proceedings and Transactions of the Nova Scotia Institute of Science, Halifax, 1903, Vol. x), pp. 183-4.

[13]Douglas McKay, *The Honourable Company—A History of the Hudson's Bay Company* (London, 1937), pp. 92-3.

[14]Moberly and Cameron, pp. 35-6.

[15]W. M. Beauchamp, *Wampum and Shell Articles used by the New York Indians* (Bulletin of the New York State Museum No. 41, Vol. viii, Albany, 1901). Quoted by Jenness, p. 114.

[16]*Hudson's Bay Company, Churchill River Journal.* Quoted by James F. Kennay, *The Foundling of Churchill: Being a Journal of Captain James Knight, Governor-in-Chief, Hudson Bay, in* 1717 (Toronto, 1932), pp. 90-1.

[17]G. P. Murdock, *Our Primitive Contemporaries* (New York, 1934), p. 239.

[18]Merrithew, *op. cit.* Quoted by Davidson, p. 184.

Edmonton, rum was a favourite medium of exchange.[19] Slaves were used as a monetary unit for large transactions on the Pacific Coast and they became a recognized form of wealth. Copper shields, too, were used as a store of value,[20] but not as a medium of exchange.

As a result of contact with whites, blankets had gradually taken the place of furs and *wampum* as the monetary unit of the Indians. The unit with the Kwakiutl Indians of Vancouver Island was a cheap white wollen blanket valued at fifty cents.[21] These blankets formed the means of exchange and everything was paid for in blankets, or in objects the value of which was measured by blankets.[22]

Above all, blankets served as a standard of deferred payments. An extensive and elaborate credit system was developed in many Indian communities in Western Canada, all based on debts in blankets. Interest was charged according to the kindness of the lender and the credit of the borrower. As a rule a hundred per cent was charged for a year.[23] This credit system was closely related to the system of competitive gift exchanges best known under its Indian name of *Potlatch*.[24] Until it was prohibited by the Canadian Government it constituted a most important function, affecting fundamentally the economic, political and social system of the Indians. In substance it amounted to the ceremonial distribution of gifts on the understanding that the recipients have to return larger gifts (usually at least double of the value received) on the next occasion. It was the ambition of Indians to be able to distribute the largest possible number of blankets. Their social standing and political power depended on being able to outshine their rivals within the tribe and in other tribes in this respect. To that end, many Indians spent years of hard toil, living in poverty, denying themselves the necessities of life, in order that they might be able to save a sufficient number of blankets to hold an impressive *Potlatch*.[25] If the amount of blankets thus saved at considerable sacrifice did not suffice then they borrowed more right to the limit of their credit.

The copper shields mentioned above also changed hands on the occasion of the festivities. They were bought and sold frequently, and

[19]Moberly and Cameron, p. 36.

[20]P. H. Godsell, *Red Hunters of the Snow* (London, 1938), p. 18.

[21]Franz Boas, *The Social Organization and the Secret Societies of the Kwakiutl Indians* (Report of the United States National Museum for 1895, Washington, 1897; A. L. Kroeber and T. T. Waterman, *Source Book for Anthropology*, Berkeley, 1920), p. 389. On the other hand, according to Davidson (p. 185), the blanket used on the British Columbia coast as monetary unit was worth $1.50.

[22]Boas, p. 389.   [23]Boas, pp. 389-90.

[24]*Potlatch* is a Chinook word (there are equivalent terms in the vocabulary of other Indian tribes) and means "gift". Its meaning has, however—to quote Halliday— "an elastic string attached to it, so that the gift will come back with interest."

[25]McLean, p. 14. One of the Vancouver Island chiefs gave once an immense *Potlatch* to 2,500 guests, lasting over a month, and sent his guests home with gifts that exhausted the wealth he accumulated during the five previous years. He was sure, however, of recovering what he spent, with a hundred per cent profit. (T. S. Foster, *From Savagery to Commerce*, London, 1930, pp. 168-9.)

their sentimental value increased with every transaction. The higher the rank of the purchaser the larger number of blankets he had to pay for the coppers. It has been suggested that these coppers may be regarded as the equivalents of large bank notes, worth thousands of blankets. Their sole function was to play a part at the ceremonial exchanges. Many of them had names of their own and had no fixed value.

Under the system of *Potlatch* a rich man who had a large number of accumulated blankets was in a position to loan out his property to others at ruinous rates of interest; as the recipient of the loan might be called upon at any time to repay the full amount with accrued interest, the rate of interest worked out at times as high as two hundred per cent. "Gradually the privilege of giving began to be abused and distorted," writes Halliday, "until it resembled a huge octopus which held all customs and habits of the Indians in its embrace. It was a particularly wasteful and destructive custom and created ill-feeling, jealousy, and in most cases great poverty, and it was only after having considered the matter from every angle and for a long time, that the Government of Canada passed a Statute forbidding it."[26]

There is, however, another side to the story. The Canadian Government's action in outlawing *Potlatch* met with criticism on the part of more than one ethnologist. They held the view that the system was a necessary evil, at any rate until the Indians had reached a sufficiently advanced stage to discard it. It was these competitive exchanges which had provided practically the only incentive for the Indians to exert themselves beyond covering the bare necessities of life. Without it their economic activities tended to slacken, their standard of living to decline. This was in fact what actually happened in many instances after the prohibition of *Potlatch*.

There were various local currencies which circulated in addition to the inter-tribal currencies such as furs or blankets. For instance, among the interior Salish of British Columbia, standard bundles of hemp bark were called a "package" and were a medium of exchange.[27]

[26]W. M. Halliday, *Potlatch and Totem* (London, 1935), p. 4.
[27]F. W. Hodge (editor), *Handbook of American Indians North of Mexico* (Bureau American Ethnology, Bulletin No. 30, Washington, 1907), p. 448.

CHAPTER 47

WAMPUM AND OTHER SHELL CURRENCIES IN THE UNITED STATES

This chapter, as the chapter dealing with Canada, is confined to primitive currencies used by aborigines or by white people in their dealings with them; those used by the white inhabitants in their trading with each other are dealt with in the Historical Section. Some overlapping is inevitable, since *wampum*, for instance, was used extensively by the colonists not only in their dealings with Indians, but also in their dealings with each other.

In the greater part of Canada shell money was eliminated together with fur money as and when the Hudson's Bay Company introduced blankets as the new monetary unit. In the United States, however, Indians continued to use shell money for some time after their use was discontinued in territories within the sphere of the fur trading posts of the Hudson's Bay Company.[1]

Shells are claimed to have been a currency in America long before the advent of the Europeans. Many small shells, evidently unsuitable for ornaments, have been found in mounds and graves in the Mississippi Valley. There is no concrete evidence for their monetary use before contact with Europeans.[2] Early travellers testify, however, that at the time of their arrival in America, shell money was already in full use. Cartier, writing in 1535, tells us about shell beads that were used in his time as we use gold and silver.[3]

In the Eastern parts of the United States shell money assumed the form of *wampum*; in the Western part *dentalium*, *olivella* and other shells were used for monetary purposes in various forms. Throughout the United States Indian tribes used other subsidiary local currencies in addition to their shell money. Among the primitive currencies of North America *wampum* is by far the most important. It has a rich literature in the United States, which is not surprising considering that *wampum* was used for a long time also by the culturally and economically advanced communities of the colonists. The early settlers of New England found *wampum* already in use by the Indians. Its production required considerable skill and, in the absence of adequate tools, involved an almost incredible amount of labour. Lindstrom in *Smith's History of New Jersey* says that the Indian's utmost output of shell money amounted only to a few pence a day. Its high cost of production was one of the reasons why it maintained a high value for a long time. Owing to its relative scarcity its possession conferred high prestige on its holder,

---

[1]E. Ingersoll, *Wampum and its History* (American Naturalist, May 1883, Vol. XVII), p. 477. J. K. Lord, an American member of the British North-American Boundary Commission of 1858-62, wrote: "Since the introduction of blankets by the Hudson Bay Co., the use of these shells (*dentalia*) as a medium of purchase has to a great extent died out, the blankets having become the money, as it were, or the means by which everything is now reckoned and paid for by the savages. A slave, a canoe, or a squaw is worth in these days so many blankets: but it used to be so many strings of dentalia." (Quoted by R. E. C. Stearns, *Shell-Money*. The American Naturalist, Vol. III, March, 1869.)

[2]Ingersoll, p. 469. According to P. S. Martin, G. I. Quimby and D. Collier, *Indians before Columbus* (Chicago, 1947), p. 68, while the use of *wampum* as currency developed largely after the first contact with Europeans, there is some evidence of the prehistoric monetary use of *dentalium* and other shell strings in the West.

[3]S. H. Stites, *Economics of the Iroquois* (Bryn Mawr, Pennsylvania, 1905), p. 83.

[4]Ingersoll, p. 468.

apart altogether from its value as an ornament. Among the Iroquois a rich man was referred to as "the owner of much *wampum*."[5]

Long after *wampum* ceased to serve as a currency it remained to some extent a store of value. According to Ingersoll even during the 'eighties young English-speaking Indians invested in a few strings, knowing that they could always sell it if necessary to old Indians. Shell money was considered to be the only thing worth offering on the funeral pyre of a famous chief.[6]

Wampum was used universally as a medium of exchange among the Indians in the Eastern half of the United States. It was qualified to perform that task, because it was largely imperishable, easily divisible, and its bulk was relatively small. It was accepted in payment for everything, from the biggest to the smallest. The Island of Conanicut, in Narragansett Bay, was sold to Coddington and his associates in 1657 for £100 in *wampum*. In this instance modern money played the part of the standard of value, while actual payment was made in shells.[7] Father Bressans, a missionary, was twice sold as a slave among the Iroquois and was ransomed through payment in *wampum*. On the other hand, quite small transactions were also settled in loose *wampum* beads measured sometimes in wooden spoons.[8] For a long time it was a general rule that, unless some other means of payment was specified, payment was made in *wampum*.[9] *Wampum* was, according to Lawson, the money "with which you may buy skins, furs, slaves or anything the Indians have; it being the Mammon (as our money is to us) that entices and persuades them to do anything and part with everything they possess except their children for slaves. As for their wives, they are often sold and their daughters violated for it. With this they buy off murders, and whatsoever a man can do that is ill, this *wampum* will quit him off and make him in their opinion good and virtuous."[10]

Wampum was also used extensively as a standard of value. Before the advent of the Europeans, there was no danger of an increase of its supply beyond the genuine requirements of trade. The only reason why it was worth the Indians' while to produce *wampum* at all was because time had no value for them. They would rarely produce it in excess of their immediate necessities.[11] Moreover, there was a certain amount of wastage through wear and tear, and a large part of the output was used up as ornament, or was destroyed at funeral feasts, or was buried with the dead. The value of *wampum* was not easily affected by the increase of its quantity among the Iroquois. Demand for it for ornamental purposes, and for possessing it for considerations of prestige, was very strong.[12] It easily absorbed any normal surplus.

[5]Stites, p. 67.   [6]Ingersoll, p. 479.
[7]Stearns (1887), p. 309.   [8]Stites, p. 83.
[9]W. B. Weeden, *Economic and Social History of New England* (Boston, 1890), Vol. I, p. 41.
[10]Ingersoll, p. 471.   [11]Ingersoll, p. 471.   [12]Stites, p. 67.

After the advent of the Europeans the supply of *wampum* increased owing to the use of more efficient tools for its production. In spite of this it retained a high value for a long time. This was due to the fact that for all practical purposes it was convertible into beaver skins for which there was a steady demand from England. As long as the natives were active and furs were plentiful *wampum* could be maintained at par.[13] It was not until the price of beaver declined in England during the 17th century that a marked depreciation of *wampum* took place in America. Its value was also subject to local fluctuations. Among the Huron after a year of famine it rose considerably as they had been obliged to part with most of their *wampum* reserves in order to buy food.[14]

The cubit was the original unit of measurement of the length of *wampum* strings among the Iroquois. Apparently this unit of measure merged into a unit of account, as easily as the English pound changed from a unit of weight into a unit of value.[15]

Wampum was extensively used for special payments such as ransom and fines. It was also used as a standard of deferred payments; debts of every kind could be expressed and discharged with it.[16] Tribute was also paid in it. The Long Islanders who manufactured *wampum* were forced to pay away most of it as tribute to the Mohawks.[17] Later, after the consolidation of the European rule, the Indian tribes were made to pay tribute in that form to the colonists.[18]

The Delawares had a tribal treasury of *wampum* out of which were paid the expenses of public affairs.[19] In addition to packs of skins and furs, the public treasury of the tribes of the Iroquois League consisted largely of *wampum*.[20]

Among the other kinds of shells which served as money in the United States, *dentalium* was the most important. In California and other States near the West coast it played more or less the same part as *wampum* did in the Eastern States. The shells are found round Vancouver Island and Queen Charlotte's Island, also along the mainland coast north of the 49th Parallel. They were never used as an ornament, and had no non-monetary utility. The value of *dentalium* was not so standardized as that of *wampum*; while there were only two kinds of *wampum*—white and purple—there were a number of kinds of *dentalia*, according to the size of the individual shells. The more shells went on a string of standard length, the less the value of each individual shell and also of the whole string. Kroeber quotes the following early valuation of *dentalium:*

[13]W. B. Weeden, *Indian Money as a Factor in New England Civilization* (Baltimore, 1884), p. 19.
[14]*Jesuit Relations*, Vol. xvii, p. 77. Quoted by Stites, p. 83.
[15]Weeden (1884), p. 18.   [16]Stites, p. 83.   [17]Weeden (1884), p. 6.
[18]Weeden (1884), p. 27.   [19]Ingersoll, p. 471.
[20]J. N. B. Hewitt, *Wampum* (Handbook of American Indians North of Mexico, Bureau of American Ethnology, Bulletin 30, Washington, 1910), Part ii, p. 908.

Shells to String.	Value of each Shell.	Total Value of String.
11	$5	$50
12	$2	$20
13	$1	$10
14	50 cents	$5
15	25 cents	$2.50

This means that a string of eleven shells is equivalent to twenty strings of fifteen shells each.[21]

The value of *dentalia* was higher in California than among the northern tribes situated nearer its source of supply. In Northern Oregon or among the Yurok a slave was worth one string. Among the Nootka, it took five fathoms to buy a slave.[22]

Other shells used as currency in the Western States included *olivella* and pieces of *haliotis*. The latter was in various denominations according to its size. There were dollar pieces and fragments worth twenty-five cents. The value of pieces of the same size varied according to the degree of their brilliancy.[23] There was a time when one single shell bought a horse in New Mexico, according to E. Palmer.[24] Clamshell beads were also used as currency in some parts of California, in addition to *dentalia*, and in other districts instead of them.[25]

The unit of value on the Great Plains was the horse.[26] It was also used as a medium of exchange and as bride money. A doctor charged his fees in horses, anything between one and five according to the patient's means.[27] Doeskin was extensively used as a store of value and also to some extent as a means of exchange. As its value varied greatly according to colour, size, etc., it could not be regarded as money.[28]

Of articles other than shells those that approached nearest to the character of money were woodpecker scalps. There were two different sizes, the larger being worth between $1 and $1.50, and the smaller between 10 cents and 25 cents. They were also used as material for ornaments.[29]

Unhusked corn in sacks of standard weight played the part of the medium of exchange among agricultural tribes, but usually other foodstuffs were also used in exchange.[30]

Furs and skins played the part of a medium of exchange and a standard of value among a number of tribes. After the advent of white

[21]A. L. Kroeber, *Handbook of the Indians of California* (Bureau of American Ethnology, Bulletin 78, Washington, 1925), p. 24.

[22]Kroeber, p. 24.

[23]R. E. C. Stearns, *Aboriginal Shell Money* (The American Naturalist, June, 1877), Vol. xi, pp. 345-347.

[24]Stearns (1877), p. 329.   [25]Kroeber, p. 824.

[26]J. R. Swanton, *Media of Exchange* (Handbook of American Indians), p. 448.

[27]F. W. Hodge, *Handbook of American Indians* (Bureau of American Ethnology, Bulletin 30, Washington, 1907), p. 570.

[28]Kroeber, p. 26.   [29]Kroeber, p. 26.

[30]E. Beaglehole, *Ownership and Inheritance in an American Indian Tribe* (Iowa Law Review, Vol. x , No. 2, January, 1935), p. 83.

settlers, the Chinooks adopted beaver skins as their currency.[31] Subsequently blankets took the part of furs and skins.[32] Among the Sound Indians on the north-west coast the blanket was generally the unit of value.[33] Likewise the Pueblo Indian in New Mexico used blankets in addition to beads, skins and a kind of blue stone.[34] This blue stone, often referred to as turquoise, is also mentioned as having served as the currency of the Opatas and Yaquis in New Mexico. The same tribes are alleged to have used also pearls, emeralds, coral, feathers and gold as currencies.[35]

The use of stone money among Californian Indians is mentioned by Yates, according to whom the "gold coin" of the aborigines was a long bead made of a peculiar kind of rock, the locality of which was kept secret by the Indians. It appears to be *manganesium silicate*. It was produced in a cylindrical form and its value varied between $2.50 and $25 according to its length, beauty, finish and colouring. Its manufacture required much time and patience.[36] Obsidian blades were also mentioned as the currency of Indians in North-Western California. In reality, their value varied so widely that they must be regarded as precious stones rather than money.[37]

Right to the early years of this century everything was valued by the Dakota in skins, but a skin had come to be regarded as being equal to fifty cents.[38] Pieces of cedar bark prepared for roofing sometimes appeared also as units of value.[39] According to Burke, eagle feathers were an article of commerce with a fixed value among the Pueblo Indians.

Long after the dollar had been adopted as the monetary unit, Indian tribes of the Upper Missouri continued to transact barter based on dollar values.[40]

[31]Bancroft, p. 239.
[32]The use of blankets by Indians as a standard of deferred payments is described in the chapter on Canada. *Potlatch* was practised by some Indian tribes of the United States in the same way as it was by the Canadian Indians.
[33]Bancroft, p. 217.   [34]Bancroft, p. 545.   [35]Bancroft, p. 583.
[36]L. G. Yates, *Notes on the Aboriginal Money of California* (American Naturalist, Vol. XI, January, 1877), p. 32. See also Kroeber (p. 176). According to Walter Krickeberg, *Einige Neuerwerbungen der nordamerikanischen Sammlung des Königl. Museum für Völkerkunde* (*Zeitschrift für Ethnologie*, Vol. XLVI, 1914), there were standardized units worth $1, $2.50, $5 and $10. The Pomo tribe used them as standard of value.
[37]Kroeber, p. 825.   [38]Hodge, p. 448.   [39]Hodge, p. 448.
[40]E. T. Denig, *Indian Tribes of the Upper Missouri* (46th Annual Report of the Bureau of American Ethnology for 1928-9, Washington, 1930), p. 458.

CHAPTER 48

COCOA BEAN CURRENCY OF MEXICO

At the time of the Spanish conquest, Mexico possessed a highly advanced economic system. Commerce played a very important part in Aztec civilization and the turnover of goods was very large. It is only natural therefore that, even before the Spaniards introduced coined money, Mexico should have possessed a highly developed system of primitive currencies.

Gold dust was one of the media of exchange. It was kept in transparent quills to show the quantity,[1] and was not weighed but changed hands according to the size of the quills.[2] In that form, or cast into bars, gold was used in payment of tribute by the Southern provinces of the Aztec Empire before the Spanish conquest.[3]

More important than gold dust in the ancient Mexican monetary system were cocoa beans which constituted the principal currency of the Aztecs, and indeed of the entire sub-continent of Central America. Its monetary use was noticed by early writers and inspired Peter Martyr to make the following observation: "Oh, blessed money which yieldeth sweete and profitable drinke for mankinde, and preserveth the possessors thereof free from the hellish pestilence of avarice because it cannot be long kept or hid underground."[4] Prescott reproduces a story about Emperor Nazahualcoyotl (15th century) who, visiting the market place of Tezenco in disguise, overheard the complaints of poor woodmen. "He then ordered his officers to bring a quantity of cloth, and a generous supply of cacao (the coin of the country)."[5] Cocoa beans were usually kept in bags containing 24,000.[6] Colombus came across a ship from Yucatan carrying goods to exchange for cocoa. A traveller of the 18th century reported that cocoa beans were used as money, and that their value was kept high through the restriction of the cultivation of cocoa in the country.[7]

There were even debased cocoa beans; their stone was removed and its place was filled with earth. Cocoa beans continued to serve as currency right to the 19th century. Some Mexican and other Central American Indian tribes used until recently cocoa beans as small change, the smallest silver coin being equal to forty cocoa beans.[8]

Maize was another land product that served as a currency in Mexico.[9] Yet another kind of currency was a small piece of cotton cloth called *Patolquachtli*, used for the purchase of articles of immediate necessity or of little value.[10] Possibly this was the cloth referred to above in connection with the Aztec emperor's gift to the woodmen.

[1]W. H. Prescott, *The Conquest of Mexico* (Everyman Edn., London, 1909), Vol. i, p. 96.
[2]F. A. Ober, *Travels in Mexico* (Boston, 1884), p. 328.
[3]Prescott, Vol. i, pp. 91-2.
[4]J. Eric Thompson, *Mexico Before Cortez* (New York, 1933), p. 67.
[5]Prescott, Vol. i, p. 123.   [6]Bancroft, Vol. ii, pp. 381-2.
[7]B. Nicolas Joseph Thierry de Menonville, *Travels to Guaxaca* (Pinkerton's Voyages, Vol. xiii, London, 1812), p. 858.
[8]Ilwof, pp. 77-8.
[9]T. Joyce, *Central American Archaeology* (London, 1916), p. 40.
[10]Bancroft, Vol. ii, p. 382. See also de Oviedo y Valdes, quoted by Joyce, p. 40.

Mexico had also metallic currencies other than gold dust. When Bernal Diaz landed at the Tonala River in 1518 the Indians brought hatchets of copper to pay for the beads and other objects the Spaniards had for sale. In three days the Spaniards got more than six hundred, believing them to be low-grade gold.[11] Cortez, in a letter to the King of Spain, dated 15th October, 1524, referred to the hatchets used by the Aztecs as money. Its value was 8,000 cocoa beans.[12] Cogolludo mentioned copper hatchets as one of the currencies of the Yucatan Indians.[13] Copper and tin cut in small T-shaped pieces was the nearest approach to coined money.[14] Cortez found pieces of tin circulating in several provinces. Brasseur believed that the golden quoits with which Montezuma paid his gambling losses also served as money.[15]

In addition to cash transactions, the Aztecs granted loans on security though without interest. For failure to pay a debt the penalty was enslavement.[16]

An American journalist, George Wilkins Kendall, who spent some time in Mexico in 1841 and 1842, published a detailed account of the use of soap money in that country. Soap was apparently the only form of small change obtainable in some districts. "However singular it may appear, soap is really a lawful tender in the payment of all debts," he wrote. "The cakes are about the size of the common Windsor shaving-soap, and each is worth one cent and a half—in fact, a fraction more, as eight of them pass for twelve and a half cents, or sixteen for a quarter of a dollar. Each cake is stamped with the name of the town where it is issued, and also with the name of the person who is authorized by law to manufacture it as a circulating medium; yet Celaya soap—for it also circulates in that city—will not pass at Queretaro. The reason I cannot divine, as the size and intrinsic value appear to be the same. The municipal authorities of either town appear to have made no provision for equalizing the exchanges between the two pieces, and there are no brokers' offices for the buying and selling of uncurrent soap in Mexico. Many of the cakes in circulation were partially worn, and showed indisputable evidence of an acquaintance with the wash-tub; but all were current so long as the stamp was visible."[17]

[11]*Tribes and Temples—A Record of the Expedition to Middle America conducted by the Tulane University of Louisana in* 1925 (New Orleans, 1926), Vol. I, p. 79.
[12]Chase National Bank Collection of Moneys (Plate 202).
[13]Bancroft, Vol. II, p. 737.   [14]Prescott, p. 96.   [15]Bancroft, Vol. II, p. 382.
[16]Murdock, p. 372.
[17]G. W. Kendall, *Narrative of the Texan Santa Fé Expedition* (New York, 1844). Quoted by a paper read at a meeting of the New York Numismatic Club by Farran Zerbe.

CHAPTER 49

MAIZE MONEY OF GUATEMALA

Cocoa beans were used both before and after the conquest as a sub-stitute for coin. According to Benzoni, writing in 1572, cocoa constituted the riches of the Spanish inhabitants.[1] In the same year, a merchant named Henry Hawks, who lived for five years in Spanish Central America, wrote to Hakluyt that in Guatemala cocoa "goeth currently for money in any market or faire, and may buy any flesh, fish, bread or cheese, or other things."[2] Thomas Cavendish on his voyage around the world landed at Aguatulco in 1587 and found in the Customs House four hundred bags of cocoa "every bag whereof is worth ten crownes."[3] Master Francis Petty who described the voyage wrote: "These cacaos goe among them for meate and money. For a hundred and fifty of them are in the value of one rial of plate." About 1600 an ordinance was issued forbidding the export of cocoa except against payment in coin, presumably in order to avoid depleting the country's supply of currency.[4]

Other forms of articles of trade which had come to pass commonly as money included maize and coconuts.[5] Some of the primitive cur-rencies continued to play a part in the Guatemalan economic system until recently. The Chorti-speaking Indians used cocoa beans until about the end of the 19th century. They are still used in formal gift making and their limited present-day ceremonial use is probably a survival of their wider monetary use in the past.[6]

To this day maize is extensively used as a medium of exchange. The unit is usually a gourdful weighing about a pound and reckoned as one peso. Indians are always ready to accept maize in payment for anything they have to sell, since it is consumed every day and is easily exchange-able for other things. The maize-sellers in the market-place usually buy the things they need with the aid of shelled maize without first selling their maize for pesos. Indian buyers often ask sellers whether they wish pesos or maize for their articles, or state that they have maize but no pesos. The seller is usually willing to take either, with a slight preference for pesos as they are more negotiable and more easily transportable. Almost any seller will accept, however, maize for his wares towards the close of a bad market day. Nor is the use of maize as a medium of exchange confined to the internal trade of the Indian villages. The Ladino merchants also accept payment in maize.[7]

---

[1]Girolamo Benzoni, *Travels in America* (Hakluyt Society, Vol. XXI, 1857). Quoted by Chester Lloyd Jones, *Guatemala Past and Present* (Minneapolis, 1940), p. 197.
[2]*Hakluyt's Voyages* (Everyman Edn.), Vol. VI, p. 284.
[3]*Hakluyt's Voyages*, Vol. XVI, p. 31. Quoted by Lloyd Jones, p. 198.
[4]Lloyd Jones, p. 198.
[5]J. P. Young, *Central American Currency and Finance* (Princeton, 1925), pp. 11-12.
[6]Charles Wisdom, *The Chorti Indians of Guatemala* (Chicago, 1940), p. 34.
[7]Wisdom, pp. 34-5.

The use of maize-money and trade by means of barter increased in the 'twenties and 'thirties owing to the change in the monetary system of Guatemala. The Government wanted to withdraw the small Guatemalan silver peso and replace it by a new currency, but the Indians refused to part with their pesos to which they had grown used. In 1933 the Government announced that after a certain date the old pesos would be valueless, "but the Indians were slow to believe that their money could lose its value simply by Government decree."[8] They were even more reluctant to realize that the new money had value through a Government decree.[9]

In backward parts of Guatemala eggs are still used extensively as a medium of exchange, especially in small transactions which constitute the large majority of everyday purchases.[10] In remote villages money is very scarce, and change for even such a small coin as twenty-five cents is almost impossible to obtain. At Lubnantan most trade was transacted by barter, the egg being used as the most convenient unit. So many eggs would buy so much corncake, rice or cocoa. In large commercial transactions sacks of beans and corn or hogs represented the unit of account. Many of the people seemed to have almost forgotten the use of coined money, and to give change for a dollar bill was to them quite a complicated arithmetical problem.[11] Poultry was also used for making payment.[12]

[8]Wisdom, p. 33.   [9]Wisdom, p. 36.
[10]Robert Redfield and Alphonso Billa, *Chan Kom—A Maya Village* (Washington, 1934), pp. 60-1.
[11]Thomas Gann, *Ancient Cities and Modern Tribes—Exploration and Adventure in Maya Lands* (London, 1926), p. 211.
[12]Redfield and Billa, p. 61.

CHAPTER 50

CATTLE STANDARD IN COLOMBIA

The Goajira Indians of Colombia have developed a fairly advanced form of cattle standard. It is of relatively recent origin, as cattle was unknown in Central America until it was first introduced by the Spanish Conquistadores. While in Africa the cattle standard is linked with a form of religious reverence for cattle, there is no trace of any such attitude towards cattle in Colombia.[1] Nevertheless, the Goajira Indians are as reluctant to kill cattle as those pastoral tribes for which the monetary use of their livestock has religious associations.

Cattle serves as the favourite store of value among the Goajira Indians. When one hears of a very rich Indian, that simply means that he owns

[1]Julian A. Weston, *The Cactus Eaters* (London, 1937), p. 142.

vast herds of animals of various kinds. It was calculated some years before the second World War that the Goajiras possessed at least 100,000 head of cattle besides many other domestic animals.[2] To some extent gold is also used as store of value, but not as a circulating medium. Whenever an odd gold coin reaches an Indian, he promptly converts it into an ornament instead of using it as a currency.

Payments of various kinds are made in cattle. Itinerant Colombian and Venezuelan traders who visit the Goajiras readily accept payment in this form and have to engage three or four cowboys to return the proceeds of their sales to the towns.[3]

Cattle is generally used as bride money. There is no way for any Indian to get married except through purchasing his bride with the aid of cattle. Even the population of neighbouring towns, instead of exercising a civilizing influence, has got into the habit of marrying girls by purchase for cattle in the Indian style.[4] From time to time Weston's expedition was invited to purchase young girls at bargain prices, for three or four head of cattle, equivalent to about twenty-five or thirty dollars.[5] The daughter of a poor man may be worth only two or three head of cattle, but if the parents are rich or of high rank, then her price is a hundred or even two hundred head of cattle.[6] Apparently, the value of a woman among the Goajira depends not so much on her beauty or other accomplishments as on her social standing, which again depends on the number of head of cattle owned by her parents.

Cattle is also used as a currency for the purpose of paying ransom. In one instance missionaries averted bloodshed through negotiating with the would-be aggressors the payment of a large ransom, mainly in the form of cattle.[7] If someone is killed, the family of the victim demands blood money in cattle.[8]

Overstocking, due to the monetary use of cattle, provides the main cause of inter-tribal wars which occur from time to time among the Goajiras. The necessity of being constantly on the move in order to feed and water their excessively large herds of cattle leads to frequent clashes.[9]

Although coined money has penetrated into most parts of Colombia, in some remote districts it is used as if it were primitive money. The currency of Narino, for instance, consisted of an odd assortment of silver coins of every kind. The nationality, nominal value or silver contents of these coins was of no importance. They were graded according to their size. Coins were accepted even if they were perforated or if their inscription had become too illegible to make their identification possible. Nothing could induce the population of Narino to accept gold coins.[10]

[2]Weston, p. 212.   [3]Weston, pp. 113, 129.   [4]Weston, p. 41.
[5]Weston, p. 103.   [6]Weston, p. 106.   [7]Weston, p. 50.
[8]Weston, p. 160.   [9]Weston, pp. 127, 129.
[10]A. C. Veatch, *Quito to Bogota* (London, 1917), pp. 95-8.

CHAPTER 51

ARROWS AND GUNS AS CURRENCY IN BRAZIL

During the early period of colonization cattle served as a medium of exchange in a large part of Brazil. Even in comparatively recent times it was the currency of the Sertam Indians. Hawkers who travelled about from village to village sold their wares mostly against horned cattle and hired people to assist in conveying the cattle to the nearest market.[1] The use of cattle as a store of value in Ega is indicated by the fact that, although there was at the time of the journey of Bates a large quantity of cattle in the neighbourhood, beef could only be had when an animal was killed by accident.[2] Wealth among the Obydo was reckoned in oxen and slaves. A dozen slaves or a few hundred head of cattle were considered a great fortune.[3]

In 1726 cocoa, sugar and tobacco served as money in Maranhao. In 1712 cloves, cocoa, sugar and tobacco circulated as money by Royal Decree and the salaries of the troops were paid in this form. Cotton was money in Northern Brazil and its withdrawal from commerce for monetary purposes gave rise to much complaint.[4]

Beads were first introduced by the Portuguese and for some time were readily accepted by the Indians in payment for supplies and wages. In remote regions they are still accepted.[5]

After the development of rubber plantations, trade guns became a favourite means of payment. They were very inferior weapons so constructed that they would be worthless after forty or fifty shots at the most, compelling their owners to start working again for the possession of a new one. Once in possession of a high-grade gun, no Indian would have ever worked on rubber plantations again.[6]

The Karaja Indians employed arrows as a means of payment, also in inter-tribal trade. Owing to this, Indians usually possessed a large variety of different kinds of arrows. In their trade with whites tobacco was used, the unit being a bar of three inches; also glass beads in strings containing a hundred.[7]

The Bororo used arrows for monetary purposes. Girls who came to men's houses were paid in that form.[8]

Among the Parresi in Matto Grosso it was the privilege of the upper

[1]Henry Coster, *Travels in Brazil* (2nd Edn., London, 1817), pp. 245-6.
[2]H. W. Bates, *A Naturalist on the Amazon* (Everyman Edn., London, 1910), p. 287.
[3]Bates, p. 133.
[4]J. F. Normano, *Brazil—A Study of Economic Types* (Chapel Hill, 1935), p. 166.
[5]Alexander Marchant, *From Barter to Slavery—The Economic Relations of Portuguese and Indians in the Settlement of Brazil*, 1500-1580 (Baltimore, 1942), p. 21.
[6]F. W. Up de Graff, *Head Hunters of the Amazon* (London, 1923), p. 73.
[7]F. Krause, *In die Wildnisse Brasiliens* (Leipzig, 1911), p. 279.
[8]K. v. Steinen, *Unter den Naturvölkern Centralbrasiliens*, p. 333. Quoted by Schurtz, p. 179.

classes to own necklaces of stringed beads. They were in the character of a currency and were taken off the bearer when they were used for payment for a purchase.[9]

Chickens are still said to be used to some extent as a medium of exchange. Some tribes of Brazilian Indians never eat chickens—they keep them as household pets and trade them. Their value is about two cents.[10]

Wax cakes weighing one pound are also said to have been used as currency on the Amazon.[11]

[9]Max Schmidt, *Die Aruaken*, p. 54. Quoted by Sven Loven, *Origins of the Tanian Culture, West Indies* (Goteborg, 1935), p. 478.
[10]E. P. Hanson, *Journey to Manaos* (London, 1938), p. 186.
[11]Smyth, *Journey from Lima to Para*, 1836. Quoted by Roscher, p. 357.

CHAPTER 52

SNAIL SHELL CURRENCY IN PARAGUAY

Under the early period of the Spanish rule Paraguay had no currency. Her economic system was organized as a planned economy under the benevolent despotism of Jesuits, and the primitive communities thus organized managed to exist without money. More will be said about this system in the Theoretical Section.

Long after the rule of the Jesuits came to an end, Paraguay remained a largely moneyless community. During the late 18th century trade was transacted largely by means of barter on the basis of fixed rates. All goods were exchanged against each other. Taxes were collected in kind. Salaries of bishops, priests, Government officials were paid in kind. In Asuncion everything had its fixed price; buyers and sellers knew these prices and observed them. When a housewife wanted to purchase candles, she took to the shop a basket containing various goods, such as cotton, tea, tobacco, sugar, salt, etc. The seller of candles chose among these goods a quantity corresponding to the fixed value of the candles.[1] Modern money existed, but was used only to a limited extent, mainly as a standard of value. Even for that purpose oxen were also used. Dobrizhofer quotes an instance of an altar having been valued at 30,000 oxen.[2]

It is impossible to confirm Acosta's claim that the Indians of Paraguay had "stamps of yron for coine."[3]

Very little information is available about the primitive currencies in more recent periods. During the early part of this century, compen-

[1]M. Dobrizhofer, *Geschichte der Abiponer* (Vienna, 1783), Vol. I, p. 140.
[2]Dobrizhofer, p. 274.
[3]Father Joseph de Acosta, *The Natural and Moral History of the Indies* (Hakluyt Society, London, 1880), p. 189.

sation for theft was paid in skins and feathers in the Paraguayan Chaco. Buttons cut out of snail shells to a size of an ordinary shirt button are claimed to have been used as currency. A necklace of six yards containing some hundred buttons was the unit and it represented the value of one sheep. The scope of this currency was, however, necessarily limited because of the Communistic character of the social system of the Indian tribes. It was the duty of everybody to share his possessions with everybody else.[4]

While most authorities agree that under Jesuit rule Paraguay was completely moneyless (apart from the use of money by the Jesuits themselves in payment for imports) Dobrizhofer claims that tea was used as a currency, and that taxes were paid in that form.

[4]W. B. Grubb, *An Unknown People in an Unknown Land* (London, 1911), p. 71.

CHAPTER 53

OTHER LATIN AMERICAN CURRENCIES

Cocoa beans were the principal currency of Nicaragua. Their value was fairly high. According to Bancroft, a hundred beans bought a tolerably good slave.[1]

Copper bells and rattles of different sizes, red shells on string and precious stones are said to have served as money.[2] There seems to be more foundation to the claim that coconuts passed from hand to hand as a currency in the early days.[3]

Among the Venezuelan Indians shells served as money. They were used in the form of strings.[4]

In Guiana, Amazon stones in the shape of fish or other animals were the nearest thing to money the Caribs possessed. One of such stones was the price of a slave. Sir Walter Raleigh noticed them on the Orinoco. Laurence Keymis says of the Caribs and other tribes who dwell on the Arawari below the Oyapok: "Their money is white and green stones." He encountered the same use of such stones on the Corentyn.[5]

It has been suggested that tamed wild birds served as a currency in Guiana.[6]

According to Father Joseph de Acosta, woven cotton was the currency in Santa Cruz de la Sierra, Bolivia.[7]

[1]Bancroft, II, 737.   [2]Bancroft, II, p. 737.   [3]J. P. Young, p. 119.
[4]*Verhandlungen der Berliner Gesellschaft für Anthropologie* (Vol. IV, p. 306). Quoted by Schurtz, p. 100.
[5]R. Schomburgk, *Travels in British Guiana during the Years* 1840-1844 (Leipzig, 1848), Vol. II, pp. 263-4.
[6]P. E. Ehrenreich, *Südamerikanische Stromfahrten* (Globus, Vol. LXII, Brawnschweig, 1892). Quoted by G. Thilenius, *Primitives Geld.* Archiv für Anthropologie, XVIII, p. 12.
[7]Acosta, p. 189.

According to most historians Peru possessed no currency whatsoever before the Spanish conquest. The Inca Empire was the most advanced Socialist States ever devised and was based on a system of planned economy, which obviated the necessity for systematic commercial transactions, and there was therefore no need for any currency.[8] The system is discussed in the Theoretical Section.

It has been suggested, however, that coca leaves were used in Peru as currency. Father Joseph de Acosta who lived in Peru during the 16th century says: "We finde not that the Indians in former times used gold, silver or any other mettall for money and for the price of things but only for ornament . . . they used no gold nor silver to trafficke or buy withall and did change and trucke one thing for another as Homer and Plinie report of the Ancients. They had some other things of greater esteeme which went current amongst them for price and in steede of coine . . . in Peru they used coca to the same end, the which is a leafe the Indians esteeme much."[9] It was also suggested that under the Inca Empire pepper, dried fish, copper, cotton, maize, feathers, salt and shells served as currency, but no reliable evidence was put forward in support of this statement, which seems to be contradicted by the evidence of most of the recognized Spanish historians of the 16th century.[10]

The Araucan Indians in Chile value green jadeite beads very highly. They play the part of a currency.[11]

On various Chilean islands along the Pacific modern money is not much in evidence. Darwin recorded that at Caylon and Lemmy tobacco was a favourite medium of barter for which the crew of his ship bought local products. On Chiloe Island the inhabitants reverted to pure barter owing to the scarcity of money.[12]

On the Tierra del Fuego the cheapest variety of Antwerp gin became the recognized trade currency during the 19th century.[13]

[8]For detailed description of the moneyless economic system of the Inca Empire, see Prescott, *History of the Conquest of Peru* (Everyman Edn., London, 1908), and Thomas A. Joyce, *South American Archaeology* (London, 1912), pp. 101-4.
[9]Acosta, p. 189.
[10]Baudin, *L'Empire Socialiste de l'Inca* (L'Institut d'Ethnologie, Travaux et Memoirs, Vol. v, Paris, 1928), pp. 174-5. Quoted by P. A. Means, *Ancient Civilizations of the Andes* (New York, 1931), p. 350.
[11]Max Schmidt, *Die Aruaken.* Quoted by Loven, p. 475.
[12]Charles Darwin, *The Voyage of the Beagle* (Everyman Edn., London, 1906), pp. 262 and 266.
[13]W. S. Barclay, *The Land of Magellan* (New York, 1924). Quoted by F. Riesenberg, *Cape Horn* (London, 1941), p. 314.

BOOK II

HISTORICAL

PART I: ANCIENT PERIOD

CHAPTER 1

PREHISTORIC CURRENCIES

THE object of this chapter is to provide some characteristic instances of prehistoric currencies and to discuss them in a general way. More detailed treatment of some of these and of many others is reserved for the chapters on particular countries. It is outside our present scope to build up hypotheses on the prehistoric evolution of money. That will be the task of the Theoretical Section.

Prehistory may be defined as the period in evolution of the "historic races" concerning which no contemporary written records have survived, even though their existence as races or nations is indicated by other forms of evidence. On this basis, monetary prehistory should be defined as the period in the evolution of the money of historic races and nations for which we have no contemporary written evidence, even though its existence is indicated by various other forms of evidence. This definition can be accepted with the reservation that it only applies to uncoined money. Coins always belong to the historical period even if their monetary use is not supported by contemporary documentary evidence, because their monetary use is self-evident. In fact, coins may themselves be considered as documentary evidence. In the monetary sphere the line between prehistory and history is particularly vague. In many instances monetary prehistory continues well into early historical periods for which written contemporary evidence exists on subjects other than money.

Material concerning prehistoric currencies is gained through archæological finds or through written evidence produced in later periods. It is difficult to decide which objects found in prehistoric graves or other deposits were used for monetary purposes, because the monetary character of currencies other than coins is not self-evident. Tools, weapons, ornaments or utensils which have survived are to some extent self-explanatory. Even in the absence of written records their purpose is usually obvious. This is not so in the case of most primitive currencies. Many objects presumed to have been used for monetary purposes may have been used for a totally different purpose. Thus, rings may have been ornaments, rudimentary tools or weapons may have been unfinished manufactures; bars of metal may have been stocks of the metal trade. Nevertheless, there may be certain indications which reinforce the assumption that they served as currency.

1. It is sometimes possible to infer the monetary use of an object from its appearance. Occasionally objects are found which do not seem to be suitable for non-monetary use, because of their size or shape or some other peculiar quality. Certain utensils, weapons, tools or ornaments were produced in too large or small sizes for practical use, or in a very rudimentary form, or in a corrupted form. If these objects are found in relatively large numbers and are more or less uniform, or appear to conform to some standard regarding weight or size, it may reasonably be supposed that they had served monetary purposes.

2. The circumstances in which the objects are found may also strengthen the likelihood of their monetary use, if large numbers of identical objects, or objects conforming to a weight standard, are found together, or if they are found in a room known or assumed to have been a treasury or if they are found together with coins or other objects known to have served monetary purposes, or if unused and used objects are found together in fairly large numbers, a circumstance which makes their commercial or industrial use appear unlikely.

3. Similarity of objects presumed to have served as a primitive currency with those known to have so served in historical times or in present-day primitive communities is additional circumstantial evidence.

4. Historians of the classical period, known to be reliable, occasionally refer to the use of primitive currencies during the period for which no contemporary records existed. It may be reasonable to assume that they based their reference on written records which existed in their day but which have disappeared since. Or they may have based their reference on information which had survived in tradition during the comparatively brief period which had separated them from the time of the alleged use of the currencies concerned.

5. The mythology of early races contains frequent references to prehistoric currencies. Likewise, epics or legends, the historical foundations of which are partly obscure, contain such references. Without accepting them uncritically, they may indicate the nature of monetary systems during the periods concerned. For example, the *Iliad* and *Odyssey*, the *Old Testament*, the *Niebelungenlied*, etc., contain references to media of exchange and standards of value. Even folklore which does not pretend to be anything but fiction may have its use as a source of corroborative evidence.

6. Etymological evidence provides valuable indications pointing towards the monetary use of certain objects in prehistoric times. When the name of a monetary unit is identical with that of some object which is believed to havè served as currency, there is a strong presumption in favour of the monetary use of that object.

7. The designs on early coins often represent animals or objects which **are** believed to have served as currencies in the communities concerned

before they adopted coinage. It is possible, however, that the design represented merely the emblem of the community concerned, or that it was chosen for some other reason. In fact, some animals appearing on coins could not possibly have served as a currency.

8. The use of certain objects during the historical period for making symbolic or token payments (such as the use of the *aes rude* by Romans during the Empire as a token of clinching a bargain) points towards their early use as a currency.

Non-metallic prehistoric currencies could not survive the passage of centuries unless they were made of stone, bone, shells, beads or other durable substances. Shells are found in prehistoric mounds all over Europe, but there is no evidence to show whether they were used for ornamental or monetary purposes. The same is true concerning the scarabs of burnt clay and *aggri* beads found in Egyptian graves. Occasionally in prehistoric finds there is a remarkable abundance of stone weapons of a small size or of a shape which precludes their use as weapons.[1] For instance, small arrowheads of valuable stone found in Japan are believed to have served as a currency during the prehistoric period, since they would have been too precious to be shot away, and in many instances they were in any case unsuitable for that purpose.[2] Another prehistoric non-metallic monetary system the existence of which is supported by adequate evidence is the ox standard of the Aegean civilization and Ancient India.

There is a great deal of material available concerning metallic prehistoric currencies. Archæologists have unearthed a large number of specimens in the Aegean, in France, Italy, Great Britain and elsewhere. These can be divided into three categories:

1. Useful objects, usable for non-monetary as well as monetary purposes.

2. Metals changing hands by weight.

3. Standardized objects of no practical use which change hands by number, by weight, or by size.

Useful objects include cauldrons and tripods which are frequently mentioned in Homer. There is no evidence that such objects passed by weight.[3] They are more likely to have passed by their capacity which appears to have been standardized.

In a very large number of instances weapons, especially axes and double axes, are presumed to have been used as currency. Their monetary character can seldom be accepted with full certainty. Archæologists and metrologists have tried to establish claims that such axes conform to some weight standard, but they have not always been convincing.

[1]Luigi Carnivali, *Probabile uso delli armi preistoriche quali monete* (Mantua, 1885), p. 14.

[2]N. G. Munro, *Coins in Japan* (London, 1905), p. 5-6.

[3]*Cambridge Ancient History* (Cambridge, 1926), Vol. IV, p. 125.

Many of them are inclined to adjust the actual weight rather arbitrarily to allow for deterioration. The only instances where there is a fair degree of probability that axes had been used are those in which the weapons appear to be unsuitable for practical use. For instance, in Serbia six silver bars in the form of double axes were found without a hole in them for a handle.[4]

Mounds situated in a number of places between the Département Indre in France and Berlin contained a number of double copper axes with very inadequate holes to be of practical use.[5] Various prehistoric sites in Central European have furnished bronze double axes pierced with holes too small for a practical handle, obviously only intended for stringing them together.[6] The extreme abundance of axes in the prehistoric deposits in Brittany and Normandy led Déchellette to the conclusion that they were used for currency. This assumption was based on the fact that many specimens were too weak for practical use.[7] In the Côtes-du-Nord alone some four thousand of such axes were found, many of them tied together with metal wire. It is also possible, however, to account for the abundance of such axes by their use for sacrificial purposes alone; but then, the regular use of objects for such purposes was apt to develop their monetary use.

Ingots shaped like double axes were among the most generally acknowledged forms of prehistoric currency. According to some archæologists they were not meant to be rudimentary double axes at all, but imitations of the shapes of ox hides, replacing the latter as a more advanced form of primitive currency. Such ingots were found in Mycenæ, in Cyprus, in Sardinia and on Eubœa in Greece. They also appeared on a wall painting in Egypt on the tomb of Thutmosis III (1501-1447 B.C.) showing the receipt of tribute in that form. There is evidence that appears to indicate the monetary use of axes. Schliemann found among the treasures of Mycenæ two very small thin gold axes.[8] This appears to confirm that stores of value or symbols of value assumed the form of a battle-axe during the Mycenæan period (2nd millenium). According to Hesychius a certain unit of weight in ancient Cyprus was called "axe." This seems to indicate that it was originally the weight of an axe of standard size which served as a weight standard for monetary metal.[9] At Bennwitz, Germany, 294 queer-shaped almost identical axe blades were found in an earthenware jar.[10]

[4]A. Lissauer, *Doppeläxte der Kupferzeit im Westlichen Europa. Zeitschrift für Ethnologie* (Berlin, 1905), Vol. XXXVII, p. 523.

[5]*Cambridge Ancient History*, Vol. IV, p. 125.

[6]Lissauer, pp. 519-525.

[7]J. Déchelette, *Manuel d'Archéologie Préhistorique Celtique et Gallo-Romaine*, Part IV, Vol. III (Paris, 1918), p. 254.

[8]H. Schliemann, *Mykenæ* (Leipzig, 1878), p. 290.

[9]T. Reinach, *L'histoire par les monnaies* (Paris, 1902), p. 26.

[10]A. Götze, *Die trojanische Silberbarren der Schliemann-Sammlung. Globus*, Vol. LXXI, No. 14 (1897), pp. 218-9.

Rings are also a very important form of prehistoric currency, possibly the most important form. They appear to have been used in Egypt since the pre-dynastic period (4th millenium B.C.). They were found in the treasuries of Mycenæ[11] and in the Palace of Knossos in Crete. Ancient German mythology contains references to rings serving as payment of reward, tribute and ransom.[12] Bronze rings have been found in large numbers in prehistoric deposits. Some 700 were found in Silesia, 1,200 in Hauteville, Switzerland and 542 in Krendorf, Bohemia.[13] In Ireland, brass rings were found in immense quantities.[14] Indeed, rings have been found among prehistoric remains in most countries of Europe and the Near East. In Bohemia and Hungary open bronze and copper rings were found which were too large for ornamental use.[15]

The claim that such rings had served as money is by no means uncontested. According to many archæologists they were merely ornaments, or a convenient way of storing metals. In some cases the fact that the rings are very crudely finished reduces, however, the likelihood of their ornamental use. Another piece of evidence tending to reinforce the claim the prehistoric rings were used for monetary purposes is their known monetary use in historical times in Egypt and elsewhere. The large number of rings found in the same spot in many deposits seems to indicate that they served at any rate as a store of value. Last but by no means least, the use of rings in present-day or recent primitive communities appears to confirm their monetary use in prehistoric periods. In particular, open rings known as *manillas* used as currency throughout West Africa are nearly identical with those used in Ireland in Celtic times. Some of the open rings simply consist of bent pieces of wire. In Ireland, for instance, a number of small gold rings were made of gold wire of even thickness cut into lengths of equal weight and bent into shape.[16] In many instances the wire is not made into the shape of plain rings but into spirals or coils. In Mycenæ, together with gold rings, gold wire, both round and square, was also found.[17] Gold, bronze and sometimes silver spirals were found together with bars and Roman coins in various deposits in Central Europe.[18] In Sweden, too, gold wire in spirals was found buried, obviously serving monetary purposes.[19]

[11]Schliemann, p. 403.

[12]M. Much, *Baugen und Ringen—Eine Studie über das Ringgeld und seinen Gebrauch bei den Germanen. Mitteilungen der Anthropologischen Gesellschaft* (Vienna, 1879), Vol. IX, p. 118.

[13]K. Regling, p. 215.

[14]Sir William Betham, *On the Ring Money of the Celtae and their System of Weights* (Transactions of the Royal Irish Academy, May 23rd and June 27th, 1836) (Dublin, 1837), Vol. XVII, p. 11.

[15]R. Forrer, *Die aegyptischen, kretischen, phoenikischen, etc. Gewichte und Masse der europäischen Kupfer-, Bronze-, und Eisengeit. Grundlagen zur Schaffung einer prähistorischen Metrologie (Jahrbuch der Gesellschaft für lotharingische Geschichte und Altertumskunde.* Metz, 1906), Vol. XVIII, p. 46.

[16]Betham, p. 10.   [17]Schliemann, p. 403.   [18]Regling, p. 215.

[19]Oscar Montelius, *Die Kultur Schwedens in Vorchristlicher Zeit.* 2nd Edn. (Berlin, 1885), p. 125.

Unstamped metallic bars are yet other instances of prehistoric currencies. The best-known instance is the discovery of six silver bars by
Schliemann in the second lowest layer of the Hill of Hissarlik. He considered this layer to be the remains of Homeric Troy, so that on this
assumption the bars must have originated around the 14th century B.C.
These bars are tongue shaped.[20] In Ancient Britain (1st century B.C.) the
iron bars referred to by Julius Cæsar as serving for currency assumed the
form of unfinished swords.[21] Dumps and drops of precious metals may
also be included among the various forms of ingot currency.[22] There
were, for example, what Robert Eisler describes as proto-monetary
silver dumps found in Knossos.[23] Finally, broken or chopped metals
are also assumed to have been used as a medium of exchange by weight
during prehistoric periods.

North Alpine Celtic finds include gold dumps which may have been
used for monetary purposes. Among the objects left behind by the lake
dwellers of La Tène, Switzerland, there are date-shaped lumps of gold,
and also similarly shaped lumps of bronze, which are believed to have
been used as currency during the 1st century B.C.[24]

An even more advanced form of prehistoric currency is represented
by the various discs and roundels found by Schliemann in Mycenæ,[25]
and by other archæologists. These objects indicate a distinct progress
towards coinage. They do not appear to have served any practical non-
monetary purpose, and approach therefore the idea of modern money.
All that was needed to achieve this end was the seal of some authority
to guarantee the weight and fineness of these primitive coins. Indeed, it
is conceivable that the uniform design of these discs and roundels implied such a guarantee. This guarantee was actually expressed by means
of a punchmark in the 7th century B.C. in Lydia. And since King Gyges
(686-656 B.C.), to whom the invention of the first coins is attributed, is a
legendary rather than an historical figure, it may be said that coinage
actually originated in prehistory.

The evidence referred to above is admittedly too scant and too vague
to indicate the way in which the various supposed monetary systems
worked. But then, by its very nature prehistory cannot be expected to
convey information of a character that can be conveyed only by
written text. For this reason, prehistoric currencies are of archæological

[20]Götze, pp. 215-6.

[21]Julius Cæsar, De Bello Gallico, V, XII.

[22]Sir Arthur Evans, Minoan Weights and Mediums of Currency from Crete,
Mycenæ and Cyprus (Corolla Numismatica—Essays in honour of Barclay V. Head,
London, 1906), p. 354.

[23]Robert Eisler, The introduction of the Cadmeian Alphabet into the Ancient
world (Journal of the Royal Asiatic Society, 1923), p. 54.

[24]R. Forrer, Keltisches Münzwesen (Reallexikon der Vorgeschichte, Berlin, 1926),
Vol. VI, p. 303.

[25]I. N. Svoronos, Les premiers monnaies (Revue Belge de Numismatique, Brussels,
1908), p. 440.

rather than of economic interest, even though they assist towards the elaboration of theories on the origin of money and the early phases of its evolution.

CHAPTER 2

COPPER UNIT OF ACCOUNT IN ANCIENT EGYPT

Information about the monetary system of Ancient Egypt leaves much to be desired. Egyptologists dealing with the subject base their conclusions mostly on a small number of instances shown by documentary evidence, spread over the entire period of Ancient Egypt covering over 3,000 years. In most instances some uncertainty prevails even about the meaning of the scant texts available on the subject, owing to discrepancies in transliteration and translation. In any case there are big blanks between the facts; for periods running into many centuries no information whatever survived concerning the monetary system.

All students of Ancient Egypt agree that money played a very limited part in her economic life. The large majority of the ordinary people had probably existed without the use of money in any form, and it must have played a subordinate part even in the life of the minority that employed it to some extent. While during the more advanced period contact with other countries must have led to the use of money in foreign trade to some extent, in internal economy money remained of relatively small importance almost until the end of the Empire. The reason usually given for this is that Ancient Egypt had a controlled economy under which the productive activities of the population were planned by the Government which also managed the distribution of the proceeds of production.

Taxation was levied in kind, presumably because it was easier to collect. Everybody had to contribute to the Treasury a certain percentage of his output, whatever that happened to be. As a result of this system the Government accumulated vast quantities of goods of every kind, and these supplies were distributed among those dependent on the Government.[1] The possession of large reserves of goods gave the Government immense economic power in addition to its political power. The redistribution of the wide variety of objects collected in taxation constituted one of the most important functions of the Egyptian State. The word which Egyptologists usually translated "subject" means literally "eater of rations."[2] This does not mean that in Egypt everybody depended on the rations distributed by the Government. The peasants lived on the products of their labour—whatever was left over after the ruthless collection of heavy taxation in kind. There were independent

[1] G. Maspero, *The Dawn of Civilization* (London, 1894), p. 284.
[2] E. J. Simcox, *Primitive Civilizations* (London, 1894), Vol. I, p. 68.

merchants, artisans, artists. There were autonomous feudal estates, more or less self-sufficient. It was the army of scribes, priests, soldiers, artisans in the cities, Court functionaries and the town populations in general, that were recipients of rations allocated to them by the administrative machine of Pharaoh.

Above all, the large number of workmen engaged in public works, slaves or conscripts, were fed and clothed with the aid of these allocations. By far the most important of these public works during the old Empire was, apart from the construction of dams and other works for the irrigation of the Nile, the construction of the Pyramids and temples.

It is a frequently repeated commonplace that the Kings of the IVth Dynasty (c. 3100-2965 B.C.) had reduced their country to poverty by exhausting the Treasury in building pyramids, temples and other non-productive monuments. The meaning of this statement should be clearly understood. Under the Egyptian economic system there was no need for the kings to use financial resources to finance such public works. They were executed with the aid of slave labour or conscript labour, and the workmen were fed out of the proceeds of taxation in kind. Financial resources proper did not have to play any part, except in so far as the decoration of temples or tombs required imported materials or the work of free artists or artisans.

Nevertheless, the view that excessive public works had exhausted the resources of the Empire and had led to the downfall of the IVth Dynasty is substantially correct. It simply means that the granaries and other storehouses of the Treasury had become depleted, because an unduly large proportion of workmen was engaged in public works instead of being engaged in agricultural or industrial production, and an unduly large proportion of the goods collected from the rest of the population had to be used up in feeding them.[3] In this respect Ancient Egypt's position did not differ fundamentally from that of modern communities with a fully developed money economy. In our days, as then, a country is apt to become depleted of consumers' goods if an unduly large proportion of its productive capacity is devoted to unproductive public expenditure, or even on productive capital expenditure if it does not increase immediately the output of consumers' goods. The difference is that, thanks to our modern methods of production, it now takes less time to make good the deficiency in consumers' supplies than it did in Ancient Egypt.

To judge by the above description, it might appear as though the economy of Ancient Egypt was entirely moneyless. In reality this was not so. Money played a certain part in Egyptian economy. There was a fair amount of trade, judging by the frequent representation of market scenes on wall paintings and references to them in documents. Most of

[3]This aspect of the economics of Pyramid building was clearly brought out by Simcox (pp. 68-70).

the objects which changed hands at markets were goods for simple everyday requirements; they changed hands mainly by way of barter. For instance, a pair of sandals was offered for a string of beads or for some measures of grain.[4] To a large extent, however, a common denominator was used to facilitate the barter. This common denominator was the unit of weight of copper, the *uten*, or *utnu*, or *deben*, or *tabnu*, (as it is variously called by various writers), and its sub-division the *kit*, or *chat*, or *kedet*.

Writers dealing with this subject disagree about the role played by this unit. According to Maspero, copper and gold rings representing a multiple or sub-division of the units of weight, actually served as a medium of exchange.[5] In small transactions payment was made, he claims, in the form of such rings. It was only in large transactions that payment was made in goods specified in a sort of invoice in which beds, sticks, honey, oil, big axes, and garments all figured as equivalents for a bull.[6] All these objects were reduced to the common denominator, their value in terms of *deben* or *chat*. For instance, an ox was purchased for a hundred and twenty *deben*; payment included an ornamental stick worth twenty-five *deben*, a simpler stick worth twelve *deben*, eleven jugs of oil worth ten *deben*, etc. Various types of sticks or staves recur so regularly in these invoices of barter[7] that it is permissible to speculate whether they constituted a limited medium of exchange. A widely-quoted transaction was the sale of a house by a scribe to a priest. The price was paid in various pieces of furniture valued in terms of *chat*.[8]

It is thus beyond doubt that metals played the part of a standard of value. The question is to what extent metals, either in the form of rings or in other form, played the part of a medium of exchange. According to some authors both *deben* and *chat* were units of weight pure and simple. This seems somewhat doubtful, however, in view of the fact that in many inventories the units representing the weight of various kinds of metals and other objects or materials are added together in a grand total.[9] There would be no point in adding together the weight of gold, silver, copper and malachite without allowing for the difference in their

[4]P. Montet, *Les Scènes de la Vie Privée dans les Tombeaux Egyptiens de l'Ancien Empire* (Paris, 1925), pp. 323-325.

[5]Maspero, p. 324. According to E. Meyer, *Kleine Schriften* (Halle, 1924) stone weights of 3, 4, 6, 50 rings were found. According to Brandis (*Das Münz-, Mass-, und Gewichtswesen in Vorderasien*, Berlin, 1866, p. 182), rings of gold, such as those in the Leyden Museum, were used as a basis of exchange. Montet (*La vie quotidienne en Egypte au temps des Ramsès*, Paris, 1946, p. 168) thinks the monetary use of metals increased after the release of large accumulations through the pillage of tombs and temples during the period of decline.

[6]Maspero, p. 324.

[7]A. Ermann and H. Ranke, *Aegypten und aegyptisches Leben im Altertum* (Tübingen, 1924), p. 590.

[8]J. Pirenne, *Histoire des Institutions et du Droit Privé de l'Ancienne Egypte* (Brussels, 1934), Vol. II, p. 343.

[9]J. H. Breasted, *Ancient Records of Egypt* (Chicago, 1906), Vol. IV, pp. 365-6.

relative value. It seems more probable that the unit represented the weight of one metal only and the figures relating to the other metals represented their equivalent in terms of the weight of that metal.[10]

All authors agree that when metals were actually used in payment they were weighed on each occasion. There were no stamped rings or ingots which were accepted by tale. Egypt was very late in adopting coinage and continued to use uncoined metal in her commercial transactions long after other Mediterranean countries had adopted coinage. It was not until her invasion by Persia (525 B.C.) and subsequently by Alexander (322 B.C.) that coinage was introduced. Until then, and to a large extent even during the period of Persian occupation, coins that found their way into Egypt were chopped up and changed hands according to weight, in the same way as in Madagascar in modern times.

Originally copper was probably the main, if not the only, monetary metal. Several writers on the subject conceived the notion that copper in the form of rings or bent wire, constituted the circulating medium of Egypt. They based this view on a mistaken idea about the volume of copper that was available for monetary purposes, or indeed for any purpose. The German Egyptologist Lepsius was largely responsible for giving rise to this misconception by making an exaggerated estimate of the copper output of the Sinai Peninsula. Subsequent investigations of the slack heaps by mining and metallurgical experts have led to the conclusion, however, that these copper mines could only have yielded relatively modest quantities of metal.[11] Some experts even hold the view that the total output of these mines over the entire period could not have exceeded a few thousand tons.[12] Evidently, even though copper was a precious metal, such a relatively small quantity could not have sufficed to serve as a circulating medium in the Egyptian Empire during a long period, especially as a large part of the output was used for non-monetary purposes.

There is also written evidence to indicate that in one period at any rate copper was a very scarce metal in Egypt. In a letter of the King of Elishah (Cyprus) to the King of Egypt, written during the 14th century B.C., the former informed the latter that "a present to my brother I have sent . . . as copper (or bronze) is not common in thy midst."[13] In this and many other texts, copper and bronze is expressed by the same word, so that it is impossible to say which metal was referred to.

[10]J. B. McLean takes the view that the *deben* expressed not only weight but the result of a calculation of weight and bulk, indicating the gold contents of the objects. (*The Origin of Weight*. Numismatic Chronicle, 4th Series, London, 1912, Vol. XII, pp. 340-1.)

[11]This question was carefully re-examined by Rickard, J. de Morgan, and more recently by A. Lucas, *Copper in Ancient Egypt* (Journal of Egyptian Archæology, Vol. XIII, 1927).

[12]A. Lucas, *op. cit.*, claims that the total of copper objects found in Egypt by archæological research weighs barely a few tons.

[13]C. R. Conder, *The Tell el Amarna Tablets* (London. 1893), pp. 171-3.

To some extent at any rate copper was actually used, however, as a means of payment. According to the Papyrus Anastasi a grant of a hundred *uten* of copper was distributed to the garrison of the fortified town of Pa-Ramses in lower Egypt in order to enable the men to celebrate the visit of King Minephtah (XIXth Dynasty, c. 1225 B.C.).[14] In all probability, however, the volume of copper available was not nearly sufficient to cover the requirements of the limited volume of trade transacted. This may account for the fact that copper was used mainly as a standard of value in which payments were calculated but not actually made.

The fact that copper was not widely used for payment seems to be indicated by its complete absence from the only tax list we possess. It was found in the tomb of Rekhmire, Vizier during the reign of Thutmosis III (15th century B.C.) near Thebes. The taxes paid over to him by local officials in Upper Egypt included gold, hides, apes, bows, staves of cedarwood, chests of linen, oxen, silver, bead necklaces, garments, grain, calves, pigeons, honey, loaves and many other objects, but no copper.[15] It stands to reason that, had copper been in common monetary use, some of the taxpayers would have contributed their dues in that form.

Evidence of actual payment in copper is indeed very scant. There is the instance of Amenem Epe's letter instructing his pupil Pives to pay over to the Temple of Heliopolis fifty *debens* of copper.[16] It seems possible that the various wall-paintings showing market scenes in which metal rings were exchanged are concerned with payment made in copper rings. During the New Empire (c. 1580-525 B.C.) there was evidence of increased use of copper, judging by the large quantities shown in lists of Pharaoh's contributions to the Temple.[17]

Regarding the shape in which copper was used as currency, there is reason to believe that originally it was coils of copper wire. The hieroglyphic sign for money is, in fact, the ideograph of a bent wire. Nevertheless the ring form must have been adopted at any early stage, in fact the term *deben* which was already in use in the Old Empire, means "circular" or "encircling."[18] In tombs of the first four Dynasties stone weights were found in terms of *deben*.[19] The rings were not stamped but weighed on each occasion, even though they conformed to some standard. A wall painting in Thebes from the time of Thutmosis III (1501-1447 B.C.) shows the weighing of such rings. They continued to be used during the Middle Kingdom and the New Empire.[20] Subsequently ingots of various shape were used, also chopped coins and scrap metal.

[14]François Lenormant, *La Monnaie dans l'Antiquité* (Paris, 1878), Vol. I, p. 95.
[15]Breasted, Vol. II, pp. 718-745.   [16]Ermann and Ranke, p. 137.
[17]Breasted, Vol. IV, pp. 363-5.
[18]Arthur E. B. Weigall, *Catalogue Général des Antiquités Egyptiennes du Musée de Caire* (Cairo, 1908), p. III.
[19]Regling, p. 214. The stone weights bore the sign of the ring and a figure showing the number of rings they represented.
[20]Regling, p. 214.

There is much evidence for the quotation of prices in terms of copper. Lenormant has compiled a list of prices from various original sources showing that an ox was worth a hundred and nineteen *uten* (or *deben*); a goat two *deben*; a pair of ducks a quarter of a *deben*; a knife three *deben*; a razor ten *deben*; ten pieces of cloth twenty-five *deben*; five measures of honey four *deben*; eleven measures of oil ten *deben*; a tanned hide two *deben*; etc.[31] A bronze vase weighing twenty *deben* was valued at fifty *deben*, the difference being accounted for by the labour expended on it. The valuation in itself shows that *deben* was not a mere unit of weight. The wages of workmen engaged by temples were given at five *deben* per month in addition to rations of grain.[32] Temple servants are on record as having complained in the reign of Ramses IV (1172–1167 B.C.) that over a period of thirty-one years they had to deliver skins, sticks, paper, hoes, corn and flour, mostly valued in *deben*.[33] The ease with which it is possible to find instances of price quotations in copper unit seems to show that copper was widely used as a unit of account.

It seems probable, on the other hand, that gold was used more extensively as a medium of exchange than copper. Egypt was the leading gold producing country of that period. In addition to the gold resources of the Eastern Desert, large quantities were obtained from the mines of Nubia (Northern Sudan) and Kush (Southern Sudan). The mining of gold and of copper was a Government monopoly. Egypt also received vast quantities of gold in the form of tribute from defeated or intimidated kings. Gold was used very extensively also for ornaments. While the quantity of copper objects found in ancient remains was relatively small, very large amounts of gold objects were found in those tombs which escaped the greed of tomb robbers. Judging by the lists of presents contained in various documents, gold was used for the manufacture of ordinary implements and arms, even though owing to its softness it was most unsuitable for such purposes.

Above all, gold was extensively used in foreign trade, which during the greater part of the Old and Middle Kingdoms consisted mostly of exchanges of presents between Kings of Egypt and other rulers. The Tell el Amarna correspondence (14th century B.C.) contains a wealth of material concerning these exchanges. These archives of the "Foreign Office" of the Middle Kingdom are full of begging letters by various princes who looked upon Egypt in the same way as the United States is looked upon in our days by less richly endowed countries: as the chief source of financial assistance.

A letter by Burraburias II of Babylonia to Amenophis IV (c. 1367–1350 B.C.) of Egypt contains the following passage: "Let my brother send me much good gold that I may use it for my work. And the gold which my brother will send, let not my brother leave it to the officer.

[31]Lenormant, Vol. I, pp. 95-6.
[32]Lenormant, Vol. I, p. 97.   [33]Ermann and Ranke, p. 138.

But let the eyes of my brother see it and let my brother seal it and send it. The former gold which my brother sent, because my brother did not look to it but an officer of my brother sealed and sent it . . . when I put them in the furnace did not give out full weight."[24] It is not quite clear from this text whether it was the actual rings or ingots that were supposed to be sealed by Pharaoh. If so, they would provide a very early instance of State-guaranteed bullion.

Tusratta, King of Mitanni, in a letter to Amenophis III (c. 1400-1367 B.C.) demanded in no uncertain terms a great deal of gold: "So let my brother send gold in very great quantity without measure . . . for in my brother's land gold is as plentiful as dust. May the Gods so direct that although now in the land of my brother gold is so plentiful, he may have gold ten times more plentiful than now."[25]

That there was a definite system of reciprocity in this exchange of presents is indicated by a letter from an unknown Syrian Prince, containing the following passage: "And as far as gold is needful and my father has brought gold, and whatever my lord and father has said to be needful I am pledged to send it."[26]

Evidently gold was a kind of currency for international trade, even though that trade assumed the primitive form of exchange of presents. There is considerably less evidence to show what exact part it played in the internal trade of Egypt. Already in the Old Kingdom under the 2nd Dynasty (c. 3350-3200 B.C.), an annual inventory was made for fiscal purposes of everybody's holding of land and gold. From this bare fact Dykmans has inferred some extremely far-reaching conclusions about the monetary part played by gold during those early days.[27] While gold must have changed hands extensively in large transactions, there is no evidence to show whether it was considered a commodity or a currency. During the New Empire silver began to play an increasing part, but in this respect again there is no adequate evidence to enable us to ascertain its monetary functions. The records of Temple incomes in the Harris Papyrus contain an item of 4,203 *deben*, 7⅜ *kit* representing the silver received in exchange for objects of imposts sold by the Temples over a period of thirty-one years.[28]

The question is how far the monetary metals affected economic life in Ancient Egypt, and how far they constituted the factor making for progress and power. Beyond doubt there is some connection between the output of monetary metals, as far as it can be estimated, and the general conditions in Ancient Egypt. The periods during which mining activity appears to have been at its highest were the reigns of the 4th (c. 3100-2965 B.C.), 12th (c. 2200-2000 B.C.), 18th (c. 1580-1350

[24]*Tell el Amarna Tablets*, edited by S. A. B. Mercer (Toronto, 1939), pp. 24-5.
[25]Mercer, p. 71.   [26]Conder, p. 176.
[27]G. Dykmans, *Histoire Economique et Sociale de l'Ancienne Egypte* (Paris, 1936).
[28]Breasted, Vol. IV, p. 99.

B.C.) and 19th (c. 1350-1200 B.C.) Dynasties.[29] It is very tempting to infer from these facts the conclusion that, as Egypt's power was also at its highest under these Dynasties, the Pharaohs concerned owed their power to the increased volume of money in their possession and that their country was prosperous because of the larger volume of money available to finance production and consumption. We have to be careful, however, to avoid an uncritical application of modern economic experience to the totally different conditions prevailing in Ancient Egypt. For there is no possible means of knowing how far the increase of mining output was a cause of the power of the Pharaohs and how far it was an effect.

Mining in those days was a difficult undertaking. It required the despatch of an expedition, usually headed by the Vizier or Pharaoh himself, to the Sinai Peninsula or to Nubia beyond the Cataracts, or across the Eastern Desert, or even further afield across difficult countries inhabited by hostile peoples. Until a comparatively late period the working of the copper mines in Sinai or of the gold mines in Nubia was far from continuous. Only a strong Pharaoh was in a position to send a big expedition with adequate military escort to work the mines for a limited period. Elaborate road building and the digging of water holes in the desert was also necessary in order to secure the safe arrival of the expedition to its destination, and its safe return with the output. Under weak rulers Egypt was not in a position to carry out such undertakings, and consequently her resources of gold and copper inevitably declined. As a result, weak rulers tended to become weaker, while strong rulers tended to become richer owing to the revival of the mining activity which they were able to bring about thanks to their power that had already existed prior to the increase of their mining output.

Beyond this, it would be unwise to accept superficial conclusions on the connection between the changes in the volume of gold and copper resources of Egypt and the ups and down of her fortunes. As we saw at the beginning of this chapter, owing to a peculiar economic and social system that operated in the country for thousands of years, money necessarily played a relatively subordinate role as an economic factor. Its system of production did not require the stimulus of an increasing volume of currency, and consumption was largely regulated by the Government. Nevertheless, money was required in Ancient Egypt, not so much for internal economic purposes as for the requirements of wars and of foreign policy. Armies operating abroad and garrisons occupying conquered countries which had some kind of money economy were obviously in need of money. This is clearly indicated in the Tell el Amarna correspondence. The hapless Rib Addi, Governor of Gebal,

[29]For detailed accounts of mining activities during these periods the reader is referred to T. A. Rickard, *Man and Metals—A History of Mining in Relation to Civilization* (New York, 1932), Vol. I, *passim*.

Syria, bitterly complained in a series of letters about lack of financial assistance by Ikhnaton (c. 1386-1369 B.C.). In one of his letters he says: "There is no silver to give for horses . . . I have no chariots and I have no horses to proceed against the King's enemy."[30]

Gold played a very important part in the relations between Pharaoh and the kings of the Asiatic mainland. Their support often depended on Pharaoh's ability to satisfy their greed for gold. Internally, too, the supply of monetary metal at Pharaoh's disposal necessarily influenced his political position. A large part of his revenue consisted of the output of mines and of tributes paid by subject races. In possession of large metallic resources he was able to reward his supporters generously, and, above all, he was able to keep on the right side of the all-powerful Priesthood by means of generous presents to the Temples. As some Pharaohs had to learn to their cost, this was an essential condition of political stability. In this sense, the quantity of the monetary metals, limited as their monetary role was, played an important part in determining external and internal political power and stability. And since economic prosperity largely depended on such political factors, it must have been also influenced indirectly by the fluctuation of metallic output. But this does not mean that the metallic output determined economic trends in the modern sense—in the Keynesian sense, we may say— by leading to corresponding trends in the volume of production, through its effect on the volume of money available for trade.

That the absence of a highly developed monetary system was not due to lack of knowledge of the existence and working of such a system is evident from the fact that foreign invaders of Egypt found it difficult to popularize the use of coins. The Persians, and subsequently the Greeks, introduced their own coinage, but its circulation remained confined to foreign colonies and to the wealthiest classes. The large masses of the population continued to base their economy on the old system.

When the Ptolemies (323-30 B.C.) sought to introduce their own coinage, they encountered a similarly unresponsive attitude. Realizing the impossibility of popularizing coinage, the State authority under the Ptolemies endeavoured to make the best of the monetary use of grain which was highly developed during their era. Various obligations to the Government were made dischargeable by payments in grain (wheat or barley). It seems reasonable to assume that some monetary use was made of grain long before the Ptolemies, but there is no adequate evidence in support of this assumption. On the other hand, there is ample documentary material about the activities of the grain banks introduced by the Government during the 4th century B.C. By that time private banks dealing in coined money were already highly developed. The Government granaries engaged also in credit transactions of an even

[30]Mercer, p. 363.

o

more diversified character than those of the private banks.[31] These Government granaries were scattered all over the country and the Ptolemies converted them into an elaborate banking system with its centre in Alexandria. They received taxes and rents in grain and effected payment in grain on behalf of the Government. They also acted as agents for private persons. They accepted deposits and effected transfers of corn on behalf of their clients.[32] The transfers were made mostly in wheat, less often in barley. In the numerous documents dealing with these transfers no reference was made to quality. The only differentiation was between the produce of the various seasons' harvests.[33] Private persons wanting to open an account had first to pay in a grain deposit. They were then entitled to issue cheques against these deposits in terms of grain. The cheques were negotiable and their bearer was entitled to present them to any Government granary.[34] The system continued also during the Roman period (30 B.C.-A.D. 639), at any rate during the early centuries.

The example of the Egyptian grain banks shows that a primitive currency lends itself to a high degree of development in the hands of a culturally advanced people. The probable reason why the Egyptian people preferred this system to the universal adoption of coined money was partly conservatism and partly the shortage of coins.[35] The extent to which grain played a monetary part is shown by the fact that in the archives of a large Egyptian estate under the Ptolemies money accounts and grain accounts were almost equal in importance. Since Egyptian economy was based on grain from the very early days, it stands to reason that grain must have played an important part in barter and may have risen to the rank of the leading medium of exchange, or at any rate of a subsidiary commodity-currency of a kind adopted in Babylonia during the same period.

It has been suggested by various writers that scarabs and *aggri* beads found in Egyptian tombs, many of them originating from the predynastic period, had served as currencies. This is, however, pure conjecture without any evidence, whether documentary or circumstantial, in support of the claims.

[31]M. Rostovtzeff, *The Social and Economic History of the Hellenistic World* (Oxford, 1941), Vol. I, p. 403.
[32]Rostovtzeff, Vol. III, p. 1286.
[33]F. Preisigke, *Girowesen in Griechischen Aegypten* (Strasbourg, 1910), p. 69.
[34]Preisigke, pp. 128-9.   [35]Rostovtzeff, Vol. I, p. 403.

CHAPTER 3

BARLEY AND SILVER MONEY OF BABYLONIA AND ASSYRIA

Money was much more highly developed in the valley of the Tigris and Euphrates than in the Nile valley. Babylonia had also a highly advanced

legal system during the 3rd millenium, which contained elaborate provisions on various monetary transactions.

There was much more free commerce in Babylonia and Assyria than
in Egypt. Foreign trade was more highly developed. By her geographical
position, Babylonia was bound to be in close contact with the neighbouring states. Home trade, too, was highly developed, as shown by a
wealth of documentary material inherited by posterity. The use of a
unit of account developed at a very early stage. The transition from
natural economy to monetary economy advanced very far already during the 3rd millenium, and by the time of the 1st Dynasty of Babel (c.
2225-1926 B.C.) the process was largely completed.[1] Not only did the
monetary use of grain and metals develop considerably, but it led also
to the evolution of a remarkably advanced credit system. Above all, the
currency became legal tender, and there is evidence that in many instances silver ingots were actually stamped—though apparently not by
State authority—to testify their weight or fineness.

Babylonia provided a characteristic instance of the existence of a
dual system of currency. Copper, and subsequently silver, and at a later
phase gold, played the part of the principal currency, but barley also
fulfilled an important role. The fact that the weight of the *shekel* was
equal to that of 180 grains of barley seems to indicate that barley preceded silver as the principal monetary unit. From the beginning of the
historic period the two currencies functioned side by side both as a
standard of value and as a medium of exchange. They were used for
special payments and served to an almost equal degree as a standard of
deferred payments. A ratio was officially fixed between them, and in
many instances payment was allowed to be made in either, at the payer's
option. Nevertheless, over a long period silver was definitely the principal currency and barley an important subsidiary currency employed
to facilitate business transactions, especially in rural districts, in face of
a shortage of silver. Copper preceded silver as the monetary metal, and
remained a subsidiary currency right to Assyrian times.

It is difficult to form an opinion whether the use of silver as a standard
of value preceded its use as a medium of exchange. Evidence on its
former use dates back to the 28th century B.C. On a stele of Manishtusu
(c. 2792-2784 B.C.), of the Dynasty of Akkad (c. 2872-2575 B.C.) there is
detailed information about land bought by that king. The price of each
field was first given in grain, then converted into silver at the rate of one
gur of grain being equal to one *shekel* of silver. For instance, the value
of one field is given as 12,780 *gur* of grain and its silver value is three
talents and thirty-three *minæ* of silver.[2] This calculation is made in each

[1]W. Schwenzner, *Das geschäftliches Leben im alten Babylonien* (*Der Alter
Orient*, Vol. XVI, No. 1, Leipzig, 1916), p. 5.
[2]Jacques de Morgan, *Délégation en Perse*, Vol. II, p. 24. Vol. VIII, p. 19 *et. seq.*
Quoted by B. Meissner, *Babylonien und Assyrien* (Heidelberg, 1920), Vol. I, p. 355.

case of land purchase, but the price of movables such as wool, oil, slaves and copper implements is given in silver only.[3] On the other hand, documents dating from the Ur Dynasty (c. 2400-2100 B.C.), contain conversions also of the price of movable goods.[4]

As in Egypt so in Babylonia and Assyria business was largely transacted by barter, especially during the early period; and the money value of the goods bartered was only reckoned in order to facilitate the transaction. On a slab of black basalt dating from the reign of Marduk-Nadin-Akle (1106-1101 B.C.) details are given of the purchase of a field for "760 silver" (the name of the unit is not given). Payment was made according to a detailed list including a chariot valued at a hundred units of silver, six harnesses reckoned as three hundred units, a cow, thirty units; thirty measures of wheat and other products, a hundred and thirty-seven units; two dogs and ten puppies, twelve units, etc.[5] In another instance eight slaves were sold for fifty-eight gold *shekels* and were paid for in the form of a hundred and twenty *gur* of grain, five young oxen, five donkeys and one and a half *talent* of wool.[6]

Evidence showing the use of metals, especially silver, as a medium of exchange is plentiful. The metal used for that purpose was not cut into rings or coils of wire as in Egypt, but was melted into small ingots which were passed from hand to hand by weight and were tested for fineness on each occasion. "To weigh" was the term used for payment in metal, while "to measure" indicated that payment was made in grain.[7] The standard unit of weight was the *shekel*; sixty *shekels* were a *mina* and sixty *minæ* a *talent*. The *shekel* and the *talent* which came to be known subsequently as coins or monetary units, first originated as units of weight just as the pound was a unit of weight long before it became a monetary unit.

As a general rule, silver was used mainly in transactions in towns and grain was used in rural economy.[8] Their use as means of payment was regulated by the Code of Hammurabi (c. 2123-2081 B.C.), that remarkable legal system elaborated during the 3rd millenium B.C. According to this Code, payment for hiring oxen or field labourers was made in grain; but surgeons, veterinary surgeons, artisans, brick-makers and

[3] The price of a slave girl is given as 13 *shekels*. *Cambridge Ancient History. The Golden Age of Hammurabi*, by R. Campbell-Thompson (Cambridge, 1924), Vol. I, p. 520.

[4] G. Reisner, *Temple Urkunden aus Telloh*, Nos. 102 and 103, quoted by Meissner, p. 355.

[5] J. Oppert and J. Menant, *Documents juridiques de la Syrée et de la Chaldée* (Paris, 1877), pp. 122-3.

[6] *Ungnad Orientalistische Litteraturzeitung*, October, 1906. Quoted by E. Meyer, *Kleine Schriften* (Halle, 1924), pp. 90-1.

[7] Maspero, pp. 749-50.

[8] M. Jastrow, *The Civilization of Babylonia and Assyria* (Philadelphia, 1915), p. 326. According to Sir Leonard Woolley, *The Sumerians* (Oxford, 1925), p. 117, for local dealings values were generally reckoned in barley, but for large sums and for distant trade, gold and silver were more workable standards.

tailors were paid in silver. In at least one instance drastic penalty is enacted against merchants insisting on payment in the wrong currency. According to Article 108: "If a wine-seller does not receive grain as the price of traffic but have wish to receive money (or silver) . . . they shall call that wine-seller to account and they shall throw her into the water."[9]

The fact that the price of grain in terms of silver fluctuated in sympathy with the price of other commodities seems to indicate that silver was the main currency. Meissner compiled some interesting information, based on documentary evidence, about the fluctuations of the ratio between grain and silver. Officially one *shekel* of silver was supposed to be equal to one *gur* of grain. In reality this ratio seldom corresponded to the market price of grain. During the earliest period recorded only 240 *sila* of grain was obtainable for one *shekel* (300 *sila* being equal to one *gur*). At the time of Hammurabi this figure declined to between 150 and 180, while during the turmoil towards the closing phase of the 1st Dynasty (20th century B.C.), it was down at 90. During periods of famine the price of grain rose to 20 *sila* per *shekel* at the time of Nabu-Mukir-Apal. When Babylon was beseiged by the Assyrians under Tukulti-Ninurta (1256-1233 B.C.) only three *sila* was obtained for one *shekel* of silver in the "black market." Under the régime of Assurbanipal (668-626 B.C.) the purchasing power of silver recovered to 234 *sila*, while in the new Babylonian Empire (626-539 B.C.) the ratio was on the average 180. After the conquest of Babylonia by Persia (539 B.C.) the price of grain rose to between 15 and 40 *sila* per *shekel*.[10] The price of dates showed similar fluctuations. Likewise the price of oil tended to rise in terms of silver currency.[11] In general it seems to be correct to say that, in the long run, silver tended to depreciate in terms of commodities, including grain.

The monetary character of silver was reinforced by the stamping of the ingots to guarantee their weight and/or fineness. The exact significance of the stamping of silver ingots to which reference is made in many contracts is far from clear. It has been suggested that reference to sealed silver in various cuneiform texts only meant that the ingots were enclosed in sealed sacks. This seems to be unlikely, however, since often the word "sealed" was used with reference to very small sums.[12] Reference is made in documents originating during the 1st Dynasty to silver stamped with the seal of Babylon or of certain other towns. Whether it means that the authorities of these towns guaranteed the silver content of the ingots or simply that the weight given in the document conformed to the standard of weight used in those towns, cannot be ascertained.[13] Some 1,500 years before the supposed invention of coinage by Lydia,

[9]R. F. Harper, *The Code of Hammurabi* (Chicago, 1904), p. 37.
[10]Meissner, Vol. I, p. 362.   [11]Meissner, Vol. I, p. 363.
[12]C. H. W. Johns, *Babylonian and Assyrian Laws, Contracts and Letters* (Edinburgh, 1904), p. 253.
[13]Meissner, Vol. I, p. 356.

silver ingots in Babylonia were stamped in many instances with the image or superscription of the god whose temple is supposed to have guaranteed their fineness.[14] If both weight and fineness were guaranteed by the State authority, the ingots would constitute, for all practical purposes, coined money, so that it would be correct to claim that money in the modern sense of the term was invented not by Lydia in the 7th century B.C., but by Babylonia in the 3rd millenium. The evidence so far available seems to indicate, however, that the guarantors were local authorities, temples or private merchants. It was only in Cappadocia (a dependency of Assyria) that we have come across early instances of State-sealed ingots.

There is a reference in a Babylonian contract to payment of "fifty *shekels* of white silver in single *shekel* pieces."[15] This clearly indicates that silver ingots were cut into equal pieces representing a *shekel* and multiples of the *shekel*.

Another striking feature of the Babylonian system was the highly developed credit system. In this respect Babylonia reached a very advanced stage already during the 3rd millenium. This is indicated by the provisions contained in the Code of Hammurabi about debts and deposits. Judging by documentary evidence from a period preceding Hammurabi's reign, it seems that his Code merely regulated an existing practice which may have already been in operation for centuries. Loans were granted regularly both in silver and in grain. Payment was usually due at the next harvest.[16] Loans were granted in many instances by the temples, which appear to have played the part of banks. In the commercial city of Sippar, the Sun God (acting through his priests) was the chief banker. Special Priestesses, amongst them Royal Princesses, kept the Sun God's accounts and did business also on their own account. Very frequently the loans were free of interest.[17] The temples lent goods from their enormous stores, and these loans were repayable in kind. Particularly frequent were advances of corn, oil, wine, wool and slaves. Interest was only charged on overdue accounts, but judging by documentary evidence, most loans were repaid punctually.[18]

Merchants, too, were systematically engaged in lending both in silver and in grain.[19] Interest was usually charged on such loans, the statutory

[14]A. T. Olmstead, *History of Assyria* (New York, 1923), p. 537.

[15]J. H. Stevenson, *Assyrian and Babylonian Contracts* (New York, 1902), p. 97.

[16]*Cambridge Ancient History* (Cambridge, 1924), Vol. I, p. 528.

[17]B. Meissner, *Aus den Altbabylonischen Recht* (*Der Alter Orient*, Vol. VII, No. 1., Leipzig, 1905), pp. 14-5.

[18]C. H. W. Johns, *Cuneiform Inscriptions Chaldean, Babylonian and Assyrian*. Collections contained in the library of J. P. Morgan (New York, 1908), p. 18. According to Bernhard Laum (*Die Banken im Altertum* Handworterbuch der Staatswissenschaften, Jena, 1924, Vol. VI, p. 106), during the Kassite period remittances were made out of grain accounts with temples.

[19]In a judgment of Hammurabi, a Governor is ordered to repay 30 *gur* of corn he borrowed from the merchant Ilisu-ibi for three years, and interest thereon (L. W. King, *The Letters and Inscriptions of Hammurabi*, London, 1903, p. 32).

rate being twenty per cent per annum. In practice interest rates were at times higher and it was usual to charge twenty-five per cent on loans in silver and thirty-three and a third per cent on loans in grain.[20]

There were some remarkable instances of a combination of barter and credit transaction with an option to the debtor to pay in money. For example, a slave dealer sold slaves for future delivery, against immediate payment in oil by the Temple Treasury of the Sun God. The value of the oil and of the slaves was assessed at one-third *mina* and two-thirds *shekel*. If the slaves were not delivered in one month their money value had to be paid instead.[21]

Bills of exchange were in regular use in Babylonia. They were written on clay tablets. Lenormant reproduced the translation of a number of such bills,[22] which contained the essential features of modern bills:— the name of the drawer and the drawee, the amount involved, the place of payment, the date of maturity and the amount of interest. In some instances the documents assumed the character of a cheque rather than a bill.

In Assyria lead was the original currency and remained in use long after Babylonia advanced from copper to silver currency. At Assur, the capital of Assyria during the 14th and 13th centuries B.C., Andræ found lumps of lead stamped as if for use as currency. He also found roundels of buttons that apparently were used as token money by temple courtesans.[23] Olmstead claims that Assyria used proper coins long before their adoption by Lydia. Possibly he may have in mind the sealed ingots of Cappadocia referred to above.[24]

In Assyria as in Babylonia bills of exchange were widely used. An unusual feature of Assyrian business deals was the inclusion of a paragraph in the contract under which any of the parties starting a legal action arising from the deal had to deposit a large amount of silver and gold for the duration of the action. These clauses indicate that gold, too, was used as a currency in the later phases of Assyrian history. Assyrian contracts frequently substitute for a given weight of silver a number of "Ishtar heads," that is, ingots molten in the image of the god Ishtar.[25]

To what extent did the economic life of Babylonia and Assyria depend on their very elaborate monetary and credit systems? Owing to the fact that the economic system was not State-controlled to the same extent as in Ancient Egypt, its smooth functioning undoubtedly required an adequate volume of currency. There are several passages in the Tell el Amarna correspondence which might easily be interpreted as indicating that public works in the 14th century B.C. were held up unless the rulers of Babylonia or Assyria succeeded in receiving gold from Egypt. In a letter to Amenophis III (c. 1400 B.C.), Kadasman-Enhil I

[20]Woolley, pp. 117-8.   [21]Meissner (1905), p. 9.
[22]Lenormant, Vol. I, pp. 113-122.   [23]Rickard, Vol. I, pp. 153-4.
[24]Olmstead, pp. 537-8.   [25]Stevenson, pp. 43, 73, 77, 79, 81.

of Babylonia says: "And as to the gold of which I have written thee, gold as much as (there is), which, before thy messenger comes to me, now quickly, during this harvest either in Tammiz or in Ab, send it, that I may complete the work which I have undertaken. . . . And if thou do not, in Tammiz or Ab, send the gold (so that) I cannot complete the work which I have undertaken, why shouldst thou then later send anything. When I have completed the work which I have undertaken why should I then desire gold? If thou shouldst send me then 3,000 *talents* of gold I would not receive it and would send it back to thee and I would not give thee my daughter to wife."[26] There are similar passages also in other letters asking for gold.

It is tempting to infer from such passages that in Babylonia, just as under the modern gold standard, the execution of public works was frequently dependent on the possibility of financing them with the aid of gold imported from abroad. Fortunately a letter by Assurballit I (1380-1335 B.C.) to Amenophis IV (c. 1375-1360 B.C.) corrects this false impression: "A new Palace which I am beginning I will finish. Gold as much as its decoration and its requisites demand send."[27] In this instance, at any rate, gold is obviously needed not for the financing of the construction of the Palace but simply for the purpose of being physically used for its decorations. It is, to say the least, possible, and even probable, that the demands for gold in other instances served a similar purpose. The Kings of Babylonia, as the Kings of Egypt, were in a position to build palaces and temples by the use of slave or conscript labour and with the aid of materials collected in taxation. The gold they received from Egypt was not used for the payment of wages, or for the purchase of food to feed the slave workmen, or for the purchase of bricks, but simply for decorative purposes, and for "requisites," which may mean golden dishes, goblets, etc.

That the gold received from Egypt was not wanted in Babylonia for monetary purposes seems to be indicated by the following letter from Burraburias to Amenophis IV: "Now my brother has sent two *manahs* of gold as my present. Now behold there is plenty of gold sent by thy father and as there is enough sent which thy father sent, why should you send two *manahs* of gold? I have received now much and exceeding much gold piled up in the Temples of the Gods. Gold enough is sent but thou, whatever is needed in thy land, send and let it be taken by thee."[28]

If the gold had been regarded as a monetary reserve, there could never have been enough of it, let alone too much. It is presumably because during that period gold in Babylonia was used mainly for ornamental purpose that Burraburias—who on other occasions was not at all reluctant to ask Amenophis for more gold—felt he had more than enough

26Mercer, p. 15.   27Mercer, pp. 60-1.
28Conder, p. 176.

of this costly raw material for temple decoration. As the concluding sentence in his letter implies, the principle of reciprocity was in operation, and gold could not be imported without having to part with something for which there may have been more pressing need at home.

It was not until a later period that gold increased in importance as a monetary metal in Babylonia and Assyria. Already earlier in the Kassite period (c. 1743-1187 B.C.) in many instances prices were given in gold, but payment was made mostly in kind.[29]

It seems probable that, although silver was the main monetary metal, the quantity of silver available for monetary purposes did not play a vital part in the economic life of Babylonia. After all, if the Government or private individuals were short of silver, they could always fall back upon barley as a means of payment, and if they were short of barley too, they could transact business by means of barter based on values expressed in silver. In fact, following on the sack of Babylon by the Hittites (c. 1758 B.C.), silver became a mere unit of account (probably because there was not enough of it left to go round) and payment was made in grain, and to some extent in slaves, domestic animals, weapons and garments.[30] As we saw above, a large part of the credit transactions was not in terms of silver, nor even in terms of grain, but in non-monetary commodities, oil, wine, wool, bricks and even slaves. Under such a system monetary requirements must have been highly elastic. They could easily be adapted to the quantity of silver available. Nevertheless, judging by the rising secular trend of commodity prices in silver, it seems probable that, taking a long view, the quantity theory of money was valid.

While in Ancient Egypt the State refrained from intervening in the monetary system which was allowed to develop without official interference, the Babylonian and Assyrian rulers took an active hand from very early times. They were anxious to regulate prices, and made efforts to prevent rises by means of price control.

[29]E. Meyer, p. 90.
[30]G. Glotz, *Aegean Civilization* (London, 1925), p. 195.

CHAPTER 4

SEALED INGOTS IN CAPPADOCIA

Cappadocia is believed to have been the first country which is known to have used ingots stamped by the State authority. There is documentary evidence to show that between 2250 and 2150 B.C. such ingots were employed regularly in commercial transactions.[1]

[1]Sidney Smith, *A Pre-Greek Coinage in the Near East* (*Numismatic Chronicle*, London, 1922. 5th Series, Vol. ii), pp. 178-184.

Early documents from Cappadocia frequently refer to payments of sums that have been paid or are to be paid in money "of my seal," "of your seal," "of the seal of so-and-so."[2] Sidney Smith suggests that some ingots were stamped by the state, and that they changed hands above their actual metallic value. He bases this claim on the text of a bill of exchange which stipulates that if payment of the sum of forty-two *minæ* of refined silver is not made in two hundred and thirty days after a certain date, interest shall be paid at the rate of one *shekel* per *mina* per month. "On a *mina* of the house of Garu (a kind of magistrate) they shall return one and one-eighth *shekels* and pay the silver."[3] This seems to indicate that for officially stamped silver there is an additional interest or premium of one-eighth *shekel* per *mina*. If this interpretation is correct it means that at that early period there were silver ingots in use with official seals.

On the ground of this evidence, credit for the invention of State-guaranteed money must be given to Cappadocia. Her stamped silver ingots differ from the gold dumps produced by the King of Lydia 1,500 years later in degree only. There is no evidence whether the officially stamped Cappadocian ingots aimed at uniformity in weight, and whether the seal of the magistrate guaranteed a certain standard fineness. In any case, since the early coins changed hands mostly by weight they did not differ fundamentally from officially sealed ingots; and the fineness of early coins also varied widely.

Although there is no evidence to show whether the officially stamped silver ingots were legal tender in Cappadocia, there was obviously no need for making their acceptance compulsory, since they actually commanded a premium against privately stamped ingots.

The metals used for monetary purposes were pre-eminently silver and copper. Although lead was an important article of commerce, it does not appear to have assumed, as in Assyria, the character of money.[4]

[2]Smith, p. 182.
[3]*Cuneiform Texts from Cappadocian Tablets.* Plates 2, 11, pp. 1-20. Quoted by Smith, p. 183.
[4]Sidney Smith, *Early History of Assyria* (London, 1928), p. 160.

CHAPTER 5

SHEEP AND SILVER CURRENCY IN THE HITTITE EMPIRE

To judge by a code of law originating from the 14th century B.C., weighed silver played the part of currency during that period in the Hittite Empire.[1] A very advanced system of price fixing appears to have been in force. The unit was the *shekel*, or rather the half-*shekel*, in terms

[1]F. Hrozny, *Code Hittite, provenant de l'Asie Mineure* (Paris, 1922).

of which prices and wages were fixed in the code.[2] The price of meat provided the only noteworthy exception from this rule. It was fixed in terms of sheep and fractions of sheep instead of silver. This seems to indicate the existence of a sheep-unit during an earlier period. Since the price of the sheep itself was fixed by the code in silver, in practice the difference between the fixing of the price of meat and other objects was only a matter of form.

The price of domestic animals was fixed in fractions of half-*shekels*[3] (Articles 185B and 186). So was the price of agricultural products (Article 185A), though certain payments were made in grain. For instance, blacksmiths were paid in grain for copper plates according to the weight of the utensil (Articles 160-161). The wages of most free artisans were ten half-*shekels* (Article 176A), those of slave artisans six half-*shekels* (Article 239). On the other hand, agricultural labourers were paid in measures of barley (Article 158).

Penalties were fixed in some instances in terms of slaves, but in most instances in weights of silver, in terms of half-*shekels* or, in the case of larger amounts, in *minæ*.[4]

Gold seems to have been reckoned also in half-*shekels*. Correspondence between a Hittite King and a Syrian King refers to a tribute of three hundred half-*shekels* of gold, payable every year.[5]

The Hittite Empire provides an outstanding example for the multiple currency system during the ancient period. Although silver was the main currency, sheep, grain and, to some extent, slaves played the part of subsidiary currencies.

[2]While Hrozny's translation gives all price and wage quotations in *shekels*, a more recent work by L. Delaporte, *Les Hittites* (Paris, 1936), quotes everything in half-*shekels*.

[3]Delaporte, p. 237, remarks that Babylonia and Assyria counted in whole *shekels*. Some six centuries later, however, a much-quoted observation of Senacherib refers to the ease with which he could mint half-*shekels*, which seems to indicate that by that time at any rate the half-*shekel* was a popular unit in Assyria.

[4]Delaporte, pp. 222, 226.

[5]K. Bittel, *Die Ruinen von Bogazkoj* (Berlin, 1937), pp. 77-78.

CHAPTER 6

LIVESTOCK AND WEIGHED SILVER MONEY OF THE JEWS

The Jews of the early biblical period were mainly pastoral and it would seem possible, therefore, that at some time in their early history the sheep or the lamb constituted a monetary unit. The only evidence pointing in that direction is etymological: the word *kesitah* (lamb) is used in the *Old Testament* on some occasions in a sense indicating a monetary unit.[1] It has been suggested that the *kesitah* was a coin bearing the impression of a lamb or a sheep, but there is no evidence of the Jews having used any

[1]*Genesis*, XXXIII, 19; *Joshua*, XXIV, 32.

coins at all during such early periods. It seems much more likely that *kesitah* meant a certain weight of silver equal to the price of a lamb, and that its use was a survival from the period when the monetary unit was the lamb. The fact that the word *mikhne* means "purchase" and also "livestock"[2] appears to support this theory.

It seems probable that livestock constituted the principal store of value of the early Jews. On his return from Egypt Abraham (c. 2000 B.C.) was described as having been "very rich in cattle, in silver and in gold."[3] The various forms of wealth were possibly mentioned here in their order of importance. There is further evidence in the *Old Testament* to show that Abraham's tribe was becoming over-stocked with livestock, which is almost invariably the difficulty of pastoral communities using their livestock as their currency, or at least as their store of value. In a well-known passage in *Genesis*, it is stated that the grazing land in Canaan was becoming inadequate for the flocks and herds of both Abraham and Lot and, to avoid strife between their herdsmen, Abraham suggested that they should part company and move their herds in opposite directions.[4]

The quotation concerning Abraham's wealth on his return from Egypt shows that already during that early period (c. 2000 B.C.) the Jews used metals as a store of value. There is also evidence in the *Old Testament* indicating the use of silver as a medium of exchange. When Abraham purchased the cave of Machpelah, he "weighed to Ephron the silver, which he had named in the audience of the sons of Heth, four hundred *shekels* of silver current with the merchants."[5] That slaves were paid for in silver is indicated by a reference in *Genesis*: "He that is born in thy house and he that is bought with thy money (or silver) must needs be circumcised."[6] The Ishmælites, on their way from Gilead to Egypt, to whom the sons of Jacob sold Joseph, paid for him "twenty of silver."[7] At a much later period Solomon (c. 970 to 933 B.C.) purchased chariots from Egypt for "six hundred of silver" each and horses for "hundred and fifty" each.[8]

According to the laws of Moses, the value of men and cattle, houses, fields and provisions, was expressed in silver.[9] This is the nearest indi-

---

[2]S. Ejges, *Das Geld im Talmud* (Vilna, 1930), p. 14.

[3]*Genesis*, XIII, 2, also *Genesis*, XXIV, 35.   [4]*Genesis*, XIII, 6-9.

[5]*Genesis*, XXIII, 16. As this frequently quoted passage is sometimes translated as "four hundred *shekels* money current with the merchants" it is well to recall that in Semitic languages "money" and "silver" are identical. It is perhaps also advisable to point out in this connection that, owing to the possibility of anachronism through the corruption of texts of the *Old Testament* by more recent interpolations, conclusions based on it must be treated with some reserve.

[6]*Genesis*, XVII, 13.

[7]*Genesis*, XXXVII, 28. In this instance as in a number of other instances, the unit is not named in the text.

[8]*I Kings*, X, 29.

[9]*Leviticus*, XXVII, 3 *et seq.*; *Leviticus*, XXVII, 14 *et seq.*; *Numbers* III, 47 *et seq.*; *Deuteronomy*, II, 6, 28; XIV, 25-26.

cation to show that silver was also used as a standard of value, though there is no evidence that it was used as a unit of account to facilitate barter, as was the practice in Babylonia and Assyria; nor did it serve as a standard for deferred payments to anything like the extent as it did in those countries.

Silver was used extensively as a means of unilateral payments. Abimelech, King of Gerar, gave Abraham "thousand of silver."[10] The Philistines bribed Delilah with "eleven hundred of silver" to find out the source of Samson's strength.[11] Fines and compensations were regulated in terms of silver.[12] Contributions to the Temple were also made in the same form.[13] Tribute also was paid mostly in the form of silver or gold.[14] In the 7th century B.C. the Kingdom of Judah paid to Egypt a tribute of "hundred *talents* of silver and a *talent* of gold."[15] King Solomon was alleged to have received yearly "six hundred three score and six *talents* of gold."[16]

Gold was used extensively as a store of value, but its main use was decorative rather than monetary. Hiram, King of Tyre, supplied Solomon with gold for the decoration of the Temple of Jerusalem on two occasions, to the amounts of a hundred and twenty and four hundred and twenty *talents* respectively.[17] The second amount was said to have come from the mysterious gold producing land of Ophir, to which the Phœnicians sent expeditions from time to time. There is no evidence that this vast influx of gold led to any increase in its monetary use. Silver remained throughout the principal medium of exchange.

The *shekel*, which was the monetary unit, was originally a unit of weight, as in Babylonia. Presumably when in the text of the *Old Testament* no unit is named in connection with payments of silver the figures referred to are *shekels*. Until a very late period, coins were unknown in the Kingdoms of Israel and Judah.[18] Silver, and to some extent gold, assumed the form of ingots changing hands by weight. The Jews are known to have possessed scales which may be presumed to have served solely for weighing precious metals. This was the practice also in other countries of Western Asia where ordinary merchandize changed hands by hollow measure, by number or by size, and only gold and silver and possibly other metals were weighed. Nevertheless, it is believed that ring money was not altogether unknown. The servant of Abraham gave to

---

[10]*Genesis*, xx, 16.
[12]*Exodus*, xxi, xxii.
[14]II *Chronicles*, xvii, 11.
[15]II *Kings*, xxiii, 33; II *Chronicles*, xxxvi, 3.

[11]*Judges*, xvi, 5, 18.
[13]*Exodus*, xxx, 13, 15; xxxviii, 26.

[16]I *Kings*, x, 14; II *Chronicles*, ix, 13. The amount of six hundred and sixty-six is probably figurative; it must have been chosen to indicate what was considered a very large amount. It is not likely to be correct, for it would be larger than the revenues of the whole Persian Empire under Darius, according to the estimates of Madden.
[17]I *Kings*, ix, 11, 14, 28. These amounts, too, appear to be exaggerated.
[18]T. Reinach, *Jewish Coins* (London, 1903), p. 2.

Rebecca "a golden ear-ring of half a *shekel* weight and two bracelets for her hands of ten (*shekels*) weight."[19] The fact that the ring and the bracelets conformed to the *shekel* standard appears to indicate the possibility of their monetary use. This does not mean that these rings changed hands by tale; in all probability they were weighed on each occasion. Nevertheless the fact that they were produced to represent a fraction or a multiple of the *shekel* must have faciliated transactions in them. Another indication that rings were a medium of exchange, or at any rate a store of value, is contained in the *Book of Job*, where it is stated that when Job was visited by his friends, each gave him a piece of money and an ear-ring of gold.[20] It stands to reason that such a number of rings as he may be presumed to have received was not meant for his personal use as ornament.

There are also indications that pieces of silver were cut to conform to the *shekel* standard. While coins were not known to have been issued until after the return of the Jews from their Babylonian captivity (537 B.C.), there must have been in fairly common use pieces of silver of equal size, presumably without any stamp guaranteeing their weight or fineness, but possibly stamped by the seal of merchants. The existence of such unofficial "coins" appears to be indicated by various references in the *Old Testament* to the use of purses.[21] There is a reference in the *Old Testament* to quarter-*shekels*.[22] Contributions to "men of God" were made in the form of such pieces of silver. That the pieces of silver used as money were weighed is indicated by the passage in *Genesis* on the return of the money taken by the sons of Jacob when coming to Egypt to purchase grain. They found the money "of (full) weight."[23]

References to pieces of gold also occur in the *Old Testament*. An emissary sent by the King of Syria to the King of Israel "took with him ten *talents* of silver and six thousand pieces of gold and ten changes of raiment."[24] The change of raiment must have been a popular unit for the purpose of presents or payments, but it has not been suggested that it was a monetary unit.

It seems that the monetary system of the Jews prior to the adoption of coinage reached a fairly advanced stage. No reliable information is available how its evolution had affected prices and the economic system in general. It seems that the Temple was used during the early period largely as treasury,[25] but also as a bank as in Babylonia, at any rate to the extent of receiving money for safe keeping, and that the lavish use of gold for decorative purposes in the Temple served partly the object of accumulating a monetary reserve for emergency. When Hezekiah had

[19]*Genesis*, XXIV, 22.   [20]*Job*, XLII, 11.
[21]*Kings*, V, 23; XII, 10; *Proverbs*, I, 14.
[22]I *Samuel*, IX, 8. "Behold I have here at hand the fourth part of a shekel of silver."
[23]*Genesis*, XLIII, 21;   [24]II *Kings*, V, 5.
[25]*Joshua*, VI, 19, 24.

to pay a tribute of three hundred *talents* of silver and thirty *talents* of gold to the King of Assyria (around 700 B.C.) he "cut the gold from the doors of the Temple of the Lord, and from the pillars."[26] Banking and credit was not developed to any extent comparable to that of Babylonia and Assyria—indeed the Jewish system under which the charging of interest was forbidden[27] did not encourage the development of a credit system. The explanation of the ban on interest was that lending was supposed to be regarded as charity, not business.[28] In cash transactions, however, a fairly advanced form of money was used, which only differed from coins by the absence of an official seal that would make them acceptable by tale instead of having to be weighed on each occasion.

International trade was transacted largely if not exclusively by means of barter. King David (about 1010-970 B.C.) paid King Hiram in wheat, barley, wine and oil for timber and other materials needed for building the Temple of Jerusalem.[29]

[26]II *Kings*, xviii, 16.
[27]*Exodus*, xxii, 25; *Leviticus*, xxv, 36; *Deuteronomy*, xxiii, 20.
[28]A. Bertholet, *A History of Hebrew Civilization* (London, 1926), p. 221.
[29]Rickard, Vol. I, p. 266.

CHAPTER 7

SLOW DEVELOPMENT OF COINAGE IN PHŒNICIA AND CARTHAGE

Information about the early monetary system of Phœnicia is scant. Coins were not used until the middle of the 5th century B.C. Prior to that, it is assumed that in Phœnicia, as in the neighbouring countries, goods were bartered according to their value in terms of weighed metals, and that subsequently ingots, weighed at each transaction, became the medium of exchange.[1] Babelon's assumption is that the monetary system of the Phœnicians, as that of the Syrians, was substantially the same as that of the Jews. There is evidence to show that tribute was paid by the Phœnicians to Egypt during the reign of Thutmosis III in the form of gold rings and bars. The *Old Testament* abounds in references to the vast wealth of Phœnicia in gold and silver and to transactions carried out in gold with the Jews.[2]

Vast quantities of gold were imported by Phœnician seamen from distant lands including the mysterious Ophir. For the most part they were used for the production of ornaments, especially bracelets. One end of the Phœnician bracelets was left open. Such objects were exported in large quantities to Celtic Ireland, to the west coast of Africa and other

[1]G. Contenau, *La Civilization Phœnicienne* (Paris, 1926), p. 214.
[2]I *Kings*, ix, 11, 14, 28; x, 11; II *Chronicles*, viii, 18; *Zaccharias*, ix, 3; *Ezekiel*, xxviii.

distant overseas countries. There is no reason to suppose, however, that they played then the part of money in trading relations between the Phœnicians and the importing countries. Presumably they were simply objects of barter. It is only subsequently that they appear to have been adopted for internal monetary purposes by the importing countries.

Many historians and numismatists have commented on the fact that Phœnicia was comparatively late in adopting coinage. They consider it strange that coins should have been invented by Lydia, a predominantly pastoral community, instead of Phœnicia, one of the most highly commercialized communities of all times. Various theories have been put forward about the reason why the Phœnicians preferred to do their international trade without the use of coin. According to Lenormant Phœnicia traded, for the most part, not with civilized peoples who would understand the use of coin, but with primitive savages.[3] This explanation does not seem to be convincing for the Phœnicians did not use coined money even in their trade with the most advanced peoples of their period; nor was it adopted for their internal use until a comparatively late period.

According to Burns the reason was that, while Lydia and other nations which preceded Phœnicia in adopting coinage had transacted most of their foreign trade by land, Phœnicia traded almost entirely by sea. When trading by means of caravans it was important to keep down the bulk and weight of the means of payment intended to pay for the goods to be purchased abroad. This consideration did not play such an important part in sea-borne traffic.[4] It is even argued by several authors that from the point of view of sea transport it was positively an advantage to carry a substantial cargo both ways instead of carrying money one way and a goods cargo the other way only. This argument again is not very convincing. Phœnicia was actively engaged in gold trade with other countries, and from the point of view of the weight or the bulk of the cargo it does not make any difference whether the gold was transported in the form of dust or bars or bracelets or coins.

The real reason is presumably that during the centuries separating the invention of coins and their adoption by Phœnicia coins were of relatively little use in foreign trade. Confidence in the primitive coins of that period was not sufficiently established to induce foreign nations to accept them by tale. Nor would the Phœnicians, with their reputation for exceptional sharpness in business dealings, have inspired sufficient confidence abroad to initiate the practice. Throughout the Hellenic world and also in other parts of the Mediterranean area their name stood, rightly or wrongly, for unscrupulous dealing, and their seal might not have been accepted too freely as a guarantee of fineness. As a general rule only subject nations accepted the coins of their rulers without

[3]Lenormant, Vol. I, p. 124.
[4]A. R. Burns, *Money and Monetary Policy in Early Times* (London, 1927), p. 53.

questioning their weight and fineness. In trade between independent parties, gold coins, and even silver coins, were invariably weighed on each occasion, and their fineness was also tested. That being so, there seemed to be little advantage to be gained in international trade by taking the trouble to coin the metal instead of using it as means of exchange in forms less expensive to produce.

Admittedly this theory does not account for the absence of coins in Phœnician internal trade; but then her internal trade was a bare fraction of her foreign trade. The explanation put forward by Burns[5] that Phœnician inland trade was well served by the method of using metals by weight is probably correct.

Even after the adoption of coined money in Phœnicia, her colony, Carthage (9th to 2nd century B.C.), continued to trade without the use of coins. Her first coins were minted in Sicily in about 410 B.C., and were based on Sicilian standards; their sole object was to finance military operations on that island. It was not until much later (about 340 B.C.) that Carthage began to issue coins for internal use in Africa.[6]

According to Aristide,[7] Æschines[8] and other classical sources, Carthage had adopted a strange type of leather currency. An object, the nature of which was unknown to the classical authors writing on the subject, was said to have been wrapped into leather and sealed, and circulated as a currency. Modern historians disagree whether it was a mere emergency currency similar to the leather money used at sieges on various occasions in Medieval Europe, or whether it was a normal medium of exchange. Nor is there any indication whether it was used internally only or whether it circulated throughout the dependencies of Carthage, as Bosworth Smith suggests.[9]

It is certain that Carthage, like Phœnicia, transacted foreign trade largely, if not exclusively, on the basis of barter. Classical authors give an account of an instance of "silent barter" between Carthaginian merchants and African natives.[10]

---

[5]Burns, p. 53. [6]Lenormant, Vol. I, pp. 139-140.
[7]Aristide, *Orat. Platon.*, II, 145. Quoted by Lenormant, Vol. I, p. 220.
[8]Æschines, *Dial. Socrat.*, 78. Quoted by R. Bosworth Smith, *Carthage and the Carthaginians* (London, 1913), p. 31.
[9]Bosworth Smith, p. 31. [10]Herodotus IV, 196.

CHAPTER 8

INVENTION OF COINAGE IN LYDIA

Most historians from Herodotus onwards agree that Lydia was the first country to use coined money at the beginning of the 7th century B.C. The only rival to the somewhat nebulous King Gyges (?686-656 B.C.), the founder of the Mermnade Dynasty, for the claim for the honour of having invented coinage, is King Pheidon of Argos (?748-680 B.C.). The difference between the time of the assumed appearance of coins in Lydia and in Argos is hardly likely to have been more than a few decades, and the chronology of that period is far from being an exact science. In any case, the development of the first coin was such a gradual process that it is by no means easy to be too categorical about the precise moment when rudimentary ingots or dumps of precious metal assumed the character of a crude coin. Long before the primitive punchmarked dumps of electrum came into circulation in Lydia, such dumps were already in circulation either without a seal or with private seals in various countries, notably in Knossos during the 2nd millenium B.C. Silver dumps of more or less uniform weight found in the Palace Knossos bore signs indicating their weight. There is, however, no evidence to show that, even if these signs served as a guarantee of weight and fineness, the Minoan State authority was responsible for engraving them on the rudimentary "coins." The importance of the Lydian coins lies precisely in the fact that they provided the first *known* instance of uniform sealed ingots—or at any rate ingots aiming at uniformity— issued under the authority of the State.

Some historians are rather puzzled why Lydia of all countries should have been the first to use coinage. According to Hall it is probable that the idea was given to the King of Lydia by the Ionian Greeks settled on the mainland of Asia Minor. "One could hardly imagine Lydians," he says, "a pastoral people ruled by country squires, inventing anything but a new tune on the pipes."[1] Other authorities maintain, however, that Lydia was a centre of land-borne international trade, and seek to explain the invention of coinage by commercial necessity. However this may be, the fact is that Lydia was one of the leading gold producing countries of her period. Gold was washed mostly from river-beds and contained a large percentage of silver which explains why the first Lydian coins were not pure gold but electrum.

It is worth noting that the art of ascertaining the fineness of gold reached a comparatively advanced stage in Lydia. The touchstone that served the purpose of assaying before the invention of more reliable methods was known for a long time under the name of Lydian stone.[2]

It would be a mistake to imagine that the Lydian coins bore much resemblance to modern coins or even to coins issued by the Greeks and other Mediterranean nations during the 6th and 5th centuries B.C. They were crude bean-shaped ingots, rather too large for convenient circulation[3] and much too rudimentary to be accepted by tale. All they bore

---

[1]H. R. Hall, *The Ancient History of the Near East*, 8th Edition (London, 1932), pp. 533-534.

[2]*Encyclopaedia Britannica*. Article on "Assaying." 14th Edn., Vol. II, p. 555. See also J. L. Myres, *Precious Metals* (Lectures at the Royal Anthropological Institute, London, 1931), p. 149.

[3]Babelon, p. 226.

was a primitive punchmark and there is a difference of opinion whether it guaranteed weight or fineness only, or both. It seems reasonable to assume that notwithstanding this punchmark, these primitive coins continued to change hands by weight and were weighed on most occasions even in internal trade. For this reason they may be considered to be on the border-line between primitive and modern money.

We have the evidence of Herodotus to show that long after the adoption of coinage gold bars of uniform size continued to be produced in Lydia. Crœsus (560-546 B.C.), caused "a vast quantity of gold to be melted down, and ran it into ingots, making them six palms long, three palms broad, and one palm in thickness."[4]

[4]Herodotus, I, 50.

CHAPTER 9

LIVESTOCK STANDARD IN ANCIENT PERSIA

Oxen and sheep were the original standard of value in Ancient Persia and were also used as medium of exchange. There is evidence in the *Zend Avesta* that they were continued to be used as currency concurrently with metals. A doctor's fees were fixed in terms of animals or parts of animals according to the standard of the patient.[1]

The Persian Empire adopted the gold *stater* as its monetary unit, and it became the first gold coin of international standing. Nevertheless primitive currencies continued to be used to a large degree in various parts of the vast Persian Empire. Monetary conditions were far from uniform. The Kings of Persia allowed various conquered territories to retain their own monetary systems in accordance with the widely divergent economic conditions prevailing there. While in the Western provinces coins were used, in the province of Babylonia trade continued to be transacted largely on the basis of uncoined gold and silver bars weighed at each transaction. The same was probably true about Syria and Phœnicia, and in Egypt in particular the attempt to introduce Persian coinage met with very limited success. Even the central administration of the Empire made only limited use of coinage. Government officials and Oriental troops received payment in kind, only Greek mercenaries had to be paid in coin.[2] Gold coins were widely used in the auriferous and civilized districts of India under Persian rule.

The bulk of the immense gold resources accumulated by the Kings in Persia through booty and tribute as well as the mineral resources of the Empire was not coined but was simply melted into earthenware vessels.

[1]Babelon, p. 27.
[2]*Encyclopaedia Britannica*, 14th Edn., Vol. XVII, p. 569.

When the King required money he minted as much as was necessary.[3] After the capture by Alexander of the vast Persian treasures hoarded in Suse and Persepolis (331 B.C.), the gold resources of the defeated Persian Empire became dispersed all over Western Asia and Europe, partly in the form of Macedonian *staters*, but largely in the form of bullion, in which form they continued to circulate and act as the monetary medium in Magna Græcia and later in the Roman Empire.

[3]Herodotus, III, p. 96.

CHAPTER 10

OX AND BASE METAL CURRENCIES IN GREECE

Copper ingots the shape of which is believed by some to be that of a double axe and by others to be that of an ox-hide, found in various Ægian countries such as Crete, Eubœa, Cilicia, etc., are believed to have constituted an important currency during the era of the Middle and Late Minoan Civilization (c. 2250-1300 B.C.). There is evidence to indicate that such ingots formed part of the treasure of the kings of Knossos during the late Minoan period. Scribes weighed them and recorded their value in *talents* on clay tablets. A tablet was discovered showing the picture of a copper ingot followed by six marks signifying the figure of sixty; after this is a picture of a balance and marks representing fifty-two and a half.[1] In Knossos there have also been found cast pieces of silver, marked with the sign of H or the sign of ⊢, the one being half of the weight of the other.[2] There were other objects both in the Palace of Knossos and in the Palace of Mycenæ which might conceivably have played a monetary role. There were also the uniform ingots and metal discs referred to in the chapter on Prehistoric Currencies.

The monetary use of the ox was highly developed in Ancient Greece. There are many references in the *Iliad* and the *Odyssey* to the use of oxen as a unit of account. The first prize at a competition was a big tripod "that the Achæans prized amongst themselves at the worth of twelve oxen." The second prize was "a woman of manifold skill in handiwork worth four oxen."[3] A cauldron that the fire had not yet touched is valued at one ox.[4] The shield of Pallas has been described by Homer as having "a hundred tassels hung, rare works of art, all gold, each one a hundred oxen's price."[5] There is also a much-quoted passage about the exchange of arms between Glaucus whose arms were worth a hundred oxen and Diomede whose arms were only worth nine oxen.[6]

[1]C. Seltman, *Greek Coins* (London, 1933), pp. 7, 10.
[2]Glotz, p. 196.   [3]*Iliad*, XXIII, 703.
[4]*Iliad*, XXIII, 885.   [5]*Iliad*, II, 448-9.   [6]*Iliad*, VI, 236.

In all these passages cattle is evidently referred to as a standard of value. There are, however, other passages which might conceivably indicate the use of a cattle as a medium of exchange. For instance, when Lycaon, Priam's son, was sold as a captive, he "fetched the price of a hundred oxen. Subsequently he was redeemed for thrice that."[7] Even this passage probably refers to the use of the ox unit as a standard of value, and that the price expressed in terms of oxen was actually supposed to have been paid in other form. In the *Odyssey* reference is made to the purchase of a slave girl by Lærtes who gave for her "the price of twenty oxen."[8] It is not clear whether Homer meant that twenty oxen were actually paid over or that the payment was merely the equivalent of twenty oxen. The latter interpretation seems more convincing. Fortunately there is at least one instance in which the separation of the functions of the unit of account and those of the metallic media of exchange is quite distinct. In the *Odyssey*, when Ulysses, after his return to Ithaca, was about to slay his wife's suitors their spokesman, Eurymachus, sought to appease him by offering a ransom:—"We will each bring a contribution to the value of twenty oxen and repay you in bronze and gold."[9]

Evidence indicating the existence of cattle-money is not confined to Homeric quotations. The description of a man who has been bribed into silence as having "an ox on his tongue" had been in current use during the 6th and 5th centuries B.C.[10] The prizes at the Delian festivities were announced in heads of oxen, even though actual payment was made in coined money, at the rate of two drachmæ per ox.[11] One of the few instances known to us in which payment was actually made in oxen was that of the purchase of a house from the widow of Polydore, King of Sparta.[12]

It seems probable that under the system described by Homer oxen were not used regularly as a medium of exchange—though they may have been so used during an earlier period—but mainly as a standard of value. Trade was conducted largely by barter, and the favourite medium of exchange consisted of metal utensils and raw metals or ingots. The Greeks besieging Troy were said to have bought wine against iron and copper.[13] There is no indication of the form of the metals used in trade.[14] Ransom was offered in the form of bronze, gold and iron.

---

[7]*Iliad*, XXI, 79.   [8]*Odyssey*, I, 435.

[9]*Odyssey*, XXII 58.

[10]Theognis, 815-6; Æschylus, *Agamemnon*, 36.

[11]Pollux, *Onomasticon*, IX, 61. Quoted by Seltman, p. 10.

[12]Pausanias, III, 12, 3. "On this street there is, as I have said, what is called the Booneta: it was once the house of King Polydorus, and when he died they bought it from his widow, and paid the price in oxen. For as yet there was no silver or gold money, but after the ancient fashion people bartered oxen and slaves, and ingots of silver and gold."

[13]*Iliad*, VII, 473.   [14]Regling, (1910), p. 972.   [15]*Iliad*, VI, 48.

There are repeated references to tripods and cauldrons in the *Iliad*, and rich people possessed large numbers of them, far in excess of any conceivable non-monetary requirements. During that period there were no facilities to weigh base metals; they were, therefore, cast in the form of utensils of current use, conforming, presumably, to a number of standard sizes. The value of the metal was estimated, not by weighing but by the dimensions or approximate capacity of the utensils.[16] One of the prizes offered by Achilles was a cauldron of four measures,[17] another a tripod of twenty-two measures.[18] Fines were fixed in such utensils. They did not constitute, however, units of account in which prices were expressed. There are references in Homer to cauldrons and tripods worth so many oxen,[19] but no oxen are quoted as being worth so many cauldrons. Reinach observes that even their use as a medium of exchange is only referred to in the most recent verses of the epic which, it is now assumed by many authorities, must have been written over a very long period.[20]

Indeed, quite conceivably the references to oxen as a standard of value and to cauldrons and tripods as media of exchange during the siege of Troy constituted one of the frequent instances of anachronism in which writers dealing with an earlier period think in terms of their own period. The only piece of concrete documentary evidence for the monetary use of cauldrons and tripods was provided by the discovery by Halbherr, at Knossos and Gortynos, of a tariff of fines expressed in those utensils, believed to have originated in the 6th century B.C., long after the Homeric period.[21] Such utensils appear to have constituted a store of value, in addition to being medium of exchange.

The question is, was the system described by Homer in operation during the period of the Trojan war (about the 13th century B.C.) or during the much later period when the *Iliad* and the *Odyssey* was written (about the 8th century B.C.). We now know that the late Minoan and Mycenæan civilizations (16th to 12th century B.C.) had succeeded in developing an advanced form of metallic monetary system approaching the stage of coined money. Indeed, it is even conceivable that in Knossos and Mycenæ the uniform pieces of metal found in large numbers by archæologists constituted coins issued and guaranteed by implication by the State authority. Yet Homer, writing about a period corresponding to the most advanced phase of the Ægean civilization prior to the classical era of Hellas, describes a much more primitive system as having been in operation during the lifetime of Agamemnon of Mycenæ.

The apparent contradiction may presumably be accounted for by the fact that during the centuries that passed between the events and con-

---

[16]T. Reinach, *L'Histoire par les Monnaies* (Paris, 1902), p. 26.
[17]*Iliad*, XXIII, 268.   [18]*Iliad*, XXIII, 264.
[19]*Iliad*, XXIII, 703, 885.
[20]Reinach, p. 26.   [21]Reinach, p. 27.

ditions described in the *Iliad* and the *Odyssey* and their recording by Homer there was an all-round deterioration of civilization in the Ægean area as a result of the Doric invasion. Quite possibly during the Dark Ages, from which Hellas had just emerged when the *Iliad* and the *Odyssey* came to be produced in the form known by us, Greece may have reverted to the use of the primitive monetary system described by Homer, after having progressed to the verge of the adoption of modern money or the eve of the Doric invasion. Coinage which may possibly have been invented in Knossos and Mycenæ, had to be invented over again by Lydia many centuries later. In Homer's own time livestock was possibly still the standard of value, and it was reasonable for him to assume that this crude form of money must have existed five centuries earlier. The system he described was probably in operation a century or two before his time, so that it was still vaguely remembered, but the memory of the much more advanced system that existed a few centuries earlier had faded by then into oblivion and was not revived until the excavations of Schliemann, Evans and other modern archæologists.

The ox continued to exist as a unit of account long after it had been replaced by metals and implements as a medium of exchange. According to Ridgeway,[22] the monetary unit of the *talent* originated from the use of the ox as a monetary unit, one *talent* being equal to one ox. This seems to be, however, most unlikely. The *talent* was a unit of very high value, and was probably always worth many oxen.

In Athens fines and rewards were fixed by Draco (621 B.C.) in cattle.[23] One of the reforms of Solon (594 B.C.) was the computation of the fines and bounties in coined money instead of livestock.

Iron assumed an important part as monetary material during the Dark Ages after the Doric invasion (about the 12th to 10th century B.C.). Pheidon of Argos (estimates of date vary; *c.* 748-680 B.C.) dedicated iron spits in the Heræum, and a bundle of such spits was actually found on the occasion of excavations on the site of the Temple of Hera.[24] They are believed to have been a currency and it is assumed that they were dedicated to the Temple on the occasion of the adoption of coinage. Even after the introduction of coined money spits remained in circulation as small change in various parts of Greece. Six of them were made equal to a silver drachma, so that the original primitive iron currency was thus linked to the modern currency system.

Sparta provided the best-known instance of the use of iron currency in Ancient Greece. Plutarch recorded that iron bars were introduced in Sparta by Lycurgus (c. 825 B.C.?) as the sole currency.[25] Each bar weighed an Eubœan *mina* and the transport of even a moderate amount

[22]Ridgeway, *The Origin of Metallic Currency*, passim.
[23]Dionysius Halicarnassensis, x, 50. Quoted by Seltman, p. 10.
[24]Burns, p. 27. A bundle, containing 180 iron spits, was actually found at the Heræum.
[25]Plutarch, *Lycurgus*, 9; *Lysander*, 20.

required a cart with two oxen. These iron bars had been made deliberately useless for any practical non-monetary purpose by dipping them into vinegar while in a red-hot state, which process is supposed to make iron too brittle for industrial use.[26]

It is popularly believed that the choice of such an austere type of currency was largely responsible for the development of the austere Spartan character. Beyond doubt, it must have discouraged commerce and the accumulation of wealth, and it may have tended to make the Spartans disinterested in furthering their own financial advantages. The system was, however, far from watertight. In theory the State had the exclusive right to import and accumulate precious metals for the requirements of external trade and other external payments, but in practice this rule was frequently circumvented. The discovery of "owl's nests"— the popular name for illicit hoards of silver coins of Athens bearing the effigy of the owl—was a fairly frequent occurrence, in spite of the capital punishment it entailed. And the fact that Spartan generals (Pausanias was corrupted by the Persians) and even kings (Plistsanaxa was alleged to have been bribed by Pericles to keep Sparta neutral while Athens was dealing with Eubœa) were liable to be corrupted by foreign powers is in itself held to cast doubt on the effectiveness of iron bar currency as a character-building device.

Nor is it even likely that the system was adopted primarily for the purpose of enforcing austerity. Indeed, it is possible that at the time of its adoption iron was still a comparatively rare metal with a relatively high value. It was not until later centuries that its value had fallen to such an extent that large quantities came to be required even for small payments.

It seems reasonable to suggest tentatively that Sparta had adopted iron currency simply because she happened to be a producer of iron. She produced neither gold nor silver nor copper, but the most important iron mines of Greece were on her territory in the mountains or the Malean Cape and in the Tænarian promontory.[27] Possibly Sparta originally resorted to iron currency largely out of sheer economic nationalism. Her leaders had no wish to import foreign monetary metals since there was an ample supply of iron available at home for monetary purposes. Once the iron currency was adopted it tended to make for austerity, owing to the difficulty of spending it or hoarding it on a large scale. Whether the adoption of the iron currency was the cause or the effect of the austere Spartan character, both austere character and austere currency may have been the effect of the distribution of mineral resources in Greece.

[26]Other classical writers maintain that only inferior iron, unsuitable for other purposes, was used (A. Boeckh, *Die Staatshaushalt der Athener*. 3rd. Edn., Berlin, 1886), Vol. I, p. 693.

[27]C. T. Seltman, *Athens—Its History and Coinage before the Persian Invasion* (Cambridge, 1924), p. 121.

No information is available to show whether the Spartan iron bars were stamped by the Government.[28] If so they could hardly be classed among the primitive currencies in spite of their cumbersome character. Another interesting question is whether they circulated at their full metallic value or whether they were a fiduciary currency which had to be accepted above their metallic value. If the uncorroborated statement by Plutarch according to which the iron bars were rendered deliberately useless for practical purposes is correct, then these bars represent one of the outstanding historical instances of early fiduciary currency.

One of the reasons why such a primitive currency remained in force in Sparta over a long period[29] while other parts of Greece had an advanced form of currency, was that Sparta was to a large extent a self-sufficient totalitarian State. Her political and social system was based on a controlled economy. Commerce played a much more subordinate part in Sparta than in other States of Greece. There is evidence that iron currency had been in use also elsewhere in Greece[30] but nowhere did it assume such an importance as in Sparta, nor did it remain in existence for such a long period. Iron currency appeared to have suited Sparta's primitive and controlled economy to a sufficient extent to make it tolerable over a long period. Nor did the limitations of that currency prevent Sparta from embarking on costly and prolonged external military undertakings such as the Peloponnesian wars. On the eve of these wars, Pericles, in order to reassure his fellow-citizens of Athens, declared that there was no need to worry about Sparta since she is such a poor country that she could not possibly afford a prolonged war.[31] The inadequacy of Sparta's currency, and the relative poverty of her resources, was no more able to prevent her from waging a prolonged war, however, than was in our time the somewhat similar handicap under which Germany worked in 1939.

It seems probable that a credit system developed in Greece as in other

[28]Bœckh, I, p. 693, is of the opinion that the iron bars bore Government stamps.

[29]It remained official medium of exchange till the 3rd century B.C. (E. S. G. Robinson, *Money—A Companion to Greek Studies* (Cambridge, 1931), p. 537.

[30]Epaminondas, the national hero of Thebes, only possessed one iron spit after his death, according to Plutarch. Herodotus (II, 135), quotes the instance of the courtesan Rhodopis, presented to the oracle of Delphi one-tenth of her possessions in the form of iron spits.

[31]Thucydides, *The History of the Peloponnesian War* (Everyman Edn.), pp. 70-71. Archidamus, the King of Sparta, who was against the war, argued on similar lines as Pericles. He laid stress on the lack of monetary resources of Lacadæmon, and urged the meeting he was addressing that before embarking on a war it would be necessary to procure the money (pp. 40-41). On the other hand, the Corinthian ambassadors, who were anxious to secure the alliance of Sparta against Athens, argued that the necessary monetary resources could be obtained through a loan from Olympia and Delphi and by the contributions of Sparta's allies (p. 59). However, all this only meant that, while Sparta was expected to be able to prepare, with her internal resources, an invasion of enemy territories, she could not expect to finance the external expenses of the war (such as the hiring of mercenary sailors to man her fleet) with the aid of her iron bar currency (to which Thucydides made no reference). For that purpose Sparta needed external financial assistance.

parts of the ancient world long before the adoption of coinage. For this reason the view taken by Zimmern that the adoption of coinage made a fundamental difference to Greek economic and social life in that it induced the rural population to contract heavy indebtedness is probably exaggerated.[32] In fact, as a general rule, interest charged on loans in primitive money, or on loans in kind, has always been much higher than interest on loans in modern money. There is no reason to suppose that it was otherwise in Ancient Greece.

[32]Sir Alfred Zimmern, *The Greek Commonwealth* 2nd Edn. (Oxford, 1922), p. 117.

CHAPTER 11

CRUDE BRONZE CURRENCY OF ANCIENT ITALY AND ROME

In Rome and in pre-Roman Ancient Italy, cattle constituted the earliest known form of currency. The word *pecunia* originated from the word *pecus* (cattle). According to Festus, one head of cattle was equal to ten sheep.[1] Fines were fixed in terms of livestock. For minor offences the fine was two sheep, while for grave offences it amounted to anything up to thirty oxen.[2] Litigating parties had to deposit with the judge five heads of cattle if the value of the claim in question was over ten heads of cattle, and five sheep if the value was less. The losing party forfeited his deposit and his animals were sacrificed to the gods.[3] In pre-Roman Sicily the cow formed the basis of assessments during the reign of Dionysius (405-367 B.C.)[4] The use of cattle continued for a long time in early Rome, as is indicated by the fact that the laws passed in the years 454 and 452 B.C.—the Lex Aternia-Tarpeia and the Lex Menenia-Sestia —fixed fines in cattle and sheep at the same time as their equivalent in metallic money.[5] The Constitution of the Twelve Tables (around 450 B.C.) stipulated fines in copper and gold units, but makes no mention of cattle. The Lex Iulia Papiria (430 B.C.) definitely provides for the replacement of payment in cattle by payment in more advanced forms of currency.[6]

The use of stamped leather as currency by the early Romans was affirmed by Seneca and Eusebius, the latter alleging that it was employed in the reign of Numa Pompilius, second King of Rome (c. 715 B.C.).

Other non-metallic materials which are alleged to have served monetary purposes were clay and wood, but, as Burns remarked, "the evi-

[1]*Festi Epit.*, p. 24. Quoted by E. Babelon, *Monnaies de la République Romaine* (Paris, 1885), Vol. I, p. II.
[2]*Festus*, p. 202. Quoted by Babelon (1885), Vol. I, p. II.
[3]E. Speck, *Handelsgeschichte des Altertums* (Leipzig, 1906), Vol. III, Part II, p. 1047. Th. Mommsen, *Geschichte des Römischen Münzwesens* (Berlin, 1860), p. 197.
[4]Pseudo-Aristotle, *Œconomica* II, 21. Quoted by Ridgeway, *Roman Money— A Companion to Latin Studies* (Cambridge, 1943), p. 442.
[5]Babelon (1885), Vol. I, p. II.   [6]E. A. Sydenham, *Æs Grave* (London, 1926), p. 13.

dence is too unsubstantial to be worth consideration."[7] There is more substance in the claim that salt was used as money in Rome; hence the use of the term *salarium*. Originally it meant an allowance of salt for soldiers and officers, and also for civil administrators, but later it came to be used as a term for military pay in general, and for the pay of the civil service in the provinces, even though that pay no longer assumed the form of salt. It is not known to what extent salt was used by its recipients as a medium of exchange instead of being consumed.

According to Mommsen the change from the cattle standard to the metallic standard had been the result of the change from pastoral to agricultural economy. The metals that had come to be adopted were those needed by peasants for their implements. In Italy this metal was copper.[8] By far the most important primitive currency of pre-Roman Sicily and Italy and of early Rome was, in fact, raw copper or bronze.[9] It was known under the name of *æs rude*, or, less frequently, *æs infectum*. Its use developed while cattle currency was still in use.[10] According to Pliny its use was preserved till the régime of Servius Tullius in the 6th century B.C.

Æs rude consisted of shapeless lumps of raw copper or bronze of varying size. In the central Italian districts, including Rome, this form of money continued to be used long after Greek influence had led to the adoption of silver coins in the South. Sometimes the fragments show signs of having been roughly cast or hammered into irregular cubes or bars, and occasionally they are circular, elliptical or oblong. The assumption is that these were a later and more advanced form of currency. The weight of the known monetary specimens vary between less than an ounce to several pounds.[11] The ingots were broken in accordance with requirements. The word *æstimare* (to estimate) is believed to have originated from the use of *æs rude* as a unit of account.[12] Attempts to prove that the fragments of *æs rude* or the ingots of which they formed part conformed to certain weight standards failed completely.[13] Their size and weight was purely a matter of chance, and in any case it was of no consequence since they changed hands by weight. The unit of weight was the *libra* (pound)—in Sicily the *litra*—but this unit itself was subject to many changes in the course of centuries.

Sydenham warns against the assumption that all fragments of bronze found in Italy served the purpose of money. Numismatists are in general satisfied, however, that many of them were surviving specimens of *æs rude* referred to by Pliny. The explanation of the choice of bronze is that

[7]Burns, p. 293.   [8]Mommsen, p. 169.
[9]Since the word *aes* is used to indicate both bronze and copper, it is difficult to ascertain from contemporary references which of the two was meant.
[10]Babelon (1885), Vol. I, p. II.   [11]Sydenham, pp. 10-11.
[12]Marquardt, *Römische Staatsverwaltung*, Vol. II, p. 5. Quoted by Babelon (1885), Vol. I, p. II.
[13]E. J. Hæberlin, *Æs Grave*, Vol. I (Frankfurt, 1910), p. 6.

gold was almost unknown in central Italy, and silver was also a very scarce article of import.[14]

Bronze remained the monetary standard of Rome right to the end of the Republic. *Æs rude* was, however, superseded progressively by more highly developed forms of bronze currency. The early bronze discs, a number of which have been discovered in Etruria, closely resemble large cast coins without, however, any official stamp or marking.[15]

The next stage in the development of ancient Roman currency was the adoption of *æs signatum*, which consisted of fairly regular shaped copper and bronze bars with branch-like or fishbone-like markings. Even more advanced varieties of this type consisted of oblong or brick-shaped bronze ingots marked by animals, especially by oxen or sheep, which fact is claimed to indicate the existence of a link between this form of currency and the original livestock currency.[16] Pliny states that King Servius Tullius was the first to stamp the bronze. "Timæus hands down the tradition that aforetime they employed it in a rough state in Rome. It was stamped with the figures of animals whence it was termed pecunia."[17] The accuracy of this statement has been called in question by recent historians.

In many instances the ingots bore the mark of a tripod, sword, anchor, etc., while the word ROMANOM appears on other specimens together with the Roman eagle. This leads to the theory that the *æs signatum* was issued by the State. Mommsen does not believe, however, that the State went beyond stipulating the use of *æs signatum* as means of payment and perhaps guaranteeing the purity of the metal. Its weight was not guaranteed and had to be ascertained at each transaction.[18]

Æs signatum was found in many instances together with *æs rude* and with coins in central and northern Italy.[19] *Æs signatum* continued to circulate even after the adoption of bronze coins, for large payments, especially during periods of debasements.[20] Even *æs rude* remained in use for a long time after the adoption of coinage. The fact that many pieces that are believed to have served as currency contained zinc seems to indicate that *æs rude* was used under the Empire, since zinc is not known to have been produced in Rome before that period.[21]

[14]Babelon (1885), Vol. I, p. II.   [15]Sydenham, p. 10.
[16]Babelon (1885), Vol. I, p IV.   [17]Pliny, *Hist. Natur.*, XXXIII, 3, 12.
[18]Mommsen, p. 173.
[19]K. Regling, *Geld vor Einführung der Münze. Pauly's Real-Encyclopoedie der klassischen Altertumswissenschaften* (Stuttgart, 1910), Vol. XIII, p. 980.
[20]Regling (1910), p. 980.
[21]Over 10,000 pieces were found in the Apollo Baths, Vicarello, in association with a large number of coins. An analysis of these pieces disclosed a content of 95.2 per cent of copper and 4.8 per cent of zinc. The assumption, based on the nature of the finding-place, is that during the Empire the *æs rude* was used mainly for offerings to the gods (Mommsen, p. 170). Soldiers of Hannibal consecrated vast quantities of raw copper in the wood of the goddess Feronia. After the retreat of the Carthaginian Army, the Roman soldiers recovered this treasure (Titus Livius, XXVI, II, 9. Quoted by Babelon (1885), Vol. I, p. III.

The next stage was that of *æs grave*. This currency consisted of cast copper coins weighing one pound each, or the multiple or fraction of one pound. These were issued definitely under State authority, and, in spite of their clumsy and cumbersome character, they cannot be considered primitive currencies. One of the reasons why *æs rude* and *æs signatum* remained in use even after the adoption of coinage was that during the Punic wars the coins were gradually debased to a fraction of their original weight. Within the space of little more than half a century from the date of their introduction, the weight of the standard coins had fallen from a pound to two ounces during the first Punic war (264-241 B.C.).[22] The second Punic war (218-201 B.C.) led to its further debasement to one ounce. Since *æs rude* and *æs signatum* continued to change hands by weight they were not affected by the debasements, and their use as a standard of value and as a medium of exchange was preferred to that of the debased *æs grave* which the payees were forced to accept at a face value in excess of its metallic value.

Expansion of foreign trade had led to the adoption of precious metals for monetary purposes. It took a long time, however, before gold and silver became monetary metals. Whether through sheer conservatism or for other reasons, Rome stubbornly resisted the innovation. The effect of the maintenance of the almost Spartan system of heavy copper currency was that the home market was secured for home production.[23] Whether this was accidental or deliberate it is impossible to say. There is certainly no reason to suppose, however, that the heavy bronze currency was adopted or maintained for considerations of austerity.

So long as trade was confined to central Italy the cumbersome *æs grave* sufficed as a medium of exchange. With development of trade with Greeks, Sicilians and other Mediterranean peoples, Rome found it necessary, however, to adopt a more convenient form of money.[24] At first both silver and gold changed hands by weight. Gold circulated regularly in the form of bars and was weighed though not assayed on the occasion of every transaction. Although the bars were issued by the State they were not stamped, in order not to make their division difficult. They were produced in recognizable forms. The law passed by Sulla (138-78 B.C.) against counterfeiting applies also against the debasement of gold bars.[25] Reckoning in copper continued, however, especially in Sicily, long after silver coins became the medium of exchange.[26]

Even after the replacement of *æs grave* by silver and gold coins and more advanced copper coins, the primitive forms of copper currency never ceased altogether to play a part in Roman life. For one thing, *æs rude* continued to be used for ceremonial and symbolic payments, and also for religious purposes. Moreover, under the Empire every now and again currency crises developed and the distrust in the coinage tended

[22]Sydenham, p. 29. [23]Speck, p. 1048. [24]Sydenham, p. 35.
[25]Mommsen, p. 402. [26]Speck, p. 1049.

to encourage the use of metals by weight. In any case natural economy never disappeared altogether in Rome. Taxes were collected largely in kind.

The 3rd and 4th centuries A.D. witnessed a marked return towards primitive money. Silver coins became debased to the utmost limit of possibility. Their silver content was gradually reduced to a negligible fraction. As a result they ceased to be convenient for commercial purposes. On the other hand, for some inexplicable reason, none of the Emperors dared to take similar liberties with gold coinage. While their weight was reduced, this did not affect their use by weight as a medium of exchange and a standard of value, because their fineness remained unaffected. The only explanation of this attitude towards gold is that it was regarded as the *sacra moneta*. Even during the period when Rome lost much of her ancient prestige, an Indian traveller observed that trade all over the world was operated with the aid of Roman gold coins which were accepted and admired everywhere.[27] Gold by weight became the principal unit of account in the Roman Empire during the 3rd century A.D.[28]

The value of gold coins was too big for everyday transactions. For that purpose wheat was used in some of the dependencies of Rome, especially in Egypt.[29] Loans were granted in wheat, but also in other commodities. During the 4th century A.D. almost the whole economy of the great estates in Egypt was based on wine which was the chief currency on the estate of Alypius, metallic money being very little used.[30]

In recent years it has become fashionable among historians to seek to minimize the extent to which the debasement of Roman silver coinage led to the abandonment of the use of coined money. There can be little doubt, however, that, to a large degree, the Roman Empire reverted to natural economy or the use of primitive currencies during the period of debasements. Among the various countries under Roman rule, Egypt provided the most satisfactory documentary evidence relating to the subject, thanks to the survival of a number of papyri from this period. From this evidence Mickwitz compiled an interesting table showing the relative extent to which land rents were payable in money and in kind during the first centuries of our era. The following are the percentages[31]:—

[27]A. Engel and R. Serrure, *Traité de Numismatique du Moyen Age* (Paris, 1891), pp. 3-4.
[28]G. Mickwitz, *Gold und Wirtschaft im Römischen Reich des vierten Jahrhunderts nach Christ* (Helsinki, 1932), p. 80. For international political payments—such as tribute to Alaric and Attila, or subsidy to barbaric allies—the recognized unit was the pound (weight) of gold (Edward Gibbon, *The Decline and Fall of the Roman Empire*, Everyman Edn., London, 1910), *passim*.
[29]Mickwitz, p. 119.
[30]M. Rostovtzeff, *Social and Economic History of the Roman Empire* (Oxford, 1926), p. 439.
[31]Mickwitz, p. 120.

	Payment in money.	Payment in kind.	Mixed payment.
1st century	23	57	20
2nd century	15	53	33
3rd century	22	46	32
4th century	16	77	7
5th century	—	—	—
6th-7th century	34	46	21

Possibly the figures relating to Egypt do not give a reliable indication about the state of affairs in other parts of the Empire for, as we saw in the chapter dealing with that country, money economy had never taken root among the ancient Egyptians. Nevertheless, there is evidence also from other parts of the Empire, showing a tendency towards reverting to payments in kind. For example, soldiers and officers received once more their salt rations in kind, and the term *salarium* which for centuries was used in a metaphorical sense, may have assumed once more a concrete meaning.

CHAPTER 12

BRONZE AXES AND WHEELS AS CURRENCIES IN GAUL

While the Celts on territories adjacent to races of higher civilization adopted coinage at a comparatively early period, those of the interior continued for centuries the use of primitive means of payment—cattle, metal bars, rings, etc.[1] According to Polybius, when the Gauls invaded Italy their wealth consisted chiefly of cattle and gold ornaments. On taking Rome in 300 B.C. their leader Brennus demanded and received a tribute of 1,000 lbs. of gold—plus the weight of his sword which he threw into the scales when the Romans objected to the use of false weights.

Peculiar-shaped axes known in archæology under the name of "celts" are believed to have served as currency in the interior of Gaul. More than 300 deposits of axes have been discovered.[2] The 240 axes found at Plurien (Côtes-du-Nord), were too thin and also otherwise unsuitable to be of any non-monetary use.[3] At Maure-de-Bretagne (Ille-et-Villeine) about 4,000 very small bronze celts tied together by a wire were found.[4] One of the reasons why it is assumed that these axes were not trading stocks but monetary hoards is that, in addition to their small

[1] Forrer (1926), Vol. VI, p. 302.
[2] A. Blanchet, *Traité de Monnaies Gauloises* (Part I, Paris, 1905), p. 21.
[3] Blanchet, p. 22. The same deposit contained some twenty celts with ornamental designs which would have been worn off by practical use. (Jules Lemoine, *Trouvaille d'objets en bronze de l'époque larnaudienne*, 1888, p. 7. Quoted by Blanchet, p. 22).
[4] Blanchet, pp. 22-23.

size and peculiar shape, unused and used axes were found mixed together. Had the deposits constituted stocks-in-trade they would probably have been kept apart.[5] There is also the fact that many of these celts were found in earthenware jars, a favourite hiding place for coins and other treasures during troubled periods. Finally, some hatchets of lead were found, which could obviously serve no practical non-monetary purpose.[6] There is, of course, the possibility that the axes served purely sacrificial requirements.[7] But then, regular demand created by such requirements does often qualify various objects in primitive communities to assume the role of money.

At the French Archæological Congress of 1887, J. Pilloy stated that at Brécy several kilos of scraps of axes and other instruments were found. All fractions, which appeared to have been broken deliberately, had roughly the same weight, "which appears to indicate that they might have served as current money."[8] Possibly the fractions have changed hands by weight.

Gold and brass rings were found in numerous deposits, and some archæologists claim that they had served monetary purposes. This theory is not accepted by other authors who believe that the rings may have been ornaments or utensils.[9] Two golden rings were found in a Gallic tomb and preserved in the Museum of Chartres. One of them has two dots and the other four dots, the latter weighing exactly twice as much as the former. These rings, conforming as they do to some weight standard, may possibly have served as currency.[10] At Fontenay-le-Comte some thirty golden rings were found together with gold coins, which fact may indicate their monetary use.[11]

According to Déchelette, small bronze wheels which have been found in large numbers probably constituted a pre-coinage currency in Gaul, and remained in monetary use even after the adoption of coinage. The wheels were found in a number of instances together with coins and rings.[12] Blanchet strongly opposes the theory however.

From the 3rd century B.C., onward, local imitations of Macedonian *staters* came to be used in Gaul, and after the Roman conquest Roman coinage penetrated into the country. During the period of the debasement of the Roman coinage, in Gaul under Postumus (3rd century A.D.), gold was used as medium of exchange by weight.[13] In a lake at Nesmy, gold bars were found, marked by notches dividing them into twelve

[5]Blanchet, p. 23.
[6]J. Déchelette, *Manuel d'Archéologie Préhistorique Celtique et Gallo-Romaine* (Paris, 1918), Part II, Vol. I, p. 255.
[7]Déchelette, p. 256.   [8]Blanchet, p. 23.
[9]Blanchet, pp. 25-27.
[10]Comte H. de Widranges, *Des anneaux et des rouelles, antique monnaie des Gaoulois* (Bar-le-Duc, 1861) p. 16. Quoted by Blanchet, p. 26.
[11]Blanchet, p. 27.   [12]Dechelette, Part II, Vol. III, p. 1299.
[13]H. Mattingly and E. A. Sydenham, *The Roman Imperial Coinage* (London, 1933, Vol. II, Part II), p. 322.

equal parts, each of which was equal to the weight of the gold *stater*
which was in circulation in Western Gaul. It is reasonable to infer that
these bars had been used as currency.[14]

[14]Blanchet, p. 25.

CHAPTER 13

CATTLE CURRENCY OF THE ANCIENT GERMANS

As the Germanic tribes were primarily pastoral communities, it is only
natural that cattle should constitute their earliest form of currency.
Tacitus remarked that their livestock was rather undersized, adding:
"The pride of the people is rather in the number of their beasts, which
constitute the only wealth they welcome."[1] It is usual for races which
have adopted cattle or other livestock as currency to neglect the quality
of their animals for the sake of securing the largest possible number of
them. In the Gothic translation of the Bible by Ulfilas (A.D. 340-388)
the word "money" is always rendered by *faihu* (cattle).[2]

Metallic money was well known to the Ancient Germans by the time
the Romans had come into contact with them. During recent decades
some German historians and archæologists have sought to prove that
the Teutons had achieved a high stage of civilization, and to that end
they have been at pains to argue that the monetary use of Roman coins
—as distinct from their ornamental or hoarding use—was widespread
already at an early period. In this respect, however, it is necessary to
draw a distinction between the frontier tribes and those of the interior.
"Although the border tribes for the purpose of traffic treat gold and
silver as precious metals," Tacitus observed, "and recognize and collect
certain coins of our money, the tribes of the interior practice barter in
the simplest and oldest fashions. The coinage which appeals to them is
the old and long-familiar."[3] The Germans willingly accepted gold coins
in trading with the Romans. As many of the coins had reached them in
a mutilated state they were accepted by weight. In this respect they conformed to the custom of the period. On the other hand, according to
evidence quoted by German authorities, the Teutons practised the
custom of melting down the imported coins, and turned them into rings
and spirals, which were used also for ornamental purposes.[4]

The use of bracelets as a means of payment towards the close of the
Ancient period may possibly be inferred from a passage in the *Niebelungenlied*. When Siegfried brought to Kriemhild the news of the success

[1]Tacitus, *Germania*, VI (Loeb. Ed.) (London, 1937), p. 271.
[2]C. F. Keary, *The Coinage of Western Europe* (London, 1879), p. 6.
[3]Tacitus, VI (Loeb Ed.), p. 271.
[4]G. Grupp, *Kultur der alten Kelten und Germanen* (Munich, 1905), p. 218.

Q

of her brother's mission, she replied: "I would fain give thee the envoy's guerdon, wert thou not too rich to receive it." Siegfried said he would be proud to take a gift from her hand, whereupon she bade the chamberlain "to fetch the envoy's mead. She gave him four and twenty bracelets with precious stones for his fee."[5] Although the precious stones constitute a departure from the practice of payment in plain bracelets, the reference to the practice of fixing fees in bracelets is not without interest. The practice was also referred to in the *Waltharlied* which, though written by Ekkehard in the 10th century A.D., covers the same period as the *Niebelungenlied* (5th century A.D.). It contains a reference to two offers made by Walthar to King Gunther, to pay 100 and even 200 "bracelets of red gold," in return for his safe passage through Burgundy.[6]

Broken or cut pieces of rings are supposed to have been used in internal trade before, during and after the Roman period.[7] Considering that this practice of payment in rings and fragments of rings continued to prevail in various parts of Northern Europe throughout the early Middle Ages, its existence in Ancient Germany need not be regarded as an indication of inferior civilization.

[5]The *Niebelungenlied*. Translated in prose by M. Armour (London, 1908), p. 53,
[6]*The Song of Walthari*. Translated by Helena Eassen (J. Scheffel, *Ekkehard* Everyman Edn., London, 1911), pp. 363-4.
[7]W. Stein, *Handel (Deutscher)*. Reallexikon der Germanischen Altertumskunde (Strassburg, 1918-19), Vol. II, p. 386.

CHAPTER 14

IRON SWORD CURRENCY OF BRITAIN

There is very little documentary evidence concerning the primitive currencies used by the early Britons. In Ancient Wales the primitive system of slave-currency appears to have been linked to the metallic currency. A young male slave was equated to one *libra* (pound) of silver.[1] It is assumed that throughout the British Isles cattle played the part of currency, though there is no actual evidence of it until the early Middle Ages. Practically the only written evidence on early British primitive currency is contained in Julius Cæsar's *De Bello Gallico* (V, XII, 18). Unfortunately there is a discrepancy between the text of the various manuscripts in existence. Authorities are divided whether it refers to iron rings or iron bars. There are other obscurities and discrepancies in the text, as a result of which no two translations are identical.

For a long time the accepted version was the following: "*Utuntur aut ære aut nummo aures aut annulis ferreis ad certum pondus examinates pro*

[1]*Ancient Laws of Wales*, p. 795. Quoted by Ridgeway, pp. 32-3.

nummo." (They use either brass money or gold money or instead of money, iron rings adjusted to a certain weight.) This version was accepted by such early authorities as Ruding and Akerman. The latter connected the supposed iron ring currency of Britain with the proved bronze and gold ring currencies of Ireland.[2] The complete absence of iron rings that could be regarded as early British currency is attributed by E. Hawkins to oxidation[3]—an argument which in view of the discovery of many other iron objects originating from the same period does not sound altogether convincing.

Even among the early numismatists there were some, however, who preferred to accept the version of Julius Cæsar's text which contains the word *tælis* (bars) instead of *annulis* (rings). Among others, Eckhel believed in that version, which has now come to be regarded as authentic by most archæologists and numismatists.

The bars found in early Iron Age sites, which were believed to have been used for monetary purposes assumed the form of badly finished sword blades.[4] According to R. A. Smith: "Such bars have often been found secreted in considerable numbers in a manner recalling the familiar hoards of coins. They have been found in the centre of British camps, and it seems much more probable that the Ancient Britons would conceal their money at a crisis than that they would bury half-made swords. It must be remembered that in such a society division of labour was not in an advanced stage, and the smith who shaped these bars would have himself produced the finished article if swords they were to be. He would not have prepared a large number to hand on to another for the finishing process. Again, there is too much metal in them for the manufacture of the swords of the period, which had a thin blade. . . . There was a smaller series of the same form, evidently meant to represent half the value of the original specimen, and a larger series four times the weight of the smallest."[5]

Metrologists claim the unit to be about eleven ounces; there are presumed to be pieces weighing a quarter, half, two and four units, the most common being the double unit. Smith believes that the "swords" probably did not change hands by weight, but according to approximate size, and minor variations of weight were disregarded.[6] Against this, Hulme, who contests the claim that the "swords" played a monetary role, pointed out that there is no correlation between their length and

[2]Akerman in *Numismatic Journal*. Vol. I, 1836-7. Quoted by R. A. Smith, *Paper on the Ancient British Iron Currency*. Proceedings of the Society of Antiquaries, 2nd Series, Vol. xx, 1905, p. 186.

[3]E. Hawkins in *Numismatic Chronicle*, Vol. I, p. 13. Quoted by R. A. Smith, *op. cit.*

[4]R. C. Collingwood, *Roman Britain* (in *An Economic Survey of Ancient Rome*. Edited by T. Frank, Vol. III, 1904-5, p. 60), quotes the following instances for finds of supposed currency-bars: 17 at Hod Hill (Dorset), 394 at Meon Hill (Glos.), 147 at Bourton-on-the-Water (Glos.) and 300 near Malvern (Worcs.).

[5]Smith p. 182.   [6]Smith, p. 188.

weight,[7] though in this respect, again, the unknown factor of loss of weight through varying degree of deterioration ought to be borne in mind. Hulme, like so many historians and archæologists, appears to have been sub-consciously influenced by the desire to clear the early inhabitants of his country of the charge of having used primitive currencies during a period when other races were already using coins. His remark that if iron bars had been used as currency "the inference is unavoidable that the Celtic tribes who used this form of currency were a race endowed with a very low mentality"[8] is characteristic of this attitude. In reality, since in various parts of Ancient Greece iron spits were used as currency at a fairly advanced phase of civilization, there is no reason for Britons to be ashamed of a similar use of iron swords during the 1st century B.C. on the British Isles.

In any case, to reassure those who, like Mr. Hulme, regard this matter as one of national prestige, it is necessary to point out that the unfinished swords had only been used by a minority of the early inhabitants of the British Isles. Coins are now known to have been used in various parts of pre-Roman Britain.

R. A. Smith in reply to Hulme's argument that no "currency bars" were found in graves, pointed out that very few Iron Age graves have so far been found in the currency bar area, and that no British or Gallic coins have been found in pre-Roman graves, even though they are now known to have existed.[9] He also quoted possible parallel instances in the Celtic area outside Britain. According to Déchelette, there were two denominations in the iron spits found in Saone at Chalon.[10] Smith believes that finds in Etruria may also have provided similar instances.

It is worth noting that, although according to Cæsar iron was obtainable in the maritime provinces of Britain,[11] the use of iron currency bars was confined to interior districts. Possibly this is one of the numerous instances of the choice of a scarce material for monetary use. The finding places of the currency bars are almost exclusively in South-Western England, and they are regarded as an indication of the sphere

[7]E. Wyndham Hulme. *Currency Bars and Water Clocks* (Antiquity, VII, 1933, Gloucester), p. 62.

[8]Hulme, p. 61.

[9]R. A. Smith, *Currency Bars and Water Clocks* (Antiquity, VII, 1933). Ruding was satisfied that the reason why Julius Cæsar (*De Bello Gallico*, V, XXII), did not state the nature of the tribute which he imposed upon Cassivellanus was that he was unable to collect any gold or silver and the form in which he had to accept the tribute "was of a kind too mean to be particularized." (*Annals of the Coinage of Great Britain*, 3rd Ed., 1840, Vol. I, p. 97.) As a matter of fact, it is now known that more than a century before the arrival of Julius Cæsar in Britain, the Britons were issuing coins which were imitations of those in use since the 3rd century B.C. in Gaul. (Burns, p. 47.) In any case, *De Bello Gallico* contains several references to tribute from Gallic races without specifying its form, yet it is safe to assume that in Gaul gold and silver were in monetary use at that time.

[10]Déchelette, *La Collection Millon*, pp. 191-243, refers to "iron spits of the Gallic period, serving as primitive money."

[11]Julius Cæsar, *De Bello Gallico*, V, XII.

in which La Têne culture entered Britain from Brittany.[12] In South-Eastern England where tin coinage was in use during the Iron Age, no iron currency bars have been found.[13]

Gold rings found in various parts of England are considered by some archæologists to have been used as currency. Among others in Grunta Fen, Cambridgeshire, five small rings attached to a larger gold ring were found.[14]

There are some references of dubious value to the use of leather money in Ancient Scotland. According to the *Historie of Scotland* written in Latin by Johne Leslie, Bishop of Rosse,[15] the mythical Reutha King of Scotland, alleged to have reigned between 187 and 173 B.C., caused pennies to be coined, "of a buffill hyde, to wit sik kynde of lathir, because afor him in Albion was na vsse for stricken or cuinzet money." This remark is reproduced here for what it is worth.

Among the objects which have been claimed to have served monetary purpose in Early Britain are small coal discs found in Dorset. Reference to them is found in Hutchins' *History of Dorsetshire*: "Near Smedmore is found what the county people call coal money. It is generally discovered on the top of the cliff two or three feet below the surface and closed between two stones set edgeways and covered with a third . . . and mingled with a few bones of some animal. . . . They are of a round form one to two or three inches and a half in diameter and a quarter of an inch thick; one side is flat, the other convex on which are several mouldings; on the other side are two, sometimes four, small round holes near the rim (perhaps the centre holes by which they were fixed to the turning press) but they do not penetrate through the piece. Antiquaries conclude them to be British antiquities but whether amulets or money is not agreed. . . . It may be observed that coal is the cant word for money, whence 'down with your coal' is a common expression in some countries for 'pay your money'."[16] This last piece of "evidence" shows the length to which zealots of a theory are prepared to go in quest of support for their argument.

W. A. Miles, an archæologist in the early 19th century who spent some months in the Wareham district and purchased from local labourers all pieces that were available, gave a detailed description of the circumstances in which these coal discs were found, circumstances which appear to indicate that they were used in connection with funerals, or for

[12]R. C. Collingwood and J. N. L. Myers, *Roman Britain and the English Settlements* (Oxford, 1936), p. 29. See also D. Kendrick and C. F. C. Hawkes, *Archaeology in England and Wales* (London, 1932), p. 176.

[13]Derek Allen, *British Tin Coinage of the Iron Age* (Transactions of the International Numismatic Congress, London, 1936, London, 1938), p. 854.

[14]*Numismatic Chronicle* (Vol. XIV, London, 1852), p. 63 ff.

[15]Translated from Latin by Jas. Dalrymple in 1596 (Scottish Text Society, 1885), p. 326.

[16]*Hutchins' History of Dorsetshire*, Vol. I, p. 197. Quoted by Ruding, Vol. I, p. 4.

sacrificial rather than monetary purposes.[17] The discs had been turned in a lathe and the mouldings and ornaments had been formed with great neatness and precision. Some years previous to Miles's investigations "coal money" was more abundant and several large pieces were found on which, according to fishermen, some characters were visible, but no such specimens had been preserved.

Miles is of the opinion that these coal discs were produced and used not by the Ancient Britons, but by some Phœnician or Carthagenean colony.[18] Other authorities also feel that it is not probable that the Britons had the necessary machines or the skill to use them in so remarkable a manner.[19] It stands to reason that these objects could not have been used as a circulating medium, as they would not have remained intact if they had passed from hand to hand. The fact that they were invariably found with animal remains certainly does indicate some mysterical use in sacrifice or sepulchural rites.[20]

The reason why so much space has been devoted here to the discussion of an object which, on the face of the evidence, is unlikely to have served a monetary purpose lies in the fact that specimens of this coal money have been included in the Knox Collection of Moneys, Buffalo Museum of Science; and in the Catalogue of that Collection it is stated that it was used as currency between the 1st century B.C. and the 5th century A.D.[21] Stuart Mosher's book which includes the Catalogue contains no further evidence to confirm the monetary use of these coal discs, still less any reference to justify the claim that they were used during the period indicated by the Catalogue. On the basis of the evidence available, it seems difficult to accept the claim. Nevertheless, the Catalogue and Mosher were right in recording it, if only to encourage further enquiry into the matter.

Copper ingots may possibly have served as a currency in Ancient Wales. According to R. A. Smith, the term _ære_ in Julius Cæsar's remark may possibly have referred to such currency. Cakes of copper, dating from the Roman period have also been found near Andesey, in Kent, and elsewhere.[22]

It should be emphasized that, although various kinds of primitive money were used in Ancient Britain even after the Roman régime, already before the Roman conquest both foreign and local coins were in use. There is not sufficient material of evidence to indicate the relative importance of primitive and modern money, or the nature of the former's monetary functions. As indicated above, various areas of Britain did not progress at the same pace towards the adoption of modern money.

[17]W. A. Miles, _A Minute Account of the Kimmeridge Coal Money_ (London, 1826). [18]Miles, p. 64.   [19]Ruding, Vol. I, p. 4.   [20]Miles, pp. 49-51. [21]Stuart Mosher, _The Story of Money as told by the Knox Collection._ (Bulletin of the Buffalo Society of Natural Sciences, Vol. XVII, No. 2, Buffalo, 1936), p. 71. [22]R. A. Smith, p. 187.

CHAPTER 15

SLAVE GIRL MONEY OF IRELAND

A full-grown cow or ox was in ancient times a very general standard of value in Ireland. It was used both in actual payment and in estimating amounts.[1] There is ample evidence in support of this statement in the text of the Brehon Laws which are believed to have originated during the 5th century A.D. and may be assumed therefore to reflect conditions prevailing even earlier. The Brehon Laws contain many instances of the use of the cow standard in connection with payment of rents and blood money. Values are expressed in cows, also rates of wages. Poets, builders, etc., received payment in cows.[2]

As Ridgeway pointed out, Irish tradition in respect of the use of the cow as a monetary unit goes back far beyond the date at which the Brehon Laws were compiled; and from it we get a glimpse of a system almost Homeric. Thus the Annals of the Four Masters, originating from A.D. 106, state that the tribute (*Boroimhe* meaning literally "cow-tax") paid by the King of Leinster consisted of 150 cows, 150 pigs, 150 couples of men and women in servitude, 150 girls and 150 cauldrons.[3] Cattle was loaned extensively in early Ireland. The recipients of such loans became the vassal of their creditor.[4]

Another favourite monetary unit in Ancient Ireland was the slave girl or bondsmaid (*kumal*). Fines were fixed in *kumals*. There is a reference in Ancient Irish literature to a king, said to have lived during the 1st century A.D., who had a chessboard, each piece of which was worth six *kumals*.[5] The oldest epic poem of Western Europe, the *Tain*, which is supposed to have originated just before the beginning of the Christian era, refers to a chariot belonging to Queen Mæve which was worth thrice seven bondsmaids.[6] There is a reference in St. Patrick's *Confessions* to a payment that he had to make for his safe conduct when visiting Western Ireland in the following terms:—"You know by experience how much I have paid out to those who were judges in all the regions which I have often visited; for I think that I have given away to them not less than the price of fifteen humans (*pretium quindecim hominum*)."[7] Now this may mean that he actually surrendered fifteen slaves or slave girls, or merely

---

[1] Joyce, *Social History of Ireland*, Vol. II, p. 385. Quoted by Patrick Nolan, *A Monetary History of Ireland* (London, 1926), Part I, p. 93.
[2] Nolan, Vol. I, pp. 93-4, 98-9, 102-3.
[3] *Annals of the Four Masters* (O'Donovan's edition). Quoted by Ridgeway, pp. 31-2.
[4] Lujo Brentano, *Eine Geschichte der wirtschaftlichen Entwickelung Englands*. Vol. I (Jena, 1927), p. 14.
[5] Nolan, Vol. I, pp. 117-8. The value of a *kumal* was equal to three milch cows. (W. F. Skene, *Celtic Scotland* 2nd Edn., Edinburgh, 1890, Vol. III, p. 153).
[6] Nolan, Vol. I, p. 128.
[7] *Tripartite Life of St. Patrick*, II, 372. Quoted by F. Seebohm, *Tribal Custom in Anglo-Saxon Law* (London, 1911), p. 100.

that he made payment of some form to an amount equal to their price. As he was strongly opposed to slavery, the latter explanation, according to which he used slaves merely as a standard of value and not as a means of payment, seems much more likely to be right. On another occasion St. Patrick is represented as putting the alternative between the death of a transgressor and the payment of seven slaves.[8] The Hibernian Synod, which sat under him in the 5th century, decreed that he who sheds the blood of a bishop or a high prince or a scribe "shall be crucified or pay seven *ancillæ*." The text adds that if paid in specie, one-third of the fine must be paid in silver.[9] This clearly indicates that the unit of slave girl merely served, on that occasion at any rate, as a standard of value.

It is believed that the *kumal* became an abstract unit of account by the 2nd century A.D. In the *Senchus Mor*, dealing with the law of distress, reference is made to the payment of blood money consisting of "seven *kumals* of silver" and "seven *kumals* of land" for killing someone who was under the protection of Fegus, King of Uladh.[10] Seven *kumals* appear to be the popular unit, and there are also references to payments of half of seven *kumals*,[11] which conclusively proves that *kumal* was during that period a standard of value, not a medium of exchange.

From a passage in the *Senchus Mor*[12] and the *Book of Aicill* the following table of values is evolved:—

8 wheat-grains	=	1 pinginn of silver.
3 pinginns	=	1 screpall.
3 screpalls	=	1 sheep.
4 sheep	=	1 heifer.
6 heifers	=	1 cow.
3 cows	=	1 *kumal*.

Yet another favourite means of payment and standard of value was the bag of grain, containing usually oats or barley. Presumably it was used for smaller values than the *kumal* or the cow. Judging by several passages in the Brehon Laws, a bag of grain of standard size must have been equal to a screpall of silver.[13] Rents for grazing rights, fines for trespassing were fixed in the Brehon Laws in bags of grain. The legal text refers at times to half and quarter bags, while the smallest unit was the handful.[14] Poems, much older even than the Brehon Laws, indicate the practice of reckoning in bags of grain.[15]

According to Joyce, from the very beginning of the records of Ireland, gold and silver were used as a medium of exchange, sometimes as ingots, and more commonly in the form of rings, bracelets and other orna-

[8]*Tripartite Life*, I, 212.

[9]Wasserschleben, *Die Bussordnungen der abendländischen Kirche*, p. 136. Quoted by Seebohm, p. 101.

[10]*Brehon Laws*, IV, I, 65-77. Quoted by Nolan, Vol. I, pp. 120-3.

[11]Seebohm, p. 103.   [12]Seebohm, p. 97.   [13]Nolan, Vol. I, p. 124

[14]Nolan, Vol. I, p. 125.   [15]Nolan, Vol. I, p. 126.

ments.[16] Silver and gold by weight were used as means of payment. Cormac Cass, who lived during the first half of the 3rd century A.D., is recorded to have given nine ounces and 500 ounces of silver to bards and learned men for praising him.[17]

Rings and other ornaments of standard weight were used as a medium of exchange. Gold, iron and brass rings existed in Ireland for ages prior to our era.[18] Open rings were the most common form of smaller gold ring money found in Ireland. They were made of gold wire of the required thickness and cut into lengths of equal weights.[19] Vast quantities of gold, silver and brass rings have been dug up in Ireland. The uniformity of the weight of a large number of them is quoted as evidence that they served monetary purposes. Betham states that they are all different multiples of the half-penny weight, but this claim, like other similar claims, must be regarded with some doubt. In addition to the gold rings, an immense number of brass rings were found in the County Monaghan and elsewhere in the early 19th century. A number of brass rings were intended to be counterfeits of gold rings—they are exactly the same shape and size, neatly covered over with a coating of gold plate and defy detection unless weighed.[20] The rings are believed to have been the principal circulating medium till the arrival of the Danes (11th century), when coined money came to be adopted.[21]

The similarity of these rings to the *manillas* which until recently constituted the principal currency along the West African coast, was often pointed out. According to Betham, the term *manilla* is of Celto-Phœnician-Irish origin. *Main* is "value" or "worth" and *aillech* is "cattle," or any kind of property.[22] The etymological evidence seems somewhat far-fetched in this instance as in many other instances.

[16]Joyce, Vol. II, p. 383. Quoted by Nolan, Vol. I, p. 146.
[17]Nolan, Vol. I, p. 128.
[18]Sir Wm. Betham, *On the Ring Money of the Celtæ and their System of Weights* Transactions of the Royal Irish Academy, 1836, Vol. XVII, 1837, p. 9).
[19]Betham, p. 10.   [20]Betham, p. 11.
[21]J. Lindsay, *A View of the Coinage of Ireland* (Cork, 1839), p. 5.
[22]Sir Wm. Betham, *On Modern and Ancient Ring Money* (Proceedings of the Royal Irish Academy, Vol. I, pp. 20-21).

CHAPTER 16

CATTLE CURRENCY OF INDIA

In India, as in many other parts of Asia, livestock was probably one of the earliest forms of currency. Cows, goats and sheep were media of exchange during the period of the Brahman literature. The salary of performers of sacred ceremonies was fixed in cattle. Dowries were paid in cows or cloth or slave girls.[1] At the time of Buddha (6th century B.C.)

[1]Pran Nath, *Tausch und Geld in Altindien* (Leipzig, 1924), p. 7.

the price of a slave girl was four to five cows or six oxen. Ancient legal texts contained many references to cattle as means of payment. According to the laws of Manu (about 900 B.C.), if one of the highest of the twice-born Brahman class slew one of the Warrior class involuntarily, he might cleanse himself by paying to the Brahmans or priests 1,000 cows and a bull. If he slew one of the agricultural or trading class, the payment was 100 cows and a bull; if the victim was one of the servile class, ten cows and a bull was payable.[2]

Judging by the epic poem *Mahabharata* (7th to 4th century B.C.), cattle was the main form of wealth.[3] At the same time cows served also as a standard of value to facilitate direct barter, according to evidence contained in the Buddhist literature.[4] According to a text in the *Rig-Veda* (about 1400 B.C.), ten cows were the price of an image of Indra.[5] The monetary use of cattle is also confirmed by etymological evidence. The modern monetary unit *rupee* originated from the Sanskrit word *rupa* which means "cattle."

Rice was also one of the principal standards of value over a long period.[6] It was also a medium of exchange. Other alleged early media of exchange are claimed to have included clay and lacquer.[7]

Cowries constituted an early form of currency. The early Indian mathematic treatise Bhascara Aharaya's *Lilivati*, portions of which were written A.D. 628, contains reference to their monetary use. The Chinese traveller and scholar Fa Hsien, who spent several years in India at the beginning of the 5th century A.D., states that cowries formed the ordinary currency.[8] Even earlier, from the 3rd century B.C., cowries were a currency and had a very high purchasing power in India. Twenty of them sufficed to pay for the daily wants of a man. Even one single cowrie had a fair purchasing power in fruits and vegetables.[9]

A wide variety of goods was used as means of payment. Taxes were paid largely in kind. In a treatise on political economy written in the 4th century B.C., Tsanakia, Finance Minister of Tsandragupta, gives details of the mixed economy that was in operation. The King's revenue consisted partly of money but included also grain and other goods.[10] The provincial treasuries, like those of Ancient Egypt, became depositories of an immense variety of products. In transactions between private

[2]*Ordinances of Manu*, XI, pp. 128-131. Quoted by Seebohm, p. 3.
[3]Pran Nath, p. 23.
[4]Caroline Foley Rhys Davids, *Notes on Early Economic Conditions in Northern India* (Journal of the Royal Asiatic Society, London, 1901), p. 876.
[5]*Rig-Veda*, IV, 24, 10. Quoted by R. K. Mookerji, *Hindu Civilization* (London, 1936).
[6]Rhys Davids, p. 876.
[7]Pramathanath Banerja, *A Study of Indian Economics*, 2nd Edn. (London, 1915), pp. 167-8.
[8]V. A. Smith, *The Early History of India*, 4th Edn. (Oxford, 1924), p. 314.
[9]Pran Nath, p. 1.
[10]Extracts of this early work on ecnomics appeared in English translation in the *India Antiquary of* 1905.

ndividuals, too, both money and commodities were used for payments. The rule was similar to that prevailing in Ancient Babylonia—payment was in metallic money in towns and in commodities in villages. While, however, in Babylonia barley largely served as means of payment in villages, performing distinct monetary functions, in Ancient India the multiplicity of the goods serving as means of payment materially reduced the monetary role of any one of them. Nevertheless, it is possible to claim that grain was a primitive currency in large parts of India. At weddings the bride paid the priest in grain.[11] Loans were granted in terms of grain. Interest rate was even higher than on loans granted in metallic money. Some law books laid down that no debtor should ever be compelled to repay more than double the amount borrowed if the loan was in gold, and three times the amount if the loan was in grain. *Vasistha* II, 44).[12] During the 4th century A.D. one per cent per month on loans of grain by the King to farmers was considered the ideal rate. In practice up to five per cent per month was often charged to low-caste borrowers, or if security was inadequate. Even Brahmans had to pay two per cent.[13]

India had metallic currencies from a very early period. Gold played a very important role in Ancient India. According to W. J. Perry, every place mentioned in the *Rig-Veda* which Sanskrit scholars have been able to identify happens to be a site where gold was found. In Southern India most ancient stone structures, indicating early civilization, are found in vast numbers in certain regions of the States of Hyderabad, Mysore, etc., always in close association with extensive and long-forgotten gold mines revealed by recent archæological exploration.

Notwithstanding this, gold was not the earliest monetary metal used in Ancient India. Excavations at Mohenjo Daro (Sind) have brought to light certain oblong bars of copper which their discoverer assumes to have been coins.[14] Buddhist literature contains frequent reference to metallic money pieces, but there is no evidence to show that these pieces conformed to any standard or that they were regulated by any state authority. They appear to have been cut into regular shapes and the punchmark they bore was probably that of traders in metals.[15] Long before the Greek invasion such pieces of metals appear to have been in use. Oblong, square or round pieces have been found in all parts of India. They were believed to have been employed as measures of value.[16] These pieces of metals commonly, but not always, bear on them rude

[11]Pran Nath, p. 7.
[12]Pramathanath Banerja, *Public Administration in Ancient India* (London, 1916), p. 274.
[13]L. D. Barnett, *Antiquities of India* (London, 1913), p. 211.
[14]Sir John Marshall, Director of Archæology in India in the *Illustrated London News*, 20th September, 1924, p. 528. Quoted by Burns, p. 37.
[15]Thomas, *Ancient Indian Weights*, p. 4. Quoted by Rhys Davids, p. 877.
[16]Prof. Wilson, *Asiatic Reseaches*, Vol. XVII, p. 596. Quoted by Brijkishore Bhargava, *Indigenous Banking in Ancient and Medieval India* (Bombay, 1935), pp. 276-7.

symbols of the sun, the moon, the star, or some nondescript mark to
which it is not easy to assign a definite significance.[17] Some pieces o
metals were cut out of hammered sheets of copper or silver, and were i
many instances clipped to conform to uniform weight standards.[18] The
are known under the name of *puranas*. There is no information to
indicate whether the punchmarks on them indicated State guarantee.

At Singavaram (Madras Presidency), silver blocks and spiral coil
of thick silver wire were found together with small silver coins. Ther
were six square blocks, weighing each about fifteen and a half *tolas*
bearing the symbol of a bull in well-marked relief. Their uniformit
suggests their use as currency. There were also spiral rings of silver, on
and a half inches in diameter, six inches long, and of a thickness of abou
a quarter of an inch. The assumption is that uniform lengths of wir
were clipped off whenever necessary, hammered into flans, then struc
into primitive coins.[19]

As elsewhere, metals were used for payment by weight. Fines of 100
500, 1,000, etc., *panas* were fixed in legal texts. The unit of weight i
believed to have become gradually a monetary unit.[20] Gold and silve
bars were often sealed by merchants; frequently many merchants pu
their seals on these bars, as and when they exchanged hands.[21] In th
Rig-Veda there are instances of Vedic bards acknowledging the gift o
"100 pieces of gold." There is, however, no distinct allusion to coine
money.[22] The word *nishki* is often used in the *Rig-Veda* and while i
some passages it is taken to mean money, in others it implies a golde
ornament for the neck. Jackson points out the two interpretations ar
not necessarily contradictory for in India pieces of gold serving a
money have been used as ornaments for the neck from times immemorial.[?]
Pran Nath suggests that the pieces of metals which were in circulatio
at the time of the Vedas served primarily for payment to Brahmans fo
performing sacrifices and they were stamped with a sign in commemora
tion of these sacrifices.[24]

Although there can be no doubt that various kinds of primitive cur
rencies were in existence since early times, the bulk of trade was done b
barter. In fact, early legislation imposed deliberate limitations to the us
of money. Many objects were excluded from money traffic and wer
only allowed to be traded through barter. The list of these goods quote
by Pran Nath is very long, and its application must have reduce
considerably the sphere in which money could function.[25] According t

[17]Prof. Wilson, *Ariana Antiqua*, p. 364. Quoted by Bhargava, p. 277.
[18]C. J. Brown, *The Coins of India* (Calcutta, 1922), p. 15.
[19]Prof. Wilson, *Essay on Indian Antiquities*. Quoted by Bhargava, p. 277.
[20]T. G. Aravamuthan, *A New Type of Punchmarked Coin* (Transactions of th
International Numismatic Congress, 1936) (London, 1938), pp. 393-4.
[21]E. Thomas, *Ancient Indian Weights*. Quoted by Babelon, p. 100.
[22]A. V. Williams Jackson, *History of India* (London, 1906), Vol. I, p. 19.
[23]Jackson, p. 20.   [24]Pran Nath, p. 22.
[25]Pran Nath, p. 4.

other interpretations, however, these restrictions only applied to Brahmans.[26]

Judging by the high purchasing power of the monetary units in early times, the volume of currency must have been rather short of requirements. The *Atharvaveda* contains a prayer for the increase in the volume of currency brought by the merchants to the market so as to be able to earn money with the aid of money.[27]

There is no evidence of the use of fiduciary currencies; all objects used for monetary purposes were either useful or ornamental, and had therefore an intrinsic value apart altogether from the value conferred on them by their monetary use.[28]

[26]Pran Nath, p. 5.
[27]Quoted by Alfons Dopsch, *Naturalwirtschaft und Geldwirtschaft in der Welt geschichte* (Vienna, 1930), pp. 40-1.
[28]Rhys Davids, p. 881.

CHAPTER 17

SHELL, SILK AND METAL CURRENCIES OF CHINA

China is practically the only country about which we possess detailed evidence concerning the early evolution of her primitive currency. We owe it to Terrien de Lacouperie who, in his *Catalogue of Chinese Coins*,[1] produces a chronological list of the outstanding numismatic events from the earliest time to the 7th century A.D. Unfortunately, in many instances he does not quote his authorities. Nevertheless, he is accepted by all numismatists and monetary historians as the leading authority on Ancient Chinese currency, even though some Chinese scholars are not altogether satisfied about the authenticity of some of his information. The present chapter is based largely on his material.

The pre-Chinese population of China had used cowrie shells as a medium of exchange. When the Chinese arrived on the scene (24th century B.C.) they found cowries in general use. The Chinese invaders, who for many centuries constituted a minority of the population, regulated the circulation of cowries as well as that of tortoise-shells and other shells.[2] Reference to cowries appear in *Ya-King*, the oldest Chinese book.[3] The same book also mentioned tortoise-shell currency, used for large payments which would have required too many cowries. The use of cowries and other shells by the early Chinese as currency is also indicated by etymological evidence. The words denoting "buying,"

[1]Terrien de Lacouperie, *Catalogue of Chinese Coins from the 7th century* B.C. *to* A.D. 621 *including the series in the British Museum* (London, 1892).
[2]Terrien de Lacouperie, *The Metallic Cowries of Ancient China* (The Journal of the Royal Asiatic Society, Vol. xx, London, 1888), p. 438.
[3]Ridgeway, p. 21.

"selling," "riches," "prices," "cheap," "dear," and many others referring to money and wealth contain the ideographic sign denoting the word "shell."[4]

There is evidence indicating the use of cowries as store of wealth in the 14th century B.C. In 1375 B.C. P'An Keng of the Shang Dynasty rebuked his Ministers for their greed in hoarding cowries and gems. By then the Chinese had adopted and regulated for their own requirements cowries and tortoise-shells of various sizes used as currency by the pre-Chinese tribes.[5] By 852 B.C. supplies of tortoise-shells and cowries became distinctly scarce,[6] and by the end of the 7th century B.C., they had become too scarce to satisfy monetary requirements.[7]

In 221 B.C. the first Emperor of China forbade the use of cowries and tortoise-shells, and also of gems, pearls and tin, as currency.[8] In A.D. 10, however, Wang Mang, wishing to return to the ancient state of things in every way, attempted among other changes to restore the use of shell currency. He instituted a system under which there were five different varieties of shells serving as monetary units at an arbitrary value.[9] The largest type of cowries was equal to 216 ordinary cowries a pair. Cowries which were smaller than sixth-tenths of an inch were not used for currency. Of tortoise-shells there were four different sorts, of various sizes and denominations, with different values.[10] The intelligent section of the population, especially the merchants, objected to this revival of an antiquated system. They gave vent to their feelings in a seditious popular little song. Four years later Wang Mang realized his mistake at last and discontinued the system of shell money.[11]

In addition to cowries and tortoise-shells, pearl oyster shells were also used in Ancient China, the unit being a pair.[12] The popularity of cowries as currency led to the use of metallic cowries around 600 B.C. in order to combine the time-honoured shape of the currency with the advantage of the use of metals for monetary purposes.[13] It has also been said that the idea of a hole in the Chinese "knife money" (which subsequently developed into a round coin with a square hole) was suggested by the practice of stringing the cowrie shells.[14] There are, however, alternative explanations, as we shall see below.

Metals by weight were in use from very early times. In the 23rd century B.C. goods were traded against wrought and unwrought metals by weight.[15] In the 11th century B.C. the amount of metal to be paid by those convicted of crimes as an alternative to their punishment was

[4]Lord Avebury, *Inaugural Presidential Address at the Institute of Bankers* (Journal of the Institute of Bankers, June, 1879), p. 2.
[5]Lacouperie, *Catalogue of Chinese Coins*, p. IX.
[6]Lacouperie, p. X.   [7]Lacouperie, p. XII.   [8]Lacouperie, p. XIV.
[9]Lord Avebury, p. 2.   [10]Lacouperie, pp. 381-2.   [11]Lacouperie, p. 383.
[12]Lacouperie, p. XX.
[13]Lacouperie (1888), pp. 438-9.
[14]Wen Pin Wei, *The Currency Problem in China* (New York, 1914), p. 12.
[15]Lacouperie, p. VIII.

fixed.[16] Copper was in use from the 3rd millenium.[17] Gold and silver was also used, though, according to some students of Ancient China, only at a much later period. Unwrought metals continued to be used in the more backward parts of China as currency even after the adoption of coinage.[18] Gold was used in cubes and bronze in rings, in ingots or in plates circulating by weight.[19] It has been suggested that the gold cubes were only used for the purchase of jewels or as presents from Princes to wealthy persons.[20] Later silver was used as a medium of exchange in the shape of ingots.[21]

As in Ancient Egypt, metallic money often assumed the form of rings. In the middle of the 10th century penalties were expressed in terms of rings of copper weighing six ounces.[22] Culprits were allowed to escape their punishment by paying 100, 200, 500 or 1,000 pieces of ring money. It is believed to have originated in the 11th century when Tcheng, King of Tchou, established special Treasury Offices to regulate the metal and silk currency.[23] It was not until 655 B.C.—about the same time as in Lydia and in Argos—that the ring money of the Central Kingdom of Tchou came to be stamped.[24]

The use of implement money was not slow to follow that of raw metals. In 1954 B.C. the founder of the Hia Dynasty cast metal implements which were easy to barter for the relief of his people in distress during the floods of the Hwang-Ho.[25] Towards the end of the 2nd millenium small implements of bronze in daily use such as hoes, spades and sickles, exchanged by weight, became a favourite currency.[26] It is only natural that among agricultural people the implements most likely to develop a monetary use should be agricultural tools.[27] By the 7th century knives, sickles, hoes or adzes formed the lower currency in China.

Knives became by far the most important type of early currency. Their introduction is attributed in a rather legendary way to the dis-content caused among the soldiers of Prince Hwan by the stringent monetary conditions in the 7th century B.C. Their general, to allay the disaffection, authorized them to make use of their metal knives for barter. The people were delighted with the innovation and found the knife a convenient medium of exchange.[28] Another version of the origin of knife money was that Prince Hwan authorized the payment of fines for slight offences in metal knives instead of the legal ring currency.[29] According to yet another version, it was sea traders of the Indian Ocean who had established a colony in Shantung who started issuing large bronze knives of regular weight for currency with a distinct mark or emblem around 670 B.C. The issue of knife coins remained largely in the

[16]Lacouperie, p. IX.
[17]A. Dopsch, p. 30.
[18]Lacouperie, p. XIV.
[19]Lacouperie, p. X.
[20]Burns, p. 23.
[21]Dopsch, p. 31.
[22]Burns, p. 14.
[23]Lacouperie, p. X, p. 319.
[24]Lacouperie, p. XII.
[25]Lacouperie, p. IX.
[26]Lacouperie, p. X.
[27]Burns, p. 28.
[28]Lacouperie, p. 213.
[29]Lacouperie, p. XI.

hands of merchants, merchant guilds or local authorities. As they circulated without State authority they cannot be regarded as coins proper.
After a time the word *tao* (knife) lost its proper meaning and was used
simply as a unit of currency.[30] Knife money had a round ring for handle
with a square hole in it. Subsequently the knife part was abandoned and
only the round disc with a square hole remained as the traditional
Chinese coin. Incidentally, neither the knives nor the various other
implements used as currency were usuable for non-monetary purposes.
After a while they became merely symbols of the objects out of which
they originated. In particular hoe money came to assume such a curious
shape that many numismatists refer to it as "shirt money," since it
resembles the shape of a shirt.

The nearest thing to State regulation of knife money was the enact-
ment of rules for the weights of metallic currency between 670-655 B.C.
by Prince Hwan. He also caused implement money to be cast in order
to make known the models and weights to the people.[31] Gradually,
however, the various Chinese rulers came to adopt coins of their own,
though it was not until 135 B.C. that free coinage was forbidden. At the
same time implement money of every kind was also demonetized.

Grain constituted another early primitive currency in Ancient China.
It was displaced by metallic currencies, but on three occasions between
the 1st century B.C. and the 5th century A.D. attempts were made by
conservative Emperors to revert to it. In 48 B.C. counterfeiting had
brought the metallic currency into such disrepute that the revival of the
use of grain, silk, hempen and silk cloth, and shells as media of exchange
was seriously considered.[32] In A.D. 24 grain was actually adopted as
currency, and so was silk and hempen cloth and metal in lumps by
weight. The experiment did not last long,[33] but it was repeated once
more in A.D. 402, again because the metallic currency had been hopelessly debased by counterfeiting. It was found, however, that even
commodity currencies were not immune from debasement. Much
hardship was caused to the people because of the introduction of moist
grain and flimsy, loosely woven silk as currency. It was decided therefore
to revert to metallic coinage.[34]

Silk was a popular form of currency in China. The word *pu*, which
originally meant cloth, subsequently assumed the meaning of "money."
Pieces of hemp or silk cloth were used as a medium of exchange during
the 2nd millenium and were regulated into a currency system in 1091
B.C. Tcheng, second King of Tchou, circulated silk in pieces of regular
size.[35] Such was the popularity of silk as currency that in the 6th century
B.C., when coins were already well known, payment in coinage was
refused by the Prince of Ts'In for the release of an officer; he insisted

[30]Lacouperie, p. 331.   [31]Lacouperie, pp. XI, XII.
[32]Lacouperie, p. xv.   [33]Lacouperie, p. 369.
[34]Lacouperie, p. 403.   [35]Lacouperie, pp. X, XVIII.

that the coins must first be exchanged for silk.[36] In 460 B.C. the King of Ts'U established three boards for the management of the currency, one being in charge of gems, the second of gold and the third of coins and silk. With the popularization of metallic coinage, silk currency fell in disuse, but, as we saw above, attempts were made at times to revive its monetary use. Apart from the instances referred to above, in A.D. 347, the old currency of silk and hempen cloth was substituted for copper coin in Western Shensi.[37] Pieces of closely woven silk and hempen cloth were ripped up to be employed as currency even though in doing so they were made unfit for use as clothing and their intrinsic value was destroyed. Before long copper coinage was restored, however.

Salt was yet another material which served as money in Ancient China.[38] In the 7th century B.C. the States of Liang, Tchou, Sung, Wei and others used salt extensively and the authorities were in great trouble when the usual supply was not forthcoming at the proper time.[39] Other materials which are claimed to have played the part of currency include clay. In A.D. 513-516 some clay money was said to have been issued about which we have no particulars.[40] Cardboard is also said to have been used as currency, though Terrien de Lacouperie does not give any details. Finally, the use of deerskin as currency is mentioned.[41] In reality, on Terrien de Lacouperie's own evidence, the so-called deerskin currency issued in 119 B.C. was merely a sort of token or badge for which the Kings, Feudal Princes and noblemen had to pay the Emperor 400,000 copper cash pieces. They were compelled to wear them as badges of honour without which entrance to Court and audience by the Emperor could not be obtained. It is characteristic of the loose employment of the term "money" that these obviously non-monetary objects should come to be described as such.

Credit was highly developed in Ancient China. During the Tchou Dynasty (1122-256 B.C.) an institution was established to make advances both for purposes of production and consumption.[42] Early Chinese texts contain many references to laws concerning lending.

The role played by the various Chinese Governments was much more active than that played by the State in Ancient Egypt or even in Babylonia. Money as a medium of exchange evidently played a much more active part in Ancient China than in either of these two Empires. The part played by money in Chinese economic life during the early period is not adequately indicated by the material available and it is a pity that

[36]Lacouperie, p. XIII.
[37]Lacouperie, p. XIV.
[38]Lacouperie, p. XX.
[39]Lacouperie, p. XII.
[40]Lacouperie, p. 424. Similar currency was issued after the T'Ang Dynasty in the 10th century.
[41]Lacouperie, pp. 358-9.
[42]Kin-Wei Shaw, *Chinese Banking* (*The China Critic*, 19th July, 1928). Quoted by F. M. Tamagna, *Banking and Finance in China* (New York, 1942), p. 13.

R

Chinese students of economic history have not made more facts accessible to those unacquainted with their language.

The above survey of primitive currencies in Ancient China shows a remarkable contrast between the high degree of development of Ancient Chinese civilization and the backward and untidy currency situation that prevailed most of the time. We must bear in mind, however, that Ancient China was a conglomeration of races at various stages of cultural development, and that very often a primitive form of currency was maintained by the more advanced sections of the community for the sake of being able to trade with a more backward community which knew no other currency.

PART II: MEDIEVAL PERIOD

CHAPTER 18

RINGS AND WEIGHED METAL CURRENCIES OF THE BRITISH ISLES

IN Anglo-Saxon and Norman England coins were in general use. Nevertheless, various forms of primitive money continued to be used simultaneously with modern money, partly owing to the scarcity of coins and partly owing to the distrust that arose from time to time as a result of debasement or counterfeiting.

The English word "fee" originated from the German word *vieh* (cattle) through the intermediary of the Anglo-Saxon word *feoh*, meaning cattle, property, treasure, price, reward, levy, tribute, money.[1] This itself seems to indicate that in early England cattle was a favourite means of payment. In fact, the wergeld was fixed in the early laws both in terms of cattle and in metal currency. Ine's Law at the end of the 7th century gives fines in terms of cattle.[2] In Wessex the wergeld varied between two hundred and thirty-three and a third oxen. The quotations in fractions of oxen shows that the ox was a unit of account rather than a means of payment. In the Code of Athelstan (895-940), the value of the ox was fixed at thirty pence for the purpose of wergeld.[3] The value of a sheep was fixed at a shilling which at that time was equal to four pence.[4] Among the early English, cattle and slaves were always taken as payment, and consequently estimates of value were commonly made in terms of cattle, and occasionally in slaves.[5]

There is no direct evidence to show that skins were used at any time as a currency in England. But the fact that they had been used as token payment—in the Domesday Book (1085-86) the rent of Chester is given as forty-five pounds and three marten skins—makes it appear at least possible that at an early period they played a monetary role.[6] There is some evidence of doubtful value about the use of leather money in

---

[1]Matzerath, *Die altenglischen Namen der Geldwerte, Masse und Gewichte* (Bonn, 1913), p. 2.

[2]Keary (1879), p. 7.

[3]H. M. Chadwick, *Studies on Anglo-Saxon Institutions* (Cambridge, 1905), p. 156.

[4]Chadwick, p. 62.

[5]W. Cunningham, *The Growth of English Industry and Commerce during the Middle Ages* (3rd Edn., Cambridge, 1896), p. 122.

[6]W. Charlton, *Leather Currency* (Brit. Numismatic Journal, Vol. III, 1906), p. 315.

the time of King Edgar (942-975). Ruding quotes from *The Wits*, Act 5, Scene 1, the following passage:—

> "Why this was such a firk of piety
> I ne'er heard of: bury her gold with her
> 'Tis strange her old shoes were not interred too,
> For fear the days of Edgar should return,
> When they coin'd leather."[7]

Ruding also quotes the *History of Allchester*, written in 1622, according to which King Edward I (1272-1307) issued leather money bearing his name, stamp and picture, which he used for financing the building of Carnarvon, Beaumaris and Conway Castles, "to spare better bullion." Specimens of this currency are alleged to have been preserved and kept for some time in one of the towers of Carnarvon Castle. Ruding remarks that there is no evidence in support of this statement. In his opinion, they may have been promissory notes.[8] In the author's opinion, this and many other references to "leather money" may have referred to rudimentary paper money consisting of sealed pieces of parchment and which, being made of animal skin, may be described as being "leather."

In England during the early Middle Ages, as in other Northern European countries, rings were also used as currency. In the Anglo-Saxon Chronicles, under the year 937, a poem describes Athelstan as "the ring-giver of warriors." In 975 King Edgar is similarly described.[9] The Saxon word *beag* or *beah*, the literal meaning of which is ring or armlet, is used in the laws of Ethelbert to indicate fines.[10]

In addition to rings, metals by weight served as a medium of exchange. William the Conqueror allowed Edgar Atheling (1066-1107) a pound weight of silver every day.[11] Uncoined precious metals were used for hoarding. The units of weights used in various periods came to be regarded as units of value. Thus the words *mancus*, *ore* and *mark*, often used in expressing early English amounts of money, were originally Danish weights of silver and gold.[12] These units were never coined in England. The word *pound*, which originated from the Latin *pondus*, was also originally used for indicating a pound's weight of silver. This was, to begin with, purely a money of account, as no coin representing this value was ever struck by any Anglo-Saxon King.[13]

The word *shilling* is believed to have originated from *scylan* (to divide), owing to the fact that a shilling was originally a portion of some silver ornament, broken off and cast into the scale for payment by

---

[7]Ruding, 3rd Edn., Vol. I, p. 131.
[8]Ruding, Vol. I, p. 206.   [9]Nolan, Vol. I, p. 160.   [10]Keary (1879), p. 8.
[11]Speed's *History of England*, p. 504. Quoted by J. Simon, *An Essay Towards an Historical Account of Irish Coins* (2nd Edn., Dublin, 1810), p. 4.
[12]Chadwick, p. 12.
[13]T. Hodkin, *The History of England from the Earliest Times to the Norman Conquest* (London, 1931), p. 233.

weight. St. Oswald is said to have ordered his beautiful silver dish to be broken up and distributed to the starving crowd who would take these *scyllingas* into the market and exchange them for the needed food.[14] The name *scilling* meaning "a piece cut off" was given by the Saxons to pieces of broken silver which it was the practice to throw into the scale to make up the loss of weight of the coins when payment in coins was made by weight.[15]

In his *Catalogue of English Coins in the British Museum*, Keary quotes the translation of the ancient *Traveller's Tales*, according to which a Gothic King gave a ring of pure gold marked as worth six hundred *scillings*.[16] This quotation seems to indicate that the *scillingas* served not only as a medium of payment, but also as a standard of value.

The only money which appears to have been coined during the early period was the silver penny, of which two hundred and forty weighed a pound. Its original name was *sceatt*, derived presumably from the Gothic word *skatts*, its original meaning was "cattle" but it had come to signify "wealth" or "treasure." It corresponds to the German word *Schatz*. In ancient legal texts, sometimes two hundred and fifty pennies were reckoned to be equal to the pound. According to Chadwick the explanation is that it was customary even in the 9th century to pay large sums of money by weight even if they consisted of coins. The extra ten pence to the pound represented an allowance for worn coins.[17]

In Scotland, too, cattle was the early means of payment for wergeld. In the *Leges inter Brettos et Scotos*, which is attributed to King David I (1124-1153), the wergeld was fixed in shillings and in cows, the amount varying according to the victim's rank, between sixteen and a thousand cows.[18] According to the law of William the Lion (1165-1214) the fine imposed on a thief was fixed at thirty-three and a half cows.[19] Under the Statutes of Alexander II, dated 1220, those who held the King's land and absented themselves from the army had to pay a fine fixed in cows and sheep.[20] In the Scottish treatise entitled *Regiam majestam*, reflecting conditions during the early 13th century, the cow is equated to six shillings for the purpose of fines.[21]

Metals were also used in various forms in Scotland. Simple gold pellets, usually marked by a cross in relief, constituted the transitional stage to coinage.[22]

---

[14]Hodkin, p. 233.
[15]A. E. Feavearyear, *The Pound Sterling—A History of English Money* (Oxford, 1931), p. 8.
[16]Keary (1887), Vol. I, p. IX; Keary (1879), pp. 8-9.
[17]Chadwick, p. 30. Reference to "half a pound of pennies," is made by Turner, *Anglo-Saxons*, Vol. II, p. 128. Quoted by Cunningham, p. 123.
[18]Chadwick, p. 63; Seebohm, pp. 311-4.
[19]Nolan, Vol. I, p. 92. "Of every thief through all Scotland the weregehede is XXXIII ky and one half."
[20]Seebohm, p. 300.   [21]Seebohm, p. 305.
[22]Daniel Wilson, *The Archæology and Prehistoric Annals of Scotland* (1851), p. 520.

In Wales, too, the wergeld was fixed in cows, the blood money for killing a king being a thousand cows.[23] The payment in case of murder of a free tribesman was a hundred and twenty-six cows—a hundred and twenty for the murder itself and six for the insult implied by the murder.[24] The cow used in payment was defined in the Venedotian Code as being of normal value when in full milk and until the fifth calf. Even the quantity of the milk of the standard cow was strictly defined.[25] The standard cow was equal in the Code to "three scores of silver," which expression is translated in the Latin version of the Dimetian Code as *uncia argenti*. The assumption is, therefore, that the score of silver was equal to an ounce.[26]

The records of the donations to the Monastry of St. Cadoc contain frequent references to swords, horses and garments, always valued in cows. According to Seebohm gold-hilted swords, vestments and "best horses" were used as means of payment and cows were the standard of value. He believes this system was a survival from an earlier period when all payments were made in cattle.[27]

Under the Dimetian Code which dates from the 8th century, payment of wergeld is fixed in slaves. "If anyone by intention shall have committed homicide, let him pay three *ancillæ* and three *servi* and acquire safety."[28]

Ever since the time of Edward I the rent for the Scilly Isles was paid to the Crown in puffins.[29] There is a memorandum added to a Conveyance of Scilly to the heirs of Golshull, dated 1440, which says that "the Islands of Scilly were held of the King . . . and at the rent of fifty puffins, or six shillings and eightpence yearly."[30] There is no evidence, however, for the use of puffins as currency between the islanders. Quite possibly the above facts merely constitute an instance of the payment of rent in kind or, since the value of the fifty puffins was negligible even for conditions prevailing in the 15th century, their annual surrender to the Crown may have merely constituted a token payment (such as the payment of a peppercorn as the ground rent in many instances in our days) aimed at upholding the Crown's rights of ownership.

[23]Seebohm, pp. 314-5.   [24]Seebohm, p. 43.   [25]Seebohm, p. 48.
[26]Seebohm, p. 49.
[27]F. Seebohm, *The Tribal System in Wales* (London, 1904), pp. 217-25.
[28]Seebohm (1911), p. 108.
[29]W. Borlase, *Observations on the Ancient and Present State of the Islands of Scilly* (Oxford, 1756), pp. 80-1.
[30]Borlase, p. 109.

CHAPTER 19

CATTLE MONEY IN IRELAND

The primitive monetary standards described in the chapter on Ancient Ireland continued to be used during the early Middle Ages and, to some extent, even in later centuries, right up to the days of Queen Elizabeth. Although foreign coins found their way into the country, no Irish coins were known to have been minted until the Danish invasion (11th century). Even after the use of coins became established, cows, slaves and slave girls, grain and metals by weight or in the form of rings continued to serve as currencies or at any rate as units of account.

Cattle remained a favourite means of payment and also a unit of account throughout the Middle Ages. The Annals of Ulster indicate that in the 12th century there was a fixed parity between silver and oxen. In the year 1161 "seven score oxen were given but it is their value that was presented, namely, 420 ounces of white silver, to wit, three ounces in every ox."[1] In 1157, gifts to the Church were recorded to have consisted of eight scores of cows, three score ounces of gold, etc. Nolan observes that the cattle here mentioned may or may not have been given in kind. It was a standard of value, and possibly it was the equivalent of 160 cows that was given.[2]

At the end of the 14th century under the reign of Richard II, a French scribe accompanying the Royal progress through Leinster, makes special mention of the valuable horse of the Irish Commander, Mac-Murrough Kavanagh. According to his account, the horse cost 400 cows. The French observer, commenting on this fact, stated that in Ireland they generally bought and sold by means of beasts only:—

> "*Un cheval, et sans sele ne arcon*
> *Qui lui avoit coste, ce disoiton,*
> *Quatre cent vaches, tant estoit bel et bon;*
> *Par pour argent*
> *A on pais, pour ce communement*
> *Merchandent eulx a bestes seulment.*"

Nolan, who quotes the above verse, remarks that there was in fact a shortage of coin in Ireland during that period, due to export of large quantities of gold and silver through trade. Hence the reversion to trading on the basis of cattle.[3]

Even in the 15th century, poets were rewarded by the gift of cows. Teig O'Higgins (died 1484) in his verse on the death of Cathal O'Connor of Sligo, said that the deceased never gave him less than two cows for a poem.[4]

Bondsmaids (*kumals*) also continued to be used as a medium of exchange and standard of value during the Middle Ages. In A.D. 889 the payment of a fine of thirty times seven *kumals* is recorded. The ratio between slave girls and cows was fixed at three cows per head.[5] In the

[1]Nolan, Vol. I, p. 106. [2]Nolan, Vol. I, pp. 131-2.
[3]Nolan, Vol. II, p. 51. [4]Nolan, Vol. I, p. 107.
[5]Nolan, Vol. I, p. 112. The *Book of Aicil* (*Ancient Laws on Ireland*) states that two times seven *kumals* are equal to forty-two cows (Nolan, p. 113).

ancient law of service or tenancy (Brehon Laws, Vol. II) mention is made of half a *kumal* and quarter of a *kumal*. Seven *kumals* were the recognized large units.[6]

There are many instances to show that the practice of using precious metals by weight as currency continued during the Middle Ages. Cormac MacGuileannan, King-Bishop of Munster (c. 885-903), left legacies expressed in ounces of silver and gold. In 988, the terms of surrender of Dublin Fortress included the payment to the King of one ounce of gold for every garden on Christmas night for ever.[7] In 1004, Brian-Boruma, King of Ireland, offered twenty ounces of gold to the altar of St. Patrick in the cathedral of Armagh.[8] In 1029 a ransom included one thousand cows, sixty ounces of gold and sixty ounces of silver. In 1156, the will of Turlough O'Connor, King of Ireland, contained legacies of five hundred and forty ounces of gold and forty marks of silver.[9] In 1152 he received for the ransom of the chieftain of Munster, sixty ounces of gold.[10] In 1157, Maurice O'Loghlin, King of Ireland, upon the dedication of the church of Mellifont, gave likewise sixty ounces of gold to the monks of that house; to whom Donat O'Carrol, King of Ergal, founder of that church, gave also sixty ounces of gold; and Dervorgilla, wife of Tierna O'Ruark, contributed the same amount.[11] Apparently, sixty ounces constituted a widely used unit. Its multiples are frequently encountered in Medieval Irish records. In 1161, four hundred and twenty ounces of pure silver were collected in the diocese of Cory.

Maurice O'Loghlin, King of Ireland, granted land to the Monastery of Ardbraccen at a yearly rent of three ounces of gold.[12] In an ancient registry of St. Thomas's Abbey near Dublin there is an entry dated 1199:—"For this grant, the said Roger has given to us an ounce of gold, to be expended on the repairs of the walls of this city."[13]

Rings are believed to have circulated as currency down to the 11th or 12th century. According to Betham these rings were all standard weight. Their use as a substitute for coins may account for the fact that very few ancient coins have been found in Ireland.[14] Although the kings of Ireland had minted coins, they changed hands largely by weight, owing to the wide discrepancies between the weight of the individual coins.[15]

[6]Nolan, Vol. i, pp. 114-5.   [7]Nolan, Vol. i, pp. 128-9.   [8]Simon, p. 3.
[9]Nolan, Vol. i, p. 130.   [10]Lindsay, p. 4.   [11]Simon, p. 3.
[12]Lindsay, p. 5; Simon, p. 3.
[13]Simon, p. 11.   [14]Lindsay, p. 5.   [15]Simon, p. 10.

CHAPTER 20

CATTLE, CLOTH AND WEIGHED METAL MONEY IN GERMANY

Pre-Christian Prussians used pieces of cloth with bronze rings as their currency.[1] In Austrasia the gold *solidus* and the silver *denar* were not used much in commerce as a medium of exchange, but largely as a unit of account.

Cattle was frequently the actual medium of exchange in the early Middle Ages.[2] In early Germanic legal texts there are frequent references to cattle, in terms of which the wergeld was often fixed. In the *Lex Ribuaria*, the *Lex Salica* and the *Capitulare Saxonicum* the wergeld was fixed both in coined money and in cattle. Up to the time of Dagobert I (602-639) the Franks collected tribute from the Saxons in cattle.[3]

Under the *Lex Salica* and the *Lex Ribuaria* the wergeld was fixed in the monetary unit in gold *solidus*, but actual payment could be made in livestock under Tit. XXXVI of the *Lex Ribuaria*. Oxen and cows, "horned, seeing and sound," were reckoned as two *solidi* and one *solidus* respectively. Horses and mares "seeing and sound" were reckoned as six and three *solidi*.[4] Under the *Lex Saxonicum* the four-year-old oxen were acceptable at two *solidi*, bullocks at one and a half *solidi*.[5] Slaves, arms, grain, etc., were also accepted in payment. During the Carolingian period it was stipulated, however, that swords and falcons were no longer acceptable.[6]

Charlemagne, in his dealings with the Saxons, found it necessary to define the value of his *solidus* by equating it to the value of a one-year-old ox.[7] According to Dopsch, this fact does not indicate the use of cattle as a currency. He explains that the adoption of the dual system of currency was due to the confusion arising from the existence of two different kinds of *solidi* during that period, as a result of which it was expedient in legal texts to state the equivalents of wergeld in terms of cattle.[8] This explanation appears to be in keeping with the endeavour of Dopsch to prove that throughout that period an advanced money economy existed in Europe in general and in Germany in particular. The development of this school of thought was a reaction from the earlier exaggerated conception that after the collapse of the Roman Empire Medieval Europe reverted entirely to natural economy. The truth probably lies somewhere between the two extremes. The admitted

---

[1]Ilwof, p. 48.
[2]H. Brunner, *Deutsche Rechtsgeschichte*, 2nd Edn. (Leipzig, 1906), p. 314.
[3]Keary (1879), p. 6.   [4]Seebohm (1911), p. 171.
[5]Seebohm (1911), pp. 217-8.
[6]Brunner, p. 322.   [7]Ridgeway, p. 34.
[8]A. Dopsch, *Wirtschaftliche und soziale Grundlagen der europäischen Kulturent-wickelung aus der Zeit von Caesar bis auf Karl der Grossen* (Vienna, 1930), pp. 518-21. See also Seebohm (1911), *passim*.

fact that it was considered expedient, for no matter what reasons, to stipulate in legal texts an option of payment or reckoning in cattle is in itself sufficient to indicate its widespread monetary use.

That cattle was used extensively as a store of value in Germany is indicated by the origin of the word *Schatz* (treasure, wealth) which is supposed to have been derived from the Gothic *skatts* (cattle) or the Frisian *sket*, which latter word retained for a long time its meaning of cattle.[9]

In a large number of instances legal texts prescribe payment in eggs, chickens, etc., as an alternative to money payment.[10] It is difficult to ascertain to what extent these goods served monetary purposes. On the whole it seems safer to regard their use as payment in kind. Grain alone among the land products may be considered to have played the part of a currency to any considerable extent. It must have been used frequently and regularly as a means of payment, judging by the fact that contracts often stipulated payment in *Korngeld* or *Pfenniggeld*.[11] Tille gives instances from the 8th century in which payment was fixed in grain. In case of difficulties in making payment in grain, the possibility of payment in the form of other commodities was provided for. From the end of the 8th century rye and oats had a fixed value for the purpose of statutory payments, though their ratio was liable to changes.[12] In the *Capitulare Saxonicum* (Chapter XI) the value of oxen, oats, rye and honey was fixed in terms of *solidi* for the purpose of payment, while other commodities were acceptable in payment according to valuation.[13] According to Tille, grain was widely used as a store of value and a means of saving.[14] Even in the 15th century grain retained its monetary function in rural districts in many parts of Germany, in the sense that if no coins were available payment in grain had to be accepted.[15]

In Medieval Brandenburg chickens, wax and pepper changed hands at a fixed price, and are claimed to have played a limited monetary role. There was also a unit called *frustrum* (provisions). Details of this system are lacking, but the unit was presumably some definite assortment of goods, or at any rate an assortment liable to variation but corresponding to certain requirements.

In Friesland the wergeld was fixed in cloth. The *wede* was four and a half ells; four *wede* were equal to one *reilmark* or *gewandmark*; three of this unit was equal to one *linmark*.[16] The value of the *wede* was fixed at

[9]W. Stanley Jevons, *Money and the Mechanism of Exchange* (London, 1875), p. 23.
[10]J. Kulischer, *Allgemeine Wirtschaftsgeschichte des Mittelalters und der Neuzeit* (Munich, 1926), p. 94. Customs were often payable in wine, cheese, herrings or pepper. Merchants had to carry these commodities with them for the purpose of discharging customs dues (Ilwof, p. 36).
[11]Kulischer, p. 317. See also A. Tille, *Getreide als Geld. Jahrbuch fur National-ökonomie und Statistik*, 3rd Series, Vol. xx (Jena, 1900), p. 721 *et seq.*
[12]Tille, p. 726.   [13]Tille, p. 727.   [14]Tille, p. 728.
[15]Tille, p. 731.
[16]Brunner, pp. 230-31.

one *schilling* or twelve *pfennige*.[17] The Fries people also reckoned in terms of barrels of beer.[18]

Rings, such as were used for monetary purposes during the final phase of the Ancient Period covered by the *Niebelungenlied*, continued to be so used during the early centuries of the Middle Ages. Metals in bars, and especially in the form of scrap, were used for payment by weight. In 572 the Franks forced an invading Saxon army to ransom itself when cut off at the Rhone. Payment was fixed, according to Gregor de Tours, in bars of gold which were subsequently found, however, to have been brass.[19] Fines were often fixed in terms of weighed gold or silver, according to the Merovingian Formulæ and the early charters of St. Gall.[20] Gibbon's *Decline and Fall* contains many instances of the payment of tribute by Byzantium to Barbaric invaders in terms of weights of gold.

There were in a later period legal regulations fixing the standard quality of scrap silver, and limiting the permitted percentage of alloys. The term frequently employed was *marca usualis argenti*.[21] Payment was prescribed in such weighed metals in Bavarian and Austrian documents dating from the 13th and 14th centuries. Another method of payment was in coins which were no longer valid, and which were accepted by weight.[22] The use of scrap silver for payment during a period when the art of coinage had reached a relatively advanced stage was partly due to the multiplicity of coins issued by the dwarf principalities. It saved minting costs and the loss on the exchange of coins. In particular for travelling expenses and in wholesale trade it was found more advantageous to use scrap silver.[23] Coins were often cut, partly to ascertain their fineness by the colour of the freshly cut metal, and partly to provide small change.[24]

The fine imposed on the Franconian Prince Eberhard for revolting against King Otto I (912-973) was a hundred pounds (presumably silver by weight) payable in horses.[25] Apparently, metal served as a standard of value, while actual payment was made in livestock. Horses were known, however, to have served also as a limited medium of exchange two centuries earlier when even land was exchanged for them.[26]

[17]Robert Eisler, *Das Geld. Seine geschichtliche Entstehung und gesellschaftliche Bedeutung* (Munich, 1924), p. 94.
[18]Kulischer, p. 317.
[19]Gregory of Tours, *Historia Francorum*, IV, 42 (Oxford, 1927).
[20]Seebohm (1911), p. 14.
[21]Luschin v.Ebengreuth,*Allgemeine Münzkunde und Geldgeschichte des Mittelalters und der Neueren Zeit* (Munich, 1904), p. 141.
[22]Luschin v. Ebengreuth, p. 143.
[23]Luschin v. Ebengreuth, Article on *Silber in the Reallexikon der Germanischen Altertumskunde* (Strassburg, 1918-19), Vol. IV, p. 178.
[24]Luschin v. Ebengreuth, Article on *Hacksilber in the Reallexikon der Germanischen Altertumskunde* (Strassburg, 1913-15), Vol. II, p. 350.
[25]Eisler, p. 71.
[26]Babelon, pp. 16-17.

CHAPTER 21

LEATHER CURRENCY IN ITALY AND FRANCE

Roman currency continued to circulate in Medieval Italy for a long time after the collapse of the Western Empire. At the same time, the practice of payment in precious metals by weight that became popular during the period of the decline of Rome, continued to prevail throughout the early Middle Ages, especially in large political payments.

Italy, with the traditions of the money economy of Rome behind her and with her highly developed commerce, was among the first countries to develop an advanced monetary system after the collapse of the Roman Empire. There is, therefore, very little evidence of any extensive use of primitive money in Italy. In a number of instances coined monetary units served as a standard of value to facilitate barter transactions. Thus at Teramo in 1052 the sale of land against payment in objects to the value of a hundred *solidi* was recorded.[1] In 1108 the Duke of Cagliari undertook to pay to the Mary Church of Pisa an annual contribution of one pound of gold or of goods to an equal value.[2] King Peter of Cagliari granted to the Genoese in 1174 for five years an annual subsidy of five hundred pounds payable in goods valued according to current prices.[3] Barter is claimed to have prevailed to a large extent in Venice and elsewhere in Italy even in the 14th century. The role of modern money was largely that of a unit of account.[4]

Pepper appeared to be a standard of value. In 1378 Genoa issued a pepper loan, repayable at the option of the holders in pepper or in gold.[5] In Milan during the 13th century payment in contracts was often fixed in cash or grain.[6]

Leather money was used on various occasions as emergency currency. Thus in 1122 Doge Domenico Michæle used stamped pieces of leather to pay his fleet and his troops during the crusade.[7] In this instance leather was, however, a rather advanced form of currency, a forerunner of paper money. The same was the case with the leather money with which Emperor Frederick II paid his troops in 1237 at the sieges of Milan and Faventia; afterwards the leather was exchanged for silver. Leather money was used also at the siege of Parma in 1248.[8] All these instances were purely temporary emergency situations. Presumably

---

[1]F. Savini, *Il Cartulario delle Chiesa Teramana* (Rome, 1910), p. 115. Quoted by W. Täuber, *Geld und Kredit im Mittelalter* (Berlin, 1933), p. 98.

[2]*Historiæ Patriæ Monumenta*, Vol. x (No. 257), p. 180. Quoted by Täuber, p. 98.

[3]*Historiæ Patriæ Monumenta*, p. 248. Quoted by Tauber, p. 98.

[4]Dopsch, p. 189.

[5]Kulischer, p. 317.

[6]J. Wackernagel, *Vierteljahrschrift für Sozial—und Wirtschafts—geschichte*, Beiheft II (Stuttgart, 1924), p. 15. Quoted by Robert Eisler, p. 70.

[7]Charlton, p. 316.　　　　　　　　[8]Charlton, p. 316.

the leather moneys were stamped, and they were, therefore, on the borderline of being modern money.

In France, as in Italy, the general use of money in the modern sense of the term developed at a much earlier stage of Medieval history than in Northern and Eastern Europe, and there is little evidence of any widespread use of primitive currencies after the end of the Frankish Empire. Nevertheless, during the early Middle Ages it must have been a widespread practice to grant loans in produce, especially in grain and wine, judging by the fact that the Council of Paris in 829 condemned it as usury if the creditor stipulated coined money as the measure of value in the case of loans in produce.[9]

In Normandy marten or weasel skins were used for payment of tribute in the 11th and 12th centuries, which seems to indicate their limited monetary use. Philippe I (1060-1108) issued pieces of leather with a small silver nail in the centre.[10] Louis IX (1226-1270), John the Good (1350-64) and Charles the Wise (1364-1380) also issued leather currencies, the last two probably as a result of the impoverishment of France, the country having been denuded of its metallic currency in connection with the payment of ransom for John.[11] It is not known how far these leather currencies were really promissory notes. If they bore the seal of State authority they may have been the forerunners of paper currency.

[9]Täuber, p. 42.   [10]Charlton, p. 315.   [11]Charlton, p. 315.

CHAPTER 22

CATTLE, CLOTH AND FISH CURRENCY OF ICELAND

Medieval Iceland had possessed a remarkably advanced system of primitive currencies. Her cattle standard, and later her cloth standard and her fish standard, was very elaborate. As in the Scandinavian countries in general, cattle is believed to have served as currency from the prehistoric period. It continued to perform monetary functions right up to the late Middle Ages. The standard of value was the cow of three to ten winters. It had to be at least of medium size; it had to have had less than three calves, and it had to be without blemish, horned, and milking. The cow fulfilling all these conditions was the monetary unit known under the name kugildi.[1]

Interest-bearing loans were granted in terms of kugildi.[2] There was an elaborate tariff of the value of cattle of various kinds and ages in terms of the standard unit, expressed in fractions. For instance, a sterile cow

[1]K. V. Amira, Nordgermanisches Obligationsrecht (Leipzig, 1882), Vol. II, p. 522.
[2]Luschin v. Ebengreuth, p. 135.

was worth two-thirds *kugildi*, a five-year-old ox one and a quarter *kugildi*, a six-year-old ox one and a half *kugildi*. A horse of medium quality aged between four and ten years was worth one *kugildi*, a two-year-old horse half a *kugildi* only. Twelve one-year-old rams or six ewes were worth one *kugildi*. The value of various types of sheep, goats, pigs, etc., was all fixed by law in terms of the cow unit.[3]

The *kugildi* remained a unit of account long after it ceased to be a medium of exchange.[4] Indeed, judging by the elaborate requirements which the cow that was used as a unit had to fulfil, it seems doubtful whether it could ever play the part of a medium of exchange on an extensive scale; for the number of cows corresponding to the ideal unit could never be sufficiently large in any Icelandic community to satisfy the requirements of a medium of exchange. In documents it is often expressly stated that payment fixed in *kugildi* was actually to be made in metallic money or in other form.[5] Ordinary cattle were probably used as a medium of exchange on the basis of their official value fixed in *kugildi*.

Throughout the historic period cloth was also used as currency. The plain home-woven woollen cloth (*wadmal*) served as a general standard of value. It was used for wergeld and for the valuation of damage.[6] Taxes were fixed in *wadmal*.[7] The unit was a piece one ell long and two wide. There were two standard qualities, brown or brown-stripped, and plain white, the former being more valuable than the latter.[8] The use for currency of a material as easily produced as *wadmal* was a great boon to the poor, and made for their economic independence, for there was, so to speak, a mint on virtually every farm; the money was "coined" on the hand-loom.[9] Even in modern times, in some parts of Iceland the value of land was at times expressed in terms of *wadmal*.[10]

There was a fixed legal ratio between the cow and the cloth currency. In the 12th century 120 ells of *wadmal* were equal to one *kugildi*.[11] Rugs, too, are alleged to have passed as currency to some extent, their value depending on the size and thickness of the nap.[12]

Grain and bread are also said to have been early means of payment.[13] The latter, however, was probably only a favourite medium of barter.

[3]K. Weinhold, *Altnordisches Leben* (Berlin, 1856), pp. 52-3.
[4]Weinhold, p. 117.
[5]Luschin v. Ebengreuth, p. 135.   [6]Amira, p. 510.
[7]K. Gjerset, *History of Iceland* (London, 1922), p. 206.
[8]Schönfeld, *Der Isländische Bauernhof*, pp. 223-4. Quoted by M. W. Williams, *Social Scandinavia in the Viking Age* (New York, 1920), p. 228.
[9]Williams, p. 228.
[10]Annandale and Nelson, *The Faroes and Iceland*, p. 136. Quoted by Williams, p. 228.
[11]Amira, p. 523. Strangely enough, 120 ells were called as "the big hundred" and 60 were reckoned as "half a hundred."
[12]*Origines Islandicæ*, Vol. II, pp. 129, 395. Quoted by Williams, p. 228.
[13]Max Wirth, *Das Geld. Geschichte des Umlaufmittels von der ältesten Zeit bis in der Gegenwart* (Leipzig, 1884), p. 5.

From an early period silver by weight was used for monetary purposes. The original parity was 120 ells of *wadmal* equal to one-third mark of silver, but by 1280 the cloth equivalent was reduced to 96 ells of *wadmal*.[14] Silver and to a lesser extent gold changed hands largely in the form of bars which were often drawn out in the shape of long, thick wires, from which small parts could be cut or broken or used for payment by weight.[15]

To a very large extent silver and gold were used as money also in the form of rings known under the ancient name of *baugr*, corresponding to the ancient Irish word of *boge*. The term is still used in Iceland to-day for a plain stoneless ring. It had also in ancient times the metaphorical meaning of money. In olden times, before gold or silver coins came into use, the metals were rolled up in spiral-formed rings and pieces cut off were weighed and used as medium of payment.[16] Ancient Icelandic poems make frequent reference to breakers or scatterers of rings (rich men generous with their wealth), haters of rings (those who scorn wealth), etc.[17] The Icelandic epic poem Burnt Njal, for instance, praised the generosity of its hero in these words: "He that lavisheth rings in largesse."[18] The editor of the poem of *Rigs Mal* appended to a reference to rings a footnote saying "many of these massy rings of gold are preserved in the North, some of them having similar rings hanging on them: those were used as money and given either whole or in parts as presents or for other purposes."[19]

Scrap metals, and precious metals in general, by weight served as means of payment. In the 10th century Arnkill was sentenced to pay twelve ounces of silver for the death of each domestic of Thorolf.[20] It is not only rings or bars that were broken into small pieces for use for small payments. Even jewels and other objects made of precious metals were thus employed, also imported foreign coins. Such coins always changed hands by weight.[21]

During the more advanced period of the Middle Ages, in the 15th century, dried stockfish seems to have served extensively as a medium of exchange and unit of account, owing to its great commercial importance especially in the export trade.[22] A contemporary document issued some time between 1413 and 1426 and quoted *in extenso* by Ridgeway[23] gives a long tariff of prices in dried stockfish fixed by an Icelandic Chief for the purpose of regulating trade between English traders and the Icelandic people. The following are some of the items:—

[14]Amira, p. 524.   [15]Williams, p. 229.
[16]R. Cleasby and G. Vigfusson, *Icelandic-English Dictionary* (Oxford, 1874).
[17]Nolan, Vol. I, p. 160.
[18]*The Story of Burnt Njal.* Translated by Sir G. W. Dasent (Everyman Edn., London, 1944), p. 139. There is also a reference to "Lord of Rings", meaning a chief.
[19]*Illustrated North Antiquary*, p. 456. Quoted by Lindsay, p. 5.
[20]Abstract of the *Eyrbiggia Saga* (*Illustrated North Antiquary*), p. 495. Quoted by Lindsay, p. 5.
[21]Weinhold, p. 118.   [22]Roscher, p. 357.   [23]Ridgeway, pp. 18-20.

		Stockfish
48 *alen* (ells) of good and full-width trade cloth ..		120
3 *tonder* (tons) of wheat		120
4 *tonder* (tons) of beer		120
1 *tonde* of clean and clear butter		120
1 *tonde* of wine		100
⅛ *tonde* of honey		15
1 pair of black (leather) shoes		4
⅛ *tonde* of salt		5

The assumption is that payment was not actually made in stockfish in the majority of transactions, but barter was conducted on the basis of the above values, so that fish served as a unit of account rather than a medium of exchange.

The price fixing system was in operation from early times; also the various types of currencies bore fixed relation to each other.[24] In Iceland as in other Nordic countries, the development of an advanced primitive monetary system had been largely the result of the requirements of the highly developed wergeld system.

[24] Williams, pp. 231-2.

CHAPTER 23

RING MONEY OF DENMARK

In the earliest times the wergeld was fixed in cattle. Goods were exchanged for goods, or were paid for in gold and silver rings.[1] The monetary use of finds of rings with one end open is indicated by their size: many of them are about two inches in diameter, too small for bracelets, too big for finger rings.[2] Very large silver rings, worn on the head or neck, were frequently used as money in commercial transactions.[3] To a large extent pieces of silver and gold, broken or cut off from rings or bars, were used as a medium of exchange. They changed hands according to weight.[4] It was not till about A.D. 1000 that King Swend Tweskideg, father of King Canute, began to coin money in Denmark.[5]

When the Danes adopted grain as their monetary unit instead of cattle, they fixed the new unit to correspond to the value of a cow or a

[1] J. M. S. Birch, *Denmark in History* (London, 1938), pp. 12-13.
[2] Gesellschaft für Nordische Altertumskunde, *Leitfaden zur nordischer Alter-tumskunde* (Copenhagen, 1837), p. 44.
[3] J. J. A. Worsæ, *The Primeval Antiquities of Denmark* (London, 1849), p. 59. In the *Gudrun Saga* repeated references were made to gifts of a number of bracelets. (*Gudrun*, Translated by Margaret Armour, Everyman Edn., London, 1932, pp. 138 and 154.)
[4] Worsæ, p. 66.   [5] Worsæ, p. 66.

sheep.[6] Grain and loaves served as means of payments for some time.[7] During the rule of the Aristocracy (13th and 14th centuries) in Denmark, prices of all commodities were fixed in terms of barley or rye.[8]

Weighed metals subsequently came to be used as a medium of exchange and standard of value. The units were the *ore* (alleged to have meant originally the ears of animals whose skins are said to have served as currency) and the mark. The latter was originally a measure of length. 448 ells of cloth was equal to a mark. Subsequently the unit became identified with a quantity of monetary metals.[9] It served also as a standard of value for payments actually made in kind. In the *Gudrun Saga* King Hetel of Denmark gave instructions to make a payment "to the value of a hundred marks."[10]

[6]Roscher, p. 352. [7]Max Wirth, p. 5. [8]Roscher, p. 342.
[9]Ridgeway, p. 397. [10]*Gudrun*, p. 56.

CHAPTER 24

CATTLE AND CLOTH CURRENCY OF SWEDEN

In Sweden coined money did not appear until the 11th century. Until then cattle and cloth were the most widely used currencies. In the early Middle Ages cattle was the general standard of value in which all property was estimated. Fines and debts were expressed in terms of cattle. It was also the medium of exchange with which even land could be purchased and with the aid of which slaves were able to purchase their freedom. This system survived to some extent even during the 12th century, in spite of the adoption of coinage.[1]

Woollen home-woven cloth called *wadmal* served as a currency up to the 14th century. In legal texts the value of stolen goods was estimated in terms of cloth. Debts, fines and fees were expressed either in coined money or in lengths of cloth. In some districts of Sweden cloth was actually legal tender and had a fixed ratio with coined money. Even in the 14th century creditors were under legal obligation to accept cloth in settlement of money debts, at the rate of one ell of cloth per *Ortung pfennig*. According to a legal text the purchase of the freedom of a slave could be achieved against payment in a fixed quantity of cloth, or in a fixed number of oxen, or in an amount of coined money:[2] the exchange rate was ninety-six ells of cloth per silver mark.[3] In addition to the use of *wadmal*, linen, measured by the ell, also served as a monetary unit. In the laws of some Swedish districts there is reckoning in terms of this unit, called *lerept*. It was considerably more valuable than *wadmal*, twenty-four ells were equal to a mark.[4]

[1]Amira, Vol. I, p. 442. [2]Amira, Vol. I, p. 478. [3]Amira, Vol. I, p. 480.
[4]Weinhold, pp. 121-2.

It has been suggested that skins served as a currency in Sweden till the late Middle Ages.[5] According to von Amira, this is doubtful. What is certain is that skins or furs were used as money in the Baltic countries under Swedish control. In 1338 the Bishop of Abo, Finland, pledged a field for a loan of one and a half "packets," the packet of forty skins being the unit.[6]

In spite of the widespread use of non-metallic currencies, the monetary use of metals was known in Sweden since the earliest times. During the early centuries after the collapse of the Roman Empire metals by weight changed hands as currency. Gold wire in the form of spirals was found in various places and the assumption is that it had served monetary purposes.[7] During the historic period weighed metals in the form of spiral rings and later bars and plates were known to have served as currency.[8] Ring money was in circulation in Sweden until the 13th century.[9] In Visby there were sworn silver weighers and assayers to supervise the traffic.[10]

Coined money appears to have changed hands by weight, judging by the provision whereby a slave could buy his freedom by paying three marks (unit of weight) of woollen goods or six marks of *pfennige*, or four good oxen. An identical fine was payable for killing a slave.[11]

[5]Luschin v. Ebengreuth, p. 139.
[6]Amira, Vol. I, p. 478.   [7]Amira, Vol. I, p. 478.
[8]Amira, Vol. I, p. 478. According to Montelius (*Kulturgeschichte Schwedens*, Leipzig, 1906, pp. 180-81), a number of plain gold rings found in medieval deposits weighed exactly 191½ grammes, or at any rate between 190 and 200 grammes. He attributes the differences in their weight partly to inaccuracy of scales in the early days, and partly to varying degrees of wear. The Sagas of the pre-Christian period speak of rings of one mark and a half mark.
[9]Mosher, p. 48.   [10]Luschin v. Ebengreuth, p. 178.
[11]Montelius, p. 125.

CHAPTER 25

BUTTER AS CURRENCY IN NORWAY

Cows of between five and eight winters were a medium of exchange in Norway from prehistoric days to the late Middle Ages. Under the laws of Haakon the Good (940-963), fines were payable in cows, provided they were not too old, in slaves of over fifteen years of age, in cloth or in weapons.[1] Clause 223 of the Gulathing Law stipulates that wergeld is payable in cows instead of silver, at the rate of one cow for two and a

[1]Schive and Holmboe, *Norges Mynter* (Oslo, 1865), pp. 1-111. Quoted by Ridgeway, pp. 34-5.

half *ores* of silver.[2] After the adoption of coinage, payments could be discharged in cows or in coins, though in many commercial documents it is specifically stipulated whether payment should be made in cows or in coined money.[3]

Fines, fees, purchase prices, loans and insurance amounts were often expressed in cloth.[4] In some Norwegian districts, cloth was made legal tender. In the 13th century the cow was at a fixed ratio to metallic money, one cow being equal to one-third of a mark in silver.[5]

Butter was used for valuation in many commercial documents, the unit being a basket. Rents were often payable wholly or partly in butter.[6] There was also a strange unit represented by a month's upkeep of a man (*manadamater*). It was equal to one basket of butter. In 1309 ten of these units bought a horse worth three cows.[7]

In the late Middle Ages skins were used as currency in Telemarken for the purpose of valuations and also for actual exchanges. Rents were expressed in *hud* (skins). In the 14th century ten skins were equal to one mark of fine silver.[8]

According to Mosher, during the Middle Ages iron bars were used as money by the Norsemen, being the principal medium of exchange except for wire money of gold. The bars were about one foot in length and half inch thick. There is a specimen in the Knox Collection, Buffalo, dating from about A.D. 1000. Forty of such bars was the price of a horse and a hundred would purchase a slave.[9]

Precious metals by weight were used extensively as a medium of exchange. Gold and silver pieces were cut to a certain weight. They were not stamped until a considerable time after the establishment of Christianity. Gold rings of different size and weight passed in ancient times in Norway from man to man, like our money passes now.[10] In 1220 a Norse law was enacted which required each ring of a series to be of a definite weight. Large amounts were expressed in rings. Some of the rings found were of a shape and weight that excludes non-monetary use. The terms "ring-breaker" or "gold-breaker" applied in ancient Norwegian language to rich and generous men.[11] The fine for homicide was three rings.[12]

[2]Seebohm, pp. 246-7.
[3]Amira, Vol. II, pp. 522-23.
[4]Amira, Vol. II, p. 511.
[5]Amira, Vol. II, p. 523.
[6]Amira, Vol. II, pp. 524-5.
[7]Amira, Vol. II, p. 525.
[8]Amira, Vol. II, p. 525.
[9]Mosher, p. III, and Plate V.
[10]Baden, *History of Norway*. Quoted by Lindsay, p. 4.
[11]Amira, Vol. II, p. 528.
[12]V. Görnberg, *The Culture of the Teutons* (London, 1931), p. 355. Seebohm (1911, p. 241) gives a list of wergelds for wounding payable in rings of twelve *ores* of silver under the Gulathing Law, varying to one ring in the case of a slave to forty-eight rings in the case of a king.

CHAPTER 26

CALVES AS MONETARY UNIT IN HUNGARY

According to the early Arabic writer Ibn Rosteh, and the early Persian writer Gardezi, even before the Hungarians settled in the Danube valley cattle constituted their chief store of value during their temporary stay in Lebedia, in the 8th century. It seems, however, that fur-lined garments constituted a kind of standard of value, judging by a reference to a bride's father having displayed his wealth in skins, furs and silk cloth, "to the value of ten fur-lined garments."[1]

In the early period after the establishment of Hungary in the Danube valley in 896, the calf was the principal unit of account in Hungary. According to legal texts from the 11th century, in particular in the laws of King St. Stephen (997-1038), the wergeld was fixed at five calves or the multiples of that number which was the generally used unit.[2] At the same time, skins and fur-lined garments are claimed to have constituted currency units.[3] The monetary use of skins seems to be indicated by the fact that until the reign of King Béla IV (1235-1270) the Slavs had to pay tribute to the Kings of Hungary in skins.[4]

Gold was adopted as a monetary metal at an early period. The unit was the *pensa auri*. Authorities disagree about the nature of this unit; according to one theory it was a certain unit of weight of uncoined gold, changing hands by weight, since the original meaning of the Latin verb *penso* was "weighing," even though subsequently it was also used to convey "purchasing" or "paying." *Pensa auri* was also suggested to mean uniform pieces of unstamped gold of a definite weight.[5] There is, however, no evidence that such uniform pieces had actually been in use, and the view is held by some experts that the term *pensa* indicated "coin" or "money." This theory seems to be supported by the fact that the Hungarian word for "money" is *pénz*. It has also been suggested that *pensa auri* meant simply the Byzantine gold coin *bezant*, which was then in widespread use in that part of Europe.

In the laws of the 11th century, one calf was equal to one *pensa auri*. The wergeld was fixed in both units. Towards the end of that century the wergeld was fixed in *pensa auri* only, but even in the laws of King Ladislaus I (1077-1095) there is a clause fixing the fine at "ten *pensa auri*, worth ten calves."[6] Subsequently the *pensa auri* was made equal to forty silver denars, the denar being the current coin in retail trade during the early period of coined money.[7]

---

[1]Pauler and Szilágyi, *A Magyar Hofoglalás Kútföi* (Budapest, 1900), pp. 169-173. Quoted by B. Hóman, *Magyar Pénztörténet*, 1000-1325 (Budapest, 1916), pp. 156-7.
[2]Hóman, pp. 157-8.   [3]Hóman, p. 167.
[4]Rupp, *Numai Hungariæ* (Buda, 1846), ii, p. 156. Quoted by Luschin v. Ebengreuth, p. 137.
[5]Hóman, pp. 158-60.   [6]Hóman, p. 167.   [7]Hóman, p. 273.

The wide use of cattle as a store of value is indicated by the fact that the term *marha* (cattle) had come to be used for every form of mobile wealth. This use of the term continued to the end of the Middle Ages, and to some extent even in the 16th century and after.

In large transactions silver was used by weight as the currency. During the second half of the 12th century and in the 13th century silver bars became the principal medium of exchange and standard of value, owing to the debasement of coined money. Coins came to be taken by tale in small transactions only; in larger transactions they changed hands by weight.[8] To a large extent silver only served as a unit of account to estimate the value of payments in kind which continued to be prevalent throughout Medieval Hungary. Documents from the 13th and 14th centuries show that payment was often fixed partly in money and partly in kind, though the value of the latter was fixed in marks of silver, the mark being the accepted unit of weight. In many instances the objects to be accepted in payment were stipulated, or certain objects were expressly excluded. Presumably there was a fixed or agreed tariff on the basis of which the value of the payments in kind was reckoned.[9]

When payment in silver by weight was stipulated, the fineness of the metal was often indicated. Terms such as "fine silver," "superfine silver," "pure silver" presumably had their definite meaning.[10] Uncoined gold was not used regularly as a medium of exchange.

[8]Hóman, pp. 273-5.   [9]Hóman, pp. 275-8.   [10]Hóman, pp. 281-84

CHAPTER 27

FUR MONEY OF RUSSIA

Cattle must have served as a currency in early times in Russia; the evidence indicating this is largely etymological. The oldest name for money is *skot* which means "cattle" and also "treasure." The word *skotniza* means "cattle yard" or "stable," but also "treasury." Under Jaroslav in 1018 *skot* was collected from the people. In a contract between Novgorod and German merchants at the end of the 12th century, payment was fixed in *skot*. In the oldest Russian code of law Articles 21, 24 and 25 refer to *skot* as the unit of payment. As a survival of the use of livestock as a medium of exchange the practice of adding a horse, cow or sheep to the purchase price continued right up to the 16th century.[1] The term *skot* must have been imported into Russia by Viking traders who had penetrated deep into the country. This, at any rate, appears to

[1]J. Kulischer, *Russische Wirtschaftesgeschichte*, Vol. I (Jena, 1925), pp. 115-6. See also O. Schrader, *Geld* (Reallexikon der Germanischen Altertumskunde, Berlin, 1917-21), Vol. I, p. 372.

be a reasonable inference from the fact that similar terms had been put
to similar dual use in Scandinavian and Germanic languages.

It is conceivable that flint arrowheads may have served as a currency
in Neolithic Russia. In various places large numbers of such arrow-
heads of very beautiful finish were found.[2] It is permissible to suggest
tentatively that the labour spent on their finish would have been wasted
if they had been shot away, so that possibly they may have been meant
to be media of exchange. In the Volga Valley a number of very small
arrowheads were found, too small for ordinary use.[3]

Furs were said to have been in monetary use ever since the 8th century
A.D.[4] In the 10th century tribute was known to have been paid in that
form. Ambassadors sent abroad by the Grand Dukes of Muscovy
received furs for their travelling expenses,[5] though, of course, outside
Russia they could only be sold as merchandise. Ahmed de Tours,
writing in 1160, says that squirrel skins were the current money of the
Russians who had no coined money.[6]

The Franciscan friar de Rubruquis who crossed Russia on his visit
to Mongolia as Ambassador of Louis IX of France in 1253, and who is
considered to have been a most reliable observer, remarked that among
the Russians the money in circulation consisted of small pieces of furs,
"marquetées de couleur."[7]

The *Russkaya Prawda*, which codifies the Russian laws of the 11th
and 12th centuries, contains evidence that there was a fixed ratio between fur currency and silver currency. The fine for certain offences was
fixed at five metal *kuna* or two skins. The same ratio existed among the
Volga Bulgars during the 10th century. The Arab traveller Ibn Dasta,
writing during the first half of that century, says that the Volga Bulgars
paid small change in marten skins, each skin being equal to two and a
half *dirhem* (an Arab silver coin then current in Southern Russia).[8]

In addition to contemporary written evidence there is also etymological evidence in support of the claim that furs and skins were the currency
of Medieval Russia. The word *kuna*, which was used to express money in
general, originated from the skin of the marten (*kunitza*).[9] In fact,
marten skins were the monetary unit in Russia till the late Middle Ages.

[2]John Abercromby, *The Pre- and Proto-historic Finns, Both Eastern and Western*
(London, 1898), Vol. I, p. 71.
[3]Abercromby, p. 74.
[4]Charlton, p. 317. According to the Persian writer, Gardezi, the Bulgars along
the Volga had no metallic currencies, and payment was made in fur money (Pauler
& Szilágyi, p. 157). Gibbon, in his *Decline and Fall* (v, p. 523 of Everyman Edn.),
refers to payment of tribute in white squirrel skins by the Russians of the Lake Ladoga.
[5]Baron S. de Chaudoir, *Aperçu sur les Monnaies Russes* (St. Petersburg, 1836),
pp. 7-8.
[6]J. de Hammer, *Sur les Origines Russes* (St. Petersburg, 1825), pp. 37, 101.
Quoted by Chaudoir, p. 9.
[7]Quoted by Chaudoir, p. 9.
[8]W. Kliutshewskij, *Geschichte Russlands* (Berlin, 1925), Vol. I, p. 221.
[9]Chaudoir, p. 26.

It was not until 1409 that the *kuna* standard was abolished in Pskow, and it existed till 1411 in Novgorod.[10] During an early phase of the use of this money, skins had to be complete with snouts and paws; if claws were missing they were considered invalid.[11]

The unit, in the case of squirrel skins, was a *griwna kun*, representing a certain number of squirrel skins. Tolls and customs were paid in skins. Priests received payment in that form, and donations to the Church were made in it. The archæologist Troutovskij found miniatures showing parts of skins being exchanged for money. The presumption is that the pictures represent the exchange of skins when Novgorod adopted coined money.[12]

Apparently the supply of skins failed to keep pace with the expanding monetary requirements. To remedy the situation, the use of whole skins was discontinued. Snouts, ears and claws were substituted for them. These are claimed to have given place later to pieces of skin or leather, at first of irregular shape one inch square, afterwards of circular form, impressed with Government stamp.[13] It is alleged that these pieces were convertible at Government depots into whole skins. There seems to be, however, no adequate evidence to confirm this.[14]

In old Russian law books, attributed to Grand Dukes Jaroslav and Vladimir, there are frequent references to squirrel skins, and subdivisions of squirrel skins. The use of marten skins was particularly popular in Western Russia. There was a fixed parity between the *kuna* and fine silver, but the rate did not remain stable.[15]

In the late Middle Ages furs of gibelines and *bieki* (petit gris) were still in use. In 1489 Grand Duke Ivan Vasilievich gave to his Ambassador to Emperor Frederick quantities of these furs.[16] In 1426 the inhabitants of the Dwina province paid contribution in these furs.[17]

Hare skins are also believed to have served as a currency. This is deduced from the name of the smallest of early Russian coins, the *polushka* (quarter copeck). *Ushka* means "hare skin," *pol* signifies "half," therefore *polushka* must have been equated to two coins per hare's skin; the latter is said to have been one of the lowest units of exchange before the use of metallic money.[18]

Baron de Chaudoir, to whom we owe most of the information on Russian fur money, is of the opinion that it provided a most suitable material to serve as money. It was useful, fairly scarce, easy to transport

---

[10]Chaudoir, p. 27.

[11]Chaudoir, p. 9. Several contemporary German writers seek to discredit evidence on the monetary use of skins in Russia. None of them have produced so far any convincing evidence in refutation of Chaudoir and other Russian writers, even though the monetary use of stamped pieces of furs remains yet to be confirmed.

[12]Kulischer (1925), p. 116.   [13]Charlton, p. 317.

[14]Luschin v. Ebengreuth, p. 137.   [15]Luschin v. Ebengreuth, p. 137.

[16]Chaudoir, p. 7.   [17]Chaudoir, p. 44.

[18]E. D. Clarke, *Travels in Various Countries in Europe, Asia and Africa*, 4th Edn. (London, 1817), Vol. I.

and was of diverse value for various units.[19] A crisis is said to have occurred, however, when the Mongol invaders of Russia refused to recognize the small bits of fur serving as money. There was general bankruptcy among the merchants. Thereupon North Eastern Russia reverted to the use of whole skins with full intrinsic value, in the place of pieces.[20]

Furs and skins remained in monetary use long after the adoption of metallic money, between the 14th and 16th centuries, because there was not enough gold and silver to cover requirements.[21]

Bronze rings are claimed to have been an early currency in Caucasia, Russian Armenia, part of the Ural district, and along the banks of the Volga, judging by finds in prehistoric graves. Specimens found there in burial grounds are regular and graduated, according to a system of weight.[22]

In the Middle Ages metals in Russia were largely commodities. Nevertheless, for large purchases silver was used. Silver bars, marked with eagles and other signs, were used as currency. They were broken, according to requirements, and changed hands by weight.[23]

[19]Chaudoir, p. 8.   [20]Wirth, pp. 9, 10.
[21]Ilwof, p. 59.   [22]Burns, p. 18.
[23]F. Friedensburg, *Münzkunde und Geldgeschichte der Einzelstaaten des Mittelalters und der Neueren Zeit* (Munchen, 1926), p. 86.

CHAPTER 28

OTHER EUROPEAN CURRENCIES

In the 10th century Ibrahim ibn Jakub, the famous traveller, reported that small pieces of linen of very thin texture which could not be used for any practical purpose served as a currency in Bohemia. They had a fixed value of one-tenth *Pense*. They served as a medium of exchange, against which it was possible to buy anything, even high valuable objects such as slaves, horses, gold, silver, etc. They also served as a store of value, and people possessed cases full of them.[1] Even in the 13th century textile money of a different kind was in limited use. The rent of the Moravian mint was paid in scarlet cloth.[2]

Grain, horses, cattle and salt were also claimed to have performed a monetary role. When the Czechs revolted against Charlemagne (805-6) after their subjection they had to pay an annual tribute of a hundred and twenty heads of cattle and five hundred marks in silver.[3]

[1]G. Haas, *Über den Bericht des Ibrahim Ibn Jakub von den Slaven aus dem Jahre 973.* Baltische Studien, Vol. xxxvii (Stettin, 1881). Quoted by Thilenius, p. 21.
[2]Juritsch, *Handel und Handelsrecht in Boehmen bis zur Hussiten Revolution*, p. 14. Quoted by Kulischer (1926), p. 317.
[3]Ilwof, p. 47.

In Poland in the 13th century squirrel skins, limbs and heads, are claimed to have been used as a currency, according to the contemporary writers. Towards 1298 the *groschen* coins of Prague began to replace them as a medium of exchange.[4] Some modern writers have called in question, however, the monetary use of skins. There can be no doubt that they had been used for certain payments. The Polish King Casimir (1427-1492) imposed a tribute in furs on Novgorod in 1471.[5] Under the laws of the same ruler, plaintiffs in courts of justice had to deposit with the judge three marten or sable skins, which were returned if the action was won.[6]

Scrap silver served as means of payment from Silesia to the Baltic coast during the 10th and 11th centuries. Slavs east of Germany only accepted precious metals by weight, and coins were cut up and weighed.[7]

The Baltic Slavs used pieces of linen as their currency. On the Island of Rügen, gold and silver was only used for women's jewellery and temple decoration. In commerce, only linen was used as a means of payment.[8] The monetary use of linen among Northern Slavs is supported by etymological evidence. The word *platni* means "linen," while *platiti* means "to pay." According to Brueckner, the Slavs did not know coins originally, and when they did not transact pure barter "they paid with small pieces of thin textiles which served in general as their coin."[9]

In Lithuania and Livonia skins of squirrels and foxes were used as money up to the 13th century.[10] In Estonian language *raha* means "money," in Lapland it means "fur." In the Swedish colonies along the east coast of the Baltic, furs served as currency. A bundle of forty furs, called *zimmer* was the unit.[11]

Pepper is said to have been used as currency on the Baltic sea coast during the 15th century. It was accepted for tax payment at a fixed rate.[12]

[4]Chaudoir, pp. 9-10.
[5]Chaudoir, p. 8.   [6]Charlton, p. 314.
[7]Luschin v. Ebengreuth, p. 139.
[8]Helmoldi, *Chronica Slavorum*, Vol. I, cap. 38. Quoted by Luschin v. Ebengreuth, p. 136.
[9]A. Brueckner, *Cywilizacja i jezyek*. 2nd Edn. (Warsaw, 1901). Quoted by Luschin v. Ebengreuth, p. 136.
[10]Ilwof, p. 48.   [11]Luschin v. Ebengreuth, p. 139.
[12]Chase National Bank Collection of Moneys (Case No. 201).

CHAPTER 29

COWRIES AS CURRENCY IN INDIA

In many parts of Medieval India the line of demarcation between medium of exchange and commodity was altogether indefinite. Money was "not yet a thing unto itself, in contradistinction to all other goods."[1]

[1]A. Appadorai, *Economic Conditions in Southern India*, A.D. 1000-1500 (Madras, 1936), p. 703.

In the 11th century in Tanjore many things could be bought for paddy, though others could only be bought for metallic money.[2] Wheat also served as a medium of exchange.

Clay, lacquer and cowries are claimed to have served as currency.[3] Among these only cowries are known to have assumed considerable importance. According to Pyrard de Laval, who visited India in the 16th century, the people of Bengal used cowries for ordinary money, although they had gold and silver and plenty of other metals; and kings and "great lords" had houses built expressly to store their shells, and treat them as part of their treasure. All the merchants from other places in India took large quantities of cowries to Bengal, where they were always in demand. They were put in parcels or baskets of 12,000. In dealings between merchants these parcels were taken as counted.[4]

According to Conti, in some regions stones called "cat's eyes" were used as currency.[5] Bitter almonds unsuitable for consumption constituted small change.

One of the early forms of metallic currencies consisted of pieces of iron, worked into large needles. Silver rods were used as currency in Travancore, with or without Government stamp. In Southern India during the 14th century, barter was based on values in gold and silver. Gold ingots of certain weight were used as money in the beginning of the 15th century, in the neighbourhood of Vijanazar.[6]

[2]Appadorai, pp. 703-4.
[3]Pramathanath Banerja, pp. 167-8.
[4]Albert Gray, *The Voyage of François Pyrard de Laval* (Hakluyt Society, London, 1887), Vol. I, pp. 238-240.
[5]Appadorai, p. 703.   [6]Appadorai, p. 703.

CHAPTER 30

LIVESTOCK STANDARD OF THE MONGOLS

Although the Mongolian Empire played a most important historical part during the Middle Ages, subsequently its civilization declined, its state-craft deteriorated and in modern China it became for all practical purposes an unhistoric race. For this reason the primitive currencies it used in recent times are dealt with in the Ethnological Section. Its currency system during the heights of its power in the 13th century deserves, however, to be dealt with in the Historical Section, especially as it was one of the factors that contributed towards the aggressive expansionary policy pursued by Jenghiz Khan and his successors.[1]

[1]In a broader sense the Mongolian race covers practically the entire population of Central and Eastern Asia. Here we confine ourselves to Mongolians in the narrower sense, that is the Mongolian-speaking races which inhabited in the 13th century the territories which are to-day Asiatic Russia and the outlying parts of China.

In the early period of Mongolian history taxes are said to have been paid in skins and cloth.[2] By far the most important primitive currency used by the Mongols since the dawn of their history was, however, livestock, in particular sheep. "Instead of our gold and silver coinage," writes Peisker, "they have a sheep coinage in which all valuations are made. Of course, they were acquainted with foreign coins from the earliest times and obtained countless millions of pounds from tributes, plunder and ransom of prisoners and they used coins now and then in external trading, but among them they still barter and conclude all their business in sheep, cattle, horses and camels."[3] Fines were fixed in livestock. While disobedience to the Khan or his subordinates was punished by death, other offences were punished by payment in cattle, sheep or camels to the sufferer or his group.[4]

Livestock constituted the store of value of the Mongols. As they were an almost entirely pastoral community, their possessions consisted almost entirely of their flocks and herds.[5] As is indicated by the remarks of Peisker quoted above, livestock was also used as a medium of exchange though in this respect this claim would require factual support. To a much larger extent it was used as a standard of value. This is confirmed by de Rubruquis. "Among the Kirghiz whom I met on the Pamirs," he writes, "the difficulty always was for a young fellow to find the hundred sheep which was the usual price paid for a girl, and one of my hunters, when paid off, counted his wages as representing so many sheep."[6] This remark also indicates the use of sheep as bride money.

The monetary use of livestock necessarily resulted in overstocking. The Mongols, like other nomadic races, hardly ever slaughtered cattle.[7] The result was that the grazing lands of Central Asia proved to be inadequate eventually to meet the requirements of the Mongols' livestock. Consequently, there was a hard struggle between Mongols and other nomadic races, in particular for the winter pastures, as a result of which the relatively weakest horde was pushed out of the steppe and had to conquer a new home.[8]

There can be no doubt that this search for new grazing lands was largely responsible for the aggressive expansionary policy of the pastoral races which were surging westward towards the end of the Ancient Period, and in particular of the Mongols towards the middle of the 13th century. It was largely because they chose to use livestock as their

[2]E. H. Parker, *A Thousand Years of the Tartars* (London, 1924), p. 54.
[3]Peisker, *The Asiatic Background. Cambridge Medieval History*, Vol. I, p. 343.
[4]L. H. D. Buxton, *Mongolia. Encyclopædia Britannica*, 1945 Edn., Vol. xv, p. 709.
[5]Heinrich Schurtz, *Central Asia and Siberia* (Helmolt, *The World's History*, London, 1904), p. 145.
[6]Sir Percy Sykes, *The Quest for Cathay* (London, 1936), p. 103.
[7]R. Hildebrand, *Recht und Sitte* (Jena, 1896), p. 23. Quoted by J. Peisker, *Die älteren Beziehungen der Slaven zu Turko-Tataren und Germanen und ihre sozialge-schichtliche Bedeutung* (Stuttgart, 1905), p. 13.
[8]Peisker, *The Asiatic Background*, p. 349.

currency that they had to find more and more room for their livestock which tended to be well in excess of normal economic requirements.

The ruthless savagery with which the Mongolian invaders exterminated and devastated the communities in Eastern and Central Europe which they conquered was also the consequence of this tendency of holding excessive livestock. According to Gibbon, after the conquest of Northern China, "it was seriously proposed, not in the hour of victory and passion, but in calm deliberate council, to exterminate all the inhabitants of that populous country, that the vacant land might be converted to the pasture of cattle."[9] Even though this suggestion was not followed, the mere fact that it was under consideration seems to indicate one of the main reasons why the Mongol hordes systematically exterminated the population of towns and the agricultural population of other conquered territories. It was not primarily their bloodthirsty nature, cruelty for its own sake, but as an economic motive: the desire to turn the land into steppe on which their surplus livestock could graze. This theory is in accordance with the modern historic conception of Jenghiz Khan which is inclined to discard the old belief that the Mongols indulged in senseless slaughter solely for its own sake. Their brutality was cold and calculated, like that of Hitler's decision to exterminate the Poles, not for the sake of the satisfaction derived from doing so but in order to make room for the eastward expansion of the German race. The reason why the Mongols devastated towns and villages, and slaughtered their population was that they wanted all the cultivated land to relapse into a state in which it would become once more suitable for pasture.

The existence of livestock currency did not exclude the use of metallic currency for commercial purposes. According to a Chinese traveller in Mongolia in 1221-24, "the money they use in commerce is of gold but has no hole,"[10] the absence of which must have appeared strange, viewed through Chinese eyes. There is no adequate evidence of the relative extent to which coins and livestock were a medium of exchange and a standard of value, but there can be no doubt that livestock was the chief form of store of value and that it was extensively used for bride money, fines, tribute and blood money.

[9] Gibbon, Vol. III, p. 354. See also Schurtz (1904), p. 128.
[10] E. Bretschneider, *Medieval Research from Eastern Asiatic Sources* (London, 1888), Vol. I, p. 90.

CHAPTER 31

SALT MONEY OF CHINA

Rice played the part of a standard of value, and possibly also a medium of exchange from time to time, in Medieval China. According to Friar Odoric's account, in the 14th century the rich man's income in China was estimated in heavy ass-loads of rice.[1] Tea also constituted a form of currency.[2]

We have it on the evidence of Marco Polo that salt served as small change during the 13th century. Salt water was boiled and set it in a mould, and every piece from the mould weighed half a pound. The exchange rate of salt cakes increased in the mountains where forty salt bars were equal to a gold bar, against eighty salt bars at the salt springs. The inhabitants of the cities used for food the broken fragments of the salt cakes, putting the whole cakes into circulation as money. The bars were stamped by the State.[3]

Cowries, which were used as currency during the Ancient Period, continued to serve that purpose throughout the Middle Ages. In Marco Polo's time "white porcelains found in the sea" were in full use in the Province of Yunnan.[4]

In 702 pieces of iron and tin were used for monetary purposes, to relieve the shortage of copper coins which had disappeared from circulation owing to the demand for the casting of idols that developed as a result of the spreading of Buddhism.[5]

In 1282 and 1283 permission was given to use iron as a medium of exchange in ports in dealing with foreign merchants, but the use of gold and silver was prohibited. It is not clear whether this measure refers to amorphous iron, bars or coins.[6] By far the most important metallic currency in Medieval China, in addition to the copper coins, was the *sycee* or shoe-shaped ingot of silver. It was said to have been first made in this shape under Kublai Khan (1260-1295), but according to a memorandum on currency reform submitted by the Minister of Finance to the President of the Chinese Republic in 1918, *sycee* was known to have existed during the Sung Dynasty (960-1280). While copper coins were used for retail traffic wholesale traffic was served almost exclusively with *sycee*.[7] It changed hands by weight, the unit being the *tael*, which had been for many centuries an abstract unit of account.

Apparently, silk and wheat, which were used for monetary purposes for long periods in Ancient China continued to be so used during the early Middle Ages, judging by the fact that in A.D. 739 the Emperor had to forbid their monetary use.[8]

[1]R. C. Temple (1899), p. 108. [2]Dopsch, p. 30.
[3]Marco Polo (Everyman Edn.), p. 241. [4]Marco Polo, p. 245.
[5]E. Biot, *Mémoire sur le Système Monétaire des Chinois* (Paris, 1837), p. 61.
[6]Rockhill, p. 424. [7]Kann, p. 65. [8]Biot, p. 63.

CHAPTER 32

GOLD DUST MONEY OF JAPAN

Japanese history begins in the 8th century A.D. Objects which are claimed to have served as a currency before the existence of contemporary records include copper rings covered with gold or silver, which are found in ancient stone graves of Japan. Crystal beads, which are found in large numbers, and claw-shaped agate and jade may also have been money.[1] Munro is inclined to believe that the small arrow-heads of agate and other superior stone may have been a form of primitive money, since they were too precious to be shot away, and many of them were not suitable for shooting.[2]

Horses and swords figure so frequently as wergeld in early Japanese documents that they are claimed to have served as means of payment.[3] In Yokohama fines and taxes were paid in textiles in the early Middle Ages.[4] During the Nara period (8th century) cloth was used even in the comparatively advanced provinces as a medium of exchange.[5]

Nevertheless, rice was the only primitive currency that was known to have been in general use. Its monetary use is supported by etymological evidence, as most Japanese words expressing value are related to "rice."[6] In 900 the prices of goods were quoted in terms of rice, the unit being the bundle of unhusked rice.[7] The salaries of Court officials were fixed in rice and cloth.[8]

Metallic money was not, however, unknown. In A.D. 713 tax was payable in copper. In the 10th century gold dust became a medium of exchange.[9] At first it was put into a small bag of convenient size (ten *ryo*). But later it was realized that gold dust often dripped from the mouth of the bag, so it was melted into gold bars and used by weight, the bars being cut as required.[10] The use of gold dust and gold bars continued even after the adoption of coinage, as there were not enough coins. Merchants adopted the practice of wrapping gold dust in small paper packets, the units being the *ryo*, the *bu* and the *shu*. Silver, too, was used as a medium of exchange in lumps and bars.[11]

---

[1]Munro, p. 5.
[2]Munro, p. 6.
[3]Nakada, *Public Law*, p. 47. Quoted by Koichi Miyashita, *Beiträge zur japanischen Geldgeschichte* (Vienna, 1931), p. 36.
[4]Miyashita, p. 39.
[5]Y. Takekoshi, *The Economic Aspects of the History of the Civilization of Japan* (London, 1930), Vol. I, p. 74.
[6]K. Hamada, *Ancient Japanese Money*, pp. 42 ff. Quoted by Miyashita, p. 40.
[7]Takekoshi, p. 95.　　　　　　　　[8]Takekoshi, p. 16.
[9]M. Takizawa, *The Penetration of Money Economy in Japan* (New York, 1927), p. 31.
[10]Phra Sarasas, *Money and Banking in Japan* (London, 1940), p. 54.
[11]Phra Sarasas, pp. 55-6.

PART III: MODERN PERIOD

CHAPTER 33

COMMODITY-CURRENCIES OF THE UNITED STATES

THE early monetary history of the British, French and Dutch North American colonies which subsequently became the U.S.A. provides an unequalled wealth of material on the uses of primitive money. The large variety of objects which were used by the various colonies includes furs, *wampum*, tobacco, rice, grain, beef, flour, hemp, peas, timber, fish, tar, pitch, cattle, dairy produce, musket balls, etc. There is an immense volume of documentary evidence concerning them, largely in the form of legislation passed in order to make these objects legal tender, to fix and alter their ratio to coined money, or to modify the scope and nature of their monetary use. Strangely enough, the American economic literature of the period concerned paid relatively little attention to the theoretical aspect of these currencies. Most economists of the Colonial period writing on the origin of money were concerned with the abstract rather than with the actual and illustrative emergence of money.[1]

As in other early colonies, the development of commodity-currencies was due to the extreme shortage of coins. Apart from the economic factors causing this shortage, it was aggravated by the prohibition of the export of coins by England and, after 1684, by the prohibition of the operation of mints in the colonies.[2]

According to some authors, the economic system of the North American Colonies in the early period was too primitive to make the use of coined money indispensable. The economy of rural districts was simple. Most settlers moved within a small radius and did not buy many things from outside it. In the opinion of Nettels, early social arrangements were such as to make for the elimination of the use of modern money wherever possible.[3]

Beer goes so far as to suggest that, as the use of gold and silver as a circulating medium implies an advanced and complex economic civilization, their employment in Virginia for instance would have been actually abnormal.[4] But allowing for these considerations, it is never-

---

[1] E. A. Johnson, *American Economic Thought in the 17th Century* (London, 1932), p. 161.
[2] C. P. Nettels, *The Monetary Supply of the American Colonies before 1720.* (Madison, Wisconsin, 1936), p. 212.
[3] Nettels, p. 223.
[4] G. L. Beer, *The Origin of the British Colonial System, 1578-1660* (London, 1908), p. 252.

theless certain that the extreme scarcity of coins must have caused grave inconvenience to the early colonists. In his standard work on the subject, Nettels makes the observation that the reason why the colonists chose to supplement the inadequate supply of coins by the monetary use of commodities was that they must have felt it imperative to prevent the prices of their staple products from being depressed by the scarcity of money.[5] But for the monetary use of commodities, the inadequacy of the supply of coins would have unduly depressed local prices, and would have influenced the terms of trade strongly against the colonies: that is, larger amounts of exports would have been required to pay for the same amounts of imports. Whether this fact was actually realized in each instance by those responsible for the adoption of commodity-currency, or whether the expedient was simply resorted to owing to a practical need due to the scarcity of means of payment is open to question.

Another major consideration was that metallic money would have been an expensive tool for a poor community to possess. The early settlers had very little capital and preferred to put as little as possible in the shape of money and as much as possible into food, clothing and implements. In the words of Horace White: "They could not have both a metallic currency and an axe."[6]

Yet another motive was the desire to raise the prices of the staple products and to secure a steady demand at a fixed price. In other words, the adoption of commodity-currencies acted as a "valorization scheme" for the benefit of the producers of the commodities turned to monetary use. In the predominant majority of instances—in fact with the sole exception of *wampum*—it was always a staple product that was chosen. Its price was raised usually well above the natural level corresponding to commercial supply and demand. This was done partly by artificial means by legislation; but to a great extent the additional demand for the commodity concerned created through its monetary use justified in itself a rise in its price, or, alternatively, an increase of production without a corresponding fall in its price.

Yet another reason was the desire of the authorities to collect large amounts in taxation, which would have been impossible if payment in commodities had not been accepted. The budgetary problem of the colonial administrations would have been incapable of solution unless the commodity-currencies had been made acceptable by the local creditors of the colonies and recipients of official payments. Salaries of the Colonial Government officials were for a long time paid partly in commodity-currencies. To be able to do so these currencies had to be made generally acceptable. The fact that the commodities concerned could be used for tax payments in itself went a long way to assuring

[5]Nettels, p. 203. There was of course an alternative: trading by barter, but the colonists had reached a too advanced stage in progress for reverting to that system.
[6]Horace White, *Money and Banking* (New York, 1908), p. 14.

their monetary use.[7] But it was necessary to declare them legal tender to ensure their acceptability.

Wampum was used for monetary purposes by the settlers because it was the chief currency of the Red Indians. In their trade with the Indians the colonists had to use *wampum*, and since the possession of this currency enabled them to obtain from the Indians various objects they needed for use or for export, it soon became generally acceptable also in dealings among the colonists themselves. In Massachusetts *wampum* was introduced as a currency in 1627. Contracts were made payable at will in *wampum* or in silver or in beaver skins. In 1637 *wampum* was made legal tender at the rate of six white or three black beads per penny for sums under one shilling.[8] In 1643 *wampum* was made legal tender for sums not exceeding forty shillings.

In 1641 in New Amsterdam the Council passed an Ordinance fixing the value of *wampum*, well strung, at six to the stuyver, and well-polished beads at four to a stuyver.[9] Large quantities of forgeries, made of stone, bone, glass or porcelain, circulated among the colonists, and these were refused by the Indians. Director-General Stuyvesant tried to stop counterfeiting, and issued an Ordinance in 1650 according to which loose and unstrung *wampum* ceased to be legal tender. The measure was not, however, a success. The scarcity of well-strung *wampum* threatened financial disaster, so that less than four months after the Ordinance, loose and imperfect beads had to be admitted once more as legal tender. Seven years later, this deflationary crisis was followed by the development of a *wampum* inflation. The supply of *wampum* became by then so large that its value had to be reduced.[10] As Bradford pointed out at the time the monetary use of *wampum* had led to an increase in its quantity.[11]

For a long period, *wampum* played a most important part in the monetary history of the British and Dutch colonies in North America. In New England their value which was fixed in 1637 at six white beads to a penny was subsequently altered to four white *wampums* or two black *wampums* to a penny. In 1661, *wampum* ceased to be legal tender.[12] On the other hand, in New York it was still the chief currency in 1672. In 1693 the ferry charge from New York to Brooklyn was fixed at eight stuyvers in *wampum* or one penny in silver. In Newcastle, Delaware, the import duty on rum was payable in *wampum*.[13]

The main reason why *wampum* maintained its monetary role for so long was that it was freely convertible into beaver skins which were in

[7]Nettels, p. 209.

[8]A. F. Dodd, *History of Money in the British Empire and the United States* (London, 1911), p. 228.

[9]A. Barton Hepburn, *A History of Currency in the United States* (New York, 1915), p. 5.

[10]N. Vreeland, *Wampums: The Native Substitute for Money in North America* (British Numismatic Journal, 1910), Vol. 7, pp. 345-6.

[11]Johnson, p. 131.   [12]Vreeland, p. 346.   [13]Vreeland, p. 350.

T

constant demand in Europe. It was the decline of the beaver skin trade which led to the decline of the monetary use of *wampum* among settlers[14] Gresham's Law also came into operation. Since the Indians only accepted the best *wampum* there was a tendency for the worst specimens and counterfeits to remain in circulation in the New England towns.[15] The monetary use of *wampum* as small change among white people lingered on during the early years of the 18th century, long after it ceased to be legal tender. Its value was subject to violent fluctuations.[16]

Tobacco was the most important among the commodity-currencies in Virginia and in the other Southern States. The first law passed by the first General Assembly of Virginia in 1619 was to fix the price of tobacco at three shillings for the best and at eighteenpence for the second grade, per pound. It appears that at that time tobacco was already a local currency. In 1642 an Act was passed forbidding the conclusion of contracts in which payment in modern money was stipulated. As a result, tobacco became virtually the sole currency. This Act was repealed in 1656, but practically all the trading in the colony continued to be done with tobacco as a medium of exchange.[17]

The price of tobacco which was 3s. 6d. in 1628 fell, as a result of increased cultivation, to 6d. by 1631. Efforts were made to restrict the amounts grown, and to improve quality. Artisans who had got into the habit of growing tobacco in their back gardens for monetary purpose were forbidden to plant tobacco. Notwithstanding these measures the price continued to fall and reached 3d. in 1639. It was then enacted that half of the supply of good tobacco and all of the bad was to be destroyed and creditors were to accept 40 lb. for each 100 lb. owed to them. An effort was made to raise the price in stages to 2s. per lb. This law, too, was quite ineffective, and by 1665, tobacco depreciated to 1d. per lb. In the following year Virginia concluded a treaty with the other colonies producing tobacco, Maryland and Carolina, to stop planting tobacco for one year, in order to raise the price. During this period public dues and private debts could be paid in various country produce at specified rates.

Subsequently tobacco notes were issued. They were certificates of deposit in government warehouses, and were declared to be acceptable for all tobacco debts within the warehouse district where they were issued. In 1727, they were made legal tender.[18] The Marquis of Chastelleux, after visiting the colonies, wrote: "The tobacco warehouses, of which there is a number in Virginia, are under the direction of public authority. There are inspectors, nominated to prove the quality of the tobacco brought by the planters and if found good they give a receipt for the quantity. The tobacco may then be considered as sold, the authenticated receipts circulating as money in the country. For example,

[14]White, p. 3.   [15]Nettels, p. 212.   [16]White, p. 3.
[17]White, p. 4.   [18]White, p. 5.

COMMODITY-CURRENCIES OF THE UNITED STATES 291

suppose I have deposited twenty hogsheads of tobacco in Petersburg. I may go fifty leagues thence to Alexandria or Fredericksburg, and buy horses, clothes or any other article with those receipts, which circulate through a number of hands before they reach the merchants who purchase the tobacco for exportation." Such receipts performed the office of currency right to the eve of the 19th century.[19]

The monetary use of tobacco resulted in a marked deterioration of its quality. Tobacco currency was debased by giving an inferior grade a deceitful appearance of good quality.[20] The stimulus given to tobacco-growing by its use as money led to overproduction and the demand abroad did not keep pace with the American supply. The remedy would have been to switch over to other branches of production, but the monetary use of tobacco made such a change difficult. The practice actually made most planters dependent for their "cash" supply on the continuity of their supplies of tobacco. A district which did not grow tobacco had to obtain its supply from other districts for its monetary requirements. It was stated in the Maryland Assembly that traders who did not grow tobacco had to buy it for monetary purposes, and that this inconvenience caused many to forsake the province. Since most payments were made in tobacco, anyone who failed to grow it failed to supply himself with the accepted currency.[21]

Owing to the wide and frequent changes in its value, tobacco did not satisfactorily play the part of the standard of value. Nor was it very satisfactory as a medium of exchange. It was too bulky. Sheriffs collecting public moneys in tobacco had to be granted by the State of Virginia ten per cent and more to meet the cost of transport. A discount of eight per cent was allowed to planters who delivered tobacco directly to the auditors.[22]

Beaver skins were one of the earliest forms of currency in New England. They were legal tender from an early date. In 1631 the General Court of Massachusetts ordered that corn should be accepted for debt payments at its current price, unless money or beaver skins were expressly stipulated. This order remained in force for over half a century but from time to time other articles were also put to monetary use.[23] To such an extent were beaver skins needed for money that a law had to be passed in Massachusetts decreeing that no planter returning to England should carry either money or beaver skins with him without permission from the Governor.[24]

In 1635 it was ordered that musket bullets "of a full boare shall pass

[19]Hepburn, p. 4.   [20]Nettels, p. 213.   [21]Nettels, p. 218.
[22]Nettels, p. 221.
[23]White, p. 6. The following is a judgment of the Massachusetts Court: "Sir Richard Saltonstall is fyned four bushells of malte for his absence from Court. Chickatanbott is fyned a skyn of beaver for shooteing a swine of Sir Richard Saltonstall." (Hepburn, p. 3).
[24]Hepburn, p. 3.

currantly for a ¼d. a peece provided that noe man be compelled to take above 12d. att a tyme of them."[25]

In 1640 Indian corn was made currency at a fixed rate of 4s. a bushel, wheat at 6s., rye and barley at 5s. and peas at 6s. Dried fish was also made acceptable for tax payments, and so was cattle, according to valuation.[26]

In 1690 the monetary products of Massachusetts were wheat, Indian corn, barley, peas, oats, pork and beef.[27] In Connecticut, wheat, peas, Indian corn, rye, pork and beef were used as currency. Although the monetary use of these commodities was suspended between 1710 and 1720 the result of the scarcity of coins was that the General Court again agreed to receive wheat, rye and Indian corn in tax payment.[28] Newhaven decreed in 1641 that commodities might be purchased by labour.[29]

In New Hampshire during 1701-9 eight kinds of boards or staves and four kinds of fish, as well as pork, beef, peas and Indian corn were listed as currencies.[30] Rhode Island currencies included wool.[31] The currencies of North Carolina, in addition to tobacco, included corn, pork, pitch and tar. These products were called "specie" and were readily accepted as currency, more so than paper money.[32]

In South Carolina rice was the principal commodity-currency. In 1739 the Assembly of South Carolina made it receivable for taxes. In the following year a tax of 1,200,000 lbs. of rice was levied and commissioners were appointed to issue rice orders to public creditors in anticipation of collection at the rate of 30s. per 100 lbs. These rice orders were made receivable for all purposes.[33] After the currency depreciation in South Carolina all considerable contracts were concluded in terms of rice.[34] Wheat, peas, pork, beef, tobacco and tar were also "monetary commodities" at varying rates.[35]

In Maryland, in addition to tobacco, flour and hemp were used as currencies.[36]

On various occasions, colonial authorities devalued their currency. For instance, they made debts of 100 "weight of tobacco" repayable with the aid of notes worth not more than 50 "weight of tobacco."[37]

In New York the list of monetary commodities at the end of the 17th century included pork, beef and winter wheat. New Jersey used wheat, Indian corn, butter, beef and pork.[38] The commodity-currencies of

[25]Hepburn, p. 3.   [26]White, p. 6.
[27]Nettels, p. 208.   [28]Nettels, p. 227.
[29]H. Bronson, *A Historical Account of Connecticut Currency.* Paper of the Newhaven Historical Society (Newhaven, 1865), Vol. i, p. 38. Quoted by Nettels, p. 208.
[30]Nettels, p. 208.   [31]Nettels, p. 208.
[32]A. McFarlane Davis, *Colonial Currency Reports* 1687-1751 (Boston, 1911), Vol. iii, p. 226. "An Essay concerning silver and paper currency more especially with regard to the British colonies in New England."
[33]White, p. 8.   [34]Davis, p. 226.   [35]Nettels, p. 208.
[36]Nettels, p. 208.   [37]Davis, p. 239.   [38]Nettels, p. 208.

Pennyslvania included hemp, flax, wheat, rye, oats, barley, Indian corn, tobacco, beef, pork and hides.[39]

Commodity-currencies had the grave defect that they tended to encourage a policy of over-valuation which caused much trouble. The invariable practice of the Assemblies in valuing commodities for public payments was to set the legal prices higher than the prevailing market rates.[40] The over-valuation of commodity-currencies produced an effect similar to that of inflation. It amounted to a scaling down of local debts contracted in the legal tender.[41] The dice were loaded against creditors to a particularly high degree when debtors had the choice of several commodities with which to discharge their liabilities. The general practice in such situations was to choose the commodity that was the cheapest at the time when payment was due.[42] The possibility of choosing the cheapest commodity-currency tended to cause a rise in prices, for sellers, having to envisage the likelihood of receiving payment in the worst currency, had to cover themselves by raising their prices accordingly. In Connecticut towards the close of the 17th century the merchants adopted the practice of asking their customers in what form they would pay before stating their price.[43]

English exporters to the American colonies, confronted with the over-valuation of tobacco, etc., were forced to demand very large nominal profits on their goods sold there, in order to be able to pay the statutory price for commodity-currencies. This had led to much friction. In 1626 Virginia complained that the profits made by English exporters were exorbitant. Governor Wyatt and the Council asked the Privy Council for a depot to be set up which would take tobacco at 3s. a lb. in return for English commodities valued at twenty-five per cent above their cost price in England.[44] Since tobacco was worth considerably less than 3s. in England, this plan was rejected. English merchants, too, were dissatisfied with the system of over-valued tobacco-currency. With the further decline in its market value, relations between planter and trader grew increasingly strained.

In 1631-32 the Virginia Legislation passed an Act imposing heavy penalties on those who contracted to buy imports for tobacco at a lower rate than 6d. per lb. This effort to force English exporters to pay higher prices for tobacco failed, since they in turn raised their prices for British goods. In 1633 it was decreed that imported goods should be bought against tobacco at a rate of 6d. per lb. at a price corresponding to the goods' cost of production in England. Some months later the price of tobacco was raised to 9d. As this price was well in excess of the market value of tobacco in England the law could not be enforced. In 1634

[39]Nettels, p. 208.   [40]Nettels, p. 212.
[41]Nettels, p. 229.
[42]W. S. Sumner, *A History of American Currency* (New York, 1874), p. 7
[43]Sumner, pp. 15-16.
[44]*Virginia Magazine*, Vol. II, pp. 53-4. Quoted by Beer, p. 253.

Governor Harvey complained that all English goods were sold in the colonies for at least three times their original price.[45] But English merchants had to do so, in order to be able to accept payment in tobacco at its over-valued parity, without suffering losses.

One of the gravest defects of commodity-currencies was that they were perishable. Sooner or later their quality deteriorated to such an extent that they ceased to be acceptable as currency and the last receiver had to sell them as a merchandise at its low market price.[46] There was a strong inducement for the payer to deliver his most inferior product. The settlers were apt to use their worst products in local payments, withholding the best grades for sale abroad.[47] There was a widespread tendency to pay taxes in inferior products. Treasuries often had to rid themselves of redundant merchandise by selling it at a loss when the market price fell below the official rates.[48]

Another grave disadvantage was caused by the existence of different qualities of commodity-currencies leading to a different value for the same goods in the same place. Tobacco, for instance, in Virginia was of four different kinds. There were also differences in values according to the dependability of inspectors. Some inspectors were more efficient and skilful than others, and, as a result, tobacco certified by their receipts commanded a higher price than that guaranteed by less skilful or slacker men. Differences were also due to discrepancies between the quality of the crops of different seasons and those of different cultivators. In Virginia the value of tobacco notes differed according to the location of the warehouses in which the tobacco was deposited. Efforts were made legislatively to suppress the monetary use of inferior tobacco.[49] There was so much shrinkage and deterioration in tobacco that notes issued against it could not be safely kept for more than a year.[50]

The use of certain types of primitive money gradually led to the evolution of more advanced types. *Wampum* shells were strung together to represent various denominations easily recognizable. In 1649 an order was issued in Massachusetts that the beads "should be entire, without breaches, both the white and the black without deforming spotts" and that they should be properly strung into eight different sizes of parcels: the white beads into parcels to the value of 1d., 3d., 1s. and 5s., and the black beads into parcels of 2d., 6d., 2s. 6d., and 10s.[51]

When hogsheads of tobacco were marked by an inspector of standing they passed at their face value without any re-weighing or re-examination.[52] Such stamped units accepted on the authority of a stamp may be regarded as the primitive equivalent of coined money, while tobacco notes and similar receipts were a primitive form of paper money.

In respect of the development of paper money America was ahead of

[45]Beer, p. 254.   [46]Nettels, p. 213.   [47]Nettels, p. 212.
[48]Dodd, p. 229.   [49]White, pp. 10-11.   [50]White, p. 11.
[51]Dodd, p. 228.   [52]White, p. 12.

Europe, even though it was far behind China. The issue of paper money was grossly abused, however. Though it was in most respects less inconvenient than commodity-currencies, as a result of its depreciation it soon became so unpopular that contemporary writers came to regard commodity-money as the lesser evil, and in many instances the sale of goods was refused against paper money while commodity-money was accepted.[53] On the other hand, writers defending the issue of paper money argued that it was much more suitable than staple commodities as a means of paying debts. "Why," asked Blackwell, "may not Paper-Money be as good as Tobacco-Money, Potato-Money and Sugar-Money?"[54] A Massachusetts committee in 1684 pointed out that money overcame the inconveniences which resulted from the use of staple commodities as a means of paying debts. Fish and corn, the committee said, were "so cumbersome and troublesome as could not be borne."[55]

From time to time, after a spell of inflation of paper money in various colonies they were, nevertheless, only too pleased to revert to commodity-money in spite of its disadvantages. While the regular use of commodity-money ceased during the 18th century, in backward areas it survived till the early part of our century.

In Eastern Tennessee deer skins and racoon skins were receivable as taxes and served the purpose of currency early in the 19th century.[56] European immigrants into Texas in the 1820's used cattle for money because they had plenty of it and no money. Everything was reckoned in cattle which was a general medium of exchange. The doctor was paid in cattle and the lawyer and the butcher.[57] In California during the gold rush lumps of gold and gold dust in bags were used as currency.

Right to the end of the 19th century, coon, rabbit and squirrel skins, in that order of precedence in value, were freely used as currency by the mountaineers of Kentucky.[58]

[53]Davis, p. 121.   [54]Johnson, p. 170.
[55]*Archeologia Americana*, Vol. III, p. 282. Political MSS., Vol. I. Massachusetts Archives.
[56]White, p. 8.   [57]Wirth, p. 3.
[58]J. Laurence Laughlin, *Principles of Money* (New York, 1903), p. 11.

CHAPTER 34

LEATHER MONEY ON THE BRITISH ISLES

The draft of a speech delivered by Thomas Cromwell in Parliament in 1523 contains a reference to the use of leather as currency. Explaining the difficulty of furnishing coin or bullion for the expenses of the army of 40,000 that was to be despatched to France he stated: "Thus we should soon he made incapable of hurting anyone, and be compelled,

as we once did, to coin leather. This, for my part, I could be content
with; but if the King will go over in person and should happen to fall
into the hands of the enemy—which God forbid—how should we be
able to redeem him? If they will naught for their wine but gold they
would think great scorn to take leather for our Prince."[1] There is no
indication whether the leather currency referred to was used during the
period of Henry VIII or during an earlier period; nor is it clear whether
it was stamped.

Leather is claimed to have been used as currency during a later period
in the Isle of Man. George Weldron's description of the Isle of Man
during the first part of the 18th century, published in 1726, states:
"Formerly their current money was leather which every man of substance was entitled to make, not exceeding a certain quantity limited by
a law then in force; this had no other impression than that of the
maker's name and date of the year."[2] According to Bishop Merrick's
letter to Camden, leather money appears to have been used for local
purposes on the Isle of Man in 1570. Some doubt has arisen, however,
whether this alleged leather money, which was stamped with the Manx
trie cassyn, was really money or whether the stamp was merely a mark
on hides and skins.[3]

In the time of Mary Stuart, Scottish people estimated land in "cauldrons of victuals."[4] According to Adam Smith, iron nails were used as a
currency in Scottish villages in the 18th century.[5] Even in our days in
some of the islands of the Outer Hebrides crofters pay village grocers
regularly in eggs, owing to the scarcity of modern money, the inadequate
supply of which is reserved for payments which must be made in that
form. A similar practice prevails to some extent on the Outer Scilly
Islands where payment is in local produce. Small and remote communities possessing little money are apt to revert to the use of produce for
monetary purposes.

During the 18th century the rent of some of the Western Islands of
Scotland was said to have been paid in birds.[6] This in itself would not
justify us in regarding birds as a currency there, unless we succeeded
in finding evidence for their use for other kinds of payments.

Oatmeal was used extensively in Scotland as a means of payment even
in comparatively recent times, and to some extent agricultural wages are

---

[1]State Letters and Papers, Henry VIII, No. 2958. Quoted by Charlton, p. 322.
[2]*Manx Society's Transactions*, 1864, Vol. IX. Quoted by Charlton, p. 327.
[3]Charlton, p. 327.
[4]Fynes Moryson, *Itinerary* 1617, Vol. III, p. 155. Quoted by Roscher, p. 350.
[5]Adam Smith, *The Wealth of Nations* (McCulloch's Edn., Edinburgh, 1843),
p. 11. "There is at this day a village in Scotland where it is not uncommon, I am
told, for a workman to carry nails instead of money, to the baker's shop or the ale
house."
[6]Borlase, p. 81. For discussion of the question whether puffins used for the
payment of rents on the Scilly Islands constituted a primitive currency, see p. 262
in the chapter on Medieval England.

still paid in that form. When in 1946 oatmeal was included in the bread rationing scheme, there were strong protests from Scotland on the ground that it would prevent farmers from meeting their contractual liabilities to pay their labourers in oatmeal. It is difficult to say to what extent oatmeal is used by its recipients for making payments in their turn.

CHAPTER 35

CATTLE CURRENCY OF IRELAND

Even after the end of the Middle Ages, cattle continued to play a limited monetary role in Ireland. In the 16th century MacMahon of Monaghan was told he could not have an interview with the Deputy of Dublin (the rogue Fitzwilliam) unless he promised to pay 600 or 700 cows. "For such and no other are the Irish bribes," remarked Fynes Moryson.[1]

During the reign of Elizabeth in 1567, Donel O'Madden was made Captain of his tribe by patent of the Queen, on condition of paying a fee of eighty fat cows. Nolan observes that cows were still regarded, even at this advanced period, "as a medium of exchange or a medium of value, as a sort of money, in fact, and they passed current for a pound sterling."[2] He quotes an article of agreement between the Earl of Tyrone and Sir Turlough O'Neill dated 1593, by virtue of which the former was to pay to the latter "so many cows yearly as shall after the rate of twenty shillings sterling the cow, make up the sum of 2,000 l. sterling . . . or in default of money, a choice cow for every twenty shillings sterling . . . the said money or cows to be paid at Strabane or Bynnvorb."[3]

Even at the beginning of the 17th century rents were paid in cows. In 1613 Sir Niall Garve O'Donnell wrote from his prison in the Tower of Chichester for the restoration of three scores of cows or pounds which had been lent out as stock to his clansmen in Ullster.[4]

[1]Nolan, Vol. I, p. 108.   [2]Nolan, Vol. I, p. 108.
[3]Nolan, Vol. I, pp. 108-9.   [4]Nolan, Vol. I, p. 109.

CHAPTER 36

RUM CURRENCY IN AUSTRALIA

The scarcity of coins during the early period of British colonization in Australia compelled the settlers and convicts to revert to barter and this led to the use of primitive currencies in their everyday dealings. During the later 18th and early 19th centuries most trade was done by barter, and deferred payments were settled in rum, corn, meat and other marketable produce.[1]

Rum, which formed a portion of every cargo that arrived, was the principal commodity used as a medium of exchange, to such an extent that the period is still referred to as the period of the "rum currency." It was possible to purchase anything for rum, which was even used as a reward for bringing offenders to justice. It was for long regarded as a universal medium of exchange.[2] For twenty years or more, rum remained the customary means of paying wages. Convicts were willing to do extra work against payment in rum. It has been said that there was nothing which the people would not do for rum. Settlers willingly sold their produce for it. It was not, however, a very satisfactory currency, for it did not encourage provident habits. Most recipients were unable to resist the temptation of consuming it themselves instead of preserving it for future payments.[3] It certainly did not serve to any large extent as a store of value. Nor was its value very stable to satisfy the requirements of a standard of value; it fluctuated according to supply and demand which was affected by the arrival of each cargo.

Notwithstanding these conditions, Whitehall did not think a convict colony had to be provided with money, and metallic currency came to be used mainly through the import of Spanish dollars. Owing to the scarcity of these coins, their centre was cut out and this circulated as a separate coin.[4] Since, however, the silver coins had to be used for the purchase of goods from incoming ships, as a general rule they did not stay in circulation for any length of time. The scarcity of metallic currency was relieved mainly through the issue of promissory notes even for amounts of a few pence only.

The aborigines are not known to have devised any system of currency. While credit is known by some tribes, they are not known to have devised any medium of exchange or standard of value. The same may be said to be true about the much more advanced New Zealand Maoris, though in their case some authors claim that greenstone had served as a currency. This claim is strongly contested by Firth who states that greenstones were merely a favourite medium of barter.

[1]F. Gardner, *Some Notes on Australian Currencies*. British Numismatic Journal, Vol. xxii, p. 17.

[2]Gardner, p. 18; A. Chitty, *Early Australian Coinage*. British Numismatic Journal, 1907, Vol. iv, p. 179; E. Shann, *An Economic History of Australia* (Cambridge, 1930), p. 22.

[3]Shann, p. 21.   [4]Chitty, p. 181.

CHAPTER 37

FUR AND WHEAT CURRENCY IN CANADA

Under French rule, coins in Canada were very scarce, and furs and grain were extensively used as currency. Trade was carried on for a time by means of negotiable notes payable in furs, grain or farm produce.[1]

A decree issued by Louis XIV in 1670, ordered the creation of a separate money for the French American Colonies: "*afin d'aider les artisans et gens de journée qui n'eut estée jusques a présent payez de leur travail qu'en sucre et petuns qu'ils sont obligez d'envoyer en France pour en tirer la valeur et denvrées néecessaire pour leur subsistance.*"[2]

At a session of the Council on 29th May, 1665, reference was made to a decree by which wheat was ordered to be rated at 100 sols in payment of old debts, "in order to assist the credit of the country." This was found disadvantageous and a decision was taken that in future wheat should be taken in payment according to its current value. Four years later this decision was reversed, as it was found that creditors accepted payment at a very low rate only. On 19th March, 1669, it was enacted, therefore, that as a provisional measure for three months wheat was to be accepted at four *livres* per one *minot*.[3]

In 1673 the Council of Quebec ordered that bear skins could be tendered in payment at their current value.[4]

The Council decreed on 27th September, 1674, that moose skins "shall be currency at their current value and that no one is entitled to refuse them in payment of debts." An Order dated 24th October, 1682, made wheat, Indian corn and peas, legal tender, and decreed that salt and pork must be accepted at their customary price for the purchase of firearms.[5]

Maple sugar was used as currency in Nova Scotia.[6] As late as 1846 the practice of issuing promissory notes payable in timber, country produce and other special articles, prevailed to a great extent in Nova Scotia.[7]

The monetary use of skins and blankets in dealings with Indians and Eskimos is discussed in detail in our chapter on Canada in the Ethnological Section of this book.

Dried codfish was widely used on certain parts of the Newfoundland coast during the 19th century. In the Regulations on Fisheries in the

[1]Francis Parkman, *Old Regime in Canada* (London, 1884). Quoted by Chalmers, pp. 175-6. E. Zay, *Histoire monétaire des colonies françaises* (Paris, 1892), p. 5.
[2]Zay, p. 41.
[3]*Documents relating to Canadian Currency Exchange and Finance during the French Period.* Edited by Adam Shortt (1925-6), Vol. I, p. 15.
[4]Kingsford, *History of Canada*, Vol. I, p. 156. Quoted by Davidson, p. 187.
[5]Documents, pp. 53-55.   [6]Documents, p. 187.
[7]Act 9, Victoria c.52. Quoted by Chalmers, p. 190.

Terra Nuova issued on 18th August, 1825, fish played the part of official money which served for the payment of wages and of procuring all that the fishers desired and could obtain.[8]

An article appeared in the *Westminster Review* of March, 1889, which states that, to that day, on the north-east coast of Newfoundland, cod alone was currency.[9]

[8]Dalloz, *Jurisprudence Générale.* Repertoire V. Obligat, No. 1751. Quoted by Babelon, p. 9.
[9]Davidson, p. 182.

CHAPTER 38

SUGAR MONEY OF BARBADOS

The West Indies like other early colonies had suffered a great deal through scarcity of coins, which, owing to the adverse trade balance, could not be kept in the colonies for any length of time. They had reverted therefore to the use of their various staple produces as means of payment.

The existence and operation of primitive currencies in the West Indies received scant attention in economic literature. Jevons made a passing reference to the peculiar currency laws of some of the West Indian Islands in which it was provided that the successful plaintiff in a lawsuit should be obliged to accept various kinds of raw produce such as sugar, rum, molasses, ginger, indigo or tobacco.[1] We owe most of our information on the subject to Chalmers who deals in great detail with the primitive currencies of Barbados and the Leeward Islands, and to a less extent with those of the other British colonial possessions in the West Indies and Latin America.

During the early period penalties in Barbados were expressed in cotton and tobacco, which were then the staple produce. They were supplanted after about 1640 by sugar, which became the principal medium of exchange. Describing the traffic of a merchant, Ligon says: "He makes his exchanges and he receives his sugars."[2] Ligon observes that wages are expressed in "sterling or the value of such goods as grown upon the plantation."[3] Foreign merchants reproached the Islanders for having no money except brown sugar. Lord (Francis) Willoughby of Parham stated in 1664 that "the current medium of the Island consisted of goods for they had no money."

There was a legal ratio between Muscavado or brown sugar and the pound sterling. The earliest ratio appears to have been ten shillings per

[1]Jevons, p. 27.
[2]Richard Ligon, *The True and Exact History of the Island of Barbados* (London, 1673), p. 111. Quoted by Chalmers, p. 46.
[3]Ligon, p. 40. Quoted by Chalmers, p. 46.

100 lb., but in 1667 according to Lord (William) Willoughby the Assembly "had raised their coin—that is Muscavado—from ten shillings per 100 lb. to pass in payment for sixteen shillings."[4]

From time to time the ratio was changed. In early legislation penalties are expressed in sugar. In the "Act concerning morning and evening prayers in families," it is provided that "whosoever shall swear or curse, if a master or a freedman, he shall forfeit for every such offence four pounds of sugar, if a servant, two pounds of sugar." In the Act of 19th December, 1688, marshals of markets were ordered to charge their fees in sugar instead of insisting on payment in money "which proves very inconvenient."[5]

Towards the close of the 17th century coin displaced commodities to a considerable extent as a medium of exchange. At the beginning of the 18th century between 1704-1715, Barbados reverted temporarily to the use of commodities as money.[6] There was not enough coined money to meet the requirements of trade. "The merchants bartered the commodities they imported for sugar, cotton, ginger and the products of the Island, Muscavado sugar being a general medium of commerce."[7]

[4]Chalmers, p. 47.   [5]Chalmers, p. 47.
[6]Oldmixon, *British Empire in America* (London, 1708), p. 14. Quoted by Chalmers, p. 47.
[7]Chalmers, p. 50.

CHAPTER 39

TOBACCO MONEY OF THE BERMUDAS

The currency of the Bermudas under the domination of the Summer Islands Company was mainly tobacco. Salaries and wages were paid in this currency from the early part of the 17th century. Fines were fixed in it. The penalty for the sale of fig drink to apprentices was fixed in 1627 at 10 lb. of tobacco. Housewives reckoned their purchases and tenants paid their rents in this currency. Waller, in *The Battle of the Summer Islands*, says:

"Such is the Mould that the blest Tenant feeds
On precious Fruits, and pays his rent in Weeds."[1]

The "martial officers" of St. George's were paid in tobacco from 1620 onwards, and artificers in 1623. From 1658, coins tended to replace tobacco as a currency for external payments.[2]

An order was issued in 1670 in St. George according to which tobacco must not be refused when tendered in current payment on the basis of its annual rating. In 1694 the pay of soldiers was fixed in current money or tobacco at the current price. Four years later, however, a fixed rate

[1]Chalmers, p. 151.   [2]Chalmers, p. 151.

was established. The Act of 31st October, 1698, provides that all tobacco being "marchantable . . . shall and may go and pass current payment and full satisfie all debts contracted from and after publication thereof at the rate of current value of 3d. per lb." The Act openly admits that this measure is taken in order to assist the producers of tobacco presumably because they were adversely affected by Virginian competition.[3]

[3]Chalmers, p. 152.

CHAPTER 40

TOBACCO AND SUGAR MONEY OF THE LEEWARD ISLANDS

According to Governor Codrington, writing from Antigua in 1691: "In ye Leeward Islands there is very little money and ye trade drove in them almost whooly by way of Truck of the severall Especies of ye produce of the Islands in exchange for others. . . . Nor is money so much as the standard of Trade, ye Merchants keeping all their books and accounts in shuggar or other of ye produce of ye Islands, and in these doe state all ye Debts to and from them."

In 1740 the Secretary of the Leeward Islands wrote, "When I speak of 'currency' without the addition of 'coin,' you will please observe, I always mean the Value that is put on Sugar, Rum, Cotton and other Commodities, the growth of the Leeward Islands, which is called Currency in contradistinction to Gold and Silver."[1]

During the early period tobacco constituted the monetary standard. Fines were imposed in terms of "good Marchantable tobacco in Rolls," under the Antiguar Act of November, 1644. For commerce with the heathen a fine of 1,000 lbs. of such tobacco was imposed by a Montserrat Act, also for Sabbath breaking "by unlawful gaming, immoderate and uncivil drinking . . . or any other prophane or illicious Labours of the Weekdays, as digging, houghing, baking, crabbing, shooting or such like indecent Actions."[2]

From about 1670 onwards sugar became the monetary commodity. For about thirty years the parity was 12s. 6d. for "five score pound weight of good dry merchantable Muscavado Sugar." This was in excess of the current market value, which fact discouraged the import of coin owing to the losses suffered on the exchange.

According to Oldmixon sugar served for all the uses of money on Nevis. "All the trade of the Island is managed by sugar. Pounds of sugar and not pounds of sterling is the balance of all their accounts; and exchanging that commodity for others did the inhabitants business as well as if they had silver."[3]

[1]Chalmers, p. 60.   [2]Chalmers, pp. 60-1.
[3]Oldmixon. Quoted by Chalmers, p. 63.

Various Colonial Acts levied taxes, prescribed fees and imposed fines in sugar. Property was valued in the same commodity. Sugar was used in the Leeward Islands not only as a medium of exchange but also as a unit of account. In 1668, Montserrat decided to engage "an able preaching Orthodox Minister" with a salary of "fourteen thousand pounds of sugar, or the value thereof in Tobacco, Cotton Wool, or Indigo." For solemnizing marriages, the Minister was entitled to charge "100 pounds of sugar or the value thereof in Tobacco, Cotton Wool or Indigo."[4]

In 1698 an estimate of an estate in St. Christopher contained the following item: "600 akers of good manurable land att least att 1,000 li. Sugar—the usual price of Sugar at 12s. 6d. per hundred . . . £3,750."[5]

Up to the end of the 17th century commodities formed the sole internal currency and the major part of the remittances of the Leeward Islands.[6] At the turn of the century, however, there was an influx of metallic money, with the result that the use of commodity-money declined. One of the effects of the influx of coins was the rise in value of commodities, with the consequence that, while debtors wished to discharge their obligations in coins, creditors insisted on maintaining the old practice of collecting payment in commodities. An Act passed in 1700 put an end to such disputes by deciding that money might be tendered in lieu of commodities at the following rates:

12s. 6d. for every 100 lbs. Muscavado.
2s. for every lb. of Indigo.
9d. for every lb. of Cotton Wool.
1½d. for every lb. of Tobacco or Ginger.[7]

After the adoption of the gold standard in England under Queen Anne (1702-1714), sugar lost further ground as a circulating medium. It continued to be accepted in payment, not at a fixed rate but at the current price. In cases of dispute, the value of the commodity tendered in payment was determined by arbitration. For a long time during the 18th century sugar continued to play a limited monetary part. The Assembly of Nevis on the 15th June, 1752, arranged for the appraisal of all sugar, rum and molasses paid for debts. And the same authority suggested, on the 24th August, 1753, an Act to make the commodities of the country legal tender owing to the scarcity of metallic money that developed during this period. It was explained that commodities should be made acceptable according to their current value for internal payments, but not for the payment of any debts contracted in England. No legislation seems to have been passed, however.

In 1756, in Antigua, taxes were payable to the extent of two-thirds in "good Marchantable Muscavado Sugar." This practice was discontinued by an Act of 1760. To a limited extent, however, sugar con-

[4]Chalmers, p. 61.   [5]Chalmers, p. 61.   [6]Chalmers, p. 62.
[7]Chalmers, p. 62.

tinued to be accepted for certain purposes. As late as 1784, a revenue Act was passed in St. Christopher which stated: "And whereas it may be burdensome and oppressive to the inhabitants of this Island to pay the amount in specie, be it enacted that the payment of the taxes aforesaid may be in cash, sugar or rum at the option of the person or persons liable to pay the same."[8]

Coins appear to have completely replaced commodities by the end of the 18th century.

[8]Chalmers, p. 63.

CHAPTER 41

MAHOGANY LOGS AS CURRENCY IN BRITISH HONDURAS

Mahogany logs constituted the principal currency of British Honduras during the 18th century. Bulky as this article was, it was used as a medium of exchange, partly owing to the lack of metallic currency and partly in order to secure a steady demand at a fixed price for the country's staple produce. Indeed, as was the case with various islands in the West Indies, it was grossly over-valued, and its over-valuation became one of the reasons for the continued acute shortage of coins, owing to the loss which would have been incurred through the import of coins and their disposal on the basis of the official rate.

The first legal provision concerning logwood currency was contained in Act 1 of the popular Convention of 9th April, 1765, providing that: "whoever shall be found guilty of profane cursing or swearing shall . . . forfeit and pay for every such offence the sum of 2s. 6d. in Jamaica currency or the same value in merchantable unchipped logwood."[1]

In May 1766, it was provided that all debts contracted in the Bay of Honduras shall be payable in logwood in the absence of special agreement to the contrary. Penalties of £5 or £50 in logwood currency were fixed in the same year.[2] The extent to which this logwood currency was over-valued compared with the current value of mahogany logs in terms of Jamaica currency is estimated by Chalmers at about three hundred per cent. The disadvantage of this was realized in 1784 when it was resolved that all business in future should be kept and transacted in Jamaica currency. Payment in logwood was to be made on the basis of the current prices which was to be fixed officially.[3]

"Cut money" was used extensively in Demerara and Essequibo at the beginning of the 19th century. A round bit was cut out of the Spanish dollar, and circulated independently.[4]

Primitive currency was adopted unofficially in British Guiana owing to the gross over-valuation of the token money in circulation towards the middle of the 19th century.

[1]Chalmers, p. 169.   [2]Chalmers, p. 13.   [3]Chalmers, p. 140.
[4]Chalmers, p. 127.

Retail traders established among themselves a currency of empty bottles and jugs of sugar cane, according to Governor Barkley.[5]

[5]Chalmers, pp. 135-6.

CHAPTER 42

UNCOINED SILVER MONEY IN RUSSIA

The use of furs as currency which was adopted during the early Middle Ages continued in Russia to some extent during the 16th and 17th centuries. Herbertstein, Ambassador of the German Emperor to the Russian Grand Duke Ivan Vassilyovitch, at the beginning of the 16th century, states that the Russians used heads and ears of squirrels and other animals, instead of money.[1] In 1514 Grand Duke Ivan Vassilyovitch fixed the value of the *kuna* (marten skin) at six *groschen* for the purposes of marriage money.[2] In 1610 a Russian war chest was captured by the enemy containing 5,450 *roubles* in silver and 7,000 *roubles* in furs. The fact that fur money was in use in the Kaluga district right to the end of the 17th century is proved by a ukase issued by Peter the Great in March, 1700, forbidding its monetary use.[3]

Throughout this period the use of coined money was on the increase. At the same time, however, uncoined silver continued to play an important monetary part. Herbertstein mentions that when silver was imported into Russia it was made into small, oblong ingots without stamp or inscription. In collections there are many such ingots, some round, others cylindrical or cone shaped. They are called ingots of Kiew or Novgorod, because they remained in circulation in those cities longer than elsewhere. Some bear the punchmarks of bankers through whose hands they had passed. Ingots worth a *rouble* or multiples of it had been issued by goldsmiths, merchants and bankers.[4]

In districts engaged in trade with Asia scrap silver, cut coins, and amorphous silver was still used for monetary purposes until comparatively recently. Centuries ago this practice prevailed all over Russia. According to Grempler, the meaning of the word *rouble* originated from *rubit* which meant "to chop."[5] According to Georgi, however, the *rouble* originated through the use of bars with deep notches (*rubli*) which enabled the possessor to detach as much of the bar as his payments required. Such bars were in fact introduced into Moscow in 1654.[6]

[1]Chaudoir, p. 10. [2]Chaudoir, p. 32.
[3]Ilwof, p. 6. [4]Babelon, p. 83.
[5]W. Grempler, *Über Hacksilberfunde* (Mitteilungen der Anthropologischen Gesellschaft in Wien, 1889), Vol. XIX, Neue Folge, p. 124.
[6]Georgi, *Description de St. Petersburg* (St. Petersburg, 1793), p. 187. Quoted from E. D. Clarke, Vol. I, p. XIII.

U

CHAPTER 43

GRAIN MONEY IN FRANCE

Considering the degree to which the *assignat* depreciated during the advanced period of the French Revolution, there is relatively little information available about the use of commodities for monetary purposes. By 1795 the *assignat* had ceased to be the standard of value. Precious metals were the recognized standard of value. The fluctuations in the price of gold and that of grain in terms of *assignats* were practically the same, while the prices of other commodities rose to a different degree. According to a speech by Député Cresson on 25th November, 1795, in the Convention, the price of gold and grain had risen 150 fold while that of meat had risen only 40 fold. In 1785 Député Jean Bon-St.-André proposed to the Convention that the value of goods should be based on grain, the unit to be a quintal of grain. Prices and wages should be reckoned in terms of wheat but paid in *assignats* on the basis of the current wheat prices during the month in question in the locality concerned. He wanted to separate the two principal functions of money by making grain the standard of value, while *assignats* were to remain the medium of exchange.[1]

To some extent, grain was in fact adopted for the purpose of tax payments. The degree of 3. Thermidor III (21st July, 1795) stipulated that land tax was to be payable half in *assignats* and half in grain. The determination of its quality and quantity was to be made on the basis of grain prices in 1790. The Act of 24. Fructidor III (10th September, 1795) raised the proportion of payment in grain to seventy-five per cent. Landlords were authorized to collect half the rents due to them in grain in order to be able to discharge their liability of tax payment in grain. A degree of 8. Messidor IV (26th June, 1796) realized to some extent Jean Bon-St.-André's idea. Under it, taxpayers had to pay for each franc of the tax the value of 10 lb. of wheat in paper money.[2]

A forced loan raised in 1796 could be paid in metallic money at its nominal value, in *assignats* at one per cent of their nominal value or in grain on the basis of the 1790 prices. Article 7 of the decree of 19. Frimaire IV (10th December, 1796). As a matter of fact, this experiment failed as three quarters of the proceeds of the loan were paid in *assignats* and practically nothing in grain.[3]

In a speech delivered before the Convention on 17th May, 1795, Jean Bon-St.-André pleaded that, in order to overcome the consequence of distrust in the monetary unit, the values expressed in contracts should be fixed in products. He wanted the Convention to apply this to all

---

[1] S. A. Falkner, *Das Papiergeld des franzoesischen Revolution*, 1789-1795 (Munich, 1924), p. 94.
[2] Falkner, p. 95.   [3] Falkner, p. 96.

public and private business and wished that contracts should be based on a schedule of values. Ten days later, Député Desermon introduced a Bill to establish the schedule on which contractual payments were to be based.[4]

Hand-made nails, which, according to Adam Smith, served as currency in some Scottish villages during the 18th century, were put to similar use, according to Chevalier, in one of the French coalfields during the 19th century.[5]

During the concluding month of the second World War, and during the first few post-war months coffee served to a great extent as a kind of medium of exchange in parts of France. Such was the shortage that practically anything could be bought for coffee. Cigarettes were also used both as a medium of exchange and as a standard of value, but to a lesser extent than in some other liberated continental countries. Contracts were concluded in terms of various commodities in preference to being concluded in terms of depreciating francs.

[4]Falkner, p. 97.   [5]Jevons, p. 28.

CHAPTER 44

COMMODITY UNITS OF ACCOUNT IN GERMANY AND AUSTRIA

For a long time after the advent of money economy in the Tyrol, land continued to serve as the standard of value and cattle and land products as the medium of exchange.[1]

During the inflationary period which followed the first World War various commodities were adopted as a medium of exchange or as a standard of value. In November, 1922, the Medical Association of Allgaus decided that doctors' fees should be charged on the basis of the butter standard. The fee for a consultation was the equivalent of one pound of butter, that for a visit one and a half pounds of butter. The daily wages of dressmakers in Hof was the value of six litres of milk. The bootmakers in Upper Swabia received as wages the equivalent of twenty-four litres of milk for eight hours' work. Builders in Berlin received as daily wages one and three-quarter pounds of butter, which compared with the equivalent of eight pounds of butter in 1914.[2] Vienna doctors asked their farmer patients in 1922 for payment in flour instead of in kronen. The consultation fee was seven kilos of wheat, a visit ten kilos. For distant calls an addition of three kilos per kilometre

[1]Arnold, Geschichte des Eigentums, p. 207. Quoted by Roscher, p. 350.
[2]Frankfurter Zeitung, 7th November, 1922. Quoted by Eisler, p. 55.

was made.[3] Rural schools charged their fees in the Weimar districts in rye.[4]

A large number of loans in terms of commodities were issued in Germany in 1922-3 by public and private borrowers, or they carried an option clause in which lenders were entitled to demand commodities in payment. Some of them had a wheat option, or a coal or lignite option, a timber or a potash option, etc. In one instance the price of benzol and in another the charge for electricity current per kilowatt hour was made the adjusting factor.[5] In 1923 Bastfaserkolter A.G. issued a loan of 200,000 kilogrammes of flax. Interest was payable in marks according to the market price of flax. The bonds served as a means of payment between firms growing flax and industries consuming it.[6] The State of Oldenburg issued in 1922 rye bonds. Holders were repaid the amount originally subscribed, allowing for changes in the price of rye between the date of subscription and that of the maturity of the bonds.[7] The rye note issue of the famous Roggenrentenbank is a widely-quoted instance of the use of the commodity-currency unit of account.

During the later stages of the second World War barter developed extensively in Germany but no unit appears to have been adopted to any great extent. In prison camps, on the other hand, the cigarette standard became very highly developed. It fulfilled all the functions of modern money. It became the principal medium of exchange with the aid of which it was possible to buy anything within the camp. It was largely used as a unit of account to facilitate barter transactions. It was used extensively as a standard of value for deferred payments. Prisoners were able to spend in advance their future cigarette rations by contracting debts. Considerable gambling debts were run up in terms of cigarettes. Cigarettes were also used as a store of value. Prisoners accumulated their savings in them. Those who acquired cigarettes did not necessarily consume them but kept them for the purposes of making purchases. Finally cigarettes were also used to pay for sundry services performed by prisoners for each other and also as bribes in order to obtain favours from the prison guards.[8]

Cigarettes served a monetary purpose so well partly because there was usually a good but not excessive supply, and a possibility of a replacement of quantities consumed; and because there was a steady consumers' demand, so that any cigarette owner could rely on being able to use it in payment. They are comparatively non-perishable. The units varied according to the size of the packets which, if needs be,

---

[3]*Frankfurter Zeitung*, 2nd August, 1922. Quoted by Eisler, p. 55.
[4]*Frankfurter Zeitung*, 20th September, 1922. Quoted by Eisler, p. 68.
[5]The author is indebted for this information to Mr. G. Stern, of the Union Corporation.
[6]*Textilwoche*, June, 1923, p. 12. Quoted by Eisler, p. 95.
[7]*Frankfurter Zeitung*, 20th September, 1922. Quoted b sler, p. 68.
[8]Paul Einzig, *The Cigarette Standard* (The Banker, Sy Eieptember, 1945).

could be opened and sub-divided to obtain small change. Gresham's Law came into operation in many instances, as there was a tendency for the inferior cigarettes to remain in circulation. The currency was often deliberately debased by putting inferior material in the cigarettes.

According to the account of an ex-prisoner of war, at the slightest sign of a shortage in cigarettes, the velocity of circulation of this currency declined almost to zero, as the supplies were all hoarded. Prices in terms of cigarettes slumped, and trading came almost to a halt. With an influx, or even rumoured influx of new supplies, the velocity of circulation greatly increased. Spending was much more free and prices in terms of cigarettes soared.[9] Supply and demand also affected the relative value of the cigarettes of various tobacco firms, and attempts to fix exchange rates between them failed.[10]

In order to prevent the deterioration of cigarettes, which is inevitable if the packets change hands too frequently, a bank was established in the camp, to issue notes convertible into cigarettes. It was difficult, however, to produce notes reasonably safe from forgery.[11] Eventually a Communal Store was established, with a share capital in cigarettes. The profits were paid out in dividends, presumably in the same form.[12]

In post-war Germany the cigarette standard became very widely adopted. Prices in terms of cigarettes were very low. Soap, which was also in short supply, became another primitive currency. Although both cigarettes and soap came into circulation primarily through the purchases made by the British and American troops, they continued to serve as currencies in dealings between Germans.

At a later phase a fictitious money called barter unit came to be adopted in Berlin and other big cities. The price of everything in the market where barter was transacted was fixed in such units. Even cigarettes changed hands on the basis of their barter unit value.[13]

[9]G. B. Clarke, *The Experiment*. Clare Market Review (Summer, 1946), p. 29.
[10]Clarke, p. 30. [11]Clarke, p. 30. [12]Clarke, p. 31.
[13]Herbert M. Bratter, *Germany's Financial Problems* (*Commercial and Financial Chronicle*, 12th September, 1946), p. 1388. *An Economy based on Cigarettes* (*Nation's Business*, June, 1947), pp. 42-3, 77, 79.

CHAPTER 45

OTHER EUROPEAN CURRENCIES

During the siege of Leyden by the Spaniards (1574) leather money was issued. It did not remain in circulation, however, for the half-starved population boiled the pieces of leather and ate them.

After the liberation of the Netherlands from German occupation in 1945 a craze for smoking seized a very large part of the population. Since the available supply of tobacco was not sufficient to satisfy more than a fraction of the demand, it became possible to buy almost anything against payment in cigarettes. Prices in cigarettes were exceedingly low. Highly valuable objects, such as jewels, optical instruments, and even houses, were sold for amounts of cigarettes which represented a negligible fraction of their value.

After the Allied occupation of Sicily the cigarette standard became widely adopted, especially in dealings between troops and civilians. The Italian population was not keen to accept military lira notes any more than notes of the Bank of Italy, but only too willing to part with farm products, fruit, etc., against payment in army cigarettes.

Hawkers in Sicily arrived with cartloads of farm produce at some military camp and departed with bags of cigarettes. They did not smoke these cigarettes, which constituted their working capital, but used them for acquiring further supplies of farm produce at a considerable profit. This practice was extended to the Italian mainland to a large extent after the extension of Allied occupation.

Olive oil, which is one of the staple articles of produce and consumption throughout the Near East, has long served as currency in the Ionian Islands, Mytilene, etc.[1] It is fairly uniform in quality, durable, and easily divisible, so that it is suitable for the purposes of being primitive money.

During the inflationary period at the end of 1944 olive oil and wheat came to be adopted as a standard of value used to facilitate barter. Olive oil in particular was important, being a staple commodity, especially in some of the Islands of the Ægean. This practice of relying on olive oil or wheat as a standard of value continued even after the first attempt at stabilization was made. All prices tended to be adjusted to fluctuations in the price of olive oil.[2]

During 1945 olive oil and wheat were largely replaced by sovereigns as the standard of value. Prices came to be adjusted to the daily quotation of sovereigns on the black market. Before the quotation became available at about 11 a.m. it was practically impossible to buy anything as sellers were reluctant to fix prices.

In Lapland cheese served as a currency up to the 19th Century.[3]

In Iceland the monetary use of products such as wool and butter continued during the modern period.

[1] Jevons, pp. 25-6.
[2] The author is indebted for this information to Sir David Waley who was financial advisor to the Greek Government during that period.
[3] Ilwof, p. 41.

CHAPTER 46

ALMONDS AS CURRENCY IN INDIA

The use of various primitive currencies in the backward parts of India is dealt with in our Ethnological Section. Here we only refer to currencies used also in the highly developed cities during the modern period.

Cowries were extensively used as a currency in India until comparatively recently. Various early travellers in the 16th and 17th centuries remarked on the use of bitter almonds as small change. Tavernier, among others, stated that for small change they used small almonds brought from Ormus. They gave forty almonds for the smallest monetary unit, but the parity changed according to the quality of the almonds. Other authors confirmed this information and pointed out that these almonds were too bitter to eat.[1] Evidence about the monetary use of bitter almonds in Surat is contained in Hamilton's *New Account*[2] which states that thirty-two almonds were equal to a pice (the smallest coin at the time). The same author also refers to the use of cowries as small change in other parts of India.

[1] *The Book of Duarte Barbosa*. Hakluyt Society (London, 1918), Series II, Vol. XLIV, p. 156.
[2] Ed. 1744, Vol. II, p. 314. Quoted by *The Book of Duarte Barbosa*, p. 156.

CHAPTER 47

FICTITIOUS MONETARY UNIT IN CHINA

The use of primitive money such as sheep, tea bricks, salt, etc., in the backward parts of China is dealt with in the Ethnological Section. Opium appeared to circulate during the 19th century as currency on Hainan Island.[1]

Reference was made in the chapter on Medieval China to the use of shoe-shaped silver ingots as a principal medium of exchange. The *tael* was the fictitious unit of account. Its equally fictitious sub-divisions were: ten *mace*=1 *tael*; ten *candareens*=1 *mace*. A *tael* is equal to about an ounce of silver of a given fineness. This system remained in use throughout the modern period until quite recently. With the development of foreign trade during the 16th and 17th centuries with the Portuguese and other seafaring nations, there came a heavy influx of silver as a result of the large exports in tea and silk. Thus the use of silver as a medium of exchange was further increased. It was used especially in wholesale trade, while the currency of the ordinary people for everyday transactions remained the so-called "cash"—the copper coins.

For many centuries silver was used as a currency without any Government regulation of its use. Therefore a confused system developed. The monetary unit, the *tael*, varied not only from place to place but to a large extent also according to the nature of the payment. The Imperial Treasury had for its standard the *Ku'ping tael*. Each city or commercial guild had a *tael* for its own use. The principal local *taels* were in Tient-

[1] Schurtz, p. 143.

sin, Peking, Canton and Shanghai *taels*. The most important from the
point of view of the foreign trader was the Customs *tael*, or *Hai kuan
tael*, in terms of which duties on imports were fixed in commercial
treaties.[2] The price of salt was reckoned in different *taels* according to
its origin. There was a different unit of account for cotton cloth, cotton
yarn and raw cotton. In addition, complications were caused by differences in fineness of the silver. As a result at a given moment in 1905
there were in use in Chungking alone at least sixty different currency
units in silver.[3]

The confused state of Chinese silver bullion currency continued until
the concluding years of the Empire. The State abstained from interfering and left it entirely to local authorities and private trading interests
to run their own monetary system. This situation handicapped trade.
Much time was lost through having to weigh the metal in every transaction and having to apply some rudimentary form of assaying.

It was not until the early years of this century that silver coins began
to be issued in large quantities, and it was not until after the Revolution
that the modern monetary system began to take root. The use of silver
bullion as a medium of exchange in wholesale trade survived, however,
until the silver crisis of the 1930's and still survives in remote districts.

Until recently taxes were partly collected in silver. In addition to the
discrepancies between various units, and the confusion arising from
differences in the fineness of the silver, the fluctuation of silver in terms
of copper cash was an additional source of complication. No wonder
that there had been strong agitation in favour of doing away with this
system. In a memoir, the Chinese Minister at St. Petersburg in 1904
declared that "the use of uncoined silver for money is like using un-
cooked rice for food, or uncut cloth for clothing."[4]

During and after the second World War, China reverted to a large
degree to the use of primitive currencies. This was due partly to the
progressive depreciation of the Chungking *yuan* owing to the increasing
output of the printing press. Another factor was the extreme scarcity
of most kinds of goods, as a result of which many sellers were reluctant
to part with their goods in return for paper money which could only be
spent on a limited range of goods. Finally, there was a shortage even in
the supply of paper money, owing to the difficulty of securing the ever-
increasing volume of paper required for that purpose.

In accordance with her ancient traditions, China adopted an immense
variety of primitive currencies. The cigarette was, of course, amongst
them, but it served as a short-term store of value rather than a medium
of exchange or a standard of value. To a large degree the Chungking

[2]Wen Pin Wei, *The Currency Problem in China* (New York, 1914), p. 36.
[3]H. B. Morse, *Trade and Administration of the Chinese Empire* (1907), p. 145.
Quoted by Wei, p. 37.
[4]Wei, p. 75.

notes were accepted in payment, but prices were based on the latest black market quotation of the United States dollar. When the Chinese peasant sold his products on the market against payment in paper money, he promptly converted his takings into cigarettes, even if he intended to spend the money in a few days, or even in a few hours. Cigarettes, tinned food and other objects served as a "hedge" against a depreciation of the *yuan* in the interval.

Various drugs and cosmetics, among other articles, served as a local medium of exchange in towns which happened to possess a sufficient supply to satisfy monetary requirements even in a limited sphere. For instance, in districts adjoining French Indo-China a fair supply of lipsticks was secured before communications had been interrupted by the Japanese occupation of that country. In some towns lipsticks became a favourite medium of exchange. Almost anything could be bought against payment in scores of lipsticks which changed hands many times without being used.

Lorry tyres and rickshaw tyres constituted a favourite store of value and standard of deferred payments. There were many other kinds of local primitive currencies. Needless to say, precious metals by weight recovered their old monetary role which, as far as silver is concerned, had never been relinquished altogether.[5]

[5]For most of the information on Chinese primitive currencies during the second World War the author is indebted to Mr. W. Fletcher, M.P., who spent some years in China during the war.

CHAPTER 48

RICE MONEY IN JAPAN

The feudalistic period during which rice constituted the principal means of payment, continued in Japan during the 16th century, and even later, although metallic money was gradually penetrating into economic life.

The wealth of feudal lords, which was based mainly on rice collected from the peasants, was estimated in terms of rice. At the beginning of the 17th century the national wealth was calculated at 28,000,000 *koku* of rice.[1] Part of the rice appropriated by the lord was consumed in his household, or expended on wages of artisans. But the greater part served for the payment of stipends of his retainers and attendants.[2] The latter usually sold part of the rice, in order to purchase town products, payment for which was in coin.

As for the peasants, they could not afford to make rice their staple food, for part of what was left to them after the lord had appropriated

[1]M. Takizawa, p. 20. One *koku* is equal to 5.12 bushels.
[2]Takizawa, pp. 28-9.

his share had to be used for the purchase of necessities which they could not produce themselves.

The common people, especially in rural districts, rarely saw gold coins even at the beginning of the 17th century. They were still accustomed to use rice for monetary purpose, and continued to do so to some extent even in subsequent centuries. Debts were contracted and paid in terms of rice. For small transactions copper money and rice were used indiscriminately. In some districts copper coins were scarce even at the end of the 17th century and at the beginning of the 18th century, so that everything had to be bought with rice.[3] Taxation was payable partly in money and partly in rice.

Rice was extensively used during the 17th century as a unit of account. The people were more accustomed to measure values in terms of rice than in terms of gold and silver coins. In various accounts of revenue and expenditure amounts in metallic money were expressed also in terms of rice in order to make their meaning clear.[4]

The practice of raising money by means of issuing rice notes also developed. These notes were freely convertible into rice whenever presented for conversion to the large landowners who usually had large supplies of rice in their store houses. It was the custom for the landowners to call in the notes issued every year in exchange for their stocks of rice in order to make room for the new crop, and thus to turn over the stocks. In the course of time they realized, however, that holders of the notes did not clear their rice all at once and that it was safe to issue more notes than the amount of rice available. Abuse of this practice induced the Tokugawa government to prohibit it in 1760, but the practice continued, nevertheless, in secret. It continued even during the 19th century, and forged notes were often discovered to be in circulation.[5]

The price of rice was fixed officially. From time to time the Government changed the official price.

Although rice played an important monetary part its price fluctuated more or less in sympathy with other commodities instead of moving in an opposite direction. This is probably due to the fact that, in addition to serving as a medium of exchange, rice was a staple article of consumption of overwhelming importance. Consequently, when its price rose through a bad crop, the cost of living rose instead of falling as it would do in a country with a currency that does not serve such dual purpose. Moreover, rice was not the sole currency. Its value in terms of metallic money necessarily fluctuated in sympathy with that of other goods whenever the value of metallic money changed, through debasement or inflation.[6]

With the expansion of trade during the Tokugawa regime rice became

[3]Takizawa, p. 34.   [4]Takizawa, p. 35.
[5]Takizawa, pp. 88-9.   [6]Takizawa, pp. 40-1.

too bulky for commercial transactions, and money came into general use with the merchant class.[7] The gradual replacement of payment in rice by payment in money was strongly deplored by the political philosophers of the period who considered that the development of the use of metallic money was an unmitigated evil. They were imbued with Chinese philosophy in which stability of society was glorified. For this reason they were alarmed by the disintegrating tendencies brought about by the development of a modern monetary system. Nevertheless, by the 18th century metallic money had become a pivot of economic life in Japan, and it became impossible to live without it no matter how much rice one might have in one's store-house. The feudal institutions based on a rice economy became gradually undermined by the new factors brought into being by metallic money.[8]

While in the towns rice long ceased to play any monetary part, in remote villages it remained the principal currency. Even in recent times according to evidence secured a few years before the second World War, rice performed monetary functions within many villages, although modern money was needed for trading with the outside world, and its use was gaining ground also in internal traffic. In his description of the village Suye Mura, J. F. Embree made frequent references to the monetary use of rice during his stay there in 1935-36. It is used for local purchases by the farmers,[9] even though the lower middle-class elements that have settled in the village use modern money.[10] Wages of agricultural labourers are paid in rice. Independent artisans, such as blacksmiths, roof-makers, etc., also receive their payment in that form.[11] Veterinary surgeons are paid in rice once a year.[12] Rent of land is a percentage of the rice crop,[13] but this role of rice may be regarded as payment in kind rather than a monetary function.

Rice plays a most important part in the activities of the co-operative credit clubs in such backward villages. They grant loans to members either in modern money or in rice. In some villages these credit transactions are mostly done in rice. Members of the club usually meet in the eleventh and twelfth month of the lunar calendar, because at that time the harvest is usually gathered, and everybody has ample supplies of rice. The rice is measured out under supervision of the leaders of the club, and checked in a book. While the reckoning is usually in rice, actual payment is sometimes made in money equivalent. The debtor repays the loan in instalments. These credit transactions are usually combined with a lottery.[14] The monetary use of rice in Suye Mura provides a remarkable instance for the use of primitive money in our time by remote sections of a modern community.

[7]J. F. Embree, *A Japanese Village* (London, 1946), pp. 3-4.
[8]Takizawa, p. 49. [9]Embree, p. 84. [10]Embree, p. 121.
[11]Embree, p. 101. [12]Embree, pp. 39-40. [13]Embree, p. 84.
[14]Embree, pp. 103-5.

BOOK III

THEORETICAL

PART I: WHAT IS PRIMITIVE MONEY?

CHAPTER 1

DEFINITION OF PRIMITIVE MONEY

THE great use of definitions, according to Shield Nicholson, is "to lay bare the meanings of the terms employed, to clear up the ideas for which they stand and thus to get rid of all ambiguities."[1] Their great danger is that one is liable to impose unwarranted limitations to the scope of one's enquiry, and to prejudice one's conclusions. Nevertheless, for theoretical discussions definitions are essential. The author abstained from applying any rigid preconceived definition in the Ethnological and Historical Sections, in order to be able to register all claims put forward from serious quarters instead of having to reject out of hand a large percentage of them. Before undertaking the examination of the theoretical aspects of primitive money it is necessary, however, to try at this stage to arrive at a definition of the meaning of the term.

In this task we can expect relatively little direct help from economists. Even those amongst them who have devoted some thought to primitive money have not attempted to define its precise meaning; most of them confined themselves to a few instances and have allowed the range of their haphazard choice to imply their concept of primitive money. Many economists do not regard primitive money as money at all. The instances they quote are merely meant to illustrate what they consider to have been the pre-monetary phase of economic evolution.

Nor is the majority of anthropologists dealing with the subject of primitive money very helpful. Many of them are reluctant to commit themselves to a cut-and-dried definition, and are inclined to attribute monetary status to many objects which obviously cannot be described as money. On the other hand, most of those anthropologists who *are* prepared to commit themselves are in favour of a strict and narrow definition. Indeed, they are at times inclined to be even more royalist than the king. In many instances they refuse to recognize the monetary status of objects which many economists are willing to regard as money. This in spite of the fact that it is the anthropologists' job to think in terms of primitive conditions; they are more in a position than

[1] J. Shield Nicholson, *A Treatise on Money and Essays on Monetary Problems*, 3rd Edn. (London, 1895), p. 13.

economists to allow for the difference between primitive and modern conditions.

There are, admittedly, anthropologists who favour an elastic definition. This latter attitude is in accordance with that of many economists towards the definition of modern money. Marshall remarks that "the need for elasticity in the use of the term 'money' is somewhat greater than in most economic terms," and that there are some enquiries for which the definition of money may with advantage be used narrowly and others for which a broad use of it is appropriate.[2] Among anthropologists Herskovits in particular favoured a broad and elastic definition.[3]

What matters is that we should not forget that we are the masters of our definition, not its servant. We must always bear in mind that, after all, it is we who have brought it into existence and consequently we are entitled to interpret it in a sense suitable to our enquiry, adjust it, and even depart from it if necessary. We must never consider ourselves to be rigidly bound by our self-imposed limitations. As Rist rightly observed: "A definition is never interesting in itself, but solely in virtue of the help it can render to enquiry."[4] The fetish-worship of a definition involves, according to Jevons, "the logical blunder of supposing that we may, by settling the meaning of a single word, avoid all the complex differences and various conditions of many things."[5] We must consider definition as a necessary evil the disadvantages of which can be mitigated by its liberal and elastic interpretation.

Before attempting to define the term "primitive money," we must first select a suitable definition of the term "money" itself. While our difficulty in arriving at a direct definition of primitive money is lack of guidance, in trying to select an appropriate definition of money we are faced with an *embarras de richesse*. It has far too many definitions, and it is by no means easy to choose one that can be applied to primitive money without having to surround it with too many reservations. Most monetary economists have been fully alive to the difficulty of defining such an elusive notion as money. Some of them sought to overcome it by making their definition simply a catalogue of the essential functions, qualities and requirements of money. Helfferich rightly objects to this method. "We cannot admit," he says, "a mere stringing together of separate functions to be a correct definition."[6] He feels that a definition should only include the fundamental characteristics of the phenomenon to be defined, and should not include derivates and incidental items of secondary importance. Indeed, in matters of definition brevity is a highly valued virtue. The danger is that in an effort to avoid making the definition too long and clumsy one runs the risk of omitting something

[2]Alfred Marshall, *Money Credit and Commerce* (London, 1923), p. 13.
[3]Herskovits, p. 216.
[4]Charles Rist, *History of Monetary and Credit Theory* (London, 1940), p. 33
[5]Jevons p. 248.   [6]Helfferich, Vol. I, p. 277.

essential. As a general rule, most monetary theorists deliberately confine their definition to one single aspect or very few aspects of money, in order to emphasize those aspects in accordance with their favourite theories. They adapt their definition to their preconceived theory.

The majority of definitions of money may be classed in two main categories: those which regard money as a commodity and those which regard it as an abstract unit. The former category of definitions is based on the function of money as a medium of exchange. Its most prominent exponent is Menger who considers "money" to be virtually synonymous with "medium of exchange" and rules out any means of payment which does not play that part.[7] Such a restricted use of the term would, of course, exclude all non-commercial means of payments. But, as Schurtz observes, this attitude does not in the least solve the problem. "Whether we call money the first beginnings of what we now regard as money, or whether we give it some other name is utterly unessential compared with the real problem involved."[8] Jevons points out that "by calling some money and some not, we do not save ourselves from the consideration of their complex legal and economical conditions."[9] Admittedly, we could save ourselves a good deal of trouble if we narrowed down the scope of our enquiry by ruling out in advance anything that does not fit in with our preconceived theory. But it is an ostrich-like policy to try to ignore out of existence the inconvenient and difficult instances. It was frequently resorted to until recently by monetary theorists of the metallist school who confined their definition to metallic money and treated paper money as a freak development or an emergency measure. It is only since the end of the 19th century that the idea that a good definition of money must cover not only metallic currency but also inconvertible paper currency came to be widely accepted.[10] On the other hand, Menger's narrow attitude in identifying money with medium of exchange and excluding from its definition anything that does not adequately fulfil that function is still firmly held by an important school of thought.

The terminology of monetary science is none too rich and we can ill afford to use more than one term for the same notion. If "money" is nothing else than "medium of exchange," it would simplify matters if we simply called it medium of exchange. Since, however, money has also other functions and since in many instances those functions are more important than that of the medium of exchange, it seems to be unjustified to use the term as a mere synonym for "medium of exchange." Even if we accepted Menger's definition and excluded the means of non-commercial payment from the range of monetary objects,

[7]Karl Menger, Article on *Geld* in the *Handworterbuch der Staatswissenschaften* (Reprinted by the London School of Economics. Collected Works, Vol. IV, London, 1936), pp. 93-4.

[8]Schurtz, p. 2.   [9]Jevons, p. 248.

[10]Rist. p. 334.

V

those means would exist nevertheless and would call for theoretical examination. It would not facilitate our task in any way if we simply denied their monetary status. The acceptance of Menger's definition would also exclude from our enquiry units which served as standards of value without at the same time serving as media of exchange. Yet the function of standard of value is a very important monetary function and no investigation of primitive money could be complete without covering the abstract units of account for the use of which we have much historical and ethnological evidence.

In one respect Menger's definition is sufficiently elastic to be applicable to primitive conditions. "In certain instances," he says, "money acts as such only in certain sections of the community or for certain transactions."[11] Evidently Menger, having studied primitive currencies more thoroughly than most monetary theorists, does not insist on the universal acceptability of money as a medium of exchange as an indispensable condition of the monetary status.

One of the variants of the class of definitions based on the medium of exchange functions of money describes money as an object which confers on its holder general purchasing power. In Locke's words: "Money represents a pledge whereby men were assured of obtaining valuable things equal to those with which they parted." We frequently encounter descriptions of money as "a voucher to purchase" or a bond used against the aggregate of existing wealth giving the bearer the right to have delivered to him any portion whatever of this wealth at his option up to the amount of the money he holds.[12] These definitions imply general and unconditional acceptability of money. Therefore, they are inapplicable to the large majority of primitive communities where the right of holders of money to make indiscriminate purchases and to require sellers to accept payment in it does not exist in law or in practice.

Definitions which are based exclusively on the use of money as a unit of account are as unsuitable for application to primitive money as those based solely on its functions as a medium of exchange. If we defined money as the common denominator in terms of which the prices of goods and services are expressed, we would rule out objects which served as media of exchange without being at the same time units of account, such as the cauldrons and tripods used in Homeric Greece as media of exchange without being used as standards of value, or the stores vouchers used in parts of Congo and accepted by the Africans in payment for their goods and services, since they do not serve as units of account but are valued, like everything else, in terms of slaves, salt or some other form of primitive money.

In yet another category of definitions stress is laid on the standard of

[11]Menger, p. 93.
[12]Charles Gide, *Principes d'Economie Politique*. 12th Edn. (Paris, 1910), p. 629.

deferred payments function of money. According to these definitions, "money is the object which is acceptable in discharge of liabilities."[13] This is not generally applicable to primitive conditions, since in many instances certain objects may serve that purpose while different objects may be used at the same time for other monetary purpose.

The overwhelming importance of unilateral non-commercial payments in primitive life as compared with payments arising from trade is altogether overlooked by practically all definitions. It is assumed that money must be essentially commercial in character and that any object which serves the purposes of non-commercial payments may safely be disregarded even if its use is of first-rate importance in the economic, political and social life of primitive communities. The more closely primitive communities are investigated, however, the more evident it must be that objects used solely for non-commercial payments perform a social function similar to that played in modern communities by objects used for commercial payments.

According to John Stuart Mill, "money is the medium through which the incomes of the different members of the community are distributed to them and the measure by which they estimate their possessions."[14] In many primitive communities, however, a large part of the income of its members is distributed in kind in spite of the existence of money. As for the function of measuring possessions, it is certainly an important one in primitive conditions. We encounter instances in which an object is used for that purpose without being used as a standard of value in trade. Nevertheless, this function is in itself not important enough to serve as a basis for a definition of primitive money.

Hitherto, we have been dealing with the definitions arising from the basic functions of money. Let us now examine briefly some definitions arising from its nature, qualities or peculiarities to which various authors have attached sufficient importance to use them as the basis of definitions. Outstanding amongst them is the definition according to which money is an object which is accepted not for direct consumption but for the purpose of subsequent use for purchases or payments. Helfferich lays particular stress on this requirement. According to him, whether an object may or may not be regarded as money depends on whether it was intended for consumption or whether it fulfils its purpose by passing from hand to hand.[15] He admits that the two functions can be fulfilled by the same object, though not at the same time. What matters in his opinion is the recipient's intention at the time when he

[13]R. G. Hawtrey, *Currency and Credit* (London, 1928), 3rd Edn., p. 2. This class of definition is sometimes combined with the one based on the medium of exchange function. Thus D. H. Robertson defines money as "anything which is widely accepted in payment for goods or in discharge of other kinds of obligations." (*Money*, London, 1922), p. 2.

[14]J. S. Mill, *Principles of Political Economy* (London, 1878), p. 8.

[15]Helfferich, p. 2.

accepts payment in money. This point may certainly be accepted as a useful element in the definition of primitive money, but in itself it is not adequate for our purpose. We also ought to bear in mind that merchants accept goods which they can keep as their stock in trade instead of consuming or using them directly; such goods certainly cannot be regarded as money.

Several ethnologists laid stress on the difference between objects which are used exclusively for monetary purposes and those which fulfil a dual function. Thus, Ilwof describes the latter class as money substitutes (*Geldsurrogate*). Temple distinguishes between "money" and "currency," the latter term including, according to his definition, objects which have a non-monetary use in addition to their monetary use. This distinction is, however, artificial from the point of view of the definition of money.

The separation of monetary and non-monetary functions is also behind the definition according to which money must be a thing unto itself in contradistinction to all other objects.[16] Those who use this definition visualize a huge balance with all the money in one of the scales and all goods and services in the other. This picture does not in the least fit primitive conditions where the majority of currencies have some non-monetary use and the same quantity, therefore, are apt to appear in both scales of the balance, though not necessarily at the same time. Moreover, the simultaneous existence of several currencies have made it difficult to apply a clear-cut distinction between money and goods.

The existence of a price-mechanism through the functioning of the monetary system is yet another basis for the definition of money. It links up with the definition based on a sharp distinction between money and goods, since price-mechanism in the modern sense can only work on the basis of such a distinction. In a primitive community, however, the operation of price-mechanism is interfered with in many ways. The limitation of the role of money often prevents the smooth working of the quantity theory on which the price-mechanism in a modern community rests.

Acceptance by tale is also considered by some authors as the criterion of money. According to Ellis, money exists when amongst primitive peoples tradition attaches a symbolic meaning to certain objects so that they are merely counted out in payment. On the other hand, objects such as tobacco, cattle, corn, etc., cannot properly be called money because their relative value was determined by weighing and measuring, and they were not passed by tale.[17] This definition cannot be accepted, since it would rule out not only all commodity-currencies but even metals changing hands by weight—especially if they were assayed every time they changed hands—which for many centuries played an important

[16]Menger, p. 93.
[17]H. S. Ellis, *German Monetary Theory*, 1905-1933 (Cambridge, Mass., 1934), p. 24.

monetary part in Western Asia and most parts of Europe and which constituted in monetary evolution a phase not far removed from the adoption of coinage. It would even rule out early coins which were weighed and assayed for many centuries.

Indiscriminate acceptance is again considered by many authors an essential element in the definition of money. Marshall defines money as the objects which are generally current without doubt or special enquiry as means of purchasing goods and services and of defraying commercial obligations.[18] Wicksell, too, defines the general medium of exchange as a commodity which is habitually and without hesitation taken by anybody in exchange for any commodity.[19] These and other similar definitions imply two conditions. The one is that the object serving monetary purpose must be taken without regard for the character or credit of the payer. The other is that it should be accepted as a matter of course without any agreement to ensure its acceptance. The first condition does not arise in a primitive community except in the infrequent instances of the use of credit instruments as currency. The second condition cannot be applied to a large proportion of primitive currencies, for in a great many instances the choice or acceptance of the currency is a matter of negotiation.

From the foregoing it is evident that for our purpose the definition of money must necessarily be both broader and more elastic than that applied by economists to modern money. Otherwise we run the risk of excluding, for the sake of adhering to our definition, a wide range of objects which call for enquiry. The alternative to making our definition sufficiently broad and elastic for their inclusion would be to discuss them in a separate treatise, a course which would have obvious inconveniences.

The main difficulty which the monetary theorist has to face in defining modern money is how to include within the scope of his definition abstract instruments of credit which have come to play a monetary role. Our main difficulty here is how to include under our definition objects which the monetary theorists dealing with modern conditions can well afford to ignore, but which in conditions prevailing in primitive communities play a distinct if limited monetary role. A definition of primitive money must allow for the frequent instances of separation of the main monetary functions encountered in primitive communities. It is justifiable and indeed necessary to include among primitive currencies any object that fulfils to a reasonable degree either the function of a medium of exchange or that of a standard of value, standard of deferred payment or means of unilateral payments. An object that performs solely the functions of a store of value does not on that account qualify for being considered a money.

[18]Marshall, p. 317.
[19]Knut Wicksell, *Lectures of Political Economy* (London, 1935), Vol. II, p. 16.

After the above preliminaries, the author now ventures to suggest a concrete definition of primitive money. It may be defined as *a unit or object conforming to a reasonable degree to some standard of uniformity, which is employed for reckoning or for making a large proportion of the payments customary in the community concerned, and which is accepted in payment largely with the intention of employing it for making payments.*

Insistence on uniformity does not mean that the units or objects serving as money must necessarily be of uniform quantity, weight or outward appearance. Objects which do not possess the required degree of uniformity can be reduced to some recognized standard by weighing or measuring. The definition does not claim absolute uniformity, only a reasonable degree of uniformity. That degree varies according to the sense of value developed in the community using the money in question. In many communities livestock possessed a sufficient degree of uniformity, while in others it was considered necessary to define a standard unit of livestock for monetary purposes. The reason why it is essential to insist on a certain degree of uniformity is in order to draw a line between monetary payments and payments in kind. If the State authority prescribes the acceptance of sundry goods in settlement of claims on the basis of their current market value when the claims mature, the goods which are thus used for payment do not constitute money because they do not possess the required degree of uniformity. It is true, wheat can be reduced to the required standard of uniformity by expressing it in terms of weight or hollow measure. But if the unit of weight or measure is not acceptable at a definite value then it is incapable of being reduced to the required standard of uniformity for monetary purposes.

The definition covers the units used in reckoning payments as well as the objects used for making payments, in order that units used solely as a standard of value or a standard of deferred payments should be included in the scope of our enquiry. By payment we mean any kind of payment customary within the community concerned and not only commercial payments. The definition makes an essential qualification of money its acceptance with the intention of use for future payments.

Even this definition, broad and elastic as it is meant to be, should not be applied too literally. Owing to the immense variety of objects serving as primitive money and the diversity of conditions in which they play that role, it may appear justified at times to disregard our self-imposed limitations in what seem to be borderline cases. It would indeed be idle to devise a watertight definition which would necessarily cover every conceivable kind of primitive money. Such definition, according to Rist, would be so general in character that it would cease to have any meaning in the same way as a general definition of "living beings" which tries to cover the fundamental characteristics common to the protozoa, the elephant and the man would be entirely useless.[20] Admittedly, the

[20]Rist, p. 329.

adoption of a broad and elastic definition which allows for exceptions flavours of empiricism. Nevertheless, it seems preferable either to the acceptance of a too rigid definition or to dispensing with definition altogether. A plan of campaign often has to be adapted in the field to meet new situations as and when they arise to such an extent as to make it unrecognizable. In spite of this, it is essential to start with a plan of campaign, if only in order to have something from which we can depart. Definitions must be conceived and applied in the same spirit.

We cannot conclude this chapter without defining the difference between "money" and "currency." The two terms are often used indiscriminately, while in many instances the discrimination between them is unreasonable. To the author's mind, "currency," as its name implies, is "current money," that is, money actually in physical circulation, or capable of being put into circulation. Credit-money does not belong to this category, nor do abstract units of account. Both are money, but they are not currencies. Every currency is money, but only those moneys which are actual circulating media are currencies.

CHAPTER 2

WHAT IS NOT PRIMITIVE MONEY?

In the last chapter an attempt was made to define primitive money. The author is, however, only too well aware of the inadequacy of his effort. Owing to the immense difficulties of defining primitive money in a positive sense, it is essential to try to define it also in a negative sense by indicating the objects which are *not* primitive money. To that end we have to try to draw a line between primitive money and barter, and also between primitive money and modern money. Neither of these tasks is easy, for in both directions the difference is often one of degree. Barter merges into primitive money and primitive money into modern money through barely perceptible shades of distinction.

In many instances a transaction may constitute barter from the point of view of one party and purchase or sale from the point of view of the other. In other instances each of the two parties considers that it is he who paid with money for the goods supplied by the other party. Since even those directly concerned are apt to disagree whether a transaction is a purchase or a barter, it must be very difficult for the outside observer to make up his mind about it. Nevertheless, it is possible to lay down a few broad and tentative rules:—

1. If an object or an abstract unit serves as a unit of account to facilitate barter, it may be regarded as money but the system cannot be considered to be monetary economy. It is described sometimes as "money-barter."

2. It is necessary to draw a distinction between a favourite medium of barter (an object which figures frequently in barter transactions and is readily accepted for non-monetary uses by most if not all people in a community) and primitive money. The former is accepted for direct consumption, while the latter is accepted in order that it should be used in exchange for other goods and services.

3. Though the simultaneous use of several kinds of primitive moneys does not necessarily disqualify any one of them from being regarded as a money, if the multiplicity of objects used at the same time in exchanges reduces the scope of each one of them beyond a certain limit none of them can be regarded as being anything but a medium of barter.

4. Though changes in the choice of primitive currencies used in a primitive community are apt to be more frequent than in a modern community, if they are so frequent that the monetary use of the objects in question cannot be depended upon at all they must be considered as media of barter.

5. Though the use of a medium of exchange in primitive communities is not necessarily as general as in modern communities, if it is accepted in payment for one or two kinds of goods and services only it must be considered as a medium of barter. In this respect, however, we must bear in mind that the total number of categories of goods or services to be paid for in a primitive community is itself apt to be very small.

6. Foodstuffs or other objects of small value given as small change cannot be regarded as money unless they are accepted with the definite object of making payments with them.

7. Means of non-commercial payments may be considered as money under the broad definition adopted by the author. If, however, their sole use is the ceremonial exchange of units against each other without any direct or indirect economic objective, they cannot be considered as money.

The borderline between primitive and modern money is equally hard to draw. The broad rule that coins, sealed ingots, notes and credit money are modern and everything else is primitive grossly over-simplifies the problem. For one thing, the transition between metals changing hands by weight and coins or sealed ingots is very gradual. In any case, for a long time after the adoption of coinage, gold coins and to some extent also silver coins changed hands mostly by weight instead of by tale. Moreover, it is a matter of opinion whether ingots bearing the seal of merchants, temples or townships should be regarded as modern or primitive money. It is also arguable whether the fish-hook money of the Persian Gulf or the knife money of Ancient China may be considered modern, in spite of their strange shape, on the ground that they were sealed by the State authority. The practice of cutting up coins and using the pieces separately either by tale or according to weight also introduces an element of complication.

Beyond doubt, paper money is essentially modern. There are, however, borderline cases such as those of the rice notes in Japan or the tobacco notes in Virginia. If notes are printed not on paper but on pieces of leather, furs, blankets, mats, canvas, etc., then their modern character may be open to argument. Likewise, if tea-bricks, hogsheads of tobacco, etc., change hands by tale on the strength of a Government guarantee of their quantity and quality by means of a seal or certificate, it is arguable whether they are an advanced commodity money or a rudimentary form of modern money.

The following are a few tentative rules for the purpose of determining limits between primitive and modern money:—

1. Every kind of non-metallic money with the exception of paper money and credit money may be considered to be primitive.

2. All metallic currencies which do not bear a seal or insignia implying a guarantee of weight and fineness by a State authority are primitive.

3. All paper currencies issued in terms of primitive currencies are themselves primitive.

4. When coins change hands by weight they may be considered primitive money unless the purpose of weighing individual coins is merely to ascertain whether they are full weight or not.

5. All cut coins may be considered primitive money, even if they change hands by tale.

6. All commodity-currencies are primitive, even if they change hands by tale on the strength of a Government guarantee.

7. Credit money need not necessarily be modern money. If credit is granted in terms of goods, then it is nearer to natural economy than money economy and must be regarded as primitive.

The term "primitive money" is often applied to objects which cannot be regarded as money in any sense. Travellers are usually the worst offenders in this respect. They are all too ready to call money any object which they happen to have used in barter. Ethnologists who have not specialized in the economic aspects of their subject are often guilty of the same error. The following are instances of objects which should be excluded from the range of primitive currencies:—

1. Objects which, while used regularly in exchanges or in payments, do not conform to any standard and have to be valued individually in each case. Such objects include precious stones, the value of which cannot be determined solely by their weight or size.

2. Objects which have special individual value owing to sentimental, religious, social or historical associations.

3. Objects which are of such high value or which are so scarce that they hardly ever change hands at all.

4. Objects which are accepted in payment not on the basis of any fixed value but on the basis of their current market value at the time when the payment is due.

5. Objects serving for payment of wages in kind on the basis of the "truck" system. Such objects may, however, become currencies if their recipients use them systematically for the purchase of other goods.

6. Objects used for the payment of rent in kind by their producers.

7. Objects used for the payment of taxes in kind by their producers.

From the foregoing it is evident that a definition of primitive money in a negative sense must also be necessarily vague and far from adequate. In the following chapter we shall try to go a step further in the task of determining the limits of our subject with the aid of ascertaining the essential requirements or qualities of primitive money.

CHAPTER 3

REQUIREMENTS OF PRIMITIVE MONEY

According to Turgot, an object need not possess any special qualifications in order to be suitable for monetary use. He believed that any commodity had the qualities enabling it to measure and transmit value.[1] This view is not shared by the overwhelming majority of economists who maintain that in order that an object or material should be suitable for performing the functions of money it has to possess certain very definite qualifications. Economists have compiled various lists of what they regard as indispensable requirements of money. The extent to which these requirements are indispensable differs widely. An object need not possess all of them in order to qualify for being regarded as money, though their possession increases its suitability to perform that role. After all, even a bad money is undoubtedly money.

The most generally accepted list of requirements is that of Jevons,[2] according to whom money must have the following requirements, in the order of importance given here:—

1. Utility and Value.
2. Portability.
3. Indestructibility.
4. Homogeneity.
5. Divisibility.
6. Stability of Value.
7. Cognizability.

By its very nature primitive money cannot and is not expected to possess these requirements to anything like the extent to which modern money possesses them. Conditions prevailing in primitive communities do not necessarily call for such a degree of perfection of the monetary

[1] Turgot, *Valeurs et Monnaies* (Œuvres de Turgot), Vol. I, p. 75.
[2] Jevons, p. 31.

system as modern conditions do.[3] Most of the above requirements do not apply to primitive money which only plays the part of an abstract unit of account; stability of value is the only quality which such a limited money must possess. Nor are the requirements of currencies used for political and other unilateral payments necessarily as exacting as those of currencies used for bilateral transactions. As there is no direct *quid pro quo* for unilateral payments, the payees may not be quite so strict in insisting on the qualifications as sellers of goods and services or creditors would be. Finally, the requirements that qualify an object to serve as a store of value are also comparatively lenient. The observations contained in this chapter mainly concern currencies acting as media of exchange or standards of deferred payment, though fundamentally their requirements are similar to those of the means of unilateral payments.

1. There is no absolute need for primitive money to possess utility (by which Jevons probably means non-monetary utility). While the overwhelming majority of primitive currencies can be used for other purposes, there are many instances for the monetary use of utterly useless objects. This is fully realized by Jevons, but he thinks that when the various useless objects were first adopted as money they were of practical use even though subsequently they came to be considered acceptable merely because the recipients were able to use them for further purchases. In some instances we know that objects which in the course of monetary use became corrupted into useless shapes, were originally useful implements, or weapons, or ornaments. According to Jevons, if we were acquainted with the history of all types of useless money, similar explanations would be found in other cases.[4] Even if this were so—and there is no possibility of ascertaining it—the fact remains that objects which may conceivably have had originally some non-monetary utility continued in monetary use long after they had ceased to possess any such utility.

On the other hand, the rule laid down by Jevons that money must have value obviously applies to primitive as well as to modern money, provided that by "value" we mean "purchasing power," not non-monetary intrinsic value. Primitive money, like modern money, can only perform monetary functions if, for no matter what reason, it is considered sufficiently valuable to be acceptable in payment for goods and services. If by value Jevons meant intrinsic value, then his view cannot be accepted as necessarily valid for primitive money any more than for modern money.

2. Primitive money, like modern money, must possess as a rule the

[3]According to F. A. Walker (Palgrave's *Dictionary of Political Economy*, 1923), Vol. ɪɪ, p. 788, "cattle and sheep may be a good money or inconvenient money, according to the circumstances of the community. In a pastoral community they present many advantages."
[4]Jevons, p. 32.

quality of portability. The largest specimens of millstones in Yap would provide one of the rare known exceptions—if they could be considered as money. Anyhow, their ownership can be transferred without actually moving the objects. It is possible that similar systems existed in other primitive communities. In any case, portability is largely a matter of degree. It seems that primitive peoples attach less importance to a high degree of transportability than modern peoples, judging by their frequent choice of very heavy or bulky substances for monetary purposes. Commodity-currencies are also almost invariably bulky and not easy to transport over long distances, though they possess the required degree of portability for use within the confines of a small community.

Portability in a broader sense means the possibility of transport without disproportionate effort, expense, risk or sacrifice. The commodity-currencies used in the early American colonies did not adequately fulfil the requirements of transportability, as their transport absorbed a high proportion of their value. The inadequate portability of African currencies constituted one of the major difficulties of explorers and traders until comparatively recent times. Even cowrie shells, which possessed a high degree of portability so long as their value was high, became too bulky after they had depreciated and had in consequence to be transferred in vast quantities. Many commodity-currencies were liable to deteriorate through being transported.

3. Indestructibility is not an essential requirement of primitive money any more than of modern money. Paper money is essentially destructible, and so are many kinds of primitive currencies. Indeed, some of the latter have a very limited degree of durability and are apt to deteriorate either by their very nature or through the wear and tear caused by their monetary use. While many of them are relatively durable, others such as grain and food products in general must be consumed within a more or less short period in order to avoid their total deterioration. Provided that a currency is freely acceptable its limited durability does not necessarily disqualify it, since recipients assume that they may pass it on before it deteriorates; and holders can always consume it or turn it over if they feel that it is approaching the limit of its durability. Hence the occasional use of eggs, cheese, butter and meat as currency. It is quite safe to use wheat or rice as a store of value, for the existing stock can always be replaced out of the new crop without undue loss or expense.

4. Homogeneity of money means that the money in use must consist of the same material and that the quality of that material must be uniform. This is an essential quality of modern money, but primitive money need not possess it to the same degree. While its quality has to conform to some standard of uniformity, sense of value or the capacity to assay it or otherwise ascertain its quality may not be sufficiently deve-

loped in many primitive communities to necessitate absolute uniformity. In many communities grain or rice used as currency was accepted by weight or measure without regard to discrepancies of quality. Extreme diversity, however, bars any object from being considered as a primitive money, even if it is accepted freely as a medium of barter.

Homogeneity in a broader sense implies not only identical quality of material, but also a certain degree of uniformity of the object serving as currency, or at any rate the absence of such a degree of discrepancies as to lead to discrimination in its acceptance. Good money must be accepted indiscriminately, whether by weight, by size, or by tale, in discharge of current or deferred liabilities. Even modern money does not, however, always fully conform to this requirement. A new note is always slightly preferred to an old one, even though the latter must be in a thoroughly bad state before it is rejected by a recipient who is in a sufficiently strong position to pick and choose. One denomination may be preferred to another, and instances are known of the development of a discount on the less favoured denomination. Since even modern money is not always accepted indiscriminately, it is not surprising that there should be instances of discrimination in the acceptance of primitive moneys. Amidst primitive conditions a high degree of such discrimination may in fact exist, without disqualifying the objects concerned from being regarded as money.

5. All primitive currencies do not conform to the requirement of divisibility. The livestock standard almost completely lacks this quality even though in the communities which use it as a standard of value rather than a medium of exchange it is possible to reckon in fractions of cows. Likewise, they reckon in fractions of slaves, even though slaves are more or less indivisible.[5] In other instances division of the monetary unit such as furs or skins is physically possible, but would entail a considerable reduction of their value. On the other hand, there are innumerable instances of primitive currencies which are easily divisible. There are strings of shells of every description, and metals changing hands by weight. In the case of the latter there is no need for the division to be accurate, since the broken pieces are taken at a value that is in exact proportion to their weight. In many primitive communities the lack of divisibility of the monetary unit is made good by the simultaneous use of other types of currency representing smaller units.

6. The extent to which primitive currencies correspond to the requirements of stability of value varies widely. Force of tradition is apt to maintain the value of the unit in some communities over long periods. On the other hand, since the majority of primitive currencies

---

[5]There are a few instances for actual payments in parts of animals in Ancient India and elsewhere. And cannibals, for whom human life was of small account, and who used human currency largely because of its meat value, may possibly have slaughtered slaves when in need of small change.

have a more or less extensive non-monetary use the change in the non-monetary requirements and the volume of supply to satisfy them are likely to affect the value of the unit.

The question of the stability of the value of primitive money may arise also in a different sense. In several instances in the early North American colonies and in the West Indies, commodities serving as a medium of exchange were made legal tender for the discharge of debts, but had no fixed value. They were acceptable on the basis of their current market value. It is doubtful whether any object which is not acceptable at a fixed value for the settlement of liabilities can be regarded as money. It would appear to be more correct to class it among the media of barter. On the other hand, it must be remembered that during periods of extreme inflation even paper currencies are sometimes only accepted at their current market value.

7. Most primitive currencies satisfy the requirement of cognizability to a considerable degree. The object chosen is usually something very well known within the community and easily distinguishable from other objects. There is, of course, always the possibility of passing on objects of inferior quality; such objects are usually accepted not under the mistaken belief that their quality is up to the standard but because the recipient may reasonably hope to unload them in turn by making purchases. In the case of shells and other ornamental types of money, many primitive peoples developed a very high faculty for distinguishing between the genuine article and imitations which European traders tried to dump on them. In some instances the cognizability of the object accepted as currency is increased through the impression of a seal or design on them.

There are, in addition to the above requirements of money, other qualifications which are worth considering. There is the "impersonal" character of money which means that it must change hands without regard to the personal qualifications of the payer or the recipient. Under this requirement, certain credit instruments such as bills or cheques may not be regarded as money. In primitive communities the requirement of acceptance without discrimination according to the standing of the payer is not so highly developed, as in many instances the use of certain currencies is confined to certain types of people.

We have seen above that, generally speaking, primitive currency does not conform to the requirements of good money to anything like the extent modern money must. This in itself does not disqualify it from being regarded as a money even though it may not fulfil all monetary functions quite so satisfactory.

Above all, money has a requirement, without which even the full possession of all the above qualifications would not assure its monetary functions; and in possession of which any object or material may serve as a medium of exchange, though it may not correspond to any adequate degree to any of the recognized requirements. It is its acceptability. An object may function as a primitive money, in spite of all its defects, if a sufficiently large proportion of the community is prepared, for no matter what reason, to accept it in payment for goods and services and in settlement of debts. This may be stating the obvious. But then, the obvious is at times liable to be overlooked, and needs occasionally to be stated.

CHAPTER 4

CLASSIFICATION OF PRIMITIVE MONEY

Classification is no real substitute for definition, but is useful in supplementing the latter, especially if, as in our case, the definition has to be sufficiently vague to correspond to the requirements of pure theory and sufficiently elastic to correspond to the requirements of the subject it covers. It is almost impossible to devise a definition that would give an adequate idea of the range of objects that are to come under it. This end can be achieved much more satisfactorily with the aid of classification. Although a device of descriptive science, it should never be despised by analytic science as a complementary device.

Classification of primitive money may be effected on an almost infinite variety of bases. The following are some of the most important among them:—

1. Has it a concrete existence or is it an abstract unit?
2. Does it assume the form of currency or credit?
3. What material does it consist of, and what form does it assume?
4. Has it full intrinsic value or is it a fiduciary currency?
5. Is it used exclusively for monetary purposes?
6. Is it a luxury or a necessity?
7. Is its use confined largely to commercial or non-commercial payments?
8. Is its use universal or is it limited to certain categories of members of the community using it?
9. Is its commercial use universal, or is it confined to certain categories of goods?
10. Is it used for internal or external payments?
11. Is it produced locally or is it imported?
12. Is its use conventional or is it imposed by State authority?
13. Is it convertible into other objects?
14. Does it change hands by tale or by measured quantity?
15. Which of the monetary functions does it perform?

1. While the term "currency" implies concrete objects in current circulation, the term "money" includes also objects which have no concrete

existence but are "abstract," "fictitious," or "ideal" units (as they are variously called), and also credit which though expressed in terms of currency, has no concrete existence. Abstract units are used as standards of value to facilitate barter or to determine various forms of payments and long-term liabilities, and to represent various forms of credit. Even if the term of the unit in question indicates some object which has a concrete existence, actual payment is made in many instances in different objects. It is not easy to draw a rigid line between such abstract units and concrete currencies, for very often a money that is mainly a unit of account is also used to some extent as a medium of exchange and a store of value.

2. "Money" includes both currency and credit. The name "currency" implies objects of physical existence in current circulation. Credit-money consists of documents representing a definite amount of money, such as the Japanese rice notes or the Virginian tobacco notes, or the Babylonian bills of exchange, or the alleged early Russian stamped pieces of leather convertible into whole pieces. Or it may consist of book entries, such as the wheat deposits in Egypt between the 2nd century B.C. and the 3rd century A.D. Or it may consist of mere verbal undertakings, entered into between members of illiterate communities, usually on occasions of public functions when the presence of a large number of witnesses takes the place of written evidence.

3. The most popular form of classification is according to material. Therefore, primitive currencies are divided into non-metallic and metallic currencies; or between raw materials and finished products; or they are classified according to whether they consist of food-stuffs, clothing, ornaments, implements, weapons, etc.; or according to whether they are objects produced by hunting, pastoral, agricultural or industrial communities.[1] The interest attached to such classification is primarily ethnological. The kind of material chosen by primitive peoples for their currencies is necessarily of considerable interest to the ethnologist studying their material culture. From an economic point of view the importance of the material chosen lies in the question whether the material is home-produced or imported; whether it is apt to be scarce or plentiful; whether it has intrinsic value, etc. The material chosen is also of importance from a point of view of general economic history, as an indication of the stage of economic development of the community concerned.

[1]The most elaborate classification on such lines was provided by Terrien de Lacouperie, in the Introductory Chapter to his *Catalogue of Chinese Coins*. He classifies primitive currencies according to whether the objects used are natural, commercial, or industrial. The latter category is again divided according to whether the industrial products serving as currencies are finished products or not. A more simplified version of classification on the basis of the form of the material serving as a currency is that of Wundt, according to whom money is either *Naturgeld* (objects used for monetary purposes in their natural state) or *Kulturgeld* (objects transformed in order to render them suitable for monetary purposes).

Primitive currencies may be classified according to their material in two main groups: non-metallic and metallic currencies. The non-metallic currencies again may be grouped according to whether they consist of material produced by hunting, pastoral, agricultural or industrial communities. This is the classification adopted by Jevons in his classical chapter on *The Early History of Currency*. In hunting communities it consists mostly of the skins of wild animals. In pastoral communities the skins of domestic animals are sometimes used but the main form of currency is livestock. In agricultural States grain and a variety of other land products—mostly foodstuffs—are used. In industrial communities an almost infinite variety of industrial semi-products, such as yarn or cloth, or finished articles, such as utensils, weapons and ornaments serve as currency.

The metallic primitive currencies, too, may be utensils, weapons or ornaments or raw metals, scrap metals or other forms of amorphous metal. Or the metals may assume the form of ingots cut into definite shape aiming at uniformity in weight. The choice of metals indicates the phase of economic and cultural development of a community.

4. A more important basis of classification from an economic point of view is the nature of the value of the primitive currency—whether it has full intrinsic value or is a fiduciary currency. The difficulty in the way of this classification lies in ascertaining when the intrinsic value of money is really equal to its nominal value; for its intrinsic value is apt to be artificially increased by the monetary use of the material concerned. The demand created through such use puts up its value above the level justified by its non-monetary use. On the other hand, it is equally true that its artificial value together with its unlimited market tends to increase its production which again tends to bring down its value. There are a number of instances where an object of full intrinsic value is adopted for monetary purposes but becomes corrupted into an object of no practical use, the nominal value of which becomes divorced from its intrinsic value. In other instances artificial value is fixed by law or convention well above the intrinsic value of the primitive currency.

5. A very important consideration is whether primitive money can be used for non-monetary purposes or not. Some authors are inclined to attach exaggerated rigidity to classification based on this consideration, not realizing that non-monetary use is largely a matter of degree. Even gold coins can be converted for industrial use by melting.

6. Another basis of classification is whether an object chosen for monetary use is a luxury or a necessity. This again concerns the ethnologist rather than the economist, though it would be a mistake to minimize its economic implication.

7. Primitive money can also be classified according to whether it is in universal or limited use. Some currencies are used solely for commerce,

W

others solely for payments to the State or tribal authority, or for religious, matrimonial or ceremonial payments.

8. There are instances in which the use of certain kinds of money are limited to certain social classes. Certain currencies can only be used by chiefs or members of ruling classes, either because other classes do not possess them or because they are forbidden, by tribal law or tradition, from using them. In several instances there are separate currencies for men and women. In other instances invaders allow the conquered people to retain their own currency, so that there are separate currencies for the conqueror and the conquered.

9. Currencies that serve as a medium of exchange can again be classified according to whether they are so used universally or for certain specific uses only. Some currencies can only be used for large purchases, others only for small purchases. Some can only be used for the purchase of certain classes of goods.

10. Primitive currencies may also be classified according to whether they serve for internal or external payments. There are many instances in which an object regularly used for purchases abroad does not serve as a currency in internal circulation. In some of these instances, the foreign recipient of the "external" currency regards the objects received as goods, but in others it is regarded as a true international currency which can be used for purchases in third countries. A large proportion of primitive currencies are by their very nature only suitable for internal trade. In so far as these objects or materials find their way abroad they constitute goods and not money.

11. Another basis of distinction lies between locally produced and imported currencies. There are several instances in the Pacific Islands where primitive communities use each others' products as currency instead of their own. In some instances the import of the monetary material, whether in raw or finished state, is a tribal monopoly.

12. This brings us to a most important basis of classification of primitive currencies, according to which their monetary use is either purely conventional or else effected by the political authority. In a large proportion of primitive communities currencies are adopted, used, changed and abandoned in a haphazard way, without any apparent deliberate interference on the part of the political authority. There are, however, many instances for some form of intervention. There are, for example, currencies made acceptable for payment of dues to the tribal or State authority. In some instances the choice of currency for that purpose is not made merely permissible but compulsory. Other primitive currencies are prescribed as legal tender in private dealings. In some instances the State prescribes the material, shape, weight, etc., of the currency, while in others it goes so far as to stamp the objects chosen for monetary purposes either as a guarantee of quality or quantity, or to

enable recipents to discriminate against objects not qualified for monetary use.

13. Primitive currencies are either convertible (interchangeable) or inconvertible (non-interchangeable). In many instances more or less rigid parities become established by tradition or through intervention by the State authorities on the basis of which it is possible to use several currencies as alternative means of payment at a fixed rate. Some primitive communities have established an elaborate system of fixed parities.

14. Some materials serving as primitive currency are taken by weight or measure while others are accepted by tale. This is an important basis of classification, for the acceptance of a money by tale usually represents an advanced phase in monetary evolution, though in many instances it merely indicates an absence of a developed sense of value.

15. An even more important distinction is between moneys performing particular monetary functions. There are moneys which are largely, if not exclusively, media of exchange; others which are primarily or exclusively standards of value, standards of deferred payments or means of non-commercial payments.

PART II: THE ORIGIN OF MONEY

CHAPTER 5

MONEYLESS COMMUNITIES

IT has often been suggested, not only by economists and economic
historians but even by some anthropologists who ought to know
better, that communities without any rudimentary forms of money
have never been found. This assertion is in striking conflict with the
factual evidence relating to both past and present-day primitive communities. To be exact, there are many historical and ethnological
instances in which it has so far been impossible to find any evidence for
the use of any form of money by the communities concerned prior to
their contact with advanced civilizations. Admittedly, this does not
necessarily mean that these communities had no money. Possibly a more
thorough investigation might disclose the existence of some rudimentary form of money that has so far escaped our attention. But on the
basis of the present state of the study of the subject those communities
must be regarded as moneyless. While those authors who deny the
existence of instances of moneyless communities are entitled to insist
that final judgment should be withheld pending closer investigation,
they are certainly not justified in stating categorically that moneyless
communities have never been found. The onus of proving the existence
of money in communities which are at present claimed to be moneyless
rests with them.

Much depends, of course, on the definition of money that we choose
to accept. If an unduly rigid definition is applied it is, of course, possible
to quote a very large number of historical and ethnological instances
of moneyless communities. By excluding objects used mainly as means
of unilateral payments and not as universal media of exchange, anthropologists such as Malinowski and Firth have arrived at the conclusion
that there were practically no primitive currencies in the Pacific area.
The other extreme is represented by the school which applies an unduly
elastic definition for money as a result of which any favourite medium of
barter is claimed to be the currency of the community. On such a basis
there is bound to be found a "currency" in practically every community
in the same way as there is bound to be an oldest inhabitant in every
village. However, in some instances at any rate the absence of money
has been sufficiently firmly established to satisfy all but the most
extreme school favouring an elastic definition.

The term "moneyless economy" is used in two different senses and this is liable to lead to argument at cross-purposes. It may mean a community with absolutely no money, or it may mean a community where some medium of exchange or unit of account existed but formed no part of the every-day life of the ordinary people and was only used by a small section of the community. It may be a matter of opinion as to what extent the restricted use of money in a community justifies the claim that it is moneyless. We do not propose to enter here into this controversy and shall in this chapter concern ourselves exclusively with the absolutely moneyless communities in which no money whatsoever is known to have existed, at any rate for internal purposes.

A community may be moneyless for any of the following reasons:—

1. Low general standard of intelligence.
2. Absence of an adequate sense of values.
3. Low stage of economic development.
4. Absence of a developed system of non-commercial payments.
5. Absence of a system of private possession of goods.
6. Existence of a totalitarian planned economy.
7. Religious objections to the use of money.
8. Existence of closed self-sufficient economic units.
9. Extreme scarcity of money.
10. Extreme distrust in the monetary system as a result of its abuse.
11. Existence of pure barter.

1. Judging by many ethnological instances, the adoption and use of money requires very little intelligence. The human species did not always possess, however, even that limited degree of intelligence. There can be little doubt that during the early phase of their existence, many races must have been at a too low intellectual level to be capable of using even the most rudimentary form of money. That this is so seems to be indicated by the existence of present-day or recent primitive communities at such a stage of intellectual level. Those who studied the natives of Tierra del Fuego, for instance, during the first half of the 19th century and other tribes of a similarly low standard of intelligence must have realized that such backward races are intellectually incapable of using money. There are other instances in which savages reached a comparatively advanced stage in several directions but were unable to develop even the most primitive form of currency system. Amongst such communities are the Australian aborigines. Even though in some ways they have a highly developed social system, none of those who investigated their economies at the time when they were first contacted by Europeans succeeded in discovering any trace of a medium of exchange or a standard of value.

The same is true concerning some Negrito tribes in Malaya and some of the Indian tribes in backward parts of South America. The Andamanese, too, were until recently incapable of developing a monetary system. It was recorded that the absence of a standard of value gave rise to frequent and violent conflicts between groups engaged in exchanges of gifts arising from disputes concerning the relative value of goods to be exchanged.[1] In many other instances of communities in which ethnological research has failed so far to discover any trace of a monetary system, its absence must be attributed to the low standard of intelligence. In order to be able to employ money, whether as a medium of exchange or a unit of account, man must first develop a certain minimum degree of arthimetical faculty. Yet even nowadays there are backward communities where no one can count more than five, or even two. At such a phase of development the use of money is out of the question.

2. In other primitive communities the standard of intelligence may be high enough for the use of money, and economic and political development may have reached a relatively advanced phase, but notwithstanding this there is no scope of money owing to the absence of an adequate sense of values. The use of money implies a faculty of ascertaining equivalents. During the phase when objective values are non-existent and exchanges are effected on the basis of subjective values—that is, on the basis of the relative urgency of needs of the individual directly concerned in any one particular exchange transaction—there is little scope for the use of money.

Again, in other instances there is an absence of any desire to receive equivalent values in exchange for the goods offered. In many primitive communities it is the ambition of every party to outbid the other when reciprocating gifts or even when engaged in barter transactions. In such circumstances any instrument aiming at the measurement of value and at the effecting of equivalent exchanges is clearly superfluous.

3. Another reason for the absence of money lies in the low stage of economic evolution. In communities at their earliest stage there was no systematic exchange of goods, and such occasional exchanges as may have occurred could be effected without money. There may have been some exchange of presents within the community or between the communities, but such turnover of goods does not call for the use of money.

4. At the earliest phase of evolution non-commercial payments were not sufficiently developed to call for the adoption of any standardized means of payment. Religious sacrifices or bride money were not yet standardized. Nor did such political authority as existed regulate either unilateral payments or the means of settlement of claims arising from trade.

5. Another obstacle to the evolution of a monetary system is the absence of any system of exclusive possession of goods. In a loose way

[1]Foster, p. 89.

such communities were at times described as Communistic, but that need not necessarily be the case. On many islands in Polynesia, for instance, there is no Communism in the sense of common ownership of the means of production, nor is there any systematic equalitarian distribution of the goods produced; but members of these communities and even strangers are entitled to be provided for if they have not enough for their elementary requirements. Moreover, anyone is entitled to ask for the gift of anybody else's property which cannot be refused without grave breach of etiquette. It is the general custom of members of some communities to help themselves as a matter of course to anything they covet without the owners' knowledge or permission. Such systems do not provide a good scope for the use of money.

6. In communities where there is a thorough-going planned economy on Communistic lines the use of money is not indispensable and, in some known instances, it has in fact been dispensed with. The outstanding instance is, of course, that of the Inca Empire before the Spanish conquest of Peru. Practically all authorities agree that the Peruvians had no knowledge of money.[2] Although the country was exceptionally rich in gold and silver, these metals were not used either as a medium of exchange or as a store of value, but only for purposes of decoration.[3] There was no need for any means of payment of even a standard of value, for the simple reason that every phase of the economic activities of the population was regulated by the State authority. The life of the people was planned from cradle to grave. On the basis of statistical material regularly collected, the central administration at Cuzco prescribed in minute detail what everybody was to produce and how their products were to be allocated. Money did not come into the production or distribution of goods at all. The producers of food, cloth, etc., had to surrender a determined share of their output to the political and religious authorities, and the State provided for the requirements of those who did not take a direct part in production. There was no profit motive and no individual initiative. Wages and salaries as such were unknown. Everybody was entitled to be provided for adequately even if through some misfortune he had lost his working capacity. Possessions were redistributed from time to time, so that there was no scope even for using a standardized store of value, although ornamental objects were in fact accumulated by those who could afford it.

There was a limited amount of barter. The Indians "knew nothing of buying or selling, having no money, they exchanged one article of food for another."[4] On the other hand, they were not allowed to sell

[2]W. H. Prescott, *History of the Conquest of Peru* (Everyman Edn., London, 1908), p. 93.

[3]Ynca Garcillasso de la Vega, *Royal Commentaries of the Yncas* (Hakluyt Society, London, 1871), Vol. ii, p. 21. Even a generation after the conquest by the Spaniards, in 1560, "there was no regular money in the country" (p. 28).

[4]Garcillasso de la Vega, p. 123.

clothes (which were allotted to everybody either in the form of raw material or in the form of finished product) or houses or land.

Judging by the high stage achieved by the Inca civilization at the time of the Conquest, the absence of money had certainly not been an obstacle to progress. Indeed, the buildings, roads, bridges, etc., found by the conquerors indicated a very advanced stage of economic and technical progress. In no other instance before or since is planned moneyless economy ever known to have been carried to such an advanced stage.

The nearest approach to the moneyless system that existed in the Inca Empire was the totalitarian system operating during the 16th and 17th centuries in the Jesuit Republic of Paraguay. Within the community, which was fairly large, no money of any sort is said to have been used, though it has been suggested that tea was a kind of limited medium of exchange. This claim has never been substantiated. The Jesuit Fathers themselves transacted a certain amount of foreign trade with the aid of money, but organized the country under their control on a planned moneyless basis. The idea was to protect the Indians from exploitation and extermination by ruthless and greedy adventurers who in other parts of Latin America followed in the footsteps of the *Conquistadores*. There is less detailed information available about the working of this system than about the Inca Empire. It seems probable that planning was not carried to such an advanced phase as in Peru and that the moneyless economy operated largely with the aid of barter in addition to the distribution of goods by the central authority.

Whether it was because of the inadequacy of the system or in spite of its adequacy, the fact remains that under this regime the country showed very little vitality and had become depopulated to about the same extent as conquered Peru and other Latin American territories which had been ruled by more ruthless masters. Nevertheless, the fact that moneyless economy continued for many generations shows that it was feasible. Indeed, it continued to a large degree even after the Jesuit Fathers lost their unrestricted authority. At the end of the 18th century all goods were exchanged against each other; the salaries of bishops, priests, Government officials and all taxes were payable in kind. In Asuncion when a housewife went shopping she took with her a basket containing various goods such as cotton, tea, tobacco, sugar, salt, etc. The sellers of objects she wanted to buy chose amongst her goods the equivalent of their wares.[5]

The experiment of Robert Owen in New Lanark during the early part of the 19th century cannot be classed among the planned moneyless economies, since it merely aimed at the substitution of a new standard of value for the old one through the adoption of labour tickets instead of the conventional form of money.

[5]Dobrizhofer, Vol. I, p. 274.

After the Communist revolution of 1917 it was believed that Soviet Russia would put a moneyless economy into operation. This at any rate was inferred from the way in which the existing monetary system was reduced to absurdity through extreme inflation. That was done, however, not as a deliberate policy but as the only possible way in which the deficit could be financed in the then existing circumstances. In fact, after the end of the civil war when political and economic conditions became consolidated the money of the civil war period was replaced by a monetary system which, in outward form at any rate, conformed to the rules operating in capitalist countries. There is no reason to believe that it is still the ultimate aim of Communist policy to eliminate money. While to do so would be possible, it is now considered convenient to retain a monetary system.

7. Certain religious communities, especially in the United States, set out to adopt moneyless systems. Such communities are still in operation also in other countries. They never developed beyond the stage of small closed economies.

8. During the Middle Ages there were many instances of small closed economies which were for all practical purposes moneyless in their internal working, even though they may have had to use money in their contact with the outside world. Such units were the monastries and the baronial estates. To a large extent they were self-sufficient and under an authoritarian regime their production and distribution was planned without the need of money. Everyone within these communities had very precisely defined functions to perform, not in return for payment in money but as a duty to the community which in return provided them with the necessities of life. During more recent periods there were similar limited closed economies in Latin America where certain large estates—the *pueblo* and the *hacienda*—achieved almost complete self-sufficiency and no money passed in their internal economy. All such communities may be regarded as enlarged families within the members of which no money had to change hands.

9. Extreme scarcity of money during various periods of history was responsible for the development of moneyless barter. In other instances, however, scarcity of modern money led to the adoption of primitive moneys.

10. Extreme distrust in the monetary system owing to debasement or inflation induced large sections of communities in various historical periods to revert to barter.

11. Apart from such conditions of emergency, moneyless economy based on barter is encountered in many primitive communities which are intellectually sufficiently advanced to adopt a money economy and where the other preliminary conditions for the use of money also exist. Out of conservatism or for other reasons they prefer, however, barter. Cassel was entirely wrong in claiming that barter and the scale

of measurement necessarily developed together and that developed trade without scale of measurement never existed.[6]

Moneyless economy is not always a preliminary phase of evolution of money. In a large proportion of instances referred to above it was resorted to after a more or less advanced type of money had been in use for many centuries. Nevertheless, the system provides the obvious starting point for the investigation of the origin of money. We only have to concern ourselves closely, however, with moneyless barter economy which will be dealt with in the next chapter.

[6]Gustav Cassel, *Theory of Social Economy* (London, 1923) p. 349.

CHAPTER 6

EVOLUTION OF BARTER

Before dealing with the popular assumption that money necessarily originated through barter, it is essential to examine the evolution of barter itself. It is a commonplace of textbooks that barter came about as a result of the development of division of labour and of private ownership. In this respect, however, as in so many others, it is difficult to say which came first, the hen or the egg. In any case the popular formula over-simplifies matters. It is widely assumed that, after the phase of food-gathering by isolated individuals or families, original Communism was the earliest stage of evolution. There was division of labour within the family, but since the family is regarded as one single economic unit this division of labour is not generally accepted as such in the economic sense of the term. Gradually the family expanded into the tribe which was, to begin with, just a larger family, and the head of which assigned among his relatives the work to be executed. It was not until the tribe became much larger and the family ties looser that a certain degree of division of labour in the generally accepted sense— that is, between independent economic units—was supposed to have developed. Such a specialization of occupations was accompanied by barter. Members of the primitive community no longer contributed the proceeds of their labour into a common pool, but came to exchange their surpluses with each other. Before this stage was reached, the output of the small communities was divided up between its members according to the proportion fixed by tradition or by the head of the family or chief of the tribe. Any booty or the proceeds of exchanges of presents with other communities were divided in a similar way.

According to the popular conception of barter, it is first supposed to have developed between various communities before it existed within the communities concerned. This was because, while each community was supposed to have specialized mostly in one culture, the difference between tribal cultures provided the scope for barter. This contention, according to which foreign trade preceded home trade, is based on a mistaken notion of the division of labour, and on the idea that division of labour, in the sense of specialization in particular branches of production, must necessarily precede barter. It is a concept accepted uncritically by many economists and economic historians as well as anthropologists. Yet it stands to reason that although a community may be entirely pastoral there may be individuals within it who specialize in breeding cattle or goats or sheep or horses. This in itself provides ample scope for barter within a pastoral community. Even if the whole community were engaged in cattle-breeding, there is scope for bartering one kind of cattle against another. One tribesman may want more oxen, another more cows. Young animals may be offered in exchange for matured ones. Some may prefer quality, another quantity, and so on, and so forth. Likewise, in a hunting or fishing community there may be division of labour. And, even if there were none, by sheer accident one fisherman might catch one type of fish and another fisherman another type. As both naturally prefer variety in their diet, they may want to exchange part of their catch. In agricultural communities, too, there is a wide scope for barter without any division of labour. Even assuming that all the families within the community grow precisely the same kinds of products—which is not very likely—it is always possible that the potato crop of one grower fails while his beans do well, while another grower has a good potato crop and a poor bean crop. In such a case they may swap the surplus of beans of the one grower for the other grower's surplus potatoes.

Indeed, a certain degree of barter can exist not only before the development of division of labour but even before the development of private property in the generally accepted sense of the term, which is the individual ownership of the means of production. Primitive public and private ownership is an extremely complicated subject which cannot be dealt with here in detail. Most people who talk about the original Communism of primitive peoples have only the haziest notion of the immense variety of shades that exist in forms of primitive property, ranging from absolute collectivism to extreme individual ownership leading to the burial or destruction of the goods owned by the deceased. What matters for the purpose of our argument is that in most Communistic systems consumers' goods, once distributed, become the property of the individuals, and can be bartered against each other.[1] As a matter of fact, in many instances, while land, livestock and other capital assets are owned by the entire community or by the chief of the tribe, the whole or part of the products of these means of production used by particular families belong to them, and are exchangeable.

[1]As we saw in the previous chapter, however, the Inca Empire provided an exception as there the Indians were not allowed to barter their clothes, even though they were allowed to exchange foodstuffs.

Primitive religion provides a strong motive for barter before the development of either private property or division of labour. The innumerable variety of temporary or permanent taboos imposed on the consumption of various foodstuffs by certain individuals, families or groups is apt to lead to the exchange of the products affected against products which the tribesmen are entitled to consume. Totemism leads to exchanges between the various totemic groups.

In a very large number of known instances early barter took the form of the exchange of presents. This may have been due to a lack of a sense of equivalent among primitive peoples, or perhaps in some instances to a primitive sense of dignity which looked down on business-like bargaining; or, in many instances, to a highly developed sense of prestige by which the primitive man sought to gain reputation as a generous giver. Foreign trade between Egypt and other countries during the 2nd millenium B.C. was conducted almost entirely by the exchange of presents between kings. The giver very often indicated what he wished to receive in exchange.

Exchange of presents may be considered a primitive form of barter, owing to the impelling need for reciprocating the gifts received. No member of a primitive tribe could afford to disregard this obligation, and for this reason in many instances the difference between exchange of gifts and barter was largely one of form. In fact, the border-line is apt to disappear altogether. For example, the easy-going Loyalty Islanders, when they foregather to exchange their goods, often tell each other: "Give me as much as you wish," and at the end of the day the undisposed-of surpluses are simply given away. Primitive barter is not confined to exchanges of goods. There are also many instances of exchange of services.

Another primitive form of barter was the so-called "silent trade" or "dumb barter." Each party leaves the merchandise he wishes to exchange in a fixed place and if the other party is satisfied with quantity and quality he removes the goods offered; if not, he leaves them in order to give the other party an opportunity to increase his offer. If no agreement can be reached each party withdraws his goods. This practice continued over a period of thousands of years in backward countries, even in some parts of Europe. Its cause may lie in the difference between the stage of civilization of the two parties; or in distrust due to recent hostilities, in a desire to avoid conflict arising from heated bargaining, or in many other considerations.[2]

---

[2]In some known instances silent trading continued even after the adoption of money economy. Nor was it necessarily confined to the exchange of goods. According to the popular legend of Wayland's smithy, riders or coachmen left their horses at a certain place, together with the cost of shoeing them, and departed; when returning late they found their horses shod and the money gone. Various forms of this legend are encountered in many countries. They indicate the probable existence of silent trading in services.

Although in form very primitive, silent barter is in substance more advanced than the exchange of presents, for it is based on the strict principle of give-and-take resulting from hard (if silent) bargaining. It has never been suggested that silent barter is a necessary phase in the evolution of barter, though, owing to the frequent instances encountered, it must be considered to be decidedly more than a freak phenomenon. Nor can it be claimed that in every community, or even in the majority of instances, an exchange of presents necessarily preceded barter proper. Indeed, there are instances in which exchange of presents developed after a more "businesslike" form of exchange of goods had existed for some time, as a result of the establishment of closer and friendlier relations between the parties.[3] In general, however, it is probably true to say that barter proper succeeded in chronological order the exchange of presents, and that silent trade eventually gave way to ordinary barter.

Nor is it easy to answer categorically the question whether barter on the basis of prices arrived at through bargaining represents a higher phase than barter based on prices fixed by tradition or tribal law. Much depends on the character of the community concerned. It is arguable that, since free bargaining implies individualist spirits, the chances are that rigid ratios between goods preceded fluctuating ratios. The fact, however, that even in a totalitarian state such as Ancient Egypt barter was done on the basis of freely negotiated fluctuating ratios is well worth bearing in mind. In particular it seems probable that the elaborate tariffs of fixed barter ratios which travellers in Africa and Oceania encountered even in recent years represented a high phase in the evolution of barter.

The creation of markets contributed towards the improvement of the system of barter. In these markets everybody knew where to find the goods he needed, and also where to find the individuals who need the goods; and the chances for matching supply and demand were relatively high. Remarkably elaborate arrangements were made at some of the primitive markets in Africa and elsewhere to assist in the exchange of goods and safeguard the interests of the parties.

The existence of pure barter does not necessarily indicate a very primitive form of civilization. Often the system survives long after the community has progressed considerably in other respects. This may be due to conservatism, since primitive peoples are reluctant to change their trading methods, even though they be sufficiently intelligent and advanced to adopt more convenient methods. In some cases there is prejudice against the adoption of a monetary economy, though such prejudice is usually directed against the use of coins rather than against

[3]An instance for such a relapse into exchange of presents is quoted by Rosemary Firth, *Housekeeping among the Malayan Peasants* (London School of Economics Monographs on Social Anthropology, Vol. vii, London, 1943), p. 52.

primitive money. In many cases barter continues to be the principal method of trading long after the adoption of some form of money, for the simple reason that there is not enough money to go round. And a decline in the supply of money often causes a relapse into barter. Distrust in money has also been responsible for reversion to the barter system; such distrust may have been caused by debasement or inflation.

In innumerable instances the bulk of trade continued to be transacted almost entirely, or at any rate largely, by means of barter even though the communities concerned possessed some kind of monetary system for non-commercial payments. In such instances goods continued to be exchanged against each other, and payments for services were made in kind, not by necessity but evidently by choice.

In the light of the stock phrases used by many economists about the inconvenience of barter it may appear puzzling to the student that any community which was sufficiently advanced to realize the possibilities of a monetary system should continue to practise such an inconvenient method. The explanation is that in a primitive community barter is not nearly so inconvenient as it appears through modern eyes. Economists are inclined to exaggerate its inconvenience because they look at it from the point of view of modern man. The instances—real or imaginary—they quote are calculated to make their readers wonder how any community could possibly have existed under barter except in extremely primitive conditions. Some of them seek to demonstrate the absurdity of barter by describing the difficulties that would arise if our modern communities were to attempt to practise it. It is, of course, easy for a lecturer to earn the laughter of his audience by telling them about the pathetic efforts of some market gardener who has to find a barber in need of radishes before he can have his hair cut. What the lecturer and his audience do not realize is that in a primitive community the grower of radishes usually cuts his own hair, or has it cut by a member of his family or household; and that even in primitive communities with barbers as an independent profession the barber and the gardener have a fair idea about each other's requirements, and have no difficulty in suiting each other. If the barber does not happen to require to-day any of the products the gardener is in a position to offer, he simply performs his service in return for the future delivery of products he is expected to need sooner or later.

Even the genuine instances quoted by economists to illustrate the absurdity of barter are apt to be misleading in their implication. There is, for instance, the well-known experience of Mlle. Zélie, singer at the Théâtre Lyrique in Paris, who, in the course of a tour round the world, gave a concert on one of the Society Islands, and received the fee of three pigs, twenty-three turkeys, forty-four chickens, five thousand coconuts and considerable quantities of bananas, lemons and oranges, representing one-third of the box office takings. In a letter published by

Wolowski and quoted to boredom by economists ever since, she says that, although this amount of livestock and vegetables would have been worth about four thousand francs in Paris, in the Society Islands it was of very little use to her. Another much-quoted experience is that of Cameron in Tanganyika, when in order to buy an urgently needed boat he first had to swap brass wire against cloth, then cloth against ivory and finally ivory against the boat. Jevons refers to the difficulties encountered by Wallace in some islands of the Malay Archipelago: if the vendors of food did not happen to want his goods they would pass on, and Wallace had to do without dinner. He had to keep a selection of supplies to multiply the chances of suiting the seller's requirements.[4] Barth complained that in Central Africa his servant in trying to acquire the goods needed through indirect barter became utterly exhausted in the process.[5]

What the economists quoting these and other similar instances do not appear to realize is that the difficulties complained of are not inherent in the system of barter. They are largely anomalies arising from sudden contact between two different civilizations. A native singer in the Society Islands would not have been embarrassed at receiving payment in kind, since she would have known ways in which to dispose of her takings, or store them for future use. Nor would a native of Tanganyika have found the system of barter prevailing there at the time of Cameron's visit nearly so difficult as Cameron did. Knowing local conditions, he would have been prepared for the difficulties and, before embarking on a major capital transaction such as the purchase of a boat, he would have made his arrangements accordingly. In any case, the fact that the goods required could not be obtained by a single transaction would not have worried him unduly. The majority of primitive peoples enjoy bartering and bargaining, and the time lost in putting through three transactions instead of one would not matter to them nearly as much as to modern man living at high speed, especially to an explorer in a hurry to proceed on his journey. And while Cameron must have suffered a loss in each of the three transactions, a local man with adequate time at his disposal and with a thorough knowledge of his market would have chosen the right moment for effecting the necessary exchanges on terms reasonably advantageous to him.

In many communities the necessities of life were exchanged against each other as a matter of routine. Economic units within a tribe, or even belonging to different tribes, came to be complementary to each other. In the Pacific, or on the Malayan Peninsula, fishing villages and inland villages exchanged fish against land products regularly, often at prices that remained unchanged for generations. This arrangement suited their primitive requirements. When as a result of internal progress or through increased contact with the outside world their requirements

[4]Jevons, p. 2.   [5]Barth, II, p. 312.

became more diversified, the need for a medium of exchange or at least a common denominator became more evident. Nevertheless, the conditions in which barter operated were even then far from being necessarily intolerable. The existence of fixed price ratios referred to above went a long way towards assisting. Likewise, the possibility of credit in connection with barter—delivering goods in return for future deliveries of other goods—must have also helped to no slight degree. John Stuart Mill's much-quoted imaginary instance of a harassed tailor on the verge of starvation, trying frantically to find a baker who happens to be in need of a jacket, in order to be able to secure his daily bread in exchange for it,[6] existed only in the imagination of a 19th century economist who, however distinguished in his own line, appears to have been unacquainted with the elements of anthropology. Fortunately for themselves and for the progress of mankind, savages had enough common sense to make the best of a system which, while far from being ideal, was capable of being adapted to the needs of the situation. The tailor could easily make arrangements with the baker to secure the supply of bread over a period in return for the sale of a jacket.

The difficulty of "marrying" barter transactions in primitive communities, even after the development of a certain degree of division of labour, should not be exaggerated. The "double coincidence" (to quote the word of Jevons) that must arise is by no means difficult to achieve in a small community where everybody knows a great deal about everybody else's products and requirements. Jevons admits the possibility of the achievement of such double coincidence in modern communities being assisted by advertising.[7] Even in the absence of such devices, primitive man usually knows where to find a counterpart to his proposed transaction. Nor is the difference between the value of the objects to be exchanged an unsurmountable obstacle. It could be overcome by accepting deferred payments. In African villages the blacksmith is often paid after harvest for all the services he rendered between harvests.

For the above reasons it seems to be a mistake to assume that barter became reduced to absurdity at an early phase of economic progress. The chances are that in the majority of communities it survived long after its replacement by some form of monetary system became possible through technical and intellectual progress.

[6]"A tailor who has nothing but coats might starve before he could find any person having bread to sell who wanted a coat; besides he would not want as much bread at a time as would be worth a coat, and the coat could not be divided." (Mill, p. 4).

[7]Jevons, pp. 3-5.

CHAPTER 7

ORIGIN OF MONEY—THE MEDIUM OF EXCHANGE THEORY

In the last chapter the author sought to prove that the picture drawn by economists about the inconvenience of barter in primitive communities is grossly exaggerated. It would seem that the assumption that money necessarily arose from the realization of the inconveniences of barter, popular as it is among economists, needs careful re-examination.

The medium of exchange theory of the origin of money appears sometimes in an extreme form which suggests that at a certain moment a deliberate decision to adopt money was made, when the increase in the volume of trade made barter conditions intolerable. Economic historians and anthropologists rightly denounce the idea of a deliberate decision thus to change the system of commercial exchanges as being fully as unrealistic as Rousseau's conception of the conclusion of a *contrat social*. The suggestion made by Crowther that currency must have been the invention of a "lazy genius" who could not be bothered with the complications arising from barter[1] appears to be equally divorced from reality. While it is just possible that some communities out of untold thousands may have adopted money through the deliberate invention of one person or the deliberate decision of the community, the chances are that in the overwhelming majority of instances the evolution of money was an unconscious and gradual process. It is important that economists writing on the subject should duly realize that institutions such as division of labour, or private property, or money, are not invented by some genius, lazy or otherwise, on a dull Sunday afternoon.

It is equally important to bear in mind that money was not invented once for all for the entire globe. While in many instances the institution may have been copied by various communities from others, very often each community worked out its own salvation independently in its own way, without knowing anything about identical or similar solutions arrived at in other parts of the world. It is impossible to accept the application to money of the diffusionist conception implied in Crowther's remarks.

It seems certain that, while in many communities barter without the use of any kind of money continued long after the system had become cumbersome owing to increase in the commercial turnover, in other communities some form of money was adopted long before this became absolutely necessary or even particularly advantageous from the point of view of the interchange of goods. Apart from instances in which money was first adopted for purposes other than trade, even its premature development out of barter is conceivable at a stage when the community could well have retained the more primitive method of

---

[1]Geoffrey Crowther, *An Outline of Money* (London, 1940), p. 15.

moneyless trading. Money tends to develop automatically out of barter, through the fact that favourite means of barter are apt to arise. A stage is usually reached when the use of one of these means of barter becomes so widespread that it may be said to have become a medium of exchange. This process was ably described by Menger[2] who realized the inadequacy of the conception under which pure barter is supposed to have continued until it reduced itself to absurdity through the expansion of turnover, and was then replaced by money. He ridiculed the assumption that primitive communities are necessarily gravely handicapped in trade by the difficulty in effecting direct exchanges between the original producer and the ultimate consumer. He pointed out that if the would-be buyer of certain goods was unable to find a seller to accept his goods, he could always improve his bargaining position by swapping his goods against others which were more easily exchangeable. If even these goods did not serve his purpose adequately he could swap them against other goods even more easily acceptable until he gained possession of the right kind of goods with the aid of which he could acquire the goods he really needed.

An intermediate stage in the progress from pure barter economy—under which goods are acquired for direct consumption only—to money economy is the employment of some favourite medium of barter. This is some object which is accepted in return for goods or services, not for direct consumption by its recipient but because he expects to be able to obtain for it the goods or services he requires. Frequently it is an object which is so widely accepted for direct consumption that anyone not requiring it for that purpose is safe in accepting it, in the certain knowledge that he will have no difficulty in passing it on. In so far as money developed from barter, the favourite medium of barter preceded the medium of exchange. The increasingly frequent use of one particular medium of barter tended to raise its status gradually and imperceptibly to that of a medium of exchange.

It seems probable that when money developed out of barter it did so not because barter had become intolerable through an increase in the commercial turnover, but because more and more people found it convenient to use the same intermediate goods in their transactions. This may appear to be saying the same things in a different way. In reality there is an essential difference between the negative approach used by many generations of economists who attributed the origin of money to the intolerable inconvenience of barter that forced the community to adopt a reform, and the positive approach suggested here, according to which the method of exchange was improved upon before the old method became intolerable and before an impelling need for the reforms had arisen.

There is ample ethnological evidence to show that most primitive

[2]Menger, pp. 8-11.

communities had a number of favourite media of barter in use at any given moment. Many of these communities could get on very well without the adoption of a common medium of exchange, as their trade was limited, and barter with the aid of media of barter suited their requirements tolerably well. Nevertheless, they gradually came to adopt a medium of exchange—not because they came to realize that this was the right thing to do, nor because the old system of barter was becoming intolerable, but simply because in practice they found this more convenient.

The objects chosen, first as a favourite medium of barter and later as a medium of exchange, were chosen because those accepting them could rely on being able to find others willing to accept them. Possibly the reason why certain objects qualified for such a purpose was that they were a generally desired article of consumption or ornament, or a staple article of export, or because they were a standard of deferred payments often in demand by debtors. But the steady demand for an object, and the high degree of acceptability arising from it, may have been due to non-commercial considerations. Many people may have been willing to accept it because it could be used for religious sacrifices, for political payments (fines, tribute, blood money) or for bride money. All these and other non-commercial requirements must have led in innumerable instances to a widespread and systematic demand for objects eminently qualified to fulfil the functions of a medium of exchange, long before the need for the employment of a medium of exchange was sufficiently strong to overcome conservatism and other factors responsible for the survival of pure barter. It seems probable that when the growing diversity of goods and services and the growing division of labour made the use of a medium of exchange increasingly necessary, the object chosen as an intermediary was very often not a favourite medium of barter but the ready-made medium of payment which was already widely used in the community for non-commercial purposes.

Conversely, it seems also possible that in many instances, when an object was chosen for the purposes of religious or political payments or for the payment of bride money, preference was given to favourite media of barter. Whether it was the means of unilateral payments that became media of exchange or media of barter that was adopted as means of unilateral payments depended largely on the degree of commercial spirit that the various races possessed. A tribe with a strong inclination to trade was liable to develop a medium of barter before it came to adopt any definite standardized means of unilateral payments. The chances are, however, that religious sacrifices, political payment and payment for brides preceded in the majority of instances the development of favourite media of barter.

Even in so far as money developed from barter, Menger's theory does not provide the only conceivable explanation of its evolution.

Schurtz put forward the view that the way from barter economy to money economy led through the system of exchanges on the basis of traditionally or officially fixed prices.[3] Thurnwald is also in favour of this explanation.[4] Their arguments are not altogether convincing. We possess evidence about the existence of many fixed "tariffs" or "ratios" between various goods, both locally produced and imported. But it is difficult to see why the fact that certain exchange rates were kept artificially rigid should in itself have led to the monetary adoption of any of the goods concerned. On the contrary, in so far as the existence of fixed barter ratios facilitated barter it contributed towards the survival of the moneyless system of trading.

Hitherto we have been dealing with the origin of money through its function as a medium of exchange. Barter can, however, give rise to money also through necessitating the use of a standard of value even before calling for the use of a medium of exchange. This aspect of the origin of money through barter will be dealt with later. Our next task is to ascertain whether, in so far as money originated through its function as a medium of exchange, it arose from internal trade or external trade.

[3]Schurtz, p. 79.   [4]Thurnwald, p. 264.

CHAPTER 8

ORIGIN THROUGH EXTERNAL TRADE

It is a widespread belief that external trade had developed before internal trade. This assumption should not be accepted without close scrutiny; for it has arisen largely through the fact that prehistoric external trade is more easily traced than prehistoric internal trade. In the absence of written records there is no safe way of ascertaining whether and to what extent goods were exchanged within any one prehistoric community. On the other hand, prehistoric deposits contain ample evidence of foreign trade during the Neolithic period, and even during the late Paleolithic period. Shells, amber, instruments and weapons of flint, etc., have been found hundreds and even thousands of miles from their places of origin. It is no wonder that, in the absence of any corresponding evidence about the exchange of goods inside prehistoric communities, many students should have arrived at the conclusion that external trade must have preceded internal trade, both in chronological order and in order of importance.

On the surface, ethnological evidence on trade in primitive communities explored in modern times also appears to support this one-sided conclusion. Explorers, early travellers and pioneer traders, in their accounts of economic conditions of savage races, give much more information on external trade than on internal trade.[1] This is only natural, since most of these visitors were only interested in their own trade with the natives. Their diaries abound with instances in which they were forced to make payments in various forms to native chiefs for supplies or for free passage through their territory. The extortionate methods applied by the chiefs, the difficulties arising from the acquisition and transport of primitive moneys, and the complications caused by their change from village to village, and even within the same village at short notice, was a subject that necessarily forced itself to the attention of travellers, even if they were not particularly interested in primitive money. The information they gathered for the benefit of later travellers referred to the trade practices of the natives with strangers. Their stay in these communities was usually not sufficiently prolonged to enable them to investigate the less obvious turnover of goods within the community, even if they had been sufficiently interested in the subject. Even ethnologists whose aim was to investigate the mode of life of primitive peoples showed until recently very little interest in internal trade.

The result is that most of material published on the trade of primitive peoples deals with their external trade only, and this must have been largely responsible for the assumption that their internal trade must have been either non-existent or quite insignificant. On the basis of this assumption the view is taken by many writers that primitive money must have developed primarily from external trade. It is widely assumed that money is not required in primitive communities for internal purposes in the early stages of their economic development, either because "everyone produces the same thing and there is no scope for exchange," or because "each economic unit is self-sufficient," or because "in original Communism production and distribution is effected by the tribal authorities without the intervention of money."

We saw in Chapter 6 that the idea that barter is absent inside primitive communities at an early stage of economic evolution is entirely false, as there is ample scope for the exchange of goods even in the absence of private property or division of labour in the generally accepted sense of the term. Indeed, there must be a good deal of traffic internally even in communities which have practically no external trade owing to geographical difficulties or the hostility of the neighbouring tribes. It is, to say the least, possible to argue, therefore, that there was a modest amount of trade within the communities at a time when the acquisition of goods from other communities assumed almost entirely the form of booty or tribute.

It is even reasonable to assume that in a large proportion of instances

[1]Speke refers scores of times to payment to natives of Tanganyika and Uganda in the form of wire or other European goods; there is only one single reference in his book to payment in a similar form between natives.

internal trade as a systematic activity preceded foreign trade. This does not necessarily mean, however, that money for internal use preceded money for external use. For internal trade the system of barter based on tariffs fixed by tribal authority or tradition may have obviated the need for the use of currency. The exchange rate between goods bartered between tribes, on the other hand, must usually have been a matter of bargaining, and the use of a common denominator or a medium of exchange may have been found necessary at a relatively early stage.

Economic historians or anthropologists, when claiming that the development of money arising from external trade preceded that of money arising from internal trade, often fail to define the meaning of the two terms. There can be four kinds of money arising through external trade:—

1. Imported objects which are in general non-monetary use within the importing community and which have a relative scarcity value, and which tend to become a favourite medium of barter or a means of non-commercial payment.

2. Imported objects which are imported with the specific purpose of their monetary use, and which have no non-monetary use in the importing community, apart possibly from their employment as ornaments arising mainly from their monetary use.

3. Exportable staple products which are in strong and systematic monetary or non-monetary demand outside the exporting community.

4. Imported objects which are in general monetary or non-monetary use in the importing community or in third communities, so that the importing community is in a position to re-export them and use them for purchases abroad.

Salt-money in Ethiopia and elsewhere is one of the characteristic instances of the choice of an imported object as primitive currency on account of its general acceptability for non-monetary use within the importing community. Demand for salt usually exceeds supply in primitive communities far removed from its places of origin. Anyone accepting salt in payment for his goods and services is safe in assuming that he is able to buy with it practically anything that is for sale. Salt becomes a medium of exchange as a result of its scarcity value. There are many similar instances most of them by far concern the monetary choice of objects imported from a community with a more advanced civilization. Brass rods, cloth, gin in various parts of Africa became currencies because they were subject to a strong non-monetary demand which could only be met by import, and because, for this reason, these goods had a scarcity value.

According to Bücher, all primitive money originated in this way. He refuses to admit that it could possibly have originated in any other way. "*Now with regard to money,*" he writes. "*How much has been written and enquired about the many species of money among primitive peoples,*" *and yet, how simple the explanation of their origin. The money of each tribe is that trading commodity which it does not itself produce but which it regularly acquires from other tribes by way of exchange.* For such an article naturally becomes for it a universal medium of exchange for which it surrenders its wares. It is its measure of value according to which it values its property which would in no other way be made interchangeable. It is its wealth, for it cannot increase it at will. Fellow tribesmen soon come to employ it also for transferring value, because of its scarcity it is equally welcome to all. Thus is explained what our travellers have frequently observed that in each tribe, and often indeed from village to village a different money is current."[2] (Italics are Bücher's.)

Bücher's theory provides an outstanding example of that dogmatism and over-simplification that is encountered so frequently in the study of primitive money. Beyond doubt it contains a great deal that is acceptable. Relative scarcity is certainly one of the requirements of money which tends to secure its universal acceptance. In a very large number of instances the use of primitive currency undoubtedly developed on the lines indicated by Bücher. On the other hand, it is equally easy to find many instances to show that the rule laid down by Bücher with such uncompromising emphasis is by no means universally applicable. Had he been less dogmatic he could not have helped realizing that there are many instances in which monetary material is not selected from among imported goods but from among local products. It is indeed astonishing that an economic historian of his standing should have chosen to ignore obvious facts simply because they did not suit his favourite theory. It is impossible to take the charitable view that Bücher, in the course of his elaborate investigations into the economic systems of primitive communities, did not come across many instances contradicting his one-sided view. And apart from any factual evidence that must have come to his notice, it is inconceivable that he should have ignored the existence of an extensive literature on the subject elaborating the opposite extreme hypothesis—namely, that primitive communities always choose their own staple products as their currencies.

The choice of imported currencies is explained by Schurtz on the ground of the desire of "vested interests" within the tribes to retain their strong position. "The more important money became, and the more social standing depended on its possession, the less was it appropriate that it should be produced within the tribe. If everybody were in a position to manufacture money the position of the wealthy tribesmen and of the chiefs could easily be weakened and the social structure of the community disturbed."[3] On the basis of these observations it seems that it would not always be correct to claim that money adopted with this object in view necessarily originated through foreign trade. In

[2]Bücher, pp. 67-8.   [3]Schurtz, pp. 20-1.

many instances it was probably the desire to possess such money that led to the development of external trade.

The third type of external money includes easily exportable staple products. There is ample evidence to show that staple products were chosen as primitive currency in a great many instances. Until comparatively recently it was, in fact, the recognized classical view that communities at primitive stages of evolution chose, as a matter of course, their staple products for currency. It is a commonplace of textbooks on money that the currency of pastoral communities was livestock or its products; that of agricultural communities grain and other land products; that of hunting communities skins and furs; that of fishing communities dried fish. It is to Bücher's credit to have undermined the formerly implicit faith in this one-sided view, even though he replaced it by one equally one-sided.

There can be no doubt that many—though by no means all—communities in all periods chose their staple products for their currencies. A question of importance is whether such products were chosen because of home consumers' demand or because of foreign demand. According to one theory the choice of a staple domestic product necessarily presupposes a steady foreign demand. This argument will be dealt with in greater detail in the next chapter dealing with the origin of money through internal trade. From our present point of view it is sufficient to observe that the existence of a persistent foreign demand for the product in question undoubtedly facilitates its monetary use within the producer community. Various objects would not have been adopted in many instances for monetary use had it not been for the existence of an external demand. While a staple product which is also a staple article of consumption within the producer community may become currency even in the absence of export, if the output is far in excess of normal domestic needs then the existence of an external outlet for the surplus is unquestionably helpful towards its monetary use.

Even if a staple product is also the staple article of consumption, the existence of an elastic market to absorb the surplus greatly facilitates the monetary use of that article. Everybody accepts it because there can be no doubt about the possibility of using it for purchases, whether at home or abroad. Moreover, the existence of a steady foreign market tends to reduce fluctuations in the value of the product concerned due to variations in the local supply. Nevertheless, it would be a mistake to generalize and claim that only those staple products which have an external market are suitable for monetary use, or that their monetary adoption is necessarily primarily due to the demand for export purposes. This theory, like Bücher's, contains part of the truth and contributes usefully to the theory of the development of money without, however, supplying a complete explanation.

The fourth type of "external" currency includes the objects which are accepted in payment abroad not because the importing community wants to consume them, but because it is in a position to re-export them. A community may accept in payment for its exports an object for which it has no non-monetary use at home, but which is freely accepted by other communities for monetary or non-monetary purposes. There are several instances of such "international" primitive currencies. There is, for example, the mat currency of Micronesia, or the *diwara* in the Bismarck Archipelago, or the *wampum* among a large number of North American Indian tribes. Some of such "international" currencies serve only the purpose of foreign trade; for the requirements of home trade there are different currencies. On the other hand, there are also instances of the use of the same currency for both home and foreign trade. And it is, to say the least, conceivable that such a currency was adopted for internal requirements as a result of its use for international requirements.

It is equally possible that an imported object is adopted for internal monetary purposes by the importing community because it can easily be re-exported to meet non-monetary requirements. In many known instances primitive communities play systematically the part of the intermediary between two other communities. They accept certain articles in payment for their goods, not because they need those articles for their own non-monetary requirements, but because they can depend on being able to exchange them for goods they want to import from other communities. If the objects in question enjoy a high degree of acceptability abroad, the chances are that they come to assume monetary functions also internally.

There are many instances of the replacement of a primitive currency by a more advanced form of currency as a result of foreign trade and contact with the outside world. Beyond doubt, trade with other communities played a very important part in the origin and development of money—though not so all-important as many authors would like us to believe.

CHAPTER 9

ORIGIN THROUGH INTERNAL TRADE

There is a strong tendency in modern economic literature, due to the influence of free trade doctrines, to underrate the relative importance of home trade compared with foreign trade. This tendency is evident also in writings on primitive trade. We discussed in the last chapter the widespread conception that external trade necessarily preceded internal trade, and that for a long time the latter was far too insignificant to give rise to the use of currency. If by "trade" we mean a systematic commercial exchange of goods on a relatively large scale by a class of professional traders, then the assumption is probably largely correct. If, however, we include also the non-professional bartering of goods between individuals and households producing them and those consuming them, then in all probability the volume of home trade has always been much larger than that of foreign trade.

The question is, can non-professional barter between producers and consumers give rise to currency? Or was it only professional barter that tended to produce such a result? Professional traders were of course better qualified for initiating the use of currency than individuals engaging in an occasional barter transaction. On the other hand, the need for developing a monetary system was not so strong in professional traders in primitive communities at an early stage of development, since they were in a better position than private individuals to engage in pure barter and to overcome its inconveniences, while benefiting by its advantages. Indeed, in recent times those engaged professionally in barter transactions were often opposed to the introduction of money in African primitive communities, on the ground that under a barter system they stood to make a profit both ways. The trader is certainly better placed than the private individual for the disposal of goods received in barter. It is possible to imagine, therefore, that in the majority of instances money may have originated through the needs of non-professional trade rather than through that of the professional trade. If we accept this view then it would appear possible and even probable that, more often than not, when money originated through trade it was through home rather than through foreign trade.

In the last chapter reference was made to the theory according to which the staple product of a community could not serve as its currency unless there were a steady demand for it for export. This need not be so, however, if the product in question were also a staple article of consumption. There is bound to be a strong and steady demand for such articles within the community, and the existence of that demand alone should be sufficient to secure for the product in question general acceptability in payment for goods and services of every kind. Thus in wheat-growing communities wheat is the staple product of consumption and this is the reason why it often assumes the functions of primitive currency. Those who have something to sell accept wheat in payment even in excess of their own needs, because they know that there will be no difficulty in finding someone to accept their wheat in payment for purchases. The position is the same for rice in communities where it is the staple article of consumption, and for other land products. Systematic home consumption of animals and their products, of clothing, tools, utensils, weapons and ornaments also appears to be a suitable basis for the selection of these articles as local currencies.

It is important to consider the question as to what extent home consumption is capable of absorbing the home production. It is generally argued that unless the whole output can be absorbed at home there is always a danger of a depreciation of the object chosen as currency, owing to the existence of a growing unwanted surplus. In reality, primitive communities have more than one way of neutralizing such surpluses. They can be partly absorbed by sacrificial requirements, or through the accumulation of large stocks by tribal authorities, or through their use as a store of value by private individuals. Large quantities are usually destroyed or consumed on occasions of festivities, or are burned or buried with the dead. Nature prevents an unlimited increase of stocks of perishable goods. There is much wastage of clothing, utensils, etc., through wear and tear. Much primitive money is buried for safe keeping and is never found. On the other hand, it must also be borne in mind that the certainty of being able to dispose of large quantities of the monetary object is bound to tend towards an increase in production. That increase may assume such proportions as to exceed the absorbing capacity of the community.

It does not necessarily follow, however, that the quantity of an object, merely because it is home-produced, can be increased to an unlimited extent. Very often there are physical limitations, such as inadequacy of its supply, or the difficulty of making it available. The cost of production may also become a limiting factor, since as soon as the increase of the quantity of the primitive currency has brought about its depreciation beyond a certain point its further production ceases to be profitable. Or, in communities where prices are too rigid to adapt themselves to supply and demand, once the goods available for sale are absorbed by possessors of primitive money, further addition to the monetary supply ceases to be worth while.

There are instances in which the purely internal character of the primitive money is quite obvious. Cattle, which is the principal currency of the Ankole of Uganda, can only circulate within the tribe. It is not allowed to leave the tribe except in extreme emergency. This practice prevails to a larger or lesser extent throughout the parts of East Africa and South Africa where cattle constitutes the main primitive currency. It is open to question, however, whether cattle assumed that role through having been a medium of barter, or whether its use for religious and political payments and for bride money preceded its use in home trade.

Other known instances of currencies which developed for the requirements of home trade and which did not owe their acceptability to any demand for export include the iron currency of Sparta and the scrap copper currency of Ancient Italy and Sicily and of early Rome. There were also highly perishable foodstuffs (which did not become exportable until modern times), such as butter, eggs, cheese, etc., which served as media of exchange in various communities, within the limitations imposed on their monetary use by their perishable character. Finally, many home-produced objects serving as ornaments became a medium of exchange, even though, owing to the difference in taste determining the choice of ornaments, they were not exportable.

From the foregoing it appears that in a by no means negligible proportion of instances an object produced locally was chosen for monetary purposes even in the complete absence of any demand for export. It is, therefore, evidently incorrect to claim that a home-produced object can only become a currency if it constitutes a staple export. Admittedly the possibility of unloading the surplus outside the community tends to increase the acceptability of a medium of barter. But demand for export is by no means the only possible steadying influence, nor even necessarily the best possible steadying influence. If an object that serves as a medium of barter becomes a generally employed store of value this in itself secures for it an almost unlimited demand; for there is virtually no limit to the desire to accumulate wealth. The accumulation of cattle as a store of value is only limited by grazing facilities and water supply. The accumulation of furs is only limited by storage facilities. The accumulation of grain is only limited by the extent to which the reserve can be turned over to safeguard it from deterioration; thus the supply must not exceed the yield of so many years of crops.

If in addition to the domestic demand for the purposes of store of wealth we allow for the domestic demand for religious and political purposes and for bride money, then it is evident that internal demand for an object is fully capable of ensuring a sufficient degree of acceptability to make possible its choice for monetary purposes.

CHAPTER 10

THE STANDARD OF VALUE THEORY

In the last three chapters we have been dealing with the origin of media of exchange through barter. There is, however, another way in which barter has contributed towards the origin of money, namely, by giving rise to the use of a standard of value. Most economists agree that medium of exchange and standard of value are the most important monetary functions. Indeed, most economists hold the view that they are the only fundamental functions and that all other functions arise either from one or from the other. Where they disagree is on the question which of the two is more important and which of them preceded the other. In this respect the controversy is to some extent identical with the conflict between the materialist and the nominalist conception of money. Most of those who believe that money must have intrinsic value naturally attach more importance to its medium of exchange function than to its standard of value function and believe that money must have originated through the former function.

Helfferich, being a leading exponent of the 20th century German materialist monetary school, stated that the function of the standard of value derived from that of the medium of exchange without any question of reciprocity arising.[1] It is not apparent to him how any object, merely by reason of serving as a measure of value, should be clothed with the function of acting as a medium of exchange. He accuses those who hold the opposite view of putting the cart before the horse. Menger goes even further. He thinks that money has only one fundamental function—that of the medium of exchange, and that its function of standard of value developed from its function of medium of exchange.[2] On the other hand, Keynes, being a leading exponent of the nominalist school which regards money primarily as a unit of account, attaches more importance to its standard of value function, stating that in itself the use of a mere medium of exchange would hardly have made us emerge from the phase of barter.[3] He believes that real money comes into existence only when it becomes "money of account."

Although as a general rule the materialist school supports wholeheartedly the medium of exchange theory of the origin of money a few of its members endorsed the standard of value theory. Thus Laughlin, a leading monetary materialist, stated that as soon as two or three articles entered the field of exchange, reference to a common denominator became imperative. "So natural is this operation of the human mind," he said, "that the evolution of the standard concept must have preceded the concept of the medium of exchange. In fact, the whole history of money seems to show the existence of a tendency to use as a medium of exchange the article first chosen as a standard of value."[4] No nominalist could have put the case for the standard of value theory more forcefully. Another prominent member of the "hard money school," Gregory, takes a similar line. "The difficulties of pure barter," he writes, "were first overcome by the expression of values in terms of some common prized object before that object or any other object served as a medium of exchange, and the qualities which fitted the commodity to serve as a common denominator of values would not necessarily fit it to serve as a given medium of exchange."[5]

According to the standard of value theory of the origin of money, it is difficult to see how the medium of exchange could possibly have preceded in chronological order the standard of value, considering that the use of a medium of exchange necessarily implies the use of a

[1]Helfferich, Vol. I, pp. 329-30.
[2]Menger, p. 94.
[3]J. M. Keynes, *A Treatise on Money* (London, 1930), Vol. I, p. 1.
[4]Laughlin, p. 7.
[5]T. E. Gregory, *Money*. Encyclopædia of Social Sciences (New York, 1933), Vol. X, p. 603.

standard of value. If an object comes to be used systematically as an intermediary in the exchange of goods and services, by its function its use implies consciously or otherwise the expression of prices in terms of the object concerned. It fulfils, therefore, the function of the standard of value. On the other hand, the use of a standard of value evidently does not necessarily imply the use of a medium of exchange. Indeed, as Gregory rightly pointed out, the need for a common denominator to facilitate barter must have been felt long before the increase in the volume and diversity of goods made the use of a medium of exchange imperative.

So long as there were fixed exchange parities between the principal objects bartered against each other systematically, there was no imperative need for a standard of value. With the diversification of products, services and requirements, however, the tariffs of fixed parities tended to become too involved, and the use of some common unit of account became increasingly necessary. There was a tendency to fix ratios in one particular unit or in several units convertible to each other on the basis of fixed parities. Thus in Iceland during the 14th century there existed an elaborate tariff of fixed prices expressed in terms of stockfish on the basis of which all barter transactions were effected.

In communities where barter was based on free bargaining the need for a common denominator must have made itself felt at a relatively early stage. It seems probable that, in many instances, long before primitive man felt impelled to accept for his goods or services an object he did not require for his direct needs, he must have come to be induced to value goods and services in terms of some fairly widely used object. This view is contested by Menger who believes that at a primitive stage a common denominator was not necessary because primitive barter was not done for the sake of obtaining equal value, but for the sake of securing what was needed in return for what was in superfluity.[6] He may be right so far as the very early phases are concerned. But then at such early phases the medium of exchange was equally unnecessary. The turnover of goods consisted at that stage largely of exchanges of presents. Once the stage was reached at which the exchange of goods and services became a matter of bargaining, the sense of value of primitive man must have developed sufficiently to try to secure goods sufficiently valuable to make it worth his while to part with his own goods. It is true there is a biblical instance of the sale by Esau of his birthright for a mess of pottage. There are more recent instances in the experience of travellers in backward countries who have found that savages are prepared to give away valuable ivory, gold or precious stones in return for worthless trinkets. But communities which are at that stage do not as a rule use a medium of exchange any more than they use a standard of value.

---

[6]Menger, p. 62.

Menger admits that standards of value may have been employed by primitive communities before the adoption of a medium of exchange, though not for the requirements of trade. According to him they were employed even before the development of barter, for the purpose of valuing wealth which required the use of a common denominator.[1] We propose to return to this point later when dealing with the non-commercial origin of the standard of value function of money.

In a large number of instances the units serving as a standard of value could not possibly have been used as media of exchange, for the simple reason that they were merely ideal units without any concrete existence. Admittedly it is possible that in the remote past those abstract units were represented by concrete objects serving as media of exchange. It is, to say the least, conceivable that some units of account at any rate were purely imaginary from the outset.

What seems much more likely is that many objects with real existence were chosen as units of account to facilitate barter, not because they had acted as media of exchange or even as media of barter, but for non-commercial reasons. We have already referred to the possibility of the origin of the standard of value through its use for the valuing of wealth. Even Menger recognizes that this stage may have been reached long before there was any barter, and therefore decidedly before there could be any question of adopting any medium of exchange. Wealth was accumulated from a very early stage of evolution, with the aid of various forms of stores of value. Human nature being what it is, there must always have been a natural desire to compare the size of the wealth of one chief against that of another chief. Unless they kept their wealth in precisely the same form there could be no comparison without the use of some form of common denominator in terms of which the various forms of wealth could be expressed for the sake of comparison. Among pastoral races, for instance, all possessions were expressed in terms of oxen, sheep, camels, etc. It stands to reason that when in subsequent stages these races began to feel the need for a unit of account to facilitate barter they used the same unit previously adopted for the valuation of wealth, and that when the growing volume of barter and its increasing complexity gave rise to the necessity for a medium of exchange there was a tendency to choose the same animal for that purpose. In this way a medium of exchange may have originated through the function of the standard of value. It seems reasonable to assume that in many instances the use of a standard of value for the sole purpose of comparing wealth preceded its commercial use for the purpose of facilitating barter. It is also conceivable, however, that some units which were used for comparing wealth never came to be used for facilitating barter.

Beyond doubt the adoption of a standard of value must have been

[1] Menger, p. 67.

hampered at an early stage by the lack of an arithmetical faculty in savages. It may be easier to swap goods against a concrete medium of exchange than to reckon in terms of an abstract unit of account.

Allowing for all considerations, on balance it seems probable that more often than not the standard of value preceded the medium of exchange. This in itself should not in any way prejudice opinions on the question whether the one function is more important than the other. Precedence in chronological order does not necessarily determine the order of importance.

CHAPTER 11

THE STORE OF VALUE THEORY

While economists are engaged in a controversy on the question whether the function of money as a medium of exchange preceded its functions as a standard of value, they are inclined to overlook or under-rate the claim of the store of value function. This is probably due to the fact that an object that is used as a store of value cannot, by that reason alone, be considered as money. It need not necessarily be suitable even subsequently to assume the role of money; many non-monetary objects which are capable of fulfilling the function of a store of value are precluded by their nature from assuming that role. Nevertheless, the part played by the store of value in the origin of primitive money deserves attention.

Jevons was among the few economists who realized the full significance of the store of value function of money and the possibility that chronologically it may have preceded the other monetary functions. "The use of esteemed articles as a medium for conserving value may in some cases precede their employment as currency," he writes. "Historically speaking, such a generally esteemed substance as gold seems to have served firstly as a commodity valuable for ornamental purposes; secondly as store of wealth; thirdly as medium of exchange, and lastly as a measure of value."[1] He quotes instances for the use of gold in the Homeric period as a store of value and points out that it was not until a later period that it replaced oxen as a common measure of value. His observations convey the impression that he considered it essential for an article to be used for ornamental purposes before it could become a store of value. This is by no means necessarily so. Goods such as wheat, oxen, smoked fibre mats, etc., were used as a store of value even though they could not be described as ornamental.

Menger, although a leading exponent of the medium of barter theory of the origin of money, admitted that hoarding must have preceded

[1] Jevons, p. 16.

barter. Even in self-sufficient household economies certain goods were hoarded; their possession was valued for possession's sake, or for the prestige it conferred on its owner. Subsequently, according to Menger, these goods came to be used for unilateral payments, and in due course they became media of barter and media of exchange.[2] This sequence of the phases of evolution is supported by ethnological evidence. Many African chiefs accumulated ivory even before it became a medium of exchange following on the appearance of European traders on the scene.[3]

A detailed examination of the origin of money through its function as a store of value is provided by Rist: "Money has a third function," he writes after dealing with its functions as a medium of exchange and a standard of value, "the most important of all, which is probably the origin of its other functions—that of serving as store of value, as an insurance against the uncertainties of the future."[4] He quotes in support of his assumption a remark by Keynes: "The importance of money essentially flows from its being a link between the present and the future."[5]

Rist rightly points out that when money loses its capacity to serve as a store of value—the day paper money begins to depreciate at a rapid pace—it becomes less suitable for acting as a medium of exchange, even though it does not altogether lose its capacity of serving that purpose.[6] After both World Wars people in various countries reverted largely to barter, or to the use of primitive money, because their paper money ceased to be suitable to fulfil the function of store of value. Holders of goods were reluctant to accept notes even for a few hours and preferred to employ as a medium of exchange goods capable of playing the part of a store of value.

Although Rist's remarks concern exclusively modern money, there is no reason why they should not be applied also to primitive money. It seems that Rist realizes, and possibly even exaggerates, the importance of the store of value functions of money and the historical precedence of that function. He makes it quite clear that an object cannot *satisfactorily* fulfil the function of a medium of exchange unless the recipients are prepared to hold it temporarily at any rate in its capacity of a store of value. There are, it is true, primitive currencies which, owing to their perishable nature, are accepted not because they are stores of value but because there is a possibility of their direct consumption by the recipient if he should be unable to use them in payment to others before they begin to deteriorate. The predominant majority of primitive

[2]Menger, p. 55.
[3]Casati, *Zehn Jahre in Aequatoria*, Vol. I, p. 136. Quoted by Schurtz, p. 23.
[4]Rist, p. 325.
[5]J. M. Keynes, *The General Theory of Employment, Interest and Money* (London, 1936), p. 293.
[6]Rist, p. 328.

Y

currencies, however, is suitable for use at least as a temporary store of value.

This does not necessarily mean, however, that the function of store of value is always the origin of its other functions. Beyond doubt in a great many instances money originated in the widespread adoption of a certain object as a store of value. The fact that an object serves that purpose materially increases the possibility of inducing sellers of goods and services to accept it in payment even if they have no direct use for it, because they can be assured of realizing their holdings without difficulty. The practice of accumulating large stocks of goods serving as a store of value greatly facilitates their acceptability in commercial transactions. Indeed, since a time-lag must necessarily elapse between the acceptance of money in payment and its subsequent use in payment, be it only a few days, or a few hours, or even a few minutes, in that broad sense Rist is right in claiming that every medium of exchange must be also a store of value. During the second World War the depreciation of the Chinese paper money assumed such proportions that sellers of goods were unwilling to keep it as a store of value even for the briefest possible period. The Chinese peasant, having disposed of his products in the market, promptly re-invested the day's takings into cigarettes which he would re-sell next day, or even on the same day, when he wanted to spend the proceeds of his sales. It was because cigarettes were thus able to serve as a store of value that they also came to be considered to be more suitable than paper money for serving as a medium of exchange and a standard of value.

As we pointed out at the beginning of this chapter, the mere fact that an object serves as a store of value does not in itself qualify it for serving as a currency. Unless the object in question conforms to a certain standard of uniformity it is not suitable for monetary functions. We have already dealt with this point in Chapter I in discussing the definition of money. Jewels or objects of art may well serve as store of value but can never assume the character of money owing to their lack of uniformity and the impossibility of valuing them solely according to their weight or size. The largest stones of Yap, or the highest values among the beads of Pelew or the shells of Rossel may serve as stores of value, but could not act as currencies. In Nicobar silver-plated spoons and forks are the most highly valued possessions of the natives who invest most of their savings in such objects. Owing to this, the spoons and forks are the principal store of value in that community. But they are not currency; that part is played by coconuts. Likewise in Ashanti, the highly valuable aggri beads were until recently a favourite store of value, but they did not play the part either of a medium of exchange or of a standard of value.

Objects can fufil the function of standard of value without necessarily being a store of value. In many instances the function of standard of value must have preceded that of store of value. In fact, there were instances where an "ideal" unit which could not possibly have fulfilled the function of store of value, was used as a standard of value. On the other hand, there were instances in which the object serving as a store of value was selected to fulfil the function of standard of value even though it was not used as a medium of exchange. This was the case with the ox unit in the Homeric period.

It would be dogmatic to assume the precedence of the function of store of value over that of medium of exchange; indeed, it is never easy to ascertain which function was the cause and which was the effect. In many cases an object may have become a store of value because of its use as a medium of exchange. Possibly in some instances the function of medium of exchange and store of value developed simultaneously and assisted each other reciprocally. On the other hand, in many instances it is reasonable to assume that the store of value function preceded that of the medium of exchange.

Circumstances resulting in the choice of an object as a store of value might, in given circumstances, work actually against its choice as a medium of exchange. For example, in many East African communities cattle constitutes the principal store of value. But, precisely because cattle are valued so high, their owners are utterly reluctant to part with them. As a result, while cattle may be a standard of value in spite of this attitude they often cannot adequately fulfil the functions of a medium of exchange, because they do not circulate freely enough.

Even in instances when the monetary use of an object has originated in its use as a store of value it is necessary to examine whether such use has not in turn originated in its use for religious sacrifices, political payments, ornamental use, ceremonial functions, or bride money. This question will be dealt with in subsequent chapters which will show that objects which are used for such purposes are apt to be hoarded in order to have them handy to meet future requirements, anticipated or unforeseen. It is conceivable, however, that the religious, political or matrimonial use of certain means of payment led in some instances to their use as media of exchange or standards of value without their necessarily passing through the intermediate stage of a store of value.

Notwithstanding the limitations of the store of value theory of the origin of money, it undoubtedly contains a large part of the truth, and it is indispensable for an understanding of the evolution of money. Rist may have exaggerated when he says that the circulatory function of money implies the function of store of value, "the two being as inseparable as the obverse and reverse of a medal."[7] Nevertheless, it is essential to realize that the store of value function is of first-rate importance among the causes leading to the adoption of money.

[7]Rist, p. 329.

CHAPTER 12

ORIGIN FROM STANDARD OF DEFERRED PAYMENTS

Deferred payments played an important part in the life of primitive communities from a very early stage. As was pointed out in an earlier chapter, the conception of Hildebrand according to which there were three stages of evolution, natural economy, money economy and credit economy, is entirely false. Credit existed on a fairly extensive scale long before the stage of money economy was reached. There are many ethnological instances of credit in kind in communities where no trace of any medium of exchange or even standard of value could be discovered.

The cause of the development of deferred payments during the pre-monetary phase are as follows:—

1. Discrepancies in the value of the goods or services bartered. It is not always possible to return immediately for the objects received objects of approximately equal value, and often the difference has to be delivered at some future date. Such deferred deliveries constitute loans in kind. The possibility of such transactions must have gone a long way towards making the system of barter workable, notwithstanding the inevitable discrepancies in the value of objects bartered. To return to J. S. Mill's much-quoted imaginary instance, it enables tailors and bakers to engage in barter, even though no tailor can possibly consume at once all the loaves given in exchange for a coat.

2. Deferred deliveries due to natural conditions. Sowing seed was often lent in agricultural communities and was repayable out of the next crop. Blacksmiths and other artisans were paid after harvest. Food was lent between crops. Hunters and fishers borrowed goods and repaid them when the result of their activities enabled them to do so.

3. Loans were granted to enable the borrower to pay ransom fines, tribute, blood money, bride money, etc.

4. Rents were fixed in kind in advance for long periods.

5. Loans in kind may have been granted for trading purposes.

Even during the most primitive phase of barter when the exchange of goods assumed the form of reciprocal presents or services, there was often a discrepancy between the time of making the original payment or rendering the original service and reciprocation. In a sense, it is therefore true to say that credit existed from the very earliest phases of economic activity, even before the evolution of barter proper.

Nor were loans and credits the only forms of deferred liabilities in kind before the adoption of money. Land was rented during the pre-monetary stage. Liabilities arising from marriage payments were often deferred. Tribute was usually fixed for a long period ahead.

In all these instances repayment or payment was originally made in kind. From a very early stage primitive man must have realized the difficulties that were liable to arise from such a system. Debtors may have been prevented from making payment in the form stipulated by the terms of their contracts through the failure of the harvest, cattle diseases or inadequate yield from hunting or fishing. In such situations payment was only possible through acquiring the objects in question at the cost of exorbitant sacrifices, if indeed it was possible at all. The debtors were therefore liable to be placed at a grave disadvantage. According to the system prevailing in Babylonia and many other early civilizations, and also in many present-day primitive communities, the original loans were either interest free or bore a relatively low rate of interest, but in case of inability to pay on maturity the debtors were charged something like a hundred per cent interest. Postponement of payment through adverse contingencies was therefore apt to be ruinous to the debtors. Non-payment meant in most primitive communities the enslavement of the defaulter or of members of his family. The need for provisions by which to ease the task of repayment must have been therefore obvious at a very early stage.

In many instances alternative means of payment were agreed upon between the debtor and creditor, either in advance or at any rate when the impossibility of discharging the liability in its original form became evident. From such agreements traditional alternative methods of payment must have arisen. At a very early stage the tribal authority must have realized the necessity for adopting or regulating such systems of alternative payments; or possibly the practice in this respect developed so definitely that even in the absence of intervention by the primitive State authority it came to be applied universally in the community.

Legislation in various States in the Ancient and Medieval Periods provides for such alternative payment of liabilities in kind. There are similar provisions in the tribal laws and customs of many present-day primitive communities. This in itself does not mean that the object in which creditors are obliged to accept payment necessarily constitutes a primitive money. Very often the acceptance of a large selection of objects for payment of deferred liabilities was made obligatory, and neither of them was therefore used sufficiently generally to justify us in regarding them as a standard of deferred payments. There must have been a tendency, however, towards a reduction in the number of primitive legal tenders in any given community, until eventually a single object, or a small number of objects, came to assume the role of standards of deferred payment. In many instances this stage must have been achieved before a medium of exchange came into existence, indeed before even a standard of value was adopted for current trade transactions. In such instances money must have originated through its functions as a standard of deferred payments.

Several theoretical economists have realized the possibility of money originating through debts. Among others, Knapp, in his *State Theory of Money* postulated the existence of debts before the existence of money. His theory is not very useful for our present purpose. Since according to Knapp, money comes into existence by State legislation concerning the settlement of liabilities, it stands to reason that on the basis of his hypothesis debts had to precede money.[1] Knapp's theory cannot, however, be quoted in support of the claim that money originated through its function of standard of deferred payments, except in the narrow sense in which Knapp himself defines money.

The argument put forward by F. M. Taylor is more helpful from the point of view of tracing the origin of money in pre-monetary debts. "Some one money will become the standard money of debts and then take for itself also the place of standard money in prices. This follows because the standard means of payment is free to move while that of debts is not."[2] There can be no doubt that it is much easier to switch over from one medium of exchange to another than from one standard of deferred payment to another. We saw in the Ethnological Section, especially in the part dealing with Africa, how primitive communities were in the habit of changing frequently their medium of exchange. On the other hand, since existing long-term liabilities are expressed in terms of the standard of deferred payments its change is necessarily an important and difficult matter and is usually either a very gradual process or is brought about by intervention of the primitive State authority. While this argument is concerned with changing from one existing monetary system to another, it may also apply to the adoption of a monetary system in moneyless communities. If a community possesses both a rudimentary standard of deferred payment and a popular medium of barter, there seems to be more likelihood of changing the latter to adapt it to the former than of changing the former to adapt it to the latter. Moreover, in all probability the State authority intervened to regulate the standard of deferred payments long before any intervention for fixing a medium of exchange came to be considered necessary.

Another argument by Taylor in favour of the theory that medium of exchange may have been preceded in many instances by standard of deferred payments is that "voluntary acceptability is created by compulsory acceptability."[3] This means that if by tradition or tribal legislation a certain object has been made compulsorily acceptable in payment of debts, members of the community concerned are likely to be willing to accept it voluntarily also in payment for goods and services. Cumpulsory acceptance does not only mean the adoption of a legal tender for debt repayment but also the adoption of means in which

[1] G. F. Knapp, *The State Theory of Money* (London, 1924), *passim*.
[2] F. M. Taylor, *Chapters of Money* (Michigan, 1906), p. 158.
[3] Taylor, p. 83.

political payments can be discharged. This aspect of the question will
be dealt with in the chapter dealing with political payments. According
to Ellis, it would be difficult to decide whether payments to the State or
legal tender in private trade is the more essential.[4] Beyond doubt, many
authors were inclined to exaggerate the importance of legal tender in
private payments and underrate the importance of political payments
from the point of view of the evolution of money. There can be no
doubt, however, that the adoption of a rule, whether through tradition
or by deliberate tribal legislation that a certain object must be accepted
in discharge of debts went a long way towards qualifying that object for
subsequent adoption as a medium of exchange.

Among the contributions of theoretical economists to the question
whether money may have originated through its function of standard of
deferred payments, that of Hawtrey deserves particular attention. In
Chapter I of his *Currency and Credit*, entitled "Credit without Money,"
he argues that money is not the only alternative to barter. He puts forward the tentative suggestion that a society might have existed without
the use of money provided that it was possible to buy and sell against
debts. "Goods are brought to market and exchanged," he writes, "but
even though there is no medium of exchange it does not follow that they
must be bartered directly for one another. If a man sells a ton of coal
to another, this will create a debt from the buyer to the seller. But the
buyer will have been himself a seller to someone else and the seller will
have been himself also a buyer. The dealers in the market can meet
together and set off their debts and credits. But for this purpose the
debts and credits which represent the purchase and sale of a variety of
goods must be reduced to some common measure. In fact, a unit for the
measurement of debts is indispensable."[5] Needless to say, this is a purely
hypothetical situation, and Mr. Hawtrey is careful to make it plain that
he does not claim it to be anything else. He does not present it as his
theory of the origin of money but merely as an imaginary system to
illustrate the theoretical possibility of money having originated in some
such way. This is in accordance with his definition of money as the
means for the settlement of debts. While Hawtrey's hypothesis deals
with a rather advanced imaginary community, it nevertheless indicates
the theoretical possibility of the existence of a premonetary system
under which the difficulties of barter are overcome by the development
of credit before the development of currency.

Such theoretical confirmation of the possibility that money had
originated through its use as a standard of deferred payments as has
been provided by Hawtrey, Taylor and Ellis is useful owing to the
impossibility of securing adequate historical or ethnological evidence on

[4]Howard S. Ellis, p. 33.
[5]Hawtrey, p. 2.

this point. The only kind of ethnological evidence we can put forward is that in primitive communities such as the Banks Islands, for instance, there is a primitive currency which is used very extensively as a standard of deferred payments and much less extensively as a medium of exchange. It seems reasonable to presume that the latter use was largely due to its adoption as a standard of deferred payment in the first instance.

In many other instances, on the other hand, the chronological order may have been reversed, and objects which were first adopted as media of exchange came subsequently to be adopted as standards of deferred payments. It is also certain that in many instances the objects which were first adopted for political or other unilateral payments came to be used subsequently for debt payments. It seems probable, however, that in a fair proportion of instances at any rate money originated through the role it played as a standard of deferred commercial payments.

CHAPTER 13

ORIGIN THROUGH ORNAMENTAL AND CEREMONIAL FUNCTIONS

Ornamental requirements must have played a very important part in the origin of money. Indeed, there is reason to believe that shells, which were among the earliest currencies in many parts of the world, served as ornaments before they were put to monetary use. The idea that, owing to his extreme poverty, primitive man could only afford to use as currency objects that were capable of being turned to practical use in satisfaction of primary requirements, is entirely false. Even in our society, man does not as a rule satisfy his needs in the strict order of their importance. Very often even the poorest is inclined to do without some necessity in order to satisfy a craving for some luxury. It does not seem reasonable, therefore, to assume that primitive man is an essentially rational human being who is fully aware of the correct order in which he ought to meet his needs, and who, on the basis of this knowledge, always listens to the sober voice of reason in deciding which of his needs should be satisfied before the others out of the limited means at his disposal. Babelon is not far wrong in his delightfully French paradoxical remark that it is the superfluous which, by instinct, seems to man the most necessary.

It is, therefore, conceivable that a primitive fishing community, instead of devoting all its time to fishing, might devote part of its time to collecting attractive-looking shells for ornamental use. In any case, shells could be collected without necessarily neglecting fishing, either by sacrificing hours of rest or recreation, or by collecting them when fishing is impossible, or by picking them up casually. Non-productive members of the community can also collect them.

Shells must first have been valued because of their ornamental use, and their comparative durability and uniformity made them suitable subsequently to undertake monetary functions. Steady demand for them for ornamental purposes must have subsequently made them acceptable as a medium of exchange. What is true of shells may be equally true of beads, feathers, ornamental articles of clothing, animal teeth, etc. It is probable that the use of precious metals as a store of value and medium of exchange originated through their ornamental use.

There is indeed an impressive selection of arguments in favour of the ornamental origin of money. According to Helfferich, ornaments qualify for monetary use because there is no limit to the desire for accumulating them. Vanity, ostentation and the desire for decoration are never fully satisfied. Those possessing a surplus stock of necessities would, therefore, gladly exchange them for precious metals.[1] Laughlin pointed out that in the tropics where clothing is not the main want, and where it is easy to satisfy requirements of housing and food, ornaments appear as the most desired wealth.[2]

In early Communistic or semi-Communistic societies food and other necessities had to be shared. On the other hand, as Schurtz points out, ornaments were allowed to be individual possessions.[3] This accounts for the choice of whales' teeth as the currency of Fiji where notions of private ownership are not established very firmly. Yet another consideration is that primitive man must endeavour to avoid at all cost acquiring the reputation of meanness. Social opinion forces him to distribute his possessions generously. One of the few forms in which he could hoard wealth without being accused of meanness is through the display of ornaments.[4]

The claim of the theory of the ornamental origin of money is evidently a strong one. It is, however, equally possible that objects which had become valued possessions because of their monetary use came to be regarded subsequently as attractive ornaments. This is certainly in accordance with the primitive desire to display wealth. One of the difficulties which colonizing powers have in inducing natives to appreciate the use of paper money and of banks is that notes cannot be worn as ornaments and bank balances are invisible. This difficulty could be mitigated if banks in primitive countries adopted the practice of issuing to the clients ornamental badges indicating the approximate amount of their deposits.

Money and ornament was in earlier times—and still is in many backward communities—so completely identical that it is often difficult to form an opinion which preceded the other. Only a few hundred years ago the gold plates which adorned the dinner tables of England's stately

---

[1]Helfferich, Vol. I, p. 15.   [2]Laughlin, p. 11.   [3]Schurtz, p. 14.
[4]W. W. Carlile, *Monetary Economics* (London, 1912), p. 136.

homes were considered as monetary reserves and frequently used as such.[5]

In addition to personal ornaments, objects used for decorative purposes were also apt to play a monetary part. Whether the stone money of Yap, the smoked mats of the New Hebrides, or the display of human or animal skulls in New Guinea, Borneo or Assam correspond to our ideas of the ornamental, they were certainly viewed as such by the communities concerned. They may have become a kind of currency as a result of their ornamental use, or vice-versa.

On the whole, it seems probable that in the majority of instances the ornamental use of various objects preceded their monetary use. This seems to be indicated by the adoption for monetary use of objects which, while themselves not particularly ornamental, symbolize similar objects of high ornamental or ceremonial value. This is the case with the small stones in Yap, the ordinary mats in Samoa, and the ordinary wampum among the North American Indians. The specially valuable pieces do not circulate as money, but the much larger number of ordinary specimens benefit by their reflected glory derived from the ornamental or sentimental value attached to the former.

Ethnologists studying primitive communities in various parts of the world have given accounts of certain types of "currency" used solely for ceremonial purposes. They lay stress on the fact that these currencies—if they can be called currencies—are not exchanged against goods but are used for the sole purpose of ceremonial exchanges without any apparent economic benefit accruing to either part. The outstanding example of such ceremonial exchanges is the Kula on the Tobriand Islands described by Malinowski. He gives a detailed account of the journeys undertaken by the islanders for the purpose of exchanging shell ornaments for other kinds of shell ornaments purely as acts of friendship and courtesy. The shells thus exchanged eventually return to their original owners, and the only benefit derived from the series of transactions is increased prestige gained by the decorum with which the exchanges are effected. Some types of money on the Rossel Islands are also used for somewhat similar purposes. In Alor in the Dutch East Indies the exchange of drums proceeds similarly, even though drums are used also for bride money. Among North American Indians the potlatch consists partly in the ceremonial exchange of copper plates while the more practical turnover in blankets is also largely ceremonial in character.

In many communities it is difficult to draw the line between ceremonial and economic exchange. The factor of social prestige plays in

[5]A proclamation issued by Charles II in 1661 declared:—"The nation had flourished for many hundreds of years, famous for her constant sterling standard and renowned for her plenteous stock of monies and magnificence of plate." (Ruding, II, p. 3). There is no indication, however, that gold plates had been used as actual circulating media, though they must have been used as bullion in large transactions.

these exchanges at least as an important part as economic considerations. If an object is only used for the purpose of exchange in the course of ceremonial acts, then it performs no economic function. However, even though such objects are valued not because they can be used for the purchase of goods and services, but because of their ceremonial use and the social prestige their possession carries, sooner or later members of the community will come to consider it worth while to accept them in payment for goods and services. There must be many instances of ceremonial "money" developing into money proper. It is, of course, difficult to determine how far the ceremonial use preceded the commercial use of such money.

CHAPTER 14

RELIGIOUS ORIGIN

The importance of non-commercial factors in the origin of money cannot be sufficiently emphasized. In a great many primitive communities trade in the form of systematic exchange of goods was for a long time of relatively small significance. This was partly because the early economic unit, the household, tended to be largely self-sufficient, and partly because the circulation of goods within the tribal economic unit was effected on the basis of participation in the proceeds of economic activity in proportions determined by the tribal chief, or council of elders, or by tradition. Even after the State had replaced the tribe as the economic unit in many instances an authoritarian system provided for the non-commercial distribution of goods in the form of rations. This was done in Ancient Egypt to a large extent.

In his work *Heiliges Geld*, dealing with the religious aspect of the origin of money, Laum lays particular stress on the insignificance of trade in the Homeric period. He says that trade in those days assumed largely the form of the disposal of booty.[1] Slave trade, which was relatively active in primitive communities, consisted usually of the exchange of unwanted surplus captives against other goods. The reason why Laum lays stress on this point is because it forms part of his thesis that the ox monetary unit did not originate in trade but in religion.

Among the non-commercial factors leading to the use of money the religious factor deserves undoubtedly special attention, if only because before Laum it was neglected almost completely by economists, and was not treated in accordance with its importance even by ethnologists.[2]

[1] Bernhard Laum, *Heiliges Geld* (Tübingen, 1924), p. 13.
[2] There are a few exceptions. Carlile, for instance, observed that the intervention of the religious impulse was found to have brought with it a fresh stimulus to the "quasi-monetary use" of ornaments. Helfferich (p. 10) remarked that "the bringing of the money from distant parts accompanied with definite ceremonies, some sort of connection with the cult of the dead or belief in spirits—all these have frequently brought it about that semi-savage races clothed certain commodities, in themselves useless, with a mysterious dignity."

Yet any student of the ethnology of Oceania and to a lesser degree of various regions in Asia, Africa and America, can hardly help being struck by the frequent association between primitive money and primitive religion. Students of ancient history, and even of medieval history, too, had ample opportunity to note the connection.

The religious aspects of money may be summed up under the following headings:—

1. Money may have originated in many instances through regular requirements for specific standardized objects for the purpose of sacrifices to deities.

2. In many communities the creation of money is attributed to supernatural powers.

3. In other communities the (admittedly) human producers of money have to observe certain religious rites or rules in executing their "sacred" task.

4. Magic qualities attributed to certain objects have led to their adoption for monetary use.

5. The use of certain objects in connection with religious purposes other than sacrifices, such as death rites, may have contributed towards their adoption for monetary use.

6. The fixing of fines for breaking taboos, and of fees for performers of religious rites, gave rise to the need for a standardized unit.

Laum's theory about the origin of money through religious sacrifices came as a reaction against the materialistic conception which sought to explain the origin of money on pure utilitarian legal and commercial grounds. Until recently it was widely believed that primitive man was essentially utilitarian—in fact, he was supposed to be the ideal type of the "economic man," that favourite creation of classical economists. As it was argued in an earlier chapter, nothing could be further from the truth. Recent ethnological research has revealed the fact that the savage is chiefly guided by non-economic considerations. Among these is the belief in, and fear of, supernatural forces, that is, a primitive form of religion, or magic, or superstition. This factor plays an overwhelmingly important part in the life of primitive man, and for this reason religious requirements are in many instances apt to play a more important part in the origin of money than economic requirements. The evolution of the economic system in general was itself largely influenced by the religious factor. According to Eduard Hahn the evolution of pastoral economy, for instance, was largely due to sacrificial requirements. Tribes in the hunting stage developed the habit of sacrificing captured animals; in order to be able to provide animals for that purpose at short notice, they adopted the practice of keeping large stocks of them. It was, according to Hahn, as a result of this practice that the formerly wild animals gradually became domesticated through their close, if originally enforced, association with man.

Every phase of the economic life of many savage communities is riddled with taboos and other religious rules. Regligion often plays a most important part in determining what to produce, when to produce it and how to produce it. Distribution is also largely affected by religious influences. As for consumption, the survival, right to our days, of food taboos among strict adherents of various religious creeds in our civilized generation should give us an idea of their strength in primitive communities. It would be unnatural if of all economic institutions money had escaped the influence of the religious factor. And it is only natural that the religious factor should exercise its influence largely through the urge of primitive man to sacrifice to the supernatural beings he fears or worships.

Laum has evolved the theory that the practice of making sacrifices to deity was to a large extent a form of barter between man and his gods. Sacrifices were made either in payment for blessings already received, or more often in anticipation of blessings requested, or in an effort to conciliate the offended gods. Consideration of prestige reinforced the religious motive for sacrificing to the gods on a generous scale. In the New Hebrides, not only does social standing depend on the number of pigs sacrificed, but, it is firmly believed, even after death the rank of the departed in the spirit world is determined by it. Likewise in Scandinavian mythology the position of dead heroes in the Valhalla depended on the amount of gold they brought with them on their funeral pyres or in their graves.[3] Apparently in these and other primitive communities it was thought to be easier for a camel to go through the eye of a needle than for a poor man to enter the kingdom of heaven —or at any rate its more select sections.

In many cases the god responsible for certain activities received in the form of sacrifice, the goods produced in his "department." For instance, during the classical era, Demeter, the giver of grain, received grain sacrifices. But Laum himself admits that man only returned to god a small proportion of the goods received from him.[4] So there was no question of any barter between man and god—unless it is assumed that the difference between value received and given was made up in prayers and various forms of rites designed to please the deity who, on a strictly commercial basis, came second best out of the bargain.

The economic importance of religious sacrifices lies in the fact that they create an almost unlimited demand for the surpluses in staple products of the communities concerned. In a primitive community which has no adequate external markets to absorb regularly its surpluses an unusually good crop would be almost as disastrous as the failure of the crop—but for the possibility of disposing of the unwanted

[3]Sumner and Keller, *The Science of Society* (Vol. II, Chapter XVIII). Quoted by Viljoen, p. 254.

[4]Laum, pp. 23-4.

surplus by making generous sacrifices to the gods. Otherwise the existence of excessive supplies, beyond any reasonable requirements for reserves, might upset the economic equilibrium. So when in years of excellent crops or of unusually large increase in the livestock the community expressed its gratitude to the deity to whom the good result was attributed, in reality it unconsciously took measures to safeguard its economic stability. The difference between this practice and the burning of coffee, cotton, wheat, etc., under "valorization schemes" in modern communities in order to prevent a fall of the price of their staple product, is merely one of form. Owing to the ever-present demand for sacrificial purposes—demand which conveniently increases when supplies become uncomfortably large—the general acceptability of the commodity-currency need not depend on foreign buying, even in communities where everybody produces more than enough of it for his present and future economic requirements.

A point to which Laum attributes much importance is that the State authority in Ancient Greece and elsewhere laid down rules determining the precise quality of animals suitable for sacrifice and guaranteed this quality, thereby providing early instances of State-guaranteed units of value.[5] What is more important than this rather far-fetched theory is that the Greek States were in the habit of making official sacrifices in addition to those made by private individuals, and the necessity for acquiring and maintaining livestock for that purpose created a steady demand for it. That demand alone could account for the adoption of oxen or other sacrificial objects as monetary units. Admittedly the determination of the quality of sacrificial animals must have contributed to some extent to the development of a unit of account. It was an early form in which an attempt was made towards the development of a standard unit under State authority. The reason why this was the starting point of the evolution of the unit of account was that oxen were not the only form in which sacrifices were made. Often they were made in the form of other animals or in various implements connected with sacrifice such as tripods, cauldrons, axes, sacrificial knives or spits. The value of these objects was reckoned in standard oxen.[6] This was so not only in Greece but also in Ancient India.

Another piece of evidence quoted by Laum in support of his theory that religious sacrifice played a part in the development of the unit of account was that, to judge by Homer, the numbers of oxen quoted frequently as the value of various objects was often identical with the numbers of animals used for sacrifice. Thus the numbers of 100, 20, 12, 9, 4, appear in the *Iliad* and in *Odyssey* as customary units of value, and 100, 12, 9, as the number of oxen sacrificed on various occasions.[7]

The next step, according to Laum's theory of the evolution of money

[5]Laum, p. 29.   [6]Laum, pp. 59-61.   [7]Laum, pp. 17-8.

through religion, was the payment to priests performing sacrifices of fees in terms of oxen or their equivalent. He thinks that it was in this form that oxen were first used in payments between man and man. In Ancient India part of the fee for the performance of sacrifices, determined in terms of cattle, was paid in terms of other objects and it was for this purpose that equivalents of cattle in other goods had to be fixed. It was thus that cattle are supposed to have become a standard of value in India.[8] It was from this religious use that the practice of quoting prices in terms of cattle may have arisen. The tariffs of fees to those officiating at religious sacrifices are amongst the earliest documentary evidence concerning the existence of fixed means of payment.

At a more advanced stage sacrifices of animals were replaced by donations to the gods, mainly in the form of metals. By this time, however, metals may have already assumed the role of a medium of exchange. In Argos a bundle of spits found in the excavation of the Heræum is assumed to have been used for currency before it was placed at the disposal of deity; in fact, the assumption is that it was so disposed of only after it ceased to be used for monetary purposes.

One-sided and exaggerated as Laum's theory is, it has served a very valuable purpose. His thesis, stated with force and with clarity, may be opposed but cannot be ignored. It would be possible to make out an even stronger case than that presented by Laum by basing his conclusions on broader factual foundations. He purposely narrowed down the factual basis of his theory by ruling out all ethnological evidence on the ground that it would not be justified to judge the behaviour of advanced races at an early phase of their evolution by that of present-day backward races. While he is right in refusing to accept ethnological evidence as conclusive, he is wrong in rejecting it *en bloc* out of hand. It is fully as dogmatic to lay down the hard and fast rule that the early behaviour of the advanced races was different from that of present-day savages as to assume that it was identical. The happy middle course is to use ethnological evidence, subject to reservations, for the corroboration of historical evidence instead of relying entirely on the latter.

Had Laum adopted this view he could have quoted the instance of the pig currency of the New Hebrides, a highly developed primitive monetary system that owes its existence entirely to the sacrificial use of certain types of pigs. There the standard animal suitable to be sacrificed is strictly defined; its value is determined by a well-established scale. This, together with the steady demand for pigs for sacrificial purposes, has led to the development of the use of the sacrificial pigs as a store of value, medium of exchange, standard of value, and especially standard of deferred payments. And while it would be irreverent to the memory of the Homeric heroes to bracket them with the savages of Oceania, the fact that the latter had worked out an elaborate monetary

[8]Laum, p. 61.

system on lines in accordance with Laum's theory could well be used in support of the theory that at a much earlier pre-Homeric stage of the Ægean civilization monetary evolution proceeded on similar lines. After all, during the period described by Homer the system appears to have been well established and it may have taken a thousand years to reach that stage. In this connection it is worth mentioning that in parts of French Indo-China the primitive currencies used until comparatively recently by backward races were cattle, tripods and cauldrons, which is identical with the system that operated in the Homeric age; this fact also indicates the possibility of the Homeric system originating through sacrificial requirements.

In various islands of the Pacific the primitive money in use is believed to be of supernatural origin. Thus in Pelew the high-valued units of the bead money are considered to be of divine origin; that is why man-made imitations are rejected.[9] On the Duke of York Island the *diwara* shell-money is believed to have been created by the spirits. On Rossel Island the *ndap* money is claimed to have been created by the chief god. On Yap, even though most specimens of the famous stone money were known to have been produced and shipped by human beings, there is a legend that attributes the origin of that money to a mischievous god who introduced it in order to cause dissension.

The fact that money is believed to be of divine origin does not in itself necessarily indicate, however, that it had originated in connection with sacrificial or other requirements. There is no such suggestion in connection with three of the four instances given above. Nevertheless, it indicates the presence of a strong religious element in the origin of money and its early use by primitive peoples. This is also indicated by the number of instances in which the production or collection of the monetary objects is subject to religious rules or has to be effected in connection with religious rites. On some of the Solomon Islands the hunting of porpoises for the purpose of producing tooth money is only permitted in connection with the death feasts of priests. In the Maldives in early days cowries were only allowed to be collected at certain phases of the moon. The men who produce in Lawongai the *Tsera* shell-money used in Lesu must be continent while engaged in that task.

In many primitive communities money is looked upon with religious reverence. Throughout Melanesia red mats, shells, or feathers serving as currency are more valuable than the corresponding currencies of other colouring, because red is the sacred colour. In the Solomons the name of one type of shell-money is *rongo* which means "sacred." The shell-money of the Gazelle Peninsula in New Britain is called *tambu* which is a variant of the well-known term *taboo*, meaning "sacred" or

[9]Nevertheless, Kubary's suggestion that the premium on the higher (and therefore more sacred) units of Pelew money is paid to reconcile the hurt feelings of the money, resenting the change of ownership, must not be taken too seriously.

"forbidden for religious reasons." Likewise, in Fiji the sperm whale's teeth serving as currency are called *tambua*. On the Solomons it is believed that the spirits of ancestors dwell on the packets of a hundred fathoms of shell-money deposited in sleeping houses. On Rossel certain of the high-valued units of the shell-money can only be handled in a crouching position. On parts of the Philippines the storehouse where rice money is kept is considered a sacred place and no woman is allowed to enter. Likewise, in many African communities where cattle serves as a currency women are not allowed to touch the beasts during periods of menstruation or pregnancy.[10]

In Uganda much of the tribal cattle that serves as a currency is believed to belong to a god who exercises his proprietary rights through his priests. In Angola the monetary use of a certain type of cotton cloth is known to have originated through its religious use as shrouds at funerals. The beaver, whose skin was at one time the principal currency in the northern half of North America, was regarded as a sacred animal; though admittedly in the case of some Indian tribes at any rate the monetary use of beaver skins can be traced to the commercial demand by European colonists. One of the reasons why *wampum* was valued so highly was that it was required for the funeral pyre of famous chiefs. The pieces of metals that circulated as money in Vedic times in Ancient India owed their use to the fact that payment to Brahmans for performing sacrifices were made in them. The signs these pieces bore were supposed to commemorate sacrifices.

It also seems a reasonable assumption that cowries and precious metals were worn as amulets long before they were used as currencies,[11] and their subsequent adoption as a store of value, means of unilateral payment and medium of exchange was in many instances largely influenced by their use as charms which created a steady demand for them. This may conceivably have been true of many other types of ornament-currencies.

Beyond doubt, Laum has rendered a great service by drawing attention to the neglected religious aspect of the origin of money. But while in many instances he is probably right in claiming religious sacrifice as the origin of money, he is apt to overlook many other instances in which money developed through other factors. Primitive man had other requirements besides religious ones, and in many instances these and not religious requirements must have accounted for the adoption of money. Nor is it always easy to divorce the religious and worldly motives. Sayce is right in observing that "in primitive societies the distinction between the religious and the secular is much less sharply drawn than it often appears to be among modern civilized peoples."[12]

---

[10] Schapera and Goodwin, p. 140.
[11] Viljoen, p. 278.
[12] R. U. Sayce, *Primitive Arts and Crafts* (Cambridge, 1933), p. 6.

z

The evidence showing the connection between religion and primitive money at its earliest phases is, beyond doubt, conclusive. The possibility that in many instances money first arose through non-religious causes—commercial or non-commercial—and only became "sanctified" as a result of the prestige it achieved for very worldly considerations prior to its assumption of a holy character cannot, however, be ruled out. Even allowing for this possibility there is enough to be said in favour of the religious explanation of the origin of money to justify its acceptance as part of the theory of monetary evolution. It certainly contains part of the truth, but it must be studied in conjunction with other theories.

CHAPTER 15

POLITICAL ORIGIN

The last chapter dealt with the important part played by religion in the evolution of money, through the desire it aroused in primitive man to earn the goodwill of supernatural powers by making sacrifices to them. It seems reasonable to assume that the rudimentary political authority which already existed at the early stage also made demands on primitive man. It is probable that sacrifices were made even before the existence of any distinct political authority beyond the authority of the head of the family. The chances are, however, that by the time the sacrificial objects became sufficiently standardized to be able to assume a monetary character there must have been some kind of tribal authority in existence. And it stands to reason that, from an early phase, tribal authority imposed certain political payments on members of its community. Having rendered unto deity what was deity's, primitive man had to render unto Cæsar what was Cæsar's.

The role of the State authority—or rather its rudimentary predecessor, the chief of the clan or tribe—in contributing towards the origin of a means of payment was acknowledged by various authors. They were aware that political payments preceded trade,[1] and that for a long time the turnover in goods consisted largely, if not exclusively, of the collection of such payments by chiefs and their subsequent redistribution to their subjects.[2] Menger realized that non-commercial payments (primarily political payments) constituted the earliest form of payments, and preceded barter, or at any rate they preceded systematic large-scale barter calling for a medium of exchange. He held the view, however, that such payments were made in kind until a medium of exchange had developed through trade, after which they were made in money.[3] In

---

[1] See among others K. Knies, *Das Geld* (Vol. I, of *Geld und Kredit*, Berlin, 1885), p.12.

[2] Somló, p. 64.   [3] Menger, pp. 47-8.

this conclusion, however, he was obviously begging the question. Since he assumed that money could only originate from a favourite medium of barter, he concluded that no object used for political payments prior to the existence of such a favourite medium of barter could be described as money.

Among other economists, Cassel endorsed the view that the means of political payment preceded the medium of exchange. "Probably authoritative decisions determining the commodities to be given in discharge of unilateral obligations have been of great importance in fixing the value of suitable medium of exchange."[4] Among economic historians, Max Weber, in his *General Economic History*, laid particular stress on the importance of political payments in the origin of money.

It is, however, to the credit of Knapp to have drawn general attention to the role of the State as the chief originator of money. His contribution to the study of the origin of money is of a highly doctrinaire character. Like Menger, he is inclined to beg the question. He lays down the rule that "money is the creature of law," and from this preconceived assumption he infers that anything that is not decreed money by legislative measure is not money. From the point of view of the subject of the present chapter, this principle is of small use, especially since Knapp and most of his followers have only the advanced form of the State and of law and of money in mind. What is more helpful to us is the stress he laid on the importance of the form of payments made to the State and by the State, from the point of view of confirming, if not establishing, the monetary character of the objects in which such payments are made.

Political payments during the early phases of civilization may have assumed the following forms:—

1. Payments to the political authority.
    (a) Tribute to the chief by members of his community.
    (b) Tribute, ransom or blood money to the chief by other communities.
    (c) Payment to the chief by members of his community, representing their contribution towards tribute, ransom or blood money payable to another tribe.
    (d) Fines.

2. Payments by the political authority.
    (a) Payments or reward by the chief to those serving him.
    (b) Payment of tribute, ransom or blood money to another tribe.
    (c) Payment to his own subjects of their share in ransom or tribute received, or booty captured from other tribes.

[4]Cassel, p. 352.

3. Payments between members of the tribe, or between members of different tribes, regulated by the political authority.

    (a) Ransom.
    (b) Blood money.
    (c) Compensation.
    (d) Subscriptions to secret societies.

Tribute by tribesmen to their chief was the first form of taxation. Originally it may have assumed the outward form of voluntary presents, or of a compulsory levy representing a certain proportion of their products. This latter method survived in Ancient Egypt, even after statecraft and economy had attained a relatively advanced stage. In other communities at a much less advanced phase of evolution the disadvantage of collecting tribute in the form of sundry objects must have been realized, and the means in which the tribute was payable came to be prescribed by the chief. Or even if that stage was not reached the chief may have assessed in some unit of account the amount payable, even though actual payment was continued to be made in sundry products. According to Cassel, "the exacting of tribute of various kinds probably led very early to a definite tariff scheme of certain commodities which were accepted in payment."[5]

Tribute and booty secured from other tribes is of considerable importance from the point of view of the origin of money. According to Laum, it was much more important than trade even at such an advanced stage of civilization as during the Homeric period.[6] Indeed, Helfferich goes so far as to say that trade only developed when two tribes found that their strength was approximately equal, so that neither was able to secure the goods of the other by force of arms.[7] The form in which tribute was to be paid was usually prescribed by the recipient. It tended to be a standardized form.

When a tribe had to pay tribute, ransom or blood money to another tribe, the amount was usually assessed among members of the tribe. Since all of them did not necessarily possess the objects in which payment was to be made, they were possibly allowed to contribute their own products on the basis of fixed ratios to the object in which the tribe had to pay.

Even before a definite means of payment or unit of account had emerged from the payment or receipt of tribute, the imposition of fines necessitated the determination of some units. While tribute may have been allowed to be paid in kind—that is, in the form of the produce the payer happened to possess—fines must have been fixed in a standardized form from an early stage. Etymological evidence supports the view that the fixing of fines was in some instances at any rate the origin of money. According to Semper, on the Pelew Islands every kind of payment is

[5]Cassel, p. 346.   [6]Laum, pp. 12-13.
[7]Helfferich, Vol. I, p. 6,

still called "penalty."[8] Nearer home, the German word *Geld* is said to
have originated from *Vergeltung* which word, as Londoners have reason
to remember from the days of "V" weapons, implies the settling of
scores, or revenge.

The fixing of the means of payment for fines must have largely contributed towards the adoption of a store of value. It is conceivable that
if it became known that a wealthy member of the community was fined,
and had to find a large number of oxen as an alternative to being executed, imprisoned or enslaved the price of oxen would be raised against
him. If he had enemies, they would seek to ensure that he paid an
exorbitant price, if indeed he was able to buy the oxen at all. And since
in primitive communities the reasons or excuses for fining a man were
manifold, it was advisable for anyone who could afford it to keep oxen
(or other objects in which fines were fixed) in order that he should be
prepared for that eventuality. Steady demand for such objects for such
payments was apt to lead to their adoption as a medium of exchange.

In a primitive community a chief can only uphold his prestige by
being liberal in giving away what he accumulates. Once his receipts
have become largely standardized he will make his payments also in the
form of the means fixed for his receipts. Or if he pays out different
objects in reward of the same services, the need for a unit of account
arises, in order to ensure more or less equal distribution.

Blood money is an extremely important institution in primitive
communities. It constituted practically the only brake to incessant
blood feuds when the State authority was not strong enough to prevent
individuals from taking the law into their own hands. The principle
under which every injury, from minor insults to murder, could be made
good through the payment of compensation to the injured party or his
relatives may appear to us mercenary, but amidst the then prevailing
conditions it had much to recommend it. Within the tribe or the nation,
the State authority confined itself to fixing the unit in which payment
was to be made or reckoned, to fixing the amounts payable for various
injuries and to enforcing the payment thus determined. Owing to the
frequency of injuries that had to be made good through the payment of
blood money, the object chosen as a means of payment was bound to be
in constant demand, if not for actual payments then at any rate for
provision for future contingencies. Blood money is a very ancient
institution; the chances are that it existed in many primitive communities long before trade conditions necessitated the adoption of a monetary unit.

The payment of blood money between tribes must have largely contributed towards the origin of inter-tribal currencies which, in turn,
must have led to the development of currencies on a nation-wide scale.
It provided probably the earliest inducement for the development of an

[8]Semper, p. 181. Quoted by Schurtz, p. 7.

agreed monetary unit between two communities. Much of our information concerning the monetary systems of the Middle Ages is derived from documentary evidence regarding the fixing of blood money, not only within the same tribe or nation but also between different tribes or nations. The conclusion of peace between two tribes was usually accompanied by a settlement of claims and counter-claims for the slaying and mutilation of members of the two tribes. This system worked out in a strange way. Since the victor usually inflicted heavier losses than the vanquished, he was called upon to pay a difference, so that for all practical purposes the victor paid reparations to the vanquished—unless the victory was so complete that terms were simply dictated by the victor.

When payment has to be made to another tribe it has to be made in some definite form prescribed by the recipient. We saw above that this necessitates assessment and collection tending to give rise to standard means of payment or at least to a standard of value. When a chief distributes booty or tribute or ransom collected from other tribes he has to apply a standard of value to secure equal distribution.

Chiefs may prescribe the means of payment for various forms of payment, either between their own subjects or between their subjects and members of another tribe. We saw above that the means of payment fixed for ransom and especially for blood money constitute an important contribution towards the evolution of money. There is also the necessity for assessing compensation paid to tribesmen who suffered a loss through hostile action by the rest of the tribe. Doughty's *Arabia Deserta* describes the way in which the tribesmen whose camels were lost in a raid were compensated by the tribe. The damage was spread over all tribesmen in proportion to their possessions, and it was assessed in camels, even though the possessions may have included also other beasts.

All these forms of political payments, or politically regulated unilateral payments must have contributed to no slight degree towards the evolution of a monetary unit. And once the means of payment have become standardized the need for securing the prescribed objects or for disposing of them must have largely contributed towards the evolution of barter. Those engaged in trade, if they felt the need for a medium of exchange or a standard of value, had only to apply to their requirements the money that was already in use for the purposes of political payments.

In South West Africa the Bergdama paid over a period an annual tribute to the Saan in the form of *dagga* cakes made of intoxicating herbs. As a result of this practice, the *dagga* cake became a medium of exchange among the Bergdama. There must have been many similar instances.

It is conceivable that in some instances at any rate the political authority fixed a means of payment for trading transactions long before the traders themselves had developed one for their own use. In case of deferred deliveries, it may have been considered necessary to fix an alternative means of discharging liabilities if, as a result of failure of crop or other contingencies, delivery became impossible. If at that stage a standardized means for political payments existed, it stands to reason that the political authority imposed it on the community for such commercial payments.

In a remarkably large number of ethnological instances, especially in the Pacific area, a means of payment has long been in use mainly for political purposes, but, even though it is suitable also for commercial purposes, trade continues to be conducted largely by barter. This fact is well worth bearing in mind. It means that in the communities concerned trade had not yet reached the stage at which it made the use of money indispensable. To the extent to which the need for a medium of exchange or a standard of value is felt, the unit used for political payments is employed. The fact that the use of that unit for political payment is general while its commercial employment is limited seems to indicate that the political use of such units preceded their commercial use. It is justified, therefore, to assume that in communities where the bulk of trade is conducted by barter in spite of the existence of a reasonably developed monetary system used mainly for political payments, money is definitely of political origin.

The political factor tends to contribute towards the origin of money also in a different way from the one vaguely indicated by Knapp's theory. In some instances units of payment appear to have been devised, not by the State authority but on private initiative mainly for the purpose of securing political influence and control. It is, of course, not easy to draw the line between political and other factors. But it seems safe to say that the primary object of the men's clubs or secret societies, which have played an important part in the origin of money in some communities in Oceania and Africa, is the acquisition of political power. Members who succeed in buying their way to leadership in such societies achieve thereby political power.

On Vanikolo, New Hebrides, smoked fibre mats were adopted primarily as means of payment for subscription to secret societies. Their other monetary functions are, admittedly, limited. On the other hand, the shell-money of the Banks Islands which was also originally adopted solely for subscription to secret societies became subsequently a medium of exchange and standard of value. Secret societies in Nigeria adopted their own currency, tin-tack-shaped iron pieces with arrow-like heads. This currency, too, became a medium of exchange to some extent. Since secret societies are a very ancient institution, it is possible that their special currencies were the first form of money used by the communities concerned.

CHAPTER 16

MATRIMONIAL ORIGIN

In addition to the possibility of commercial, religious or political origin of money, it is also necessary to consider the possibility of its origin and development from the primitive form of marriage. In many primitive communities the exchange of presents on the occasion of marriage plays a very important part in the turnover of goods. Sometimes there is a system of the reciprocal exchanges of goods between the family of the bridegroom and the bride, beginning with the betrothal and continuing long after the marriage. In most communities, however, the system is unilateral. It consists of the payment of bride money by the bridegroom to the bride's father. The origin of this system, which is the exact inverse of the equally mercenary modern system of dowries, lies in the economic value of women in primitive communities. Since their labour is transferred from their own family to that of the bridegroom it seems reasonable to primitive man that the gainer should compensate the loser. In certain parts of New Guinea bride money is paid in large earthenware jars, and the number of jars given corresponds to three years' output of jars by a woman.

Utilitarian considerations are, of course, not alone in determining the system. Payment of bride money was also influenced by questions of prestige. Bride money came to occupy such an important place in primitive social system that in many communities its non-payment could make a marriage legally invalid and children derived from it illegitimate. The opening motive of the story of Ibsen's drama *The Vikings at Helgeland*, which is based on Scandinavian mythology, is largely built on this tradition. The rule still exists, or existed until recently, among some South African tribes, in which extra-marital sexual relations could be legitimized by the payment of the required number of heads of cattle representing the bride price.

In Africa, in the Pacific Isles, among the Latin American Indians and Central Asiatic nomads, young men wanting to marry had to earn and save in order to be able to buy their bride and had to accumulate their savings in the form of the objects used for bride money. Alternatively, they had to borrow these objects and repay them later. Whichever solution was chosen, the practice largely contributed to the development of a primitive monetary system. Young men and their families would have to accumulate the objects in question for the purpose of bride money, and would, therefore, accept them in payment for goods and services in preference to most other objects. Anyone possessing such objects could safely rely on being able to acquire in exchange for them practically anything they wanted. These objects also tended to become a favourite standard of deferred payments. Even when payment was made in other forms it was often reckoned in terms of such objects, because of their importance in their capacity as means of payment of bride money.

As a general rule, only highly valued objects were accepted as bride money. Cattle, of course, were a favourite bride money among many pastoral tribes. In communities which had several types of money only that of the highest value was usually accepted as bride money. Occasionally a special money was adopted for the purpose, which, owing to the high esteem in which it was held, was not meant to be used for commercial transactions. Almost invariably the objects serving as bride money were favourite stores of value.

Bride money, like blood money or tributes, contributed towards the development of international currencies, particularly where tribes practised the system of exogamic marriage. Young men of such communities had to choose their bride from outside their tribe or group, and bride money had to be paid not in terms of bridegroom's tribal money, but in that of the bride's. And since there were brides and bridegrooms in each tribe, this gradually led to the development of monetary units usable in both communities. Possibly this system may have been responsible for the eventual adoption of the same monetary units in the wider sphere of a race or a nation.

In internal traffic the object used as bride money was liable to become a medium of exchange, precisely because of the high degree of its acceptability resulting from its use of bride money. It is, of course, not easy to ascertain in most instances whether the choice of bride money was the cause or the result of the choice of a medium of exchange. Conceivably in many cases the unit in which bride money was payable was simply the object which had already come to be adoption previously as a favourite medium of exchange, and which had thus already been performing monetary functions.

The fact that in many communities certain standardized means of payment are used systematically as bride money while trade is transacted mostly by barter seems to indicate that primitive communities are inclined to adopt standardized means of payment as bride money before they feel the need of adopting a medium of exchange. As for the precedence as between means of payment for religious, political and matrimonial purposes, the question is difficult if not impossible to decide, because in the large majority of instances the same objects were in general use for all non-commercial purposes.

In many instances certain primitive units remained in use as bride money, blood money or fine long after more advanced monetary units had been adopted for commercial exchanges. This was so in Ancient Greece where the payment of fines in sheep persisted to the days of Solon, though coins had already been in use for two centuries. Likewise, the religious and ceremonial use of primitive currencies often survived their commercial use. This fact may lead to the inference that the general use of certain primitive currencies for non-commercial purposes at a time when trade was transacted mostly by barter may simply mean that the currencies in question, having originated through trade, were subsequently adopted for non-commercial use, while their commercial use was largely discontinued. This inference is, however, false. In instances when the non-commercial use of money is known to have survived its commercial use, this was usually due to the adoption of a more advanced type of money for commercial purposes. It seems unlikely that a monetary system should have been discarded by trade for the sake of returning to barter, while it was retained for centuries for non-commercial payments.

The matrimonial factor tends to lead to the adoption of a medium of exchange in communities where affinal exchanges are practised. In many primitive communities where the profit-motive fails to provide the required stimulus to induce the savages to produce beyond their immediate requirements, an incentive has been developed through the adoption of a system under which marriage is preceded by the exchange of goods. Among the Manus in New Guinea, in Trobriand and other parts of the Pacific, the families of the bridegroom and the bride exchange certain traditionally determined objects which usually include the shell or teeth money used for non-commercial purposes in the community. The amounts involved are very considerable. This practice, even more perhaps than the unilateral payment of bride money, tends to popularize the objects in question, and, through the increase of the turnover in goods where there would otherwise be practically none, it tends to develop a commercial spirit which should prepare the way for the subsequent adoption of money for the requirements of trade.

PART III: THE VALUE OF PRIMITIVE MONEY

PRIMITIVE V. MODERN MONETARY THEORY

" J UST as the theory of value is regarded as the heart of economics, so the theory of the value of money may be considered as the central point of monetary theory."[1] We have now reached the stage at which we have to answer the question whether, and to what extent, the theories of the value of money, elaborated on the basis of the study of modern money, apply to primitive money. Our task is to examine whether there is any fundamental difference between the behaviour of primitive and modern money. Furthermore, we must examine the question whether, in so far as modern monetary theory cannot be fully applied, certain reservations will meet the case or whether the difference calls for the elaboration of a totally different set of principles.

To answer this question, we have first to examine briefly the principal modern theories of the value of money. The object of this task is two-fold. We must try to ascertain how far they are suitable for explaining changes in the value of primitive money, and also how far the evidence concerning the value of primitive money tends to confirm the theories based until now almost entirely on the behaviour of modern money in a small number of modern communities during the past century or two. It is the object of this book to extend the scope of our enquiry over a very large number of communities, and over a period of some five thousand years. The following are the theories which come under our scrutiny.

1. Supply and Demand Theory.
2. Quantity Theory.
3. Quality Theory.
4. Cost of Production Theory.
5. State Theory.
6. Gresham's Law.

To avoid overburdening this section, we have abstained from dealing with the almost infinite variety of versions that exist in respect of each of these theories. As far as possible we have presented simplified versions of them. It would be futile to try to apply to primitive conditions elaborate Keynesian theories which can obviously apply to modern conditions only.

[1]Hoyt, p. 4.

This part of our task is probably the most difficult in the entire study of our subject. "We lack nearly all the essential data for the understanding of the phenomena of prices and values in primitive society," states Herskovits, "even though the discussion of these matters has found its way into the literature of both economics and anthropology."[2] Price statistics are virtually non-existent; in a relatively few instances there is documentary evidence enabling us to follow the trend of individual prices to a reasonable degree, but means for measuring changes in the general price level are absent. But even if we possessed complete series of index numbers, it would not help us very far, owing to the absence of data about changes in the volume of primitive money. Most primitive currencies were not issued by any central authority but came into circulation through many private channels. Even in so far as the political authority was responsible for the issue of primitive money, it did not publish any returns or keep records. Changes in the quality or intrinsic value of primitive currencies are also usually less easily traceable by the student of a later generation than the degrees of debasements of coinage are. Similarly, factual material on the cost of production of primitive money is virtually unobtainable.

When we come to factors such as the volume of goods and services available for purchase, the velocity of circulation, the relative extent to which trade is transacted by barter and with the aid of primitive money, the relative extent to which each of the several primitive currencies simultaneously in circulation is used as a medium of exchange, or the relative extent to which primitive money is used for commercial and non-commercial payments, we have not even the elements of the statistical material required for our purpose. Some of these factors are virtually non-existent in a modern currency system. It is their existence in primitive currency systems that makes the examination of the latter so much more difficult from the point of view of elaborating a theory of value of money.

However, the examination of trends in primitive communities, or even in advanced communities using primitive money, does not call for statistical material to anything like the same degree as the examination of modern monetary development does. The question whether a rise in prices by five per cent or ten per cent is inflationary or not can only be discussed with the aid of an array of figures relating to note circulation, deposits, credits, wholesale and retail prices, wages, cost of living, etc. In matters of primitive currency it would be idle to attempt to investigate such minor changes in prices—even if we were in a position to ascertain them at all. And when it comes to spectacular movements, such as the depreciation of cowries in Western Sudan or of brass bars in the Congo, then the presence of an inflationary expansion of the

[2]Herskovits, p. 158.

currency is evident even in the absence of statistical material. The factual material presented in the Ethnological and Historical Sections of this book should go a long way, even in the absence of statistics, towards enabling us to examine the possibility of applying modern monetary theories to primitive money and that of applying the experience with primitive money to modern monetary theory.

It will be seen that each of the above-mentioned theories contains elements which hold good for primitive money, in spite of the difference in conditions. In many instances the difference between the extent to which they are valid concerning primitive and modern money is a matter of degree. In some respects, however, the theories elaborated to suit modern conditions cannot be fitted at all to primitive conditions. To that extent it is necessary to supplement modern theory of the value of money by the addition of rules that apply specially and exclusively to primitive money. The aspects of primitive money that have to be thus covered are as follows:—

1. Dual monetary and non-monetary role of primitive money.
2. Price levels in semi-natural economies.
3. Multiplicity of primitive money.
4. Limited scope of primitive money.

It will appear that modern monetary economics which have failed to account adequately for the origin and development of primitive money and to describe and analyse the primitive monetary system, have failed to provide a complete theoretical explanation of their behaviour relating to prices. The movements of prices in primitive communities cannot be explained fully on the basis of modern monetary theories. On the other hand, it will appear that experience with primitive money goes a long way towards confirming modern monetary theory— provided that the difference between primitive and modern conditions are duly borne in mind.

CHAPTER 18

THE SUPPLY AND DEMAND THEORY

Both the nominalist school and the commodity school of monetary theorists agree that the quantity of money is liable to affect its value. They arrived at this conclusion, however, through totally different lines of approach. According to the commodity theory, money is like any other commodity and its value is therefore naturally affected by supply and demand. According to the nominalist school, money has no intrinsic value, it is merely an abstract claim on commodities in general, and the total volume of claims determine the purchasing power of a unit. The result of the difference between the two lines of approach is that while the nominalists believe in the quantity theory of money, the commodity theorists believe in the supply and demand theory. The difference between the two theories is largely one of emphasis and method of approach. The quantity theory allows not only for the volume of money and the volume of goods, but also for the velocity of circulation of money. Even this difference is largely one of form rather than of substance; for, after all, the supply of money is determined by two factors: its quantity and the velocity of its circulation.

Many authors when discussing the supply and demand of money have in mind the supply of lendable money and the demand for it by borrowers in the money market. In this sense supply and demand affects of course the interest rates only, although in its indirect effect it may react on the value of money. We are not concerned here with this aspect of the supply and demand theory. According to the version we are dealing with here, the value of money is determinated by the supply available for spending and the demand represented by the value of goods and services available for sale, and by the requirements for noncommercial payments. The supply and demand theory links up with the cost of production theory since the cost of production of money affects its supply, and changes in the value of money due to the supply and demand factor are liable to react on the cost of production. The supply and demand theory also links up with the quality theory inasmuch as money with intrinsic value cannot depreciate for any length of time below its commodity value.

When trying to apply the supply and demand theory to primitive money, we must bear in mind that supply and demand was not originally the factor necessarily determining the value of money. It was probably preceded in many instances by the system of fixed exchange parities. The supply and demand factor developed gradually over centuries. Carlile, when dealing with this point, observes that this is not easily realized by modern minds trained through many centuries by the operation of the monetary system.[1]

The value of primitive money in its earliest stages must have been characterized by a high degree of rigidity. Even in some comparatively advanced primitive monetary systems that rigidity continues to prevail. On Rossel Island, for instance, the value of each unit of the complicated currency system is determined by custom and is unaffected by the law of supply and demand. Likewise on the Sulu Archipelago, the value of the cotton cloth currency was fixed by the Sultan and was independent of supply and demand. On the other hand, in other instances the value of primitive currencies became extremely sensitive to changes in the relation between supply and demand. Many travellers in Africa found that if the expedition that preceded them used certain type of primitive money the prices in terms of that money had risen considerably. This

[1]Carlile, p. 144.

sensitiveness of prices to relatively moderate changes in the relation between supply and demand was due partly to the smallness of the community in which the primitive currency was used. In a large country temporary or local changes of the quantity of money or of the volume of goods available for sale are moderated by the tendency towards the equalization of their effect, owing to the possibility of absorption of the surplus money by other districts of the country or of sending supplies to the district where they are short. In a small community there is, however, no opportunity for a diffusion of the effect of local changes which, however temporary, are liable to produce, therefore, their maximum effect.

Even if the currency used is largely international, its value is liable to fluctuate widely if owing to geographical conditions the community in question is to a large degree isolated. Thus the value of cowries differed widely in various parts of French West Africa owing to the distance between the various communities and the difficulty of transport, as a result of which the supply and demand factor was liable to affect cowries independently in each community which was isolated to a large extent from other communities using the same currency.

In many instances primitive currencies are liable to react particularly strongly to the supply and demand factor because they are not used to any considerable extent as stores of value. Their depreciation does not lead to any increased demand for hoarding purposes. On the other hand, in a large number of instances, when primitive money is used extensively as a store of value or as an ornament, or for sacrificial requirements, any increase of its quantity can easily be absorbed by an increase of demand for such use. Conversely, the increase in the value of a currency through its short supply is liable to lead to de-hoarding.

As Horace White reminds us, the value of money depends on the non-monetary as well as monetary demand for it.[2] While the non-monetary demand for modern money is usually negligible in modern communities, it is apt to be very substantial in primitive communities, or in modern communities using primitive currency. The dual role of primitive money is dealt with in detail in a separate chapter. It is essential to realize in dealing with the supply and demand theory that in instances in which there is a non-commercial demand for money it is liable to absorb easily any surplus of supply which in other circumstances would lead to a sharp depreciation. When money is only used for monetary purposes the absorbing capacity of the community depends on the general volume of goods and services available for sale. If, at the same time, there are non-commercial or non-monetary uses for it, then the surplus is apt to be sterilized by the specific demand for such purposes. On the other hand, non-monetary supplies are liable to

[2]Horace White, p. 10.

be converted for monetary use as a result of an appreciation. The ever-present possibility of switching from monetary to non-monetary use and *vice versa* is an important factor in primitive monetary theory.

There are many ethnological instances of the failure of an increase in the supply of money producing a corresponding depreciation of its value. For instance, the heavy influx of stone money in Yap brought about by shipments of Captain O'Keefe did not lead to its depreciation. Nor did the importation of pigs by Europeans on a large scale to the New Hebrides bring about even a halt in the rise in their price. The explanation is that on Yap the influx of stone money was easily absorbed, thanks to the strong desire of the natives to possess such stones as a symbol of wealth. In New Hebrides the increase in the number of pigs merely provided the natives with an opportunity of increasing the number used for sacrificial purposes. Any primitive money which is a favoured possession of the natives is not easily liable to depreciation simply because the desire to possess it induces the savages to work harder and thus to increase the volume of goods available for sale. In any case, the surplus of such kinds of currencies is not likely to remain long in monetary circulation. It is either destroyed through sacrifices, or hoarded for considerations of prestige or it is displayed as decoration or ornament.

On the other hand, there are many instances showing that primitive currencies, in given circumstances, are apt to be sensitive to the influence of supply and demand. For example, the relative value of slave currency and salt currency tended to change strongly in favour of the latter, whenever an inter-tribal war broke out, in anticipation of the capture of the number of defeated opponents, who would become available for monetary purposes, and also owing to the increased demand for salt currency for military requirements. There are many similar instances quoted in the next chapter examining the application of the quantity theory to primitive money.

Requirements arising from non-commercial payments are liable to affect the value of money in the same way as requirements for the purchase of goods or the payment for services. This factor is apt to be overlooked by modern monetary theory, even though it is of considerable importance even in modern conditions. In primitive communities it is of the utmost importance. The imposition of tribute on a tribe is bound to raise the value of the money in which the tribute is payable. We saw in the Ethnological Section how the value of cowries in Dahomey and elsewhere fluctuated according to requirements for tax payments. An important death feast tends to create a strong demand for the currency used for sacrificial requirements. The payment for brides is an important factor influencing the supply and demand of primitive money.

From the foregoing it is evident that the extent to which the supply and demand theory operates in the systems of primitive money varies widely. There are currencies of extreme rigidity and others of extreme elasticity. Nevertheless, as a broad principle, the supply and demand theory may be considered as being substantially valid in the large majority of instances, even though the normal working is often hampered by rigidities resulting from tribal laws or custom.

CHAPTER 19

THE QUANTITY THEORY

The quantity theory of money is in substance a sophisticated application of the old supply and demand theory. It has been formulated in various ways, but its fundamental principle is that, other things being equal, the price level changes proportionately to changes in the volume of money.[1] The main difference between this theory and the supply and demand theory is that the quantity theory lays more stress on the money factor and is inclined to ignore or underrate the goods factor. There is also a new factor introduced: the "velocity of circulation," the existence of which as a separate factor is ignored by the supply and demand theory.

The extent to which the quantity theory is valid in primitive communities varies widely. As we saw in the last chapter dealing with the supply and demand theory, in some instances it is nearly inoperative, owing to the rigidity of the exchange value of goods. The price of objects which are regularly bartered are in some communities fixed by tribal law or custom, or simply they remain unchanged over long periods through the intertia that characterizes many primitive economies. In other primitive communities, on the other hand, prices are very sensitive to the influence of supply and demand. In some relatively advanced communities employing primitive currencies, price control was at times enforced. Such was the case for instance with Babylonia, Assyria and the Hittite Empire.

In addition to the rigidities prevailing in many primitive economies, the dual role played by money in primitive communities is also apt to interfere with the normal working of the quantity theory. In a large number of instances the objects or materials used for monetary purposes are also used for non-monetary purposes. To over-simplify a complicated formula, in modern society the quantity of money is on one side of the scales and the quantity of goods available for sale is on the other. With primitive currency, on the other hand, money is not

[1] Irving Fisher, *The Purchasing Power of Money* (Revised Edition, New York, 1920), *passim*.

AA

exclusively on the monetary side of the scales but partly also on the goods side. Fluctuations in the non-monetary demand for primitive currency are apt to vitiate the working of the quantity theory. Instances of such complications were provided by the fluctuation in the silver price of barley, which was also a currency with an officially fixed parity in relation to silver in Babylonia, and by the fluctuation in the price of rice in Japan during the period when it was largely used as a currency.

It is difficult enough to provide reasonably complete statistical evidence in support of the quantity theory even if applied to a modern community. When it comes to a community with a primitive currency the task becomes as hopeless as the solution of an equation with four unknown factors. Take, for instance, the case of Babylonia. We know that there was a secular trend for the depreciation of silver in terms of all commodities. Since, however, silver was not issued as a rule by the State but was put into circulation privately, there can be no statistical information about the increase in its quantity. While the rise in prices must have been largely in accordance with the principles of the quantity theory, we can only assume this, without being able to prove it statistically.

Another disturbing factor is the multiplicity of currencies in a primitive community. If there is an increase in the quantity of one monetary material without any change in the total of all monetary materials there is no reason for a general rise in prices though there may be a rise in terms of that particular currency accompanied by a depreciation of that currency in terms of other currencies.

There are, nevertheless, many instances in primitive communities which illustrate the validity of the quantity theory of money. At the beginning of this century, dogs' teeth on the Admiralty Islands depreciated following on their large-scale import by traders from China and Turkey. Captain Cook remarked on the depreciation of red feathers following on the increase of their supply. In the interior of New Guinea Wirz registered a marked depreciation of cowries after only a few days of trading during the course of which his expedition made purchases with them. In Mongolia the value of the tea brick currency depends largely on an increase in the local supply. The ease with which the value of beads and other means of payment used by early travellers in Eastern and Central Africa responded to the volume available was frequently testified from first-hand information. In Uganda cowries were originally very valuable; the price of a woman was two cowries. Later, however, with the wholesale influx during the second half of the 19th century, they depreciated. In Bagirmi after a successful slave raid the purchasing power of the slave currency depreciated. In the Belgian Congo brass rods depreciated sharply, partly owing to their debasement but largely owing to the increase of their quantity. In North America the inflation of *wampum* resulting from the increase of its output with the aid of modern tools led to its depreciation. The tobacco-currency of the colonists, too, fell sharply in value, owing to the increase of its production.

Conversely, a decline in the volume of primitive money led in many known instances to a rise in its value. Thus, the ban on the import of gongs and drums in Alor brought about their appreciation. In Wadai at the time of Nachtigal's visit the shortage of cotton cloth currency produced a deflationary effect: goods were difficult to sell and prices were low. In Nigeria after 1900 the value of cowries recovered for a time, owing to the ban on their import.

For all but a few of the above instances statistical evidence is entirely absent, and in no case is it adequate to enable us to ascertain the approximate extent to which prices had moved in sympathy with changes in the quantity of money. Nevertheless, it is evident that in communities where the price structure was not unduly rigid there was a fundamental trend of prices behaving in accordance with the quantity theory. Indeed, large-scale inflation is known to have overcome eventually the rigidity of the price structure in more than one primitive community.

When we come to examine the influence of the velocity of circulation we are entirely in the dark. Even in a modern country it is an obscure factor. In a primitive community the velocity of circulation of money is apt to vary widely according to the use to which money is put. In communities where some form of the system of competitive exchanges is in operation the velocity of circulation is apt to be very high. This does not mean, however, that prices in such communities have necessarily a rising tendency on account of that. For a large proportion of the transactions is purely "financial" and not commercial. The same pig may change hands in the New Hebrides several times within a few hours, in settlement of debts, without affecting the price of goods in terms of pigs, any more than the high velocity of circulation of money in Wall Street or in the Monte Carlo Casino affects the price level.

In communities where primitive currency is mainly used as a store of value or as ornament (the latter is called "dead money" in West Africa), its velocity of circulation is apt to be very slow. In Pelew the velocity of circulation of the bead currency is increased artificially by social custom forcing everybody to spend freely. A similar custom prevails also in many other primitive communities. In large backward countries the velocity of circulation is apt to be slow, owing to the sparsity of the population or the high degree of self-sufficiency of household and other small economic units. In the Ancient Period and early Middle Ages the velocity of circulation was apt to be slow.

In the absence of any adequate statistical evidence for the existence of any arithmetical relation between prices and their factors under the quantity theory, we have to confine ourselves to an examination of the factors liable to affect the quantity of money in primitive communities:—

1. *The caprices of nature.* Much has been said about the extent to which modern monetary systems based on precious metals are exposed to the caprices of nature in the form of an increase or decrease of output of gold or silver mines. Primitive communities are often exposed to similar factors to an incomparably higher degree. The quantity of the annual output of gold never represents more than a small fraction of the total stocks available, so that changes in the total quantity are apt to be slow. On the other hand, the quantity of the various materials and objects used for monetary purposes in primitive communities is liable to wide fluctuation through natural causes. The results of hunting and fishing will affect that quantity of fur and fish currencies which are thus bound to be affected by the caprices of nature. The supply of livestock serving as currency is exposed to wide fluctuations through changes in the animal birthrate and even more through animal diseases, or through deficiency that might develop in the supply of animal fodder and water. The quantity of agricultural products serving as money depends, of course, on the annual crop which usually represents a large proportion of the monetary stocks of those products. Even the quantity of monetary industrial products is exposed to fluctuations, since the supply of raw materials or labour is bound to have its ups and downs. The quantity of metallic currencies naturally depends on the output of mines. Nevertheless, as a general rule, really wide fluctuations in the quantity of primitive currencies, comparable with those experienced by paper currencies, do not occur until the establishment of contact with more advanced communities which are in a position to increase considerably the production or import of the monetary material, or to reduce it considerably by acquiring it in exchange for modern goods.

2. *The degree of monetary use of the materials concerned.* The mere fact that a certain material is chosen as a primitive currency tends to increase its output—within the limits imposed by nature and by its cost of production—owing to the fact that its monetization secures for it a steady and dependable demand. The relative extent to which the material is adopted for monetary purposes is liable to changes. It is affected by the rate at which barter is abandoned for the sake of primitive money economy. When there are several monetary materials in operation their relative monetary role is apt to change from time to time and such changes are liable to affect the extent to which their monetary use affects production. As and when modern money displaces primitive money, the quantity of the latter is apt to decline owing to the decline of demand. This would not affect, however, its purchasing power, for simultaneously with the decline of its volume there is also a narrowing of its sphere of use.

3. *The valuation of monetary materials.* The quantity of monetary materials is likely to be affected according to whether it is overvalued or undervalued in terms of commodities, or in terms of other primitive

currencies. Over-valuation tends to encourage its production and import since those who possess it can get better value for their over-valued money. Under-valuation tends to reduce production and encourage export and hoarding, as holders do not get the full value for their money when they spend it. Advanced communities using primitive money are particularly apt to react to over-valuation or under-valuation. Over-production of tobacco in the early American colonies was due to the high official value fixed for that currency.

4. *Technical progress.* Improved methods of production enable primitive communities to increase their output of monetary materials, and the same result is achieved by better economic organization. The increase of the quantity of *wampum* as a result of the introduction of modern tools to manufacture it is the best-known instance for the working of this factor.

5. *Influx of primitive currencies.* This is usually effected by trade with more advanced communities. In many instances advanced traders took advantage of the existence of primitive currencies for the acquisition of the goods of primitive communities at a low cost, by supplying them on a large scale with that currency. Apart from the advantage of being able to produce such objects with the aid of modern machinery, the advanced community also stands to benefit by the additional value derived by that article out of its monetary use. While in its country of origin its value is determined by its non-monetary employment, in its country of destination its value derived from non-monetary use is increased through its over-valuation due to its monetary use.

6. *Export of primitive currencies.* In so far as a primitive currency is purely internal its quantity is unaffected by the trade balance. If, however, it happens to be an exportable commodity, with or without monetary use abroad, the effect of changes in foreign demand is apt to be strong. If the foreign demand for a primitive currency falls, larger supplies accumulate at home, and its purchasing power declines. This was the case with beaver skins in the American colonies during the 17th century.

7. *The consumption of the monetary material.* Since a large proportion of primitive currencies can be used for non-monetary purposes, monetary supplies are naturally affected by the degree to which they are consumed or otherwise diverted for non-monetary purposes. Over-valuation tends to discourage non-monetary use, under-valuation tends to encourage it. Increase or decrease of the ornamental use of monetary materials is an important factor affecting the quantity of primitive currencies.

8. *Wastage.* Many primitive monetary materials are far from being non-perishable, and even though they may be consumed before they perish, a proportion of them is liable to be held for monetary use too long to be fit to be converted for non-monetary use. Wear and tear

through monetary use is also an important cause of wastage. Shells and ornamental currencies in general are apt to lose their monetary character after a while through wear and tear. In addition to natural wastage, primitive currencies are apt to be destroyed through sacrifices, or burial with the dead.

9. *Hoarding.* In so far as a primitive currency fulfils the function of store of value the fluctuation in the hoarding demand affects the quantity available for current monetary purposes. As in modern communities using modern money, the quantity hoarded is, however, liable to affect the purchasing power of the primitive currency, even if it is not in actual use, by its mere existence. Large quantities of primitive money are apt to disappear altogether as a result of hoarding.

10. *Incentive to increase the quantity of primitive currency.* Apart from the degree of over-valuation there may be other factors stimulating the production or import of primitive currencies. New kinds of goods may become available or purchasable with that currency.

11. *The political factor.* The quantity of primitive currency is apt to be affected by war. The victorious tribes may return home laden with spoils which may include quantities of the monetary material. They may also impose a tribute on the vanquished. The latter's monetary stock may thus become depleted. Changes of territory are apt to lead to increase the relative supplies of money. A conqueror may absorb populations which did not possess this currency.[2] As a result, the volume of money which until then was adequate may become insufficient to cover the increased requirements, unless the conquered race can continue to use its own currency.

12. *Debasement.* In many instances it is possible to increase the quantity of primitive currency by a deterioration in its quality or by reducing its size. The reduction in the length of brass rods in the Congo is an outstanding example. Another form of debasement is the sacrificing of quality in the production of monetary material, for the sake of quantity.

13. *Adoption of additional types of money.* If a community adopts new types of primitive currency without at the same time displacing wholly or partly the old currency, the total volume of its monetary circulation increases. This device is often resorted to by advanced communities, in preference to suffering the disadvantages of an inadequate supply of modern money.

14. *Development of credit.* The development of a credit system in certain primitive communities tends to lead to an increase in the volume of its money. In many cases the total amount of credit outstanding at any given moment is several times larger than the volume of its currency. There are indications that such credit inflation tends to depreciate the purchasing power of the unit, even if an expanded volume of credit

[2]Burns, pp. 315-6.

is not used for the purchase of goods. The savages grow used to thinking in terms of large figures, and prices rise accordingly.

All the above factors, through their influence on the quantity of primitive currencies tend to influence the price level in primitive communities. In addition, in many instances the monetary policy followed by the State authorities also affects the price level through its influence on the volume of primitive currencies. This subject will be dealt with in a later chapter.

CHAPTER 20

THE QUALITY THEORY

According to the quality theory of money the purchasing power of a currency is determined by its intrinsic value. In modern monetary literature this theory is better known under the name of "metallistic" theory, according to which the value of money is determined by the commodity value of the metal it contains. It is also known as "commodity theory." Applied to paper money, this conception is expressed in the metallist theory by the principle that the purchasing power of coins depends on the value of the precious metals they contain, and the purchasing power of notes depends on their convertibility, or their prospect of convertibility, into precious metals.

As often as not primitive money is non-metallic. Therefore the name of "metallistic" theory could not apply generally. Nor is the name "commodity" theory adequate for primitive money. For the intrinsic value of primitive currencies is not always represented by their commodity value. Often it is a prestige value, or sentimental value, or religious value.[1] Such currencies cannot be described as commodities, but so long as they possess a value that is not derived from their monetary use they may be said to have intrinsic value.

Barter is necessarily based on intrinsic values, or at any rate on the subjective estimate of relative intrinsic values by the parties concerned, influenced by the importance and urgency of requirements and the degree of superfluity of the goods offered, by considerations of supply and demand and cost of production. So long as a primitive currency is on the borderline between medium of barter and medium of exchange, its purchasing power is claimed to depend on its intrinsic value in this sense of the term. Many economists hold the view that communities using primitive currencies have not yet emerged from the state of natural economy and that the use of primitive currencies is an advanced form of barter. Those who accept this conception must logically conclude from it that intrinsic value must determine the purchasing power of all

[1]"Wampum did not command regard because used as money. It was used as money because for other reasons it already commanded regard." Laughlin, p. 12.

primitive currencies. For in barter neither the goods given nor those received are over-valued on account of any additional demand due to monetary use. In so far as their exchange rates deviate from the arithmetical ratio between their intrinsic values this is attributed to their relative scarcity or abundance, or to various other circumstances, but not to any supplementary value due to their monetization—for the simple reason that they have not become monetized.

The application of this conception to primitive money is in contradiction to irrefutable factual evidence. Beyond doubt, primitive currencies tend to have a high degree of intrinsic value—that is, a high percentage of their value is due to their non-monetary use. Livestock standards, for instance, are based on the high valuation of livestock in pastoral and agricultural communities. All commodity currencies have arisen because of the high esteem in which the staple products of the community concerned stood, either because these products were also staple articles of consumption or because they were staple exports with practically unlimited marketing possibilities. Utensils, weapons or ornaments assumed the role of money because of the non-monetary use of these objects. Textiles assumed the role of a medium of exchange because of their practical value. Metals by weight or size were accepted in payment because they had a full intrinsic value as raw materials.

This does not necessarily mean, however, that in all instances these currencies necessarily changed hands on the basis of their commodity values. In any case, their monetary use tended to increase their commodity value beyond the level justified by non-monetary use alone, through diverting from non-monetary use a large proportion of the available supplies. In the long run this tendency was often offset by the effects of an increased output due to the over-valuation of the objects in question. During a transition period, however, their commodity value is apt to be above the level justified by non-monetary supply and demand. It is open to argument whether currencies changing hands on the basis of this increased commodity value may be claimed to have full intrinsic value, or whether that part of their value which is due to their monetary use must be considered to be of a fiduciary character. Since gold coins are considered to possess full intrinsic value, notwithstanding the fact that monetary demand is responsible for a large proportion of their value, it seems reasonable to apply the same principle to primitive currencies. This means that only currencies accepted at a value in excess of their commodity value, irrespective of whether this latter is due to non-monetary or monetary demand, may be said to be partly fiduciary in character.

There are many instances in which primitive currencies are accepted at a value in excess of their commodity value even in this sense of the term. In the application of the livestock standards, for example, there was an inevitable tendency to use the most inferior animals. This in itself did not necessarily increase the nominal value of the livestock currency above its intrinsic value, for the prices of other goods in terms of livestock tended to adjust themselves to the deterioration of the cattle. On the other hand, there are instances of commodity currencies where a produce which has deteriorated in quality yet remained acceptable at full commodity value. This was the case with the rice currency in Burma in the 19th century. Even though only the worst quality of broken rice, unsuitable either for consumption or for seed, was used for monetary purposes, it was accepted as if the bags contained good rice. In the majority of instances, however, the debased produce became unacceptable sooner or later, or changed hands at a lower value. This happened with the tobacco currency of the American colonies.

Since prehistoric times there have been instances of utensils and weapons which were obviously not suitable for practical use owing to their shape or size. While the objects may possess some intrinsic value as raw materials, in view of the fact that some labour was spent on their manufacture they must have exchanged hands at a value above the commodity value of the raw material they contained. Therefore, they were in part at least fiduciary currencies. According to one theory, these currencies were originally useful objects with full intrinsic value. From being useful objects, changing hands at their full commodity value, they became mere symbols changing hands at above their commodity value because the recipient could use them for monetary purposes. Any recipient who chose to melt them down was apt to be out of pocket. Admittedly this was also the case with modern coinage in most countries where the cost of minting was added to the mint's purchase price of the precious metal in determining the face value of the coins. For that reason even such coined money in such countries must be regarded as being of partly fiduciary nature.

In many instances the strips of textile materials serving as currencies were cut so narrowly that their practical use became impossible without a considerable amount of labour. Shirts used as a currency in Central Africa were often too small even for children, or were of an extremely coarse texture scarcely fit to be used for dress.[2]

Metals changing hands by weight retained largely their full intrinsic value. An exception to this rule was provided by Sparta, which country, it was alleged, treated her iron bar currency in a special way in order to render it useless for all practical purposes.

There are many instances of primitive currencies which obviously could not have full intrinsic value. Indeed, some primitive communities came to use for monetary purposes objects which had no practical non-monetary use, and the value of which rested solely on their acceptability as currency. Some of the mat, shell and feather currencies were neither

[2]Barth, Vol. II, p. 446.

useful nor ornamental. Nor is it possible to assume that they deteriorated from some object that had originally a commodity value. They were valuable because their owners could depend on being able to use them for payments. For instance, the leather money of Carthage was obviously not the corruption of some former money which had full intrinsic value but was deliberately devised to be fiduciary currency.

In some instances a currency without full intrinsic value was adopted because of the possibility of converting it into objects with full intrinsic value. There was the shell money on the Solomon Islands which, according to Thurnwald, was freely accepted as currency owing to the possibility of its conversion into pigs.

From the point of view of the quality theory of money there seems to be no fundamental difference between primitive and modern money. In both cases the theory only holds good in part of the instances. In other instances currencies had no full instrinsic value, if indeed they had any at all. It is not even possible to ascertain any definite trend in monetary history indicating an increase or decrease of the fiduciary character of money in the course of the progress of civilization. Communities in the most diverse stage of civilization used currencies with or without full intrinsic value. Nevertheless, the quality theory is undoubtedly valid as a broad rule in a large proportion of instances. The commodity value is obviously the fundamental determining factor of the monetary value of metals changing hands by weight, and also that of the majority of staple product currencies.

In many instances the value of the primitive currencies declined as their quality deteriorated. Thus the feather money of Santa Cruz depreciated when the coils showed signs of wear. On the Solomon Islands old shell strings depreciate, and are exchanged for new at the rate of two for one. In Ethiopia the Galla examine salt bars carefully, to ensure that they are not broken or even cracked, before accepting them as currency.[3] There is, however, in most instances no way of ascertaining whether any definite ratio exists between the deterioration of the quality of primitive moneys and the price level in the communities using them. While it is possible to trace statistically the effect of the debasement of coinage on prices, any effort to elaborate similar statistical material in connection with the debasement or deterioration of primitive currencies would in most instances stand but little chance of succeeding. There was presumably in many communities a broad tendency for the price level to adapt itself to the decline of the intrinsic value of primitive currencies. Conservatism and inertia must have introduced, however, a degree of rigidity that excluded the possibility of close and speedy adjustment.

The extent to which the quality theory is valid varies from community

[3] E. Marno, *Reisen im Gebiete der Blauen und Weissen Nil* (Vienna, 1874), pp. 39 and 80. Quoted by Thilenius, p. 20.

to community, and from period to period. The notion that it is one of the fundamental laws of primitive human nature to insist on currencies with full intrinsic value cannot be upheld in the light of experience any more than the opposite notion that the adoption of full-valued currencies has been an unnatural product of civilization.

CHAPTER 21

THE COST OF PRODUCTION THEORY

According to the cost of production theory, the value of money is determined by its cost of production in the broadest sense of the term, which includes the cost of transport. Ricardo and Nassau Senior were among the early exponents of this theory which was also fully endorsed by Marx. In accordance with his theory of value, the latter maintained that the value of money is determined by the amount of labour devoted to its production, or, to be exact, by the ratio between the amount of labour required for the production of money and that required for the production of goods. This theory clearly implies the acceptance of the commodity theory of value, since the intrinsic value of money is largely determined by its cost of production. Modern Socialist writers have discarded this application of the Marxian theory of value to the value of money and give their preference to the claims theory, in particular Knapp's version of it, since the State theory of money is in keeping with the Socialist attitude towards the role of the State in economic life. On the other hand, many non-Socialist authors still adhere to some extent to the cost of production theory.

"Money is always the production of labour," writes Horace White. "Nobody would give that which has cost him labour in exchange for something which he could obtain without labour."[1] This view is, of course, contested by the adherents of the claims theory who hold the view that, irrespective of whether the object has cost labour or not, it would be accepted if the recipient were satisfied that he in turn could use it for the purchase of goods and services. Thus, the production of paper currency costs very little labour relative to its value, while the production of credit money costs practically no labour at all. The answer of the commodity theorists to this argument is that paper money and credit are not money at all.

The question is whether there is any strict or even approximate ratio between the cost of production of money recognized as such by the commodity theorists and its value. Various attempts have been made to apply the cost of production theory to explain the value of gold. There can be no doubt that there is a broad tendency towards the adjustment

[1]White, p. 9.

of the value of gold to its cost of production, owing to the fact that the profit made by goldfields working under relatively unfavourable conditions largely determines the volume of production, which again under the gold standard largely determines the purchasing power of money based on gold.

This tendency also affects primitive money to a large degree. The opinion expressed by White undoubtedly holds good concerning primitive currencies. They certainly have to be the production of labour in order to command a value. This is so even if there is an almost unlimited supply of the monetary objects available within easy reach of the community using it for monetary purposes. Even then, the monetary objects have to be collected, which involves labour. The coconut currency of Nicobar is available in practically unlimited supply, growing on the palm trees, and is accessible to anyone who wishes to take the trouble to collect it. Nevertheless, its collection is an effort and the natives would not undertake it unless its value were sufficiently high to make it worth their while. Similarly, shells used for monetary purposes are frequently available on not too distant beaches. Even so their collection needs effort and must be made worth while. These are the extreme instances in which the cost of labour involved in the production of primitive money is low. There are many instances in which the production of primitive money requires very considerable labour, and skilled labour at that. There are, for example, the fine mats serving as money in Samoa. Months and even years are spent in their production. Their value increased in recent years, because labour has become more expensive. In Mævo, New Hebrides, the value of smoked mats which serve as a limited currency tends to rise because of the cost of labour involved in supervising the smoking process. In Yap, the value of the large stones serving as a form of currency has increased because the cost of production and transport is now higher. The feather money of Santa Cruz is very valuable because of the immense trouble taken over its production. Even though shells can easily be found, the shell strings or shell rings serving as currencies in various parts of the Pacific are valuable because their production involves much skilled labour. This also accounted for the value of *wampum* and other shell currencies of the North American Indians.

It would be very difficult, however, to establish any strict arithmetical relationship between the cost of production of these and other primitive currencies and their value. In some instances some such relationship appears to be noticeable. For example, as was pointed out earlier, in certain parts of New Guinea the bride money is large earthenware pots representing the equivalent of the loss of a woman's work for three years. On the other hand, there are many instances of wide discrepancies between the cost of production and the value of primitive money. On the Banks Islands a woman can produce one fathom of shell string in a day, yet the value of a fathom is enough to pay for her vegetable food for five weeks. This is explained in part by the fact that while most shell strings used for monetary purposes in the Pacific are very carefully finished, on the Banks Islands quality is disregarded in favour of quantity, so that the production of shell money can proceed speedily and involves relatively little skilled labour. Shell money is grossly overvalued in relation to its cost of production on the Banks Islands. It was definitely under-valued, on the other hand, in New Jersey during the early period of colonization, because the cost of production of *wampum* which required much skilled labour was evidently above its value. It was only possible to produce a few pennyworth a day. The reason why *wampum* was produced in spite of this was that time had little or no value for the Red Indians engaged in its production. When European settlers introduced modern tools, the cost of production of *wampum* declined considerably. It became possible to produce it in much larger quantities, and its value depreciated. It is an arguable point whether the depreciation was primarily due to its lower cost or to its increased quantity. Even if the latter view is accepted, the fact remains that the increase of its quantity was the direct consequence of the lowering of the cost of production. It is a matter of opinion whether the lowering of cost of production would in itself have been able to reduce the value of *wampum* even if its quantity had remained unchanged owing to an inadequacy of the supply of shells available.

It was pointed out earlier in this chapter that the term cost of production is meant in the broadest sense of the term; it allows for the extent of skill and risk involved in the production of money. Above all, it includes the cost of transport which, with the backward conditions prevailing in countries using primitive money, is apt to be many times larger than the actual cost of production.

Senior, in considering the cost of production of money, allowed for this factor, for which he deserves credit, since in the case of gold, which he must have primarily had in mind, the cost of transport is but a negligible fraction of the cost of production proper. Even for silver the cost of transport is relatively small. When we come to primitive currencies other than precious metals it is apt to be very high indeed. It naturally tends to affect their value. In Yap the stone money imported from Guam is more valuable than the specimens imported from Pelew, because of the larger distance and higher cost of transport. The value of cloth, brass wire, beads and other currencies used until comparatively recently in East Africa, depended largely on the distance from Zanzibar or from the major mainland ports which supplied travellers with these currencies. The salt money of Ethiopia increases in value with the distance from the salt mines where it is produced. Marco Polo observed a similar increase in the value of salt money used in Medieval China. The value of cowries in Nigeria, the French Sudan and other parts of

West Africa rose with the distance from Lagos or other West African ports over which they were imported. Throughout Africa the cowries imported from the Maldives are more valuable than those imported from Zanzibar, partly because the cost of transport was much higher and partly because the Maldives shells are much smaller and therefore the inland transport of the same number of them is much less costly.

It would be idle, however, to try to establish a strict relation between the cost of transport and the value of primitive currencies. In Congo, the value of iron bars failed to keep pace with its exorbitant cost of transport which was so high that a porter was required for every eight shillings' worth of rods, and a few days' transport cost was equal to the full value of the currency transported. Brass bars in the Congo depreciated to such extent that travellers found life in primitive villages more expensive than in any luxury hotel in civilized cities. Their high cost of transport failed to maintain a corresponding purchasing power. On the other hand, in French Indo-China the iron bar currency was grossly over-valued even allowing for cost of transport. Cowries in various parts of Africa depreciated towards the end of the 19th century and the beginning of this century well below their cost of transport. As a result they became entirely confined to local use as currencies and could not be used for the requirements of distant trade, since the cost of transport would have absorbed their full value. Beyond doubt, the cost of transport constitutes a brake on the unlimited production of those kinds of primitive money which could otherwise be produced in practically unlimited quantities.

Marshall expressed the view that a money cannot be perfectly satisfactory unless its supply is controlled by the cost of production or by some other cause less unstable than custom or public ordinance.[2] Yet it is a generally recognized fact that the adoption of an object for monetary use tends to increase its value above its cost of production. This again tends to increase the volume of its production, at times to an embarrassing extent. The experience of the tobacco currency of Virginia and of other North American colonies provides a clear instance to illustrate this. At first the value of tobacco for monetary purposes was far too high and the result was such an increase of its production that its value slumped to a fraction of its original level. Since its supply was not adequately controlled by its cost of production, artificial methods had to be resorted to, not very successfully, for limiting the output. Marshall's principle asserts itself in the long run, but over fairly long transition periods over-valuation compared with cost of production is apt to increase the supply of currencies.

The reason why *wadmal* served satisfactorily as a currency for centuries in the Scandinavian countries in spite of the fact that anybody

[2]Marshall, p. 16.

was at liberty to produce it in unlimited quantities was probably the fact that its value was not abnormally higher than its cost of production. Had it been possible to produce it with the aid of modern machinery at a much lower cost, it would soon have reduced itself to absurdity.

This brings us to the consideration of the application of the marginal utility theory of value to the value of primitive money. Attempts to apply this theory to modern money have not been very successful. Indeed, it is perhaps permissible to suggest that they merely resulted in a "marginal futility theory," since many arguments used were on the borderline of being too futile to be worth discussing. On the other hand, there is a fair scope for the application of the marginal utility theory to the value of primitive money in conjunction with the cost of production theory. In a community where anybody is in a position to produce money for his requirements in unlimited quantities, the value of money is determined by the lowest level of purchasing power at which its production is still considered to be profitable. In order that the output of money should be maintained in accordance with the normal growth of requirements, there must be a sufficient margin of profit on its production to make its production just worth while. If the profit increases beyond that margin, the quantity of the output increases accordingly and the value of money declines. The profit on its production declines in consequence. If the profit declines below the margin at which it is just worth while to produce the currency, then the least efficient producers working at highest cost stop producing, the quantity of money declines, its value increases, thereby restoring the margin of profit.

The reason why the marginal utility theory is more capable of being applied to primitive money than to modern money is that the output of the former responds in many instances more freely to changes in the relation between value and cost of production. Modern currency legislation introduces an element of rigidity into the changes of the value of metallic currency, especially under the international gold standard which keeps price levels in various countries at a fair degree of equilibrium with each other. There is also the factor of vested interests at work. Owing to the large capital invested in gold mines, they are apt to be continued to be worked rather than being abandoned even if the margin of profit declines to a very low level.

Needless to say, in practice the system does not work so smoothly and flawlessly even in relation to primitive money. Changes in supply and demand are apt to cause the value of money to deviate considerably from the level determined by its marginal utility to the producers. It must also be borne in mind that the marginal utility theory is not applicable to the same extent to primitive money as to objects which do not fulfil any monetary functions, for money is wanted for other purposes than the purchase of goods and services. Its possession carries substantial advantages for the sake of which many people would be prepared to produce it even though the operation is not strictly economic. In the old American colonies it was found that tobacco was produced when it could not be produced profitably, simply in order to procure cash. The need for ugent repayment of debts may also induce debtors to produce money irrespective of cost. Finally, in primitive communities where the prestige value of the possession of money is exceptionally high, it is apt to be produced at a high level of cost compared with its value. When money is produced not by individuals but by the political authority, this marginal utility theory and the cost of production theory in general may be vitiated by the compelling necessity for these authorities to supply the community with currency even at a loss. Allowing for these considerations, it is nevertheless worth while to regard the cost of production theory and the marginal utility theory as contributing towards the theory of primitive money.

CHAPTER 22

THE STATE THEORY

The theory according to which money is the creation of the State is founded on the general nominalist conception under which money has no intrinsic value but is merely a claim on goods, and it circulates because it is generally acceptable as a medium of exchange. The acceptance of this principle does not necessarily lead, however, to the acceptance of the State theory. Many nominalists hold the view that money originated, not through a proclamation of State, but through social usage or trade practices. Marshall, in an attempt to combine the two nominalist conceptions, stated that the requirements of money "can be satisfied by anything which has obtained adequate prestige from custom or from the edict of a public authority, even though it is not capable of performing any other direct service and would be valueless but for this prestige."[1]

Knapp's State theory of money succeeded in overshadowing however, the other aspects of the nominalist conception. It was endorsed by many leading monetary theorists in Germany and abroad. Knapp's fundamental principle according to which "money is a creature of law" has already been dealt with to some extent in our chapter on the political origin of money. In the present chapter we are not concerned with the role of State in the origin of money but with its influence on the value of money. From the point of view with which we are concerned, Knapp's theory is interpreted in two different ways. According to some interpretations, Knapp's State theory merely claims that the State is

[1]Marshall, pp. 15-16.

able to determine the nominal value of a newly created monetary unit and to link it to the old unit by means of a fixed parity. According to another interpretation, Knapp implies that the State is in a position actually to determine the purchasing power of its monetary unit by accepting it in payment at a fixed value, by making payments with the aid of it at a fixed value, and by making its acceptance by private individuals compulsory.

In reality Knapp was more concerned with providing an explanation for the *validity* of money than for its value. His basic theory does not claim that the State has the power to fix the value of its currency. Such a claim would have become reduced to absurdity in the light of the German inflationist experience after the first World War. All he claims is that the State alone can secure the free acceptance of an object in discharge of liabilities.

Even this less ambitious claim is not borne out by the facts of the evidence concerning primitive money. There are innumerable historical and ethnological instances to show that both primitive and advanced communities used various primitive currencies with or without any intrinsic value in the absence of any act of State decreeing these objects to be legally money. Nevertheless, there can be no doubt that an act of State is capable of increasing greatly the acceptability of a monetary object. Even if a currency has no intrinsic value whatever, the possibility of its use for payments to the political authority goes a long way towards making it acceptable. If it has also some intrinsic value, then its validity for political payments should greatly increase its acceptability for non-political payments at a nominal value in excess of its intrinsic value, and even in excess of the value it would have possessed on the basis of purely commercial supply and demand.

This argument is carried very far by some monetary theorists who claim that acceptance of a money in taxation virtually amounts to its convertibility by the State.[2] Although this argument may be exaggerated there can be no doubt that the acceptance of an object for political payment tends materially to increase its value, whether it is a fiduciary currency or a currency with full intrinsic value.

Payments made by the State to its employees and others also tends to reinforce the acceptability of the unit in which the payment is made. A much more important factor is the intervention of the State to make its acceptance compulsory in payments between private individuals. Together with its acceptance in political payments and with its use for payments by the State, this role should ensure the acceptability of a monetary object in all but extremely abnormal circumstances. It should also largely contribute towards influencing its purchasing power, increasing it above its intrinsic value.

[2]Rudolf Kaulla, *Die Grundlagen des Geldwertes*, p. 36. Quoted by Ellis, p. 39.

Having said all that, it is necessary to emphasize, however, that far-reaching as the powers of the State are in the monetary sphere, it is not in a position to determine the purchasing power of money merely by accepting it, making payments in it and decreeing it acceptable to others. Although by such means the State is in a position to increase the acceptability of money, and also to raise its value above the level at which it would have been in the absence of such measures, this does not mean that the State has an entirely free hand in determining its value at will. In normal or even moderately abnormal conditions this end could be achieved to a high degree if the assistance of price control and various devices of monetary policy were also enlisted. When, however, powerful economic forces are at work against the maintenance of the purchasing power of money at the level desired by the State, then all these means are powerless to enforce its will. All it can ensure is that liabilities can and must be discharged with the aid of legal tender money at par. The contraction of new liabilities, however, might take place at prices which would materially alter the purchasing power of the legal tender money.

The above observations are in accordance with experience with primitive money. The earliest amongst them is the experience of Babylonia. All the efforts made by the State to maintain the value of silver at an artificial parity in relation to barley failed under the pressure of economic influences which were stronger than the will of the State.

In all fairness to Knapp it must be admitted that while some of his followers sought to claim omnipotence for the State in the sphere of determining the value of money, he himself never put forward such ambitious claims. What he claimed was that the State was in a position to determine the value of new monetary units in terms of the old monetary unit. This is beyond doubt correct as far as primitive moneys are concerned. During the 19th century, the native rulers of Uganda adopted a new currency in the form of very badly finished blue beads. They equated it to the old currency at the rate of one bead to one ivory disk, in spite of the fact that the intrinsic value of the ivory disk was incomparably higher than that of the beads.

In instances in which the new unit replaced altogether the old one, the State by fixing a parity between them was in a position to determine the number of new units required for the discharge of liabilities in old units. At the actual moment of the adoption of the new unit, prices probably corresponded to the official parity. This did not prevent prices, however, from rising or falling a few weeks, or a few days, or even a few minutes after the change. The fact that the State has the power to determine the parity between the new unit and the old does not mean that it has the power to determine the purchasing power of the new unit any more than it could determine that of the old unit. In Ancient Greece when two sheep were equated to one drachma, it meant that liabilities that existed at the moment of the change could be discharged at that rate. It did not mean that from that time onwards prices remained for any length of time exactly as they were before allowing for the parity of two to one.

From the foregoing it appears that the most important aspect of Knapp's theory from the point of view of its bearing on primitive money is that action by the State is capable of raising the value of a currency by increasing its acceptability. Those who make the State theory their special study might with benefit to themselves and to their subject make a detailed investigation of the lessons derived from experience with primitive money. The extent to which the State theory is capable of explaining the value of primitive money, as distinct from its validity, depends on the relative importance of political and nonpolitical payments in a given community. Where political payments predominate the value of money is largely derived from its acceptability for such payments. On the other hand, in highly commercialized communities, where payments arising from trade are of overwhelming importance, the supply and demand theory, quantity theory, quality theory and cost of production theory are much more capable of explaining the behaviour of primitive money than the State theory.

CHAPTER 23

GRESHAM'S LAW

The principle that bad money drives out good money operates in two distinct senses. During periods of debasement the debased currencies are apt to remain in circulation while the full-valued currencies are apt to disappear through hoarding, industrial use or export. In another sense, if two or more different kinds of currencies are legal tender, and have a fixed ratio in relation to each other, then the one which is over-valued compared with its free market price is apt to remain in circulation while the under-valued one is likely to disappear. There are many instances in the evidence on the behaviour of primitive currencies to show that Gresham's Law applies to them in both senses. On the other hand, in many other instances primitive currencies have defied Gresham's Law.

Debasement was a fairly widespread practice in communities using primitive currencies. It was practised both by the authorities and by the members of the communities themselves, according to whether the currency was issued by the State authority or not. It is well known that in African communities which use cattle as a currency there is a tendency towards deterioration in quality. Since in many communities cattle change hands by number, everyone tries to use the worst animals for payment, and to retain the better specimens. On the other hand, in communities where the unit is not actual cattle but an "ideal" standard specimen of a certain age and size, endowed with certain qualities, and livestock changes hands not simply by number but according to its value in terms of the ideal unit, bad cattle need not necessarily drive out good cattle.

Another instance of the operation of Gresham's Law is provided by Burma where until comparatively recently rice served as a medium of exchange, and only inferior rice remained in circulation. Yet another instance of the same kind is that of tobacco currency in Virginia, the use of which led to a marked deterioration of the quality of tobacco produced for the requirements of monetary circulation. Since for a long time it was the quantity that mattered, tobacco of inferior quality was grown in town back gardens, and even professional planters did not exert themselves to produce good quality tobacco. Whatever good tobacco there was produced was consumed or exported. Tobacco rejected by the merchants tended to remain in circulation. The abuse was mitigated by the supervision of tobacco bales by Government inspectors, but was not eliminated altogether. This is true also of other commodities serving as currencies in the old American colonies. There was also a tendency for inferior, badly strung or faked *wampum* to remain in circulation among the colonists, for the simple reason that in trade with the Indians only perfect specimens were accepted.

The working of the cigarette standard in prisoners' camps during the second World War also illustrated the functioning of Gresham's Law. Usually the cigarettes of favourite brands disappeared; they were either consumed or hoarded. Only less popular brands of hand-filled cigarettes remained in circulation.

The operation of Gresham's Law in primitive communities is not so clear in instances where two or more currencies were in general use. In many instances, the use of various kinds of currencies was limited to well-defined purposes. For instance, in the Code of Hammurabi certain payments were prescribed to be made in silver and others in grain. For this reason, it was possible in Babylonia to maintain both media of exchange in circulation, even though one or the other was bound to become over-valued from time to time. They could not be used alternatively, but each only in its respective sphere. Generally speaking, grain was used in rural districts and silver in towns.

In present-day or recent primitive communities a limitation on the use of various kinds of currencies circulating at the same time has been practised by tribal authority. Ivory, slaves or rifles were used for the purchase of high-glass goods, while beads, cloth or brass rods were used for cheaper purchases. They would not be used alternatively. Obviously in such situations Gresham's Law could not operate. In many instances there was a traditionally fixed ratio between various currencies in use at the same time in the same community. Such was the force of tradition that they remained in use side by side over long periods in the absence of any legal authority to enforce the parity, even though one became grossly over-valued in terms of the other. Nevertheless there are other instances in which the under-valued currency tended to disappear.

The operation of Gresham's Law in primitive communities is at times apt to be handicapped by the lack of adequate export facilities. The use of some primitive currencies is confined to a particular community and cannot be exported at all. In several instances the cost of transport is so high that arbitrage could not take advantage of the difference between the internal and external valuations of the currencies. This is particularly true of the heavy iron or brass rod currencies of Africa, or of weapons and utensils made of these materials. They represent such enormous weight that it would be impossible to export them, so that they are apt to remain in circulation even if their value is considerably lower than their commercial price outside the community. For the same reason it is impracticable for arbitrage to take advantage of over-valuation of such heavy currencies. In backward parts of Indo-China, iron bars were valued during the last century at several times the world market price of iron.

The dual character of many primitive currencies facilitates the operation of Gresham's Law. If one of the several currencies in use becomes over-valued it is apt to become diverted to non-monetary use and the under-valued currencies remain in circulation.

CHAPTER 24

PRICE LEVELS IN SEMI-NATURAL ECONOMIES

The foregoing chapters attempted to assess the extent to which the principal modern monetary theories can be applied for the explanation of changes in the value of primitive money. We saw that each one of them contains part of the explanation required, and that their combination should go a long way towards explaining price tendencies in communities using primitive money. It does not go, however, the whole way. Primitive monetary systems have several fundamental characteristics that differ materially from those of modern monetary systems. Accordingly, it is essential to elaborate the rules of the behaviour of primitive money due to those peculiar characteristics. The most important among them may be summed up as follows:—

1. In primitive communities a large proportion of trade is transacted by barter in spite of the existence of some form of money.

2. A large proportion of primitive currencies is of a dual character, as they serve both monetary and non-monetary purposes.

3. There are usually several types of primitive currencies in simultaneous use in primitive communities.

4. The scope of most primitive moneys is much more limited than that of modern money.

Our task in this chapter is to examine how in a community based partly on natural economy and partly on a primitive monetary economy changes in the volume of money tend to affect the price level. There are many instances of such mixed economies. Indeed, according to Dopsch and many other authorities, there has never been a pure state of natural economy or a pure state of monetary economy. Even to-day, and even in the most advanced communities, certain payments are still made in kind. The difference between the relative extent of natural and monetary economies in various phases of history is largely one of degree. Differences of degree should not be underrated, however, for they may be substantial enough to amount in practice to a difference in kind. At the risk of appearing paradoxical, one might even suggest that the difference between a difference of degree and one of kind is merely one of degree. The slight degree of natural economy that has survived in modern communities may safely be ignored by modern monetary theory; on the other hand, it must be taken into account in primitive communities.

There can be no question of a price level in a community with natural economy because there is no common denominator in which the prices of goods and services can be expressed. The price of each commodity in terms of other commodities, in so far as it is not determined by tradition or by law, is determined by supply and demand, relative costs of production, the degree of personal preferences of the bargaining parties, the degree of superfluity of the surplus offered for sale, and the relative urgency of their needs for each others' products. This latter factor is particularly important. Primitive man, being anything but the "economic man" of the textbooks, may allow himself to be influenced in his barter transactions by entirely unreasonable considerations, and the prices arrived at may depart widely from the supply and demand equilibrium level and from the level determined by cost of production plus reasonable profit. In any case, supply and demand only operate in reasonably good markets. Savages engaged in bargaining have often no means of knowing how far the price they ask or offer corresponds to the correct price arising from the total supply and demand in their community. Very often theirs is an isolated transaction, and neither party knows how much the next door neighbour will give for their goods. As for cost of production, any possible comparison between the working time spent on the one good and the other is bound to be quite rudimentary. No profit is likely to be added to it in their mental calculation (if any). Primitive man does not barter for the sake of profits; he barters because he has a surplus of some goods and a need of other goods. The size of his unwanted surplus and the urgency of his need for the goods of others are the determining factors.

Theoretically speaking, under barter there is not one price level but many price levels—one in terms of each commodity actively exchanged against other goods. Each price level is influenced by the volume of the respective goods in terms of which it is expressed, and also by the volume of all other goods. In this respect the difference between monetary economy and barter economy is that the volume of any particular type of goods is liable to wider fluctuations than the volume of money, unless it fulfils the role of store of value in which case hoarding and de-hoarding tends to moderate changes in its active supply. The economic significance of the multiple price levels under barter is small, unless there is one commodity of outstanding importance, in which case the chances are that it becomes adopted as a medium of exchange, or at least as a standard of value. In so far as barter is transacted with the aid of an abstract unit of account the price level cannot change for monetary causes. If, however, the unit of account is also a medium of barter, then the volume of the commodity selected for that purpose tends to affect the price level in the same way as if it were a medium of exchange.

Our present problem is to examine the behaviour of a medium of exchange which is only used for part of the trade turnover, the rest of the turnover being effected by pure barter without the intermediary of any standard of value. In such mixed economies the use of money is either limited to the purchase of certain articles, or to certain parts of the community, or it is in all-round but limited use. If the use of money is limited to certain goods then the quantity theory applies to some extent within the narrow sphere in which the money is used. In this respect the position is the same as in instances of multiple currencies, when any one of the currencies is used for certain limited purposes only.

If the use of money is limited to certain parts of the community then from a theoretical point of view it fulfils its normal functions in its narrow sphere. From the point of view of the value of money the sections of the community which use no money can be ignored. In so far as they trade with the money-using sections the transactions play the same part as do imports and exports. The position is more complicated if the same sections of the community transact business partly by barter or with the aid of money. If goods and services can be either bought or bartered then the relative prices of goods in relationship to each other need not be affected proportionately by changes in the volume of money. The extent of the effect depends mainly on the extent to which the community is based on a monetary economy. If the method of exchange is overwhelmingly one of barter, an increase in the volume of money produces a relatively strong effect, for the volume of goods on which the increase produces its effect is limited. Prices expressed in the currency concerned would soar. Since, however, the bulk of the communities' trade is done by barter such an increase would not materially affect the community as a whole.

As a rule the relative extent of monetary and natural economies is liable to changes, and changes in the volume or value of money are liable to affect it. A moderate rise in prices through an expansion in the volume of money would tend to increase the proportion of monetary economy to natural economy, because an increased number of people would be tempted by higher prices to sell against money rather than to barter their goods and services. Conversely a decline in prices due to monetary causes would lead towards an increase in the relative importance of natural economy. This phenomenon is noticeable also in primitive communities using modern money. During the depression of the 'thirties, the sharp decline of prices of native products in many parts of the world resulted in a reluctance to accept lower prices in money, and many people reverted to barter. This elasticity of the ratio between natural economy and monetary economy tends to absorb the shocks caused by the fluctuation in the volume of money. If, however, a rising trend of prices assumes considerable dimensions, it is apt to produce the opposite effect to that indicated above. Fear of further depreciation would induce sellers of goods and services to insist on payment in kind and the relative importance of money economy would thus decline. A persistent and substantial fall of prices, through leading to the realization that money is a good thing to receive, would tend to increase the relative importance of money economy.

Very often a limitation in the use of money is brought about purely by its scarcity. Any increase in its quantity would tend to remove this cause and to increase the relative importance of monetary economy in the community. Any decline in the quantity of money would force the community to revert to natural economy to an increasing extent. In this respect there is no material difference between primitive and modern communities. Even a community using modern money may be forced to revert to natural economy, if it suffers from a shortage of currency that would otherwise paralyse or hinder its economic activities. In many modern societies there are remote economically backward districts where money is scarce and where natural economy exists to a large degree even though they are at a culturally advanced stage. Money is reserved for certain payments which have to be made in money. In order to avoid the risk of being unable to meet such money liabilities, buyers are only prepared to pay with goods or services. The scarcity of money in such communities does not affect the relative prices in the turnover in kind. If, however, the supply of money is inferior to the amount that must be paid in money, then goods and services are apt to be sold at very low prices against money payment, in order to secure the urgently needed cash. Such forced sales might in given circumstances interfere with the equilibrium of barter ratios.

A rise in prices resulting from a rise in the cost of production due to non-monetary causes may produce different results from a rise caused by an increased volume of money. For the volume of money available may cease to be sufficient for paying higher prices, in which case part of the goods is bartered instead of being sold. Conversely, a fall in prices due to non-monetary causes tends to make money supplies more comfortable and tends to expand the use of money and to reduce that of barter.

In any community where barter and the payment for services in kind is practised on any noteworthy scale it would be impossible to compile even in theory an equation of exchange. The goods side of the equation would always be extremely elastic and uncertain, owing to the ever-present possibility of diverting goods and services from the realm of money economy to that of natural economy and *vice versa*.

CHAPTER 25

DUAL CHARACTER OF PRIMITIVE MONEY

We saw in the chapter on the quantity theory that the effect of changes in the quantity of money on the price level is apt to be vitiated by the dual part played by primitive money, serving, as it often does, as goods as well as money. The equation which seeks to prove that price levels are determined by the quantity of money, its velocity of circulation and the volume of trade, is often inapplicable to primitive money, for the reason that a commodity-currency is liable to appear on both sides of the equation. That is, a given quantity of commodities cannot at any given moment be both money and goods, but it might at any moment be switched over from its one use to the other. Very often holders of the monetary commodity themselves do not know whether they intend to consume their goods or to use them in payment for purchases. This means that even if we possessed full figures about the volume of the monetary commodity at a given moment, we would have no means of knowing how much of it will eventually be used for monetary purposes. In this respect many types of primitive money differ fundamentally from modern money. The fact that they are not "a thing unto themselves in contradistinction to everything else" is apt to modify their behaviour materially. This particular difference between qualities inherent in primitive and modern money is probably more important than any other from the point of view of monetary theory. Some writers have sought to overcome this difficulty by laying down the rule that any object that has a non-monetary use is thus disqualified from being regarded as money. Since, however, many objects of practical use fulfil obvious monetary functions this attitude amounts to taking an easy way out of a theoretical difficulty by simply shirking it instead of facing it. It is not very helpful to evade a problem by narrowing our definition in order to exclude an awkward point from the scope of our enquiry.

In any case, the discrimination between currencies serving exclusively monetary purposes and those serving also non-monetary purposes is largely artificial. Even coined money cannot be said to have no non-monetary use. After all, coins are used as ornaments in India and elsewhere, and they can be melted down for industrial purposes. It would be impossible to state at any given moment how much of the gold and silver coins hoarded by the Indian people is likely to serve monetary purposes, and how much retains permanently the role of ornaments. To carry this argument to extremes, it is possible to claim that even paper money has its non-monetary use since it can be pulped, or be used for wall-paper, or for the decoration of screens, as the million mark notes were used to some extent after the inflationary period in Germany in the 'twenties. There is admittedly a considerable difference in degree between the non-monetary use of primitive and modern money. Nevertheless, the fact that modern money is not disqualified by its non-monetary use from being regarded as money may be quoted against the purists who want to exclude commodity currencies from the scope of monetary theory.

If wheat or rice played exclusively a monetary role in the communities concerned, then it would behave substantially in the same way as a metallic currency. Its value would respond to the factors that influence the value of modern money. Since, however, it combines the role of money with that of the staple product, and since it is usually not the sole currency employed by the community, its behaviour is liable to be affected by factors for which modern monetary theory does not allow.

Non-monetary demand is apt to assume an important part among the factors determining the value of money. This demand may be caused by changes in the trend of home consumption and also by changes in export possibilities. Modern monetary economists occasionally engage in speculation about the effect of a cessation of demand for gold abroad, but such hypothetical questions are not likely to assume practical importance, and can be disregarded in examining the prospects of the purchasing power of a gold currency in the near future. On the other hand, 17th century monetary experts in America had good practical reason for envisaging the effect of the slackening of European demand for beaver skins on the beaver skin currency of their country. The changed situation was entirely due to non-monetary influences.

As a rule a good crop in the staple products results in an all-round increase in the local consumption of those products, if there are also staple consumers' goods. Not only are the producers themselves liable to consume more wheat owing to their increased prosperity, but also other classes benefiting indirectly by that prosperity. In that case the increase in the monetary supply of wheat, after the growers have retained their sowing seed and food reserves, and others have made their initial purchases, will be much less than the amount corresponding to the increase of the crop.

Let us now examine the effect of an increase in the crop of a staple product serving monetary purposes on the assumption that a large part of the surplus is regularly exported. If the good crop is due to local conditions then the producers and exporters of the staple product are able to satisfy their requirements for imported goods and the community will remain in possession of a large quantity of the monetary commodity for internal purposes. As a result, demand for internal non-monetary products will be high, and prices will rise. If the crop of the monetary product is bad abroad, so that the price rises and there is a strong demand, then the internal prices of non-monetary goods is likely to fall, not only because the internal monetary value of the object in question tends to move in sympathy with its external value, but also because exceptionally large exports will deplete the supply available for internal monetary purposes.

If, on the other hand, the crop of the staple monetary commodity is better abroad than at home, and its price abroad falls, then the internal price level will tend to fall, partly because producers, being unable to sell their goods profitably abroad, are prepared to part with them in return for smaller quantities of non-monetary goods at home, and partly because in the absence of large exports the internal monetary supply is likely to be relatively large.

The value of monetary commodities which have a world market price is liable to be determined largely by that price, not by the fluctuations of its quantity within the producing country. No matter how large the crop may be, if the excess can be exported at world market prices there is no reason why its value within the producing community should decline below that level. On the other hand, a drop in the world market price reacts on the purchasing power of the commodity currency within the exporting community, even if its quantity there should remain unchanged. Needless to say, in primitive conditions substantial discrepancies are apt to arise.

If several currencies are in use then the behaviour of the commodity currency is determined by its relative importance amongst them, and by the relative importance of its monetary and non-monetary functions. In Babylonia, there was a secular trend of depreciation of silver in terms of commodities. Although barley was a currency, it moved in sympathy with the other commodities, and appreciated in terms of silver. In Japan rice tended to move in sympathy with other commodities and not with modern money; even though it was a currency, its important non-monetary role as a staple product and as a staple article of consumption made it behave like a commodity.

An interesting question is whether, when a commodity plays a dual role, its monetary supply is determined by non-monetary demands, or must non-monetary requirements be satisfied with what is left over after meeting monetary requirements. There are instances in both senses. In 18th century Brazil when cotton was currency, business men complained that, owing to its monetary use, cotton was short for non-monetary requirements. On the other hand, we saw in the chapter on Gresham's Law that an under-valued commodity currency is apt to be diverted to non-monetary uses.

In many communities fluctuations in the crops fail to affect price levels in either way, owing to the strength of tradition by which prices are maintained for generations. The extent to which this factor operates varies widely, and this is one of the reasons why the working of primitive monetary systems depends so much on the nature of the community operating them. The same is true concerning the operation of Gresham's Law.

CHAPTER 26

MULTIPLE CURRENCIES

The simultaneous use of more than one type of currency in a community is not a peculiarity of primitive monetary systems. We encounter it also in communities using modern money. The bimetallist system provides an outstanding instance; the simultaneous circulation of coins and paper money provides another. The difference between these systems and the multiplicity of primitive money is that in modern conditions the different types of currency usually form part of the same system. They are related to each other with a fixed parity on the basis of which they are, in theory at any rate, convertible into each other. In normal conditions the several modern currencies in circulation can usually be used indiscriminately, and for this reason there is no buying or selling of one currency against the other. The different currencies are practically like different units of the same system. It is their grand total that is liable to determine the value of a unit in terms of goods, and the fluctuation of the relative quantities within that total does not tend to affect the price level.

Under multiple systems of primitive currencies also, there are instances in which the currencies are equated to each other by means of fixed parities. Even then the position in practice differs from that of multiple modern currencies, in so far as one or more of the primitive moneys belong to the category of commodity currencies. In that case one currency is apt to be bought and sold against the other. The total of primitive currencies in use is then not in contradistinction to the total of goods to be bought. The quantity of any one of these currencies is in contradistinction to the quantity of goods *plus* the quantity of the other currencies.

For instance, in Medieval Scandinavia cattle, cloth and precious metals by weight were used as currencies with fixed parities between them. Cattle was used for buying not only non-monetary goods but also cloth and metals. Cloth bought cattle and metals as well as non-monetary goods. And metals bought cattle and cloth in addition to non-monetary goods. Consequently an equation of exchange with cattle, cloth and metals on the money side and everything else on the goods side would present a false picture; for a large part of any of the three monetary commodities was liable to become neutralized at any time through purchases for non-monetary purposes against payment in another monetary commodity.

In spite of the existence of fixed parities between them, commodity currencies largely play the part of commodities pure and simple. The relative importance of their non-monetary character is apt to be even higher in the absence of fixed parities.

In any case, the existence of a fixed ratio under the primitive monetary system means something different from its existence under a modern monetary system. It very seldom means that the one currency is freely convertible into the other. Convertibility in practice often operates in one way but not in the other way. More frequently there is no question of real convertibility, merely of the possibility of the alternative use of the currencies, on the basis of their fixed parities, for the settlement of liabilities. Even this use is often limited. Their actual exchange value is liable to deviate materially from their official parity, in which case sellers of goods and lenders of money are inclined to stipulate payment in a definite form. If two or more currencies are legal tender and their parity is officially fixed—as in Liberia where palm oil and kernel could be used optionally for payments—then the less valuable amongst them will be used for the discharge of liabilities. This is not the same thing by any means as the free convertibility of two currencies under a modern monetary system.

If the parity fixed between primitive currencies is effective, the situation is somewhat similar to that of a modern community where partial price control is in operation. Let us take an example of an African community where salt and guinea-cloth are both currencies and are equated to each other with an effective fixed parity. If the quantity of salt currency increases the price level tends to rise. Owing to the operation of the fixed parity the price of guinea-cloth in terms of salt cannot rise, and for this reason the price of everything else in terms of salt tends to rise more than it would have risen if the price of guinea-cloth had also been allowed to rise. This situation may best be compared with that prevailing in most countries during and immediately after the second World War. Owing to the fact that the price of a number of important articles was not allowed to rise, the increased purchasing power was brought to bear on the uncontrolled goods to a much larger degree than it would have been if the price of all goods had been allowed to move freely. Since those who had more money did not have to spend more on controlled goods, they were in a position to increase their demand for uncontrolled goods, and bid up the prices of the latter to a much greater extent than they would have done if a considerable part of their larger purchasing power had been absorbed by an all-round rise in prices which would have taken place in the absence of a partial control.

When no fixed parities exist between the primitive currencies, or if the fixed parities are not effective, then in the circumstances described above guinea-cloth currency would appreciate in terms of salt currency in sympathy with the general rise in the prices in terms of salt currency. Prices in terms of guinea-cloth currency, on the other hand, would tend to remain unchanged. This means that in the absence of an effective parity there would be several independent price levels within the same community. It is conceivable that, while prices in salt currency rise, prices in guinea-cloth currency would fall.

In a modern community with gold and silver coins in circulation the effect of a rise in the volume of gold coins on the general price level might in theory be offset by a corresponding fall in the volume of silver coins, in which case there would be no change in the price level. In a country using primitive currencies without any effective parity between them the effect of a rise in the quantity of one of them on the price level is not offset by a corresponding fall in the quantity of the other. The result of such a situation is simply that the two price levels move in opposite directions, provided of course that the two currencies can be used more or less indiscriminately for the same purposes.

The situation is totally different, however, if each of the currencies is limited in scope and can only be used for the purchase of certain categories of goods. An expansion of cowries, for instance, would only affect the prices of goods of small value in a community where guinea-cloth is used for the purchase of goods of medium value and slaves for the purchase of highly valuable goods. About this aspect of multiple primitive currencies more will be said in the next chapter.

Even if there is an effective fixed parity between the currencies it is usually liable to adjustment. In face of strong pressure due to the expansion of one of the currencies the chances are that the parities will be changed sooner or later. This was done at frequent intervals during periods of cowrie inflations. In communities where cowries had fixed parities with other currencies these parities were often found to be entirely untenable and unworkable, and had to be adjusted.

Changes in the relative cost of production of the currencies used within the same community are also liable to affect their parities, though not so easily as changes in their relative quantities. Likewise, changes in the quality of one of several of the currencies through debasement or deterioration is also liable to upset the equilibrium between them. In either case Gresham's Law is likely to operate, and the least valuable of the currencies is likely to be used extensively in payment whenever possible.

It seems justified to conclude that, unless there are fixed and effective parities between currencies that can be used indiscriminately, only the least valuable, or rather the most highly over-valued, amongst them fulfills effectively the part of money. The others largely assume the role of commodities with officially but ineffectively fixed prices. In that case the price level in the community concerned is apt to be determined not by the total volume of all currencies but by that of the one currency which functions effectively.

CHAPTER 27

LIMITED CURRENCIES

The limitation of the use of a currency tends to affect its value unfavourably. As a general rule, the more restricted the use of a primitive money the smaller its surplus value in excess of its intrinsic value arising from its monetary use. We saw before that every object tends to appreciate above its non-monetary value through its adoption for monetary use. If, however, its monetary use is limited then its appreciation due to that factor also tends to be moderate.

Let us first examine the limitations in the use of money due to the separation of its functions. If an object is used as a standard of value only and has no other monetary functions, this in itself should not cause an increase in its value. In practice, however, such an object is usually employed also as a standard of deferred payments, in which case there may be a tendency towards its accumulation by debtors for the purpose of making subsequent payments to creditors. As debts are constantly maturing, and preparations for their repayment are constantly being made, a certain amount of the objects concerned would thus be permanently withheld from non-monetary circulation, and this would tend to raise their value.

The use of an object as a medium of exchange or as a store of value tends to raise its value to a much larger degree. If it serves actively as a medium of exchange then a substantial quantity is bound to be withheld for non-monetary use in order to satisfy monetary requirements.

A time lag is always bound to elapse between the acceptance of the monetary commodity and its spending. The length of this time lag is determined by the density of the population, the relative degree of commercial activity, and many other factors affecting the velocity of circulation of the currency. In many backward communities the circulation of the medium of exchange is liable to be sluggish. This means that a relatively large proportion of the supply of the monetary object is likely to remain permanently withheld, and this will tend to raise its value above its non-monetary value. The extent to which this factor is liable to affect the value of primitive money is not determined by the absolute figure of the amount withheld, but by its tendency. The value of the monetary object tends to rise when the amount withheld for monetary purposes is on the increase. The tendency may become reversed if for some reason the requirements for monetary purposes decline.

The use of the monetary object as a store of value means that considerable quantities of it are hoarded. Moreover, such a use tends to play the part of a shock-absorber. If an object is only used as a medium of exchange its value is liable to fluctuate widely, for an increase in its quantity is apt to translate itself into an increase of the demand for goods. If, on the other hand, the object in question is also a favourite store of value then it is possible that the surplus disappears sooner or later through being added to the existing hoards.

The use of an object as a means of unilateral payment also tends to increase its value, owing to the need for keeping a supply of those objects handy for the purpose of such payments. The value of an object which serves exclusively as a means of unilateral payment is not so sensitive towards changes in its quantity as the value of an object serving as a medium of exchange. Unilateral payments are usually fixed fairly rigidly and their amount does not react to such an extent to supply and demand as prices payable for goods and services do. In the long run and in face of major changes in the quantities, however, adjustment of the scales of unilateral payment is likely to be effected.

Let us now examine the effects of the limitations of the use of a monetary object as a medium of exchange on its value. If the geographical sphere in which it circulates as a medium of exchange is restricted, then its value is liable to fluctuate widely even through comparatively small changes in its quantity. On the other hand, the effect of a change in its quantity is liable to become dispersed if the money is in circulation over a wide area.

Ethnographical limitations to the use of a money are also liable to increase the degree of its sensitiveness towards unsettling factors. If a currency is used exclusively in dealings with white traders then its value is often at the mercy of the latter. The market being narrow, it can easily be influenced. If, on the other hand, a currency is used exclusively for internal purposes, the absence of an export market to act as a shock absorber is liable to render it sensitive towards changes in its quantity or quality, or in its cost of production, unless these factors are neutralized by the fundamental conservatism of a primitive community.

Social limitations to the use of primitive money tend to increase the degree of its reactions to disturbing factors by narrowing down the sphere of its use. This rule does not hold good, however, for money the use of which is confined to chiefs and members of the ruling classes in general. The possession and use of such money confers prestige on its holder and user, and for this reason there is likely to be an almost insatiable demand for it. Any surplus that reaches the community is likely to be absorbed.

As was pointed out in the last chapter, if separate currencies are used for big, medium-sized and small purchases, then changes in the quantity of any one of them only affects the prices of the categories of goods and services which can be bought with it. In that case there may be conflicting tendencies between the various sections of the price levels. If the use of a currency is limited to the purchase of a small range of goods—for instance, luxuries only—then the goods factor tending to affect prices is liable to assume considerable relative importance. The wider the range of goods which can be bought with the same currency, the higher is the relative importance of the money factor as against the goods factor. In other words, if a money can be used for buying anything, then changes in the supply of some of the categories of goods are not liable to affect its value to a high extent unless the total supply of goods is affected. If, on the other hand, the money can only buy a few kinds of goods, then changes in one or two kinds of goods are liable to affect the supply of goods to a relatively high degree, and for this reason they are apt to produce a pronounced effect on the average value of the monetary unit. There is less chance for the operation of the law of averages, through which conflicting changes in the quantities of various goods tend to offset each other, thereby largely neutralizing the effect of any one change on the value of money.

PART IV: PRIMITIVE MONETARY POLICY

CHAPTER 28

ACTIVE AND PASSIVE ATTITUDE OF THE STATE AUTHORITY

MONETARY policy may be defined as the attitude of the political authority towards the monetary system of the community under its control, aiming at furthering its own economic interests or that of the community. A policy may be either active—when it involves decisions to apply measures—or passive—when it involves decisions to abstain from applying measures. A passive attitude towards the monetary system, in order to be considered to form part of a monetary policy, must be deliberate.

The following are the principal measures included within the scope of monetary policy:—

1. Creation of a new monetary system :
   (a) by decreeing the monetary character of an object or unit;
   (b) by taking practical measures leading to the monetary use of an object or unit;
   (c) by confirming and consolidating, either by decree or by practical measures, the existence of a money developed under private initiative or found in use in a newly-conquered community.

2. Abolition of an existing monetary system :
   (a) by decreeing a change;
   (b) by taking practical measures leading to a change.

3. Alteration or regulation of the functioning of the monetary system:
   (a) by changing the quantity or quality of the unit serving as money;
   (b) by changing the unit of account;
   (c) by changing the quantity of money or preventing a change in it;
   (d) by seeking to control prices;
   (e) by seeking to control interest rates;
   (f) by fixing or altering the ratio between several moneys that may exist simultaneously;
   (g) by fixing, altering, or seeking to influence the exchange rate between the local money and outside money;
   (h) by regulating the sphere in which the money is to function.

Deliberate passive attitude of the political authorities may affect the monetary system and its functioning by allowing private initiative or local custom a free hand in adopting new money, altering it, terminating its use, regulating its functioning in any of the ways indicated under (3) above.

Although we are accustomed to think of monetary policy as something essentially modern, it is justifiable to apply the term also to primitive money in primitive as well as modern communities. Any of the problems covered in the above summary are liable to arise in primitive communities or in advanced communities using primitive money.

It seems probable that in the majority of instances new systems of primitive money came to be adopted without State intervention. It is true, during the earliest phases of monetary evolution the overwhelming importance of political transactions compared with that of commercial transactions resulted in the initiation of means of payment by the action of the political authorities. On the other hand, at a later phase, with the development of trade the initiative in originating moneys passed from the hands of the authorities to those of private interests. The question is, are we justified in claiming that the passive attitude of the tribal or State authorities in face of such adoption of new monetary systems for commercial purposes constituted passive monetary policy? It seems reasonable to assume that in most instances where money developed on private initiative the passivity of the State authority was not deliberate, and did not therefore constitute monetary policy. What probably happened was that the communities developed their money quite unconsciously, and the tribal chief or the head of the State was no more aware of what was happening than other members of the community. By the time they came to realize it, the monetary system was already well established.

It is conceivable, however, that in a number of instances the State authority did realize what was happening, and abstained from interfering with the course of evolution of a monetary system because it considered this a private matter. A similar attitude appears to have been taken even by the State authorities of some relatively advanced communities. For instance, as far as is known, in Ancient Egypt the development of the limited monetary system that was in operation for a very long period was entirely a matter of private initiative. The State authority was only concerned with the system of natural economy by which it collected taxes from the producing classes and distributed rations to the non-producers. In view of the advanced degree of civilization achieved by Ancient Egypt, and the existence of a very high degree of State intervention in the economic sphere in general, it seems reasonable to assume that the neutrality of the State in the monetary sphere was not accidental but was a matter of deliberate policy. Burns was probably right in claiming that Egypt avoided the use of coins as long as possible as a matter of deliberate policy,[1] not through the ignorance of the State authority of what was happening in the monetary sphere.

[1]Burns, p. 334.

The extent of State intervention in the adoption of a monetary system depended largely on the way in which this system had originated. Where money originated through barter there was no need for intervention if money originated in *internal* trade. Such internal development of a favourite medium of barter was probably entirely spontaneous. Likewise if money first developed in internal trade as a unit of account the chances are that it developed spontaneously. Where money originated from external trade, in the majority of instances State authority was probably indispensable for its development. More often than not, external trade was not regarded as a matter for individuals. Explorers and traders often describe their experiences with savage tribes, how they negotiated with the chiefs to establish a monetary unit as an actual medium of exchange or as a unit of account to facilitate barter. The tribes contacted by the explorers usually acted as a single trading unit under the lead of their chiefs. In many instances the tribesmen were not allowed to trade with the travellers without the chief's permission. They were not allowed to acquire modern goods except through their chief. Unauthorized possession of such goods entailed in some instances death penalty. In such circumstances the adoption of a monetary unit depended on the political authority, and was an act of monetary policy.

Where money originated through its role of a store of value its adoption was probably spontaneous. It is for individuals and not for the State to decide in what form they will preserve their capital. Nevertheless it is conceivable that the tribal chief, in choosing objects in which to store their own wealth or the tribal wealth, set a fashion followed by many individuals. As and when private property took the place of tribal common ownership, the objects constituting tribal possessions came to be accumulated and stored privately. Whether the choice of store of value by the State authority was meant deliberately to set an example to members of the tribe is open to doubt. Probably it was not a matter of monetary policy.

We saw in the chapter dealing with the religious origin of money that State authority played an important part in the adoption of a standard object acceptable for sacrifice. Since, however, the objects chosen as sacrificial units were not chosen for monetary or economic reasons, the action of Church or State, deliberate as it may have been, cannot be regarded as an act of monetary policy.

It goes without saying that the political origin of money was entirely due to active monetary policy. Even though in many instances the State may have fixed means of payment for limited purposes only, in effect it led to the development of money through deliberate acts of policy, either in the form of decreeing the use of certain units for certain purposes, or by accepting certain objects in payment and using them in payment.

Bride money developed largely on private initiative, and in so far as it gave rise to a monetary unit this cannot be said to be due to monetary policy. On the other hand, the development of ceremonial payments through which money often developed into a medium of exchange, may have been largely due to the initiative of the political authority. Even so, since the object of such payments was non-economic, such intervention cannot be said to constitute an act of monetary policy. In so far as money originated through its ornamental use, its development was due to private initiative. In this case, as in that of the store of wealth, the example set by the chief must have played an important part, but could not have been a matter of deliberate policy pursuing monetary ends.

In instances where primitive money originated through a relapse from more advanced money, its adoption was very often spontaneous. If a community returned to primitive money it was usually when they found advanced money unsatisfactory, because there was not enough of it, or because there was too much of it and was depreciating, or because it was debased by the State authority, or because of its actual or anticipated demonetization by the State authority. In such circumstances the community often took the remedy into its own hands by developing a primitive monetary system to supplement the existing monetary system or to supplant it. When in the 3rd century A.D. the Roman Empire largely reverted to the use of weighed metals owing to the debasement of coins, it is probable that this was first done by private individuals, though the State subsequently took advantage of it to fix taxes and fines in weighed metals instead of in its own debased coins.

In the West Indies and on the North American mainland during the early colonial period, a wide variety of primitive currencies was adopted spontaneously, though subsequently the monetary use of such currencies was confirmed and regulated by the State authority. It was not until after the colonists had been using *wampum* or tobacco or wheat for some time as a means of payment that the State authority took action as a matter of monetary policy.

Again, during the French Revolution the public reverted spontaneously to some extent to the monetary use of grain, but efforts were made later by the Convention to adopt the system legally. During and after the second World War, the cigarette standard was adopted everywhere spontaneously in face of the indifference or even disapproval of the State authority.

Political authority intervened in many instances to terminate the use of primitive money, in order to replace it either by another kind of primitive money or by modern money. This end is achieved either by decreeing the use of a new unit instead of the old, or by ceasing to use the old unit for payments to and by the State. The earliest historical instance of such a termination of a primitive currency was provided by

Solon's Law under which fines in Athens became payable in modern money instead of in livestock. Similar changes were brought about by early Roman legislation, and by legislation passed by various European countries during the Middle Ages. In China various primitive currencies were repeatedly demonetized by decree, only to be restored again later. In Japan the widespread monetary use of rice was terminated by State intervention.

The colonial authorities in America passed many Acts of Legislation repealing earlier laws under which various commodity currencies were made legal tender. During the 19th and early 20th centuries the European colonizing powers intervened in many instances in order to discourage, hinder, and even forbid the use of primitive currencies adopted by the native population before the advent of the colonizers, or introduced by European traders.

Primitive State authorities themselves resorted in many instances to measures aiming at the demonetization of primitive currencies. In Ashanti, for instance, the import of cowries was prohibited, in order that they should not compete with locally produced gold dust as the currency of the country. When travellers in the interior of Africa found that a certain type of primitive currency which until recently was welcomed ceased to be acceptable, in many instances this was due to the decision of the chief who wanted to change the local currency.

In many other instances, on the other hand, the political authority simply deliberately refrained from preventing the demonetization of the existing primitive currencies when they were replaced on private initiative by other systems.

Our next task is to ascertain to what extent the political authority took active interest in the maintenance, regulation and modification of monetary systems after they had been established, whether by private individuals or by the State authority itself. In many cases, the monetary system was left to take care of itself, and for a long time it operated without any grave disadvantage. But its use must have eventually led to difficulties and presumably after an acute crisis or prolonged complications State intervention often followed, in the form of changing the system or of improving it by regulations.

There are many instances of State action aiming at influencing the quantity of primitive money. They will be dealt with in the chapters on expansionary, restrictionist and stabilizationist policies. The political authority also frequently adopted policies affecting the quality of money even before the phase of coined money was reached. Usually it aimed at safeguarding the standard quality of the medium of exchange. Thus the early Roman authorities came to stamp the *æs rude* which thereby became *æs signatum*. In China a ruler issued models of the utensils which had served as a currency, in order to standardize the privately produced specimens. In many countries when metals by weight served as currency, the State authority appointed weighing masters to check the balances. Assaying, too, came under State supervision. Already in the 3rd millenium in Cappadocia preference was given to silver bearing the seal of the magistrate. On various Pacific islands the counterfeiting of the various primitive currencies was made an offence. In the early American colonies the authorities inspected and certified the quality of tobacco and other goods serving as a currency. In many instances the types of the objects serving as primitive money were subject to Government regulation. Their quantity, shape, size, quality, etc., was defined. These regulations were liable to be changed and the political authority thus influenced the monetary unit not only in the negative sense of safeguarding it but also in a positive sense.

There are several early instances of price control measures during the Ancient period. The records of Babylonia and the Hittite Empire produce much interesting documentary evidence concerning this form of monetary policy. In many primitive communities prices were rigidly fixed, though this may in many instances have been due to traditions rather than tribal laws.

Interest rates, too, were subject to control by early State authority, but unless their level was fixed very high their intervention usually failed to produce the results aimed at.

There are many instances of fixing ratios between the various primitive currencies in use simultaneously in a community, and also for fixing ratios between primitive and modern money. In Babylonia the ratio between silver and barley was fixed, and was changed from time to time. In the Hittite Empire there was a fixed ratio between silver and sheep. In Ancient Ireland the three units, slave girls, cattle and grain, were related to each other by fixed parity, also to silver. Likewise, in the Scandinavian countries cattle, woollen cloth and silver bore a fixed ratio. In the early American colonial days the commodity currencies had a fixed value in coins, and so had in some parts *wampum*.

Instances of State intervention in the exchange value of primitive currencies are reviewed in the chapter on Foreign Exchange Policy. Finally, the political authority often prescribed the sphere in which various primitive currencies are to operate. The outstanding instance for such intervention is the Code of Hammurabi which strictly defines the occasions on which barley or silver was to be used, and provided for drastic penalties in case of non-compliance with the law

CHAPTER 29

RESTRICTIONIST MONETARY POLICY

The aspects of monetary policy in a community using primitive money which are of the greatest interest to the modern student are those that concern the regulation of the quantity of primtve money. In this respect it is necessary, however, to be particularly on our guard against falling into the error frequently committed by students of modern money, that of viewing primitive conditions from a modern point of view without allowing for the differences in the general background.

It is important to realize, in the first place, that changes in the quantity of money in a primitive community are not nearly as important as in a modern community. They are not liable to affect production to anything like the same extent. Scarcity of money is not so inconvenient, because the remedy lies largely in the hands of the members of the community concerned. Whether the scarcity is due to natural causes or to deliberate policy on the part of the political authority, the community is always in a position to mitigate it by the adoption of additional primitive currencies, or by reverting to natural economy. In any case, a large percentage of the trade of communities using primitive currencies is usually done by means of barter. If the volume of currency is found to be inadequate and for some reason cannot be supplemented by the adoption of some new object for monetary use, then the proportion of trade transacted by barter is simply increased. The borderline between the use of primitive currencies and natural economy is often very vague, and to cross it is not very difficult. It is only in modern communities that economic life is at the mercy of the caprices of nature, or of those of international trade and finance, or of the policy of the political authorities or of the banking community, each one of which factors is capable of reducing the volume of money. Having departed from natural economy modern man does not nowadays find it easy to revert to it or even to the use of primitive money, in order to relieve a scarcity of money. It is usually only under the stress of extreme difficulties that he does so.

Similarly, in a primitive community an increase in the volume of money is not so essential from the point of view of stimulating production as in a modern community, precisely because the producers are in a position to increase their production even if the volume of money is inadequate by adopting additional means of payment, or by reverting to natural economy to the extent to which the existing monetary supply cannot cover increased requirements.

Even so, the policy aiming at the restriction, stabilization or expansion of the volume of primitive money is of importance, not so much from the point of view of the volume of production as from that of the level of prices. It is guided largely by this consideration rather than by a desire to stimulate or restrict output. That latter aspect of monetary policy is essentially modern, and the men exercising the political authority in the overwhelming majority of primitive communities are most unlikely to have been conscious of it. It is even open to doubt whether the colonial authorities in North America and the West Indies were aware of the effect of the adoption of various commodity currencies on the productive capacity of the countries under their administration. They merely aimed at relieving the awkward position created by the persistent shortage of coins and securing better prices for the staple products, and may not have been aware of the broader implications of their policy.

In this chapter and in the next two chapters an attempt will be made to examine the extent to which political authorities in communities using primitive money aimed consciously or otherwise at monetary restriction, expansion or stabilization.

It is a commonplace of textbooks that money, in order to be valuable, must be scarce. In their introductory chapters to monetary theory many economists suggest that, scarcity being one of the fundamental requirements of money, the choice of primitive peoples necessarily fell upon objects which fulfilled this requirement. It is easy to find examples in support of this theory. Bücher, for instance, built his theory of the origin of money entirely on a set of examples showing that the objects used were scarce in the countries where they were chosen to play the part of currency. There are, however, many examples to show the one-sidedness and falsity of this theory. Objects chosen for monetary purposes can have value not only on the ground of their scarcity in the absolute sense of the term, but also because, even if they exist in virtually unlimited quantities, their acquisition or transport costs labour. Of course, in a sense even staple products may be said to owe their value to their relative scarcity. The supply of wheat in an agricultural community where it serves as a commodity currency may well exceed non-monetary requirements. Nevertheless, it is not unlimited, and may, therefore, be claimed in theory to be scarce. But it seems much more reasonable to attribute its value to the exertions required by its production rather than to its "scarcity."

However, in a very large number of known instances the choice of communities in an early stage of development fell on objects that were definitely scarce. Their natural scarcity may have been due to the fact that the objects were not obtainable within the community, or that they were only obtainable in limited quantities, or that they required a considerable amount of labour or risk to obtain.

The choice of imported or otherwise scarce objects as currency was not always the result of deliberate policy. An object in strong demand, such as salt, for instance, tends to assume the role of currency owing to the readiness with which everyone will accept it as payment for goods and services. The State authority, realizing its high degree of acceptability, may decide to take advantage of it by securing the monopoly of salt import and distribution.

In many instances the scarcity of the monetary object is due not to any scarcity of the material but to the scarcity of skilled labour required for its preparation. This is the case with *wampum* and other shell ornaments used as money, particularly in the Pacific area. Other instances are the feather money of Santa Cruz, or the mat money of Samoa. The relative scarcity of porpoise teeth currency in the Solomons is largely due to the labour and risk involved in the expeditions to secure them.

Lastly, a primitive currency may tend to be naturally scarce owing to demand for it for non-monetary requirements, as a result of which the volume that is available for monetary purposes is apt to be inadequate.

In so far as the political authority is responsible for the adoption or maintenance of a currency that is naturally scarce, it pursues, consciously or otherwise, a restrictionist policy even though it does not itself take any steps towards reducing or keeping down the volume of currency. There are many instances, however, in which the political authority—or tribal traditions which for practical purposes have the force of law—deliberately aim at preventing an increase in the volume of currency, or even at reducing it. In this the political authority is often merged with the religious authority which is apt to be the executing hand of the monetary policy by enforcing taboos.

Beyond doubt, restrictionist monetary policy is almost as old as money itself. It is unlikely, however, that its adoption was due in many instances to any desire to lower prices or to prevent their rise. What is much more probable is that the political authority sought to maintain a scarcity in its own narrow interests. The chief and his most powerful supporters, having acquired a large quantity of the monetary object, were anxious to prevent others from sharing their power by acquiring holdings comparable to those of the members of the "ruling class." Or, at a more advanced stage, the State was anxious to retain the profitable monopoly of the production or import of the objects serving as money. These considerations must have prevailed in many instances over the desire to increase the capacity of members of the community to pay tribute and other contributions to the political and religious leaders of the community, a desire which might otherwise have led to the choice of a more easily accessible object for monetary purpose. These conflicting considerations were often reconciled by having side by side a scarce and a plentiful currency.

In most instances when the official monetary policy is restrictionist, this policy is enforced through the monopolistic position secured by State authority. This monopoly may assume the form of control of the output or import of the monetary material. In Ancient China during an early period, for instance, the mines producing metals for monetary purposes were only opened in times of distress. In other times the State authority prevented their exploitation. Or the monopoly may be enforced by the placing of taboos on the production or gathering of the monetary material even though members of the community have easy or relatively easy access to its source. Possibly the myth of the "sacred" origin of shell money was built up deliberately in order to deter tribesmen from producing or importing them. In some instances the beach where the monetary shells were found was placed under taboo. In other instances persons producing or importing unauthorized shell money were regarded as witches or wizards and treated accordingly. Again in other instances the imitation of the ancient pieces of bead or shell money was prevented by the adoption of a deeply-rooted belief that they were of divine origin, and that man-made money must be rejected.

The choice of a monetary object unobtainable within reasonable distance is a method frequently resorted to in the Pacific. It is relatively easy for the chiefs to control long-distance foreign trade. In many instances the monetary shells reach the community concerned through the intermediary of several tribes, so that nobody apart from the chiefs knows where they come from. Restrictionism may also take the form of providing a seal for the monetary object in order to exclude from circulation any quantity in excess of that desired by the State, or in order to ensure that the State alone should be in a position to put the currency into circulation. At a more advanced stage the seal of the State authority guarantees the quality or weight of the objects, in which case the borderline of modern money has been reached.

A peculiar form of State restrictionist policy exists among the East Africans where all cattle which form the principal currency belong to the chief, and even though in practice they are in the possession of members of the community they cannot transfer them without the chief's consent. This rule does not make for deflation.

A restrictionist method adopted in the interior of Africa was the frequent change in the choice of the means of payment. Travellers incensed by the difficulties caused by such incalculable changes, regarded them as manifestation of the low intellectual powers of the Africans. In reality there was method in the madness of the chiefs who were probably largely responsible for the changes. If any one type of article were retained for monetary use for any length of time, the community would have been flooded with it within a very short time. By frequently changing the currency they safeguarded themselves against inflation. Whether this was done deliberately or it just happened to work out that way is an open question.

In face of the growing requirements a stationary volume of currency would tend to become increasingly inadequate. As a matter of fact, the volume of primitive currency in monetary use, like the volume of water in a lake, tends to decline unless replenished. We saw in the chapter on the Quantity Theory that there are many ways in which primitive money tends to disappear. Apart altogether from any increasing requirements, the monetary supply tends to become inadequate through wastage and other processes of decline. Restrictionist policy may not go beyond preventing adequate replacements. In doing so it may produce a deflationary effect.

CHAPTER 30

STABILIZATIONIST POLICY

We saw in the last chapter that very often the tendency of primitive monetary policy is towards preventing inflation, and that in pursuing that aim, it is inclined towards producing deflation. This deflationary trend of primitive monetary policy would not have been justified on the ground of being a reaction to abuses of inflation. Inflationary trend is not among the original sins of the primitive monetary system. Indeed, broadly speaking, it is true to say that there is hardly any inflationary danger in a primitive community unless and until it contacts a more advanced community. The savage himself does not as a rule aim at producing large quantities of money. Even if he is in a position to do so he only produces money as and when required. We saw in an earlier chapter that the Nicobarese do not pick coconuts unless they need them for immediate purchases or debt repayments. The North American Indians only produced *wampum* as and when required.

With the advent of the European or American trader, or, for that matter, the Arab, Chinese or Indian trader, the danger of inflation appears for the first time on the horizon of the primitive community. These representatives of a superior civilization are in a position to produce many kinds of primitive currencies on a really large scale at a low cost of production. Or they are able to import it by the shipload. A quantity which in the ordinary course would have taken many decades to produce or to import can be dumped on the unsuspecting savages in a matter of months. This was done in many instances in the Pacific, in Africa and in North America.

The primitive community is usually helpless in face of such an imported inflation. Even if the chiefs were prepared to check it they would not be in a position to do so. In any case the temptation to acquire vast fortunes in primitive currencies against the sale of local products is usually too strong. It was usually the colonial authorities who sought to protect the native population against the wholesale dumping of primitive currencies. In an effort to safeguard the stability of their economies and their social systems, the British, French, German and Dutch colonial administrations introduced a series of import bans on primitive currencies.

It would be idle to pretend that the safeguarding of monetary stability was the only object of these anti-inflationary measures. Doubtless the colonial authorities were anxious to introduce modern money in order to facilitate trading with the natives. But in many instances they were also genuinely anxious to safeguard the primitive peoples against the effects of inflation, and also against exploitation by white traders through the dumping of primitive money which was bound to depreciate and become demonetized in the long run. It is mainly for the sake of safeguarding stability that the European colonial authorities in various parts of Africa checked the influx of cowries. They were rather too late in taking this step, after the influx of cowries during the 19th century had done the damage. The British colonial authorities in East Africa went so far as to destroy the large quantity of cowries which they withdrew from circulation, in an effort to repair the harm done by the delay in adopting anti-inflationary measures.

Efforts were also made in many instances to reduce the production of locally produced primitive currencies. In the Solomon Islands the output of dogs' teeth currency was restricted by limiting the number of dogs any native is entitled to own.[1] In the North American colonies, tobacco-growing was repeatedly restricted, in order to safeguard the value of the depreciating tobacco currency.

The French authorities in Sudan made an effort during the last century to maintain the stability of cowries by moving large quantities from districts where they were in super-abundance to districts where a shortage prevailed. Repeated attempts were made to hold the cowries at a fixed rate, but in face of the strong downward trend this was not very successful. Nor was the attempt at stabilizing the value of guinea-cloth much easier. The Sultans in Uganda, too, in the last century tried for some time to maintain the value of cowries by withdrawing into their Treasury the surplus and releasing it again if this was necessary.

Throughout history efforts were made to stabilize the ratio between two or more currencies in circulation at the same time in a community. Already the Law of Hammurabi sought to equate the value of silver and that of barley, but the official rate had to be revised frequently in face of the secular depreciation of silver in terms of barley. The unofficial rate was inclined, moreover, to lose touch with the official parity. There were in later periods more successful attempts at maintaining the stability of monetary units in terms of each other. The ratios between the various currencies used in Ancient and Medieval Ireland, or in Scandinavia, appears to have remained in force for long periods. Likewise, some of the ratios established in Oceania and some parts of Africa remained valid for some time.

Price control was yet another device resorted to in many communities at a comparatively backward stage of development. It was highly developed in the Hittite Empire. Among many primitive tribes prices are apt to remain stable for a long time even in face of the wholesale dumping of primitive currencies by white traders, thanks to the force of the tribal law or custom that has fixed them.

Generally speaking, it is true that primitive currencies tend to achieve

[1]Possibly this measure was in part at least due to the fact that the teeth are extracted with the aid of methods of the utmost cruelty.

stability not so much through the policy of the authorities as through conservatism and respect for tradition. Under pure barter fixed relationships developed on the basis of which goods were exchanged against each other, and this relationship remained unaltered over long periods. The same phenomenon is noticeable in price fixing in primitive currencies. In many primitive communities the commercial spirit which would bring about price fluctuation is absent to a remarkable degree. In the absence of outside interference with the working of the monetary system of primitive communities, a stabilizationist monetary policy stands a good chance of operating successfully over long periods, simply because the desire for the maintenance of the *status quo* is in accordance with the fundamental character of most primitive peoples.

CHAPTER 31

EXPANSIONIST MONETARY POLICY

The conception according to which money can only assume its functions by the maintenance of a scarcity of its volume is not borne out by the study of primitive money. It is not absolutely essential that the monetary object should be scarce, except in the broadest sense of the term. There are in fact many instances of the choice of a currency material which is plentiful, and is there ready to be picked up. In so far as the choice of such material is a result of a deliberate policy it provides an instance of primitive monetary expansionism.

Expansionism through the choice of monetary material is encountered in modern monetary history among those advocating paper money or bimetallism. In primitive communities it usually assumes the form of the choice of the staple product for monetary purposes. This may occur spontaneously, owing to the fact that there is bound to be a big commercial turnover in the staple product which is certain to be a favourable medium of barter, and also lends itself to be used as a store of value. It is possible, however, that in some instances the staple product was chosen deliberately by the political authority, or that its spontaneous adoption by the community was confirmed by the State.

It must be obvious even to a primitive mind that the choice of an object of which there are apt to be large supplies entails considerable advantages. The tribal chief must be aware that if he levies tribute and imposes fine in objects that are scarce his receipts are bound to be low, while if he determines political payments in the form of the staple product of his tribe he is assured of a substantial revenue. If he is capable of seeing beyond the narrow horizon of his immediate advantages he must realize that the choice of the staple product encourages the increase of its production, and enables the producers to find buyers for their surpluses without difficulty. This means prosperity for a large section of the community—probably the majority of tribesmen is engaged in producing the staple product—which again tends to assure the popularity of the chief. In so far as the community has reached a relatively advanced stage, the choice of an object that is plentiful greatly assists it in the transition from natural economy to money economy. In fact, if a scarce object is chosen a large section of the community is bound to retain natural economy to a high degree, or to choose some other form of primitive currency.

The adoption of a currency the supply of which is plentiful also assists in the development of capitalist production, since it is easier to accumulate capital in a currency the supply of which is plentiful than in one which is scarce.

Another advantage of the choice of the staple product as currency is that its quantity is not only large but can be increased. As we said above, the adoption of the staple product encourages the production of the monetary objects. This increase, if not excessive, should go a long way towards encouraging general economic activity.

In the majority of instances the possibilities of expanding the staple product are not sufficient to cause inflation. There are natural limits; the output of a staple product cannot be multiplied like that of paper money. Nevertheless, many communities adopting the staple product as their currency have experienced fairly advanced depreciation with all its adverse consequences. The tendency for the monetary object to depreciate is, however, offset for a long time by the opposite tendency brought about by the monetization of the staple product as a result of which the additional monetary demand tends to increase its value. Moreover, the value of an object is increased by the fact that those who can acquire it can use it freely for the purpose of acquiring with it other objects. Its liquidity compared with that of holdings of other goods constitutes an attraction that expresses itself in a rise of its value. To a very large degree, the monetization of a staple product works like a valorization scheme in modern raw material producing communities. The effect is in both cases an artificial increase of the value of the produce, above the level justified by the relation between commercial supply and demand, as a result of withholding part of the supply from the market. The difference is that while in modern valorization schemes the authorities buy up and store or destroy the unwanted supply, under the monetary use of staple products it is the members of the community who withdraw substantial quantities from the market, by using the products as a medium of exchange, means of unilateral and deferred payments, and as a store of value. Most of the members of the community benefit by such "valorization schemes," at any rate for some time.

The extent to which the monetary use of a staple product is liable to increase its value may be accentuated by artificial means. Policy aiming at that result was practised in the West Indies and in the old American colonies. The authorities of these colonies were not content with putting the staple produce to monetary use in order to relieve the shortage of coins. They fixed the parities of the commodity currencies well above their market value, in an attempt to confer the maximum benefit on the producers, and in an effort to change the terms of trade in favour of their colony. Obviously, such a policy led invariably to an increase of the output of the staple product.

Another reason why primitive State authority adopted expansionist policy was that this facilitated the accumulation of large stores of wealth by its own Treasury, and the existence of such large monetary reserves tended to give the political authority greater political power, whether the Treasury contained wheat, cattle, beaver skins or metals.

The choice of a local product for monetary material was not, however, necessarily an expansionist one. Sometimes a product was chosen the quantity of which could not be increased to any great extent. This is the case with metals. The possibilities of increasing mining output are even in our age not unlimited, and were very limited in primitive conditions.

Possibly the choice of a local product was made with the desire to avoid dependence on imports. This was presumably the case with Sparta, where the choice of iron was probably motivated largely by the desire to use the locally produced metal as the currency instead of imported silver, gold or copper.

It is difficult to draw the line between an expansionist and an antideflationist policy. On occasions the staple product was assigned a monetary role in order to avoid a deflation through the inadequacy of the supply of metallic currency. Whether this was the case with the barley currency of Babylonia it is difficult to say. The fact that wine merchants had to be forced by the threat of death penalty to accept barley in payment instead of insisting on silver seems to indicate that, at the time of the adoption of the Code of Hammurabi at any rate, it was necessary to enlist the State authority to assure the maintenance of the monetary role of barley. Hammurabi considered it necessary to intervene possibly because a demonetization of barley would have resulted in an acute scarcity of silver currency. During later periods there appeared to be a super-abundance of silver rather than a scarcity; nevertheless, barley was retained as a subsidiary currency.

An instance of anti-deflationist policy is provided by the ban in 1600 on the export of cocoa beans in Spanish Central America, in order to safeguard the currency supply of the country. In Medieval Russia the alleged practice of using parts of skins for monetary purposes instead of whole skins may have been inspired by expansionism. It may have been the result of an endeavour to adapt the volume of currency to the requirements of growing trade, and to avoid the inconveniences of an inadequate supply of money that might have handicapped the growth of trade. The ban placed in 1710 in Massachusetts on the export of beaver skins as well as coins by colonists returning to England aimed decidedly on the maintenance of an adequate monetary circulation.

Primitive monetary expansionism can be practised also with imported monetary materials. The import and accumulation of the materials may be encouraged by their adoption for monetary use. For instance, as brass forms the material of many weapons and utensils in Africa, its monetary use tends to stimulate the influx of large quantities. There are instances of State encouragement of import of monetary materials, as of encouragement to grow a product at home, through its adoption for monetary purpose.

An interesting type of primitive monetary expansionism is provided by the cloth currency of Iceland and other countries of Northern Europe in the Middle Ages. This system was expansionist, since every individual was entitled to produce as much of this local currency as he wanted within the limits of his raw material and labour resources. The same is true to a less extent of the leather money of the Isle of Man which could be produced by every "man of substance."

A curious instance of monetary expansionism is provided by the experience of the Dutch colony of New Amsterdam in North America. Governor Stuyvesant banned the monetary use of loose and badly strung *wampum*. Later, however, when an acute scarcity of currency developed, he repealed the ordinance, in order to increase the volume of currency even at the cost of admitting inferior material for monetary use.

CHAPTER 32

FOREIGN EXCHANGE POLICY

Foreign exchange policy may be defined as the attitude of the political authorities towards the value of the local currency in terms of foreign currencies, and towards the process of its conversion into such currencies. As is the case with monetary policy in general, the passive attitude of the authorities towards foreign exchanges may be considered to constitute a policy if it is deliberate. The following are the main actions taken in the course of executing an active foreign exchange policy:—

1. The fixing of exchange parities.
2. The alteration of exchange parities.
3. The adoption of measures aiming at maintaining the parities.
4. In the absence of fixed parities the adoption of measures to influence the tendency of exchange rates.

5. The adoption of measures aiming at restricting dealings in exchanges.

Whenever possible it is sought to fix the parities of primitive currency by unilateral action. If the primitive currencies consist of the staple products of the communities concerned there is a natural tendency for the official policy to aim at over-valuation of the local currency. This is simply another way of saying that every community endeavours to get as good a price as possible for its exports. Whether it can get the price aimed at depends on the external demand for its products and on the monopolistic position occupied by the producing community. We saw that in the case of the West Indian colonies and also in the colonies of the North American continent, the endeavour to over-value the local commodity currencies defeated its object by leading either to higher prices being charged by merchants exporting their goods to those colonies, or to over-production causing an inevitable fall in the price of the staple commodity.

Many circumstances may arise which make it expedient for communities using primitive currencies to alter their existing parities. Such decisions are of major importance, because they affect not only the exchange rate but also the internal value of the commodity concerned. As in modern foreign exchange policy, decisions to lower the exchange value of the commodity currency are usually inspired by the desire to increase the volume of exports, while decisions to raise the exchange value are inspired by the desire to change the terms of trade in favour of the country concerned.

While in modern foreign exchange policy the advantages of a deliberate over-valuation of the currency from the point of view of its effect upon the terms of trade were only discovered quite recently, that policy was consciously pursued in the colonies of the West Indies and North American continent throughout the 17th century. Under the influence of a desire to create employment through achieving the largest possible volume of exports, those responsible for the shaping of modern foreign exchange policy were, and in some instances still are, apt to overlook the fact that a country does not export for the sake of exporting, but for the sake of earning the means that is to enable it to import. If the means of payment required for that purpose can be earned through exporting a relatively small quantity, so much the better. The more a currency is over-valued, the smaller volume of exports is required for paying for the same amount of imports. This elementary truth which was overlooked by statesmen engaged in competitive currency depreciation during the 'thirties, was fully realized by the Colonial Governments of the Western hemisphere three hundred years earlier. It was rediscovered during the late 'thirties by Germany, in her dealings with South-Eastern Europe.

Measures for the defence of parities fixed by the political authorities of primitive communities were encountered in various African countries on the cowrie standard. Either the native ruler or the Colonial authorities often resorted to operations aiming at preventing an unwanted depreciation or appreciation. Surplus supplies were absorbed by treasuries to prevent depreciation, and they were brought out again when there was a scarcity of cowries. A much more frequent method adopted by Colonial authorities was to prevent a further depreciation of cowries prohibiting their import. In some instances the production of locally produced currency was restricted. It is difficult to decide to what extent such measures can be regarded as measures of internal monetary policy or measures of foreign exchange policy.

PART V: THE PHILOSOPHY OF PRIMITIVE MONEY

CHAPTER 33

THE ECONOMIC ROLE OF PRIMITIVE MONEY

THE period of the use of primitive money constituted an indispensable phase in economic evolution. The maxim *Natura non facit saltum*, chosen by Marshall for his *Principles of Economics*, applies in full to the progress of mankind from the crudest form of barter to the most advanced form of modern money economy. Many writers dealing superficially with earlier phases of economic history are inclined to look down with pity mingled perhaps with contempt on the inferior systems applied by inferior human beings because they knew no better. In the same way, supporters of the system of scientifically managed currency feel very superior to 19th century economists who swore by that "barbarous relic," the gold standard. Yet as those endowed with a spirit of understanding have now come to realize, mankind had to pass through that phase to achieve the present more advanced phase of scientifically managed currency. The automatic gold standard corresponded to 19th century conditions and to the stage of progress of its period. The same is true also about systems which were much less advanced than the gold standard.

It is absurd to suppose that, had by some chance Keynes lived some five thousand years earlier and had he then produced his works on scientific monetary management (which, incidentally, he could not have done without the spade-work of generations of economists), his contemporaries could have applied his monetary system. It would have been entirely out of keeping with the stage of cultural and economic progress of the day. Savage races could not be expected to jump the intermediate phases between barter and scientifically managed credit money merely because by some freak chance or anachronism a genius born long before his time happened to strike upon the idea of it. The "inevitability of gradualness" has to be regarded as a basic principle in monetary evolution.

This does not mean that at every period the monetary system necessarily corresponded to the stage of evolution of that period. There are instances of the survival of obsolete monetary systems out of conservatism or for want of knowledge of a better system. More advanced systems were at times slow in developing in comparatively advanced communities, and the maintenance of primitive systems over periods of centuries when they could and should have been removed constituted at times a grave handicap to progress. Nevertheless, thinking in terms of more than five milleniums, it is, broadly speaking, true to say that every period had the money it deserved on the ground of the prevailing stage of its economic and cultural evolution.

Between barter and modern money the gap is very wide. It had to be bridged in stages merging into each other almost imperceptibly. Primitive money was a necessary phase to prepare barter-minded races for the use of more advanced money.

Even if it had been possible to adopt modern money at a much earlier stage it would not necessarily have brought about a more rapid progress in economic evolution. Indeed, it seems probable that most communities would have had to revert to the use of some system of primitive money, as they or their economies would not have been qualified to adopt and maintain a system of modern money. The rudimentary monetary methods of primitive communities more or less corresponded to their requirements. The inconveniences of primitive money, on which so much stress is laid by modern writers wanting to emphasize the superiority of modern money, were not nearly as awkward as they seem to us when viewing it through modern eyes. Many systems of primitive money could be used, and had in fact been used, for relatively advanced purposes.

There is no reason to suppose that the absence of modern money hindered considerably the development of a rudimentary division of labour or the earliest phases in the emergence of a capitalist production. A certain degree of division of labour was already possible even under barter, and the use of money, however primitive, encouraged and facilitated further specializations. Likewise, it was possible to accumulate capital for productive purposes even under pure natural economy. The adoption of primitive money greatly faciltated, however, the process, even though it was not so convenient for the accumulation of capital as modern money. But, then, during the phases when primitive money was used there were also other causes on account of which the accumulation of capital could not proceed on a modern scale. It would not be justified to suggest that through an earlier adoption of coinage it would have been possible to accelerate materially the pace of the progress of prodution and thereby to raise the standard of living.

At the same time it must be admitted that many systems of primitive money failed to fulfil one of the main economic roles money is called upon to fulfil, namely, to relieve producers from the worry, which they have to face under barter, of finding a suitable counterpart to their sales. The great advantage of modern money and also of the more advanced forms of primitive money is that it enables producers to sell their goods without having to consider whether they will get the right type of goods in exchange for their products. Money being a mandate which can be used indiscriminately for any purpose is acceptable by producers as a matter of course. If, however, as is the position under less advanced primitive monetary systems, the means of payment that are used are not sufficiently generally acceptable, then producers are left to face the problem of ensuring that they should be paid in the right type of money or that they should have a chance of disposing of the wrong type of money. In that case their position is somewhere about half way between barter and modern money economy. Once, however, an advanced stage of primitive money is reached the difference between it and modern money from this point of view becomes largely one of degree.

It has been suggested that primitive money, while suitable for local trade, tends to handicap long-distance trade. Beyond doubt it is inconvenient to have to carry for long journeys heavy or bulky substances serving as primitive money. Even from this point of view, however, the inconveniences of primitive money from a commercial point of view are apt to be exaggerated. They are very real for travellers in backward countries who have to carry large amounts of bulky primitive currencies in order to pay their way during their expeditions. To traders this inconvenience does not operate to the same extent, for the simple reason that they have to carry bulky commodities in any case in one direction, and it is not so difficult for them to make arrangements to carry bulky commodities in both directions. The example of the Phœnicians, who were probably the most enterprising commercial race for all time, conclusively shows that it is possible to conduct long-distance trade even in the complete absence of currency, on a barter basis. Indeed, the necessity for carrying bulky and heavy cargoes in both directions instead of carrying less voluminous coins of precious metals in one direction was considered to be actually advantageous in seaborne trade, and was given by several authors, rightly or wrongly, as the reason why the Phœnicians did not invent coinage. While it would be idle to deny that the earlier adoption of modern money would have facilitated advanced trade, it would not have made a fundamental difference any more than in respect of the progress of production.

From the point of view of an equal distribution of wealth there can be no doubt that the adoption of primitive money was a step in the wrong direction and that the adoption of modern money further accentuated the maldistribution that is apt to accompany monetary economy. Generally speaking, it is true that the more advanced the type of money used by a community the easier it became to accumulate large fortunes. Apart from this, the adoption of money economy even in its primitive form tended to obscure the effects of inequalities in wealth and income. In a moneyless system, such as that of the Inca Empire, distribution of the proceeds of production was a matter of arithmetic. Those in charge of the process knew more or less the quantities at their disposal, and those receiving their share in the proceeds knew precisely what they were receiving. The adoption of even a rudimentary money economy was necessarily detrimental to the clarity of this picture. Once wages and profits came to be earned not in actual goods intended for direct consumption but in money, the recipients were no longer in a position to know precisely or even approximately what they were receiving in terms of real goods and services. It depended on the way they used their money and on the prices they had to pay. It became possible to bring about a fictitious increase of earnings which, unless accompanied by a corresponding increase in production, failed to yield to the recipients any increase of their share in real goods and services. So long as primitive currency consisted of commodities with full intrinsic value its employment did not materially obscure the true picture of distribution. With the adoption of ornament money, however, the situation changed and the further monetary system progressed towards modern money the more it obscured distribution.

Primitive money played an important economic role not only by being an indispensable intermediate phase between barter and modern money, but also by providing a useful alternative for mankind to fall back upon whenever the modern monetary system failed to function satisfactorily. But for this possibility, the extent to which inadequacy of modern money in given circumstances would have handicapped economic progress from time to time would have been considerably larger. The possibility of reverting to primitive money was particularly helpful during the early colonial period when the volume of coins was not sufficient to meet indispensable requirements. The alternative to the adoption of primitive money would have been either to revert to barter pure and simple which would have been hopelessly out of keeping with the advanced stage reached by that time, or to submit to the full extent to the grave inconveniences of the inadequate supply of modern money. In either case the solution would have been gravely detrimental to economic progress. Primitive money provided the happy medium, thanks to which a society with advanced division of labour and a large volume of trade was able to carry on, and thanks to which its productive activity was not fatally crippled by lack of currency. Beyond doubt, without being ideal by any means, the various types of primitive money used by colonists were infinitely a lesser evil than either pure barter or an acute scarcity of money. Primitive money also played an important economic role during periods when modern money became discredited for some reason.

Viewed from the perspective of economic history primitive money played an essentially constructive part, the importance of which has not been sufficiently realized. While the unfavourable effects of retaining a backward system after it ceased to be justified by the prevailing conditions must be admitted, on balance in the economic sphere primitive money helped incomparably more than it hindered.

CHAPTER 34

A SOCIAL THEORY OF MONEY

If there is one conclusion that emerges forcefully from the examination of the evidence regarding the role of primitive money, it is that the true meaning of money can only be grasped if it is viewed not as a mere technical device but as a social institution of fundamental importance. Any theory which does not regard it as such is bound to give an inadequate picture of the role money has played and is still playing in civilization. The defect of most monetary theories is that they take too narrow a view of the scope of money. Some economists regard it as a commodity employed as a convenient technical device to facilitate the exchanges of goods and services. Others regard it as a symbol and an abstract unit of account. Others again regard it as a legal instrument. This aspect of money and many of its other aspects are emphasized by various theories, which in many ways contradict each other, though they all contain part of the truth. By concentrating on a relatively narrow aspect of the subject, however, they all miss the substance.

The monetary system must be regarded as the fundmental factor responsible for providing the driving power stimulating the economic activities of all human society, except in a completely planned totalitarian system. The true significance of money can only be adequately realized if we succeed in finding a common denominator applicable to a large proportion of the systems of both modern and primitive money. Although those systems differ from each other very widely in many respects they both provide their respective communities, primitive or modern, with a stimulus for a higher degree of utilization of their productive faculties.

Let us first examine how money fulfils this role in a modern community, dependent on individual initiative and profit motive for incentive. It must be admitted that the existence of money is by no means an indispensable condition to that incentive. It can also exist under barter, but a monetary system unquestionably stimulates it. A monetary system provides wide opportunities for making, preserving and enjoying profit derived from increased productive activities. Beyond doubt, profit can be made also on direct exchanges of goods and services without the intermediary of money, but the scope for earning profit can be widened considerably by the adoption of a monetary system.

Unless a moneyless system is based on an economy that is planned to the utmost degree, it is bound to leave unutilized a large part of the factors of production simply because there is no easy means of combining them in a proper working system. Money provides that means. With its aid the owner of natural resources finds it easier to combine his productive capacity with the resources of owners of other forms of capital, or with those poessessing organizing capacity, and expert knowledge, and with labour.

It is true, modern money is essentially fictitious wealth in contradistinction to wealth consisting of real goods. But the existence of such fictitious wealth tends to increase real wealth. This is done partly by making it easier for the possessors of money to enlist the collaboration of various factors of production which might otherwise be idle. It can be done through offering them tempting remuneration. A monetary system makes possible the development of a vicious spiral of rising wages and profit, and can thereby create a fictitious feeling of prosperity. Everybody can be made to imagine that he is earning more without realizing for some time at any rate that his extra earnings are absorbed by rising costs. This feeling of prosperity, false as it is, tends to stimulate activity and thereby tends to bring about an increased volume of production which may place the originally fictitious increase of prosperity on solid material foundations. Beyond doubt the system is sheer self-deception. It is, however, constructive self-deception which, during critical periods, assists in the utilization of physical productive capacity to its utmost limit. But for the secular trend of rising prices, brought about by the operation of the monetary system, production might have lacked the adequate stimulus required to ensure its progress.

Nor is this all. The existence of a monetary system increased the possibility for accumulating the fruits of productive activity. So long as the accumulation of wealth can only be in the form of goods, it is necessarily limited, even if its limits are wide and elastic. Once it becomes possible to accumulate wealth in the form of money, its limits disappear almost completely. Finally, the enjoyment of the accumulated fruits of productive activity is also increased by the existence of money with the advantage of indiscriminate spending power that it confers on its owner.

In a primitive society money plays necessarily a totally different part. Primitive man is not as a rule interested in wealth for its own sake, nor for the sake of the additional amenities of life it is capable of providing. He is not stimulated by the profit motive to anything like the extent modern man is. In particular in tropical climates, such as that of the Pacific islands, he can secure for himself the necessary food with very little exertion; nor need he exert himself very much to secure for himself clothing and housing facilities, etc. In such circumstances it must be very tempting to lead an idle existence, conforming to the popular idea of the easy-going South Sea savage. The social system is also in many respects against making much effort to stimulate production in order to accumulate wealth. In many savage communities rich and poor live more or less in the same way. The Jabim of Simbang, for instance, have no words in their vocabulary for "rich" and "poor." Nobody is allowed to starve while the community has something to eat.[1] Everybody lives more or less in the same way. They consume the same food and they put up with the same degree of primitive discomfort. There is, moreover, a trend towards the re-distribution of accumulated wealth. Riches in a primitive community do not represent permanent possession, merely temporary power of disposal of commodities in which their owner permits the members of his group to share. "It may be considered that primitive wealth is not of an economic but of a social nature," states Thurnwald,[2] "the man who has by whatever means acquired more cattle, grain, or valuables of any kind than his neighbours has not done so in order to hoard his wealth for his own benefit, but that it may be used for the good of other members of the community." Thurnwald adds that this attitude is not entirely inspired by unselfishness. It is due also to fear of envy that makes a virtue of necessity.

The prestige value of being able to give away much is an all-important consideration. Under the prevailing social customs, chiefs and rich men of the community are fully expected to give away most of what they possess as failure to do so would not only expose them to the contempt of their community, but might even undermine their political power and endanger their personal security. A trace of this attitude towards wealth and the wealthy is surviving even in our modern society. Many, though by no means all, wealthy men spend large amounts on charitable and cutltural purposes. They do so partly in order to gain prestige and influence, and their generosity is often rewarded by honours conferred on them. To some extent they may also feel some moral obligation to return to the community at least part of the wealth they have succeeded in withdrawing from the community. Consciously or otherwise, the owner of a large fortune may feel that his contributions to charity and cultural institutions are a form of insurance premium, since they tend to disarm the feeling of hostility aroused by the evidence of his wealth. The difference between primitive and modern conditions in this respect is that such an attitude in a modern community is exceptional; it is confined to a small section of the financial Upper Ten. On the other hand, it is a fairly general rule in a primitive community. Moreover, while the modern benefactor millionaires only give away a relatively small part of what they possess, the primitive chiefs are induced by their craving for prestige or by political or moral pressure to give away most of what they have gained. They are for all practical purposes merely a clearing house of wealth through which possessions pass, possessions which they could only use temporarily during the time lag between the influx and the efflux.

What is important to realize is that the desire to give away is as powerful a motive in a primitive community as is the desire to possess

[1]Schurtz, p. 78.
[2]Thurnwald (1938), pp. 182-3.

and enjoy in a modern community. The wish to be able to increase contributions to charity seldom if ever inspires the modern man to work harder or earn more. Primitive man, on the other hand, is largely inspired by such a motive. It is the wish to be able to distribute the largest possible amount of wealth that inspires him to exert himself beyond the degree that is necessary for satisfying his simple needs. From this point of view the existence of a system of primitive money tends to stimulate his economic activities to an extent comparable with the incentive provided in modern communities by the existence of a modern monetary system, simply because primitive money provides the means through which this urge to give away can be satisfied in the most convenient form.

Beyond doubt it is possible in a primitive community to redistribute wealth even in the absence of money. This was done in fact in Ancient Egypt where the revenue of the State consisted of goods of every description, which were given away to those dependent on the State in the same form as they were received. This form of natural economy has its limits. In order to be able to satisfy more fully the desire to give away, primitive man devised various kinds of symbols of value the quantity of which is capable of being increased more easily than that of consumer goods. The existence of various types of primitive money in the Pacific and in other primitive communities considerably increased the scope for accumulating wealth in order to be able to give it away. Admittedly, in many instances, the wealth thus accumulated is largely fictitious. Such intrinsic value as the primitive money in question possess is solely due to its adoption for the purposes of being given away. But it fulfils its all-important social function to the same extent as if it consisted of objects of first-rate utility.

What is important is that the competitive fever aroused by the desire to possess these monetary objects tends to stimulate genuine productive activity. Those members of the community who are not themselves in a position to produce money have to increase their output of goods beyond their personal requirements in order to be able to acquire money from others. The process leads to an all-round increase of productive activity. It is true, part of that activity is, strictly speaking, wasteful since it is directed towards the production of monetary objects which are of no practical use. But then the same is true concerning the modern monetary system. The production of shell money in the Pacific for the sake of being piled up in the house of a chief and subsequently given away, only in order that it should find its way back eventually to the chief who would give it away once more is neither more futile nor less futile than the labour spent on the mining of gold for the sake of being able to bury it once more in the vaults of Fort Knox.

What matters is that we should realize that the monetary system both in primitive and in modern communities is a basic factor in the social structure of their respective communities, because it provides the incentive making for progress. While the nature of the incentive may differ, and there may be considerable differences of degree in its result, there is a fundamental similarity of the role played by modern money in advanced society and by primitive money in primitive society. The realization of this fact leads us to the acceptance of the social theory of money under which money, whether primitive or modern, is regarded as a motive power that tends to secure economic progress.

It must be pointed out, however, that all primitive communities are not predominently redistributionist in character. In many of them goods are accumulated not for the sake of giving them away, but for the sake of participating in affinal exchanges, or in religious sacrifices, or in secret societies. What matters is that in every instance primitive money is closely linked with the peculiar social institution which forms the centre of the political, social and economic life of the community concerned. In many instances the monetary objects are retained because of their prestige value. This is the case with many African communities on the livestock standard. In all these instances the desire to possess money constitutes a powerful driving force making for an increase of production beyond immediate requirements.

As we stated above, the only society in which money does not play such a fundamental part is a society with a totalitarian economy. In the Inca Empire, money was eliminated by a thoroughgoing system of economic planning. In Ancient Egypt the role of money was subordinate owing to the high degree of planned economy in operation. In our chapter on moneyless economies we quoted several other instances. Above all, money is bound to play a subordinate part in a modern Communist state even though in the Soviet Union it has not been eliminated altogether. It is thus possible, from our point of view, to contrast the Communistic economy not with capitalist economy, but with money economy, whether the latter be on capitalist lines as in modern communities or redistributionist lines as in many primitive communities.

CHAPTER 35

THE HISTORICAL ROLE OF PRIMITIVE MONEY

The question of the role money played in world history has never been examined systematically. Isolated instances are at times quoted, however, to show that monetary developments are liable to affect the course of history. The outstanding instance is the part the decline of monetary supplies of precious metals is alleged to have played in bringing about the decline of the Roman Empire. Another instance is the decline of the Royal power in England during the early part of the 17th century which was said to have been a result of the fall in the real value of Royal revenues brought about by the depreciation of currency that followed the influx of precious metals from the New World. There are many more similar instances, but as they concern modern money they are outside the scope of our present enquiry. Their careful examination, not as isolated instances but as manifestations of underlying trends, would be a task well worth undertaking by a historian with a sound knowledge of economics or by an economist with a sound knowledge of general history.

It stands to reason that primitive money was also able from time to time to influence the course of history. By the nature of the subject we are, to a large extent, necessarily in the realm of conjecture. Our records of the relevant facts are not nearly sufficiently complete to enable us to put forward firm views about certain monetary situations being the cause of certain military or political events. How could we be too sure of our ground, seeing that even the monetary explanation of historical events during our lifetime is the subject of heated controversy? We all know more or less the facts about the suspension of the gold standard by Great Britain in 1931. Yet there are diametrically opposite opinions about the historical effect of that monetary change. According to some, it stopped a period of decadence in Great Britain and enabled her to save Europe and world freedom in 1940. According to others, it led to currency chaos and accentuated the world economic crisis that gave Hitler his chance to seize power. If opinions are divided to such an extent when we are sure of our facts, how much more difficult it is to arrive at the absolute truth when the facts themselves are doubtful?

Nevertheless, in some instances it is possible to put forward some tentative theories. It has been suggested, for example, that the reason why the Egyptian and Chinese Empires lasted for so long was the absence of any proper monetary system. This ingenious theory was put forward, among others, by Sir Norman Angell. The assumption is presumably based consciously or otherwise on the popular feeling that "money is the root of all evil" and that the existence of a monetary system proper makes, therefore, for political and economic instability. Beyond doubt, the existence of a high degree of controlled economy in Ancient Egypt made for stable if static conditions, but there are no indications that similar conditions prevailed in Ancient China, where in any case some kind of primitive money existed ever since the dawn of history, even if it was not always Government-controlled.

Is there any reason to assume on the face of the evidence we possess that because in Egypt money served largely as a unit of account to assist barter instead of serving as a medium of exchange in everyday life this made a fundamental difference to the political stability of the Egyptian Empire? Whether through coincidence or otherwise, there are indications of an increasing gold and copper output during the periods of greatness in Ancient Egyptian history. As we pointed out in the chapter on Ancient Egypt this increase may have been effect rather than cause of the political strength of the Empire at these periods, since a weak administration would have been unable to overcome the immense difficulties that mining expeditions had to face in those times. On the other hand, the possession of a large amount of gold undoubtedly increased the power of the Pharaohs. They were able to buy the support of the priesthood with the aid of generous presents and that of foreign princes with the aid of subsidies. They were able to finance costly military operations in Western Asia. In the absence of adequate supplies of precious metals the Pharaohs became politically weak internally and externally.

It stands to reason that these ups and downs connected with the fluctuation of the output of gold or copper would have been much more pronounced if these metals had played a really important monetary part. The existence of a controlled and largely moneyless economy in Ancient Egypt necessarily reduced the part played by the monetary factor in her history. It seems reasonable to assume that the extent to which the political position of a weak Pharaoh further deteriorated through his inability to maintain the output of the monetary metals would have been even more pronounced if these metals had played a full monetary role and if, therefore, their scarcity had handicapped production. The fact that basic economic activities could be carried on to a large extent independently of the fluctuation of metallic supplies justifies us in reaching the tentative conclusion that the limited character of the role played by money was a factor making for political as well as economic stability, and in this sense it may have been to some extent responsible for the prolonged existence of the Egyptian Empire.

Another instance in which primitive money is believed to have played a historical part is that of Sparta. Beyond doubt, the choice of iron bars as currency made for isolationism not only commercially but also politically, and this again may possibly have been to some degree at any rate responsible for the Peloponnesian wars which led eventually to the decline of both opponents and of Ancient Greece as a whole. It provided an opportunity for the temporary rise of Macedonia and for the more lasting rise of Rome. Possibly if Sparta had possessed ordinary coined currency, like Athens and the rest of Greece, she might have developed also in other respects on lines similar to those of Athens, and there might have been no irreconcilable contrast between the Spartan and Athenian mentality, a contrast which accounted partly for the hatred with which the Peloponnesian wars were fought to the bitter end. However, perhaps this speculation may appear somewhat far-fetched.

The question whether the decline in metal output in Europe and the drain of precious metals through an adverse trade balance with the East was the cause of the decline of the Roman Empire does not come within the scope of this book, for by that time Rome had developed a system of modern coinage. Conceivably the reversion to natural economy in some of the outlying provinces of the Empire may to some extent have weakened its military power since the legions which came to be paid in kind lost much of their original mobility. They gradually assumed the status of land-owning militia engaged both in civilian and military life.

There is, however, another way in which a primitive monetary system enters into the picture of the decline of Rome. It provided one of the main causes of the westward surge of the pastoral races which eventually led to the overthrow of the Roman Empire. It is a commonplace of textbooks on history that the cause of this westward surge was the lack of adequate grazing land for the livestock of the races of central Asia which pushed towards Western Europe in search of new pastures, in front of them those races which had previously settled in Western Asia and Eastern Europe. What is not realized by historians is that the main cause of the inadequacy of the grazing lands during that period in the Asiatic steppes was the extensive use of livestock as a currency by the pastoral peoples.

It stands to reason that any object or material which fulfils the purpose of currency is accumulated to a considerable degree, partly for the current requirements of a medium of exchange and partly as a store of value. Livestock is apt to be kept in far larger numbers than is necessary for its economic non-monetary use. The result is that, owing to the monetary use of livestock, grazing land and water supplies are apt to be exhausted much sooner than they would be otherwise. There was undoubtedly method in the apparently sadistic madness of the Mongolian invaders who systematically exterminated the populations of conquered countries in order to turn agricultural land into pasture. This would not have been considered necessary had it not been for the excessive size of livestock kept for monetary requirements.

That pastoral races using livestock as a currency are apt to be over-stocked for this reason, and that this is apt to be the cause of inter-tribal wars, may be illustrated from conditions prevailing until recently in Africa and elsewhere. It does not seem to be unreasonable to suggest that the same reason which not so long ago induced the Masai to attack peaceful agricultural tribes may have induced the Mongols some 1,500 years ago to invade Eastern Europe and force the Vandals, Goths, etc., in turn to invade the Roman Empire. Quite possibly the reason why the Huns of Attila were not content to live in Central Asia or at any rate on the plains of Eastern Europe was political ambition. But the origin of their westward movements may well have been the desire to feed their excessive stock of horses, cattle and sheep. And were it not for the fact that these animals were not slaughtered for consumption unless they met with an accident—a symptom indicating their use as a monetary reserve—their requirements for new pastures would not have been nearly so pressing.

Primitive money played an important part in the development of colonial empires, in particular in the development of the first British Empire. The mother-country never possessed an excessive supply of coins and was not over-generous in allocating them to the Colonies. Had it not been for the adoption of primitive currencies in the West Indies and in the early colonies on the American mainland the development of those colonies would have been an incomparably slower process. In particular, the early colonies on territory that is now the United States of America would have been gravely handicapped. During the second half of the 18th century they might not have reached a sufficiently advanced stage economically or politically to aim at independence. Conceivably by the time that stage would have been reached the attitude of the mother-country might have become more liberal under the influence of 19th century political philosophy, and the break between her and the colonies might conceivably have been avoided. It is possible, therefore, to put foward a tentative and admittedly highly speculative theory that the adoption of primitive currency in Virginia, Massachusetts and elsewhere has contributed towards enabling them to reach their economic and political maturity during the period of despotic rule by England, and was therefore one of the factors leading indirectly to the War of Independence.

Primitive currency played also an important historical role in the development of the colonial empires towards the end of the 19th century. Its existence greatly aided European penetration into Africa. The savage population of the dark continent was not sufficiently advanced for the use of modern money, and their requirements were too few to make possible large scale penetration through pure barter. The existence of primitive moneys, or their adoption in the course of trade with white men, created unlimited possibilities for trading with the tribes which would not accept modern money and would accept only limited amounts of European goods for direct consumption. They acquired the habit of accumulating hoards of objects which came to be used as primitive money, whether cotton cloth, cowries, beads, brass or gin. It is largely owing to this use of primitive money as a store of value that European traders secured a stronghold in Africa. It enabled the flag to follow trade and colonization progressed much more rapidly than it would have done had trade depended on the negligible current requirements of natives for European goods for direct consumption. Had penetration been slower the changes in the balance of power in Europe in the 19th century might have resulted in a totally different share-out of Africa among European powers. During the early years of this century, Germany might have developed into a World power as a result of securing for herself a much larger place in the tropical sun instead of remaining almost entirely a continental power.

Speculation on similar lines could, of course, be continued almost indefinitely. Even though some of the instances quoted, and many others not quoted, are decidedly far-fetched, they should not be dismissed as an amusing but futile pastime. For they indicate at any rate the possibility of primitive money having played an important historical part during various periods of history. With the aid of a patient and systematic study of the subject, this possibility could in many instances become probability, even if it could never become certainty.

CHAPTER 36

MONEY AND CIVILIZATION

The Introductory Section of this book raised the question whether the evolution of the monetary system has corresponded to the requirements of the progress of civilization. This question received much attention during the last three decades. Until 1914 it was taken for granted that the monetary system of the day was in substance the logical, natural and inevitable solution of the problem which it was meant to solve. While there was from time to time much criticism of detail, the fundamental principles of the monetary system at the beginning of this century were widely assumed to be substantially in accordance with 20th century requirements. Between the two World Wars, however, a number of experts and a large section of the intelligent public came to doubt this assumption. The monetary system became subject to much fundamental criticism for its inability to secure the stability of the purchasing power of money, and even more for its inability to keep pace with technical progress and to provide the financial means with the aid of which mankind would be able to utilize in full its increased productive capacity for the benefit of all. The conclusion was reached by many that the monetary system of our generation had gravely handicapped the progress of civilization.

This leads us to the broader question whether the evolution of money in general over the whole period of its existence corresponded to contemporary requirements of civilization. The conflict lies between the school of thought which, on the basis of 19th century prosperity and stability, maintains that the monetary system, under *laisser faire*, is bound to make for progress, and the opposite school which denounces the monetary system as the root of most if not all of the difficulties man has had to face throughout his long existence.

There is also the more fundamental controversy between the school which maintains that the monetary system has throughout history been a decisive factor for good or evil, and has had a decisive influence on economic, political, social and cultural progress, and the opposite school which holds the views that so far from being the cause the monetary system has been throughout its history merely the effect of changes in the economic, political, social and cultural background. The views held by the first school rest on the materialistic conception of history according to which everything was determined by economic factors; this conception is carried a step further by those who believe that the economic system itself which determined everything is in turn determined by the monetary factor. The opposite school of thought is what we may call economic determinism under which, given a certain phase of cultural, political, technical and intellectual development, the economic system is an inevitable product of these more fundamental factors.[1] Monetary determinism carries the concept of economic determinism a step further by maintaining that the monetary system, too, is determined by social, cultural, technical and political factors and, in addition to them, by general economic factors.

The question is how far does the study of primitive money tend to confirm the views of those who consider money an all-powerful factor in the fate of mankind, and how far it tends to support the conception according to which money is a helpless passive tool under the control of more fundamental factors? To what extent were the early phases in the evolution of mankind governed by the monetary factor? Unfortunately, there are very few instances which provide adequate material to enable us to form a definite opinion. Even so, we have to try to form tentative opinions on the basis of such material as is at our disposal.

The difficulty is that the evolution of money and that of civilization are so closely interwoven that it is seldom possible to ascertain with any degree of assurance which was the cause and which the effect. Nevertheless, there are some instances in which progress in the monetary system lagged behind that of civilization.

There can be little doubt that in Ancient Egypt the prevailing monetary system was the effect and not the cause of her peculiar political, social and economic system. As a large section of her population existed on rations distributed by the authorities, there was relatively little scope for trade and for the development of a relatively advanced type of money such as existed during the period in other countries which were in many ways at a much less advanced stage of cultural progress than Egypt. Attempts to attribute the slow pace of economic progress in Egypt and the continued existence of slavery and of the caste system to the absence of a more advanced system of money are utterly unconvincing. It was because Egypt was based on a totalitarian planned economy that she did not require an advanced monetary system; it was not

[1]Some authors use the term "economic determinism" in the opposite sense, as being synonymous with the term "materialistic conception of history." In the author's view the correct meaning of the former term is that the economic system is determined by general conditions.

because of the lack of such system that she remained totalitarian.

In Babylonia and Assyria an advanced monetary system developed at an early stage, but this again was the effect and not the cause of the prevailing general conditions under which there was much more trading activity than in Ancient Egypt. It was the requirements of long distance land-borne trade that presumably led to the adoption of silver money side by side with grain money, too bulky for long-distance traffic.

There is no evidence pointing towards the influence of the monetary system in the economic, social or cultural evolution of the Ancient Jews. The relatively backward character of the Phœnician monetary system failed to prevent the remarkable development of their trade and their general cultural progress.

One of the few instances in which monetary evolution appears to have cut ahead of general evolution was provided by Lydia. It seems that the invention of coinage was succeeded rather than preceded by considerable development in trade; development which during a brief period made Lydia a relatively important factor in history. In Ancient Greece, on the other hand, the evolution of money lagged far behind that of civilization, judging by the survival of the use of livestock currency during a period when, in other respects, a highly advanced stage was achieved. The Homeric system of the ox standard of value and cauldron medium of exchange—which existed presumably at the beginning of the 1st millenium B.C.—was very similar to that of culturally backward French Indo-China in the 19th century A.D. In Sparta the adoption of a primitive form of iron currency was possibly the effect rather than the cause of the peculiar social and political system of the community.

The currency of Ancient Italy and early Rome lagged far behind cultural development. The use of crude copper as a currency long after neighbouring people had adopted gold and silver coins must to some extent have handicapped material progress.

It seems probable that in Ancient China the variety of primitive currencies which were adopted simultaneously or successively have been unable to influence general conditions to any fundamental degree. The early monetary history of China indicates a high degree of elasticity in the adaptation of a monetary system to meet requirements.

The extent to which the redistribution of the hoarded gold stock of the Persian Empire following upon its conquest by Alexander contributed towards the cultural development of the Mediterranean zone of civilization, or the effect of the scarcity of metals during the decline of the Rome Empire and during the early centuries of the Middle Ages, are outside the scope of this book since the process affected the volume of coined money. The revival of the use of primitive money in various parts of Medieval Europe must have been the effect of general conditions rather than their cause.

In Japan the use of primitive money tended to bolster up the feudal system long after it had outlived its usefulness. It must have affected general cultural development to a considerable degree.

Economic necessity dictated the adoption of primitive currencies in countries which had no adequate supplies of coins such as Medieval Russia and the early British, French, Dutch, Portuguese and Spanish colonies. The use of primitive currencies in those countries by communities at a relatively advanced stage of civilization was entirely out of keeping with the stage of cultural progress, but did not appear to affect the latter adversely. On the contrary, it facilitated the development of a material culture in accordance with the intellectual standards of the colonists.

As for the relapse into the use of primitive currencies during the modern period in Europe and elsewhere, it was due to local and temporary emergency conditions. Such temporary uses of primitive money produced any profound or lasting effects on the progress of civilization.

In the majority of present-day or recent primitive communities, the evolution of the primitive monetary system was evidently the effect rather than the cause of their social and cultural evolution. This is particularly so in the Pacific area, but also in Africa where systems were developed with the aid of imported currencies superimposed on local cultures. In some instances, however, the choice of currencies may have affected fundamentally the trend of the civilization in the communities concerned. In general there was no fundamental social upheaval until the penetration of modern money.

Even though there is no lack of instances in which the monetary system was the cause rather than the effect of the changes in the trend of civilization, it seems that in the majority of instances the prevailing primitive monetary systems were the expression of contemporary phases in civilization rather than the factor responsible for its development. In a negative sense primitive money may, to some extent, have influenced cultural progress owing to its tendency to survive its usefulness and thereby to slow down the pace of general progress. It was only during the earlier stages that monetary evolution may have cut ahead of general progress through the development of monetary systems arising from political and other unilateral payments long before the expansion of trade made such means of payment commercially necessary. At later stages the monetary system was inclined to lag behind cultural progress. It appears that the position reached during our generation, in which the monetary system was slow in adapting itself to the requirements of technical progress, must have been experienced in somewhat different forms at various stages of human progress.

No exaggerated importance must be attached, however, to this argument. While during the transition periods the backward state of primitive monetary systems must have caused much inconvenience, thinking in terms of the entire course of evolution over five thousand years there can be no doubt that the monetary system showed a remarkable degree of adaptability to changing conditions. Admittedly, from time to time it lagged behind cultural progress. There can be no doubt, however, that most of the time it was helping rather than hindering the progress of civilization.

Progress, whether cultural or economic, is not an end in itself but merely a means to the end of furthering human happiness. Has the adoption and development of primitive money made the world a better place or a worse place to live in? It has been customary since time immemorial to harp back to the "good old days" when life was much simpler and more pleasant in the absence of the complications resulting from money economy. Most of these criticisms of money are directed against the evils associated with the modern monetary system. Nevertheless, since that system developed from primitive money, the latter is also accused by implication.

The charge calls for an answer. Would the world have been a happier place if natural economy had been allowed to continue? The question is purely hypothetical. With the increasing density of population and with general progress, natural economy was bound to go and cannot possibly be expected to return. The various phases of the development of primitive money must have mitigated to no slight degree the awkwardness of the transition from natural economy to modern money economy. To some extent they combined both the advantages and the disadvantages of both systems. From the point of view of the progress of civilization they provided the necessary transitional stage. In so far as in our more advanced stage of civilization we are less happy than our ancestors, it is progress in general that is to blame and not a system which was but one of the instruments and manifestions of progress.

On the face of it there may appear to be a contraction between this chapter which does not assess very highly the importance of money in the evolution of civilization, and Chapter 34 which lays stress on the great social importance of money as a motive power in economic progress. In reality, while the earlier chapter is concerned with the role of money at any given moment, the present chapter endeavours to give a bird's-eye's view of the process of evolution as a whole. At any given moment a defective monetary system may not provide the maximum of stimulus to productive activity. It is none the less true that, with all its defects, money as a social factor has played an important part in all ages, not necessarily as an active factor making for the progress of civilization, but as a factor corresponding to the requirements of its own period and its own environment.

CHAPTER 37

THE FUTURE OF PRIMITIVE MONEY

The object of this chapter is twofold: to discuss the future prospects of
the continued existence of primitive money or of a resumption of its use,
and to discuss the future of the study of primitive money. The title of
the chapter may appear on the face of it absurd, since one would think
that primitive money has a past but not a future. It is in accordance
with the fundamental trend that the progress of civilization should
eliminate it completely. Indeed, during the 'forties this progress towards
the elimination of primitive money has become accelerated to a considerable degree, but not owing to any advance of civilization. On the
contrary, it was entirely due to the influence of the war.

War-time conditions resulted in closer contact between advanced and
primitive civilizations. Until 1941 on the majority of the small Pacific
islands, for instance, the only contacts the primitive communities had
with European civilization was through the presence of a Government
agent, a few traders, missionaries and occasional visitors. During the
war, on the other hand, many of these islands were heavily occupied
either by Japanese or by Allied troops. This meant that the military
authorities in charge paid in notes for the goods and services which the
population was compelled to supply, and the savages were forced to
accept modern money whether they liked it or not. No information is
available about what happened in this respect during the Japanese
occupation. After the liberation of the islands, however, the American
occupation forces are known to have provided goods to enable the
natives to spend the dollar notes received in payment from them. By this
means they popularized the use of modern money. In the same way,
such primitive moneys as existed at the beginning of the Far Eastern
war in the Philippines, Malaya, Burma and Assam must have suffered
an eclipse through the influence of the spendings by Allied troops in
modern money. In backward regions of New Guinea and elsewhere,
primitive money is known, however, to have survived the war.

In Africa it was particularly through the forced pace of the exploitation of natural resources of war-time requirements that the use of
modern money was extended. On the other hand, since it was impossible
to supply the colonies with adequate quantities of European goods to
enable the natives to spend their notes, modern money became largely
discredited since it was largely unspendable. The result was that many
Africans became reluctant to produce more than was required for their
own use. This state of affairs appears to have failed, however, to lead
to a revival of the use of primitive currencies to any considerable
degree.

The war, while eliminating primitive currencies or reducing their importance in the East or possibly in Africa, has at the same time brought about a reversion to the use of primitive currencies in a number of belligerent countries in Europe and South-East Asia. This trend was, however, obviously due to passing abnormal causes and was bound to be purely temporary. In fact, in the majority of instances the countries concerned soon reverted to the use of modern money. Taking the world as a whole, it is safe to say that on balance the second World War materially reduced the use of primitive money.

The odds are heavily against a reversal of this trend. It seems probable that within the next decade or two most of the remaining primitive currencies will disappear or become reduced to insignificance, retaining only a very limited use mostly for ceremonial or symbolic purposes. The reason why this can be assumed lies in the revival of interest in colonial development. It seems probable that the next few years will witness the expenditure of large sums by all Colonial Powers on the construction of roads and railways, and the penetration of modern enterprise and trade into areas hitherto practically untouched by civilization will lead to the abandonment of the use of primitive money for most purposes.

Is primitive money likely to be reverted to extensively in years to come? The answer to this question depends entirely on future monetary conditions. Should there be advanced inflation such as we witnessed since the war in Greece and Hungary, the people of countries in such a situation are likely to revert to primitive money until their currencies are stabilized. Likewise, in case of sudden changes of regime or the threat of such changes, fears that the existing currencies might become demonetized might tend to lead to increased application of barter and the use of primitive money.

What is less certain is whether a return to deflationary trend would produce a similar effect as in early colonial periods when shortage of modern money led to the adoption of primitive money by advanced communities. Should a Government decide to revert to the orthodox monetary policy by keeping its country deliberately short of currency and credit resources, it is conceivable that, instead of submitting meekly to such a policy as if it were as an Act of God, large sections of the population would take the remedy into their own hand by supplementing their meagre supplies of modern money with some form of commodity currency. On the face of it this assertion may sound incredible. After all, during the 19th century and the first part of the 20th century this was not done. The only time when modern communities during that period reverted to primitive currencies was during brief spells of currency chaos. Generally speaking, they simply accepted the shortages of money as something inevitable. In the meantime, however, this conception has greatly changed. Most people would now refuse to believe that the scarcity of money due to their Government's deflationary policy is inevitable. The monetary system no longer commands the same authority as it did before the second World War and it would be no longer considered sacrilege or *lèse-majesté* to improve on the monetary system by supplementing it through the private use of commodity currencies. Whether this would in fact be done depends on the spirit of the people concerned. The mere realization that the remedy of the inconveniences caused by the shortage of money lies largely in their own hand should go a long way towards inducing our generation to adopt deliberately a solution which earlier generations had adopted instinctively.

It is even conceivable that the Governments themselves might resort to the use of primitive currencies in order to supplement inadequate quantities of modern currencies. They may be forced to deflate the latter against their wish, either because they are precluded from pursuing an expansionary monetary policy owing to interference by the International Monetary Fund set up under the Bretton Woods scheme, or because their paper money has become so utterly discredited through earlier inflations that it has become a matter of expediency to keep its quantity restricted. In that case, it is conceivable that the Governments concerned may supplement the quantity of their note circulation by enlisting some staple products for monetary use. They may possibly find that until they have succeeded in living down the distrust caused by inflation the use of goods with intrinsic value could provide a solution to their problem. A similar situation arose in the early American colonies towards the end of the 17th century and at the beginning of the 18th century when, owing to the abuses of note issues, the public arrived at the conclusion that commodity currencies, notwithstanding their many shortcomings, constituted an improvement on the unlimited use of the printing press.

Let us now cast a glance on the prospects of the study of primitive money. It is the object of this book to stimulate interest in the subject, and the author hopes that its publication will to some extent lead to further research into its various aspects. In any case, the revival of the use of primitive money under our very noses has aroused a certain interest. In particular, the adoption of the cigarette standard received a fair amount of publicity, even though it was confined almost entirely to describing how the system worked without drawing any comparison with earlier primitive currencies and without enlarging on the theoretical implications of this limited and temporary experience. Should some of the primitive currencies adopted amidst the prevailing emergencies remain in force for some time, it is bound to stimulate enquiry into the subject.

In any case, it seems reasonable to assume that the historical and ethnological approach to economics in general and to the study of money in particular will continue to gain ground. The question is whether it will be able to do so soon enough to encourage the study of the remaining primitive monetary systems before they have disappeared. The urgency of the task of investigating conditions in primitive communities which are still using primitive currencies cannot be sufficiently emphasized. Field work for that purpose should be encouraged by every possible means. Much is spent on research into subjects which are not likely to run away, and it is of the utmost importance that a small fraction of the amounts devoted to research should be so employed as to accelerate the pace of economico-ethnological research into the use of primitive money by means of field work while it is still possible to obtain first-hand information.

It is important that ethnologists entrusted to this task should be equipped with the necessary knowledge of economics to enable them to study primitive currency systems in the right way. The first step in such investigations should be to ascertain the favourite medium of barter used in the community investigated. Many ethnologists are altogether too ready to assume that a community has no money at all merely because they work on a preconceived rigid definition of money. Such preconceptions should be discarded, and ethnologists should examine with an open mind whether any one particular type of goods is widely accepted in exchanges in preference to any other. The degree of acceptability of various goods is bound to differ at any given moment. It is possible that the ethnologists may find the use of one of them very prevalent.

The next step is to ascertain whether the most freely acceptable goods are accepted solely for the purpose of direct consumption or whether those who accept them do so partly at least with the intent of using them for future exchanges. If there is evidence that this latter is the case, then it becomes probable that the articles in question fulfil at least some of the functions of primitive currency. The ethnologist should enquire, when he discovers that members of a community hold stocks of a certain article in excess of their requirements, whether they do so for future consumption or for future purchases.

Ethnologists should also ascertain whether in case of barter there is some common denominator to facilitate the exchanges. Quite possibly they may find in many instances that this common denominator is the staple product or imported article used as a medium of barter to some limited degree. While the extent of the latter use would not in itself justify a claim that they constitute money, the fact of their use as a standard of value is conclusive.

Another question which should be investigated with care is whether the savages themselves consider the objects in question to be money. In several instances it has been ascertained that the languages of certain primitive communities have separate terms for barter and for purchase and that the natives distinguish between goods exchanged against each other and against an object or material serving as a rudimentary medium of exchange. Admittedly the distinction is often rather vague and the attitude of savages towards it is apt to be subjective rather than objective; that is, very often both parties in a barter transaction consider themselves to have made a purchase. In other instances, both parties believe they have sold their goods against payment in what they consider to be money. In such a situation the task of the ethnologist is to try to ascertain whether there is any particular article which in barter transactions is referred to as a medium of payment more frequently than others.

Investigations should not be confined to relations between the travellers and the natives. It is much more important to investigate relations between the natives. Such ethnological research can most usefully be undertaken by educated natives themselves. During recent years many members of primitive communities had received an advanced education and on their return to their native lands they were in a very good position to combine their newly acquired knowledge with their local experience and their thorough knowledge of native customs and language. In more than one instance such educated natives pronounced themselves in favour of regarding as currency certain objects the monetary status of which was not willingly recognized by European ethnologists. If the objects are considered to be money by the savages themselves it is surely not for the outside investigator to be more royalist than the king.

Those engaged in field work should not restrict the scope of their enquiry by ruling out means of unilateral payment that do not serve as media of exchange to any large extent. They should examine the importance of such media of payment as the economic drivng power of the community.

Ethnologists should define precisely the monetary functions of the objects which they consider to be primitive currencies. There has been in the past much exasperating vagueness in the writings of travellers and even ethnologists in this respect. They often remark casually that certain objects serve as the currency of a community and leave it at that without taking the trouble to explain what monetary functions that object fulfils, and to what extent. It is of the utmost importance to impress investigators and casual visitors writing on the subject with the necessity of being precise. The task of ascertaining how far an object is a medium of exchange, standard of value, store of value, standard of deferred payments, or various means of unilateral payments is not always easy. In many instances the natives themselves use the objects for monetary purposes quite unconsciously and are intellectually incapable of defining their precise use. Nevertheless, the contact between a number of natives and members of advanced civilizations should make this task easier. It should also facilitate the task of the investigator to ascertain the limitations of the various monetary uses of the objects concerned. This again requires very extensive investigation, for evidence is apt to be conflicting.

There is ample scope for research also for those who have not the opportunity of studying primitive currencies in primitive communities by means of field work. Their task is less urgent but no less important. Faculties of Economics should encourage their research students to specialize in the investigation of the primitive currencies used by one particular country or during one particular period. There is ample untapped material which would yield highly profitable rewards to patient and systematic workers. Practically every chapter of the Ethnological and Historical Sections of this book could and should be expanded into a full-sized volume by accumulating all the factual evidence available and by providing also a thorough study of the background.

Even though classical literature has been thoroughly searched for facts relating to primitive money, there is still ample scope for discovering new points through studying the immense amount of folk-lore and early literature of every kind. Students of primitive money must also follow closely the latest archæological research which from time to time produces new evidence.

Over and above all, theoretical monetary economists should study all factual evidence relating to primitive money with great care and should make good the omissions of the past by devoting more thought to the subject. A monetary theory based on broader foundations cannot be built by a single individual. It must be the result of the combined efforts of a large number of economists who between them weigh carefully every point. By learning at each other's expense, they should gradually further the knowledge of the subject step by step till it has attained, if not perfection, at any rate a stage corresponding to the general progress of economic theory.

BIBLIOGRAPHY

Works in general use, such as the ENCYCLOPÆDIA BRITANNICA, the CAMBRIDGE ANCIENT HISTORY, the CAMBRIDGE MEDIEVAL HISTORY, the OLD TESTAMENT, HOMER, etc., have been omitted.

ABERCROMBY, JOHN: *The Pre- and Proto-Historic Finns* (London, 1898).

ACOSTA, FATHER JOSEPH DE: *The Natural and Moral History of the Indies* (Hakluyt Society, London, 1880).

ADRIAN, F. O.: *Currency of the Colonies* (Colonial Office, London, 1883).

AFRICANUS, LEO: *The History and Description of Africa* (Hakluyt Society, London, 1896).

ALBERTI, J. B.: *L'Indochine d'autrefois et d'aujourd'hui* (Paris, 1934).

ALDRICH, C. R.: *The Primitive Mind and Modern Civilization* (London, 1931).

ALEXANDER, G.: *Tanganyika Memories* (London, 1936).

ALLAN, J.: *The Coinage of the Maldive Islands with some notes on the Cowrie and Larin* (Numismatic Chronicle. 4th Series. Vol. XII, 1912).

ALLDRIDGE, T. J.: *The Sherbro and its Hinterland* (London, 1901); *A Transformed Colony—Sierra Leone* (London, 1910).

ALLEN, DEREK: *British Tin Coinage of the Iron Age* (Transactions of the International Numismatic Congress of London, 1936. London, 1938).

ALVAREZ, FRANCISCO: *Narrative of the Portuguese Embassy to Abyssinia* (Hakluyt Society, London, 1881).

AMIRA, K.: *Nordgermanisches Obligationsrecht* (Leipzig, 1882).

ANDERSON, A. O.: *Early Sources of Scottish History* (Edinburgh, 1922).

ANDERSON, H. D. and ELLIS, W. C.: *Alaska Natives* (Stamford University, 1935).

ANDERSSON, J. G.: *Children of the Yellow Earth* (London, 1934).

ANDRÉE, RICHARD: *Ethnographische Parallellen und Vergleiche* (Stuttgart, 1878); *Die Metalle bei den Naturvölkern* (Leipzig, 1884).

ANDREW, A. P.: *What ought to be called Money* (*Quarterly Journal of Economics*. Vol. XIII, 1899).

ANGELL, SIR NORMAN: *The Story of Money* (London, 1930).

ANGELO, R. R. F. F. MICHAEL and CARLI, DENIS DE: *A Curious and Exact Account of a Voyage to Congo in the Years* 1666-67 (*Pinkerton's Voyages and Travels.* Vol. XVI, 1814).

APPADORAI, A.: *Economic Conditions in Southern India*, A.D. 1000-1500 (Madras, 1936).

ARAVAMUTHAN, T. G.: *A New Type of Punch-Marked Coin* (Transactions of the International Numismatic Congress in 1936, London, 1938).

ARCHER, F. B.: *The Gambia Colony and Protectorate* (London, 1906).

ARCHEY, G.: *South Sea Folk—Handbook of Maori and Oceanic Ethnology* (Auckland, 1937).

ARMSTRONG, W. E.: *Rossel Island* (Cambridge, 1928); *Rossel Island Money* (*Economic Journal*, September 1924).

ARNAUNÉ, A.: *La Monnaie, le Crédit et le Change* (Paris, 1894); *Monnaie* (*Nouveau Dictionnaire d'Economie Politique*. Vol. II, Paris, 1892).

ASMIS, DR.: *Die Stammesrechte der Bezirke Misakohe, Anecho und Lome-Land* (*Zeitschrift für Vergleichende Rechtswissenenschaften*. Vol. XXVI, 1911).

ATKINSON, F. W.: *The Philippine Islands* (Boston, 1905).

AVEBURY, LORD: Inaugural Presidential Address at the Institute of Bankers (*Journal of the Institute of Bankers*, June, 1879).

AXELSON, ERIC: *South East Africa, 1488-1530* (London, 1940).

AYMONIER, ETIENNE: *Voyage dans le Laos* (Paris, 1895); *Le Cambodge* (Paris, 1904); *Notes sur l'Annam, La Cochinchine Française* (Vol. XIII, Paris, 1885).

BABELON, E.: *Les Monnaies de la République Romaine* (Paris, 1885); *Les Origines de la Monnaie* (Paris, 1897).

BAILLAUD, E.: *Sur les Routes du Soudan* (Toulouse, 1902).

BANCROFT, H. H.: *The Native Races of the Pacific States of North America* (London, 1875).

BANERJIA, PRAMATHANATH: *A Study of Indian Economics* (2nd Edn., London, 1915); *Public Administration in Ancient India* (London, 1916)

BARNETT, L. D.: *Antiquities of India* (London, 1913).

BARTH, HENRY: *Travels and Discoveries in North and Central Africa* (London, 1857-8).

BASDEN, G. T.: *Among the Ibos of Nigeria* (London, 1921); *Niger Ibos* (London, undated).

BASTIAN, A.: *Reisen in Birma in den Jahren*, 1861-2 (Leipzig, 1866); *Reisen in Siam im Jahre* 1863 (Jena, 1867).

BATCHELOR, J.: *The Ainu of Japan* (London, 1892).

BATES, H. W.: *A Naturalist on the Amazon* (Everyman Edn., London, 1910).

BATTUTA, IBN: *Travels in Asia and Africa* (London, 1929).

BAUDESSON, H.: *Indo-China and its Primitive People* (London, 1919).

BAUMANN, H., THURNWALD, R. and WESTERMANN, D.: *Völkerkunde von Afrika* (Essen, 1940).

BAUMANN, O.: *Fernando Po und die Bubie* (Vienna, 1888).

BAUMSTARK, E.: *Die Volkswirtschaft nach Menschenrassen, Volkstämme und Völker* (*Jahrbuch für Nationalökonomie und Statistik*. Vol. V, 1865).

BEAGLEHOLE, E.: *Ownership and Inheritance in an American Indian Tribe* (*Iowa Law Review*. Vol. XX. No. 2, January, 1935).

BEER, G. L.: *The Origin of the British Colonial System*, 1578-1660 (London, 1908).

478   BIBLIOGRAPHY

BEER, M.: *Early British Economics from the 16th to the middle of the 18th century* (London, 1938).

BENTLEY, W. H.: *Pioneering on the Congo* (London, 1900).

BERNATZIK, H. A.: *Owa Raha* (Vienna, 1936).

BEROLZHEIMER, F.: *Philosophie des Vermögens* (System der Rechts und Wirtschaftsphilosophie. Vol. IV, Munich, 1907).

BERTHOLET, A.: *A History of Hebrew Civilization* (London, 1926).

BETHAM, SIR WILLIAM: *On the Ring Money of the Celtæ and their System of Weights* (Transactions of the Royal Irish Academy, 23rd May and 27th June, 1836. Vol. XVII, Dublin, 1837).

BHARGAVA, BRIJKISHORE: *Indigenous Banking in Ancient and Medieval India* (Bombay, 1935).

BIOT, E. *Mémoire sur le Système Monétaire des Chinois* (Paris, 1837).

BIRCH, J. M. S.: *Denmark in History* (London, 1938).

BIRNIE, A.: *An Economic History of the British Isles* (London, 1935).

BITTEL, K.: *Die Ruinen von Bogazköj* (Berlin, 1937).

BLACKWOOD, BEATRICE: *Both Sides of the Buka Passage* (Oxford, 1931).

BLAKE, J. W.: *Europeans in West Africa*, 1450-1560 (Hakluyt Society, London, 1942).

BLANCHET, A.: *Traité de Monnaies Gauloises* (Paris, 1905); *Une Monnaire de Fer* (*Journal International d'Archéologie Numismatique*. Vol. X, Athens, 1907).

BLUM, HANS: *Neu-Guinea und das Bismarck-Archipel. Eine Wirtschaftliche Studie* (Berlin, 1900).

BOAS, FRANZ: *Ethnology of the Kwakiutl*. 35th Annual Report of the Bureau of American Ethnology (Washington, 1921).

BOECKH, A: *Die Staatshaushalt der Athener* (3rd Edn., Berlin, 1886); *Metrologische Untersuchungen über Gewichte, Münzfusse und Masse des Altertums* (Berlin, 1839).

BOEKE, J. H.: *The Structure of Netherlands East Indies Economy* (New York, 1942).

BORLASE, W.: *Observations on the Ancient and Present State of the Islands of Scilly* (Oxford, 1756).

BOROUGH, W.: *The Natural Laws of Money* (New York, 1894).

BOSMAN, WILLIAM: *A New and Accurate Description of the Coast of Guinea*, 1700 (*Pinkerton's Travels and Voyages*. Vol. XVI, 1814).

BRANDEIS, A.: *Ethnographische Beobachtungen über die Nauru-Insulaner* (*Globus*, 31st January, 1907).

BRANDIS, J.: *Das Münz- Mass- und Gewichtswesen in Vorderasien bis auf Alexander den Grossen* (Berlin, 1866).

BREASTED, J. H.: *Ancient Records of Egypt* (Chicago, 1906-7).

BREITENSTEIN, H.: *Sumatra* (Leipzig, 1902).

BRENCHLEY, J. L.: *Jottings during the Course of H.M.S. Curacao among the South Sea Islands in 1865* (London, 1873).

BRENTANO, LUJO: *Eine Geschichte der Wirtschaftlichen Entwickelung Englands* (Jena, 1927).

BRITISH MUSEUM: Handbook to the Ethnographical Collections (London, 1910).

BROWN, C. J.: *The Coins oj India* (Calcutta, 1922).

BROWN, GEORGE: *Melanesians and Polynesians* (London, 1910).

BROWN, G. GORDON, and HUTT, A. McD. BRUCE: *Anthropology in Action—An Experiment in the Iringa District* (London, 1935).

BROWN, J. MACMILLAN: *The Riddle of the Pacific* (London, 1924).

BRUEL, G.: *La France Equatoriale Africaine* (Paris, 1935).

BRUN, WACLAW VON: *Die Wirtschaftsorganisation der Maori auf Neuseeland* (Leipzig, 1912).

BRUNNER, H.: *Deutsche Rechtsgeschichte.* 2nd. Edn. (Leipzig, 1906).

BÜCHER, KARL: *Industrial Evolution* (New York, 1901).

BUDGE, E. A. WALLIS: *The Egyptian Sudan* (London, 1907); *A History of Ethiopia* (London, 1928).

BUNZEL, R.: *The Economic Organization of Primitive Peoples* (*General Anthropology.* Edited by F. Boas, New York, 1938).

BURNS, A. C.: *History of Nigeria* (London, 1929).

BURNS, A. R.: *Money and Monetary Policy in Early Times* (London, 1927).

Burnt Njal. Translated by SIR G. W. DASENT (Everyman Edn., London, 1911).

BURTON, R. F.: *First Footsteps in East Africa or an Exploration of Harar* (London, 1856); *The Lake Regions of Central Africa* (London, 1860); *Zanzibar* (London, 1872).

BURTON, R. F. and CAMERON, V. L.: *To the Gold Coast for Gold* (London, 1883).

BUTT-THOMPSON, F. W.: *Sierra Leone in History and Tradition* (London, 1926); *West African Secret Societies* (London, 1929).

BUXTON, L. H. D.: *Peoples of Asia* (London, 1925).

CABLE, MILDRED and FRENCH, FRANCISCA: *The Gobi Desert* (London, 1942).

CAESAR, JULIUS: *De Bello Gallico.*

CAGNOLO, C.: *The Akikuyu* (Nyeri, Kenya, 1933).

CALDECOTT, J. B.: *The Spanish Dollar as adopted for Currency in our West Indian Colonies* (*British Numismatic Journal.* Vol. I, 1903-4).

CAMERON, V. L.: *Across Africa* (London, 1885).

CAMPBELL-THOMPSON, R.: *The Golden Age of Hammurabi* (Cambridge, 1924).

CARDINALL, A. W.: *The Natives of the Northern Territories of the Gold Coast* (London, 1920).

CARLILE, W. W.: *The Evolution of Modern Money* (London, 1901); *Monetary Economics* (London, 1912).

CARNIVALI, LUIGI: *Probabile uso delli armi preistoriche quali monete* (Mantua, 1885).

CASSEL, GUSTAV: *The Theory of Social Economy* (London, 1923).

Census of India, 1901. Vol. III. *The Andaman and Nicobar Islands* (Calcutta, 1903).

CHADWICK, H. M.: *Studies on Anglo-Saxon Institutions* (Cambridge, 1905).

CHALMERS, ROBERT: *A History of Currency in the British Colonies* (London, 1893).

CHARLTON, W.: *Leather Currency* (*British Numismatic Journal.* Vol. III, 1906).

CHAUDOIR, BARON S.: *Aperçu sur les Monnaies Russes* (St. Petersburg, 1836).

CHEESEMAN, EVELYN: *Backwaters of the Savage South Seas* (London, 1933).

CHEESEMAN, R. E.: *Lake Tana and the Blue Nile* (London, 1936).

CHITTY, A.: *Early Australian Coinage* (*British Numismatic Journal.* Vol. IV, 1907).

CHRISTIAN, F. W.: *Caroline Islands* (London, 1899).

CHRISTIE, E. B.: *The Subanua of Sindangan Bay* (Bureau of Science, Division of Ethnology Publications. Vol. VI, Part I, Manila, 1909).

CLARK, GRAHAM: *Prehistoric England* (London, 1940).

CLARKE, E. D.: *Travels in Various Countries in Europe, Asia and Africa.* 4th Edn. (London, 1817).

CLIFTON, MRS. TALBOT: *Pilgrims to the Isle of Penance* (London, 1911).

CLOZEL, F. J. and VILLAMUR, ROGER: *Des Coutumes Indigènes de la Côte d'Ivoire* (Paris, 1902).

CLYDE, P. H.: *Japan's Pacific Mandate* (New York, 1935).

CODRINGTON, H. W.: *Ceylon—Coins and Currency* (Colombo, 1924).

CODRINGTON, R. H.: *The Melanesians* (Oxford, 1891).

COLE, FAY COOPER: *The Tinguian—Social, Religious and Economic Life of a Philippine Tribe* (Field Museum of Natural History. Publication No. 209, Chicago, 1922).

COLLINGWOOD, R. C.: *Roman Britain* (An Economic Survey of Ancient Rome. Edited by T. Frank. Vol. III, 1904-5).

COLLINGWOOD, R. C. and MYERS, J. N. L.: *Roman Britain and the English Settlements* (Oxford, 1936).

CONANT, C. A.: *The Principles of Money and Banking* (New York, 1905).

CONDER, C. R.: *The Tell el Amarna Tablets* (London, 1893).

CONTENAU, G.: *La Civilisation Phoenicienne* (Paris, 1926).

COOMBE, FLORENCE: *Islands of Enchantment—Many-Sided Melanesia* (London, 1911).

COOTE, W.: *The Western Pacific* (London, 1883).

CORNE, G. R.: *The Voyages of Cadamosto* (London, 1937).

CORNEY, B. G.: *The Quest and Occupation of Tahiti* (Hakluyt Society. Vol. I, London, 1913).

COSTER, HENRY: *Travels in Brazil* (2nd Edn., London, 1817).

COULBORN, W. A. L.: *An Introduction to Money* (London, 1938).

COVARRUBIAS, M.: *Island of Bali* (New York, 1937).

CRABITES, PIERRE: *Gordon, The Sudan and Slavery* (London, 1933).

CRAWLEY, ERNEST: *Dress, Drinks and Drums* (London, 1931).

CRISP, JOHN: *An Account of the Inhabitants of the Poggy or Nassau Islands (Asiatic Researches.* Vol. VI. Reprinted for the Straits branch of the Royal Asiatic Society, 1886).

CROFTON, R. H.: *The Pageant of the Spice Islands* (London, 1936).

CROWTHER, G.: *An Outline of Money* (London, 1940).

CULWICK, A. T. and G. M.: *Ubena of the Rivers* (London, 1935).

CUMMING, C. F. G.: *At Home in Fiji* (Edinburgh, 1881).

CUNNINGHAM, R. W.: *The Growth of English Industry and Commerce During the Middle Ages* (3rd Edn., Cambridge, 1896); *Western Civilization in its Economic Aspects* (London, 1898).

CUREAU, A. L.: *Savage Man in Central Africa—A Study of Primitive Races in French Congo* (London, 1915).

The Currency of the British Colonies (H.M. Stationery Office, London, 1848).

CZAPLICZKA, M. A.: *Aboriginal Siberia—A Study in Social Anthropology* (Oxford, 1914); *My Siberian Years* (London, 1916).

DALLAS, ALEXANDER K.: *The Primitive Races of Mankind* (London, 1926).

DAMES, MANSEL LONGWORTH: *The Book of Duarte Barbosa* (Hakluyt Society, London, 1918-21).

DAMM, HANS: *Zentral-Karolinen (Ergebnisse der Südsee-Expedition.* II Ethnographie, B. Mikronesien, Vol. X, Part II, Hamburg, 1938).

DANKS, BENJAMIN: *On the Shell Money of New Britain (Journal of the Anthropological Institute of Great Britain and Ireland.* Vol. XVII, London, 1888).

DARWIN, CHARLES: *The Voyage of the Beagle* (Everyman Edn., London, 1906).

DAVIDS, CAROLINE FOLEY RHYS: *Notes on Early Economic Conditions in Northern India (Journal of the Royal Asiatic Society,* London, 1901).

DAVIDSON, J.: *The Natural History of Money* (Proceedings and Transactions of the Nova Scotia Institute of Science. Vol. X, Halifax, 1903).

DAVIS, A. MCFARLANE: *Colonial Currency Reprints,* 1687-1751 (Boston, 1911).

DEACON, A. BERNARD: *Malekula* (London, 1934).

DÉCHELETTE, J.: *Manuel d'Archéologie Préhistorique Celtique et Gallo-Romaine* (Paris, 1918).

DECKEN, BARON CLAAS VON DER: *Reisen in Ostafrika*, 1859-65 (Leipzig, 1869).

DELAPORTE, L.: *Les Hittites* (Paris, 1936).

DEL MAR, ALEX: *The Science of Money* (2nd Edn., London, 1896); *History of Monetary Systems* (London, 1895); *A History of the Precious Metals* (New York, 1902); *A History of Money in Ancient Countries from Earliest Times to Present* (London, 1885).

DEMAITRE, E.: *New Guinea Gold* (London, 1936).

DEMPWOLF, OTTO: *The Sandawe* (Hamburg, 1916).

DENHAM, MAJOR; CLAPPERTON, CAPTAIN and OUDNEY, DR.: *Narrative of Travels and Discoveries in Northern and Central Africa in the Years* 1822-24 (2nd Edn., London, 1826).

DENIG, E. T.: *Indian Tribes of the Upper Missouri* (46th Annual Report of the Bureau of American Ethnology for 1928-9. Washington, 1930).

DIAMOND, A. S.: *Primitive Law* (London, 1935).

DICKINS, G.: *Excavations at Sparta* (Annual of the British School at Athens, 1906-7).

DOBRIZHOFER, M.: *Geschichte der Abiponer* (Vienna, 1783).

DODD, A. F.: *History of Money in the British Empire and the United States* (London, 1911).

DOPSCH, ALFONS: *Naturalwirtschaft und Geldwirtschaft in der Weltgeschichte* (Vienna, 1930); *Wirtschaftliche und soziale Grundlagen der europäischen Kulturentwickelung aus der Zeit von Cæsar bis auf Karl der Grossen* (Vienna, 1930).

DOUGHTY, C. M.: *Wanderings in Arabia—An Abridgment of Travels in Arabia Deserta* (London, 1926).

DRACOPOLI, I. N.: *Through Jubaland to the Lorian Swamps* (London, 1914).

DRAKE-BROCKMAN, R. E.: *British Somaliland* (London, 1912).

DRIBERG, J. H.: *The Lango—a Nilotic Tribe of Uganda* (London, 1923); *The Savage as he really is* (London, 1929); *At Home with the Savage* (London, 1932).

DU BOIS, CORA: *The People of Alor* (Minneapolis, 1944).

DURKHEIM, E.: *De la Division du Travail Social* (Paris, 1893).

DYKMANS, G.: *Histoire Economique et Sociale de l'Ancienne Egypte* (Paris, 1936).

EARL, G. W.: *The Native Races of the Indian Archipelago* (London, 1853).

EBERT, M. (Editor): *Reallexikon der Vorgeschichte* (Berlin, 1924-1932).

EGERTON, F. C. C.: *African Majesty* (London, 1938).

EISLER, ROBERT: *Das Geld. Seine geschichtliche Enstehung und gesellschaftliche Bedeutung* (Munich, 1924); *The Introduction of the Cadmeian Alphabet into the Ancient world* (*Journal of the Royal Asiatic Society*, 1923).

EJGES, S.: *Das Geld im Talmud* (Vilna, 1930).

ELBERT, JOHANN: *Die Sunda-Expedition des Vereins für Geographie und Statistik zu Frankfurt am Main* (Frankfurt, 1911).

ELLIS, H. S.: *German Monetary Theory, 1905-1933* (Cambridge, Mass., 1934).

ELLIS, W.: *Three Visits to Madagascar* (London, 1859).

ELSTER, L. ; WEBER, A. and WEISER, F.: *Handwörterbuch der Staatswissenschaften* (Jena, 1923-8).

EL-TOUNSY, MOHAMMED EBN-OMAR: *Voyages au Darfour* (Paris, 1845).

EMBREE, J. F.: *A Japanese Village* (London, 1946).

ENGEL, A. and SERRURE, R.: *Traité de Numismatique du Moyen Age* (Paris, 1891).

ERMANN, A. and RANKE, H.: *Aegypten und Aegyptisches Leben im Altertum* (Tübingen, 1924).

EVANS, SIR ARTHUR: *Minoan Weights and Mediums of Currency from Crete, Mycenæ and Cyprus* (*Corolla Numismatica—Essays in honour of Barclay V. Head* (London, 1906).

EVANS, IVOR H. N.: *Among Primitive Peoples in Borneo* (London, 1922).

EVANS-PRITCHARD, E. E.: *The Nuer—A description of the Mode of Livelihood and political institutions of a Nilotic People* (Oxford, 1940).

FALKNER, S. A.: *Das Papiergeld der franzoesischen Revolution, 1789-1797* (Munich, 1924).

FARSON, NEGLEY: *Behind God's Back* (London, 1940).

FAWCETT, J.: *The Highlands of Central India* (London, 1871).

FEATHERMAN, A.: *Social History of the Races of Mankind* (London, 1887).

FEAVEARYEAR, A. E.: *The Pound Sterling—A History of English Money* (Oxford, 1931).

FERRAND, GABRIEL: *Les Poids, Mesures et Monnaies des Mers du Sud aux XVIᵉ et XVIIᵉ Siècle* (*Journal Asiatique*. July-December, 1920).

FINSCH, O: *Ethnologische Erfahrungen und Belegstücke aus der Südsee* (Descriptive catalogue of a collection in the Naturhistorische Hofmuseum. Vol. III, Vienna, 1888); *Südsee-Arbeiten. Gewerbe, Kunst, Fleiss, Tauschmittel und "Geld" der Eingeborene* (*Abhandlungen der Hamburgischen Kolonial Institute*. Vol. XIV, Hamburg, 1914).

FIRTH, RAYMOND: *Primitive Economies of the New Zealand Maori* (London, 1929); *Primitive Polynesian Economy* (London, 1939); *We the Tikopia* (London, 1936); *Currency, Primitive* (*Encyclopædia Britannica*, 14th Edn.); *Some Features of Primitive Industry* (*Economic Journal—History*, January, 1926).

FIRTH, ROSEMARY: *Housekeeping among the Malayan Peasants* (*London School of Economics Monographs on Social Anthropology*. Vol. VII, London, 1943).

FISHER, IRVING: *Elementary Principles of Economics* (New York, 1915); *The Purchasing Power of Money* (Revised Edn., New York, 1920).

FITZGERALD, W. W. A.: *Travels in the Coastlands of British East Africa and the Islands of Zanzibar and Pemba* (London, 1898).

FORAN, W. ROBERT: *African Odyssey—The Life of Verney Lovett Cameron* (London, 1937).

FORBES, H. O.: *A Naturalist's Wanderings in the Eastern Archipelago* (London, 1885).

FORBES, W. CAMERON: *The Philippine Islands* (Boston, 1928).

FORDE, C. DARYL: *Habitat, Economy and Society* (London, 1934).

FORDE, C. DARYL, and SCOTT, RICHENDA: *The Native Economies of Nigeria* (London, 1946).

FORRER, R.: *Die aegyptischen, kretischen, phoenikischen, etc. Gewichte und Masse der europäischen Kupfer, Bronze, und Eisenzeit. Grundlagen zur Schaffung einer prähistorischen Metrologie (Jahrbuch der Gesellschaft fur lotharingische Geschichte und Altertumskunde.* Vol. XVIII, Metz, 1906); *Keltisches Münzwesen (Reallexikon der Vorgeschichte.* Vol. VI, Berlin, 1926); (Editor) *Reallexikon der prähistorischen, klassischen und frühchristlichen Altertume* (Berlin, 1908).

FORTUNE, R. F.: *Manus Religion and Ethnographical Study of the Manus Natives of the Admiralty Islands* (Philadelphia, 1936); *Sorcerers of Dobu* (London, 1932).

FOSTER, T. S.: *Travels and Settlement of Early Man* (London, 1929); *From Savagery to Commerce* (London, 1930).

FOVILLE, A. DE: *La Monnaie.* 2nd Edn. (Paris, 1907).

FRAZER, SIR JAMES G.: *The Golden Bough* (Abridged Edn., London, 1932); *The Native Races of Asia and Europe* (London, 1939).

FREEMAN, R. A.: *Travels and Life in Ashanti and Jaman* (London, 1898).

FREIDENSBURG, F.: *Münzkunde und Geldgeschichte der Einzelstaaten des Mittelalters und der Neueren Zeit* (Munich, 1926).

FRIEDL, J.: *Beiträge zur Kenntniss der Wirtschaftsformen der Oceanier (Petermann's Mitteilungen.* Vol. XLIX, 1903).

FRIEND, J. NEWTON: *Iron in Antiquity* (London, 1926).

FROBENIUS, LEO: *The Childhood of Man* (London, 1909).

FRYER, JOHN: *A New Account of East India and Persia* (Hakluyt Society, London, 1912).

FÜRER-HAIMENDORF, CRISTOPH V.: *The Naked Nagas* (Calcutta, 1946).

FURNESS, W. H.: *The Island of Stone Money* (Philadelphia, 1910).

FURNIVALL, J. S.: *Netherlands India—A Study in Plural Economy* (Cambridge, 1939).

GANN, THOMAS: *Ancient Cities and Modern Tribes—Exploration and Adventure in Maya Lands* (London, 1926).

GARDNER, F.: *Some Notes on Australian Currencies (British Numismatic Journal.* Vol. XXII, 1934-35).

GARNIER, COUNT GERMAIN: *Mémoire sur la valeur des monnaies de compte chez les peuples de l'antiquité* (Paris, 1817).

GAUD, FERNAND and OVERBERGH, C. VAN: *Les Mandja (Congo Français)* (Brussels, 1911).

GEARY, SIR W. N. M.: *Nigeria Under British Rule* (London, 1927).

GERMANN, P.: *Die Völkerstämme im Norden von Liberia* (Leipzig, 1933);

GESELLSCHAFT FÜR NORDISCHE ALTERTUMSKUNDE : *Leitfaden zur nordischer Altertumskunde* (Copenhagen, 1837).

GIBBON, EDWARD: *The Decline and Fall of the Roman Empire* (Everyman Edn., London, 1910).

GIDE, CHARLES: *Principes d'Economie Politique* (12th Edn., Paris, 1910); *Communist and Co-operative Colonies* (London, 1930).

GIGLIOLI, E. H.: *Il Sale-Moneta dell'Etiopia* (*Archivio per l'Antropologia e la Etnologia*. Vol. XXXIV, Firenze, 1904).

GILES, H. A.: *The Travels of Fa Hsien, 399-414, or Record of the Buddhist Kingdoms* (Cambridge, 1923).

GJERSET, K.: *History of Iceland* (London, 1922).

GLOTZ, G.: *The Aegean Civilization* (London, 1925).

GODSELL, P. H.: *Red Hunters of the Snow* (London, 1938).

GOLDENWEISER, A. A.: *Early Civilization* (London, 1922).

GOODFELLOW, D. M.: *Principles of Economic Sociology* (London, 1939).

GÖTZE, A.: *Die Trojanische Silberbarren der Schliemann-Sammlung* (*Globus*. Vol. LXXI, No. 14, 1897).

GOULDSBURY, C. and SHEANE, H.: *The Great Plateau of Northern Rhodesia* (London, 1911).

GRAEBNER, F.: *Das Weltbild der Primitiven*. Vol. I (Munich, 1924); *Völkerkunde der Santa-Cruz Inseln* (*Ethnologica*. Vol. I, Leipzig, 1909).

GRAFF, F. W. UP DE: *Head-Hunters of the Amazon* (London, 1923).

GRAHAM, W. A.: *Siam* (London, 1924).

GRAS, N. S. B.: *Anthropology and Economics* (*Social Sciences and their Interrelations*. Edited by W. F. Ogburn and L. Goldenweiser. Cambridge, Mass. 1927).

GRAY, ALBERT (Editor): *The Voyage of François Pyrard de Laval to the East Indies, the Maldives, the Moluccas and Brazil* (Hakluyt Society, 1887-90).

GREAVES, I. C.: *Modern Production among Backward Peoples* (London, 1935).

GREGORY, T. E.: *Money—Encyclopædia of Social Sciences*. Vol. X (New York, 1933); *Currency—Encyclopædia of Social Sciences*. Vol. IV (New York, 1931).

GREIDANUS, TJARDUS: *The Value of Money* (London, 1932).

GRIERSON, P. J. H.: *The Silent Trade* (Edinburgh, 1903).

GROENEVELDT, W. B.: *Notes on the Malay Archipelago and Malacca* (Batavia, 1817).

GRÖNBERG, V.: *The Culture of the Teutons* (London, 1931).

GROSLIER, G.: *Recherches sur les Cambodgiens* (Paris, 1921).

GRUBAUER, A.: *Unter Kopfjäger in Central-Celebes* (Leipzig, 1913); *Celebes* (The Hague, 1923).

GRUBB, W. B.: *An Unknown People in an Unknown Land* (London, 1911).

Gudrun. Translated by Margaret Armour (Everyman Edn., London, 1932).

GUPPY, H. B.: *The Solomon Islands and Their Natives* (London, 1887).

HADDON, A. C.: *The Ethnography of the Western Tribe of Torres Straits* (*Journal of the Royal Anthropological Institute*. February, 1890).

HADFIELD, E.: *Among the Natives of the Loyalty Group* (London, 1920).

HAEBERLIN, E. J.: *Aes Grave* (Frankfurt, 1910).

HAHN, EDUARD: *Die Haustiere und ihre Beziehung zur Wirtschaft des Menschen* (Leipzig, 1896).

HAILEY, LORD: *African Survey* (London, 1938).

HALKIN, J. and VIAENE, E.: *Les Ababua* (*Congo Belge*) (Brussels, 1911).

HALL, H. R.: *The Ancient History of the Near East* (8th Edn. London, 1932).

HALLETT, H. S.: *A Thousand Miles on an Elephant in the Shan States* (London, 1890).

HALLIDAY, W. M.: *Potlatch and Totem* (London, 1935).

HAMBLY, W. D.: *Source Book for African Anthropology* (Chicago, 1937).

HAMBRUCH, P. and EILERS, A.: *Ponapé* (*Ergebnisse der Südsee-Expedition*. II Ethnographie, B. Mikronesien, Vol. VII, Part II, Hamburg, 1936).

HAMILTON, CAPTAIN ALEXANDER: *A New Account of the East Indies* (*Pinkerton's Travel Series*. Vol. VIII, London, 1811).

HANSON, E. P.: *Journey to Manaos* (London, 1938).

HARPER, R. F.: *The Code of Hammurabi* (Chicago, 1904).

HARRIS, W. CORNWALLIS: *The Highlands of Ethiopia* (London, 1844).

HARRISON, TOM: *Savage Civilization* (London, 1937).

HARTLAND, E. S.: *Primitive Law* (London, 1924).

HASLUND, HENNING: *Tents in Mongolia* (London, 1934).

HAWKES, C. F. C.: *The Prehistoric Foundations of Europe* (London, 1940).

HAWKINS, E.: *The Silver Coinage of England* (London, 1887).

HAWTREY, R. G.: *Currency and Credit*. 3rd Edn. (London, 1928).

HEADLAM, C.: *The Development of the Colonies under the First Georges* (*Cambridge History of the British Empire*. Vol. I, Cambridge, 1929).

HECKSCHER, ELI F.: *A Plea for Theory in Economic History* (*Economic Journal—History*, January, 1929).

HELFFERICH, KARL: *Money* (London, 1927).

HEPBURN, A. BARTON: *A History of Currency in the United States* (Revised Edn., New York, 1915).

HERNSHEIM, FRANZ: *Südsee-Erinnerungen*, 1875-1880 (Berlin, 1883).

HERODOTUS: *History*.

HERSKOVITS, MELVILLE J.: *Dahomey* (New York, 1938); *The Economic Life of Primitive Peoples* (New York, 1940); *The Cattle Complex in East Africa* (*American Anthropologist*. New Series. Vol. XXVIII, 1926).

HERTZ, J. E.: *Über Verwändung und Verbreitung der Kaurimusche*. (*Mitteilungen der Geographischen Gesellschaft in Hamburg*, 1880-81).

HESSE-WARTEGG, ERNST: *Samoa, Bismarckarchipel und Neu-Guinea* (Leipzig, 1902).

HEWITT, J. N. B.: *Wampum* (*Handbook of American Indians North of Mexico*. Bureau of American Ethnology, Bulletin 30, Vol. II, Washington, 1910).

HILDEBRAND, B.: *Natural-, Geld-, und Kreditwirtschaft* (*Jahrbuch für Nationalökonomie und Statistik*, Jena, 1864).

HILL, G. B. (Editor): *Colonel Gordon in Central Africa*, 1874-79 (2nd Edn., London, 1884).

HILTON-SIMPSON, M. W.: *Land and People of the Kasai* (London, 1911).

HIRST, FRANCIS W.: *Money* (London, 1933).

HOBBS, JEAN: *Hawaii—A Pageant of the Soil* (Stanford, California, 1935).

HOBHOUSE, L. T.: *The Historical Evolution of Property* (Essays by various writers, London, 1913).

HODGE, F. W. (Editor): *Handbook of American Indians North of Mexico* (Bureau of American Ethnology, Bulletin No. 30, Washington, 1907).

HODKIN, T.: *The History of England from the Earliest Times to the Norman Conquest* (London, 1931).

HODSON, T. C.: *The Meitheis* (London, 1908); *The Naga Tribes of Manipur* (London, 1911).

HOERNES, M.: *Primitive Man* (London, 1900); *Natur-und Urgeschichte des Menschen* (Vienna, 1909).

HOGBIN, H. IAN: *Law and Order in Polynesia* (London, 1934); *Experiments in Civilization* (London, 1939).

HÓMAN, B.: *Magyar Pénztörténet*, 1000-1325 (Budapest, 1916).

HONE, P. F.: *South Rhodesia* (London, 1909).

HOOPS, J. (Editor): *Reallexikon der Germanischen Altertumskunde* (Strassbourg, 1919).

HOPKINS, A. I.: *In the Isles of King Solomon* (London, 1928).

HORE, EDWARD C.: *On the Twelve Tribes of Tanganyika* (*Journal of the Anthropological Institute*. Vol. XII, London, 1883).

HOSE, CHARLES: *Natural Man—A Record from Borneo* (London, 1926).

HOWITT, A. W.: *The Native Tribe of South-East Australia* (London, 1904).

HOYT, ELIZABETH ELLIS: *Primitive Trade* (London, 1926).

HROZNY, F.: *Code Hittite, provenant de l'Asie Mineure* (Paris, 1922).

HULME, E. WYNDHAM: *Currency Bars and Water Clocks* (*Antiquity*. Vol. VII, Gloucester, 1933).

HULTSCH, F.: *Griechische und Römische Metrologie* (Berlin, 1882).

HUMPHRIES, C. R.: *The Southern New Hebrides* (Cambridge, 1926).

HUNTER, MONICA: *Reaction to Conquest. Effects of Contact with Europeans on the Pondo of South Africa* (Oxford, 1936).

HUPFELD, F.: *Land und Leute im Basari* (1899-1900).

HUTTON, J. H.: *The Angami Nagas* (London, 1921); *The Sema Nagas* (London, 1921).

HUXLEY, JULIAN: *Africa View* (London, 1931).

IDEN-ZELLER, OSKAR: *Ethnographische Beobachtungen bei den Tchucktschen* (*Zeitschrift für Ethnographie*. Vol. XLIII, 1911).

ILWOF, FRANZ: *Tauschhandel und Geldsurrogate in alter und neuer Zeit* (Graz, 1882).

Imperial Gazetteer. All India Provincial Series, Andaman and Nicobar Islands (Calcutta, 1909).

IM THURN, E. F.: *Among the Indians of Guiana* (London, 1883).

INGERSOLL, E.: *Wampum and its History* (*American Naturalist*. Vol. XVII, May, 1883).

INGRAMS, W. H.: *Zanzibar, its History and its People* (London, 1931).

ISERT, P. E.: *Reise nach Guinea* (Copenhagen, 1788); *Neue Reise nach Guinea* (Berlin, 1790).

IVENS, WALTER G.: *Melanesians of the South-East Solomon Islands* (London, 1927); *The Island Builders of the Pacific* (London, 1930).

JACKSON, A. V. WILLIAMS: *History of India* (London, 1906).

JACKSON, J. WILFRED: *Shells as Evidence of the Migration of Early Culture* (London, 1917).

JAIN, L. C.: *Indigenous Banking in India* (London, 1929).

JASTROW, M.: *The Civilization of Babylonia and Assyria* (Philadelphia, 1915).

JATHAR, G. B.. and BERI, S. G.: *Indian Economics* (Bombay, 1928).

JENKS, A. E.: *The Bontoc Igorot* (Department of Interior Ethnological Survey Publications. Vol. I, Manila, 1905).

JENNESS, D.: *The Indians of Canada* (National Museum of Canada, Ottawa, 1932).

JESSE, W.: *Quellenbuch zur Münz-und Geldgeschichte des Mittelalters* (Halle, 1924).

JEVONS, W. STANLEY: *Money and the Mechanism of Exchange* (London, 1875).

JOBSON, RICHARD: *The Golden Trade or a Discovery of the River Gambra and the Golden Trade of the Ethiopians* (1623—Reprinted in the Mary Kingsley Travel Books).

JOCKELSON, WALDEMAR: *Peoples of Asiatic Russia* (The American Museum of Natural History, 1928).

JOHNS, C. H. W.: *Babylonian and Assyrian Laws, Contracts and Letters* (Edinburgh, 1904); *Cuneiform Inscriptions, Chaldean, Babylonian and Assyrian.* Collections contained in the library of J. P. Morgan (New York, 1908).

JOHNSON, E. A.: *American Economic Thought in the 17th Century* (London, 1932).

JOHNSTON, SIR HARRY: *The River Congo* (London, 1884); *George Grenfell in the Congo* (London, 1908).

JONES, CHESTER LLOYD: *Guatemala Past and Present* (Minneapolis, 1940).

JOYCE, THOMAS A.: *South American Archæology* (London, 1912); *Central American Archæology* (London, 1916).

JUNOD, H. A.: *The Life of a South African Tribe* (2nd Edn. London, 1927).

KANN, EDUARD: *The Currencies of China* (2nd Edn., Shanghai, 1921).

KARAMISHEFF, W.: *Mongolia and Western China—Social and Economic Study* (Tientsin, 1925).

KARSTEN, R.: *Indian Tribes of the Argentine and Bolivian Chaco* (Helsinki, 1932).

KEARY, C. F.: *A Catalogue of English Coins in the British Museum.* Anglo-Saxon Series. Vol. I (London, 1887); *The Coinage of Western Europe* (London, 1879).

KEATE, GEORGE: *An Account of the Pelew Islands, Composed from the travels and communications of Captain Henry Wilson* (4th Edn., London, 1789).

KEESING, F. M.: *Modern Samoa* (London, 1934).

KEESING, F. M. and M.: *Taming Philippine Headhunters* (London, 1934).

KEMP, WILLIAM: *Precious Metals as Money* (Paisley, 1913).

KENDRICK, D., and HAWKES, C. F. C.: *Archæology in England and Wales* (London, 1932).

KENNAY, JAMES F.: *The Foundling of Churchill: Being a Journal of Captain James Knight, Governor-in-Chief, Hudson Bay in* 1717 (Toronto, 1932).

KENYATTA, JOMO: *Facing Mount Kenya—The Tribal Life of the Gikuyu* (London, 1938).

KEYNES, LORD: *A Treatise on Money* (London, 1930); *The General Theory of Employment, Interest and Money* (London, 1936).

KILBORNE, R. D.: *Principles of Money and Banking* (3rd Edn., New York, 1932).

KING, L. W.: *The Letters and Inscriptions of Hammurabi* (London, 1903).

KINGSLEY, MARY H.: *Travels in West Africa* (London, 1891); *West African Studies* (London, 1899).

KLIUTSHEWSKIJ, W.: *Geschichte Russlands* (Berlin, 1925).

KLOSS, G. BODEN: *In the Andamans and Nicobars* (London, 1903).

KNAPP, G. F.: *The State Theory of Money* (London, 1924).

KNIBBS, S. G. C.: *The Savage Solomons as they Were and Are* (London, 1929).

KNIES, K.: *Das Geld.* Vol. I. of *Geld und Kredit* (Berlin, 1885).

KOCH, T. GRÜNBERG: *Zwei Jahre unter den Indianen. Reisen in Nordwest-Brazilien*, 1903-5 (Berlin, 1908).

KOCK, M. H. DE: *Selected Subjects in the Economic History of South Africa* (Cape Town, 1924).

KOHLER, J.: Über das Recht der Australneger (Zeitschrift für Vergleichende Rechtswissenschaften. Vol. VII, 1887); Über das Recht der Papua auf Neu Guinea (Zeitschrift für Vergleichende Rechtswissenschaften. Vol. VII, 1887).

KOPPERS, P. W.: Die Ethnologische Wirtschaftsforschung (Anthropologia. Vol. X-XI, 1915-16, Vienna).

KRAEMER, A.: Die Samoa-Inseln (Stuttgart, 1902); Hawaii, Ostmikronesien und Samoa, 1897-9 (Stuttgart, 1906); Truk and Palau (Ergebnisse der Südsee-Expedition. II Ethnographie, B. Mikronesien, Vol. III, Part 3, Hamburg, 1926).

KRAEMER, A. and NEVERMANN, H.: Ralik-Ratak (Marshall-Inseln) (Ergebnisse der Südsee-Expedition. II Ethnographie, B. Mikronsien, Vol. II, Hamburg, 1938).

KRAUSE, F.: In den Wildnisse Brasiliens (Leipzig, 1911).

KRICKEBERG, WALTER: Einige Neuerwerbungen der nordamerikanischen Sammlung des Königl. Museum für Völkerkunde (Zeitschrift für Ethnologie. Vol. XLVI, 1914).

KRIEGER, H. W.: Island Peoples of the Western Pacific (Washington, 1943).

KRIEGER, M.: Über Handel und Verkehr auf Neu-Geuinea. Beitrag zur Kolonialpolitik und Kolonialwitrschaft (Vol. I, Berlin, 1899).

KROEBER, A. L.: Handbook of the Indians of California (Bureau of American Ethnology. Bulletin 78, Washington, 1925).

KROEBER, A. L., and WATERMAN, T. T.: Source Book for Anthropology (Berkeley, 1920).

KUBARY, J.: Ethnologische Beiträge zur Kenntnis des Karolinischen Inselgruppe und Nachbarschaft. Vol. I, Berlin, 1885; Die Palau-Inseln in der Südsee (Journal des Museums Godeffroy. Vol. IV (Hamburg, 1873); Die Bewohner der Mortlock Inseln (Mitteilungen der Geographischen Gesellschaft, Hamburg, 1878-9).

KUBARY, J., and SCHMELTZ, J. D. E.: Ethnographische Beiträge zur Kenntnis des Karolinen-Archipel (Leyden, 1889).

KULISCHER, J.: Russische Wirtschaftsgeschichte. Vol. I (Jena, 1925); Allgemeine Wirtschaftsgeschichte des Mittelalters und der Neuzeit (Munich, 1926).

KÜRCHHOFF, D.: Die Geldverhältnisse im Heutigen Afrika in ihrer Entwickelung (Mitteilungen der Geographischen 'Gesellschaft in Hamburg. Vol. XXII, 1907); Maasse und Gewichte in Afrika (Zeitschrift für Ethnologie. Vol. XL, 1908).

KUYKENDALL, R. S.: The Hawaiian Kingdom, 1778-1819 (Honolulu, 1938).

LACOUPERIE, TERRIEN DE: Catalogue of Chinese Coins from the 7th Century B.C. to A.D. 621 including the series in the British Museum (London, 1892); The Metallic Cowries of Ancient China (The Journal of the Royal Asiatic Society. Vol. XX, London, 1888).

LAMBERT, PÈRE: Moeurs et Superstitions des Néo-Calédoniens (Nouméa, 1900).

LANDTMAN, G.: *The Kiwai Papuans of British New Guinea* (London, 1927).

LANSDELL, H.: *Russian Central Asia* (London, 1885).

LAPIERE, R. T.: *Collective Behaviour* (New York, 1938).

LATTIMORE, OWEN: *High Tartary* (London, 1930).

LAUGHLIN, J. LAURENCE: *Principles of Money* (New York, 1903).

LAUM, BERNHARD: *Heiliges Geld* (Tübingen, 1924); *Das Eisengeld der Spartaner* (Tübingen, 1925); *Die Geschlossene Wirtschaft* (Tübingen, 1933); *Münzwesen* (*Handwörterbuch der Staatswissenschaften*. Vol. VI, Jena, 1925); *Die Banken im Alterum* (*Handwörterbuch der Staatswissenschaften*. Vol. II, Jena, 1924).

LAYARD, J.: *Stone Men of Malekula—The Small Island of Vao* (London, 1942).

LEAKY, M. and CRANE, M.: *The Land that Time Forgot* (New York, 1937).

LEFROY, GEN.: *The Hog Money of the Somers Islands* (*Numismatic Chronicle*. Vol. XVI. New Series, 1876).

LENORMANT, FRANÇOIS: *La Monnaie dans l'Antiquité* (Paris, 1878).

LENZ, O.: *Timbuktu* (Leipzig, 1884); *Wanderungen in Afrika* (Vienna, 1895); *Über Geld bei Naturvölkern* (Hamburg, 1895).

LETOURNEAU, C.: *Property: Its Origin and Development* (London, 1892); *L'évolution du commerce* (Paris, 1897); *La Commerce Primitif* (*Bulletin de la Société d'Anthropologie de Paris*. Vol. VII. Series IV, 1896); *La Monnaie chez les races de couleur* (*Bulletin de la Société d'Anthropologie de Paris*. Vol. X. Series IV, 1899).

LEVCHINE, A. DE: *Descriptions des hordes et des steppes des Khirgies-Kazaks* (Paris, 1840).

LEVY-BRUHL, L.: *How Natives Think* (London, 1926).

LEWIS, A. B.: *Melanesian Shell Money in the Field Museum Collection* (*Field Museum of Natural History Publication No.* 268. Chicago, 1929).

LIND, ANDREW W.: *An Island Community. Ecological Succession in Hawaii* (Chicago, 1938).

LINDSAY, J.: *A View of the Coinage of Ireland* (Cook, 1839).

LIPS, JULIUS: *Kamerun—Das Eingeborenerecht*. Edited by E. Schultz-Ewerth und Leonhardt Adam (Stuttgart, 1930).

LISSAUER, A.: *Die Doppeläxte der Kupferzeit im Westlichen Europa* (*Zeitschrift für Ethnologie*. Vol. XXXVII, Berlin, 1905).

Local Gazetteer: The Andaman and Nicobar Islands (Calcutta, 1908).

LOVEN, SVEN: *Origins of the Tanian Culture, West Indies* (Goteborg, 1935).

LOWIE, ROBERT H.: *Primitive Society* (New York, 1920); *An Introduction to Cultural Anthropology* (London, 1934); *Subsistence* (*General Anthropology*. Editor, F. Boas, New York, 1938).

LUCAS, A.: *Copper in Ancient Egypt* (*Journal of Egyptian Archæology*. Vol. XIII, 1927).

LUSCHIN VON EBENGREUTH, A.: *Allgemeine Münzkunde und Geld-geschichte des Mittelalters und der Neueren Zeit* (München, 1904).

MCCULLOCH, J. R.: *Old and Scarce Tracts on Money* (London, 1933).

MACDONALD, A. G.: *Trade, Politics and Christianity in Africa and the East* (London, 1916).

MCKAY, DOUGLAS: *The Honorable Company—A History of the Hudson's Bay Company* (London, 1937).

MCLEAN, J.: *The Indians of Canada* (London, 1892).

MCLEAN, JOHN R.: *The Elements of Primæval Finance* (*Numismatic Chronicle*. 4th Series. Vol. XII, 1912); *The Origin of Weight* (*Numismatic Chronicle*. 4th Series. Vol. XII, 1912).

MACLEOD, H. D.: *Theory and Practice of Banking*. 5th Edn. (London, 1892).

MACMICHAEL, H. A.: *The Tribes of Northern and Central Kordofan* (Cambridge, 1912); *A History of the Arabs in the Sudan* (Cambridge, 1922).

MACMILLAN, W. M.: *Complex South Africa—An Economic Footnote to History* (London, 1930); *Africa Emergent. A Survey of Social, Political and Economic Trends in British Africa* (London, 1938).

MCPHEE, ALLAN: *The Economic Revolution in British West Africa* (London, 1926).

MADDEN, F. W.: *History of Jewish Coinage and of Money in the Old and New Testament* (London, 1864); *Coins of the Jews* (London, 1903).

MAGE, M. E.: *Voyages dans le Soudan Occidental* (Paris, 1908).

MAIR, L. P.: *An African People in the Twentieth Century* (London, 1934).

MALINOWSKI, B.: *The Family among the Australian Aborigines* (London, 1913); *The Nature of Derived Needs* (*A Scientific Theory of Culture and other Essays*. Chapel Hill, N. Carolina, 1944); *Argonauts of the Western Pacific* (London, 1922); *Crime and Custom in Savage Society* (London, 1926); *Coral Gardens and Their Magic* (London, 1935); *The Natives of Mailu* (Transactions of the Society of South Australia. Vol. XXXIX, 1915); *The Primitive Economy of the Trobriand Islands* (*Economic Journal*, March, 1921).

MANN, E. H.: *The Nicobar Islands and their People* (London, 1933); *On the Aboriginal Inhabitants of the Andaman Islands* (*Journal of the Anthropological Institute*. Vol. 12, 1883).

MANSFIELD, ALFRED: *Urwald-Dokumente—Vier Jahre unter den Crossflussngern Kameruns* (Berlin, 1908).

MARAIS, J. S.: *The Cape Coloured People*, 1652-1937 (London, 1939).

MARCHANT, ALEXANDER: *From Barter to Slavery—The Economic Relations of Portuguese and Indians in the Settlement of Brazil*, 1500-1580 (Baltimore, 1942).

MARKHAM, CLEMENTS: *Narratives of the Rites and Laws of the Incas* (London, 1873).

MARSHALL, ALFRED: *Money, Credit and Commerce* (London, 1923).

MARSHALL, A. J.: *The Black Musketeers. The Work and Adventures of a Scientist on a South Sea Island* (London, 1937).

MARTIN, JOHN: *William Mariner's Account of the Natives of the Tongo Islands* (London, 1817).

MARTIN, P. S,; QUIMBY, G. I., and COLLIER, D.: *Indians before Columbus* (Chicago, 1947).

MARWICK, B. A.: *The Swazi* (Cambridge, 1940).

MASON, O. T.: *The Origins of Invention. A Study of Industry among the Primitive Peoples* (London, undated).

MASPERO, G.: *The Dawn of Civilization* (London, 1894).

MASSAM, J. A.: *The Cliff Dwellers of Kenya* (London, 1927).

MATTERS, L.: *Through the Kara Sea* (London, 1932).

MATTINGLY, H. and SYDENHAM, E. A.: *Roman Imperial Coinage*. Vol. I (London, 1923); Vol. II (London, 1933).

MATZERATH, J.: *Die altenglischen Namen der Geldwerte, Masse und Gewichte* (Bonn, 1913).

MAUNIER, RENÉ: *Sociologie Coloniale* (Paris, 1932, 1936).

MAUSS, MARCEL: *Essai sur le don* (*L'Année Sociologique*. Nouvelle Série. Vol. I, Paris, 1923-4).

MAYDON, H. C.: *Simen—its Heights and Abysses* (London, 1925).

MEAD, MARGARET: *Growing up in New Guinea* (London, 1931); *The Manus of the Admiralty Islands* and *The Arapech of New Guinea* (*Co-operation and Competition among Primitive Peoples*) (New York, 1937); *Coming of Age in Samoa* (Penguin Books, London, 1943); *Melanesian Middle Men* (*Natural History*. Vol. XXX).

MEANS, P. A.: *Ancient Civilizations of the Andes* (New York, 1931).

MEEK, A. S.: *A Naturalist in Cannibal Land* (London, 1913).

MEEK, C. K.: *A Sudanese Kingdom. An Ethnological Stuay of the Jukim Speaking Peoples of Nigeria* (London, 1931); *Tribal Studies in North Nigeria* (London, 1931); *Law and Authority in a Nigerian Tribe* (London, 1937).

MEISSNER, B. : *Beiträge zum altbabylonischen Privatrecht.* (*Leipzig,* 1898); *Babylonien und Assyrien* (Heidelberg, 1920); *Aus den altbaby-lonischen Recht.* (*Der Alter Orient.* Vol. VII. No. 1, Leipzig, 1905).

MENGER, KARL: *Grundsätze der Volkswirtschaftslehre* (Vienna, 1871); *On the Origin of Money* (*Economic Journal*, 1892); Article on " *Geld*" in the *Handwörterbuch der Staatswissenschaften*. 3rd Edn. (Reprinted by the London School of Economics. *Collected Works of Karl Menger*. Vol. IV., London, 1936).

MENONVILLE, B. NICOLAS JOSEPH THIERRY DE: *Travels to Guaxaca* (*Pinkerton's Voyages*. Vol. XIII, London, 1812).

MERCER, S. A. B.: *The Tell el Amarna Tablets* (Toronto, 1939).

METTERS, L.: *Through the Kara Sea* (London, 1932).

MEYER, EDUARD: *Geschichte des Altertums* (Stuttgart, 1884); *Kleine Schriften* (Halle, 1924).

MEYER, HANS: *Der Kilimandjaro* (Berlin, 1900); *Die Barundi—Eine völkerkundliche Studie aus Deutschostafrika* (Leipzig, 1916).

MICHELL, H.: *The Economy of Ancient Greece* (Cambridge, 1940).

MICKWITZ, G.: *Gold und Wirtschaft im Römischen Reich des Vierten Jahrhunderts nach Christ* (Helsinki, 1932); *New Papyri of Numismatic Interest* (*Numismatic Chronicle*. Series V. Vol. XVII, 1937).

MILES, W. A.: *A Minute Account of the Kimmeridge Coal Money* (London, 1826).

MILL, J. S.: *Principles of Political Economy* (London, 1878).

MILLER, CONSTANTIN: *Studien zur Geschichte der Geldlehre* (Stuttgart, 1925).

MILLIES, H. C.: *Recherches sur les monnaies indigènes de l'Archipel Indien et de la Péninsule Malaie* (The Hague, 1871).

MILLS, J. P.: *The Lhota Nagas* (London, 1922); *The Ao Nagas* (London, 1926); *The Rengma Nagas* (London, 1937).

MISES, L. VON: *The Theory of Money and Credit* (London, 1934).

MIYASHITA, KOICHI: *Beiträge zur japanischen Geldgeschichte* (Vienna, 1931).

MOBERLY, H. J., and CAMERON, W. B.: *When Fur was King* (London, 1929).

MOCKLER, A. F., and FERRYMAN: *Imperial Africa* (London, 1898).

MOMMSEN, THEODOR: *Geschichte des Römischen Münzwesens* (Berlin, 1860); *Das Geld* (*Reden und Aufsätze*. Lecture delivered 7th Feb., 1863. Berlin, 1905).

MONTEIL, CHARLES: *Les Khassonké—Monographie d'une Peuplade du Soudan Français* (Paris, 1915).

MONTELIUS, OSCAR: *Die Kultur Schwedens in Vorchristlicher Zeit* (2nd Edn., Berlin, 1885); *Kulturgeschichte Schwedens* (Leipzig, 1906).

MONTET, P: *Les Scènes de la vie privée dans les tombeaux egyptiens de l'Ancien Empire* (Paris, 1925).

MONTGOMERIE, H. S.: *The Nicobar Islands* (*Geographical Journal*, January, 1922. Vol. 59, No. 1).

MOODIE, D.: *The Record—A Series of Official Papers of the Condition and Treatment of the Native Tribes of South Africa* (Capetown, 1938).

MOOKERJI, R. K.: *The Foundation of Indian Economy* (London, 1936); *Hindu Civilization* (London, 1936).

MORGA, ANTONIO DE: *The Philippine Islands, Moluccas, Siam, Cambodia, Japan and China at the close of the 16th Century* (Hakluyt Society, London, 1868).

MORGAN, J. DE: *Les Premiers Civilizations* (Paris, 1909).

MORGAN, LEWIS H.: *Ancient Society* (New York, 1878).

MOSHER, STUART: *The Story of Money* (*Bulletin of the Buffalo Society of Natural Sciences* Vʳ' XVII. No. 2. Buffalo 1936).

Moszkowski, M.: *Auf Neuen Wege durch Sumatra* (Berlin, 1909); *L'Economie des Peuples Primitifs* (*Revue Economique Internationale.* Vol. IV., 1912).

Moulton, Harold G.: *Principles of Money and Banking* (Selected Materials) (Chicago, 1916).

Much, M.: *Baugen und Ringen—Eine Studie über das Ringgeld und seinen Gebrauch bei den Germanen* (*Mitteilungen der Anthropologischen Gesellschaft.* Vol. IX, Vienna, 1879).

Mukerjee, Radhakamal: *The Foundations of Indian Economics* (London, 1916).

Müller, W.: *Yap* (*Ergebnisse der Südsee-Expedition.* II Ethnographie, B. Mikronesien, Vol. II, Hamburg, 1917).

Muller-Lyer, F.: *The History of Social Development* (London, 1920).

Mundy, Captain R.: *The Journals of James Brooke* (London, 1848).

Munro, N. G.: *Coins in Japan* (London, 1905).

Muntz, E. E.: *The Early Development of Economic Concepts* (*Economic Journal, History,* January, 1926).

Murdock, G. P.: *Our Primitive Contemporaries* (New York, 1934).

Myres, J. L.: *Precious Metals* (Lectures at the Royal Anthropological Institute, London, 1931).

Mytinger, Caroline: *Headhunting in the Solomon Islands* (London, 1943).

Nachtigal, G.: *Sahara-Sudan* (Berlin, 1879).

Nadel, S. F.: *A Black Byzantium—The Kingdom of Nupe in Nigeria* (London, 1942).

Naskap, Frank G. Speek: *The Savage Hunters of the Labrador Peninsula* (Norman, 1935).

Nath, Pran: *Tausch und Geld in Altindien* (Leipzig, 1924).

Neel, H.: *Notes sur deux Peuplades de la Frontière Libérienne* (*L'Anthropologie.* Vol. XXV., 1913).

Nelson, E. W.: *The Eskimo About Bering Strait* (18th Annual Report of the Bureau of American Ethnology, Part I, Washington, 1899).

Nettels, C. P.: *The Money Supply of the American Colonies before 1720* (Madison, Wisconsin, 1936).

Nevermann, Dr. Hans: *Admiralitäts-Inseln* (*Ergebnisse der Südsee-Expedition,* 1908-10. II Ethnographic, Section B. Melanesien, Vol. III, Hamburg, 1934).

Newton, H.: *In Far New Guinea* (London, 1914).

Nicholson, J. Shield: *A Treatise on Money and Essays on Monetary Problems* (3rd Edn., London, 1895).

Niebelungenlied. Translated by Margaret Armour (Everyman Edn., London, 1908).

Nieboer, H. J.: *Slavery as an Industrial System* (The Hague, 1900).

Nigmann, E.: *Die Wahehe* (Berlin, 1908).

NOBACK, FRIEDRICH: *Münz-, Mass- und Gewichtsbwch.* 2nd Edn. (Leipzig, 1879).

NOLAN, PATRICK: *A Monetary History of Ireland* (London, 1926).

NORMANO, J. F.: *Brazil—A Study of Economic Types* (Chapel Hill, 1935).

OBER, F. A.: *Travels in Mexico* (Boston, 1884).

OLIVER, S. P.: *Madagascar* (London, 1886).

OLMSTEAD, A. T.: *History of Assyria* (New York, 1923).

OPPERT, ERNEST: *A Forbidden Land—Voyages to Korea* (London, 1880).

OPPERT, J. and MENANT, J.: *Documents juridiques de la Syrée et de la Chaldée* (Paris, 1877).

ORLEANS, PRINCE HENRI D': *From Tonkin to India* (London, 1898).

PAGE, J. W.: *Primitive Races of To-day* (London, 1938).

PALGRAVE, INGLIS: *Dictionary of Political Economy* (London, 1925).

PALYI, M.: *Coinage* (*Encyclopædia of Social Science.* III. New York, 1935).

PANT, S. D.: *The Social Economy of the Himalayans* (London, 1935).

PARK, MUNGO: *The Interior Regions of Africa* (London, 1799).

PARKER, E. H.: *A Thousand Years of the Tartars* (London, 1924).

PARKER, G. W.: *On the New Code of Law for the Hova Kingdom of Madagascar* (*Journal of the Anthropological Institute.* Vol. XII, London, 1883).

PARKINSON, R.: *Im Bismarck-Archipel* (Leipzig, 1887); *Dreissig Jahre in der Südsee* (Stuttgart, 1907).

PARTRIDGE, C.: *Cross River Natives* (London, 1905).

PAULY, A. F., and WISSOWA, G. (Editors): *Real-Encyclopadie der Klassischen Altertumswissenschaften* (Stuttgart, 1893-1935).

PEISKER, J.: *Die älteren Beziehungen der Slaven zu Turko-Tataren und Germanen und ihre sozialgeschichtliche Bedeutung* (Stuttgart, 1905).

PERISTANY, J. G.: *The Social Institutions of the Kipsings* (London, 1939).

PETRIE, SIR FLINDERS: *Social Life in Ancient Egypt* (London, 1923).

PFEIL, JOACHIM GRAF: *Studien und Beobachtungen aus der Südsee* (Braunschweig, 1899).

PHEAR, SIR JOHN B.: *The Aryan Village in India and Ceylon* (London, 1880).

PINTO, SERPA: *How I Crossed Africa* (London, 1880).

PIRENNE, J.: *Histoire des Institutions et du Droit Privé de l'Ancienne Egypte.* Vol. II (Brussels, 1934).

PITT-RIVERS, G. H. LANE-FOX: *The Clash of Cultures and the Contact of Races* (London, 1924).

PLUTARCH: *Lives.*

POLO, MARCO: *Travels.*

PORTEUS, S. D.: *Primitive Intelligence and Environment* (New York, 1937).

POSTAN, M. M.: *The Rise of a Money Economy* (*Economy History Review*. Vol. XIV, 1944).

POWDERMAKER, HORTENSE: *Life in Lesu* (London, 1933).

PREISIGKE, F.: *Girowesen in Griechischen Aegypten* (Strasbourg, 1910).

PREJEVALSKY, N.: *Mongolia, the Tangut Country and the Solitudes of Northern Tibet* (London, 1876).

PRESCOTT, W. H.: *The Conquest of Mexico* (Everyman Edn., London, 1909); *History of the Conquest of Peru* (Everyman Edn., London, 1908).

PRICE, J. EDWARD: *On Aggri Beads* (*Journal of the Anthropological Institute*. Vol. XII, 1883).

PRICE, M. P.: *Siberia* (London, 1912).

PRICE, WILLARD: *Japan's Islands of Mystery* (London, 1944).

PRITCHARD, W. T.: *Polynesian Reminiscences* (London, 1886).

RADIN, PAUL: *Primitive Religion* (New York, 1937).

RATZEL, FRIEDRICH: *The History of Mankind* (London, 1896).

RECHE, OTTO: *Der Kaiserin Augusta Fluss* (*Südsee-Ergebnisse*. A. Melanesian, Hamburg, 1913).

REDFIELD, ROBERT and VILLA, ALPHONSO: *Chan Kom—A Maya Village* (Washington, 1934).

REED, S. W.: *The Making of Modern New Guinea* (Philadelphia, 1943).

REGLING, K.: *Geld* (*Reallexikon der Vorgeschichte*. Vol. IV, Berlin, 1926); *Geld vor Einführung der Münze* (*Pauly's Real-Encyclopædie der Klassischen Altertumswissenschaften*. Vol. XIII, Stuttgart, 1910).

REINACH, T.: *L'histoire par les Monnaies* (Paris, 1902); *Jewish Coins* (London, 1903).

REINECKE, F.: *Samoa* (Berlin, 1902).

REY, C. F.: *In the Country of the Blue Nile* (London, 1927).

RHEINACH, LUCIEN DE: *Le Laos* (Paris, 1911).

RHYS, LLOYD: *Jungle Pimpernel. The Story of a District Officer in Central Netherlands, New Guinea* (London, 1947).

RIBBE, C.: *Zwei Jahre unter den Kannibalen der Salomo Inseln* (Dresden, 1903).

RICHARDS, AUDREY I.: *Hunger and Work in a Savage Tribe* (London. 1932); *Land, Labour and Diet in Northern Rhodesia* (London, 1939),

RICKARD, T. A.: *Man and Metals—A History of Mining in Relation to Civilization* (New York, 1932).

RIDGEWAY, WILLIAM: *The Origin of Metallic Currency and Weight Standards* (Cambridge, 1892); *Money—A Companion to Latin Studies* (Cambridge, 1943).

RIESENBERG, F.: *Cape Horn* (London, 1941).

RIST, CHARLES: *History of Monetary and Credit Theory from John Law to the Present Day* (London, 1940).

RIVERS, W. H. R.: *The History of Melanesian Society* (Cambridge, 1914); *Psychology and Ethnology* (London, 1926); *Social Organization* (London, 1932).

ROBERTSON, D. H.: *Money* (London, 1922).

ROBINSON, C. H.: *Hausaland* (London, 1896).

ROBINSON, E. S. G.: *Money—A Companion to Greek Studies* (Cambridge, 1931).

ROCKHILL, W. W.: *Notes on the Relations and Trade of China with the Eastern Archipelago and the Races of the Indian Ocean during the 14th Century* (T'Oung Pao. Vol. XV, 1914).

RODD, FRANCIS RENNELL: *People of the Veil* (London, 1926).

ROELICH, G. N.: *Trails in Inmost Asia* (New Haven, 1931).

ROEPSTORFF, F. A. DE: *Vocabulary of Dialects spoken in the Nicobar and Andaman Isles* (Calcutta, 1875).

ROGNER, EMIL: *Gesellschaft und Wirtschaft auf den Palau-Inseln* (Nürnberg, 1939).

ROHLFS, G.: *Geld in Afrika* (Dr. A. Petermann's Mitteilungen, 1889).

ROMILLY, H. H.: *The Western Pacific and New Guinea* (London, 1886).

ROSCHER, W.: *Principles of Political Economy* (Chicago, 1878).

ROSCOE, JOHN: *The Baganda* (London, 1911); *The Soul of Central Africa* (London, 1922); *The Banyankole* (Cambridge, 1923); *The Bagesu and other Tribes of the Uganda Protectorate* (Cambridge, 1924).

ROSENSTEIN-RODAN, P. N.: *The Co-ordination of the General Theories of Money and Prices* (*Economica*, August, 1936).

ROSS, W. MACGREGOR: *Kenya from Within* (London, 1927).

ROSTOVTZEFF, M.: *The Social and Economic History of the Roman Empire* (Oxford, 1926); *The Social and Economic History of the Hellenistic World* (Oxford, 1941).

ROTH, HENRY LING: *The Natives of Sarawak and British North Borneo* (London, 1896).

ROUTLEDGE, W. S. and K.: *With a Prehistoric People—The Akikuyu of East Africa* (London, 1910).

ROWE, N. A.: *Samoa Under the Sailing Gods* (London, 1930).

ROY, S. C.: *The Oraons of Chota Nagpur* (Ranchi, 1915).

RUBRUQUIS, FR. GUILLAUME DU: *Voyage en Tartarie* (*Relation des Voyages en Tartarie, recueilli par Pierre Bergeron*. Paris, 1636).

RUDIN, H. R.: *Germans in the Cameroons* (London, 1938).

RUDING, ROGERS: *Annals of the Coinage of Great Britain* (3rd Edn., London, 1840).

SARASAS, PHRA: *Money and Banking in Japan* (London, 1940).

SARASIN, P. and F.: *Reisen in Celebes* (Wiesbaden, 1905).

SARFERT, E.: *Kusaie* (*Ergebnisse der Südsee-Expedition*. II Ethnographie, B. Mikronesien. Vol. XIV, Hamburg, 1919).

SAVAGE-LANDOR, A. HENRY: *Korea* (London, 1895); *Across Wildest Africa* (London, 1907).

SAYCE, R. U.: *Primitive Arts and Crafts* (Cambridge, 1933).

SCHAPERA, I. and GOODWIN, A. J. H.: *The Bantu-Speaking Tribes of South Africa* (London, 1937).

SCHEEL, H. V.: *Der Begriff des Geldes in seiner historischökonomischen Entwickelung* (*Conrad's Jahrbüch für Nationalökonomie und Statistik*. Vol. VI, 1866).

SCHLETTWEIN, A.: *Togo* (*Das Eingeborenerecht*. Stuttgart, 1930).

SCHLIEMANN, H.: *Mykenæ* (Leipzig, 1878).

SCHMIDT, MAX.: *Grundriss der ethnologoischen Volkswirtschaftslehre* (Stuttgart, 1920-1); *Die Nama, Bergdama und Namib Buschleute* (*Das Eingeborenerecht*, Stuttgart, 1930).

SCHNEE, HEINRICH: *Bilder aus der Südsee* (Berlin, 1904); (Editor), *Deutsche Kolonial-Lexikon* (Leipzig, 1920).

SCHNEIDER, OSKAR: *Muschelgeld-Studien* (Dresden, 1905).

SCHOMBURGK, R.: *Travels in British Guiana during the Years* 1840-1844 (Leipzig, 1848).

SCHRADER, O.: *Linguistisch-Historische Forschungen zur Handelsgeschichte und Warenkunde* (Jena, 1886); *Reallexikon der Indogermanischen Altertumskunde*. (2nd. Edn. Strassbourg, 1917-28).

SCHROEDER, A.: *Annam—Etudes Numismatiques* (Paris, 1905).

SCHROTT, ADAM: *Documents relating to Canadian Currency, Exchange and Finance during the French Period* (Ottawa, 1925-6).

SCHRÖTTER, F. V. (Editor): *Wörterbuch der Münzkunde* (Berlin, 1930).

SCHULZ-EWERTH, ERICH and ADAM, LEONHARDT: *Das Eingeborenenrecht* (Stuttgart, 1930).

SCHURTZ, HEINRICH: *Das Wurfmesser der Neger* (Leyden, 1889); *Grundriss einer Entstehungsgeschichte des Geldes* (Weimar, 1898); *Urgeschichte der Kultur* (Leipzig, 1900); *Central Asia and Siberia* (*Helmolt's World History*. Vol. II, London, 1904).

SCHWABE, K.: *Mit Schwert und Pflug in Deutsch-Südwestafrika* (Berlin, 1899).

SCHWEINFURTH, GEORGE: *The Heart of Africa* (London, 1873).

SCHWEINITZ, H. GRAF VON: *Deutschostafrika im Krieg und Frieden* (Berlin, 1894).

SCHWENZNER, W.: *Das geschäftliches Leben im alten Babylonien* (*Der alter Orient*. Vol. XVI, No. 1, Leipzig, 1916).

SEEBOHM, F.: *Tribal Custom in Anglo-Saxon Law* (London, 1911).

SEECK, OTTO: *Die Entstehung des Geldes* (*Die Entwickelung der antiken Geschichtsschreibung und anderer populärer Schriften*. Berlin, 1898).

SELIGMANN, C. G.: *The Melanesians of British New Guinea* (Cambridge, 1910).

SELIGMANN, C. G. and BRENDA Z.: *The Veddas* (Cambridge, 1911); *Pagan Tribes of the Nilotic Sudan* (London, 1932).

SELTMAN, C. T.: *Athens—Its History and Coinage before the Persian Invasion* (Cambridge, 1924); *Greek Coins* (London, 1933).

SEMPER, KARL: *Die Palau Inseln* (Leipzig, 1873).

SENFFT, A.: *Marshall Insulaner* (Steinmetz); *Ethnographische Beiträge über Karolinen-Insel Yap* (*Dr. A. Petermann's Mitteilungen*, 1903. Vol. 49); *Die Rechtsitten der Yap-Eingeborenen* (*Globus*. Vol. XLI, 14th March, 1907).

SHANN, E.: *An Economic History of Australia* (Cambridge, 1930).

SHIROKOGOROFF, S. M.: *Social Organization of the Northern Tungus* (Shanghai, 1929).

SHORTT, ADAM: Documents relating to commodity currency exchange and finance during the French period (1925-6).

SIEBER, S. A., and MUELLER, F. H.: *Social Life of Primitive Man* (St. Louis, 1941).

SIEVERS, W., and HAHN, F.: *Africa* (2nd Edn., Leipzig, 1901).

SIMCOX, E. J.: *Primitive Civilizations* (London, 1894).

SIMON, J.: *An Essay towards an Historical Account of Irish Coins* (2nd Edn., Dublin, 1810).

SKEAT, W. W., and BLAGDEN, C. O.: *Pagan Races of the Malay Peninsula* (London, 1906).

SKENE, W. F.: *Celtic Scotland* (2nd Edn. Vol. III, Edinburgh, 1890).

SLATER, GILBERT: *Economic Studies*. Vol. I. *Some South Indian Villages* (London, 1918).

SMITH, E. W., and DALE, A. N.: *The Ila Speaking Peoples of Northern Rhodesia* (London, 1920).

SMITH, G. ELLIOT: *Human History* (London, 1930).

SMITH, R. A.: *Paper on the British Iron Currency. Proceedings of the Society of Antiquaries*. II. Series. Vol. XX, 1905); *Currency Bars and Water Clocks* (*Antiquary*, VII, 1933, Gloucester).

SMITH, R. BOSWORTH: *Carthage and the Carthaginians* (London, 1913).

SMITH, SIDNEY: *Early History of Assyria* (London, 1928); *A Pre-Greek Coinage in the Near East* (*Numismatic Chronicle*. 5th Series. Vol. II, London, 1922).

SMITH, V. A.: *The Early History of India* (4th Edn., Oxford, 1924).

SNETHLAGE, E. H.: *Atiko y—Meine Erlebnisse bei den Indianer des Guapore* (Berlin, 1939).

SOMLO, F.: *Der Güterverkehr in der Urgesellschaft* (*Institute Solvay, Travaux de l'Institut de Sociologie, Notes et Mémoirs*. Vol. VIII, 1909).

SORRENTO, J. MEROLLA DA: *A Voyage to the Congo and Several other Countries chiefly in Southern Africk in* 1682 (*Pinkerton's Voyages and Travels*. Vol. XVI, 1814).

SPECK, E.: *Handelsgeschichte des Altertums* (Leipzig, 1906).

SPEISER, FELIX: *Two Years with the Natives in the Western Pacific* (London, 1913); *Ethnographische Materialen aus den Neuen Hebriden und den Banks Inseln* (Berlin, 1923).

SPEKE, J. H.: *The Discovery of the Source of the Nile* (Everyman Edn., London, 1906).

STANLEY, HENRY M.: *Through the Dark Continent* (London, 1878).

STAYT, H. A.: *The Bavenda* (London, 1931).

STEARNS, R. E. C.: *Shell-Money* (*The American Naturalist.* Vol. III, March, 1869); *Aboriginal Shell Money* (*The American Naturalist.* Vol. XI, June, 1877); *Ethno-conchology—A Study of Primitive Money* (*Annual Report of the Smithsonian Institution*, 1887. Part II).

STEIN, W.: *Handel* (*Deutscher*) (*Reallexikon der Germanischen Altertumskunde*, Vol. II, Strassbourg, 1918-19).

STEINEN, K. V. DEN: *Unter den Naturvölkern Zentral-Brasiliens* (Berlin, 1894).

STEINMETZ, S. R.: *Rechtsverhältnisse von Eingeborenen Völkern in Afrika und Oceanien* (Berlin, 1903).

STEPHAN, E. and GRÄBNER, F.: *Neu-Mecklenburg* (Berlin, 1907).

STEVENSON, J. H.: *Assyrian and Babylonian Contracts* (New York, 1902).

STIGAND, H.: *To Abyssinia through an Unknown Land* (London, 1910).

STIGLAND, C. H.: *Equatoria—The Lado Enclave* (London, 1923).

STIRLING, M. W.: *The Native Peoples of New Guinea* (*Smithsonian Institute, War Background Studies No. 9*, Washington, 1943).

STITES, S. H.: *Economics of the Iroquois* (Bryn Mawr, Pennsylvania, 1905).

STRANDES, JUSTUS: *Die Portugiesenzeit von Deutsch-und Englisch-Ostafrika* (Berlin, 1899).

STUCK, HUDSON: *Ten Thousand Miles with a Dog Sledge* (London, 1914).

STUHLMANN, FRANZ: *Mit Emin Pasha ins Herz von Afrika* (Berlin, 1894).

SUMNER, W. S.: *A History of American Currency* (New York, 1874).

SVORONOS, I. N.: *Les premiers monnaies* (*Revue Belge de Numismatique*, Brussels, 1908).

SWAIN, H. G. C.: *Seventeen Trips Through Somaliland* (London, 1895).

SWANTON, J. R.: *Aboriginal Culture of the South-east* (*42nd Annual Report. Bureau of American Ethnology.* Washington, 1928); *Media of Exchange* (*Handbook of American Indians.* Washington, 1907).

SWETTENHAM, SIR FRANK: *British Malaya* (London, 1908).

SWOBODA, W.: *Die Bewohner des Nicobaren Archipels* (*Leipzig*, 1908).

SYDENHAM, E. A.: *Æs Grave* (London, 1926).

SYKES, SIR PERCY: *The Quest for Cathay* (London, 1936).

SYMES, MICHAEL: *Embassy to Ava*, 1795 (*Pinkerton's Voyages.* Vol. IX, 1811).

TAKEKOSHI, Y.: *The Economic Aspects of the History of the Civilization of Japan.* Vol. I (London, 1930).

TAKIZAWA, M.: *The Penetration of Money Economy in Japan* (N.Y., 1927).

TALBOT, P. AMAURY: *The Peoples of Southern Nigeria* (London, 1926); *Tribes of the Niger Delta* (London, 1932).

TAMAGNA, F. M.: *Banking and Finance in China* (New York, 1942).

TARACOUZIO, T. A.: *Soviets in the Arctic* (New York, 1938).

TÄUBER, W.: *Geld und Kredit im Mittelalter* (Berlin, 1933).

TAVERNIER, J. B.: *Travels in India* (Hakluyt Society, London, 1925).

TAYLOR, F. M.: *Chapters of Money* (Michigan, 1906).

TEMPLE, SIR R. C.: *The Evolution of Currency and Coinage* (T. B. Strong Lectures on the Method of Science, Oxford, 1906); *Beginnings of Currency* (*Journal of the Royal Anthropological Institute*. Vol. XXIX, London, 1899); *The Development of Currency in the Far East* (*Asiatic Quarterly Review*, April, 1899); *Notes on Currency and Coinage among the Burmese* (Reprinted from the *Indian Antiquary*. Vol. XLVIII, Bombay, 1919).

TESSMANN, G.: *Die Bubi auf Fernando Po* (Hague, 1923).

THILENIUS, G.: *Primitives Geld* (*Archiv für Anthropologie*. New Series. Vol. XVIII, 1920).

THOMAS, E. S.: *Notes on the Mining Industry of Egypt* (*The Cairo Scientific Journal*, May, 1909).

THOMAS, H. P., and SCOTT, ROBERT: *Uganda* (London, 1935).

THOMPSON, J. ERIC: *Mexico Before Cortez* (New York, 1933).

THOMPSON, J. W.: *The Commerce of France in the Ninth Century* (*Journal of Political Economy*. Vol. XXIII).

THOMPSON, LAURA: *Fijian Frontier* (San Francisco, 1940).

THOMPSON, VIRGINIA: *Thailand the New Siam* (New York, 1941).

THONNAR, ALBERT: *Essai sur le système économique des primitifs* (Brussels, 1901).

THONNER, FRANZ: *Vom Kongo zum Ubangi* (Berlin, 1910).

THURNWALD, RICHARD: *Forschungen auf den Salomo Inseln und den Bismarck Archipelago*. Vol. I. *Lieder und Sagen aus Buin* (Berlin, 1912); *Die Gemeinde der Banaro* (Stuttgart, 1921); *Werden, Wandel und Gestaltung der Wirtschaft im Lichte der Völkerforschung* (Vol. V, *Die Menschliche Gesellschaft*, Berlin, 1932); *Black and White in East Africa* (London, 1935); *Economics in Primitive Communities* (London, 1938); *Koloniale Gestaltung. Methoden und Probleme überseeischer Ausdehnung* (Hamburg, 1939); *Geheime Gesellschaft* (*Reallexikon der Vorgeschichte*. Vol. IV, 1926); *Staat und Wirtschaft im alten Agypten* (*Zeitschrift für Sozialwissenschaften*. Vol. IV, 1901); *Wirtschaft* (*Reallexikon der Vorgeschichte*. Vol. XIV, 1929); *Im Bismarckarchipel und auf den Salomon Inseln*, 1906-1909) (*Zeitschrift für Ethnologie*. Vol. XLII, 1910); *Pigs and Currency on Buin. Observations about Primitive Standard of Value and Economy* (*Oceania*. Vol. V, December, 1934).

TILLE, A.: *Getreide als Geld. Jahrbuch für Nationalökonomie und Statistik*. 3rd Series. Vol. XX (Jena, 1900).

TODD, JOHN A.: *The Mechanism of Exchange* (5th Edn., London, 1939).

TORDAY, E.: *Camp and Tramp in African Wilds* (London, 1913); *On the Trail of the Bushongo* (London, 1925).

TORDAY, E., and JOYCE, T.A.: *Notes ethnographiques sur les peuples communément appelés Bakuba ainsi que les peuplades apparentées les Bushongo* (Brussels, 1910).

TURNER, GEORGE: *Samoa a Hundred Years Ago* (London, 1884).

TYLOR, EDWARD B.: *Primitive Culture* (London, 1929).

URE, P. N.: *The Origin of Tyranny* (Cambridge, 1922).

VATTER, ERNST: *Ata Kiwan—Unbekannte Bergvölker im tropischen Holland* (Leipzig, 1932).

VEATCH, A. C.: *Quito to Bogota* (London, 1917).

VEBLEN, THORSTEIN: *The Theory of the Leisure Class. An Economic Study of Institutions* (New York, 1899).

VEDDER, HEINRICH: *Die Buschmänner—Das Eingeborenerecht* (Stuttgart, 1930); *South-West Africa in Early Times* (London, 1938).

VEGA, YNCA GARCILLASSO DE LA: *Royal Commentaries of the Yncas* (Hakluyt Society, London, 1871).

VILJOEN, S.: *The Economics of Primitive Peoples* (London, 1936).

VINCENT, FRANK: *Actual Africa* (London, 1895).

VOELTZKOW, ALFRED: *Reise in Ostafrika*, 1903-05 (Stuttgart, 1914).

VOIGT, E.: *Wirtschaftsgeschichte Niederländisch-Indiens* (Leipzig, 1931).

VOLZ, WALTER: *Reise durch das Hinterland von Liberia* (Berne, 1911).

VREELAND, N.: *Wampums—The Native Substitute for Currency in North America* (*British Numismatic Journal*. Vol. 7, 1910).

WAITZ, DR. THEODOR: *Anthropologie der Naturvölker* (Leipzig, 1859).

WALKER, F. A.: *Money in its Relation to Trade and Industry* (London, 1880); *Money* (London, 1878); *Money* (*Palgrave's Dictionary of Political Economy*, 1923).

WALKER, NANCY: *Fiji* (London, 1936).

WALLACE, A. R.: *The Malay Archipelago* (London, 1890).

WALTERSHAUSEN, A. SARTORIUS V.: *Die Entstehung des Tauschhandels in Polynesien* (*Zeitschrift für Sozial-und Wirtschaftsgeschichte*. Vol. IV, 1896).

WARNER, W. LLOYD: *A Black Civilization* (New York, 1939).

WEBER, MAX: *General Economic History* (London, 1923).

WEEDEN, W. B.: *Indian Money as a Factor in New England Civilization* (Baltimore, 1884); *Economic and Social History of New England* (Boston, 1890).

WEEKS, JOHN H.: *Among the Congo Cannibals* (London, 1913); *Among the Primitive Bakongo* (London, 1914).

WEGENER, G.: *Deutschland im Stillen Ocean* (Leipzig, 1903).

WEI, WEN PIN: *The Currency Problem in China* (New York, 1914).

WEIGALL, ARTHUR E. B.: *Catalogue Général des Antiquités Egyptiennes du Musée de Caire* (Cairo, 1908).

WEINHOLD, K.: *Altnordisches Leben* (Berlin, 1856).

WEISS, MAX: *Die Völkerstämme in Norden Deutsch-Ostafrikas* (Nürnberg, 1910).

WELCH, GALBRAITH: *The Unveiling of Timbuctoo* (London, 1938).

WESTERMANN, DIEDRICH: *Die Kpelle—Ein Negerstamm in Liberia* (Gottingen, 1921); *Africa To-day and To-morrow* (London, 1939).

WESTERMARCK, E.: *Early Beliefs and their Social Influence* (London, 1932).

WESTON, JULIAN A.: *The Cactus Eaters* (London, 1937).

WHITE, HORACE: *Money and Banking* (New York, 1908).

WHITEHEAD, GEORGE: *In the Nicobar Isles* (London, 1924).

WICKSELL, KNUT: *Lectures of Political Economy* (London, 1935).

WIESER, FRIEDRICH: *Theorie des Geldes* (*Handwörterbuch der Staatswissenschaften.* 4th Edn. Vol. IV, Jena, 1927).

WILD, R. P.: *Iron disc currency from Ashanti* (Man., May, 1936).

WILLIAMS, M. W.: *Social Scandinavia in the Viking Age* (New York, 1920).

WILLIAMSON, ROBERT W.: *The Ways of the South Sea Savage* (London, 1914); *The Social and Political Systems of Central Polynesia* (Cambridge, 1924); *The Mafulu—Mountains People of British New Guinea* (London, 1912).

WILSON, DANIEL: *The Archæology and Prehistoric Annals of Scotland* (1851).

WIRTH, MAX: *Das Geld. Geschichte des Umlaufmittels von der ältesten Zeit bis in der Gegenwart* (Leipzig, 1884).

WIRZ, P.: *Die Marind-Anim von Holländisch Süd-Neu-Guinea* (Hamburg, 1922); *Im Lande des Schneckengeldes* (Stuttgart, 1931).

WISDOM, CHARLES: *The Chorti Indians of Guatemala* (Chicago, 1940).

WODON, LOUIS: *Sur quelques erreurs de Methode dans l'étude de l'Homme Primitif* (Institut Solvay Institut Sociologique. *Notes et Mémoirs.* Vol. IV, 1906).

WOERMANN, A.: *Über Tauschandel in Afrika* (*Mitteilungen der Geographischen Gesellschaft*, Hamburg, 1880-81); *Die Entwickelungsstufen der Geldwirtschaft* (*Jahrbuch für Nationalökonomie und Statistik.* Vol. XXVI, 1876).

WOOLLASTON, A. F. K.: *Pygmies and Papuans, The Stone Age To-Day in Dutch New Guinea* (London, 1912).

WOOLLEY, SIR LEONARD: *The Sumerians* (Oxford, 1928).

WORSAE, J. J.: *The Primeval Antiquities of Denmark* (London, 1849).

WUNDT, WILHELM: *Elements of Folk Psychology* (London, 1916).

YANAIHARA, TADAO: *Pacific Islands under Japanese Mandate* (Shanghai, 1939).

YATES, L. G.: *Notes on the Aboriginal Money of California* (*American Naturalist.* Vol. XII, January, 1877).

YOUNG, J. P.: *Central American Currency and Finance* (Princeton, 1925).

YULE, SIR H. and BURNELL, A. C.: (New Edn. by W. Crooke) *Hobson-Jobson—A Glossary of Colloquial Anglo-Indian Words and Phrases* (London, 1903).

ZAHN, HEINRICH: *Die Jabim—Deutsch Neu Guinea.* Edited by R. Neuhauss (Berlin, 1911).

ZASTROV, BERENGAR V. *Die Herero* (*Das Eingeborenerecht.* Stuttgart, 1930).

ZAY, E.: *Histoire monétaire des colonies françaises* (Paris, 1892).

ZIMMERN, SIR ALFRED: *The Greek Commonwealth* (2nd Edn., Oxford, 1922).

1. MONETARY OBJECTS AND MATERIALS

ADZES, 255
Almonds, 145, 282, 311
Arrows, 67, 134, 138, 140, 152, 188, 197, 278, 286
Arrow poison, 164
Axes, 82, 90, 102, 198, 228

BARK cloth, 41-3, 46-7
Beads, 55-6, 58, 67, 91, 100, 114, 125-6, 128, 130, 132-3, 136, 140, 158-9, 168-9, 170, 172-3, 188-9, 191, 286, 377-8, 384-5, 398, 402, 403, 413, 418, 420
Beef, 292
Beer, 267
Bells, 190
Benzoe cakes, 100
Betel nuts and leaves, 54
Birds, 190
Blankets, 176-7, 182, 299, 329
Boar's tusks, 67, 90
Bottles, 305
Brass discs, 114, 136
Brass rings, 139
Brass rods, 106, 140, 160-1, 170, 358, 402, 420-1, 449.
Brass wire, 100, 128, 131, 136, 140, 413
Bread, 273
Brick dust, 128
Buffaloes, 94, 98, 100-3, 115
Buffalo hides, 100
Butter, 108, 275, 292, 307, 310, 363

CAMELS, 118-9, 125, 283, 390
Camphor, 145
Cannons, 98, 102
Cardboard, 257
Cartridges and bullets, 125, 291-2
Cattle, 102, 115, 117, 120, 125-8, 129, 132-3, 136-7, 137, 139, 141, 145, 158, 168-9, 197, 227-31, 234, 239, 241, 247, 249-50, 259, 261-3, 265-7, 269-70, 272-4, 276-7, 280, 283, 295, 297, 307, 333, 363, 368, 371, 382-5, 392-3, 419, 439, 443, 463, 467.
Cauldrons, 102, 197, 230, 322, 387, 462
Cedar bark, 182
Cheese, 310, 332, 363
Chickens, 158, 186, 189, 266
China, 94, 99, 105
Cigarettes, 104, 307, 308-10, 312, 370, 420, 438
Clay, 250, 257, 282

Cloth, 94, 100-1, 103-4, 105, 121-2, 125-6, 131, 134, 136-7, 139-41, 143-4, 146, 153-6, 158, 164, 167-8, 170-1, 183, 186-8, 190, 256-7, 265-7, 270-1, 385, 398, 403, 409, 413-5, 420, 439, 449
Cloves, 188
Coal, 245-6, 308
Coca leaves, 191
Cocoa, 183, 185, 188, 190, 448.
Coconuts, 50, 58, 71, 110-13, 185, 190, 370, 412, 444
Coffee, 100, 119, 307
Copper or bronze (ingots, rings other than Manillas, objects, scrap), 103, 122, 126, 161, 184, 197, 203-9, 211, 218, 228-9, 235-7, 246, 251, 255, 286, 363, 438, 467
Copper spelter, 106-7
Copra, 71
Cosmetics, 313
Cowries, 63, 89-90, 102, 115, 118, 125, 130, 133-4, 136, 139, 141-5, 146-8, 154-8, 250, 253-4, 273, 275, 280-83, 285, 286, 311, 332, 337, 384, 388, 399, 400, 402-3, 413, 414, 420, 445, 450-1.
Cotton, 122, 188, 300-1, 302, 428

DAGGA cakes, 169, 390
Dates, 118, 126
Discs (throwing), 141
Dog's teeth, 67, 75-7, 90, 402, 445
Donkeys, 129
Drugs, 313
Drums, 95-7, 378, 403
Dyestuff (curcuma root), 50, 59

EARTHENWARE pots, 91, 170, 391, 412
Eggs, 56, 186, 266, 297, 332, 363
Elephants, 103

FEATHERS, 62-4, 67, 164, 182, 379, 389, 410, 412, 442.
Fibre armlets, 99
Fish, 172, 271-2, 299-300, 366
Fishhooks, 56, 118, 139, 328
Flax, 293
Flour, 292, 307
Furs—see skins

GAMING counters, 104
Gin, 149-50, 165, 191, 358

Ginger, 300-1, 303
Glass jars, 107
Goats, 126-8, 129, 133, 136, 165
Gold (ingots, scrap, wire, rings) by
    weight, 105, 125, 145, 203-9, 211-2,
    217, 219, 222-3, 227, 238, 239-41, 284,
    252, 255, 260, 264, 267-8, 272, 274-6,
    282, 368
Gold (debased), 155
Gold dust, 95-7, 99-100, 104-5, 146,
    153, 156, 158, 173, 183, 286, 295
Gold nuggets, 295
Gongs, 95, 98, 102, 403
Grain, 103, 113-4, 118, 145, 181, 183,
    185-6, 209-10, 211-5, 219, 249, 256,
    266, 268, 269, 273, 280, 282, 285,
    292-3, 299, 306-7, 308, 310, 332-3,
    337, 402, 420, 426-7, 437, 439, 445,
    448, 467
Gunpowder, 134, 136, 139
Guns, 136, 139, 165, 169, 170, 188, 420

Hatchets, 100, 184
Hemp, 177, 292, 293
Hoes, 115, 120-1, 136, 140, 152, 158,
    163, 255
Horses, 103, 117, 181, 207, 280, 286

Indigo, 300, 303
Iron, 64, 102-3, 114, 121, 128, 138, 140,
    152, 154, 158-9, 161-3, 200, 231-3,
    242-5, 275, 285, 363, 414, 421, 462,
    467
Ivory, 101-2, 133, 138-9, 159, 169-70,
    369, 418, 420

Jam, 116

Knives, 114, 162, 255-6, 328
Kola nuts, 145, 158

Lacquer, 250, 282
Lead, 106, 136, 215
Leather, 225, 234, 245, 260, 268, 295-6,
    309, 329, 410, 449

Manillas, 150-2, 155, 391, 329, 378,
    384, 391, 412, 442
Mats, 41-3, 54-6, 57, 62, 140, 156, 166-7
Milk, 307
Millet, 122, 126, 131, 136-7, 144-5, 156
Molasses, 300, 303
Mulberry cakes, 117

Nails, 297, 307
Needles, 262

Oatmeal, 296
Olive oil, 310
Onions, 122
Ornaments, 17, 337, 364, 376
Ostrich feather, 156

Palm oil, 150, 158
Palm oil kernels, 153, 158
Peas, 292, 299
Pepper, 100, 266, 268
Pigs, 58-62, 67, 103, 381, 383, 400, 403
Pigs' jawbones, 67
Pitch, 292
Pork, 292, 299
Porpoise teeth, 69-72, 442
Potash, 308

Rats, 45
Rat traps, 164
Reindeer, 115-6
Rice, 93-5, 98, 101-3, 107, 109, 114, 118,
    170, 199, 250, 282, 286, 292, 313-5,
    329, 332-3, 336, 385, 402, 409, 420,
    426, 427-8, 438
Rings, 35, 117, 121, 139, 203-5, 221,
    239-40, 241-2, 245, 248-9, 255, 260,
    264, 267, 271-2, 274, 275, 281,
    296. See also Manillas.
Rubber, 158, 163
Rum, 139, 165, 175-6, 298, 300, 302

Salt, 99, 100, 104, 115, 122, 123-5,
    137, 139, 140, 144, 146, 152, 158-9,
    164, 168, 235, 239, 257, 285, 358,
    400, 410, 413.
Shawls, 118
Sheep, 108, 117-8, 127-8, 140, 218-9,
    227, 234, 272-3, 283, 393-4, 418,
    437-9, 463
Shells (other than cowries), 47, 50,
    56-90, 115, 140, 159, 163, 166-7,
    173-4, 178-81, 190, 254, 287-90, 296,
    333, 334-70, 376-8, 384-5, 391, 394,
    402-3, 407, 410, 412-3
Shields, 117
Shirts, 140, 152, 409
Sickles, 255
Silk, 145, 256-7, 285
Silver (ingots, objects, rings, wire,
    scraps) by weight, 103-6, 108, 200
    211-15, 217, 267-8, 271-2, 274, 275,
    277, 280-2, 285-6, 305, 311-3, 402,
    420, 427, 439, 445, 448, 467.
Silver coins (cut), 135
Silver leaves, 101
Sinnet, 46-7
Skins, 47, 109, 116, 169, 172, 174-5,
    181-2, 259, 274, 275, 278-80, 281,
    291, 295, 299, 305, 329-36, 337, 385,
    405, 426, 448-9

Skulls (animal), 115, 378
Skulls (human), 99, 378
Slaves, 103, 121, 141, 144, 148-9,
154-5, 158, 165, 167, 176, 188, 215,
217-22, 227-8, 235-9, 242, 248, 252,
255, 260, 262-4, 333, 400-2, 413, 420,
437, 439, 441-7, 449
Snail shells, 190
Soap, 139, 184, 309
Spades, 121, 125, 134-5, 255
Spearheads, 134, 162, 170
Spirals, 199
Spits, 231
Stones, 48-52, 62-3, 182, 190, 282, 332,
370, 378, 384, 400, 412-3
Straw, 118
Sugar, 188, 299, 300-1, 302-5
Swords, 200, 286, 295-6
Syrup, 50

Tamarind seeds, 118
Tar, 292
Taro, 50
Tea, 107, 109, 115, 329-402
Timber, 45-6, 138, 292, 304, 308

Tin, 100, 105, 121, 184, 265
Tinned food, 313
Tobacco, 50, 54, 56, 77, 79, 82, 87, 91,
116, 122, 125, 139, 141, 155, 158,
169, 170, 172, 188, 290-5, 300-3,
329, 336, 403, 405, 409, 414, 420,
437, 445
Tripods, 102, 197, 230, 32
Tyres, 313

Utensils, 17, 337, 438

Wax, 98-9, 189, 266
Weapon, 17, 337
Whale's teeth, 44, 377, 385
Wheels, 240
White metal, 125
Wine, 269
Women, 139, 247-8, 263-4
Woodpecker's scalps, 181
Wool, 118, 292, 310

Yarns, 83, 122, 153

2. MONETARY UNITS

Fictitious units are marked (f)

Bar (f), 152, 156, 159
Bu, 286

Chat, 203

Deben, 203-7.
Dirhem, 278

Fazenda (f), 168
Feoh, 259
Frustrum (f), 266

Gewandmark, 266
Grivna Kun, 279
Groschen, 281, 305
Gun (f), 165

Hud, 275

Kesitah, 219
Kit, 203, 207
Korngeld, 266
Kroo (f), 139, 155
Kugildi, 269-70
Kumal, 247-8, 263-4

Lerept, 273
Lives (f), 107
Long (f), 138, 167-8

Manadamater (f), 275
Mancus, 260
Maria Theresa dollar, 123-4, 146, 147
Mark, 260
Mina, 211-2, 215-6, 218, 219, 231
Mithkal, 212
Muk (f), 105

Ore, 260, 273

Pawn (f), 153
Pensa auri, 276
Pense, 280
Polushka, 279
Piece (f), 164-5, 167

Reilmark, 266
Rouble, 305
Rupee, 250
Rys, 286

SCEATT, 261
Scyllinga, 261
Shekel, 211-4, 218-9, 221-2
Shu, 286
Skatts, 261, 266
Sket, 266
Skot, 277
Slave (ʃ), 168
Solidus, 265-6

Spanish dollars, 46, 135, 145, 298
Staters, 227
Sycee, 285

TAEL, 107-8, 311-2
Talent, 211-2, 221-3, 228, 231

WADMAL, 270-1, 273
Wede, 266

3. AUTHORS QUOTED

ABERCROMBY, J., 278
Acosta, J. de, 189-91
Adrian, F. O., 154
Æschines, 225
Africanus, L., 141, 167
Alberti, J. B., 103
Alexander, G., 131
Alldridge, T. J., 159
Allen, D., 245
Alvarez, F., 125
Amira, K. v., 269-71, 273-5
Anderson, H. D. and Ellis, W. C., 172
Anderson, J. G., 102
Andrée, R., 23, 50, 53, 56, 115, 141,
    144, 154, 167
Angell, Sir N., 461
Angelo, M. and Carli, D. de, 167
Annadale and Nelson, 270
Appadorai, A., 281-2
Aravamuthan, T. G., 252
Archer, F. B., 156
Archey, G., 47, 63
Aristide, 225
Aristotle (Pseudo-), 234
Armstrong, W. E., 23, 72-5, 83, 90, 167
Asmis, Dr., 158
Avebury, Lord, 257
Aymonier, E., 102-3, 104

BABELON, E., 23, 102, 109, 125, 226, 227,
    234-6, 252, 267, 300, 305
Baikie, Dr., 152
Baillaud, E., 141-4
Bancroft, H. H., 174, 182-4, 190
Banerja, P., 250, 282
Barbosa, D., 102, 311
Barclay, W. S., 191
Barnett, L. D., 251
Barth, H., 140, 145, 147, 152, 153,
    351, 409
Barton, R. F., 94
Basden, G. T., 146-7, 149, 151-2
Bastian, A., 104, 106
Bates, H. W., 188
Baumann, O., 159
Beaglehole, E., 181
Beard, E., 117

Beauchamp, W. M., 175
Beer, G. L., 287, 293-4
Bentley, W. H., 161-3, 165
Benzoni, G., 188
Bernatzik, H. A., 69
Bertholet, A., 223
Betham, W., 199, 249
Bhargava, B., 251-2
Biot, E., 265
Birch, J. M. S., 272
Bittel, K., 219
Blackwood, B., 68-9, 71
Blagden, C. O., 105
Blake, J. W., 155
Blanchet, A., 239-41
Boas, F., 176
Boeckh, A., 232-3
Borlase, W., 262
Bosman, W., 155
Brandeis, A., 56
Brandis, J., 203
Bratter, H. M., 309
Breasted, J. H., 203, 205, 207
Breitenstein, H., 100
Brentano, L., 247
Bretschneider, E., 284
Bronson, H., 292
Brown, C. J., 252
Brown, G., 41-2, 85-7
Brown, G. G. and Hutt, A. M., 129, 131
Brown, J. M., 45
Brueckner, A., 281
Bruel, G., 139, 141
Brunner, H., 265-6
Bücher, K., 94-5, 99, 358-60
Budge, E. A. W., 121, 123-4
Burckhardt, 119, 125
Burns, A. C., 149
Burns, A. R., 23, 25, 224-5, 231, 235,
    255, 280, 435
Burton, R. F., 124, 126, 130, 137, 153
Butt-Thompson, F. W., 152, 159
Buxton, L. H. D., 283

CABLE, M. and French, F., 108
Cæsar, Julius, 200, 242-4
Cagnolo, C., 128

Cameron, V. L., 130, 153, 165
Campbell-Thompson, R., 212
Carlile, W. W., 377, 379, 398
Carnivali, L., 197
Cassel, G., 21, 345-6, 387-8
Chadwick, H. M., 259-61
Chalmers, R., 20, 154, 299-305
Charlton, W., 259, 268-9, 278-9, 281
Chaudoir, Baron S. de, 278-281, 305
Cheeseman, E., 59, 62
Cheeseman, R. E., 123-4
Chitty, A., 298
Christian, F. W., 49-51
Christie, E. B., 93-4
Clarke, E. D., 279, 305
Clarke, G. B., 309
Cleasby, R. and Vigfusson, G., 271
Clifton, T., 111
Clozel, F. J. and Villamur, R., 158
Clyde, P. H., 57
Codrington, H. W., 118
Codrington, R. H., 47, 63-4, 66-7
Collingwood, R. C., 243
Collingwood, R. C. and Myers, J. N. L., 245
Conder, C. R., 204, 207, 216
Contenau, G., 223
Coombe, F., 64, 66-7, 71
Cooper-Cole, F., 93
Coote, W., 62
Coster, H., 188
Courant, M., 109
Crisp, J., 100
Crowther, G., 353
Culwick, A. T. and G. M., 136
Cunningham, R. W., 259, 261
Cureau, A. L., 140
Czapliczka, M. A., 116

Dames, M. L., 102
Damm, H., 58
Danks, B., 84-6
Dapper, O., 167
Darwin, C., 191
Davidson, J., 175, 299, 300
Davis, A. McFarlane, 292, 295
Deacon, A. B., 59
Dechelette, J., 181, 240, 244
Decken, Baron C. v. d., 136
Delaporte, L., 219
Dempwolf, O., 131
Denham, Clapperton and Oudney, 140, 144, 147
Denig, E. T., 182
Dionysius Halicarnassensis, 231
Dobrizhofer, M., 189, 344
Dodd, A. F., 289, 294
Domville-Fife, C. U., 120
Dopsch, A., 253, 255, 265, 267, 285
Doughty, C. M., 119, 390
Dracopoli, I. N., 125-6

Drake-Brockman, R. E., 125
Driberg, J. H., 132-4
Du Bois, Cora, 95-7
Dykmans, G., 207

Earl, G. W., 91
Egerton, F. C. C., 139
Ehrenreich, P. E., 190
Einzig, P., 308
Eisler, R., 200, 267-8, 307-8
Ejges, S., 220
Elbert, J., 101
Ellis, H. S., 324, 375, 417
Ellis, W., 135
El-Tounsy, M. E.-O., 120-22
Embree, J. F., 315
Engel, A. and Serrure, R., 238
Ermann, A. and Ranke, H., 203, 205-6,
Evans, Sir A., 200
Evans, I. H. N., 98-9
Evans-Pritchard, E. E., 120

Fa Hsien, 250
Falkner, S. A., 306-7
Farson, N., 127
Fawcett, J., 114
Featherman, A., 58, 100, 102
Feaveryear, A. E., 261
Ferrand, G., 106, 136
Festus, 234
Finch, O., 43, 47, 56, 63, 71, 84, 86-8
Firth, Raymond, 23, 46, 65
Firth, Rosemary, 349
Fisher, I., 402
Fitzgerald, W. W. A., 128
Forbes, W. C., 95
Forde, D. and Scott, R., 148, 153
Forrer, R., 199, 200, 239
Fortune, R. F., 77, 78
Foster, T. S., 176, 342
Foville, A. de, 144, 156
Frederick, C., 106
Freeman, R. A., 154
Friedensburg, F., 280
Frobenius, L., 162-3
Fryer, J., 104
Furness, W. H., 48-9, 51
Furnivall, J. S., 101-2

Gann, T., 186
Garcillasso de la Vega, Y., 343
Gardenzi, 278
Gardner, F., 298
Gaud, F. and Overbergh, C. van, 140
Geary, Sir W. N. M., 151
Germann, P., 158
Gibbon, E., 238, 278, 284
Gide, C., 322
Gilmour, M. K., 82
Gjerset, K., 270

Glotz, G., 217, 228
Godsell, P. H., 176
Gotze, A., 198, 200
Gouldsbury, C. and Shane, H., 137-8
Graff, F. W., Up de, 188
Graham, W. A., 107
Gray, A., 118, 282
Greaves, I. C., 44
Gregory of Tours, 267
Gregory, T. E., 365
Grempler, W., 305
Grenfell, G., 100
Groeneveldt, W. B., 101
Gronberg, V., 275
Grubauer, A., 101
Grubb, W. B., 190
Grupp, G., 241
Guppy, H. B., 70

Haas, G., 280
Hadfield, E., 47
Haerberlin, E. J., 235
Haggenmacher, 126
Hahn, E., 380
Hailey, Lord, 23, 126
Hakluyt, R., 146
Halkin, J. and Viane, E., 162
Hall, H. R., 226
Hallett, H. S., 104
Halliday, W. M., 177
Hambly, W. D., 154
Hambruch, P. and Eilers, A., 57, 58
Hamilton, A., 99, 123-4
Hammer, J. de, 278
Hanson, E. P., 189
Harris, W. Cornwallis, 124
Harrison, T., 59, 61-2
Harper, R. F., 213
Haslund, H., 109
Hawkins, E., 242
Hawtrey, R. G., 323, 375
Haxthausen, W., 117
Helfferich, K., 20, 41, 320, 323, 365, 377, 388
Hepburn, A. B., 289, 291-2
Hernsheim, F., 48-9, 52
Herodotus, 225, 227-8, 233
Herskovits, M. J., 23, 48, 78-9, 120, 128, 157, 320, 396
Hertz, J. E., 63, 144
Hesse-Wartegg, E., 92
Hewitt, J. N. B., 180
Heyer, H., 131
Hildebrand, R., 283
Hilton-Simpson, M. W., 162-4
Hobbs, J., 46
Hodge, F. W., 177, 181-2
Hodkin, T., 260-1
Hodson, T. C., 115
Hogbin, H. I., 72
Homan, B., 276-7

Hose, C., 98
Hoyt, E. E., 395
Hrozny, F., 218-9
Hulme, E. W., 244
Humphreys, C. R., 59
Hunter, M., 170
Hupfield, F., 158
Hutton, J. H., 114-5
Huxley, J., 127

Ibn Batuta, 100
Ibn Rosteh, 27
Ibsen, H., 392
Iden-Zeller, O., 116
Ilwof, F., 23, 116, 135-6, 141, 146, 172, 183, 265-6, 280-1, 305, 310, 324
Ingersoll, E., 178, 179, 180
Ingrams, W. H., 137
Isert, P. E., 155
Ivens, W. G., 67, 68, 70-2

Jackson, A. V. W., 252
Jain, L. C., 114
Jastrow, M., 212
Jathar, G. B. and Beri, S. G., 114
Jenkinson, A., 117
Jenks, A. E., 93-4
Jenness, D., 173-5
Jevons, W. S., 20, 266, 300, 307, 310, 320-1, 330-1, 351-2, 368
Jobson, R., 156
Johns, C. H. W., 213-4
Johnson, E. A., 287, 289, 295
Johnston, E. A., 160, 161, 163-6
Jones, C. L., 185
Joyce, T., 183, 191
Junod, H. A., 171

Kann, E., 108, 285
Karamisheff, W., 108-9
Kaulla, R., 417
Keary, C. F., 241, 259-61, 265
Keate, G., 54
Kendall, G. W., 184
Kendrick, D. and Hawkes, C. F. C., 245
Kennay, J. F., 175
Kenyatta, J., 127-8
Keynes, Lord, 21, 24, 127, 133, 209, 365, 369
King, L. W., 214
Kingsley, Mary H., 138-9, 158-9
Kin-wei Shaw, 257
Kliutschewskij, W., 278
Kloss, G. B., 111
Knapp, G. F., 374, 387, 391, 411, 416-9
Knibbs, S. G. C., 70
Knies, K., 20, 386
Kraemer, A., 42-3, 54-7
Krause, F., 188

Krickeberg, W., 182
Krieger, H. W., 60, 63
Kroeber, A. L. and Waterman, T. L., 176, 180-2
Kubary, J., 46, 51, 53-5, 58, 384
Kulischer, J., 266-7, 277, 279-80
Kuykendall, R. S., 45

LACOUPERIE, T. de, 253-7, 336
Lambert, Père, 47
Landtman, G., 90
Lansdell, H., 117
Laughlin, J. L., 295, 365, 377, 407
Laum, B., 33, 204, 379-85, 388
Laval, Pyrard de, 282
Layard, J., 58-60, 62, 67
Lemoine, J., 239
Lenormant, F., 23, 205-6, 215, 224-5
Lenz, O., 121, 142-3, 147
Letourneau, C., 171
Levchine, A. de, 117
Lewis, A. B., 47
Ligon, R., 300
Lind, A. W., 46
Lindsay, J., 249, 264, 271, 275
Lips, J., 140
Lissauer, A., 198
Locke, J., 322
Lord, J. K., 178
Loven, S., 189, 191
Lucas, A., 204
Luschin v. Ebengreuth, A., 267, 269-70, 274, 276
Lyon, G. F., 145

MACDONALD, A. G., 150
McKay, D., 125
McLean, J., 173, 174, 176
McLean, J. B., 204
MacMichael, H. A., 120-2
MacMillan, W. M., 171
McPhee, A., 147-50
Madden, F. W., 221
Mage, M. E., 142
Mair, L. P., 134
Malinowski, B., 23, 79-83, 378
Mann, E. H., 111-3
Marais, J. S., 170
Marchant, A., 188
Marno, E., 410
Marsden, W., 100
Marshall, A., 313, 325, 414, 416, 452
Marshall, A. J., 58, 59, 60
Mauss, M., 79
Maydon, H. C., 124, 125
Mazerath, J., 259
Mead, M., 42-3, 76, 78, 81, 83, 92
Means, P. A., 191
Meek, A. S., 90, 91

Meek, C. K., 151-2
Meissner, B., 211, 213-5
Menger, K., 20, 21, 321-2, 324, 354-5, 365-9, 386
Mercer, S. A. B., 207, 209, 216
Merrithew, L., 175
Metters, L., 116
Meyer, E., 203, 217
Meyer, H., 132
Mickwitz, G., 238
Miles, W. A., 246
Mill, J. S., 323, 352
Millies, H. C., 99, 100
Mills, J. P., 114, 115
Miyashita, K., 285
Moberly, H. J. and Cameron, W. B., 175-6
Mockler, A. F. and Ferryman, F., 147, 152
Mommsen, T., 23, 234-7
Monteil, C., 144
Montet, P., 203
Montgomerie, H. S., 111, 112, 113
Moodie, D., 170
Morgan, J. de, 105, 117, 207, 211
Morier, V. A. L., 115
Morse, H. B., 312
Mosher, S., 246, 274-5
Moszkowski, E. H., 111-3
Much, M., 199
Mukerjee, R., 113
Muller, W., 48
Mundy, R., 99

NACHTIGAL, G., 141, 146
Nadel, S. F., 148
Naskap, F. G. S., 174
Nath, Pran, 249-53
Neel, H., 159
Nelson, E. W., 172
Nettels, C. P., 287-94
Nevermann, H., 75, 76
Nicholson, J. S., 319
Nieboer, H. J., 117
Noback, F., 23, 99, 100, 104, 108, 136, 138, 154, 155-6, 158-9, 169
Nolan, P., 23, 247-9, 261, 263-4, 271
Normano, J. F., 188

OBER, F. A., 183
Oldmixon, 301-2
Old Testament, 219-23
Oliver, S. P., 135
Olmstead, A. T., 214-5
Oppert, E., 110
Oppert, J. and Menant, J., 212
Orleans, Prince H. de, 108
Oviedo y Valdes, de, 185
Owen, R., 344

PALLME, J., 121
Parker, E. H., 283
Parker, G. W., 135
Parkinson, R., 76, 83-6
Parkman, F., 299
Partridge, C., 150
Pausanias, 229
Peisker, J., 283
Peristany, J. G., 128
Petty, F., 185
Pfeil, J. Graf, 87
Phear, J., 118
Pigou, A. C., 127
Pillory, J., 240
Pinto, S., 168
Pirenne, J., 203
Pitt-Rivers, G. H. L-F., 171
Pliny, 236
Plutarch, 231, 233
Pollux, 229
Polo, Marco, 285
Powdermaker, H., 87
Preisigke, F., 210
Prejevalsky, N., 109
Prescott, W. H., 183-4, 191, 343
Price, J. E., 154
Price, M. P., 109
Price, W., 49-54
Pritchard, W. T., 42

RATZEL, F., 53, 56, 58, 117, 123, 135
Reche, O., 91
Redfield, A. and Villa, A., 186
Reed, S. W., 85, 87-8
Regling, K., 23, 55, 108, 116-7, 199, 205, 236
Reinach, T., 198, 221, 230
Reinecke, F., 42-3
Reisner, G., 212
Rey, C. F., 123
Rheinach, L. de, 102-3
Rhys Davids, C. F., 250-1, 253
Rhys, Lloyd, 89
Ribbe, C., 68
Ricardo, D., 411
Richard, A. I., 138
Rickard, T. A., 204, 207, 215, 223
Ridgeway, W., 23, 108, 116-7, 119, 172, 231, 234, 247, 253, 265, 271, 273-4
Riesenberg, F., 191
Rist, C., 320-1, 326, 369-7
Rivers, W. H. R., 47, 62, 64-8
Robertson, D. H., 323
Robinson, A. E. G., 127
Robinson, C. H., 148
Robinson, E. S. G., 233
Rockhill, W. W., 100, 103, 285
Rodd, F. R., 146
Roelich, G. N., 108
Roepstroff, F. A. de, 110

Rogner, E., 53
Rohlfs, G., 153
Romilly, H. H., 87
Roscher, W., 20, 109, 117-8, 189, 271, 273, 307
Roscoe, J., 132-3
Ross, W. M., 129
Rostovtzeff, M., 210, 238
Roth, H. L., 99
Routledge, W. S. and K., 128, 129
Rowe, N. A., 43
Roy, S. C., 114
Rubruquis, G. de, 278, 282
Ruding, R., 244-6, 378

SARASAS, P., 286
Sarfert, E., 57
Savage-Landor, A. W., 110, 125
Savini, F., 268
Sayce, R. U., 385
Schapera, I., 171, 385
Scheffel, J., 242
Schlettwein, A., 157-8
Schliemann, H., 198-9
Schmidt, M., 169, 189, 191
Schnee, H., 84, 140
Schneider, O., 68-70, 76
Schomburgk, R., 190
Schrader, O., 277
Schroeder, A., 103
Schulz-Ewerth, E., 42
Schulz-Ewerth, E. and Adam, L., 140
Schurtz, H., 25, 95, 118-9, 126, 138, 145, 154, 157-8, 159, 162, 167-8, 170, 190, 283, 311, 321, 356, 359, 369, 377, 389, 458
Schwabe, K., 169
Schweinfurth, G., 121
Schweinitz, H. Graf v., 130
Schwenzner, W., 211
Scott, T. and R., 132
Seebohm, F., 119, 247-8, 261-2, 265, 267, 275
Seligmann, C. G., 82, 88, 90
Seltman, C. T., 228-9, 231-2
Semper, K., 53, 56, 388-9
Senfft, A., 50, 51, 54, 56
Senior, Nassau, 411
Shirokogoroff, S. M., 116
Shortt, A., 299
Sievers, W. and Hahn, F., 124
Simcox, E. J., 201, 202
Simon, J., 260, 264
Skeat, W. W., 105
Skene, W. F., 247
Slater, G., 114
Smith, Adam, 20
Smith, E. W. and Dale, A. N., 137
Smith, H., 119
Smith, R. A., 243-5
Smith, R. Bosworth, 225

Smith, S., 217-8
Smith, V. A., 280
Somlo, F., 386
Sorrento, J. Merolla da, 167
Spalding, W. F., 108
Speck, E., 234, 237
Speiser, F., 59, 61-3
Speke, J. H., 131, 133, 135-6
Stanley, H. M., 131
Stayt, H. A., 171
Stearns, R. E. C., 146, 173-4, 178-9, 181
Stein, W., 242
Steinen, K. v., 188
Steinmetz, S. R., 136, 139, 145
Stern, G., 308
Stevenson, J. H., 214-5
Stigland, C. H., 134
Stigland, H., 128
Stirling, M. W., 91-2
Stites, S. H., 178-80
Strandes, J., 126, 131
Stuck, H., 173, 501
Stuhlmann, F., 129-30, 133-4
Sumner, W. S., 293
Svoronos, J. N., 200
Swain, H. G. C., 126
Swanton, J. R., 181
Swettenham, Sir F., 105
Swoboda, W., 111-2
Sydenham, E. A., 234-7
Sykes, Sir P., 283
Symes, M., 106

Tacitus, 241
Takekoshi, Y., 286
Takizawa, M., 286, 313-5
Talbot, P. A., 147, 150-3
Tamagna, F. M., 257
Tauber, W., 268-9
Taylor, F. M., 374-5
Temple, R. C., 95, 99, 100, 105-7, 112, 115, 117, 285
Tessmann, G., 159
Thierry de Menonville, B. N. J., 183
Thilenius, G., 23, 102, 190, 280, 410
Thomas, E. S., 251-2
Thomas, H. P. and Scott, R., 132, 134
Thompson, J. E., 183
Thompson, L., 44
Thompson, V., 104
Thonnar, A., 160
Thucydides, 233
Thrunwald, R., 23, 68-70, 88, 91, 128-9, 131, 458
Tille, A., 266
Torday, E., 162, 164
Torday, E. and Joyce, T. A., 163
Tung Hli Ying K'An, 100
Turgot, A. R. J., 330
Turner, G., 41-2

Vatter, E., 96-7, 101
Veatch, A. C., 187
Vedder, H., 169
Vidal, M., 95
Viljoen, S., 23, 168, 170, 381, 385
Vincent, F., 135
Voeltzkow, A., 136
Volz, W., 159
Vreeland, N., 289

Wackernagel, J., 268
Walker, F. A., 331
Walker, N., 44
Wallace, A. R., 102, 351
Wauters, A. J., 160
Weber, M., 587
Weeden, W. B., 179-80
Weeks, J. H., 160-1, 163, 165
Weignall, A. E. B., 205
Weinhold, K., 270-1, 273
Weiss, M., 129, 132-5
Weldron, G., 296
Welch, G., 30, 144-5
Wen, Pin Wei, 254, 312
Westermann, D., 128, 158
Weston, J. A., 106, 187
White, Horace, 288, 290-2, 294-5, 399, 411-2
Whitehead, G., 111-3
Wicksell, K., 325
Widranges, Comte H. de, 240
Wild, R. P., 154
Williams, C., 107
Williams, M. W., 270-2
Williamson, R. W., 42, 90
Wilson, D., 261
Wirth, M., 270, 273, 280
Wirz, P., 88-9, 402
Wisdom, C., 185-6
Woermann, A., 120-2, 138, 150, 158, 163, 168
Wolowski, L. F. M. R., 351
Woollaston, A. F. K., 91
Woolley, Sir L., 212, 215
Worsae, J. J. A., 272
Wundt, W., 336

Yanaihara, T., 48, 54, 57-8
Yates, L. G., 182
Young, J. P., 185, 190

Zahn, H., 90
Zastrow, B. v., 169
Zay, E., 299
Zimmern, Sir A., 235

4. GEOGRAPHICAL INDEX OF THE THEORETICAL SECTION

ADMIRALTY ISLANDS, 402
Africa, 349, 352, 362, 380, 385, 391-2,
    398, 414, 419, 421, 429, 438, 443-5,
    449, 464, 468, 470
Africa (C.), 317, 402
Africa (E.), 363, 371, 402, 413, 445
Africa (S.), 363, 390, 392
Africa (W.), 403, 414
Alor, 378, 403
America, 380, 438
America (C.), 448
America (Latin), 344-5, 392
America (N.), 324, 345, 361, 378, 385,
    402-3, 405, 409, 412-4, 416, 420, 437,
    439, 440, 444, 448-50, 464
America (S.), 342
Andman, 342
Angola, 385
Arabia, 390
Argos, 383
Ashanti, 370, 438
Asia, 380
Asia (C.), 463
Asia (W.), 325, 462-3
Assam, 378, 470
Assyria, 400, 467
Athens, 438, 462
Australia, 341

BABYLONIA, 336, 373, 401-2, 420, 439,
    445, 448, 467
Bagirmi, 402
Banks Isle, 391, 412-3
Bismarck Archipelago, 361
Borneo, 378
Britain, 464
Burma, 420, 470

CAPPADOCIA, 439
Carthage, 410
China, 328, 336, 370, 413, 438, 442,
    461, 467
Congo, 322, 396, 402, 414
Cuzco, 343

DAHOMEY, 400
Duke of York Isle, 384

EGYPT, 336, 349, 379, 435, 461-2, 466
England, 460-1
Ethiopia, 410

FIJI, 385
France, 437
French West Africa, 399

GAZELLE PENINSULA, 384
Greece, 322, 368, 371, 379, 382-4, 388,
    393-4, 418, 462, 467, 471
Guam, 413

HITTITE EMPIRE, 401, 439, 445
Hungary, 471

ICELAND, 366, 449
Inca Empire, 343-4, 347, 457
India, 382-3, 385
Indo-China, 384, 414, 467
Ireland, 439, 445
Italy, 363, 467

JAPAN, 329, 336, 402, 467-8.

LAWONGAI, 384
Liberia, 429
Loyalty Islands, 348
Lydia, 467

MACEDONIA, 462
Maevo, 412
Malaya, 341, 349, 357, 470
Maldives, 384, 414
Massachusetts, 449, 464
Melanesia, 384
Micronesia, 361
Mongolia, 402, 463

NEW AMSTERDAM, 449
New Britain, 384
New Guinea, 378, 392, 394, 402, 412, 470
New Hebrides, 378, 381, 383, 391, 400,
    403, 412
New Jersey, 413
New Lanark, 344
Nicobars, 370, 412
Nigeria, 391, 403, 413

OCEANIA, 349, 380, 383, 391, 445

PACIFIC, 357, 384, 391, 392, 394, 413,
    439, 442, 444, 468, 470
Paraguay, 344
Pelew Islands, 370, 384, 388, 403, 413
Persian Empire, 467
Persian Gulf, 328
Peru, 343
Philippines, 385, 470
Phoenicia, 454, 467
Polynesia, 343

Rome, 363, 438, 460, 462-3, 467
Rossel Island, 370, 378, 384, 385, 398
Russia, 336, 345, 448, 460, 468

Samoa, 378, 412, 442
Santa Cruz, 410, 412, 442
Scandinavia, 381, 392, 414, 429, 445
Sicily, 363
Simbang, 457-8
Society Islands, 350-1
Solomon Islands, 384, 385, 410, 442
Sparta, 363, 409, 448, 462, 467
Sudan (W.), 396, 413, 445
Sulu Archipelago, 398

Tanganyika, 351, 357
Tierra del Fuego, 341
Trobriand, 378

Uganda, 357, 363, 385, 402, 445

Vanikolo, 391
Virginia, 329, 336, 414, 420, 464

Wadai, 403
West Indies, 334, 437, 440, 448, 480

Yap Isle, 370, 378, 384, 400, 412-3

Zanzibar, 413-4

PRINTED IN GREAT BRITAIN

Date Due

Jan 6-59		
3/31/59		
MAY 7 '60		